SHELL SCRIPTING
EXPERT RECIPES FOR LINUX, BASH, AND MORE

Continues

▶ PART IV   REFERENCE

Shell Scripting

EXPERT RECIPES FOR LINUX, BASH, AND MORE

Shell Scripting

EXPERT RECIPES FOR LINUX, BASH, AND MORE

Steve Parker

John Wiley & Sons, Inc.

Shell Scripting: Expert Recipes for Linux, Bash, and More

Published by
John Wiley & Sons, Inc.
10475 Crosspoint Boulevard
Indianapolis, IN 46256
www.wiley.com

Published by John Wiley & Sons, Inc., Indianapolis, Indiana

Published simultaneously in Canada

ISBN: 978-0-470-02448-5
ISBN: 978-1-118-16633-8 (ebk)
ISBN: 978-1-118-16632-1 (ebk)
ISBN: 978-1-118-16631-4 (ebk)

Manufactured in the United States of America

10 9 8 7 6 5 4 3 2 1

For general information on our other products and services please contact our Customer Care Department within the United States at (877) 762-2974, outside the United States at (317) 572-3993 or fax (317) 572-4002.

Wiley also publishes its books in a variety of electronic formats. Some content that appears in print may not be available in electronic books.

Library of Congress Control Number: 2011932268

For my daughters, Bethany and Emily, and my wife, Jackie. Putting up with a professional geek is never easy, particularly when it leads to a career which often means a lot of travel and time spent away from home. Also to God, from whom comes all wisdom, intelligence, and learning. The better we understand the Creation, the better chance we have of understanding the Creator.

For it is written:

"I will destroy the wisdom of the wise; the intelligence of the intelligent I will frustrate. Where is the wise man? Where is the scholar? Where is the philosopher of this age? Has not God made foolish the wisdom of the world?...For the foolishness of God is wiser than man's wisdom, and the weakness of God is stronger than man's strength."

1 Corinthians chapter 1, verses 19, 20, and 25

ABOUT THE AUTHOR

STEVE PARKER is a Unix and Linux consultant with 20 years' experience with Unix, and 15 years' experience with GNU/Linux. He wrote and maintains the online shell scripting tutorial at `http://steve-parker.org/sh/sh.shtml`.

Steve provides IT consultancy services, and can also provide training courses in shell scripting as well as Unix and Linux technologies. He can be contacted via `http://sgpit.com/`.

ABOUT THE TECHNICAL EDITOR

JOHN KENNEDY has worked with Linux (and Unix) as a system administrator since 1997. He has worked with Red Hat, SUSE, Debian, Ubuntu, Solaris, and HP-UX. He started bash scripting in 2000 because he felt he was doing too much work and wanted something to do the tedious jobs for him.

Before learning the joys of Linux and Unix, John was in the U.S. Air Force for nine years working as a communications systems operator and spent time in Germany, Texas, and England. Since leaving the military he has lived in Nebraska and Pennsylvania, and is now back in England.

John currently works as an Infrastructure Engineer for a media company based in London. He lives near Oxford with his wife, Michele, and son, Kieran. He has a daughter, Denise, who just finished her university degree in the U.S.

When John is not on his computer, he enjoys watching football (soccer) with his son, spending time with his family, and relaxing.

CREDITS

EXECUTIVE EDITOR
Mary James

PROJECT EDITOR
Christina Haviland

TECHNICAL EDITOR
John Kennedy

PRODUCTION EDITOR
Rebecca Anderson

COPY EDITOR
Nancy Rapoport

EDITORIAL MANAGER
Mary Beth Wakefield

FREELANCER EDITORIAL MANAGER
Rosemarie Graham

ASSOCIATE DIRECTOR OF MARKETING
David Mayhew

BUSINESS MANAGER
Amy Knies

PRODUCTION MANAGER
Tim Tate

VICE PRESIDENT AND EXECUTIVE GROUP PUBLISHER
Richard Swadley

VICE PRESIDENT AND EXECUTIVE PUBLISHER
Neil Edde

ASSOCIATE PUBLISHER
Jim Minatel

PROJECT COORDINATOR, COVER
Katie Crocker

COMPOSITOR
Jeff Lytle, Happenstance Type-O-Rama

PROOFREADERS
Louise Watson, Word One New York
Paul Sagan, Word One New York

INDEXER
Robert Swanson

COVER DESIGNER
Ryan Sneed

COVER IMAGE
© mika makkonen / istockphoto.com

ACKNOWLEDGMENTS

THIS BOOK WOULD NOT HAVE happened without the help (and deadlines) that the people at Wiley gave me. Every step of the process has been a new experience, and Christina Haviland has been a great mentor through each step. John Kennedy has provided feedback and encouragement throughout, and Nancy Rapoport has shown a fantastic eye for detail.

From a personal perspective, I would like to thank all of the people behind Acorn, Sinclair, and other companies in the early 1980s for making affordable computers for kids to learn real programming with. Also the BBC for their foresight in the entire BBC Micro project, the TV programs that they put behind it, and the development work that they pursued. The next generation needs something like the BBC Micro project; not using fancy IDEs to write apps for phones, but working at the bare metal with real systems. The Arduino project deserves credit for promoting this at the hardware level; it is an excellent project, making it easy to hack hardware without having to have a knowledgeable uncle on hand to translate resistor values. The Free Software infrastructure, particularly with more recent injections like the Google Summer of Code, is another ideal breeding ground for this love of hacking to develop afresh for a new (GNU?) generation. The idea of a generation growing up knowing only how to *use* devices, not how to *develop* them, is a disturbing one. The projects mentioned above provide hope for the future.

I also want to thank ICL, where I met Douglas and Capitan, Jit, and Ketan. We tested DRS/NX, and had direct access to userspace and kernel developers. That was a rare treat, and it was where I fell in love with Unix. Also the guys who used to hang out on `comp.unix.shell` back in the days when Usenet was still readable; you taught us so much, and we must have seemed so naïve (which we were).

What I gained at ICL by being employed by the same company as the kernel and userspace developers became available to everyone with the GNU/Linux operating system. In the course of writing this book, I have been able to quote e-mails written by people that I have never met (and probably will never meet) in the discussion of Unix, Linux, and shell features. Similarly, in a professional context, I have had the honor of chatting online with the key developers of specific Linux kernel features to discuss how they are implemented in different versions of the Linux kernel, none of which would be possible with a different development model. Similarly, Chet Ramey, the maintainer of the bash shell, has responded to emails about implementation details.

From a professional and IT community perspective, I would like to thank Ken Thompson, Dennis Ritchie, Brian Kernighan, Doug McIlroy, David Korn, and Steve Bourne (to name but a few) for C, Unix, and the environment that is so easily taken for granted. The concepts these visionaries came up with have lasted for 40 years and more.

I also thank Dr. Richard M. Stallman for giving the GNU project to the world, for the GPL and the Free Software Foundation, and for dedicating a lifetime to promoting software freedom. The world needs idealists, and Stallman is one of these. It is my belief that Stallman will be proved by history to be right, that it is better to share developments than to hide them. That is the scientific tradition, and it must also be applied to computer science if it is to be treated seriously as a scientific endeavor.

My thanks to all of the GNU programmers and Linux kernel developers for putting all of these Free Software pieces together into a variety of different usable and Free OSs. Also the other Unix developers, who write code under a variety of licenses for various employers.

Finally, my thanks to Bill Joy, Vinod Khosla, Andy Bechtolsheim, and Scott McNealy for Sun Microsystems and the Solaris Operating Environment. Also Jonathan Schwartz for making most of the company's software Open Source (even buying StarDivision in order to release OpenOffice.org) and the contributions that JDS made to the GNOME project, at a time when a lot of the industry didn't understand the model. RIP Sun Microsystems.

CONTENTS

PART II: RECIPES FOR USING AND EXTENDING SYSTEM TOOLS

PART III: RECIPES FOR SYSTEMS ADMINISTRATION

PART IV: REFERENCE

INTRODUCTION

The lyf so short, the craft so long to lerne.

— CHAUCER

THE SHELL IS THE STANDARD INTERFACE to every Unix and Linux system; users and administrators alike have experience with the shell, and combining commands into shell scripts is a natural progression. However, that is only the tip of the iceberg.

The shell is actually a full programming language, with variables and functions, and also more advanced structures such as arrays (including associative arrays), and being so directly linked to the kernel, it has native file I/O primitives built into its very syntax, as well as process and job control. All of the main features that Unix is best known for are available in the shell, and available to shell scripts.

This book has been written to get the most out of the shell, and should have something to surprise any reader, regardless of background and experience. This book is aimed at intermediate and experienced Unix and Linux administrators, and it may be of interest to other advanced users, too. The book assumes that you know your way around at least one flavor of Unix-like system, and have probably already written some shell scripts, but want to improve your craft.

Experienced readers will probably want to skip the first two chapters; very experienced readers may want to skip the first four chapters, although there may well be details contained there that are worth revisiting.

WHAT THIS BOOK COVERS

This book addresses shell scripting, with a focus on Bourne shell and POSIX compatibility, but a wide coverage of more recent developments, particularly the Bash shell, which is almost universal in GNU/Linux operating systems, and is included with most commercial Unices too. The KornShell is also widely available in most such operating systems, both closed and open source.

HOW THIS BOOK IS STRUCTURED

This book is in four parts; the first part covers the fundamental features and syntax of the shell; the second part looks at the tools available that a shell script can make use of; and the third part has recipes covering a fairly broad range of topics. Finally, the fourth part contains reference information.

Part One is the longest of the four sections; it looks at variables, wildcards, conditional execution, loops, functions, arrays, and processes. The theory is presented with lots of practical examples to demonstrate what is being covered. A lot of these scripts are fairly simplistic because they are concentrating on only one aspect of the shell.

Part Two covers the tools external to the shell that make shell scripts more useful; these are broken down into three chapters on text, files, and general systems administration. The examples in Part Two are a bit more real-world in their nature, and a bit longer and more complex than those in Part One.

Part Three is a set of shell scripting recipes. The hope is that you will find these recipes useful in their own right, but they have also been selected for their usefulness in demonstrating the topics covered in the first two parts of the book. They also show numerous different approaches and techniques that can be used in real-life shell scripts. The real and practical issues are dealt with in this part of the book, without making concessions to explain one specific point. These scripts do what is necessary to get init scripts written, write colorful real-time interactive games, parse HTML, control processes, translate scripts into multiple languages, write CGI scripts, create graphical reports, and more.

Finally, Part Four lists some links for further reading, as well as a glossary of terms.

WHAT YOU NEED TO USE THIS BOOK

Chapter 2 addresses some of the options that are available for getting access to a shell environment of your own and getting it set up in a way that suits you. Experimenting on live systems is one option, but not a good one. Setting up a test account is better, and running a dedicated test machine, or a virtual machine, is even better. Virtualization software, such as VirtualBox or VMWare Player, is available at no cost and provides a risk-free way of testing even the most risky of root-owned scripts.

CONVENTIONS

To help you get the most from the text and keep track of what's happening, we've used several conventions throughout the book.

- ➤ We show commands like so: **echo hello.**
- ➤ We show system output and prompts like this: `hello`.
- ➤ We show file names and code within the text like so: `/etc/hosts`.

We present code in two different ways:

```
We use bold monofont type to emphasize text that is typed in by the user.
```

```
We use a monofont type with no bolding for code content and for system output.
```

SOURCE CODE

As you work through the examples in this book, you may choose either to type in all the code manually or to use the source code files that accompany the book. All of the source code used in this book is available for download at www.wrox.com. You will find the code snippets from the source code are accompanied by a download icon and note indicating the name of the program so you know it's available for download and can easily locate it in the download file. Once at the site, simply locate the book's title (either by using the Search box or by using one of the title lists) and click the Download Code link on the book's detail page to obtain all the source code for the book.

 Because many books have similar titles, you may find it easiest to search by ISBN; this book's ISBN is 978-1-118-02448-5.

Once you download the code, just decompress it with your favorite compression tool. Alternatively, you can go to the main Wrox code download page at www.wrox.com/dynamic/books/download .aspx to see the code available for this book and all other Wrox books.

ERRATA

We make every effort to ensure that there are no errors in the text or in the code. However, no one is perfect, and mistakes do occur. If you find an error in one of our books, like a spelling mistake or faulty piece of code, we would be very grateful for your feedback. By sending in errata, you may save another reader hours of frustration, and at the same time, you will be helping us provide even higher quality information.

To find the errata page for this book, go to www.wrox.com and locate the title using the Search box or one of the title lists. Then, on the book details page, click the Book Errata link. On this page, you can view all errata that has been submitted for this book and posted by Wrox editors. A complete book list including links to each book's errata is also available at www.wrox.com/misc-pages/booklist.shtml.

If you don't spot "your" error on the Book Errata page, go to www.wrox.com/contact/techsupport .shtml and complete the form there to send us the error you have found. We'll check the information and, if appropriate, post a message to the book's errata page and fix the problem in subsequent editions of the book.

P2P.WROX.COM

For author and peer discussion, join the P2P forums at p2p.wrox.com. The forums are a Web-based system for you to post messages relating to Wrox books and related technologies and interact with other readers and technology users. The forums offer a subscription feature to e-mail you topics of interest of your choosing when new posts are made to the forums. Wrox authors, editors, other industry experts, and your fellow readers are present on these forums.

At p2p.wrox.com, you will find a number of different forums that will help you not only as you read this book, but also as you develop your own applications. To join the forums, just follow these steps:

1. Go to p2p.wrox.com and click the Register link.

2. Read the terms of use and click Agree.

3. Complete the required information to join as well as any optional information you wish to provide and click Submit.

4. You will receive an e-mail with information describing how to verify your account and complete the joining process.

 You can read messages in the forums without joining P2P but in order to post your own messages, you must join.

Once you join, you can post new messages and respond to messages other users post. You can read messages at any time on the Web. If you would like to have new messages from a particular forum e-mailed to you, click the Subscribe to this Forum icon by the forum name in the forum listing.

For more information about how to use the Wrox P2P, be sure to read the P2P FAQs for answers to questions about how the forum software works as well as many common questions specific to P2P and Wrox books. To read the FAQs, click the FAQ link on any P2P page.

Shell Scripting

EXPERT RECIPES FOR LINUX, BASH, AND MORE

PART I
About the Ingredients

1

The History of Unix, GNU, and Linux

The Unix tradition has a long history, and Linux comes from the Unix tradition, so to understand Linux one must understand Unix and to understand Unix one must understand its history. Before Unix, a developer would submit a stack of punched cards, each card representing a command, or part of a command. These cards would be read and executed sequentially by the computer. The developer would receive the generated output after the job had completed. This would often be a few days after the job had been submitted; if there was an error in the code, the output was just the error and the developer had to start again. Later, teletype and various forms of timesharing systems sped up the matter considerably, but the model was basically the same: a sequence of characters (punch cards, or keys on keyboards — it's still just a string of characters) submitted as a batch job to be run (or fail to run), and for the result to come back accordingly. This is significant today in that it is still how data is transmitted on any computerized system — it's all sequences of characters, transmitted in order. Whether a text file, a web page, a movie, or music, it is all just strings of ones and zeroes, same as it ever was. Anything that looks even slightly different is simply putting an interface over the top of a string of ones and zeroes.

Unix and various other interactive and timesharing systems came along in the mid-1960s. Unix and its conventions continue to be central to computing practices today; its influences can be seen in DOS, Linux, Mac OS X, and even Microsoft Windows.

UNIX

In 1965, Bell Labs and GE joined a Massachusetts Institute of Technology (MIT) project known as MULTICS, the Multiplexed Information and Computing System. Multics was intended to be a stable, timesharing OS. The "Multiplexed" aspect added unnecessary complexity, which eventually led Bell Labs to abandon the project in 1969. Ken Thompson, Dennis Ritchie, Doug McIlroy, and Joe Ossanna retained some of the ideas behind it, took out a lot of the complexity, and came up with Unix (a play on the word MULTICS, as this was a simplified operating system inspired by MULTICS).

An early feature of Unix was the introduction of *pipes* — something that Doug McIlroy had been thinking about for a few years and was implemented in Unix by Ken Thompson. Again, it took the same notion of streamed serial data, but pipes introduced the idea of having stdin and stdout, through which the data would flow. Similar things had been done before, and the concept is fairly simple: One process creates output, which becomes input to another command. The Unix pipes method introduced a concept that dramatically affected the design of the rest of the system.

Most commands have a file argument as well, but existing commands were modified to default to read from their "Standard Input" (stdin) and "Standard Output" (stdout); the pipe can then "stream" the data from one tool to another. This was a novel concept, and one that strongly defines the Unix shell; it makes the whole system a set of generically useful tools, as opposed to monolithic, single-purpose applications. This has been summarized as "do one thing and do it well." The GNU toolchain was written to replace Unix while maintaining compatibility with Unix tools. The developers on the GNU project often took the opportunity presented by rewriting the tool to include additional functionality, while still sticking to the "do one thing and do it well" philosophy.

 *The GNU project was started in 1983 by Richard Stallman, with the intention of replacing proprietary commercial Unices with Free Software alternatives. GNU had all but completed the task of replacing all of the userspace tools by the time the Linux kernel project started in 1991. In fact, the GNU tools generally perform the same task at least as well as their original Unix equivalents, often providing extra useful features borne of experience in the real world. Independent testing has shown that GNU tools can actually be more reliable than their traditional Unix equivalents (*http://www.gnu.org/software/reliability.html*).*

For example, the who command lists who is logged in to the system, one line per logged-in session. The wc command counts characters, words, and lines. Therefore, the following code will tell you how many people are logged in:

```
who | wc -l
```

There is no need for the who tool to have an option to count the logged-in users because the generic wc tool can do that already. This saves some small effort in who, but when that is applied across the whole range of tools, including any new tools that might be written, a lot of effort and therefore complexity, which means a greater likelihood of the introduction of additional bugs, is avoided. When this is applied to more complicated tools, such as grep or even more, the flexibility of the system is increased with every added tool.

 In the case of more, *this is actually more tricky than it seems; first it has to find out how many columns and rows are available. Again, there is a set of tools that combine to provide this information. In this way, every tool in the chain can be used by the other tools.*

Also this system means that you do not have to learn how each individual utility implements its "word count" feature. There are a few defacto standard switches; -q typically means Quiet, -v typically means Verbose, and so on, but if who -c meant "count the number of entries," then cut -c <n>, which means "cut the first *n* characters," would be inconsistent. It is better that each tool does its own job, and that wc do the counting for all of them.

For a more involved example, the sort utility just sorts text. It can sort alphabetically or numerically (the difference being that "10" comes before "9" alphabetically, but after it when sorted numerically), but it doesn't search for content or display a page at a time. grep and more can be combined with sort to achieve this in a pipeline:

```
grep foo /path/to/file | sort -n -k 3 | more
```

This pipeline will search for foo in /path/to/file. The output (stdout) from that command will then be fed into the stdin of the sort command. Imagine a garden hose, taking the output from grep and attaching it to the input for sort. The sort utility takes the filtered list from grep and outputs the sorted results into the stdin of more, which reads the filtered and sorted data and paginates it.

It is useful to understand exactly what happens here; it is the opposite of what one might intuitively assume. First, the more tool is started. Its input is attached to a pipe. Then sort is started, and its output is attached to that pipe. A second pipe is created, and the stdin for sort is attached to that. grep is then run, with its stdout attached to the pipe that will link it to the sort process.

When grep begins running and outputting data, that data gets fed down the pipe into sort, which sorts its input and outputs down the pipe to more, which paginates the whole thing. This can affect what happens in case of an error; if you mistype "more," then nothing will happen. If you mistype "grep," then more and sort will have been started by the time the error is detected. In this example, that does not matter, but if commands further down the pipeline have some kind of permanent effect (say, if they create or modify a file), then the state of the system will have changed, even though the whole pipeline was never executed.

"Everything Is a File" and Pipelines

There are a few more key concepts that grew into Unix as well. One is the famous "everything is a file" design, whereby device drivers, directories, system configuration, kernel parameters, and processes are all represented as files on the filesystem. Everything, whether a plain-text file (for example, /etc/hosts), a block or character special device driver (for example, /dev/sda), or kernel state and configuration (for example, /proc/cpuinfo) is represented as a file.

The existence of pipes leads to a system whereby tools are written to assume that they will be handling streams of text, and indeed, most of the system configuration is in text form also. Configuration files can be sorted, searched, reformatted, even differentiated and recombined, all using existing tools.

The "everything is a file" concept and the four operations (open, close, read, write) that are available on the file mean that Unix provides a really clean, simple system design. Shell scripts themselves are another example of a system utility that is also text. It means that you can write programs like this:

```
#!/bin/sh
cat $0
echo "==="
tac $0
```

This code uses the cat facility, which simply outputs a file, and the tac tool, which does the same but reverses it. (The name is therefore quite a literal interpretation of what the tool does, and quite a typical example of Unix humor.) The variable $0 is a special variable, defined by the system, and contains the name of the currently running program, as it was called.

So the output of this command is as follows:

```
#!/bin/sh
cat $0
echo "==="
tac $0
===
tac $0
echo "==="
cat $0
#!/bin/sh
```

The first four lines are the result of cat, the fifth line is the result of the echo statement, and the final four lines are the output of tac.

BSD

AT&T/Bell Labs couldn't sell Unix because it was a telecommunications monopoly, and as such was barred from extending into other industries, such as computing. So instead, AT&T gave Unix away, particularly to universities, which were naturally keen to get an operating system at no cost. The fact that the schools could also get the source code was an extra benefit, particularly for administrators but also for the students. Not only could users and administrators run the OS, they could see (and modify) the code that made it work. Providing access to the source code was an easy choice for AT&T; they were not (at that stage) particularly interested in developing and supporting it themselves, and this way users could support themselves. The end result was that many university graduates came into the industry with Unix experience, so when they needed an OS for work, they suggested Unix. The use of Unix thus spread because of its popularity with users, who liked its clean design, and because of the way it happened to be distributed.

Although it was often given away at no cost or low cost and included the source code, Unix was not Free Software according to the Free Software Foundation's definition, which is about freedom, not cost. The Unix license prohibited redistribution of Unix to others, although many users developed their own patches, and some of those shared patches with fellow Unix licensees. (The patches would be useless to someone who didn't already have a Unix license from AT&T. The core software was still Unix; any patches were simply modifications to that.) Berkeley Software Distribution (BSD) of the University of California at Berkeley created and distributed many such patches, fixing bugs, adding features, and just generally improving Unix. The terms "Free Software" and "Open Source" would not exist for a long time to come, but all this was distributed on the understanding that if something is useful, then it may as well be shared. TCP/IP, the two core protocols of the Internet, came into Unix via BSD, as did BIND, the DNS (Domain Name System) server, and the Sendmail MTA (mail transport agent). Eventually, BSD developed so many patches to Unix that the project had replaced virtually all of the original Unix source code. After a lawsuit, AT&T and BSD made peace and agreed that the few remaining AT&T components of BSD would be rewritten or relicensed so that BSD was not the property of AT&T, and could be distributed in its own right. BSD has since forked into NetBSD, OpenBSD, FreeBSD, and other variants.

GNU

As mentioned previously, the GNU project was started in 1983 as a response to the closed source software that was by then being distributed by most computer manufacturers along with their hardware. Previously, there had generally been a community that would share source code among users, such that if anyone felt that an improvement could be made, they were free to fix the code to work as they would like. This hadn't been enshrined in any legally binding paperwork; it was simply the culture in which developers naturally operated. If someone expressed an interest in a piece of software, why would you not give him a copy of it (usually in source code form, so that he could modify it to work on his system? Very few installations at the time were sufficiently similar to assume that a binary compiled on one machine would run on another). As Stallman likes to point out, "Sharing of software...is as old as computers, just as sharing of recipes is as old as cooking."[1]

Stallman had been working on the Incompatible Timesharing System (ITS) with other developers at MIT through the 1970s and early 1980s. As that generation of hardware died out, newer hardware came out, and — as the industry was developing and adding features — these new machines came with bespoke operating systems. Operating systems, at the time, were usually very hardware-specific, so ITS and CTSS died as the hardware they ran on were replaced by newer designs.

 ITS was a pun on IBM's Compatible Time Sharing System (CTSS), which was also developed at MIT around the same time. The "C" in CTSS highlighted the fact that it was somewhat compatible with older IBM mainframes. By including "Incompatible" in its name, ITS gloried in its rebellious incompatibility.

Stallman's turning point occurred when he wanted to fix a printer driver, such that when the printer jammed (which it often did), it would alert the user who had submitted the job, so that she could fix the jam. The printer would then be available for everyone else to use. The user whose job had jammed the printer wouldn't get her output until the problem was fixed, but the users who had submitted subsequent jobs would have to wait even longer. The frustration of submitting a print job, then waiting a few hours (printers were much slower then), only to discover that the printer had already stalled before you had even submitted your own print job, was too much for the users at MIT, so Stallman wanted to fix the code. He didn't expect the original developers to work on this particular feature for him; he was happy to make the changes himself, so he asked the developers for a copy of the source code. He was refused, as the driver software contained proprietary information about how the printer worked, which could be valuable competitive information to other printer manufacturers.

What offended Stallman was not the feature itself, it was that one developer was refusing to share code with another developer. That attitude was foreign to Stallman, who had taken sharing of code for granted until that stage. The problem was that the software — in particular the printer driver — was not as free (it didn't convey the same freedoms) as previous operating systems that Stallman had worked with. This problem prevailed across the industry; it was not specific to one particular platform, so changing hardware would not fix the problem.

---

[1] *Free Software, Free Society*, 2002, Chapter 1. ISBN 1-882114-98-1

GNU stands for "GNU's Not Unix," which is a recursive acronym; if you expand the acronym "IBM," you get "International Business Machines," and you're done. If you expand "GNU," you get "GNU's Not Unix's Not Unix." Expand that, and you get "GNU's Not Unix's Not Unix's Not Unix" and so on. This is an example of "hacker humor," which is usually quite a dry sense of humor, with something a little bit clever or out of the ordinary about it. At the bottom of the grep *manpage, under the section heading "NOTES" is a comment: "GNU's not Unix, but Unix is a beast; its plural form is Unixen," a friendly dig at Unix.*

Richard Stallman is a strong-willed character (he has described himself as "borderline autistic"), with a very logical mind, and he determined to fix the problem in the only way he knew how: by making a new operating system that would maintain the old unwritten freedoms to allow equal access to the system, including the code that makes it run. As no such thing existed at the time, he would have to write it. So he did.

STALLMAN CHARGES AHEAD!

From CSvax:pur-ee:inuxc!ixn5c!ihnp4!houxm!mhuxi!eagle!mit-vax!mit-eddie!RMS@MIT-OZ

Newsgroups: net.unix-wizards,net.usoft

Organization: MIT AI Lab, Cambridge, MA

From: RMS%MIT-OZ@mit-eddie

Subject: new Unix implementation

Date: Tue, 27-Sep-83 12:35:59 EST

Free Unix!

Starting this Thanksgiving I am going to write a complete Unix-compatible software system called GNU (for Gnu's Not Unix), and give it away free to everyone who can use it. Contributions of time, money, programs and equipment are greatly needed.

To begin with, GNU will be a kernel plus all the utilities needed to write and run C programs: editor, shell, C compiler, linker, assembler, and a few other things. After this we will add a text formatter, a YACC, an Empire game, a spreadsheet, and hundreds of other things. We hope to supply, eventually, everything useful that normally comes with a Unix system, and anything else useful, including on-line and hardcopy documentation.

GNU will be able to run Unix programs, but will not be identical to Unix. We will make all improvements that are convenient, based on our experience with other operating systems. In particular, we plan to have longer filenames, file version numbers, a crashproof file system, filename completion perhaps, terminal-independent display support, and eventually a Lisp-based window system through which several Lisp programs and ordinary Unix programs can share a screen. Both C and Lisp will be available as system programming languages. We will have network software based on MIT's chaosnet protocol, far superior to UUCP. We may also have something compatible with UUCP.

Who Am I?

I am Richard Stallman, inventor of the original much-imitated EMACS editor, now at the Artificial Intelligence Lab at MIT. I have worked extensively on compilers, editors, debuggers, command interpreters, the Incompatible Timesharing System and the Lisp Machine operating system. I pioneered terminal-independent display support in ITS. In addition I have implemented one crashproof file system and two window systems for Lisp machines.

Why I Must Write GNU

I consider that the golden rule requires that if I like a program I must share it with other people who like it. I cannot in good conscience sign a nondisclosure agreement or a software license agreement.

So that I can continue to use computers without violating my principles, I have decided to put together a sufficient body of free software so that I will be able to get along without any software that is not free.

How You Can Contribute

I am asking computer manufacturers for donations of machines and money. I'm asking individuals for donations of programs and work.

One computer manufacturer has already offered to provide a machine. But we could use more. One consequence you can expect if you donate machines is that GNU will run on them at an early date. The machine had better be able to operate in a residential area, and not require sophisticated cooling or power.

Individual programmers can contribute by writing a compatible duplicate of some Unix utility and giving it to me. For most projects, such part-time distributed work would be very hard to coordinate; the independently-written parts would not work together. But for the particular task of replacing Unix, this problem is absent. Most interface specifications are fixed by Unix compatibility. If each contribution works with the rest of Unix, it will probably work with the rest of GNU.

If I get donations of money, I may be able to hire a few people full or part time. The salary won't be high, but I'm looking for people for whom knowing they are helping humanity is as important as money. I view this as a way of enabling dedicated people to devote their full energies to working on GNU by sparing them the need to make a living in another way.

For more information, contact me.

Unix already existed, was quite mature, and was nicely modular. So the GNU project was started with the goal of replacing the userland tools of Unix with Free Software equivalents. The kernel was another part of the overall goal, although one can't have a kernel in isolation — the kernel needs an editor, a compiler, and a linker to be built, and some kind of initialization process in order to boot. So existing proprietary software systems were used to assemble a free ecosystem sufficient to further develop itself, and ultimately to compile a kernel. This subject had not been ignored; the Mach microkernel had been selected in line with the latest thinking on operating system kernel design, and the HURD kernel has been available for quite some time, although it has been overtaken by a newer upstart kernel, which was also developed under, and can also work with, the GNU tools.

HURD is "Hird of Unix-Replacing Daemons," because its microkernel approach uses multiple userspace background processes (known as daemons in the Unix tradition) to achieve what the Unix kernel does in one monolithic kernel. HIRD in turn stands for "Hurd of Interfaces Representing Depth." This is again a recursive acronym, like GNU ("GNU's Not Unix") but this time it is a pair of mutually recursive acronyms. It is also a play on the word "herd," the collective noun for Gnus.

As the unwritten understandings had failed, Stallman would need to create a novel way to ensure that freely distributable software remained that way. The GNU General Public License (GPL) provided that in a typically intelligent style. The GPL uses copyright to ensure that the license itself cannot be changed; the rest of the license then states that the recipient has full right to the code, so long as he grants the same rights to anybody he distributes it to (whether modified or not) and the license does not change. In that way, all developers (and users) are on a level playing field, where the code is effectively owned by all involved, but no one can change the license, which ensures that equality. The creator of a piece of software may dual-license it, under the GPL and a more restrictive license; this has been done many times — for example, by the MySQL project.

One of the tasks taken on by the GNU project was — of course — to write a shell interpreter as free software. Brian Fox wrote the bash (Bourne Again SHell) shell — its name comes from the fact that the original /bin/sh was written by Steve Bourne, and is known as the Bourne Shell. As bash takes the features of the Bourne shell, and adds new features, too, bash is, obviously, the Bourne Again Shell. Brian also wrote the readline utility, which offers flexible editing of input lines of text before submitting them for parsing. This is probably the most significant feature to make bash a great interactive shell. Brian Fox was the first employee of the Free Software Foundation, the entity set up to coordinate the GNU project.

You've probably spotted the pattern by now; although bash isn't a recursive acronym, its name is a play on the fact that it's based on the Bourne shell. It also implies that bash is an improvement on the original Bourne shell, in having been "bourne again."

LINUX

Linus Torvalds, a Finnish university student, was using Minix, a simple Unix clone written by Vrije Universiteit (Amsterdam) lecturer Andrew Tanenbaum, but Torvalds was frustrated by its lack of features and the fact that it did not make full use of the (still relatively new) Intel 80386 processor, and in particular its "protected mode," which allows for much better separation between the kernel and userspace. Relatively quickly, he got a working shell, and then got GCC, the GNU C compiler (now known as the GNU Compiler Collection, as it has been extended to compile various flavors of C, Fortran, Java, and Ada) working. At that stage, the kernel plus shell plus compiler was enough to be able to "bootstrap" the system — it could be used to build a copy of itself.

TORVALDS' NEWSGROUP POST

On August 25, 1991, Torvalds posted the following to the MINIX newsgroup `comp.os.minix`:

From: torvalds@klaava.helsinki.fi (Linus Benedict Torvalds)
To: Newsgroups: comp.os.minix
Subject: What would you like to see most in minix?
Summary: small poll for my new operating system

Hello everybody out there using minix-

I'm doing a (free) operating system (just a hobby, won't be big and professional like gnu) for 386 (486) AT clones. This has been brewing since april, and is starting to get ready. I'd like any feedback on things people like/dislike in minix, as my OS resembles it somewhat (same physical layout of the file-sytem due to practical reasons) among other things.

I've currently ported bash (1.08) an gcc (1.40), and things seem to work. This implies that i'll get something practical within a few months, and I'd like to know what features most people want.

Any suggestions are welcome, but I won't promise I'll implement them :-)

Linus Torvalds torvalds@kruuna.helsinki.fi

What is interesting is that Torvalds took the GNU project's inevitable success for granted; it had been going for eight years, and had basically implemented most of its goals (bar the kernel). Torvalds also, after initially making the mistake of trying to write his own license (generally inadvisable for those of us who are not experts in the minutiae of international application of intellectual property law), licensed the kernel under the GNU GPL (version 2) as a natural license for the project.

In practice, this book is far more about shell scripting with Unix and GNU tools than specifically about shell scripting under the Linux kernel; in general, the majority of the tools referred to are GNU tools from the Free Software Foundation: grep, ls, find, less, sed, awk, bash itself of course, diff, basename, and dirname; most of the critical commands for shell scripting on Linux are GNU tools. As such, some people prefer to use the phrase "GNU/Linux" to describe the combination of GNU userspace plus Linux kernel. For the purposes of this book, the goal is to be technically accurate while avoiding overly political zeal. RedHat Linux is what RedHat calls its distribution, so it is referred to as RedHat Linux. Debian GNU/Linux prefers to acknowledge the GNU content so we will, too, when referring specifically to Debian. When talking about the Linux kernel, we will say "Linux"; when talking about a GNU tool we will name it as such. Journalists desperate for headlines can occasionally dream up a far greater rift than actually exists in the community. Like any large family, it has its disagreements — often loudly and in public — but we will try not to stoke the fire here.

 Unix was designed with the assumption that it would be operated by engineers; that if somebody wanted to achieve anything with it, he or she would be prepared to learn how the system works and how to manipulate it. The elegant simplicity of the overall design ("everything is a file," "do one thing and do it well," etc.) means that principles learned in one part of the system can be applied to other parts.

The rise in popularity of GNU/Linux systems, and in particular, their relatively widespread use on desktop PCs and laptop systems — not just servers humming away to themselves in dark datacenters — has brought a new generation to a set of tools built on this shared philosophy, but without necessarily bringing the context of history into the equation.

Microsoft Windows has a very different philosophy: The end users need not concern themselves with how the underlying system works, and as a result, should not expect it to be discernable, even to an experienced professional, because of the closed-source license of the software. This is not a difference in quality or even quantity; this is a different approach, which assumes a hierarchy whereby the developers know everything and the users need know nothing.

As a result, many experienced Windows users have reviewed a GNU/Linux distribution and found to their disappointment that to get something configured as it "obviously" should be done, they had to edit a text file by hand, or specify a certain parameter. This flexibility is actually a strength of the system, not a weakness. In the Windows model, the user does not have to learn because they are not allowed to make any decisions of importance: which kernel scheduler, which filesystem, which window manager. These decisions have all been made to a "one size fits most" level by the developers.

SUMMARY

Although it is quite possible to administer and write shell scripts for a GNU/Linux system without knowing any of the history behind it, a lot of apparent quirks will not make sense without some appreciation of how things came to be the way they are. There is a difference between scripting for a typical Linux distribution, such as RedHat, SuSE, or Ubuntu, and scripting for an embedded device, which is more likely to be running busybox than a full GNU set of tools. Scripting for commercial Unix is slightly different again, and much as a web developer has to take care to ensure that a website works in multiple browsers on multiple platforms, a certain amount of testing is required to write solid cross-platform shell scripts.

Even when writing for a typical Linux distribution, it is useful to know what is where, and how it came to be there. Is there an `/etc/sysconfig`? Are init scripts in `/etc/rc.d/init.d` or `/etc/init.d`, or do they even exist in that way? What features can be identified to see what tradition is being followed by this particular distribution? Knowing the history of the system helps one to understand whether the syntax is `tar xzf` or `tar -xzf`; whether to use `/etc/fstab` or `/etc/vfstab`; whether running `killall httpd` will stop just your Apache processes (as it would under GNU/Linux) or halt the entire system (as it would on Solaris)!

The next chapter follows on from this checkered history to compare the variety of choices available when selecting a Unix or GNU/Linux environment.

Getting Started

Before you can work through and test the code in this book, you will need to get some kind of Unix-like environment running. Since you are reading this book, it is likely that you already have access to a Unix or Linux system, but this chapter provides an overview of some of the choices available, how to get them, and how to get up and running with your test environment. It might also be worth considering running a virtual machine, or at least creating a separate account on your existing system when working on the code in this book.

Although GNU/Linux and the Bash shell is probably the most common operating system and shell combination currently in use, and that combination is the main focus of this book, there are lots of other operating systems available, and a variety of shells, too. For shell scripting, the choice of operating system does not make a huge difference much of the time, so this chapter focuses more on operating system and editor choices.

CHOOSING AN OS

First of all, it is worth mentioning that Linux is not the only option available; other freely available operating systems include the BSDs (FreeBSD, NetBSD, OpenBSD), Solaris Express, Nexenta, and others. However, there are many GNU/Linux distributions available, and these generally have support for the widest range of hardware and software. Most of these distributions can be downloaded and used totally legally, even for production use. Of the Linux distributions mentioned here, RedHat Enterprise Linux (RHEL) and SuSE Linux Enterprise Server (SLES) have restricted availability and access to updates; Oracle Solaris is restricted to a 90-day trial period for production use.

GNU/Linux

RHEL is the commercial distribution based on Fedora. It is particularly popular in North America and much of Europe. Because the RHEL media includes RedHat trademarks and some non-Free Software (such as the RedHat Cluster), distribution of the media is restricted to licensed customers. However, the CentOS project rebuilds RHEL from source, removing

RedHat trademarks, providing a Linux distribution that is totally binary and source code–compatible with RHEL. This can be very useful as a lot of commercial software for Linux is tested and supported only on RHEL, but those vendors will often also support the application running on CentOS, even if they do not support the OS itself.

RHEL itself is available by paid subscription only. However, CentOS and Oracle Enterprise Linux are two clones built by stripping the RedHat trademarks from the source code and rebuilding in exactly the same way as the RedHat binaries are built. CentOS is available from `http://centos.org/`, and Oracle Enterprise Linux is available from `http://edelivery.oracle.com/linux`.

Fedora is the community-maintained distribution that feeds into RHEL. It has a highly active, generally very technical user base, and a lot of developments tested in Fedora first are then pushed upstream (to the relevant project, be it GNOME, KDE, the Linux kernel, and so on). Like Ubuntu, it has six-month releases, but a much shorter one-year support cycle. The technologies that have been proven in Fedora make their way into RedHat Enterprise Linux. As with Ubuntu, KDE, XFCE, and LXDE respins are available as well as the main GNOME-based desktop. DVD images can be obtained from `http://fedoraproject.org/`.

SLES is Novell's enterprise Linux. It is based on OpenSUSE, which is the community edition. SLES and OpenSUSE are particularly popular in Europe, partly due to SuSE's roots as a German company before Novell purchased it in 2004. SuSE's biggest differentiator from other Linux distributions is its YaST2 configuration tool. SLES has a fairly stable release cycle; with a new major release every 2–3 years, it is updated more frequently than RHEL but less frequently than most other Linux distributions.

SLES is available for evaluation purposes from `http://www.novell.com/products/server/`. Like RedHat Enterprise Linux, a support contract is required to use the full version.

OpenSUSE is to SLES as Fedora is to RHEL — a possibly less stable but more community-focused, cutting-edge version of its Enterprise relative. Test versions are available before the official release. OpenSUSE is available from `http://software.opensuse.org/`. The main OpenSUSE website is `http://www.opensuse.org/`.

Ubuntu is based on the Debian "testing" branch, with additional features and customizations. It is very easy to install and configure, has lots of Internet forums providing support, and is a polished GNU/Linux distribution. Ubuntu offers a Long-Term Support (LTS) release once every 2 years, which is supported for 2 years on the desktop and 5 years for servers. There are also regular releases every 6 months, which are numbered as YY-MM, so the 10-10 release (Lucid Lynx) was released in October 2010. Although widely known for its desktop OS, the server version, without the graphical features, is growing in popularity.

Ubuntu can be installed in many ways — from a CD/DVD, a USB stick, or even from within an existing Windows installation. Instructions and freely downloadable media and torrents are available from `http://ubuntu.com/`. Many rebuilds of Ubuntu are also available: Kubuntu with KDE instead of GNOME and Xubuntu with the XFCE window manager, as well Edubuntu, which includes educational software, and the Netbook Edition tailored for netbook computers.

Debian is one of the older GNU/Linux distributions in mainstream use. It has a team of over 1,000 Debian developers, providing over 30,000 packages. The stable branch is generally released every 5 years or so, so the current stable release can be rather old, although plans are to increase the frequency of stable releases. The testing branch is popular with many users, providing the latest packages but without the unpredictability of the unstable branch. Debian CD/DVD images are available for direct download, or via BitTorrent, from www.debian.org/CD/.

Many hundreds of GNU/Linux distributions are available. The website http://distrowatch.com/ is an excellent resource with information on just about every distribution that exists, as well as other Unix and Unix-like software. Some other popular distributions worth highlighting include Gentoo, Damn Small Linux, Knoppix, Slackware, and Mandriva.

The BSDs

Berkeley Software Distribution, or BSD, is one of the oldest Unix flavors. It has split into a number of different developments, the main three of which are listed here. Each flavor of BSD has a different focus which determines its development style.

FreeBSD is probably the most accessible of the BSDs, with support for a wider variety of hardware. OpenBSD is a fork of NetBSD and is generally regarded as the most secure Unix system available, and although its development is often slower, the resulting system is incredibly stable and secure. OpenBSD is widely used as a router or firewall. As for version 4.9 which was released in May 2011, only two remotely exploitable security holes have ever been found in a default install of OpenBSD. Some operating systems find that many in one month.

NetBSD is the most portable of the BSDs, running on PC, Alpha, and PowerPC, as well as ARM, HPPA, SPARC/SPARC64, Vax, and many others.

Proprietary Unix

Oracle Solaris traces its roots back to 1983, and is arguably the most feature-full and actively developed enterprise OS on the market today. SunOS was originally based on BSD, but with the move to Solaris switched to the System V flavor of Unix. Solaris today comes with the original Bourne shell as /bin/sh, as well as ksh93, bash, csh, tcsh, and zsh shells. Solaris is available for SPARC and x86 architectures.

Oracle Solaris is available for download from http://www.oracle.com/technetwork/server-storage/solaris/downloads/index.html, which can be used for free in nonproduction use, or on a 90-day trial basis. Solaris Express is a technical preview of the version of Solaris currently in development. There is also OpenIndiana, a fork of OpenSolaris available at http://openindiana.org/, and Nexenta, another fork with a GNU user space, at http://nexenta.org/.

IBM AIX is IBM's Unix for the Power architecture, based on System V Unix. It is available in an Express edition (limited to four CPU cores and 8GB RAM), the Standard Edition (which does not have the scalability limitations), and the Enterprise Edition (which adds extra monitoring tools and features). At the time of this writing, the current version is AIX 7.1, released in September 2010.

HP-UX is HP's Unix offering, based on System V Unix. It runs on PA-RISC and Intel Itanium systems. At the time of this writing, the current version of HP-UX is 11iv3, released in April 2008.

Microsoft Windows

Cygwin is an environment that runs under Microsoft Windows, providing you with a fairly comprehensive GNU toolset. If you can't change to an OS that uses a shell natively, cygwin is a convenient way to get a fully functioning bash shell and the core utilities (ls, dd, cat — just about everything you would expect in your GNU/Linux distribution) without leaving Windows. This means that you have the GNU tools such as grep, sed, awk, and sort working exactly as they do under Linux. Note that cygwin is not an emulator — it provides a Windows DLL (cygwin1.dll) and a set of (mainly GNU) utilities compiled as Microsoft Windows executables (.exe). These run natively under Windows; nothing is emulated. Figure 2-1 shows cygwin in use. Notice that some of the binaries are named with the .exe extension used by Microsoft DOS and Windows.

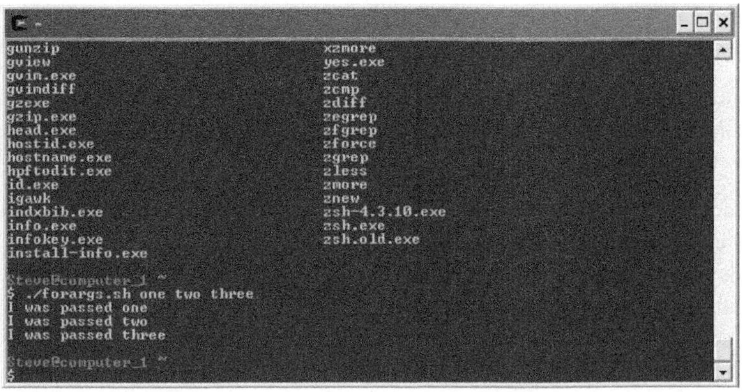

FIGURE 2-1

Cygwin is available from http://www.cygwin.com/.

CHOOSING AN EDITOR

A variety of text editors are available in most of the OSs mentioned previously. Word-processing software, such as OpenOffice.org, Abiword, or Microsoft Word, is not particularly suitable for programming, as these programs often make changes to the text, such as spell-checking, capitalization, formatting, and so on, which can break the script in unexpected ways. It is far better to use a plain-text editor, the most common of which you will look at here. Just because they do not add formatting to the actual file does not mean that these editors are at all lacking in powerful features; most offer syntax highlighting, and many offer further useful features for editing shell scripts as well as other text files.

Graphical Text Editors

For a graphical environment, a GUI-based editor can be easier to use. It is still vital to know how to use a nongraphical editor for situations where a GUI is not available (broken X Window system configuration, remote ssh to the server, serial access to server, and so on). However, for day-to-day use, some people find the convenience of a graphical editor to be useful.

Gedit

The default GNOME text editor is gedit, normally to be found under Applications ➪ Accessories ➪ gedit Text Editor. Gedit offers basic syntax highlighting, which can be useful when checking for syntax errors in your script. It also has tabbed windows and support for different text file formats (Windows, Linux, Mac OS line breaks, and character encodings). Figure 2-2 shows gedit in action.

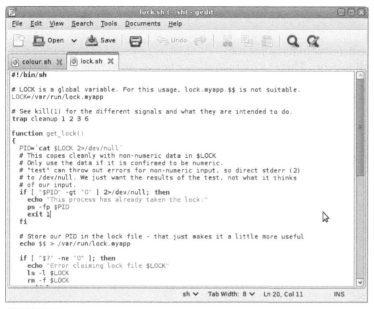

FIGURE 2-2

Kate

The default KDE text editor is kate. It offers syntax highlighting, multiple tabs, and so on, but also features a windowed shell so that you can edit your script and run it, all without leaving kate. Figure 2-3 shows kate running with a command window executing the shell script that is being edited by the editor.

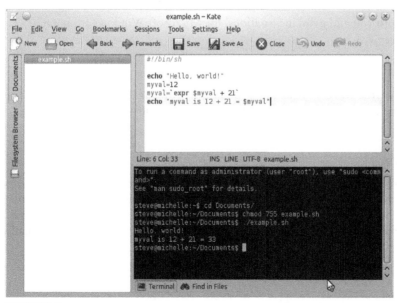

FIGURE 2-3

Kwrite is also available as part of KDE, although kwrite is more focused on writing short documents than writing code.

A graphical alternative to the hardcore commandline tool `vi` (which is provided in most Linux distributions as VIM [Vi IMproved] is gvim. This is a useful halfway house, providing some graphical features (it looks almost identical to gedit) while maintaining the familiar keystrokes of `vi` and `vim`. Figure 2-4 shows gvim in use, with two tabs editing two different scripts.

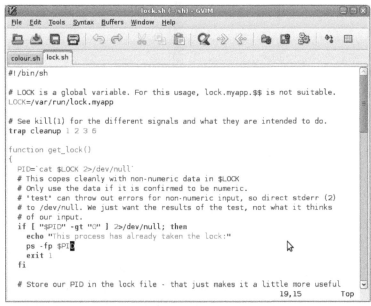

FIGURE 2-4

Vim is also available (in both vim and gvim incarnations) for Microsoft Windows from `http://www.vim.org/download.php#pc`.

Eclipse

Eclipse is a full IDE (Integrated Development Environment) by IBM. It is written with Java development in mind but can be used for shell scripting. It is overkill for most shell programming tasks, however.

Notepad++ for Windows

Notepad++ (`http://notepad-plus-plus.org/`) is a very powerful GPL (Free Software) editor for the Microsoft Windows environment. It offers syntax highlighting for many languages, powerful search options, and many additional features via the plugin infrastructure. It is very popular as a lightweight but full-featured text editor in the Windows environment. Figure 2-5 shows Notepad++ with its native Windows window decorations.

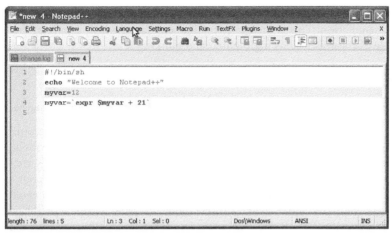

FIGURE 2-5

Terminal Emulation

GNOME has gnome-terminal; KDE has konsole. XFCE has a terminal emulator called simply "Terminal," with a stated aim of being a worthy alternative to gnome-terminal without the GNOME dependencies. There is also xterm, rxvt, and others. There is also the native "linux" terminal emulation, which is what you get when you log in to a Linux system without a graphical session.

Gnome-terminal is the default terminal in the GNOME environment. It uses profiles so you can define different appearance settings for different purposes. It also uses tabs, which can be shuffled and even detached from the original window.

Konsole is the default, and very flexible, terminal emulator in the KDE environment. It is found under the System menu. Some particularly nice things about Konsole include the ability to get a popup alert from KDE when the terminal either stays quiet for 10 full seconds (for example, when a long-running job finishes writing data to the terminal) or when the silence ends (for example, when a long-running job ends its silence and starts writing data to the terminal).

Another standout feature is the capability, through the profile settings, to define what constitutes a "word" when you double-click on it. If you want to be able to select an entire e-mail address by double-clicking it, make sure that the at sign (@) and the period (.) are in the list; if you want to be able to double-click $100 and select only the number, make sure that $ is not in the list.

If you need to run the same command on a set of systems, you can log in to each server in a different tab, and then select Edit ⇨ Copy Input To ⇨ All tabs in current window. Don't forget to deselect this as soon as you have finished.

The original terminal emulator for a graphical session is xterm. Although not as common any longer, it is well worth being familiar with xterm for those occasions when a more complete graphical environment is not available.

When you log in to a Linux system without graphical capabilities, or by pressing Ctrl+Alt+F1, you get the native Linux terminal emulation. This is the basic terminal emulator, which is part of the actual Linux OS. It is capable of color as well as highlighted and blinking text.

Nongraphical Text Editors

There are also a good number of command line–based text editors, each with different strengths.

Vi is by far the most widely used text editor among system administrators — it has quite a steep learning curve to start with, mainly because it can operate in two different modes — insert mode, where you can type text as normal in an editor, and command mode, where your keystrokes are interpreted as commands to perform on the text — and because it is difficult to tell which mode you are in at any given time. All that you really need to know about modes is to press Escape to enter command mode, and press i in command mode to enter Insert mode. Pressing Escape will always get you into command mode, so Escape+i will always get you into Insert mode. Once you have gotten the hang of that, and learned the first few of vi's many powerful commands, other editors will feel slow, awkward, and cumbersome by comparison. While vi is part of Unix, most GNU/Linux distributions include vim (Vi Improved), with vi as an alias to vim. Vim offers compatibility with vi, plus additional functionality, too. Vim comes with a `vimtutor` script, which walks you through tutorials using its many examples. Figure 2-6 shows the first page of `vimtutor`'s tutorial.

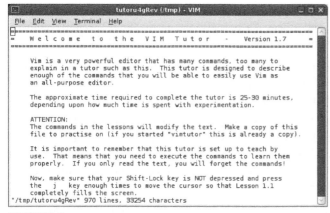

FIGURE 2-6

Emacs is another popular text editor, with an incredible amount of plugins. With a fully configured emacs setup, there is no need to ever go to the shell! It has been described as a "thermonuclear word processor." Like vim, emacs started out as a console, nongraphical text editor, but now has graphical versions, too. Being cross-platform from the start, emacs does not make any assumptions about what keys will be available on your keyboard, so the PC Ctrl key is referred to as Control, and the Alt key is known as the Meta key. These are written out as C- and M- respectively, so C-f, that is, holding down Control and the f key, moves the cursor forward by one character, while M-f, or holding down Alt and the f key, moves the cursor forward by one word. Use C-x C-s to save, and C-x C-c to quit.

There is a long-running but generally light-hearted rivalry between vi and emacs; as long as nobody is forced to use the "other" editor, vi and emacs users can generally agree to disagree. Figure 2-7 shows a graphical Emacs session running under the KDE desktop environment.

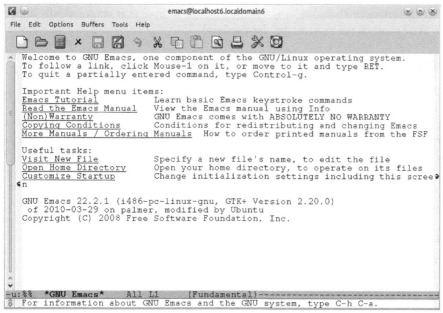

FIGURE 2-7

Pico and nano are rather more accessible text editors. Pico started as the editor for Washington University's pine e-mail client; nano is the GNU clone of pico and is the editor normally suggested on Ubuntu forums. Much like emacs, commands are sent via the Control key (for example, Ctrl-X to exit), but unlike emacs, there is always a context-sensitive menu displayed on the bottom of the screen, making the available choices much more obvious. Figure 2-8 shows nano editing an /etc/hosts file.

FIGURE 2-8

SETTING UP THE ENVIRONMENT

Unix and Linux are very customizable systems. You can set the environment (settings and variables that define how the shell behaves) to your liking in a number of ways. If there is something that you find yourself repeatedly setting or changing, it is usually possible to have that automatically done for you by the system. Here some of the most useful are explored.

The Shell Profile

One of the main places for putting your personalized tweaks is the ~/.profile ($HOME/.profile) file. When a new interactive shell is started, /etc/profile, followed by /etc/bash.bashrc (if a bash shell), ~/.profile, and finally ~/.bashrc are executed in that order. ~/.profile is read by all shells so it is best to put generic settings in there, and then bash-specific settings in ~/.bashrc. You can set variables and aliases here, and even run commands if you want to. Because the local (user-specific) versions of these files all reside in the home directory and begin with a period (.) so that a regular ls does not list them, they are often referred to as "dotfiles." There are many examples of dotfiles around the net; http://dotfiles.org/ is one useful repository.

Environment Variables

There are many environment variables that change the way the system works. You can set these interactively, or more usefully in your ~/.bashrc file.

PS1 Prompt

PS1 is the basic shell prompt; you can customize this. The default for bash is \s-\v\$, or "shell-version-dollar" — for example, bash-4.1$. Numerous settings are available — see the "Prompting" section of the bash man page for the full list. A common value for PS1 is \u@\h:\w$ — this displays the login name, the server name, and the current working directory. The following example:

```
steve@goldie:/var/log$
```

shows that you are logged in to the server "goldie" as the user "steve," and are currently in the /var/log directory.

In Debian, the default ~/.bashrc allows for color in the PS1 prompt, but it also comments that "the focus in a terminal window should be on the output of commands, not on the prompt." You can uncomment the force_color_prompt=yes line in that file if you really do want a color prompt.

PATH

You can set your PATH environment variable to tell the shell where to search for programs (and scripts) to be run. The main system commands are in /bin, /usr/bin, /sbin, and /usr/sbin, but you may have your own scripts in $HOME/bin, $HOME/scripts, /usr/local/bin, or elsewhere. Append these to the PATH so that they will be found by the shell even when you are not in that directory:

```
PATH=${PATH}:${HOME}/bin
```

Without the PATH, you will need to provide an explicit path (either absolute or relative) to the command. For example:

```
$ myscript.sh
bash: myscript.sh: command not found
$ /home/steve/bin/myscript.sh
  ... or:
$ cd /home/steve/bin
$ ./myscript.sh
```

From a security perspective, it is very bad practice to put a dot (.) in your PATH, especially at the front of the PATH. If you change into a directory and run a command (maybe ls), any program in that directory called ls will be run, and not the system /bin/ls program. Avoid having a colon at the start or end of the PATH, or a pair of colons with nothing between them, as that will have the same effect as a dot (.). Also, it is better to keep the system directories such as /usr/bin and /bin at the start of the PATH so that local scripts do not override system default ones. Therefore, use the syntax

```
PATH=$PATH:${HOME}/bin
```

rather than:

```
PATH=${HOME}/bin:$PATH
```

Tool-Specific Variables

Many system tools have their own variables; less adds the value of $LESS to its commands. ls adds $LS_OPTIONS. Your profile can therefore define useful shortcuts by setting these environment variables.

```
# define tool-specific settings
export LS_OPTIONS='--color=yes'
# Tidy up the appearance of less
export LESS='-X'
```

less also reads the $LESS_TERMCAP_* variables, which tell it about your terminal's capabilities. This is a useful sequence, which means that the codes hidden inside man pages (which are formatted by less) are interpreted as color changes.

```
# man pages in color
export LESS_TERMCAP_mb=$'\E[01;31m'
export LESS_TERMCAP_md=$'\E[01;31m'
export LESS_TERMCAP_me=$'\E[0m'
export LESS_TERMCAP_se=$'\E[0m'
export LESS_TERMCAP_so=$'\E[01;44;33m'
export LESS_TERMCAP_ue=$'\E[0m'
export LESS_TERMCAP_us=$'\E[01;32m'
```

variables

There are also a few widely recognized variables that may be used by many other tools to allow the system to be flexible to your needs. You can specify which text editor you want to use, and certain tools such as mail should use that value. You can also specify your preferred pagination tool — less and more are the two most common.

```
# define preferred tools
export EDITOR=vim
export PAGER=less
```

Your own scripts can make use of these variables to be more flexible to the user. Just use the ${EDITOR:-vim} syntax so that if $EDITOR is set then that command will be used, or if not set, you can provide a default for your application:

```
#!/bin/bash
${EDITOR:-vim} "$1"
echo "Thank you for editing the file. Here it is:"
${PAGER:-less} "$1"
```

edit.sh

This script will edit a file in your preferred $EDITOR and then display it back to you with your preferred $PAGER.

Aliases

Aliases provide mnemonics for aliases for frequently used, or hard-to-remember commands. Aliases can also be useful for specifying a default set of options where the command does not use a configuration file or environment variables for this. These can be put into your startup scripts to make everyday typing easier.

less

less has an -X option, which stops it from refreshing the screen after it has completed. This is very much a personal preference; if you wanted to less a file and then continue working with the file contents still visible in the terminal, you will want to use -X to stop the screen from being refreshed (much as if you had used cat on the file — its contents would be visible after the command has finished). However, if you want to be able to see what was displayed on the terminal before you invoked less, you would not want the -X option. Do try both and see which you prefer. If you want to use -X, you can set an alias in your ~/.bashrc file.

```
alias less="less -X"
```

Because the less command takes parameters from the $LESS environment variable mentioned previously, you can set that variable instead.

cp, rm, and mv Aliases

Because they are binary-compatible clones of RedHat Enterprise Linux, some Linux distributions — in particular RedHat, and therefore CentOS and Oracle Enterprise Linux — define some very careful aliases for the cp, rm, and mv commands. These are all aliased to their -i option, which causes them in an interactive shell to prompt for confirmation before removing or overwriting a file. This can be a very useful safety feature but quickly becomes irritating. If you find the defaults annoying, you can unset these aliases in `~/.bashrc`. The command `unalias rm` removes this aliasing, and similarly `unalias cp` and `unalias mv` reverts those commands, to their standard behavior, too.

> *If you know that a command (such as rm) is aliased, you can access the unaliased version in two ways. If you know the full path to the command is /bin/rm, you can type /bin/rm, which will bypass the alias definition. A simpler way to do this is to put a backslash before the command; \rm will call the unaliased rm command.*

ls Aliases

Because it is such a common command, there are a few popular `ls` aliases, the two most common being `ll` for `ls -l` and `la` for `ls -a`. Your distribution might even set these for you. Some popular `ls` aliases include:

```
# save fingers!
alias l='ls'
# long listing of ls
alias ll='ls -l'
# colors and file types
alias lf='ls -CF'
# sort by filename extension
alias lx='ls -lXB'
# sort by size
alias lk='ls -lSr'
# show hidden files
alias la='ls -A'
# sort by date
alias lt='ls -ltr'
```

Other Command Shortcuts

There are many other commands that you might use frequently and want to define aliases for. In a graphical session, you can launch a web browser and direct it straight to a particular website.

```
# launch webpages from terminal
alias bbc='firefox http://www.bbc.co.uk/ &'
alias sd='firefox http://slashdot.org/ &'
alias www='firefox'
```

Another very frequently used command is `ssh`. Sometimes this is as simple as `ssh hostname`, but sometimes quite complicated command lines are used with `ssh`, in which case an alias again is very useful.

Available for
download on
Wrox.com

```
# ssh to common destinations by just typing their name
# log in to 'declan'
alias declan='ssh declan'
# log in to work using a non-standard port (222)
```

```
alias work='ssh work.example.com -p 222'
# log in to work and tunnel the internal proxy to localhost:80
alias workweb='ssh work.example.com -p 222 -L 80:proxy.example.com:8080'
```

aliases

Changing History

Another feature of the shell that can be changed in your personalized settings is the history command. This is affected by some environment variables and some shell options (shopt). When you have multiple shell windows open at once, or multiple sessions logged in for the same user from different systems, the way that the history feature logs commands can get a bit complicated, and some history events may be overwritten by newer ones. You can set the histappend option to prevent this from happening.

Another potential problem with history is that it can take up a lot of disk space if you do not have much disk quota for your personal files. The HISTSIZE variable defines how many entries a shell session should store in the history file; HISTFILESIZE defines the maximum total size of the history file.

HISTIGNORE is a colon-separated list of commands that should not be stored in the history; these are often common commands such as ls, which are not generally very interesting to audit. From an auditing perspective, it is more useful to keep commands such as rm, ssh, and scp. Additionally, HISTCONTROL can tell history to ignore leading spaces (so that these two commands are both stored as rm and not as "   rm" (with the leading spaces before the command):

```
$ rm /etc/hosts
$    rm /etc/hosts
```

HISTCONTROL can also be told to ignore duplicates, so if one command was run multiple times, there may not be much point in storing that information in the history file. HISTCONTROL can be set to ignorespace, ignoredups, or ignoreboth. The history section of your ~/.bashrc could look like this:

Available for download on Wrox.com

```
# append, don't overwrite the history
shopt -s histappend

# control the size of the history file
export HISTSIZE=100000
export HISTFILESIZE=409600

# ignore common commands
export HISTIGNORE=":pwd:id:uptime:resize:ls:clear:history:"

# ignore duplicate entries
export HISTCONTROL=ignoredups
```

history

~/.inputrc and /etc/inputrc

/etc/inputrc and ~/.inputrc are used by GNU readline facility (used by bash and many other utilities to read a line of text from the terminal) to control how readline behaves. These configuration files are only used by shells that make use of the readline library (bash and dash, zsh) and are not used by any other shells — ksh, tcsh, and so on. This defines many of the handy things that bash gets credit for over Bourne shell, such as proper use of the cursor keys on today's PC keyboards. There is normally no need to edit this file, nor to create your own custom ~/.inputrc (the global /etc/inputrc normally suffices). It is useful to know what it contains in order to understand how your shell interacts with your keyboard commands. inputrc also defines 8-bit features so you may need to use this if you are working heavily with 7-bit systems.

Another useful bash option to know is

```
set completion-ignore-case On
```

which means that when you type cd foo and press the Tab key, if there is no foo* directory, the shell will search without case, so that any directories named Foo*, fOo* or fOO* will match.

Another bash option is to shut up the audible bell:

```
set bell-style visible
```

It is important to note that inputrc affects anything using the readline library, which is normally a good thing as it gives you consistency in the behavior of multiple different tools. I have never been aware of a situation where this caused a problem, but it is good to be aware of the impact of the changes.

~/.wgetrc and /etc/wgetrc

If you need to go via a proxy server, the ~/.wgetrc file can be used to set proxy settings for the wget tool. For example:

```
http_proxy = http://proxyserver.intranet.example.com:8080/
https_proxy = http://proxyserver.intranet.example.com:8080/
proxy_user = steve
proxy_password = letmein
```

You can also set equivalent variables in the shell.

The /etc/wgetrc file will be processed first, but is overruled by the user's ~/.wgetrc (if it exists).

You must use chmod 0600 ~/.wgetrc *for* ~/.wgetrc *to be processed — this is for your own protection; valid passwords should not be visible by anyone but yourself! If the permissions are any more open than 0600, wget will ignore the file.*

Vi Mode

People coming from a Unix background may be more comfortable with the ksh, both for interactive use as well as for shell scripting. Interactively, ksh scrolls back through previous commands via the Esc-k key sequence and searches history with the Esc-/ sequence. These are roughly equivalent to bash's up arrow (or ^P) and Ctrl-R key sequences, respectively. To make bash (or indeed the Bourne shell under Unix) act more like ksh, set the -o vi option:

```
bash$ set -o vi
bash$
```

Vim Settings

The following useful commands can be set in ~/.vimrc or manually from command mode. Note that vim uses the double quote (") character to mark comments. These samples should be fairly self-explanatory; these can also be set interactively from within a vim session, so typing :syntax on or :syntax off will turn syntax highlighting on or off for the rest of the current session. It can be useful to have all of your favorite settings predefined in ~/.vimrc.

```
$ cat ~/.vimrc
" This must be first, because it changes other options as a side effect.
set nocompatible

" show line numbers
set number

" display "-- INSERT --" when entering insert mode
set showmode

" incremental search
set incsearch
" highlight matching search terms
set hlsearch
" set ic means case-insensitive search; noic means case-sensitive.
set noic
" allow backspacing over any character in insert mode
set backspace=indent,eol,start
" do not wrap lines
set nowrap

" set the mouse to work in the console
set mouse=a
" keep 50 lines of command line history
set history=50
" show the cursor position
set ruler
" do incremental searching
set incsearch
" save a backup file
set backup

" the visual bell flashes the background instead of an audible bell.
```

```
set visualbell

" set sensible defaults for different types of text files.
au FileType c set cindent tw=79
au FileType sh set ai et sw=4 sts=4 noexpandtab
au FileType vim set ai et sw=2 sts=2 noexpandtab

" indent new lines to match the current indentation
set autoindent
" don't replace tabs with spaces
set noexpandtab
" use tabs at the start of a line, spaces elsewhere
set smarttab

" show syntax highlighting
syntax on

" show whitespace at the end of a line
highlight WhitespaceEOL ctermbg=blue guibg=blue
match WhitespaceEOL /\s\+$/
```

vimrc

SUMMARY

There are many operating systems, shells, and editors to choose from. In general, the choice of editor is a personal preference. The choice of operating system can be very significant in some ways, although for shell scripting purposes, many environments (all of the GNU/Linux distributions, Cygwin, and some proprietary Unixes, notably Solaris) today use GNU bash and the GNU implementations of standard Unix tools such as bc, grep, ls, diff, and so on. This book focuses on GNU/Linux, bash, and the GNU tools, but the vast majority also applies to their non-GNU equivalents.

I hope some of the customizations in the second part of the chapter will prove useful as you tweak the environment to customize the system to your personal preferences; the computer is there to make your life easier, and not the other way around, so if an alias means that you don't have to remember some complicated syntax, your mind is freed of distractions and you can concentrate on what you are actually trying to achieve, not on memorizing the exact syntax of some obscure command.

These first two introductory chapters should have prepared you to do some shell scripting; the rest of Part I covers the tools available and how to use them. The rest of the book builds on this introductory material with real-world recipes that you can use and build on, and so that you can be inspired to write your own scripts to perform real-world tasks to address situations that you face.

3

Variables

Without variables it is difficult to get much done: You can't count, loop, or read input from the user or the environment, and you can't change anything much. Without variables, you cannot write much more than a basic batch script (do one thing, then do another, then do something else). With variables, you can modify the script's behavior depending on the state of those variables, as well as modify the variables themselves to reflect the world beyond the script itself.

This chapter introduces the use of variables in the shell, and the syntax for setting and reading variables. It also lists some of the most common preset and standard shell variables and some useful shell options. Although a few of these variables are specific to bash, most of this chapter is generic across all shells. Chapter 7 goes into more depth on the more advanced things that bash (and some other shells) can do, such as arrays and more powerful parameter expansion features.

USING VARIABLES

A variable is a chunk of memory to which you can store arbitrary data, and retrieve it again, just by referencing its name. There is no need to explicitly allocate the memory required, and no need to free the memory after the need for it has gone. Although some languages have complex garbage-collection features, shell scripts generally tend to be working with relatively small amounts of data and for a reasonably short period of time, so a much simpler model suffices.

The shell is somewhat unique in the syntax for using variables. Many (such as Perl, PHP, and others) use a dollar sign prefix whenever the variable is referred to; others (such as Java or C) use no specific markup to identify a variable; the context is enough to make it clear that the code is referring to a variable.

*Sometimes you need a dollar sign to reference a variable (*echo $variable*) and sometimes you need to not have a dollar sign (*variable=foo*). Sometimes you need curly braces around the name (*echo ${variable}bar*) and sometimes it doesn't matter (*echo $variable bar*). There is logic behind these apparently arbitrary rules, so don't panic; it is all perfectly comprehensible.*

In the shell, when you refer to the value stored by a variable, you put a dollar symbol in front of the name of the variable:

```
$ echo $PATH
```

When you write to a variable, you simply use its name (the dollar sign here is just a prompt, not part of the variable reference):

```
$ PATH=/usr/sbin:/usr/bin:/sbin:/bin
```

This also means that you can refer to a variable's name and value by using the dollar sign when you want the value, but the name alone will be treated as a normal string when not part of an assignment statement:

```
$ YOUR_NAME=steve
$ echo "The variable YOUR_NAME is $YOUR_NAME"
The variable YOUR_NAME is Steve
```

Typing

In most languages, variables are associated with a "type," whether it's string, integer, boolean, float, or something else. Some languages are very strongly typed, which means that they will not allow an integer to be compared with a float, or a string to be assigned to a numeric variable, and so on (or will force you to cast them to the appropriate type, so it is at least clear what the programmer intends to happen). In the shell, there is no concept of a "type" at all; if anything, you could say that everything is a string, but that there are certain functions which will process a string as if the digits it contains were actually a number. In other languages, these errors would be caught at compile time; because a shell script is interpreted, never compiled, this is not possible.

Another peculiar thing about variables in the shell is that there is no need to explicitly declare them before using them — an unset variable is almost equivalent to a variable which contains the null string. No error is thrown when you refer to an undefined variable:

```
$ cat unset.sh
#!/bin/bash

echo "The variable YOUR_NAME is $YOUR_NAME"
YOUR_NAME="Steve"
echo "The variable YOUR_NAME is $YOUR_NAME"
$ ./unset.sh
The variable YOUR_NAME is
The variable YOUR_NAME is Steve
$
```

Assigning Values to Variables

There are three primary ways of assigning a value to a variable:

➤ Explicit definition: `VAR=value`

➤ Read: `read VAR`

➤ Command substitution: `VAR=`date``, `VAR=$(date)`

Explicit Definition: VAR=value

You can define the value of a variable (and in doing so, create the variable if it does not already exist in the environment) with the "x=y" syntax, as illustrated in the preceding `unset.sh` example. The syntax is important here, as a common mistake is to add whitespace, which changes the syntax profoundly.

No spaces are permitted around the equal sign. This can really irritate people who have a background in other languages where it makes no difference whether spaces are used or not — they generally are used to make the code clearer and easier to read. There is a reason for the shell's syntax being like this, as you will see in the next few paragraphs; the following three examples show the different ways in which spaces could be placed around the equal (=) sign, and why they are not valid variable assignments:

```
variable = foo
```

The preceding code is treated as one command (`variable`) with two arguments: = and `foo`; the syntax is exactly the same as `ls -l foo`. There is no rule which says that a command can't be called with = as its first argument, so there is no way for the shell to determine that variable assignment was intended. It may seem obvious that there is no command called `variable`, therefore variable assignment is implied. However, you don't know what commands might be available on any system which the script would run on, and you don't want your script to break just because some end user has created a file called `variable`.

```
variable =foo
```

Again, this is perfectly valid syntax equivalent to `ls =foo`, and therefore not a variable assignment.

```
variable= foo
```

This is a special case of a relatively widespread technique. To run a command with a certain environment without changing the environment of the calling shell, you can call the command prefixed by the variable assignment:

```
LD_LIBRARY_PATH=/usr/mozilla/lib firefox
```

This is a way to call Firefox and get it to run with the `LD_LIBRARY_PATH` variable set to `/usr/mozilla/lib` (the default place to look for system libraries would usually be just `/usr/lib`). So `LD_LIBRARY_PATH= firefox` would call Firefox with a blank `LD_LIBRARY_PATH`, which is exactly what would happen in the `variable= foo` syntax; the command `foo` would be called with a blank variable called `variable`.

Once you have assigned a variable in this way, you can access it by prefixing it with a dollar symbol:

```
$ variable=foo
$ echo $variable
foo
$
```

Read: read var

An interactive way to set a variable is with the read command:

```
$ cat first.sh
#!/bin/bash

read myvar
echo "myvar is $myvar"
```

If you run this script, it will prompt for one line of input, and set the myvar variable to what was typed in.

You can make this a bit easier by echoing a prompt first. The -n switch to echo tells echo not to put a newline character at the end, so the prompt and what is typed are displayed on the same line:

```
echo -n "Enter your name: "
read myvar
echo "Hello $myvar"
```

It will look like this when run interactively:

```
$ ./first.sh
Enter your name: Steve
Hello Steve
$ ./first.sh
Enter your name: Steve Parker
Hello Steve Parker
```

Notice that the entire line is read into the variable myvar — you can also use read to read in multiple variables in one go:

```
echo -n "Please enter your first name and last name: "
read firstname lastname
echo "Hello, $firstname. How is the $lastname family?"
```

The preceding code will read the two variables, ignoring any whitespace. The last variable on the line will take up any and all unread text from the line, so this inadvertently deals pretty well with double-barreled surnames:

```
$ ./firstlast.sh
Please enter your first name and last name: Steve Parker Smith
Hello, Steve. How is the Parker Smith family?
$
```

However, it doesn't cope well with too little input — the `lastname` variable will exist in the environment (which you can see by adding `set | grep name=` to the script), but it is set to the empty string:

```
$ cat firstlast.sh
#!/bin/bash

echo -n "Please enter your first name and last name: "
read firstname lastname
echo "Hello, $firstname. How is the $lastname family?"

echo "Relevant environment variables:"
set|grep "name="
$ ./firstlast.sh
Please enter your first name and last name: Steve Parker
Hello, Steve. How is the Parker family?
Relevant environment variables:
firstname=Steve
lastname=Parker
$ ./firstlast.sh
Please enter your first name and last name: Steve
Hello, Steve. How is the  family?
Relevant environment variables:
firstname=Steve
lastname=
$
```

In the preceding code there was a double space between "the" and "family," so the script displays "How is the $lastname family," but between those two spaces is a zero-length string, "$lastname." This kind of situation will be looked at more closely later in this chapter.

Reading from Files

You can also use the `read` command to read lines from files (actually, reading from the terminal is still reading from a file because in Unix everything is a file). The following code illustrates more clearly how to do this:

```
$ read message < /etc/motd
$ echo $message
Linux goldie 2.6.32-5-amd64 #1 SMP Fri Oct 15 00:56:30 UTC 2010 x86_64
$
```

However, there is more than one line in `/etc/motd`. The following code will read the line into a variable called `message`, looping around until there is no more input (`read` returns non-zero if an end-of-file was read, so the `while` loop ends — this will be looked at in greater detail in Chapter 6).

```
$ while read message
> do
>   echo $message
> done < /etc/motd
Linux goldie 2.6.32-5-amd64 #1 SMP Fri Oct 15 00:56:30 UTC 2010 x86_64

The programs included with the Debian GNU/Linux system are free software;
the exact distribution terms for each program are described in the
```

```
individual files in /usr/share/doc/*/copyright.

Debian GNU/Linux comes with ABSOLUTELY NO WARRANTY, to the extent
permitted by applicable law.
$
```

This directs the contents of /etc/motd into the loop, so the loop keeps on reading another line from /etc/motd (and echoing it out) until the message has been totally consumed. This line-by-line nature is shown better by introducing a slight pause in each step through the loop:

```
$ while read message
> do
>    echo $message
>    sleep 1
>    date
> done < /etc/motd
```

This time it takes 8 seconds to display the eight lines of text, which would be hard to show in a book, so the date command is also run every time to show that time is indeed progressing with every line read:

```
Linux goldie 2.6.32-5-amd64 #1 SMP Fri Oct 15 00:56:30 UTC 2010 x86_64
Mon Oct 25 19:49:32 BST 2010

Mon Oct 25 19:49:33 BST 2010
The programs included with the Debian GNU/Linux system are free software;
Mon Oct 25 19:49:34 BST 2010
the exact distribution terms for each program are described in the
Mon Oct 25 19:49:35 BST 2010
individual files in /usr/share/doc/*/copyright.
Mon Oct 25 19:49:36 BST 2010

Mon Oct 25 19:49:37 BST 2010
Debian GNU/Linux comes with ABSOLUTELY NO WARRANTY, to the extent
Mon Oct 25 19:49:38 BST 2010
permitted by applicable law.
Mon Oct 25 19:49:39 BST 2010
```

Command Substitution: VAR=`date`, VAR=$(date)

Another very common way of setting a variable is to set its value to the output of a given command. This is really a variant of the first format: VAR=value. If you want a variable set to "Monday" on Mondays, "Tuesday" on Tuesdays, and so on, you can use the %A flag to the date command, which tells date to give you the appropriate word for today, in the current locale. (The date command is discussed in more detail in Chapter 14.)

Most shells also allow for the VAR=$(date) syntax, but the original Bourne shell does not.

```
$ cat today.sh
#!/bin/bash

TODAY=`date +%A`
echo "Today is $TODAY"
$ ./today.sh
Today is Monday
$
```

Positional Parameters

When a shell script is called, it can be useful to pass arguments, or parameters, to the script — for example, the name of a file that you want the script to process. These are referred to within the script by the position they take on the command line: $0 is the name of the command itself, $1 is the first parameter, $2 is the second, and so on. You cannot change the values of these variables, they are a special case (normally, variables cannot start with a digit, so the shell does not interpret "1=hello" as a variable assignment at all).

A typical script using positional parameters looks like this — basename strips the path information, so ./params.sh, /usr/local/bin/params.sh, and ~/bin/params.sh will all report themselves as being params.sh:

```
$ cat params.sh
#!/bin/bash

echo "My name is `basename $0` - I was called as $0"
echo "My first parameter is: $1"
echo "My second parameter is: $2"
$ ./params.sh one two
My name is params.sh - I was called as ./params.sh
My first parameter is: one
My second parameter is: two
```

A script cannot know how many parameters it will be called with. The preceding script assumes that it will have two parameters, but it can be vital to check. This can also make scripts much more user-friendly, because they can give Usage messages if the proper usage of the script was clearly not known by the user. The $# variable tells a script how many parameters it was called with, as shown in the following examples. (The if statement would more commonly be written the other way around, if ["$#" -ne "2"] rather than if ["$#" -ne "2"], but this is hopefully more clear for this example.)

```
$ cat params.sh
#!/bin/bash

echo "My name is `basename $0` - I was called as $0"
echo "I was called with $# parameters."
if [ "$#" -eq "2" ]; then
  # The script was called with exactly two parameters, good. Let's continue.
  echo "My first parameter is: $1"
  echo "My second parameter is: $2"
else
  # The "$#" variable must tell us that we have exactly two parameters.
  # If not, we will tell the user how to run the script.
  echo "Usage: `basename $0` first second"
  echo "You provided $# parameters, but 2 are required."
```

```
fi
$ ./params.sh one two
My name is params.sh - I was called as ./params.sh
I was called with 2 parameters.
My first parameter is: one
My second parameter is: two
$ ./params.sh one two three
My name is params.sh - I was called as ./params.sh
I was called with 3 parameters.
Usage: params.sh first second
You provided 3 parameters, but 2 are required.
```

This works fine until you want to extend the script:

```
My eighth parameter is: $8
My ninth parameter is: $9
My tenth parameter is: $10
```

The variables $0 through $9 are defined, $10 does not exist and (even though this is inconsistent with other types of variables) is interpreted as $1 followed by a zero.

```
$ cat params.sh
#!/bin/bash

echo "My name is `basename $0` - I was called as $0"
echo "My first parameter is: $1"
echo "My second parameter is: $2"
echo "....."
echo "My eighth parameter is: $8"
echo "My ninth parameter is: $9"
echo "My tenth parameter is: $10"
$ ./params.sh one two three four five six seven eight nine ten eleven twelve
My name is params.sh - I was called as ./params.sh
My first parameter is: one
My second parameter is: two
.....
My eighth parameter is: eight
My ninth parameter is: nine
My tenth parameter is: one0
$
```

It has to be possible to take more than nine parameters: It is assumed that if you want a few, then $0 - $9 will be useful, but if you are dealing with many more than that it soon becomes cumbersome to have to explicitly say "$10, $11, $12, $13," and so on — you really want to say "get me the next one." The shift builtin command moves everything along by one, dropping $1, then $2, then $3, and so on, each time it gets called. You cannot get the shifted variables back, so make sure that you process them completely before calling shift!

```
$ cat manyparams.sh
#!/bin/bash

echo "My name is `basename $0` - I was called as $0"
echo "I was called with $# parameters."
count=1
while [ "$#" -ge "1" ]; do
```

```
    echo "Parameter number $count is: $1"
    let count=$count+1
    shift
done
$ ./manyparams.sh one two three
My name is manyparams.sh - I was called as ./manyparams.sh
I was called with 3 parameters.
Parameter number 1 is: one
Parameter number 2 is: two
Parameter number 3 is: three
$ ./manyparams.sh one two three four five six seven eight nine ten eleven twelve
My name is manyparams.sh - I was called as ./manyparams.sh
I was called with 12 parameters.
Parameter number 1 is: one
Parameter number 2 is: two
Parameter number 3 is: three
Parameter number 4 is: four
Parameter number 5 is: five
Parameter number 6 is: six
Parameter number 7 is: seven
Parameter number 8 is: eight
Parameter number 9 is: nine
Parameter number 10 is: ten
Parameter number 11 is: eleven
Parameter number 12 is: twelve
$
```

You can also shift a few variables at a time, with `shift n`. So to shift three variables, `shift 3` is equivalent to `shift; shift; shift`, although you may see the latter syntax more often, because it is more portable and, to some minds, a clearer expression of what is intended.

All the Parameters

The final two variables for reading the passed parameters are `$*` and `$@`. These are very similar, and are often confused. As you can see in the following code, the first four lines look identical regardless of the input, except that spaces are preserved if they are in double quotes when passed to the script, and they are also in double quotes when processed by the script. So the multiple spaces before "five" always get lost because they were not double-quoted when passed to the shell. The multiple spaces between "two" and "three" are preserved properly only when the script processes "$@" within double quotes (the last of the examples below).

```
$ cat star.sh
#!/bin/bash

echo Dollar Star is $*
echo "Dollar Star in double quotes is $*"
echo Dollar At is $@
echo "Dollar At in double quotes is $@"
echo
echo "Looping through Dollar Star"
for i in $*
do
    echo "Parameter is $i"
done
```

```
echo
echo "Looping through Dollar Star with double quotes"
for i in "$*"
do
   echo "Parameter is $i"
done
echo
echo "Looping through Dollar At"
for i in $@
do
   echo "Parameter is $i"
done
echo
echo "Looping through Dollar At with double quotes"
for i in "$@"
do
   echo "Parameter is $i"
done $ ./star.sh one "two   three" four        five  NO SPACING PRESERVED
Dollar Star is one two three four five ←━━━━━━━━━━┛
                                                          QUOTED SPACING PRESERVED
Dollar Star in double quotes is one two   three four five←━━━━━━┛
Dollar At is one two three four five ←━━━━━  NO SPACING APPARENTLY PRESERVED
Dollar At in double quotes is one two   three four five ←━━━━━┐
                                                    QUOTED SPACING PRESERVED

Looping through Dollar Star
Parameter is one  ←━━━━━━━━━  WITH $* AND NO QUOTES, EACH WORD IS
Parameter is two            TREATED AS A SEPARATE WORD
Parameter is three
Parameter is four
Parameter is five
                                        WITH "$*" THE WHOLE LIST IS TREATED
Looping through Dollar Star with double quotes  AS A SINGLE PARAMETER
Parameter is one two   three four five ←━━━━━━┛

Looping through Dollar At    $@ WITH NO QUOTES ACTS THE SAME AS $*
Parameter is one  ←━━━━┛
Parameter is two
Parameter is three
Parameter is four
Parameter is five

Looping through Dollar At with double quotes  "$@" PRESERVES WHAT THE CALLER
Parameter is one  ←━━━━━━━━━━  PRESUMABLY INTENDED; "TWO THREE" IS
                                              A SINGLE ARGUMENT, WITH THE SPACES
Parameter is two   three      BETWEEN THOSE WORDS PRESERVED
Parameter is four
Parameter is five
$
```

In the next chapter, you will see what happens if the parameters themselves contain special characters.

Return Codes

In Unix and Linux, every command returns a numeric code, between 0 and 255 — that is, 1 byte (although -1 wraps around to be the same as 255, and -2 becomes 254 and so on). This is a way of indicating success or failure, and sometimes more detailed information, too. The shell sets the $? variable to be the return code of the last-run command. For example, there are many ways that grep can fail — most commonly the string does not exist in the file:

```
$ grep nutty /etc/hosts
$ echo $?
1
$
```

Or that an error occurred, such as the file not existing, being unreadable, and so on:

```
$ grep goldie /etc/hosttable
grep: /etc/hosttable: No such file or directory
$ echo $?
2
$
```

In practice for grep, a return code of 1 means "no match" and 2 or above means that some kind of error occurred within grep itself, such as file not found.

If the command succeeds — no errors in executing and it also finds a match — then by tradition it will return an exit code of zero, indicating success:

```
$ grep goldie /etc/hosts
192.168.1.13     goldie
$ echo $?
0
$
```

This is useful for taking different action based on the results of another command. Sometimes you might want to use this to take corrective action if what you were trying to do failed. At other times, you might be quite happy that the command failed; you simply wanted to find out if it would succeed or not.

Background Processes

While background processes are dealt with in more detail in Chapter 10, it is worth mentioning here that you can run processes in the background and find their process ID (PID) in the $! variable. This can be useful for keeping track of your background processes. Do be aware that race conditions can come in here if you are not careful:

```
#!/bin/sh
ls -R /tmp &
sleep 10
strace -p $!
```

In this (admittedly artificial) example, if the ls command takes more than 10 seconds to execute, you will find yourself tracing it with strace 10 seconds into its run. However, if ls takes less time than that, the PID of your ls will be out of date — it is likely that there will be no such PID in the current process tree, so strace will fail. It is also possible, especially on a highly loaded system, that another process will have been assigned that PID while you were sleeping. You will then end up tracing an entirely unrelated process.

Reading Multiple Variables Simultaneously

As briefly mentioned earlier in this chapter, you can read multiple variables in one statement. This script reads the first line from a data file and assigns the words to the variables named:

```
$ cat datafile
the quick brown fox
$ read field1 field2 field3 < datafile
$ echo Field one is $field1
Field one is the
$ echo Field two is $field2
Field two is quick
$ echo Field three is $field3
Field three is brown fox
```

If there are not enough input fields, then some variables will be empty:

```
$ echo the quick > datafile
$ read field1 field2 field3 < datafile
$ echo Field one is $field1
Field one is the
$ echo Field two is $field2
Field two is quick
$ echo Field three is $field3
Field three is
$
```

> **GOTCHA**
>
> One common gotcha is to use a syntax like this to set $one=1, $two=2, $three=3, and $four=4:
>
> ```
> echo 1 2 3 4 | read one two three four
> ```
>
> This does not work as expected: The piped read command lives only as long as the pipeline itself, and the calling shell does not get the variables set.

Reading with While

This recipe reads the first two words from each line of /etc/hosts. Because of the way that read-line works, the aliases variable picks up any and all aliases. Note that it does not deal well with unexpected input, such as comment lines (where it says "IP is # - its name is The"). grep -v "^#" | while read would be a better method in real life.

```
$ while read ip name alias
> do
>   if [ ! -z "$name" ]; then
>       # Use echo -en here to suppress ending the line;
>       # aliases may still be added
>       echo -en "IP is $ip - its name is $name"
```

```
>     if [ ! -z "$aliases" ]; then
>       echo "   Aliases: $aliases"
>     else
>       # Just echo a blank line
>       echo
>     fi
>   fi
> done < /etc/hosts
IP is 127.0.0.1 - its name is localhost   Aliases: spo
IP is # - its name is The   Aliases: following lines are desirable for IPv6 capable
 hosts
IP is ::1 - its name is localhost   Aliases: ip6-localhost ip6-loopback
IP is fe00::0 - its name is ip6-localnet
IP is ff00::0 - its name is ip6-mcastprefix
IP is ff02::1 - its name is ip6-allnodes
IP is ff02::2 - its name is ip6-allrouters
IP is 192.168.1.3 - its name is sky
IP is 192.168.1.5 - its name is plug
IP is 192.168.1.10 - its name is declan   Aliases: declan.steve-parker.org
IP is 192.168.1.11 - its name is atomic
IP is 192.168.1.12 - its name is jackie
IP is 192.168.1.13 - its name is goldie   Aliases: smf   sgp
IP is 192.168.1.227 - its name is elvis
IP is 192.168.0.210 - its name is dgoldie   Aliases: intranet ksgp
$
```

Unsetting Variables

Sometimes you will want to unset a variable. This will free up the memory that it occupies, and will, of course, affect any subsequent references to that variable. The command is simply `unset`, and it works as follows:

```
$ echo $myvar

$ myvar=hello
$ echo $myvar
hello
$ unset myvar
$ echo $myvar

$
```

You can achieve almost the same thing by setting the variable to the null string, although as you will see later in this section, this is not always exactly the same as being unset:

```
$ myvar=hello
$ echo $myvar
hello
$ myvar=
$ echo $myvar

$
```

> *Some variables cannot be unset; these are referred to as the "read-only" variables. You can't unset $1, $2, $#, and so on.*
>
> *Some other variables (RANDOM, SECONDS, LINENO, HISTCMD, FUNCNAME, GROUPS, and DIRSTACK) can be unset, but you can't then get back the special functionality which they had before ($RANDOM will no longer return random numbers after it has been unset, and so on).*

Note that the first line of code accessed the `myvar` variable before it had been assigned a value, but no error was reported when the `echo $myvar` command was executed. There is no concept in the shell of declaring variables: Because they have no type, there is no need to specify that you need to have an int, char, float, and so on, so variables are implicitly declared when first given a value. Accessing the value of a non-existent variable simply returns the blank string, or zero, depending upon the context.

This makes shell scripting simpler and cleaner than most languages, though it does so at a great price: It is very hard to find a mis-typed variable name when debugging a script, for example. Where is the bug in the following code to calculate the length of the hypotenuse of a Pythagorean triangle?

```
$ cat hypotenuse.sh
#!/bin/sh

# calculate the length of the hypotenuse of a Pythagorean triangle
# using hypotenuse^2 = adjacent^2 + opposite^2
echo -n "Enter the Adjacent length: "
read adjacent
echo -n "Enter the Opposite length: "
read opposite
osquared=$(($opposite ** 2))          # get o^2
asquared=$(($adjacent ** 2))          # get a^2
hsquared=$(($osquered + $asquared))    # h^2 = a^2 + o^2
hypotenuse=`echo "scale=3;sqrt ($hsquared)" | bc`
   # bc does sqrt
echo "The Hypotenuse is $hypotenuse"
```

It's the kind of bug that can be hard to pin down. In this example, you know you are looking for a typo. If you don't know whether it's a typing error or a syntax error, it can be very hard to track down. Worse still, sometimes you may not even notice that there is an error, because no error is reported when the script is run, and output is produced.

The bug, if you missed it (other than the fact that this simple script takes only whole numbers), is in the line:

```
hsquared=$(($osquered + $asquared))
```

`$osquered` should be `$osquared`. There is no variable `$osquered`, so it is silently replaced with a zero. As a result, the Opposite length is canceled out entirely, and all you achieve is to square the Adjacent length, add zero to it, and then take the square root of that, which will always give you back the original value for the Adjacent.

PRESET AND STANDARD VARIABLES

There are a few variables which are provided by the shell itself. These vary in nature quite a bit: Some of them are purely informational, such as $BASH_VERSION, which tells you the version of bash that you are running (for example, 4.1.5(1)-release), but which you can override simply by setting them. Others return a different value depending on the current environment, such as $PIPESTATUS, which tells you the return codes of the commands in the last-run pipeline, and still others return a different value depending on some function of their own (such as $SECONDS, an integer which goes up by one every second). Also, some of these variables lose their special meaning if you set (or unset) them: $RANDOM will keep returning random numbers until you assign it a value, after which it will not produce random numbers again. $SECONDS will always keep counting; if you set SECONDS=35 and then read $SECONDS again 5 seconds later, it will have counted up to 40. Still others are not writeable at all; you will get an error message if you try setting UID, for instance. There are yet others, like TIMEFORMAT, which do nothing by themselves, but are used to affect how other commands work.

The following examples include some of the more common and useful predefined variables, as well as some that are less well known.

BASH_ENV

BASH_ENV is the name of a file (which may be a relative path, in which case be very careful about where you run your scripts from!) which is parsed before executing the file, much as ~/.bashrc is parsed before starting an interactive shell.

BASHOPTS

BASHOPTS is new in bash 4.1. It is a list of the enabled shell options (shopts). It gives the same information as shopt | grep -w on , but in a more easily machine-parsable manner. This is a read-only variable; you can change what it reports with the shopt builtin (-s to set a flag, -u to unset it):

```
$ shopt mailwarn
mailwarn               off
$ echo $BASHOPTS
checkwinsize:cmdhist:expand_aliases:extquote:force_fignore:hostcomplete:interactive
_comments:progcomp:promptvars:sourcepath
$ shopt -s mailwarn
$ shopt mailwarn
mailwarn               on
$ echo $BASHOPTS
checkwinsize:cmdhist:expand_aliases:extquote:force_fignore:hostcomplete:interactive
_comments:mailwarn:progcomp:promptvars:sourcepath
$ shopt -u mailwarn
$ shopt mailwarn
mailwarn               off
$ echo $BASHOPTS
checkwinsize:cmdhist:expand_aliases:extquote:force_fignore:hostcomplete:interactive
_comments:progcomp:promptvars:sourcepath
$
```

There are 40 shell options in bash 4.1, all documented in the bash man page; some of the more useful and interesting options are:

➤ **checkhash** — This will check to see if a hashed PATH entry still exists before attempting to execute the file.

➤ **checkwinsize** — This updates the LINES and COLUMNS variables after every command (effectively, as part of PROMPT_COMMAND); this means that if you resize the window and run a command which uses these variables (such as top), the running shell will automatically pick up the new window size. Without this flag, the resize command must be run manually to pick up the new window size.

➤ **cmdhist** — This reduces multi-line commands, such as:

```
$ for i in `seq 10 -1 1`
> do
>    echo -en "${i} ..."
> done ; echo "boom"
10 ...9 ...8 ...7 ...6 ...5 ...4 ...3 ...2 ...1 ...boom
$
```

which will be collapsed into a single line in the shell history, like this:

```
for i in `seq 10 -1 1`; do   echo -en "${i} ..."; done; echo "boom"
```

➤ **hostcomplete** — This is a nifty trick of bash which extends command completion to host names. If I want to log in to host declan from atomic, I can type:

```
steve@atomic:~$ ssh steve@de <tab>
```

and bash will find declan in /etc/hosts, and expand the command to ssh steve@declan. This works with /etc/hosts, but not DNS; the lookup would not be possible in the same way.

➤ **login_shell** — This is set if the current shell is a login shell; it is read-only.

SHELLOPTS

SHELLOPTS is similar to BASHOPTS; it is a list of -o options set. So if you set -o vi, then vi will appear in the list of options, and the shell will work in its vi mode (as discussed earlier in "Setting up the Environment" in Chapter 2. Like BASHOPTS, SHELLOPTS is read-only. You can use one of two different methods to set most of these; some only work with one method or the other. Here, you can use either syntax to turn the errexit feature on (-e, or -o errexit), and then off again (+e or +o errexit):

```
$ echo $SHELLOPTS
braceexpand:emacs:hashall:histexpand:history:interactive-comments:monitor
$ set -e
$ echo $SHELLOPTS
braceexpand:emacs:errexit:hashall:histexpand:history:interactive-comments:monitor
$ set +o errexit
$ echo $SHELLOPTS
braceexpand:emacs:hashall:histexpand:history:interactive-comments:monitor
$
```

Again, these are all documented in the set builtin section of the bash man page, but here are a few of the more commonly used options. A lot of these shell options also work in other shells:

➤ **-e / -o errexit** — Exit if any command returns a non-zero exit status code. This can be useful if you are sure that every single command in a script must succeed, and that exiting otherwise is the safest thing to do.

➤ **-f / -o noglob** — Disables pathname expansion.

➤ **-m / -o monitor** — If set (which it is by default), when a background command completes, you will get a line the next time bash displays a new prompt:

```
$ ls /tmp &
[1] 2922
keyring-UDudcH
orbit-steve
OSL_PIPE_1000_SingleOfficeIPC_54f1d8557767a73f9bc36a8c3028b0
pulse-Mm0m5cufbNQY
ssh-EwfFww1963
svd1b.tmp
[1]+  Done                    ls /tmp
$
```

➤ **pipefail** — This is an alternative to the PIPESTATUS variable; if off (which is the default), the return code of a pipeline will be that of the rightmost command that returned a non-zero exit status. So, if you have a pipeline that fails part way through (you have no IP addresses here starting with 192.167, so the grep fails, but the cat and cut commands work fine), it is difficult to tell if grep succeeded or not:

```
$ cat /etc/hosts | grep 192.167 | cut -f1
$ echo $?
0
```

The cut command succeeded, so you get a return code of zero (indicating success), which is probably not really what you want. However, when you set pipefail, you detect the error from any of the commands in the pipeline:

```
$ set -o pipefail
$ cat /etc/hosts | grep 192.167 | cut -f1
$ echo $?
1
$
```

➤ **-o vi** — This changes from emacs to vi mode.

➤ **-x** — This displays every command before it executes it. This is particularly useful in debugging shell scripts: #!/bin/sh -x at the start of the script, or set -x in the script (set +x disables it again), or even sh -x myscript.sh See also the BASH_XTRACEFD variable later in this section. Each line is preceded by the value of the PS4 variable, which is "+" by default:

```
$ cat x.sh
#!/bin/bash
echo "Hello, world!"
if [ "$?" -eq "0" ]; then
  # comments are ignored
```

```
        echo "Hurray, it worked!"
    else
        echo "Oh no, echo failed!"
    fi
$ sh -x x.sh
+ echo Hello, world!
Hello, world!
+ [ 0 -eq 0 ]
+ echo Hurray, it worked!
Hurray, it worked!
$
```

You can see here that the test ["$?" -eq "0"] is expanded with the values, so the test being evaluated is [0 -eq 0].

BASH_COMMAND

BASH_COMMAND is the name of the currently executing command. This is not much use most of the time, but shell builtins (such as trap) do not count. It can be useful in a trap call to explain what was happening at the time of the interrupt. This simple recipe runs a sequence of commands, and tells you what the script was doing when you pressed ^C to interrupt it. You are most likely to catch this script during a sleep call:

```
$ cat trap.sh
#!/bin/bash

trap cleanup 1 2 3 15

cleanup()
{
  echo "I was running \"$BASH_COMMAND\" when you interrupted me."
  echo "Quitting."
  exit 1
}

while :
do
  echo -en "hello. "
  sleep 1
  echo -en "my "
  sleep 1
  echo -en "name "
  sleep 1
  echo -en "is "
  sleep 1
  echo "$0"
done
$ ./trap.sh
hello. my name is ./trap.sh
hello. my ^CI was running "sleep 1" when you interrupted me.
Quitting.
$
```

If you remove the `sleep` commands, you will catch it in an `echo`, or processing the `:` test for the `while` loop:

```
$ ./trap.sh
hello. my name is ./trap.sh
hello. my name is ./trap.sh
hello. my name is ./trap.sh
^Chello. I was running "echo -en "hello. "" when you interrupted me.
Quitting.
$
```

BASH_SOURCE, FUNCNAME, LINENO and BASH_LINENO

BASH_SOURCE, FUNCNAME, LINENO and BASH_LINENO are incredibly useful debugging variables that tell you just where you are in the script, even when you have multiple files in use. LINENO simply gives you the current line number in the script:

```
$ cat lineno.sh
#!/bin/bash

echo "Hello, World"
echo "This is line $LINENO"
$ ./lineno.sh
Hello, World
This is line 4
$
```

This can be useful for debugging and indeed for getting useful information from end users. Instead of reporting "Error occurred in the fourth debugging point," your script can give the exact line number, giving you pinpoint accuracy in the diagnosis of any problems with the script. It can be useful, however, to know which function you are in at the time, and FUNCNAME tells you that and more. It also gives you the full call stack, showing how you got to be in that function in the first place:

```
$ cat funcname.sh
#!/bin/bash

function func1()
{
  echo "func1: FUNCNAME0 is ${FUNCNAME[0]}"
  echo "func1: FUNCNAME1 is ${FUNCNAME[1]}"
  echo "func1: FUNCNAME2 is ${FUNCNAME[2]}"
  echo "func1: LINENO is ${LINENO}"
  func2
}

function func2()
{
  echo "func2: FUNCNAME0 is ${FUNCNAME[0]}"
  echo "func2: FUNCNAME1 is ${FUNCNAME[1]}"
  echo "func2: FUNCNAME2 is ${FUNCNAME[2]}"
  echo "func2: LINENO is ${LINENO}"
```

```
}

func1
```

```
$ ./funcname.sh
func1: FUNCNAME0 is func1
func1: FUNCNAME1 is main
func1: FUNCNAME2 is
func1: LINENO is 8
func2: FUNCNAME0 is func2
func2: FUNCNAME1 is func1
func2: FUNCNAME2 is main
func2: LINENO is 17
$
```

So in func2, you can see that FUNCNAME[0] is the name of the function you are in, FUNCNAME[1] is the function that called you, and FUNCNAME[2] is the function (well, actually the main script, hence the special name "main") which called func1. That is all very useful and interesting, but what about when you have various library files containing different functions?

```
$ cat main1.sh
#!/bin/bash
. lib1.sh
. lib2.sh

func1
```

```
$ cat lib1.sh
function func1()
{
  echo "func1: FUNCNAME0 is ${FUNCNAME[0]}"
  echo "func1: FUNCNAME1 is ${FUNCNAME[1]}"
  echo "func1: FUNCNAME2 is ${FUNCNAME[2]}"
  echo "func1: BASH_SOURCE0 is ${BASH_SOURCE[0]}"
  echo "func1: BASH_SOURCE1 is ${BASH_SOURCE[1]}"
  echo "func1: BASH_SOURCE2 is ${BASH_SOURCE[2]}"
  echo "func1: LINENO is ${LINENO}"
  func2
}
$ cat lib2.sh
function func2()
{
  echo "func2: FUNCNAME0 is ${FUNCNAME[0]}"
  echo "func2: FUNCNAME1 is ${FUNCNAME[1]}"
  echo "func2: FUNCNAME2 is ${FUNCNAME[2]}"
  echo "func2: BASH_SOURCE0 is ${BASH_SOURCE[0]}"
  echo "func2: BASH_SOURCE1 is ${BASH_SOURCE[1]}"
  echo "func2: BASH_SOURCE2 is ${BASH_SOURCE[2]}"
  # This comment makes lib2.sh different from lib1.sh
  echo "func2: LINENO is ${LINENO}"
}
```

```
$ ./main1.sh
```

```
func1: FUNCNAME0 is func1
func1: FUNCNAME1 is main
func1: FUNCNAME2 is
func1: BASH_SOURCE0 is lib1.sh
func1: BASH_SOURCE1 is ./main1.sh
func1: BASH_SOURCE2 is
func1: LINENO is 9
func2: FUNCNAME0 is func2
func2: FUNCNAME1 is func1
func2: FUNCNAME2 is main
func2: BASH_SOURCE0 is lib2.sh
func2: BASH_SOURCE1 is lib1.sh
func2: BASH_SOURCE2 is ./main1.sh
func2: LINENO is 10
$
```

Here, func1 knows that FUNCNAME[0] is func1, and BASH_SOURCE[0] is lib1.sh, and the LINENO line is on line 9 of that file. Similarly, func2 knows that BASH_SOURCE[0] is lib2.sh, and FUNCNAME[0] is func2, and LINENO is on line 10 of that file. Here, using LINENO by itself would have been totally useless; without BASH_SOURCE, you would have to hard-code the filename into the echo statement itself, and if you're doing that you might as well hard-code the line number in — that function could easily find itself in various different files over time, and you can be sure that at some point it would not be noticed that it was displaying the name of some different file in an error message.

```
$ cat err1.sh
#!/bin/bash
. elib1.sh
. elib2.sh

func1
$ cat elib1.sh
. errlib.sh
function func1()
{
  err $LINENO this is func1, does it get it right?
  func2
}
$ cat elib2.sh
. errlib.sh
function func2()
{
  err $LINENO this is func2, does it get it right?
}
$ cat errlib.sh
function err()
{
  echo
  echo "*************************************************************"
  echo
  echo -en "error: Line $1 in function ${FUNCNAME[1]}"
  echo "which is in the file ${BASH_SOURCE[1]}"
```

```
    shift
    echo "error: Message was: $@"
    echo
    echo "*********************************************************"
    echo
}
$ ./err1.sh
*********************************************************
error: Line 4 in function func1 which is in the file elib1.sh
error: Message was: this is func1, does it get it right?
*********************************************************

*********************************************************
error: Line 4 in function func2 which is in the file elib2.sh
error: Message was: this is func2, does it get it right?
*********************************************************
$
```

Here in errlib.sh, you have a useful and fully generic error-reporting library, which can be used by many different scripts, and put in a toolkit of generic debugging tools.

LINENO has to be passed to the err() function because it does change all the time, and it is not an array, unlike the other two variables. (If it was an array, you would be able to refer to LINENO[1] as you refer to FUNCNAME[1] and BASH_SOURCE[1].) As you are passing on a parameter to the err() function, you might as well add your own customized error message along with it, too. The customized message also helps to demonstrate what is happening in the preceding output. However, you can make one final optimization: Bash adds the BASH_LINENO variable, which is an array; the bash man page says that "${BASH_LINENO[$i]} is the line number in the source file where ${FUNCNAME[$i]} was called (or ${BASH_LINENO[$i-1]} if referenced within another shell function)" so ${BASH_LINENO[0]} provides the relevant line number:

```
$ cat errlib2.sh
function err()
{
  echo
  echo "*********************************************************"
  echo
  echo -en "error: Line ${BASH_LINENO[0]} in function ${FUNCNAME[1]} "
  echo "which is in the file ${BASH_SOURCE[1]}"
  echo "error: Message was: $@"
  echo
  echo "*********************************************************"
  echo
}
$
```

 If you unset any of these variables, they lose their special function.

SHELL

SHELL is not always defined by the bash shell — although you might expect it to be! If the variable is already defined when bash starts, it will not be changed, so do not take it for granted:

```
$ SHELL=/bin/strangeshell bash
$ echo $SHELL
/bin/strangeshell
$
```

To see if you are running under bash, the following is a better test, although it is possible for that variable to have been set in any shell:

```
if [ -z "$BASH_VERSION" ]; then
  echo "This is not really Bash"
else
  echo "Yes, we are running under Bash - version $BASH_VERSION"
fi
```

HOSTNAME and HOSTTYPE

HOSTNAME is set to the name of the machine. HOSTTYPE is set to the machine type. `uname -n` and `uname -m` respectively can be more reliable, and are not changeable by the user.

Working Directory

PWD is the present working directory. You can also get this from `pwd`. OLDPWD is the previous working directory; this can save you from having to make a note of `pwd` before changing to another directory. The command cd - will change back to $OLDPWD.

PIPESTATUS

PIPESTATUS is an array of the exit status of the last-run pipeline or command. Note that using PIPESTATUS in the following way will not work:

```
echo $a | grep $b | grep $c
echo "The echo of $a returned ${PIPESTATUS[0]}"
echo "The grep for $b returned ${PIPESTATUS[1]}"
echo "The grep for $c returned ${PIPESTATUS[2]}"
```

This works for PIPESTATUS[0], but for the subsequent calls PIPESTATUS has been reset by the successful echo command. You have to grab the whole array immediately after the pipeline has ended, otherwise the subsequent echo statements are treated as single-command pipelines that overwrite the previous PIPELINE array. One useful trick to see if anything failed is the following:

```
ls $dir | grep $goodthing | grep -v $badthing
echo ${PIPESTATUS[*]} | grep -v 0 > /dev/null 2>&1
if [ "$?" -eq "0" ]; then
  echo "Something in the pipeline failed."
else
  echo "Only good things were found in $dir, no bad things were found. Phew!"
fi
```

TIMEFORMAT

The time command normally gives output in a reasonably machine-readable format, but it is not overly descriptive. It is possible to write additional scripts to interpret and reformat that data, but the TIMEFORMAT variable does that for you, for most scenarios that you might come across. It has a format similar to printf, whereby a percent (%) symbol marks a special character, which is replaced with the appropriate value. So, %U shows the amount of time the process spent in User mode (non-OS system calls), %S shows the amount of time in System mode, and %R shows the total amount of elapsed time. Each of these can then be modified by adding "l" (the lowercase letter "L"), which expands the seconds out into minutes and seconds, and/or a precision modifier (0-3) which says how many decimal places you want the seconds to be accurate to.

Standard time format looks like this:

```
$ time ls > /dev/null
real    0m0.007s
user    0m0.001s
sys     0m0.001s
```

Actually, this format is used because bash uses the following if TIMEFORMAT is unset.

```
'\nreal\t%3lR\nuser\t%3lU\nsys%3lS'
```

If TIMEFORMAT is null, time displays no output at all.

POSIX time format is similar, and is accessed via the -p switch:

```
$ time -p ls > /dev/null
real 0.00
user 0.00
sys 0.00
```

To display CPU utilization in a more easily readable format, the TIMEFORMAT variable can be set as follows.

```
$ TIMEFORMAT="%2lU user + %2lS system / %2lR elapsed = %P%% CPU Utilisation"
$ time sleep 2
0m0.00s user + 0m0.00s system / 0m2.00s elapsed = 0.04% CPU Utilisation
$ time ls -R /var > /dev/null
0m0.07s user + 0m0.05s system / 0m1.30s elapsed = 9.79% CPU Utilisation
$ time ls >/dev/null
0m0.00s user + 0m0.00s system / 0m0.00s elapsed = 100.00% CPU Utilisation
$
```

Similarly, TIMEFORMAT can be used to display elapsed time in a more natural way than the standard time output:

```
$ TIMEFORMAT="%U user + %S system = %lR total elapsed time"
$ time ls -R /var > /dev/null 2>&1
0.036 user + 0.020 system = 0m0.056s total elapsed time
$
```

sleep does not consume much User or System time, so the numbers do not quite add up. The rest of the time will have been spent waiting for the system to process the task:

```
$ time sleep 1
0.001 user + 0.000 system total = 0m1.002s total elapsed time
$ time expr 123 \* 321
39483
0.001 user + 0.002 system = 0m0.043s total elapsed time
```

Reading 512Mb from /dev/urandom consumes a fair amount of System time. This is because /dev/urandom provides random data generated from the environment, and sufficient randomness can take time to occur.

```
$ time dd if=/dev/urandom of=/tmp/randomfile bs=1024k count=512
512+0 records in
512+0 records out
536870912 bytes (537 MB) copied, 63.5919 seconds, 8.4 MB/s
0.003 user + 56.113 system = 1m3.614s total elapsed time
$
```

PPID

PPID is set to the Process ID of the process that called this shell or shell script. $$ is another special variable which provides the Process ID of this shell itself. $$ is often used for temporary files, as an almost-secure way of creating randomized, unique filenames. $$ can also be useful for a script to identify itself when multiple copies of it are running:

 mktemp (covered in Chapter 12) is often a better way of creating temporary files.

```
$ cat pid.sh
#!/bin/bash
echo "Process $$: Starting up with arguments $@ for my parent, $PPID"
sleep 10
$ ./pid.sh 1 & ./pid.sh 2 & ./pid.sh 3
[1] 2529
[2] 2530
Process 2531: Starting up with arguments 3 for my parent, 2484
Process 2529: Starting up with arguments 1 for my parent, 2484
Process 2530: Starting up with arguments 2 for my parent, 2484
[1]-  Done                    ./pid.sh 1
$
[2]+  Done                    ./pid.sh 2
$
```

RANDOM

RANDOM produces a random number between 0 and 32767. This simple recipe produces 10 random numbers between 200 and 500:

```
$ cat random.sh
#!/bin/bash
MIN=200
MAX=500
let "scope = $MAX - $MIN"
if [ "$scope" -le "0" ]; then
  echo "Error - MAX is less than MIN!"
fi

for i in `seq 1 10`
do
  let result="$RANDOM % $scope + $MIN"
  echo "A random number between $MIN and $MAX is $result"
done
$ ./random.sh
A random number between 200 and 500 is 462
A random number between 200 and 500 is 400
A random number between 200 and 500 is 350
A random number between 200 and 500 is 279
A random number between 200 and 500 is 339
A random number between 200 and 500 is 401
A random number between 200 and 500 is 465
A random number between 200 and 500 is 320
A random number between 200 and 500 is 290
A random number between 200 and 500 is 277
$
```

First it calculates the scope, or range, and uses the modulo operator to ensure that the value stays within that range. Then it adds the $MIN value to the random number, to produce a number in the required range.

REPLY

REPLY is the default variable name for read if none are supplied.

```
$ read
hello world
$ echo $REPLY
hello world
```

SECONDS

SECONDS returns a count of the number of (whole) seconds the shell has been running. In the case of a shell script, this is the time that the script itself, not the shell which called it, has been running. If you change the value of SECONDS to another integer, it will keep counting from there. Setting SECONDS to a non-integer value will set it to zero. If you unset SECONDS, it will lose its special feature and become a regular variable, even if you later set it again.

SECONDS can be useful for a number of things, not only timing: If the shell script needs the occasional unique and not totally predictable number, it can always use (`sleep 1; echo $SECONDS`) to get a number not previously used by the current script. Another use for SECONDS is a result of the fact that the `timeout(1)` command returns the exit code of the command which it executed, unless it times out, in which case it returns 124. So there is no way to know if the command actually timed out, or if it returned the number 124 itself. SECONDS can help you to more accurately determine if the command timed out:

```
#!/bin/bash

SECONDS=0
timeout 60s slow_command
timeout_res=$?
# 124 if timedout, but 124 could be the return code from slow_command
if [ "$SECONDS" -lt "60" ]; then
  # it did not time out; the value is from slow_command.
  echo "The command did not time out; it returned after $SECONDS seconds."
  cmd_res=$timeout_res
else
  # It timed out; take special action here
  echo "The command timed out."
fi
```

BASH_XTRACEFD

BASH_XTRACEFD is new to Bash version 4.1. When used with the -x feature this variable allows the script itself to define what file the output goes to (by default, it goes to stderr). This script also includes a useful tip for obtaining a new file descriptor, which can be useful if you can't keep track of how many files you have open. You use the set -x and set +x in the script to enable the -x logging feature of the shell just for that part of the script.

```
$ cat xtrace.sh
#!/bin/bash

TRACER=/tmp/tracer.txt
TRACEFD=3
# Find the next available file descriptor
ls -l /proc/$$/fd
while [ -e /proc/$$/fd/$TRACEFD ] && [ $TRACEFD -lt 255 ]; do
  let "TRACEFD += 1"
done

if [ $TRACEFD -eq 254 ]; then
  echo "Error: No more file descriptors available!"
  exit 1
fi

echo "FD is $TRACEFD"

eval "exec $TRACEFD>$TRACER"
BASH_XTRACEFD=$TRACEFD
ls -l /proc/$$/fd
# Enable logging with -x
```

```
set -x
date
echo hello world
sleep 1
date
set +x
# disable logging
eval "exec $TRACEFD>&-"
echo "The result of our tracing was in $TRACER:"
cat $TRACER
$ ./xtrace.sh
total 0
lrwx------ 1 steve steve 64 Nov 26 16:53 0 -> /dev/pts/4
lrwx------ 1 steve steve 64 Nov 26 16:53 1 -> /dev/pts/4
lrwx------ 1 steve steve 64 Nov 26 16:53 2 -> /dev/pts/4
lr-x------ 1 steve steve 64 Nov 26 16:53 255 -> /home/steve/book/part1/variables/xt
race.sh
FD is 3
total 0
lrwx------ 1 steve steve 64 Nov 26 16:53 0 -> /dev/pts/4
lrwx------ 1 steve steve 64 Nov 26 16:53 1 -> /dev/pts/4
lrwx------ 1 steve steve 64 Nov 26 16:53 2 -> /dev/pts/4
lr-x------ 1 steve steve 64 Nov 26 16:53 255 -> /home/steve/book/part1/variables/xt
race.sh
l-wx------ 1 steve steve 64 Nov 26 16:53 3 -> /tmp/tracer.txt
Fri Nov 26 16:53:27 GMT 2010
hello world
Fri Nov 26 16:53:28 GMT 2010
The result of our tracing was in /tmp/tracer.txt:
+ date
+ echo hello world
+ sleep 1
+ date
+ set +x
$
```

Here, `eval` along with `exec` was necessary for the script to parse the values of the variables in the correct way. You could use `exec 5>$TRACER` directly if you already know the value of the file descriptor you want to write to.

GLOBIGNORE

GLOBIGNORE is a special variable which is used by the globbing feature of bash, to omit certain patterns from a wildcard match. The next chapter looks at wildcards in more detail. Like many shell variables which are formatted as lists (like PATH, GLOBOPTS, and others), it is a colon-separated list of regular expressions. If any filename would match a pattern in GLOBIGNORE, it is treated as if that item did not exist. For example, Figure 3-1 shows a directory containing a few HTML, PHP, TXT, RSS, and CSS files. If you list the files starting with a, you see the first four. However, when you set GLOBIGNORE to ignore filenames matching the pattern "`*.gif`," the same command shows only the two PHP files, not the two GIF files.

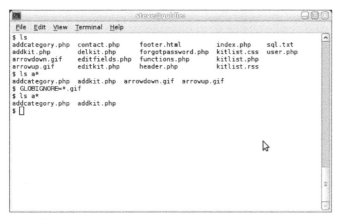

FIGURE 3-1

This is more clear with a bigger match, as shown in Figure 3-2:

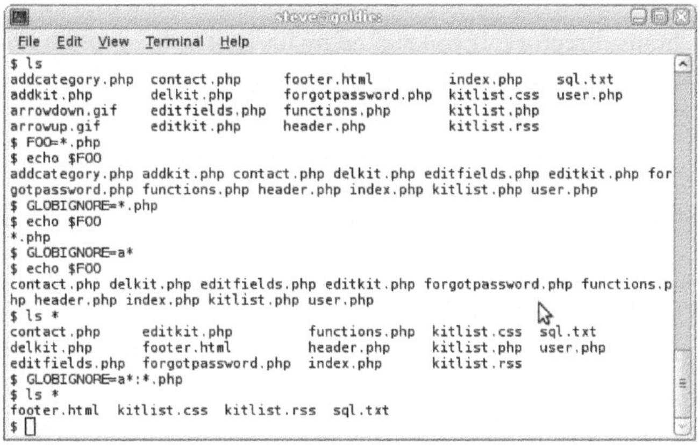

FIGURE 3-2

In Figure 3-2, the first `ls` shows you what files are in the directory. Setting FOO to "`*.php`" means that the `echo $FOO` will match all of the `.php` files. Setting `GLOBIGNORE=*.php` means that `echo $FOO` acts as if there were no matching files to be found — it outputs its actual, unexpanded value, which is the string "`*.php`".

When you then set `GLOBIGNORE=a*`, `echo $FOO` omits the files starting with "a", and setting `GLOBIGNORE=a*:*.php` results in any file which matches any of those patterns being ignored.

This can also be useful when using source control systems. For example, Figure 3-3 shows some files that have been backed up with a "~" extension:

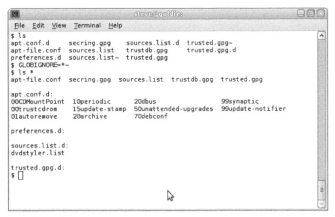

FIGURE 3-3

HOME

HOME is the path to the current user's home directory. If you run `cd` by itself, it will `cd` to the value of $HOME. In the bash shell, $HOME can also be referenced as "~", so these commands all refer to the value of the HOME variable:

```
cd ; grep proxy .wgetrc
cd $HOME ; grep proxy .wgetrc
grep proxy ~/.wgetrc
grep proxy ${HOME}/.wgetrc
```

and all will `grep` in the current user's `${HOME}/.wgetrc` file.

IFS

IFS is the Internal Field Separator: It lists the set of characters that may be used as whitespace. Its default value is <space><tab><newline>. When you looked at `read VAR` earlier in this chapter, you saw that `read firstname lastname` can be used to read in a first word (firstname) followed by none or more subsequent words (all of which were read into the lastname variable). This is due to IFS, and if you change the IFS to something else, you can change the way in which this works. This can be useful, for example, when reading the `/etc/passwd` file which is split on the colon, or reading IP addresses which are delimited by periods:

```
$ cat ifs1.sh
#!/bin/bash

# Save the original IFS
oIFS=$IFS
IFS=":"
  # /etc/passwd is delimited by colons only.
while read login pass uid gid name home shell
do
```

```
    # Ignore those with /bin/false, or home directories in /var
    if [ "$shell" != "/bin/false" ] && [ ! -z "${home%\/var\/*}" ]; then
      echo "User $login ($name) lives in $home and uses `basename $shell`"
    fi
done < /etc/passwd

# Not necessary as we're exiting the script, but it is good practice;
# subsequent commands will want the normal IFS values.
oIFS=$IFS
$ ./ifs1.sh
User root (root) lives in /root and uses bash
User daemon (daemon) lives in /usr/sbin and uses sh
User bin (bin) lives in /bin and uses sh
User sys (sys) lives in /dev and uses sh
User sync (sync) lives in /bin and uses sync
User games (games) lives in /usr/games and uses sh
User proxy (proxy) lives in /bin and uses sh
User nobody (nobody) lives in /nonexistent and uses sh
User steve (Steve Parker,,,) lives in /home/steve and uses bash
$
```

When displaying output, one instance of the first character listed in $IFS is used to pad characters, which (combined with the fact that all $IFS characters in the input are stripped away) explains why double quotes are needed around this echo statement if the spaces are to be preserved:

```
$ echo hello            world
hello world
$
```

PATH

PATH is a colon-separated list of directories used to find program files. It is searched left-to-right, so if PATH=/home/steve/bin:/usr/local/bin:/usr/bin:/bin:/usr/bin/X11, then ls (which normally lives in /bin) will be searched for as /home/steve/bin/ls, then /usr/local/bin/ls, then /usr/bin/ls, until it is found as /bin/ls. The bash shell hashes these values, so the next time you call ls, it will remember that it is /bin/ls. If you then create /home/steve/bin/ls which you want it to use instead, you can force the shell to forget its hashes by running hash -r. You can read a list of hashed paths by running hash -l.

In PATH, a period (.) is used to represent the current directory of the calling program. Less well known is that a double colon (::) will do the same, and a single colon at the beginning or end of the PATH variable will also expand to the current working directory. So if your PATH=:/usr/bin:/bin, then any file called ls in the current directory will be executed when you call ls. The effect of this can range from awkward (if a command suddenly does something different than what you expect it to do) to a major security problem (especially if you are logged in as root): An attacker could place a malicious ls in /tmp, and simply wait for the superuser to decide to list the files in /tmp; the superuser will unwittingly run the attacker's ls program. When this program also makes an effort to appear innocent (that is, it appears to do the simple task that root asked of it), this is known as a Trojan horse, after the famous wooden horse left outside Troy.

TMOUT

TMOUT is used in three different ways: by the `read` builtin command, by the `select` builtin, and by the interactive bash shell. If it is unset, or equal to zero, then it is ignored. If it has any positive value, then these three commands which make use of it will timeout after $TMOUT seconds.

The `read` builtin will exit with a value greater than 128 if it times out (it always seems to exit with a return code of 142 in that case).

```
steve@atomic:~$ TMOUT=10
steve@atomic:~$ read -p Name: name
Name:steve@atomic:~       ◀───────
$ echo $?
142
steve@atomic:~$ unset TMOUT
steve@atomic:~$ read -p Name: name
Name:Steve
steve@atomic:~$ echo $?
0
steve@atomic:~$ echo $name
Steve
steve@atomic:~$
```

THE PROMPT ("STEVE@ATOMIC")
IS DISPLAYED ON THE SAME LINE
AFTER THE "NAME:" PROMPT. THIS IS
BECAUSE THE READ COMMAND TIMED
OUT, AND THE NEXT THING THAT
THE SHELL DOES IS REDISPLAY ITS
PROMPT.

You can also call `read -t timeout` to achieve the same effect:

```
steve@atomic:~$ unset TMOUT
steve@atomic:~$ read -t 5 -p Name: name
Name:steve@atomic:~$ echo $?   ◀───────
142
steve@atomic:~$
```

AGAIN, THE PROMPT IS DISPLAYED
DIRECTLY AFTER THE PROMPT

The `select` builtin will also timeout after $TMOUT seconds, but does not break out of its loop. Here, options 1, 2, and then 3 are selected, followed by a timeout where the options and the #? prompt are redisplayed and the loop runs again. Note, however, that the body (`echo foo is $foo`) of the `select` loop does not get executed in this case.

```
steve@atomic:~$ TMOUT=5
steve@atomic:~$ select foo in one two three
> do
>   echo foo is $foo;
> done
1) one
2) two
3) three
#? 1
foo is one
#? 2
foo is two
#? 3
foo is three
#? 1) one
2) two
3) three
#? ^C
steve@atomic:~$
```

The shell will exit after TMOUT seconds; this can be a useful security feature, particularly to stop someone from leaving the console logged in as root, which happens more often than many systems administrators would care to admit in public! However, it can be incredibly irritating (and not always obvious, particularly if the prompt does not include the hostname) to come back from lunch to find that you have been logged out of the work session that you were partway through completing:

```
steve@atomic:~$ TMOUT=5
steve@atomic:~$ timed out waiting for input: auto-logout
Connection to atomic closed.
steve@declan:~$
```

You may also have to be quite a fast typist to fix a system which has been configured to set TMOUT to a value shorter than the amount of time that it takes you to change it back — it is not inactivity which it monitors for, but command execution. If TMOUT is set to a value under 10, and it takes you 10 seconds to type "unset TMOUT" or "TMOUT=0", then you are in trouble!

 Hint: Start a different shell which does not obey TMOUT, or use **scp** *or similar to copy a good config file over the bad one.*

TMPDIR

TMPDIR is used for any temporary files; if it is not set, /tmp is used. Apart from the shell itself, some application programs use TMPDIR, so if an application keeps filling up /tmp with lots of files, it can be worth changing TMPDIR for that application to make it use dedicated storage elsewhere (on external storage perhaps, away from the operating system itself).

User Identification Variables

It is often useful to be able to determine the identity of the user running a script. UID is automatically set to the user's numeric user ID when the shell launches, and is read-only, so the user cannot spoof it. GROUPS is an array of the numeric group IDs of the current user. The GROUPS array is writeable, but once it has been assigned a value, it cannot get its special properties back.

Note that $USER is not defined by the bash shell, and while it may be set and may be accurate, it could be set to any value whatsoever: It has no special meaning to the bash shell. Checking $USER is not a recommended way to accurately identify the user.

The following is often used to check that the user is root before running a privileged script:

```
#!/bin/bash
if [ "$UID" -ne "0" ]; then
  echo "Sorry, you are not root."
  exit 1
else
  echo "You are root - you may proceed."
fi
```

SUMMARY

Along with conditional execution, variables are one of the features required of a language to make it genuinely useful. The ability to read data in from the environment and execute different code as a result means that the shell is a genuinely useful programming language, not just a batch processor. The shell is slightly different from most languages, in that the syntax to assign and to read variables is not the same, and also because it has almost no concept of different types of variables.

Some variables are pre-defined by the system, and some of those (such as UID) can only be read, not written to. Others (like RANDOM) lose their special meaning if they are assigned a value.

Chapter 7 goes much more in-depth with variables, including a lot of bash-specific features. Chapter 9 deals with arrays, a special type of variable which is available in bash, ksh, and zsh.

Wildcard Expansion

Wildcards are used in two different ways when writing shell scripts. The shell itself uses wildcards for filename expansion so you can specify a* to match all files starting with the letter a, and *.txt to match all text files. Then there are the more powerful regular expressions used by many shell utilities such as sed, awk, and grep. These use a more formalized language and syntax than the shell, which is more simplistic. The bash shell does offer more powerful wildcard expansion than the standard Bourne shell, and these features are also covered in this chapter.

Also of relevance to regular expressions are the rules that affect quoting and escaping characters of special relevance to the shell. When you need to pass a* to sed, you probably do not want the shell to expand that to match the files in the current directory, but instead pass the wildcard itself directly to sed. The "Quoting" section of this chapter covers the various techniques and special characters necessary to achieve this.

FILENAME EXPANSION (GLOBBING)

The unappealing word globbing comes from the original command /etc/glob, written by Dennis Ritchie, one of the original authors of Unix. It seems that glob was short for "global" because it was intended that it would search the entire $PATH. The original implementation searched only in /bin, which was considered to be a bug. Today, the which command performs this role of glob, but it is from glob that we now have the word globbing, which means "searching for files using wildcard expansion." It still does not reference the PATH variable.

The two key characters in filename expansion are the question mark (?) and the asterisk (*). The ? matches any single character; the * matches any sequence of characters. So given a set of files containing various patterns, you can use these wildcards to find the matching files.

```
$ ls
abc    abcdef    abcdefghijk    abc.php    abc.txt    ABC.txt    def    mydoc.odt    xyz.xml
ABC    ABCDEF    abcdef.odt    abctxt    abc.TXT    alphabet    DEF    xyz
$ ls a*
abc        abcdefghijk    abc.php    abc.txt    alphabet
abcdef    abcdef.odt    abctxt    abc.TXT
$ ls A*
```

```
ABC   ABCDEF   ABC.txt
$ ls A??
ABC
$ ls a??
abc
```

This feature is often used to find all files with a given extension. Note that `*txt` is different from `*.txt`.

> *Although the convention of* `.txt`, `.sh`, *or* `.conf` *at the end of a filename is widely used in Unix and Linux, the extension itself does not have the special significance that some other operating systems (most notably Microsoft Windows) confer to it. You can rename your OpenOffice document* `myconfiguration.odt` *to* `myconfiguration.bin` *and it will still work perfectly well in OpenOffice. The* `file` *utility identifies files by their contents and is not misled by filename extensions.*

```
$ ls *.txt
abc.txt   ABC.txt
$ ls *.???
abcdef.odt   abc.php   abc.txt   abc.TXT   ABC.txt   mydoc.odt   xyz.xml
$ ls *txt
abctxt   abc.txt   ABC.txt
$
```

Because `*` matches any sequence of characters, it can also match none, unlike the question mark (`?`), which always has to match exactly one character.

```
$ ls a*b*
abc       abcdefghijk   abc.php   abc.txt   alphabet
abcdef   abcdef.odt     abctxt    abc.TXT
$ ls a?b*
ls: cannot access a?b*: No such file or directory
$
```

This example also shows that the wildcards can go anywhere, not only at the start or end of a filename. This command lists all files containing the letter h. Notice that `abc.php` is included in this; as mentioned previously, the fact that a filename contains a period has no special significance.

```
$ ls *h*
abcdefghijk   abc.php   alphabet
$
```

Although this is not filename expansion, another useful bash shell feature is the capability to expand a list of strings contained within curly brackets. This listing of `/etc/rc*.d` is more precisely matched by specifying the numbers required:

```
$ ls -ld /etc/rc{0,1,2,3,4,5,6}.d
drwxr-xr-x 2 root root 4096 Nov 25 19:38 /etc/rc0.d
drwxr-xr-x 2 root root 4096 Nov 25 19:38 /etc/rc1.d
drwxr-xr-x 2 root root 4096 Nov 25 19:38 /etc/rc2.d
```

```
drwxr-xr-x 2 root root 4096 Nov 25 19:38 /etc/rc3.d
drwxr-xr-x 2 root root 4096 Nov 25 19:38 /etc/rc4.d
drwxr-xr-x 2 root root 4096 Nov 25 19:38 /etc/rc5.d
drwxr-xr-x 2 root root 4096 Nov 25 19:38 /etc/rc6.d
$
```

This can also be particularly useful when creating multiple directories of a similar structure:

```
$ mkdir -p /opt/weblogic/domains/domain{1,2,3}/bin
$ ls -ld /opt/weblogic/domains/*/bin
drwxrwxr-x 2 steve steve 4096 Sep 22 11:40 /opt/weblogic/domains/domain1/bin
drwxrwxr-x 2 steve steve 4096 Sep 22 11:40 /opt/weblogic/domains/domain2/bin
drwxrwxr-x 2 steve steve 4096 Sep 22 11:40 /opt/weblogic/domains/domain3/bin
$
```

Although the period in a filename has no special significance, the dash (-) is used by nearly every Unix and Linux command. When faced with a file named "-rf" or worse still, "-rf .", how are you meant to remove that file? The obvious answer is `rm -rf .`, but that will remove everything from the current directory downward. Many (although not all) commands interpret two dashes (--) as indicating the end of the set of flags to the command itself, and the start of the list of filenames to operate on. So `rm -- "-rf ."` will remove the file "-rf " Similar problems can be posed by files named * or ? — it is best to avoid using these characters in filenames wherever possible.

Although ? and * are the two main metacharacters of filename expansion, there is also the [...] construct. This has three slightly different uses. Probably the most popular of these is the ability to define a range, so where `a?c.txt` would match `a1c.txt` as well as `abc.txt`, you can specify that the missing character must be between a and z by specifying the range [a-z] like this:

```
$ ls a[a-z]c.txt
abc.txt
$
```

The range can be anything you choose, but [a-z] and [0-9] are the most widely used. As an alternative to these two ranges, there are a number of defined classes that provide the same thing. [a-z] is equivalent to [[:alpha:]], and [0-9] is equivalent to [[:digit:]]. The full list of available classes appears in Table 4-1.

TABLE 4-1: Available Classes

CLASS	MEMBERS
Alnum	A-Z, a-z, 0-9
Alpha	A-Z, a-z
Blank	Space, Tab
Cntrl	ASCII characters 0-31 (nonprinting control characters)
Digit	0-9

continues

TABLE 4-1 *(continued)*

CLASS	MEMBERS
Graph	A-Z, a-z, 0-9 and punctuation
Lower	a-z
Print	ASCII characters 32-127 (printable characters)
Punct	Punctuation (printable characters other than A-Z, a-z, 0-9)
Space	Space, Tab, LF (10), VT (11), FF (12), CR (13)
Upper	A-Z
xdigit	0-9, A-F, a-f

If a range is not sufficient, you can also specify a list of characters to match by placing them between the brackets. So [aeiou] will match any one vowel, [13579] will match an odd digit, and so on. You can negate the term with an exclamation mark (!) or a caret at the start.

```
$ # files starting with a lowercase vowel
$ ls [aeiou]*
abc      abcdefghijk  abc.php  abc.txt  alphabet
abcdef  abcdef.odt   abctxt   abc.TXT
$ # files not starting with a lowercase vowel
$ ls [!aeiou]*
ABC  ABCDEF  ABC.txt  def  DEF  mydoc.odt  xyz  xyz.xml
$
```

Finally, if you need to match the character [, you have to put it first in the list, as [[aeiou]. If you have to match the character -, you can put it at the start or the end, but nowhere else, so either [-aeiou] or [aeiou-] will work.

Bash Globbing Features

Sometimes you might want to disable filename expansion completely; the bash directive set -o noglob (alternatively set -f) disables it, and set +o noglob (or set +f) re-enables it. Here you have two .odt documents; if you want to create a file called *d*.odt, filename expansion will interpret the touch *d*.odt command as touch abcdef.odt mydoc.odt. Notice that the timestamps change on the files.

```
$ ls -l *d*.odt
-rw-rw-r-- 1 steve steve 505 Nov 13 10:13 abcdef.odt
-rw-rw-r-- 1 steve steve 355 Dec 20 09:17 mydoc.odt
$ touch *d*.odt
$ ls -l *d*.odt
-rw-rw-r-- 1 steve steve 505 Dec 22 11:51 abcdef.odt
-rw-rw-r-- 1 steve steve 355 Dec 22 11:51 mydoc.odt
$
```

You can disable globbing to achieve the desired result. The `*d*.odt` is now interpreted literally.

```
$ set -o noglob
$ touch *d*.odt
$ set +o noglob
$ ls -l *d*.odt
-rw-rw-r-- 1 steve steve 505 Dec 22 11:51 abcdef.odt
-rw-rw-r-- 1 steve steve   0 Dec 22 11:52 *d*.odt
-rw-rw-r-- 1 steve steve 355 Dec 22 11:51 mydoc.odt
$
```

Shell Options

Shell options change the way in which the shell works. There are a few shell options that affect filename expansion. They are set with the command `shopt -s optionname` and unset with `shopt -u optionname`. If you need to use a shell option, you can query a setting with `shopt optionname`, or programmatically with `shopt -q optionname`, which displays nothing, but returns 0 if set and 1 if not set.

```
$ shopt nullglob
nullglob            off
$ shopt -q nullglob
$ echo $?
1
$ shopt -s nullglob
$ shopt nullglob
nullglob            on
$ shopt -q nullglob
$ echo $?
0
$
```

One feature that the shell uses to protect against inadvertent changes is that so-called "hidden" files — that is, those whose name begins with a period, such as `~/.bashrc`, `~/.ssh/`, and so on — are not matched by standard filename expansion. This can be a really useful feature as long as you understand that it exists; otherwise, it can be very frustrating. Why does `rm -rf /tmp/myfiles/*` not result in an empty directory? Because of `/tmp/myfiles/.config`. You can't use `rm -rf /tmp/myfiles/.*` because that would match `/tmp/myfiles/..`, which is `/tmp` itself. You could always use `rm -rf /tmp/myfiles`, which will remove `/tmp/myfiles` and everything in it, but if you want the directory to remain, you can use the `dotglob` shell option.

```
$ ls *
abc   abcdef  abcdefghijk  abc.php   abc.txt   ABC.txt    def  *d*.odt    xyz
ABC   ABCDEF  abcdef.odt   abctxt    abc.TXT   alphabet   DEF  mydoc.odt  xyz.xml
$ ls .*
.abc  .abcdef  .def

.:
abc   abcdef  abcdefghijk  abc.php   abc.txt   ABC.txt    def  *d*.odt    xyz
ABC   ABCDEF  abcdef.odt   abctxt    abc.TXT   alphabet   DEF  mydoc.odt  xyz.xml

..:
3204.txt  eg  glob.txt  wildcard.txt  wildcards.odt
$ shopt -s dotglob
```

```
$ ls *
abc      abcdef     abcdefghijk   abctxt    ABC.txt    .def      mydoc.odt
.abc     .abcdef    abcdef.odt    abc.txt   alphabet   DEF       xyz
ABC      ABCDEF     abc.php       abc.TXT   def        *d*.odt   xyz.xml
$
```

Another feature of the shell that can be inconvenient in certain circumstances is the fact that when a pattern does not match any files at all, it remains unchanged. So with the files listed above, a* expands to "abc abcdefghijk abc.php abc.txt alphabet abcdef abcdef.odt abctxt abc.TXT" but b* expands to "b*", the literal string including the wildcard. You can force this to expand to an empty string with the nullglob option so that you do not process the wildcard itself.

```
$ for filename in a* b*
> do
>     md5sum $filename
> done
674ea002ddbaf89619e280f7ed15560d  abc
1d48a9f8e8a42b0977ec8746cd484723  abcdef
b7f0f386f706ae1bc3c8fa3bffb0371c  abcdefghijk
8116e5ba834943c9047b6d3045f45c8c  abcdef.odt
ac100d51fbab3ca3677d59e63212cb32  abc.php
d41d8cd98f00b204e9800998ecf8427e  abctxt
e45f6583e2a3feacf82d55b5c8ae0a60  abc.txt
a60b09767be1fb8d88cbb1afbb90fb9e  abc.TXT
3df05469f6e76c3c5d084b41352fc80b  alphabet
md5sum: b*: No such file or directory
$ shopt -s nullglob
$ for filename in a* b*
> do
>     md5sum $filename
> done
674ea002ddbaf89619e280f7ed15560d  abc
1d48a9f8e8a42b0977ec8746cd484723  abcdef
b7f0f386f706ae1bc3c8fa3bffb0371c  abcdefghijk
8116e5ba834943c9047b6d3045f45c8c  abcdef.odt
ac100d51fbab3ca3677d59e63212cb32  abc.php
d41d8cd98f00b204e9800998ecf8427e  abctxt
e45f6583e2a3feacf82d55b5c8ae0a60  abc.txt
a60b09767be1fb8d88cbb1afbb90fb9e  abc.TXT
3df05469f6e76c3c5d084b41352fc80b  alphabet
$
```

This can be a very useful way to keep the output of the script nice and clean without superfluous error messages.

A similar feature is the failglob shell option. This is another way to deal with the problem of the glob pattern not matching any files at all. Setting the failglob option means that the shell itself will treat the use of a nonmatching expression as a shell error, rather than processing the command as it would normally do.

```
$ shopt failglob
failglob              off
$ ls b*
ls: cannot access b*: No such file or directory
$ shopt -s failglob
```

```
$ ls b*
bash: no match: b*
$
```

The most powerful of the globbing shell options is extglob. This provides bash with some extended pattern-matching features that exist already in ksh. These do not seem to be well documented anywhere, and at the time of this writing, the bash man page is not particularly clear about the syntax. One example that I came across recently involved dealing with a large number of disks on a Linux server. The most common disk device driver in Linux is called sd, and disks are called /dev/sda, /dev/sdb, and so on. Individual partitions on the disks are then called /dev/sda1, /dev/sda2, and so on. To list the partitions of all the disks on the system seems an easy task:

```
for disk in /dev/sd?
do
    fdisk -1 $disk
done
```

This will pick up the actual disk devices themselves — /dev/sda and /dev/sdb — but not /dev/sda1, /dev/sda2, and /dev/sdb1, which are the underlying partitions you do not want to list. However, when a Linux system has more than 26 disks, which is a common occurrence with a SAN (Storage Area Network), it loops around, so the disk after /dev/sdz is /dev/sdaa, followed by /dev/sdab, and so on. After /dev/sdaz, it is /dev/sdba, /dev/sdbb, /dev/sdbc, and so on. Here, the simple /dev/sd? pattern is insufficient. What is really needed is to express that the letters mean disks, the letters followed by numbers mean partitions, and in this case, only the disks themselves are wanted. extglob can help here. The required pattern is /dev/sd followed by one or more [a-z] characters. This is expressed as +(a-z). You can also use [:alpha:] in place of (a-z) so this example uses both.

 The extglob *patterns look a lot like normal shell filename expansion patterns, but the* (*and*) *would be illegal in normal filename expansion.*

```
shopt -s extglob
ls /dev/sd+([a-z])
for disk in /dev/sd+([[:alpha:]])
do
    fdisk -1 $disk
done
```

You could also use the GLOBIGNORE variable to find just the disks without the partitions. You can set GLOBIGNORE to a pattern that will be cut from the results of any filename expansion. This was mentioned in Chapter 3, but here we apply it to the problem of listing all disks without including their partitions. The partitions match the pattern /dev/sd*[0-9] — that is, "/dev/sd" followed by any number of any characters, and ending with a digit.

```
GLOBIGNORE=/dev/sd*[0-9]
for disk in /dev/sd*
do
    fdisk -1 $disk
done
```

With `extglob`, you can also provide a whole set of patterns to match. The full set of `extglob` wildcards is shown in Table 4-2. A pattern-list is a list of patterns, separated by a pipe (|) symbol, for example (a|bc|d).

TABLE 4-2: Wildcards

PATTERN	MATCHES
?(pattern-list)	Zero or one of the patterns
*(pattern-list)	Zero or more of the patterns
+(pattern-list)	One or more of the patterns
@(pattern-list)	Exactly one of the patterns
!(pattern-list)	Anything except one of the patterns

The question mark is used to mark the pattern list as optional.

```
$ shopt -s extglob
$ ls abc*
abc  abcdef  abcdefghijk  abcdef.odt  abc.php  abctxt  abc.txt  abc.TXT
$ ls abc?(.)txt
abctxt  abc.txt
$ ls abc?(def)
abc  abcdef
$ ls abc?(def|.txt)
abc  abcdef  abc.txt
$
```

The asterisk matches zero or more occurrences of the pattern(s), so these patterns can match an optional extension without matching all of `abc*`.

```
$ shopt -s extglob
$ ls abc*
abc  abcdef  abcdefghijk  abcdef.odt  abc.php  abctxt  abc.txt  abc.TXT
$ ls abc*(.php)
abc  abc.php
$ ls abc*(.php|.txt)
abc  abc.php  abc.txt
$
```

The plus sign requires at least one match to exist. Compared to the asterisk in the previous paragraph, this means that the file `abc` is not sufficient to match the pattern.

```
$ ls abc*(.txt|.php)
abc  abc.php  abc.txt
$ ls abc+(.txt|.php)
abc.php  abc.txt
$
```

The at (@) sign matches exactly one instance of the pattern. Creating abc.txt.txt allows comparison with the other forms already tested.

```
$ ls abc@(.txt|.php)
abc.php  abc.txt
$ touch abc.txt.txt
$ ls abc@(.txt|.php)
abc.php  abc.txt
$ ls abc+(.txt|.php)
abc.php  abc.txt  abc.txt.txt
$ ls abc*(.txt|.php)
abc  abc.php  abc.txt  abc.txt.txt
$
```

The final extglob symbol is the exclamation mark. This negates the test so it is effectively the opposite of the @ test.

```
$ ls abc*
abc        abcdefghijk  abc.php  abc.txt  abc.txt.txt
abcdef  abcdef.odt  abctxt  abc.TXT
$ ls abc@(.txt|.php)
abc.php  abc.txt
$ ls abc!(.txt|.php)
abc  abcdef  abcdefghijk  abcdef.odt  abctxt  abc.TXT  abc.txt.txt
$
```

On Unix and Linux, filenames are case sensitive. That is to say, you could have /home/steve/mydoc, /home/steve/MyDoc, and /home/steve/MYDOC, and they would all be different files. Because case is significant for filenames, filename expansion is also normally case sensitive. However, when dealing with non native filesystems, such as VFAT, it can be useful to be case insensitive. The nocaseglob shell option enables this feature.

```
$ shopt nocaseglob
nocaseglob          off
$ ls -ld /windows/program*
ls: cannot access /windows/program*: No such file or directory
$ shopt -s nocaseglob
$ ls -ld /windows/program*
drwxrwxrwx 1 root root  8192 Oct 28 19:06 /windows/ProgramData
drwxrwxrwx 1 root root  8192 Jun 11  2010 /windows/Program Files
drwxrwxrwx 1 root root 12288 Oct 28 19:04 /windows/Program Files (x86)
$
```

REGULAR EXPRESSIONS AND QUOTING

Regular expressions are different from bash wildcard expansion in that they are far more complete and clearly defined. Entire books can be (and have been) written on regular expressions. They are not directly related to the shell because other than bash's =~ syntax, only external tools such as grep, sed, and awk actually use regular expressions. Because shell expansion and regular expressions use very similar syntax, a regular expression passed from the shell to an external command could be parsed by the shell on the way; various quoting techniques can be deployed to avoid this problem.

Overview of Regular Expressions

Regular Expressions are interpreted by a command such as sed to achieve some quite powerful results. While these commands are used in various recipes in this book, the actual usage of these is beyond the scope of this book. http://sed.sourceforge.net/sed1line.txt is one excellent list of one-line sed recipes; there are many online tutorials and books available that cover these commands in great detail. Here the details will be dealt with briefly in order to discuss how to use them with the shell.

```
$ cat myfile
foo="hello is bonjour"
bar="goodbye is aureviour"
foo1=$foo
bar1=$bar
$ foo=bonjour
$ bar=aurevoir
$ sed s/$foo/$bar/g myfile
foo="hello is aurevoir"
bar="goodbye is aureviour"
foo1=$foo
bar1=$bar
$ sed s/"$foo"/"$bar"/g myfile
foo="hello is aurevoir"
bar="goodbye is aureviour"
foo1=$foo
bar1=$bar
$
```

This simple example is passed to sed as s/bonjour/aurevoir/g, which replaces any bonjour in its input with aurevoir. Using double quotes around the variables does not change this either. However, if you put single quotes around the variable references, this interpretation is not followed. Instead, the literal string $foo is replaced with $bar; the values of these variables in the calling shell is not used. The command passed to sed is s/$foo/$bar/g, and sed knows nothing about the variables in the calling shell.

 sed *is a Stream EDitor. It does not change the contents of the file on disk; it only reads the file (or standard input) and writes the modified version to its standard output. GNU* sed *has the* -i *option which updates the file in place.*

```
$ sed s/'$foo'/'$bar'/g myfile
foo="hello is bonjour"
bar="goodbye is aurevoir"
foo1=$bar
bar1=$bar
$
```

This means that understanding how different types of quoting work, and what is passed to calling commands as a result, is very significant. The rules of quoting are sometimes quite complicated and not always obvious.

Quoting

How arguments are passed from the shell to external commands is very significant. There are three main forms of quoting — the single quote, the double quote, and the backslash. Each has its place, and although there are many instances where one or another of these techniques will suffice, sometimes you will need to use the features that one of these provides, which are not available by using the others.

Single Quotes

The simplest is the single quote, which stops the shell from interpreting anything within it. Nothing other than a closing quote is parsed by the shell at all.

```
$ echo 'hello''world'
Helloworld
$ echo 'hello       world'
hello       world
$ echo '$hello'$world
$hello
$ echo 'hello
> world'
hello
world
$ echo *
cc2.ods CH3_PE.docx keyring-VH3EQr MozillaMailnews orbit-root orbit-steve plugtmp p
ulse-ca5EDFdkeDRj ssh-aRFHoS1883 virtual-steve.VQ1hrC
$ echo '*'
*
```

The first example shows that the quotes themselves are ignored, but other than that, hello and world are treated as the entire input. The second example shows that spaces are preserved within the quotes. The third line shows that $hello is treated as a literal, but the undefined variable $world (which is not within quotes) is displayed as is — that is, as a blank. The fourth line shows that even a newline does not end the echo statement — the shell knows that it is looking for a single quote to close the quotation, and nothing else is treated as significant, not even a newline.

The final two examples show that although echo * expands to all files in the current directory, echo '*' just echoes an asterisk.

Double Quotes

The second form of quoting available in the shell is to use double quotes; this way, some characters are parsed by the shell, but not all. Variables are interpreted, but filenames, as discussed in the first half of this chapter, are not expanded. Using the same examples as in the previous section, but using double quotes, demonstrates that although the two formats often seem to be equivalent, there are significant differences between the two.

```
$ echo "hello""world"
helloworld
$ echo "hello       world"
hello       world
$ echo "$hello"$world
```

```
$ echo "hello
> world"
hello
world
$ echo *
cc2.ods CH3_PE.docx keyring-VH3EQr MozillaMailnews orbit-root orbit-steve plugtmp p
ulse-ca5EDFdkeDRj ssh-aRFHoS1883 virtual-steve.VQ1hrC
$ echo "*"
*
$
```

Single quotes, too, are left alone when within double quotes. The way in which single and double quotes function independently is shown by using each to wrap around the other. Within single quotes, everything is treated literally, including the double quotes. Within double quotes, the single quote is treated as a regular character.

```
$ echo 'hello "world"'
hello "world"
$ echo "hello 'world'"
hello 'world'
$
```

One common mistake occurs when using a single quote in regular text; if you want to display a message such as Let's play a game, the lone single quote in that phrase can cause problems. These first two attempts require a closing single quote to finish the command, and neither manages to display the intended text. The correct method is to use double quotes; this ensures that the lone single quote is treated as a regular character and not anything special to the shell.

```
$ echo Let's play a game
> '
Lets play a game

$ echo 'Let's play a game'
> '
Lets play a game

$ echo "Let's play a game"
Let's play a game
$
```

Backslash

The third way to mark characters as special is to flag them individually by prefixing them with a backslash (\). When you want to include a special character in a regular string, but it would otherwise be interpreted by the shell, you can put a backslash in front of it. Here, the single quote in "can't" should not be a problem because it is surrounded by double quotes. Unfortunately as it turns out, that isn't the case.

```
$ echo "Wilde said, "Experience is one thing you can't get for nothing.""
> '
Wilde said Experience is one thing you cant get for nothing.""
```

However, the shell will interpret this string as three distinct strings:

➤ `Wilde said, "`

➤ `Experience is one thing you can`

➤ `'t get for nothing.`

➤ `",`

To display this correctly, you need to tell the shell to ignore the quotes around the actual quotation. By placing a backslash before the double quotes, they lose their special meaning.

```
$ echo "Wilde said, \"Experience is one thing you can't get for nothing.\""
Wilde said, "Experience is one thing you can't get for nothing."
$
```

Other characters you may want to escape with a backslash are the semicolon (;), which is normally used by the shell to combine multiple commands on one line; the exclamation mark (!), which is used to call back history; and the ampersand (&), which is used to run a process in the background. Within brace expansion, the special characters {, }, and , can be escaped with a backslash. To put a backslash itself on the command line, you can escape it with itself (\\).

```
$ echo the semicolon is wonderful; it is like taking a short break.
the semicolon is wonderful
-bash: it: command not found
$ echo the semicolon is wonderful\; it is like taking a short break.
the semicolon is wonderful; it is like taking a short break.
$
$ echo hope, peace & love
[1] 7517
hope, peace
-bash: love: command not found
[1]+  Done                    echo hope, peace
$ echo hope, peace \& love
hope, peace & love
$
$ echo hello
hello
$ echo !echo
echo echo hello
echo hello
$ echo \!echo
!echo
$
$ echo DOS and Windows refer to drives as C:\, D:\ and E:\.
DOS and Windows refer to drives as C:, D: and E:.
$ echo DOS and Windows refer to drives as C:\\, D:\\ and E:\\.
DOS and Windows refer to drives as C:\, D:\ and E:\.
$
```

Within double quotes, $, `, \\$, \\', \\" and \\<newline> are treated as normal; a backslash followed by anything else is not treated as special. So echo "$HOME\\&" *displays* /home/steve\\& *and not* /home/steve& *as it would without double quotes.*

Some commands require special characters as part of their own syntax; for example, sed commands normally include forward slashes. If you want to use a forward slash as part of the sed command but not part of the syntax, then you need to escape that for sed. In this case, quotes (single or double) and a backslash are required.

```
$ cat files.txt
/etc/hostnames
$ sed s/hostnames/hosts/g files.txt
/etc/hosts
$ sed s//etc/hostnames//etc/hosts/g files.txt
sed: -e expression #1, char 8: unknown option to `s'
$ sed s/"/etc/hostnames"/"/etc/hosts"/g files.txt
sed: -e expression #1, char 8: unknown option to `s'
$ sed s/\/etc\/hostnames/\/etc\/hosts/g files.txt
sed: -e expression #1, char 8: unknown option to `s'
$ sed s/"\/etc\/hostnames"/"\/etc\/hosts"/g files.txt
/etc/hosts
$
```

 This is sed *syntax, not generic shell syntax. To demonstrate this, repeat these tests replacing* sed *with* echo. echo *does not care about the forward slash, so it just treats it as a regular character.*

The backslash can also be used for line continuation. A very long command can be difficult to read, and so it is best to choose when to insert a line break. If a line ends with a backslash immediately followed by a newline, then the backslash and the newline are both removed. This applies within a shell script as well as at the command prompt.

```
$ cat cont.sh
#!/bin/bash
echo foo\
bar
$ ./cont.sh
foobar
$
```

When passing variable values to external programs, the order in which those variables are interpreted is significant. In the first example, ssh declan echo $PATH is parsed by the shell on goldie as ssh declan echo /home/steve/bin:/usr/local/bin:/usr/bin:/bin:/usr/bin/X11:/usr/games because that is the value of the PATH variable on goldie. To ensure that the string $PATH is not interpreted by the shell on goldie, you prefix it with a backslash, so that the shell on goldie does not see $PATH and replace it with the value of the variable, but the shell on declan does see $PATH and expands it appropriately, with the value that declan stores for $PATH.

```
steve@goldie:~$ echo $PATH
/home/steve/bin:/usr/local/bin:/usr/bin:/bin:/usr/bin/X11:/usr/games

steve@declan:~$ echo $PATH
/usr/local/bin:/usr/bin:/bin:/usr/bin/X11:/usr/games:/home/steve/bin
steve@declan:~$

steve@goldie:~$ ssh declan echo $PATH
steve@declan's password:
/home/steve/bin:/usr/local/bin:/usr/bin:/bin:/usr/bin/X11:/usr/games

steve@goldie:~$ ssh declan echo \$PATH
steve@declan's password:
/usr/local/bin:/usr/bin:/bin:/usr/bin/X11:/usr/games:/home/steve/bin
steve@goldie:~$
```

SUMMARY

Wildcards can be very flexible and useful, but the price of this is vigilance; whenever using any kind of nonstandard character, you will need to consider how it will be treated by the shell. In some cases it will be passed through; in others it will be interpreted as having special meaning. It is not always obvious which is which — the rules are complex and not always easy to understand.

It is very important to be sure of how you process user-generated or externally sourced input strings. For example, if you do all of your testing expecting the user to provide nice filenames without spaces in them, your script will break when the user passes it a filename including spaces if you have not quoted the filename.

The next chapter deals with Conditional Execution, which uses a variety of tests of the state of the environment to control the flow of a shell script.

5

Conditional Execution

Conditional execution means that you can choose to execute code only if certain conditions are met. Without this capability, all you would be able to do is execute one command after another after another. The ability to test a variety of things about the state of the system, and of the environment variables of the process, means that a shell script can do far more powerful things than would otherwise be possible.

IF/THEN

Almost every programming language has an if/then/else construct, and the shell is no exception. The syntax uses square brackets to perform a test, and the then and fi statements are required, acting just like the { and } curly brackets in C and some other languages.

```
if [ condition ]
then
  statement(s)
fi
```

Other than the line break after the word then, all these line breaks are required or can be replaced with semicolons. The spaces around the [and] symbols are also required, so this can be reduced at best to:

```
if [ condition ];then statement(s);fi
```

It is quite common to use the semicolon to put the then on the same line as the if. The technique of reversing a word to mean its opposite — for example, using fi to end an if statement — comes up again later in this chapter, where case statements are ended with an esac. Similarly, as you see in Chapter 12, the reverse of cat is tac.

The Unix, Linux, and Free Software traditions have a lot of (self-consciously) awful puns. In addition to the wordplay behind GNU and HURD mentioned in Chapter 1, Perlmongers attend Yet Another Perl Conference (YAPC), SuSE employs Yet Another Software Tool (YaST), and abcde is A Better CD Encoder. The Latin American GNU National User Groups are called GNU^2 (Grupos Nacionales de Usarios GNU); the list is virtually endless.

You can make this code more useful by having a section of code that will be executed only if the condition is not met:

```
if [ condition ]
then
   statements for when the condition is true
else
   statements for when the condition is false
fi
```

Here, the first set of statements will be executed if the conditional test passes, and the second set of statements will be executed if it fails. Exactly one of these blocks of code will be executed — never both, and never none of them.

You can test for failure by checking the $? return variable, which is set to zero on success, and non-zero for failure. For these tests, let's use the -r test, which returns true (zero) if, and only if, the file exists and is readable. This snippet tries to cat the file passed to it as its first parameter (putting double quotes around it to allow for filenames including spaces), and spits out an error message if it failed to do so. (cat will also display an error message of its own, to stdout.)

```
#!/bin/bash
# Test for failure
cat "$1"
if [ "$?" -ne "0" ]; then
   echo "Error: Reading $1 failed."
fi
```

This tests to see if the file exists and is readable before it attempts to access the file. This is a safer way to do it; better still would be to check for any further unforeseen failure conditions after the cat command had been run (for example, cat may not be in the $PATH).

```
#!/bin/bash
# Test for likely causes of failure

if [ ! -r "$1" ]; then
   echo "Error: $1 is not a readable file."
   echo "Quitting."
   exit 1
fi

cat "$1"
```

ELSE

It may be that you want to cat the file if at all possible, but if it can't be done, then continue execution of the script. One way to do this would be to have two tests. Here is the first test:

```
if [ -r "$1" ]; then cat "$1"; fi
```

followed by the opposite test (! reverses the result of the test):

```
if [ ! -r "$1" ]; then echo "File $1 is not readable - skipping. "; fi
```

But that is quite cumbersome and prone to errors. If you later replace the test with -s, for example, you would have to change it in two places. So, the else statement comes into play:

```
#!/bin/bash
# Check for likely causes of failure

if [ ! -r "$1" ]; then
  echo "Error: $1 is not a readable file."
else
  cat "$1"
fi
```

You can make this easier to read by taking out the exclamation point (!) and reversing the order of the statements:

```
#!/bin/bash
# Check for likely causes of failure

if [ -r "$1" ]; then
  cat "$1"
else
  echo "Error: $1 is not a readable file."
fi
```

This is more easily readable, and more robust, than the previous scripts. It is often the case that the cleanest solution is actually easier to read than a more convoluted solution.

ELIF

elif is a construct that allows you to add conditions to the else part of an if statement. It is short for "else if" so that a long string of possible actions can be written more concisely. This makes it easier to write, easier to read, and most importantly, easier to debug. A common task for a multi-platform script (such as a generic installer for various different Unixes) is to perform some parts of its task differently depending on the actual operating system it is running on. Without even including any of the actual platform-specific code, this is clearly a mess to read, edit, and debug.

```
#!/bin/bash
OS=`uname -s`

if [ "$OS" = "FreeBSD" ]; then
```

```
        echo "This Is FreeBSD"
else
    if [ "$OS" = "CYGWIN_NT-5.1" ]; then
        echo "This is Cygwin"
    else
        if [ "$OS" = "SunOS" ]; then
            echo "This is Solaris"
        else
            if [ "$OS" = "Darwin" ]; then
                echo "This is Mac OSX"
            else
                if [ "$OS" = "AIX" ]; then
                    echo "This is AIX"
                else
                    if [ "$OS" = "Minix" ]; then
                        echo "This is Minix"
                    else
                        if [ "$OS" = "Linux" ]; then
                            echo "This is Linux"
                        else
                            echo "Failed to identify this OS"
                        fi
                    fi
                fi
            fi
        fi
    fi
fi
```

elif1.sh

By using `elif`, you can make this much simpler, which not only helps the readability, but makes the script an order of magnitude more easy to maintain. To add another OS to `elif1.sh`, you would have to work out the correct indentation, or (as actually happens when these are used in practice) the indentation becomes messed up, making the whole block of code virtually impossible to read, so the task for the next person to add yet another OS is even harder again.

```
#!/bin/bash
OS=`uname -s`

if [ "$OS" = "FreeBSD" ]; then
    echo "This Is FreeBSD"
elif [ "$OS" = "CYGWIN_NT-5.1" ]; then
    echo "This is Cygwin"
elif [ "$OS" = "SunOS" ]; then
    echo "This is Solaris"
elif [ "$OS" = "Darwin" ]; then
    echo "This is Mac OSX"
elif [ "$OS" = "AIX" ]; then
    echo "This is AIX"
elif [ "$OS" = "Minix" ]; then
    echo "This is Minix"
```

```
elif [ "$OS" = "Linux" ]; then
  echo "This is Linux"
else
  echo "Failed to identify this OS"
fi
```

elif2.sh

To add a new operating system to this code, you can simply add another two lines to the script. No indentation issues, no readability issues, and the meaning is perfectly clear.

TEST ([)

The first example in this chapter used the -r test to see if a file exists and is readable. That is a useful test for that example, but there are many more, all documented in the test man page. There is no point in repeating the entire test man page here; rather, look at some useful techniques for getting the best out of test, and selecting the most appropriate test for the task at hand. With so many to choose from, it is common to see shell scripts that go out of their way to replicate the features of test, simply because the writer did not know how useful test can be.

First, let's admit to the sneaky way in which test is implemented, which explains the spacing rules mentioned at the start of this chapter. test itself is a program, which is usually implemented as a shell builtin command. So although there normally is a /usr/bin/test on the disk, it does not usually get called because the shell's builtin is found first. Another name for test is [. When [is called, it requires a] around its arguments, but otherwise, it does the same work.

```
$ type test
test is a shell builtin
$ type [
[ is a shell builtin
$ which test
/usr/bin/test
$ which [
/usr/bin/[
$ ls -il /usr/bin/test /usr/bin/[
33625 -rwxr-xr-x 1 root root 33064 Apr 28  2010 /usr/bin/[
33634 -rwxr-xr-x 1 root root 30136 Apr 28  2010 /usr/bin/test
```

This example shows that if you call test or [from bash, you will get bash's implementation of these. On the disk, you also have test and [which are very similarly sized, but different, files.

This strange configuration means that the shell can appear to have the same kind of syntax as other languages, with a much simpler parser.

The upshot of all this is that while the code looks tidy and recognizable to programmers who are used to other languages, it ends up being treated quite differently. In most languages, [and] (or their equivalents) are language constructs. In the shell, [is a program, and] is simply an argument to it, which is required, but discarded. It has no significance to the shell whatsoever.

This means that you can test that /etc/hosts is a regular file in many ways:

```
$ test -f /etc/hosts
$ echo $?
0
$ /usr/bin/test -f /etc/hosts
$ echo $?
0
$ [ -f /etc/hosts ]
$ echo $?
0
```

These are three different programs, all doing the same test, and all returning zero (indicating success). You can also test that /etc/stsoh is not a regular file:

```
$ test -f /etc/stsoh
$ echo $?
1
$ /usr/bin/test -f /etc/stsoh
$ echo $?
1
$ [ -f /etc/stsoh ]
$ echo $?
1
```

Here, the three programs all agree that the return code is 1 (any nonzero would do). Knowing what is going on behind the scenes can make test a little easier to understand.

Flags for Test

To test if a file exists, you use the -e flag (easily remembered as *e* stands for "exists"). The -a flag is a synonym for -e.

```
if [ -e /etc/resolv.conf ]; then
   echo "DNS Configuration:"
   cat /etc/resolv.conf
else
   echo "No DNS resolv.conf file exists."
fi
```

Because everything is a file in Unix, this is not quite as specific a test as it first appears; device drivers, directories, network mounts, and virtual memory space can all appear as files. A similar test is -f, which tests if the file exists and is actually a regular file. Similarly, -b tests if it is a block device and there is also -c to test for a character device. A block device is a driver for something like a hard disk, which is operated on in blocks; a character device is a driver for something that you read and write characters to, such as a terminal or the /dev/random pseudo device.

Files can also be hard or symbolic links; a hard link is effectively the actual file itself, but a symbolic link (a pointer to the actual file, which may even be on a different filesystem) is tested with the -L flag, or optionally, -h. A link to a regular file will also pass the -f test, a link to a block device will pass the -b test, and so on. The recipe that follows tests for -L before -f. Otherwise, the script would confirm that it is a regular file and never test to see if it is also a symbolic link.

Other things that a file can be in Linux are a socket (tested with the -S flag), and a named (FIFO) pipe (for which the -p flag is used). Sockets are more advanced interprocess communication features, which are beyond the scope of this book, but pipes are covered in Chapter 14.

This script tests all of these possibilities:

```
$ cat blockcharacterfile.sh
#!/bin/bash
while read -p "What file do you want to test? " filename
do
if [ ! -e "$filename" ]; then
  echo "The file does not exist."
  continue
fi

# Okay, the file exists.
ls -ld "$filename"

if [ -L "$filename" ]; then
  echo "$filename is a symbolic link"
elif [ -f "$filename" ]; then
  echo "$filename is a regular file."
elif [ -b "$filename" ]; then
  echo "$filename is a block device"
elif [ -c "$filename" ]; then
  echo "$filename is a character device"
elif [ -d "$filename" ]; then
  echo "$filename is a directory"
elif [ -p "$filename" ]; then
  echo "$filename is a named pipe"
elif [ -S "$filename" ]; then
  echo "$filename is a socket"
else
  echo "I don't know what kind of file that is. Is this a Linux system?"
fi
done
$
$ ./blockcharacterfile.sh
What file do you want to test? /etc/foo
The file does not exist.
What file do you want to test? /etc/hosts
-rw-r--r-- 1 root root 458 Dec  3 00:23 /etc/hosts
/etc/hosts is a regular file.
What file do you want to test? /dev/sda
brw-rw---- 1 root disk 8, 0 Dec 13 09:22 /dev/sda
/dev/sda is a block device
What file do you want to test? /dev/null
crw-rw-rw- 1 root root 1, 3 Dec 13 09:22 /dev/null
/dev/null is a character device
What file do you want to test? /etc
drwxr-xr-x 141 root root 12288 Dec 13 09:24 /etc
/etc is a directory
What file do you want to test? /etc/motd
lrwxrwxrwx 1 root root 13 Jun  5  2010 /etc/motd -> /var/run/motd
```

```
/etc/motd is a symbolic link
What file do you want to test? /tmp/OSL_PIPE_1000_SingleOfficeIPC_54f1d8557767a73f9
bc36a8c3028b0
srwxrwxr-x 1 steve steve 0 Dec 13 10:32 /tmp/OSL_PIPE_1000_SingleOfficeIPC_54f1d855
7767a73f9bc36a8c3028b0
/tmp/OSL_PIPE_1000_SingleOfficeIPC_54f1d8557767a73f9bc36a8c3028b0 is a socket
What file do you want to test? /tmp/myfifo
prwx------ 1 steve steve 0 Dec 14 12:47 /tmp/myfifo
/tmp/myfifo is a named pipe
What file do you want to test? ^C
$
```

blockcharacterfile.sh

Another use of the -d flag is in a /etc/profile script, which can customize a user's environment depending on what is available. This adds ~/bin to the PATH environment, but only if that directory exists:

```
if [ -d ~/bin ]; then
  PATH=$PATH:~/bin
fi
```

Files can have many other properties than the type of file that they are, including size, permissions, timestamps, and more. Unix file permissions are stored in three separate blocks, and each file has an owner, and also an owning group (which normally, but not always, overlap). Each block defines a Read, Write, and an eXecute bit; by convention these are listed as rwx, with unset bits marked as a dash (-). The very first character listed is the file type, as tested for in the preceding code. After that, nine characters indicate the permissions of the file. The first block determines what the owner of the file can do; the second block what members of the owning group can do; and the third block defines what anybody not in either of those categories can do. For example, this configuration file is owned by root, which can read and write it (the first rw-). Its owning group is the fuse group, which can only read the file (r--). The final three dashes (---) mean that nobody else can do anything to the file.

```
-rw-r----- 1 root fuse 216 Jan 31  2010 /etc/fuse.conf
```

Although it would seem obvious at first to have a fuse user to own the file, with this method the application can read its configuration from the file, but the configuration can only be modified by root, which helps to protect fuse from exploit. It is not a security measure in itself but a sensible defense-in-depth strategy, one of the many approaches taken by Unix and Linux to defend against unexpected attacks.

The first three tests here are -r, -w, and -x. These tests discover whether this particular session has permissions respectively to read, write, and execute the file in question. The ability to execute a directory is treated as the right to change into that directory. The interesting thing to note about this is that it is not really testing the file permissions directly so much as querying what this process is allowed to do with the file. The same script, running against the same file, may have different output depending on who runs it, not what file it runs against. Also, a file may have permissions of rwxrwxrwx, but if it is in a directory that the user does not have permission for, the file is entirely inaccessible.

```
$ cat rwx.sh
#!/bin/bash
while read -p "What file do you want to test? " filename
do
if [ ! -e "$filename" ]; then
  echo "The file does not exist."
  continue
fi

# Okay, the file exists.
ls -ld "$filename"
if [ -r "$filename" ]; then
  echo "$filename is readable."
fi
if [ -w "$filename" ]; then
  echo "$filename is writeable"
fi
if [ -x "$filename" ]; then
  echo "$filename is executable"
fi
done
$ ./rwx.sh
What file do you want to test? /home/steve
drwxr-xr-x 70 steve steve 4096 Dec 13 11:52 /home/steve
/home/steve is readable.
/home/steve is writeable
/home/steve is executable
What file do you want to test? /etc
drwxr-xr-x 141 root root 12288 Dec 13 11:40 /etc
/etc is readable.
/etc is executable
What file do you want to test? /etc/hosts
-rw-r--r-- 1 root root 458 Dec  3 00:23 /etc/hosts
/etc/hosts is readable.
What file do you want to test? /etc/shadow
-rw-r----- 1 root shadow 1038 Nov  4 18:32 /etc/shadow
What file do you want to test? ^C
$
```

rwx.sh

You can also find out whether a file is owned by the current user and/or group ID, with the -o and -G flags respectively. This can be much more straightforward than finding your effective user ID or group ID, getting the same information for the file, and making a comparison.

```
$ cat owner.sh
#!/bin/sh
while read -p "What file do you want to test? " filename
do
```

```
if [ ! -e "$filename" ]; then
  echo "The file does not exist."
  continue
fi

# Okay, the file exists.
  ls -ld $filename
  if [ -O $filename ]; then
    echo "You own $filename"
  else
    echo "You don't own $filename"
  fi
  if [ -G $filename ]; then
    echo "Your group owns $filename"
  else
    echo "Your group doesn't own $filename"
  fi
done
$ ./owner.sh
What file do you want to test? /home/steve
drwxr-xr-x 70 steve steve 4096 Dec 13 23:24 /home/steve
You own /home/steve
Your group owns /home/steve
What file do you want to test? /etc/hosts
-rw-r--r-- 1 root root 458 Dec  3 00:23 /etc/hosts
You don't own /etc/hosts
Your group doesn't own /etc/hosts
What file do you want to test? ^C
$
```

owner.sh

Another feature of Unix-style file permissions are the suid (Set UserID) and sgid (Set GroupID)bits.
These allow the program to be run as the user (or group), which owns the file, not necessarily the
user (or group) running the program. This is shown as an s instead of an x in the rwx style of displaying file permissions. You can test for these using the -g and -u flags respectively.

```
$ cat suid.sh
#!/bin/sh
while read -p "What file do you want to test? " filename
do
if [ ! -e "$filename" ]; then
  echo "The file does not exist."
  continue
fi

# Okay, the file exists.
  ls -ld $filename
  if [ -u $filename ]; then
    echo "$filename will run as user \"`stat --printf=%U $filename`\""
  fi
  if [ -g $filename ]; then
    echo "$filename will run as group \"`stat --printf=%G $filename`\""
  fi
```

```
done
$ ./suid.sh
What file do you want to test? /usr/bin/procmail
-rwsr-sr-x 1 root mail 89720 Apr 25  2010 /usr/bin/procmail
/usr/bin/procmail will run as user "root"
/usr/bin/procmail will run as group "mail"
What file do you want to test? /bin/ping
-rwsr-xr-x 1 root root 34248 Oct 14 07:21 /bin/ping
/bin/ping will run as user "root"
What file do you want to test? ^C
$
```

suid.sh

In some cases, such as checking whether a log file has been written to, it can be useful to find out whether a file has any content. The -s flag for test tells you if the file exists and has a size greater than zero. If the -s test passes, the file has a size greater than zero. If it fails, it either does not exist or has zero length. Depending on exactly which combination you need to know, -s alone will probably be enough, but you can combine it with -e to also see whether or not the file exists. On some systems, /var/log/mcelog contains the log of any Machine Check Exceptions that have been detected. You would want there to be none, but you can detect if there is a problem by using simple script. This example finds 18 lines in /var/log/mcelog:

Available for
download on
Wrox.com

```
$ cat mce.sh
#!/bin/sh
if [ -s /var/log/mcelog ]; then
   echo "Machine Check Exceptions found :"
   wc -l /var/log/mcelog
fi
$ ./mce.sh
Machine Check Exceptions found :
18 /var/log/mcelog
$
```

mce.sh

Sometimes you want to read a file only if it has new content. A named pipe (also known as First In, First Out, or FIFO) could be a better solution, but sometimes you do not get to choose how the data is created. The -N flag tests if a file has been modified since it was last read. This can be demonstrated this with a pair of scripts — in a graphical environment you can run this in two different windows; otherwise, use two separate sessions to the server.

Available for
download on
Wrox.com

```
$ echo hello > /tmp/myfile.log
$ echo hello world >> /tmp/myfile.log
$ cat watchfile.sh
#!/bin/bash
GAP=10                         # how long to wait
LOGFILE=$1                     # file to log to

# Get the current length of the file.
len=`wc -l $LOGFILE | awk '{ print $1 }'`
```

```
echo "Current size is $len lines"

while :
do
  if [ -N $LOGFILE ]; then
    echo "`date`: New entries in $LOGFILE:"
    newlen=`wc -l $LOGFILE | awk '{ print $1 }'`
    newlines=`expr $newlen - $len`
    tail -$newlines $LOGFILE
    len=$newlen
  fi
  sleep $GAP
done
$ ./watchfile.sh /tmp/myfile.log
Current size is 2 lines
```

watchfile.sh

Now from a separate window, run this command:

```
$ echo this is a test >> /tmp/myfile.log
```

In the first window, within $GAP seconds (which is 10 seconds in this case) you should see the following:

```
Fri Dec 17 10:56:42 GMT 2010: New entries in /tmp/myfile.log:
this is a test
```

Now from the second window, run these commands:

```
$ echo this is a two line test >> /tmp/myfile.log ; \
> echo this is the second line of it >> /tmp/myfile.log
$
```

It doesn't matter how long it takes you to type it. watchfile.sh will show data only when there is a change, so do the two echo commands on one line, and this will work. You could also increase the value of $GAP to something like 60 seconds to give you more time to type.

In the first window, you will see the following:

```
Fri Dec 17 10:57:52 GMT 2010: New entries in /tmp/myfile.log:
this is a two line test
this is the second line of it
```

Just to confirm what is in the file, cat the log file itself:

```
$ cat /tmp/myfile.log
hello
hello world
this is a test
this is a two line test
this is the second line of it
```

This can be a useful way of watching incremental changes to a file. It would be even more suitable in a cron job.

File Comparison Tests

The `test` command can also do a few basic comparisons between files. The `-ef` comparison tests if two files are actually hard links to the same inode on the same filesystem. This saves quite a bit of trouble, because although `stat --format=%i` or `ls -i` can provide the inode number of a file, you would still have to check that the two files are on the same filesystem.

```
$ cat equalfile.sh
#!/bin/bash

file1=$1
file2=$2

ls -il $file1 $file2
if [ $file1 -ef $file2 ]; then
  echo "$file1 is the same file as $file2"
else
  echo "$file1 is not the same file as $file2"
  diff -q $file1 $file2
  if [ "$?" -eq "0" ]; then
    echo "However, their contents are identical."
  fi
fi
$ echo testing > file1
$ ln file1 file2
$ echo testing > file3
$ ls -il file?
4931911 -rw-rw-r-- 2 steve steve 8 Dec 14 21:04 file1
4931911 -rw-rw-r-- 2 steve steve 8 Dec 14 21:04 file2
4931915 -rw-rw-r-- 1 steve steve 8 Dec 14 21:04 file3
$ ./equalfile.sh file1 file2
4931911 -rw-rw-r-- 2 steve steve 8 Dec 14 21:04 file1
4931911 -rw-rw-r-- 2 steve steve 8 Dec 14 21:04 file2
file1 is the same file as file2
$ ./equalfile.sh file1 file3
4931911 -rw-rw-r-- 2 steve steve 8 Dec 14 21:04 file1
4931915 -rw-rw-r-- 1 steve steve 8 Dec 14 21:04 file3
file1 is not the same file as file3
However, their contents are identical.
$ echo something different > file4
$ ./equalfile.sh file1 file4
4931911 -rw-rw-r-- 2 steve steve  8 Dec 14 21:04 file1
4931917 -rw-rw-r-- 1 steve steve 20 Dec 14 21:05 file4
file1 is not the same file as file4
Files file1 and file4 differ
$
```

equalfile.sh

The other comparison that `test` can do between two files is to find out whether one file has had its contents modified more recently than another.

Only modification time (mtime) is compared; access time (atime) and inode changes (ctime) are not used by these tests.

```
$ echo old file > old
$ sleep 60
$ echo newer file > new
$ ls -l new old
-rw-rw-r-- 1 steve steve 11 Dec 14 13:21 new
-rw-rw-r-- 1 steve steve  9 Dec 14 13:20 old
$ if [ new -nt old ]; then
>    echo "new is newer"
> else
>    echo "old is newer"
> fi
new is newer
$ if [ new -ot old ]; then
>    echo "new is older"
> else
>    echo "old is older"
> fi
old is older
$
```

 If the files have the same timestamp, both tests will report false, which is correct; they are neither newer nor older than each other. Also, if one of the files does not exist, both tests will report true. If neither file exists, both tests will also report false.

String Comparison Tests

There are four tests that can be done on strings. You can test whether they are the same, and you can test whether one comes before the other alphanumerically. This script compares two strings and reports on whether or not they are the same. If they are not the same, it then tells you which comes first alphabetically. To achieve this, you have to use a slightly different syntax from what you have seen so far. The string comparisons < and > only work within the [[...]] compound command. You can use the == and != tests within either a single or double bracket test, but the single bracket test is the only one that works with a single equal sign (=). The reason for this complexity is to maintain compatibility with the Bourne shell while adding the more powerful [[command.

```
$ cat alnum.sh
#!/bin/bash
if [ "$1" = "$2" ]; then
    echo "$1 is the same as $2"
else
    echo "$1 is not the same as $2"
```

```
        # Since they are different, let's see which comes first:
        if [[ "$1" < "$2" ]]; then
          echo "$1 comes before $2"
        else
          echo "$1 comes after $2"
        fi
fi
$ ./alnum.sh apples bananas
apples is not the same as bananas
apples comes before bananas
$ ./alnum.sh bananas apples
bananas is not the same as apples
bananas comes after apples
$ ./alnum.sh oranges oranges
oranges is the same as oranges
$
```

alnum.sh

> *The second line of* alnum.sh *uses a single = symbol to test for equality. The bash shell, and others, will also accept a double ==, which is more in line with other languages (notably C). However, this is not compliant with the POSIX standard, and the traditional Bourne shell does not recognize this syntax. It is best to use the single = as that is understood everywhere.*

Missing from this recipe is the test for inequality. This is done with the != test:

```
$ if [ "one" != "two" ]; then
>   echo "These are not the same"
> fi
These are not the same
$
```

The final two string tests are similar to the -s test for files. The -z test returns true if the string has zero length, while -n returns true if the string has nonzero length. Because you are testing a potentially empty string, you will need to put quotes around the variable name; otherwise, the test [-z $input] would reduce to [-z], which is not syntactically valid. Only [-z ""] is syntactically valid.

```
$ cat nz.sh
#!/bin/bash
# Set input to a known value as we are testing it before we set it
input=""

while [ -z "$input" ]; do
  read -p "Please give your input: " input
done
echo "Thank you for saying $input"
$ ./nz.sh
```

```
Please give your input:
Please give your input:
Please give your input: something
Thank you for saying something
$
```

<code>nz.sh</code>

Regular Expression Tests

A feature new since bash 3 is the =~ operator, which acts much like its perl equivalent. It treats the right side as an extended regular expression, so bash can now do some of the things that previously one would need to go to perl, sed, or grep to achieve. This means that you can identify file names that match the pattern *.deb by checking for [[$pkgname =~ .*\.deb]]. Note that the double-bracket syntax [[...]] is required.

```
$ cat isdeb.sh
#!/bin/bash

for deb in pkgs/*
do
  pkgname=`basename $deb`
  if [[ $pkgname =~ .*\.deb ]]; then
    echo "$pkgname is a .deb package"
  else
    echo "File \"$pkgname\" is not a .deb package."
  fi
done
$ ls pkgs/
dbus-x11_1.2.24-4_amd64.deb
firmware-linux-free_2.6.32-29_all.deb
gnome-desktop-1.023.x86_64.rpm
libgnomeprint-2.18.6-2.6.x86_64.rpm
libgnomeui2-2.24.3-1mdv2010.1.i586.rpm
linux-headers-2.6.32-5-amd64_2.6.32-29_amd64.deb
linux-headers-2.6.32-5-common_2.6.32-29_amd64.deb
linux-libc-dev_2.6.32-29_amd64.deb
linux-source-2.6.32_2.6.32-29_all.deb
README
$ ./isdeb.sh
dbus-x11_1.2.24-4_amd64.deb is a .deb package
firmware-linux-free_2.6.32-29_all.deb is a .deb package
File "gnome-desktop-1.023.x86_64.rpm" is not a .deb package.
File "libgnomeprint-2.18.6-2.6.x86_64.rpm" is not a .deb package.
File "libgnomeui2-2.24.3-1mdv2010.1.i586.rpm" is not a .deb package.
linux-headers-2.6.32-5-amd64_2.6.32-29_amd64.deb is a .deb package
linux-headers-2.6.32-5-common_2.6.32-29_amd64.deb is a .deb package
linux-libc-dev_2.6.32-29_amd64.deb is a .deb package
linux-source-2.6.32_2.6.32-29_all.deb is a .deb package
File "README" is not a .deb package.
$
```

isdeb.sh

This is quite useful, but it does not tell you what matched, or what the matching string was. To do this you can refer to the BASH_REMATCH[] array. Any expressions surrounded by parentheses () are put into this array; index 0 matches the entire string. You can read items from the array to get the exact match. By understanding a little of the .deb naming convention, which is packagename_version_architecture.deb, you can grab that data from the filename.

```
$ cat identify_debs.sh
#!/bin/bash

for deb in pkgs/*
do
  pkgname=`basename $deb`
  echo $pkgname
  if [[ $pkgname =~ (.+)_(.*)_(.*)\.deb ]]; then
    echo "Package ${BASH_REMATCH[1]} Version ${BASH_REMATCH[2]}"\
         "is for the \"${BASH_REMATCH[3]}\" architecture."
    echo
  else
    echo "File \"$pkgname\" does not appear to match the "
    echo "standard .deb naming convention."
    echo
  fi
done
$ ./identify_debs.sh
dbus-x11_1.2.24-4_amd64.deb
Package dbus-x11 Version 1.2.24-4 is for the "amd64" architecture.

firmware-linux-free_2.6.32-29_all.deb
Package firmware-linux-free Version 2.6.32-29 is for the "all" architecture.

gnome-desktop-1.023.x86_64.rpm
File "gnome-desktop-1.023.x86_64.rpm" does not appear to match the
standard .deb naming convention.
libgnomeprint-2.18.6-2.6.x86_64.rpm
File "libgnomeprint-2.18.6-2.6.x86_64.rpm" does not appear to match the
standard .deb naming convention.

libgnomeui2-2.24.3-1mdv2010.1.i586.rpm
File "libgnomeui2-2.24.3-1mdv2010.1.i586.rpm" does not appear to match the
standard .deb naming convention.

linux-headers-2.6.32-5-amd64_2.6.32-29_amd64.deb
Package linux-headers-2.6.32-5-amd64 Version 2.6.32-29 is for the "amd64" architect
ure.

linux-headers-2.6.32-5-common_2.6.32-29_amd64.deb
Package linux-headers-2.6.32-5-common Version 2.6.32-29 is for the "amd64" architec
ture.

linux-libc-dev_2.6.32-29_amd64.deb
Package linux-libc-dev Version 2.6.32-29 is for the "amd64" architecture.

linux-source-2.6.32_2.6.32-29_all.deb
```

```
Package linux-source-2.6.32 Version 2.6.32-29 is for the "all" architecture.

README
File "README" does not appear to match the
standard .deb naming convention.

$
```

identify_debs.sh

As a final example of this feature, this version of the script also identifies RPM packages by their naming convention, `packagename-version-architecture.rpm`. Notice that this copes with the gnome-desktop package including a hyphen in the package name. The script is not confused about which hyphens mark the version number and which are part of the name of the package.

```
$ cat identify_pkgs.sh
#!/bin/bash

for pkg in pkgs/*
do
    pkgname=`basename $pkg`
    echo $pkgname
    if [[ $pkgname =~ (.+)_(.*)_(.*)\.(deb) ]]; then
        echo "Package ${BASH_REMATCH[1]} Version ${BASH_REMATCH[2]} is a"
        echo "  Debian package for the ${BASH_REMATCH[3]} architecture."
        echo
    elif [[ $pkgname =~ (.+)-(.+)\.(.*)\.rpm ]]; then
        echo "Package ${BASH_REMATCH[1]} Version ${BASH_REMATCH[2]} is an"
        echo "  RPM for the ${BASH_REMATCH[3]} architecture."
        echo
    else
        echo "File \"$pkgname\" does not appear to match the"
        echo "standard .deb or .rpm naming conventions."
    fi
done
$ ./identify_pkgs.sh
dbus-x11_1.2.24-4_amd64.deb
Package dbus-x11 Version 1.2.24-4 is a
   Debian package for the amd64 architecture.

firmware-linux-free_2.6.32-29_all.deb
Package firmware-linux-free Version 2.6.32-29 is a
   Debian package for the all architecture.

gnome-desktop-1.023.x86_64.rpm
Package gnome-desktop Version 1.023 is an
   RPM for the x86_64 architecture.

libgnomeprint-2.18.6-2.6.x86_64.rpm
Package libgnomeprint-2.18.6 Version 2.6 is an
   RPM for the x86_64 architecture.

libgnomeui2-2.24.3-1mdv2010.1.i586.rpm
```

```
Package libgnomeui2-2.24.3 Version 1mdv2010.1 is an
    RPM for the i586 architecture.

linux-headers-2.6.32-5-amd64_2.6.32-29_amd64.deb
Package linux-headers-2.6.32-5-amd64 Version 2.6.32-29 is a
    Debian package for the amd64 architecture.

linux-headers-2.6.32-5-common_2.6.32-29_amd64.deb
Package linux-headers-2.6.32-5-common Version 2.6.32-29 is a
    Debian package for the amd64 architecture.

linux-libc-dev_2.6.32-29_amd64.deb
Package linux-libc-dev Version 2.6.32-29 is a
    Debian package for the amd64 architecture.

linux-source-2.6.32_2.6.32-29_all.deb
Package linux-source-2.6.32 Version 2.6.32-29 is a
    Debian package for the all architecture.

README
File "README" does not appear to match the
standard .deb or .rpm naming conventions.
$
```

identify_pkgs.sh

Numerical Tests

Six numerical comparisons are available. The -eq test returns true if the two numbers are equal, while -ne returns true if they are not equal. -lt and -gt respectively are used for comparing if one number is less than or greater than the other. If you need to test if the values are less than or equal to, -le does that test, and -ge does the complementary test to see if one number is greater or equal to the other. The following recipe is for a number-guessing game that helps you out by telling you what you have already learned from the game so far.

```
$ cat numberguess.sh
#!/bin/bash
MAX=50
guess=-1
let answer=($RANDOM % $MAX)
let answer+=1
ceiling=$MAX
floor=0
guesses=0

while [ "$guess" -ne "$answer" ]
do
  echo "The magic number is between $floor and $ceiling."
  echo -en " Make your guess:"
  read guess
  guesses=`expr $guesses + 1`
```

```
  if [ "$guess" -lt "$answer" ]; then
    echo "$guess is too low"
    if [ "$guess" -gt "$floor" ]; then
      floor=`expr $guess + 1`
    fi
  fi
  if [ "$guess" -gt "$answer" ]; then
    echo "$guess is too high"
    if [ "$guess" -lt "$ceiling" ]; then
      ceiling=`expr $guess - 1`
    fi
  fi
done
echo "You got it in $guesses guesses!"
$ ./numberguess.sh
The magic number is between 1 and 50.
Make your guess: 25
25 is too low
The magic number is between 26 and 50.
Make your guess: 37
37 is too low
The magic number is between 38 and 50.
Make your guess: 46
46 is too high
The magic number is between 38 and 45.
Make your guess: 43
43 is too low
The magic number is between 44 and 45.
Make your guess: 45
45 is too high
The magic number is between 44 and 44.
Make your guess: 44
You got it in 6 guesses!
$
```

numberguess.sh

This adjusts the "floor" and "ceiling" with every wrong guess, so you can effectively do a binary sort on the range, until you home in on the correct answer. It takes out some of the fun, but it makes a useful example of the features.

 You use -lt and -gt to exclude the possibility of the guess matching the correct answer. However, the -ge is better than -gt in if ["$guess" -gt "$floor"] *because if the player guesses the lowest possible number, and is wrong, then you still want to increase the ceiling to reflect that.*

Combining Tests

It is possible to combine tests by using the `&&` and `||` operators. These perform a Logical AND and Logical OR, respectively. To test that a file is readable, and is of nonzero length, you can combine the `-r` and `-s` tests. In this example, it does not matter which one of the tests fails; unless both conditions are true, there is really no point in calculating the md5sum of the file. `/etc/hosts` is usually readable and has content, so this recipe defaults to `/etc/hosts`. `/etc/shadow` also usually has content, but unless you are `root`, or in the group `shadow`, it is not readable. It would therefore not be possible to calculate the md5sum of this file.

```
$ cat md5-if-possible.sh
#!/bin/bash
filename=${1:-/etc/hosts}

if [ -r "$filename" ] && [ -s "$filename" ]; then
  md5sum $filename
else
  echo "$filename can not be processed"
fi

# Show the file if possible
ls -ld $filename 2>/dev/null
$ ./md5-if-possible.sh /etc/hosts
785ae781cf4a4ded403642097f90a275  /etc/hosts
-rw-r--r-- 1 root root 458 Dec  3 00:23 /etc/hosts
$ ./md5-if-possible.sh /etc/shadow
/etc/shadow can not be processed
-rw-r----- 1 root shadow 1038 Nov  4 21:04 /etc/shadow
$
```

md5-if-possible.sh

With the `[ -r "$filename" ] && [ -s "$filename" ]` syntax, if the file is not readable, the `-s` test will not be executed. This can be used to provide a convenient, although not always very easily understood, shortcut. The next snippet only works without ever displaying error messages because `echo` is only called if the `test` has already succeeded. You can also use this to speed up your scripts by performing the tests that are the quickest, or most likely to fail, first.

```
$ cat readable-and.sh
#!/bin/bash
filename=${1:-/etc/hosts}

[ -r $filename ] && echo "$filename is readable"
$ ./readable-and.sh /etc/hosts
/etc/hosts is readable
$ ./readable-and.sh /etc/shadow
$
```

readable-and.sh

The || operator performs a Logical OR, so when it only matters that one of the conditions is met, but not which one, this is the feature to use.

```
$ cat mine.sh
#!/bin/bash
filename=${1:-/etc/hosts}

if [ -O "$filename" ] || [ -G "$filename" ]; then
  echo "$filename is mine (or my group's)"
else
  echo "$filename is not mine (nor my group's)"
fi
$ ./mine.sh /etc/hosts
/etc/hosts is not mine (nor my group's)
$ ./mine.sh $HOME
/home/steve is mine (or my group's)
$
```

mine.sh

This will succeed if either the –O (Owner) or –G (Group) test passes. The || operator continues to process the tests until it finds one that passes. The useful side effect of this is that you can provide a command to run only on failure.

```
$ cat readable-or.sh
#!/bin/bash
filename=${1:-/etc/hosts}

[ -r $filename ] || echo "$filename is not readable"
$ ./readable-or.sh $HOME
$ ./readable-or.sh /etc/shadow
/etc/shadow is not readable
$
```

readable-or.sh

These shortcuts are useful and it is necessary to know about them in order to understand what many shell scripts do. I recommend that that you do not overuse these features, however, as they are not as easily readable as the longer if/then/else syntax. Some people believe that these forms, being shorter, are faster, but this is not the case.

You will notice that the shorter forms never used the if statement at all. They called test directly (in its [form). You can use this syntax with any command; it is not part of the if statement. The shell can use the && and || operators on any command, not only if and test. Here are a few examples of other commands with the && and || operators:

```
$ wc -l /etc/hosts || echo "wc failed to read /etc/hosts"
18 /etc/hosts
$ wc -l /etc/hosts.bak || echo "wc failed to read /etc/hosts.bak"
wc: /etc/hosts.bak: No such file or directory
wc failed to read /etc/hosts.bak
```

```
$ wc -l /etc/hosts | grep "^20 " && echo "/etc/hosts is a 20 line file"
$ wc -l /etc/hosts | grep "^20 " || echo "/etc/hosts is not a 20 line file"
/etc/hosts is not a 20 line file
$ wc -l /etc/hosts | grep "^18 " && echo "/etc/hosts is an 18 line file"
18 /etc/hosts
/etc/hosts is an 18 line file
$
```

CASE

case provides a much cleaner, easier-to-write, and far more readable alternative to the if/then/else construct, particularly when there are a lot of possible values to test for. With case, you list the values you want to identify and act upon, and then provide a block of code for each one. A basic case block looks like this:

Available for download on Wrox.com

```
$ cat fruit.sh
#!/bin/bash

read -p "What is your favorite fruit?: " fruit
case $fruit in
  orange) echo "The $fruit is orange" ;;
  banana) echo "The $fruit is yellow" ;;
  pear) echo "The $fruit is green" ;;
  *) echo "I don't know what color a $fruit is" ;;
esac
$ ./fruit.sh
What is your favorite fruit?: banana
The banana is yellow
$ ./fruit.sh
What is your favorite fruit?: apple
I don't know what color a apple is
$
```

fruit.sh

This displays the color of various fruits, and catches any others in the * handler. To go back to the use of elif to deal with multiple different unames, you can make this even shorter and easier to understand using case. Notice that this is not intelligent enough to correct its grammar when displaying the text "a apple."

Available for download on Wrox.com

```
$ cat uname-case.sh
#!/bin/bash
OS=`uname -s`

case "$OS" in
  FreeBSD) echo "This is FreeBSD" ;;
  CYGWIN_NT-5.1) echo "This is Cygwin" ;;
  SunOS) echo "This is Solaris" ;;
  Darwin) echo "This is Mac OSX" ;;
  AIX) echo "This is AIX" ;;
```

```
   Minix) echo "This is Minix" ;;
   Linux) echo "This is Linux" ;;
   *) echo "Failed to identify this OS" ;;
esac
```

uname-case.sh

Although it looks like a special directive, the * is simply the most generic wildcard possible, as it will match absolutely any string. This suggests that you should be able to do more advanced pattern matching, and indeed you can:

```
$ cat surname.sh
#!/bin/bash
read -p "What is your surname?: " surname

case $surname in
   [a-g]* | [A-G]*) file=1 ;;
   [h-m]* | [H-M]*) file=2 ;;
   [n-s]* | [N-S]*) file=3 ;;
   [t-z]* | [T-Z]*) file=4 ;;
   *) file=0 ;;
esac

if [ "$file" -gt "0" ]; then
   echo "$surname goes in file $file"
else
   echo "I have nowhere to put $surname"
fi
$ ./surname.sh
What is your surname?: Apple
Apple goes in file 1
$ ./surname.sh
What is your surname?: apple
apple goes in file 1
$ ./surname.sh
What is your surname?: Parker
Parker goes in file 3
$ ./surname.sh
What is your surname?: 'ougho
I have nowhere to put 'ougho
$
```

surname.sh

This allows for a filing system where customers' details are stored in a different file, depending on the first letter of their surname. It also shows matching multiple patterns, as [A-G]* or [a-g]* result in file 1. If the shell option nocasematch is set, this repetition is not necessary as such comparisons will be case insensitive in any case. By default, as with most things Unix, case does matter. You could also get around this by forcing $surname to being all uppercase or all lowercase before testing it, but this form gives flexibility in less well-defined cases.

A less well-known feature of the bash implementation of case is that you can end the statement with ;;& or ;& instead of only ;;. While ;; means that none of the other statements will be executed, if you end a statement with ;;& all subsequent cases will still be evaluated. If you end a statement with ;&, the following case will be treated as having matched. This example describes everything (categorized as uppercase, lowercase, numerical, or other) that it is given as input. A regular case statement would stop after the first match; the code that follows uses ;;& after the end of the statements from which it wants to continue testing.

This feature is specific to the bash shell; it is not a standard feature of the Bourne shell, so if you need to write a portable script, do not expect this to work. It will cause a syntax error message on other shells.

```
$ cat case1.sh
#!/bin/bash

read -p "Give me a word: " input
echo -en "You gave me some "
case $input in
  *[[:lower:]]*) echo -en "Lowercase " ;;&
  *[[:upper:]]*) echo -en "Uppercase " ;;&
  *[[:digit:]]*) echo -en "Numerical " ;;&
  *) echo "input." ;;
esac
$ ./case1.sh
Give me a word: Hello
You gave me some Lowercase Uppercase input.
$ ./case1.sh
Give me a word: hello
You gave me some Lowercase input.
$ ./case1.sh
Give me a word: HELLO
You gave me some Uppercase input.
$ ./case1.sh
Give me a word: 123
You gave me some Numerical input.
$ ./case1.sh
Give me a word: Hello 123
You gave me some Lowercase Uppercase Numerical input.
$ ./case1.sh
Give me a word: !@#
You gave me some input.
$
```

case1.sh

The other ending specific to bash is the ;& ending. This causes the following block of code to be executed as if it had been a successful match. You can use this to make "Ramsey Street" act as if it had matched the test `Melbourne | Canberra | Sydney` so that Ramsey Street is treated as being part of Australia, just as Melbourne, Canberra, and Sydney are. This example also shows some more relevant uses of the `;;&` ending. You can match against capital cities independently of matching against countries, for example.

```
$ cat case2.sh
#!/bin/bash

read -p "Which city are you closest to?: " city
case $city in
  "New York"|London|Paris|Tokyo)
          # You can identify the capital cities and still fall through to
          # match the specific country below.
          echo "That is a capital city" ;;&
  Chicago|Detroit|"New York"|Washington)
          echo "You are in the USA" ;;
  London|Edinburgh|Cardiff|Dublin)
          echo "You are in the United Kingdom" ;;
  "Ramsey Street")
          # This is a famous street in an unspecified location in Australia.
          # You can still fall through and run the generic Australian code
          # by using the ;& ending.
          echo "G'Day Neighbour!" ;&
  Melbourne|Canberra|Sydney)
          echo "You are in Australia" ;;
  Paris)
          echo "You are in France" ;;
  Tokyo)
          echo "You are in Japan" ;;
  N*)
          # We have already matched "New York" and ended it with a ;;
          # so New York will not fall through to this test. Other places
          # beginning with N will fall through to here.
          echo "Your word begins with N but is not New York" ;;
  *)
          echo "I'm sorry, I don't know anything about $city" ;;
esac
$ ./case2.sh
Which city are you closest to?: London
That is a capital city
You are in the United Kingdom
$ ./case2.sh
Which city are you closest to?: Paris
That is a capital city
You are in France
$ ./case2.sh
Which city are you closest to?: New York
That is a capital city
You are in the USA
$ ./case2.sh
Which city are you closest to?: Nottingham
Your word begins with N but is not New York
$ ./case2.sh
Which city are you closest to?: Texas
```

```
I'm sorry, I don't know anything about Texas
$ ./case2.sh
Which city are you closest to?: Sydney
You are in Australia
$ ./case2.sh
Which city are you closest to?: Ramsey Street
G'Day Neighbour!
You are in Australia
$
```

case2.sh

SUMMARY

This chapter has covered the various ways of controlling conditional execution — from the simple
if/then/else construct, through the different things that can be done with test, through to the
more flexible case statement for matching against different sets of input. The next chapter looks at
other ways of using these tests, specifically to control loops, which are a more specialized language
structure that makes use of these tests.

Flow Control Using Loops

Loops are a vital tool for writing useful code. Much of the benefit of programming, and of computers in general, is that the machine can do the mundane work faster and more efficiently than a human, so it is often the case that you spend a long time carefully writing a few lines of code, which the machine then iterates over tens, hundreds, maybe even thousands of times or more. The basic structure of a loop is that it has a block of code to execute, and something telling it when to stop going around the loop and continue execution of the program. As you will see, the shell has four different loop structures: for, while, until, and select. Each of these has its own purpose and its own strengths and weaknesses. It is often (though not always) quite obvious up front which type of loop you will want to use for a particular task.

FOR LOOPS

Unlike most loops, the for loop does not test the condition of a variable each time it goes around the loop. Instead, it starts with a list of items to iterate through and works its way through them until it has reached the end. This makes it the most deterministic of the loop structures. This does not mean that the list of items has to be written out explicitly in the script itself (although it can be, and often is). It can iterate through each of the words in a file, through the content of a variable, or even through the output of other commands. The simplest form of for is to give it a set of items to work through, however.

```
$ cat fruit.sh
#!/bin/bash
for fruit in apple orange pear
do
    echo "I really like ${fruit}s"
done
echo "Let's make a salad!"
$ ./fruit.sh
I really like apples
```

```
I really like oranges
I really like pears
Let's make a salad!
$
```

What happens here is that you define a variable, `fruit`, which is set in turn to `apple`, then `orange`, then `pear`. This loops around three times until it has exhausted its list. The first time around the loop is `fruit=apple`; the second time, `fruit=orange`; and on the third and final iteration, `fruit=pear`. Once it has completed the loop, the script continues normal execution with the next command after the `done` statement. In this case, it ends by saying "Let's make a salad!" to show that it has ended the loop, but not the script.

When to Use For Loops

The `for` loop is best when you know that you want to do the same thing to a set of items, rather than wanting to repeat something until a certain state is achieved. Altering a set of files or doing something with the same set of input all the time are tasks well suited to `for` loops. `for` loops are not so good if you expect that you will want to break out of the loop based on the outcome of some test or other.

Imaginative Ways of Feeding "For" with Data

The preceding example was fairly dull; it can be made more relevant with a few changes. First of all, the input can be the values of a variable rather than hard-coded.

```
$ cat fruit-var.sh
#!/bin/bash
fruits="apple orange pear"
for fruit in $fruits
do
  echo "I really like ${fruit}s"
done
echo "Let's make a salad!"
$ ./fruit-var.sh
I really like apples
I really like oranges
I really like pears
Let's make a salad!
$
```

This gives you the flexibility to write a more interactive script. It can take input from the user, either from reading input interactively or from the command line itself. As you saw in Chapter 3, `$*` expands to all of the parameters passed on the command line.

```
$ cat fruit-read.sh
#!/bin/bash
echo -en "Please tell me some of your favorite fruit: "
read fruits
for fruit in $fruits
```

```
do
  echo "I really like ${fruit}s"
done
echo "Let's make a salad!"
$ ./fruit-read.sh
Please tell me some of your favorite fruit: kiwi banana grape apple
I really like kiwis
I really like bananas
I really like grapes
I really like apples
Let's make a salad!
```

fruit-read.sh

 Like with "a apple" in Chapter 5, these scripts are too simplistic to cope with pluralizing the word "cherry" into "cherries" in the following example.

Available for
download on
Wrox.com

```
$ cat fruit-cmdline.sh
#!/bin/bash
for fruit in $*
do
  echo "I really like ${fruit}s"
done
$ ./fruit-cmdline.sh satsuma apricot cherry
I really like satsumas
I really like apricots
I really like cherrys
Let's make a salad!
$
```

fruit-cmdline.sh

The command-line parameters can be processed in another way; the in list part of the syntax is optional. It is perfectly valid to run the following script. It processes the $@ variables to work in the same way as fruit-cmdline.sh.

Available for
download on
Wrox.com

```
$ cat for.sh
#!/bin/bash

for fruit
do
  echo I really like $fruit
done
echo "Let's make a salad!"
$ ./for.sh apples oranges bananas
I really like apples
I really like oranges
I really like bananas
Let's make a salad!
$
```

for.sh

The same technique applies to functions. This final example of a `for` loop demonstrates the same thing within a function, where $@ is replaced with the arguments to the function itself.

Available for
download on
Wrox.com

```
$ cat for-function.sh
#!/bin/bash

do_i_like()
{
  for fruit
  do
    echo I really like $fruit
  done
}

do_i_like apples bananas oranges
do_i_like satsumas apricots cherries

echo "Let's make a salad!"
$ ./for-function.sh
I really like apples
I really like bananas
I really like oranges
I really like satsumas
I really like apricots
I really like cherries
Let's make a salad!
$
```

for-function.sh

This is still a fairly manual process — all of these loops have processed only a static list of fruits. Unix was designed with a principle that there are many tools, each of which does one thing and does it well. There are lots of small, simple tools that can be used to feed data into a `for` loop. One of the most ideal is the `seq` command, which is covered in more detail in Chapter 14. `seq` is only available on GNU-based systems, such as Linux, so although it is very useful, do be aware that it is not portable across many different operating systems. It can be used to monitor which machines on the network respond to a `ping` and which don't.

Available for
download on
Wrox.com

```
$ cat ping.sh
#!/bin/bash

UPHOSTS=/var/log/uphosts.`date +%m%d%Y`
DOWNHOSTS=/var/log/downhosts.`date +%m%d%Y`
PREFIX=192.168.1
for OCTET in `seq 1 254`
do
  echo -en "Pinging ${PREFIX}.${OCTET}...."
  ping -c1 -w1 ${PREFIX}.${OCTET} > /dev/null 2>&1
  if [ "$?" -eq "0" ]; then
    echo " OK"
    echo "${PREFIX}.${OCTET}" >> ${UPHOSTS}
  else
    echo " Failed"
    echo "${PREFIX}.${OCTET}" >> ${DOWNHOSTS}
  fi
```

```
done
$ ./ping.sh
Pinging 192.168.1.1.... OK
Pinging 192.168.1.2.... Failed
Pinging 192.168.1.3.... OK
Pinging 192.168.1.4.... OK
. . . etc
Pinging 192.168.1.252.... OK
Pinging 192.168.1.253.... OK
Pinging 192.168.1.254.... Failed
$
```

ping.sh

As you can see, the backtick (`` ` ``) takes the output from the seq command and uses it as input to the for loop. If this works for seq, it will work for any command. This opens the possibilities much wider. Here, you take the output of grep 192.168.1 and pipe that into awk to get field two, which is the name of the host. This is not totally foolproof, but assuming that the hosts file is reasonably well formatted, this should give you the names of all the machines on the 192.168.1.0/24 network. The command that produces the list of hosts is the entire pipeline of:

```
$ grep "^192\.168\.1\." /etc/hosts | awk '{ print $2 }'
```

On this particular machine, this pipeline results in the list of hosts to test:

```
router plug declan atomic jackie goldie elvis

$ cat mynet.sh
#!/bin/bash

for host in `grep "^192\.168\.1\." /etc/hosts | awk '{ print $2 }'`
do
  ping -c1 -w1 $host > /dev/null 2>&1
  if [ "$?" -eq "0" ]; then
    echo "$host is up"
  else
    echo "$host is down"
  fi
done
$ ./mynet.sh
router is up
plug is down
declan is down
atomic is down
jackie is up
goldie is up
elvis is down
$
```

Another use for this syntax is to select certain files for an operation. The mcelog utility outputs a list of any Machine Check Exceptions that have been noted since it was last run. This is often run on a regular basis, as mcelog >> /var/log/mcelog. This means that /var/log/mcelog will (hopefully) normally be empty, but if it is not empty, it could become quite large, as faulty hardware is likely to produce a great many Machine Check Exceptions. It is therefore a good idea to compress these files if they contain data, but if you gzip a zero-byte file, you end up with a 34-byte file, as gzip needs to include some headers to be able to recognize that it is a gzip file. This could end up making the problem worse, so this `for` loop will process a set of files and compress the ones that are not of zero length (those that are of zero length will have a zero followed by a space in the `wc` output).

```
$ cat mcezip.sh
#!/bin/bash

for mce in `wc -l /var/reports/mcelogs/*.log | grep -vw "0 "`
do
  gzip $mce
done
$
```

mcezip.sh

Wildcards, as discussed in Chapter 4, can also be used to feed a `for` loop. Many Linux distributions include a directory `/etc/profile.d/` where additional login scripts can be placed. The end of the `/etc/profile` script then calls each one of those scripts in turn. It uses the `.` command to source the file, rather than simply executing it, so that any environmental changes are picked up by the calling shell.

```
$ for i in /etc/profile.d/*.sh; do
>   if [ -r $i ]; then
>     . $i
>   fi
> done
```

It is worth reiterating that the `for` loop processes its command line only once. The following loop does not get stuck in an infinite loop; it only operates on the files that existed in `/tmp` at the moment the loop started executing.

```
$ cat backup.sh
#!/bin/bash

for file in /tmp/*
do
  if [ -f ${file} ]
  then
    if [ -e "${file}.bak" ]
    then
      echo "Error: Skipping ${file}.bak as it already exists"
    else
      echo "Backing up $file"
      cp "${file}" "${file}.bak"
    fi
  fi
done
$ ./backup.sh
Backing up /tmp/fizzbuzz-case.sh
Backing up /tmp/foo.bin
Backing up /tmp/todo
$ ls /tmp/*.bak
/tmp/fizzbuzz-case.sh.bak  /tmp/foo.bin.bak  /tmp/todo.bak
```

```
$ ./backup.sh
Error: Skipping /tmp/fizzbuzz-case.sh.bak as it already exists
Backing up /tmp/fizzbuzz-case.sh.bak
Error: Skipping /tmp/foo.bin.bak as it already exists
Backing up /tmp/foo.bin.bak
Error: Skipping /tmp/todo.bak as it already exists
Backing up /tmp/todo.bak
$ ls /tmp/*.bak
/tmp/fizzbuzz-case.sh.bak        /tmp/foo.bin.bak        /tmp/todo.bak
/tmp/fizzbuzz-case.sh.bak.bak    /tmp/foo.bin.bak.bak    /tmp/todo.bak.bak
$
```

backup.sh

Another useful script which makes use of the shell's ability to iterate through the values of a variable is used in the automatic installation of servers, particularly cluster nodes. It can be of vital importance that the nodes of a cluster be able to identify each other even if a centralized DNS service fails. Therefore, it is not uncommon to include the names and IP addresses of all the other cluster nodes in the local /etc/hosts file. Even though the point of DNS is that it should mean that you do not have to do this, for this particular case, it can be useful.

Available for download on Wrox.com

```
$ cat cluster.sh
#!/bin/bash

NODES="node1 node2 node3"
echo >> /etc/hosts
echo "### Cluster peers" >> /etc/hosts
echo "# Added on `date`" >> /etc/hosts
for node in $NODES
do
  getent hosts $node >> /etc/hosts
done
echo "### End of Cluster peers" >> /etc/hosts
$
```

cluster.sh

When installing multiple machines, it makes a lot of sense to script as much of the configuration as possible to ensure a consistent build as well as reduce the amount of customization required. This script will add something like this to the end of each node's /etc/hosts file:

```
### Cluster peers
# Added on Fri Apr 23 14:56:43 PST 2010
192.168.1.20    node1 node1.example.com
192.168.1.21    node2 node2.example.com
192.168.1.22    node3 node3.example.com
### End of Cluster peers
```

It is a simple thing, but well worth doing. If the application is important enough to have been clustered, it is probably also important that the cluster continues to work as expected in the case of a DNS failure.

One final thing to note about standard bash for loops is that they can cope with having no input whatsoever. In this case the body of the loop is never executed at all. Let's take a look at the `fruit-read.sh` script from the start of this chapter; you can see how it deals with a different amount of input — first two words, then one, and then none. For the final test, just press Return to give it no input at all.

```
$ ./fruit-read.sh
Please tell me some of your favorite fruits: apple banana
I really like apples
I really like bananas
Let's make a salad!
$ ./fruit-read.sh
Please tell me some of your favorite fruits: apple
I really like apples
Let's make a salad!
$ ./fruit-read.sh
Please tell me some of your favorite fruits: (just press return here)
Let's make a salad!
$
```

C-Style For Loops

The bash shell also has C-style `for` loops. Anyone familiar with the C programming language will recognize the construct `for (i=1; i<=10; i++)`. That is quite different from the shell style that you have been looking at so far. The bash version is almost the same; it adds an extra set of parentheses but is otherwise just like the C version. There is no need for the $ symbol to reference the value of variables, the `i++` operator is valid, and you can even have multiple statements separated by commas, like this:

```
$ cat cfor.sh
#!/bin/bash

for ((i=1,j=100; i<=10; i++,j-=2))
do
    printf "i=%03d j=%03d\n" $i $j
done
$ ./cfor.sh
i=001 j=100
i=002 j=098
i=003 j=096
i=004 j=094
i=005 j=092
i=006 j=090
i=007 j=088
i=008 j=086
i=009 j=084
i=010 j=082
$
```

cfor.sh

This loop starts by defining `i=1,j=100`. It then loops around for as long as the `i<=10` condition is met, and every time around the loop, it performs the modifier `i++,j-=2`, which adds 1 to `i` and takes 2 away from `j`. Each iteration of the loop then uses `printf` to display `$i` and then `$j`, each as three-digit integers.

WHILE LOOPS

The other most common form of loop in the shell is the `while` loop. As its name suggests, it keeps on executing the code in the body of the loop while the condition that it tests for remains true. This is very useful when you cannot predict when the condition that you are looking for will occur. It can also be useful when you want to keep on doing something until it makes a certain condition occur. The structure of a `while` loop is that you define the condition and then the code for it to execute while the condition remains true. This loop keeps doubling the value of a variable until it exceeds 100.

Available for
download on
Wrox.com

```
$ cat while.sh
#!/bin/bash

i=1
while [ "$i" -lt "100" ]
do
  echo "i is $i"
  i=`expr $i \* 2`
done
echo "Finished because i is now $i"
$ ./while.sh
i is 1
i is 2
i is 4
i is 8
i is 16
i is 32
i is 64
Finished because i is now 128
$
```

while.sh

Because the condition is that i is less than 100, i gets to 64 and then the loop goes back to the test, which passes. The body of the loop is entered again, sets i=128, and when execution goes back to the test for the eighth time, the test fails. The shell exits the loop, continuing with the echo statement, which displays the current value of i, which is 128. So the loop does not stop the variable from getting over 100, but refuses to run the loop while i is over 100.

When to Use While Loops

`while` loops are most useful when you don't have a list of things that you want to iterate over, but you have a testable condition for when you want to finish the loop. Mathematical calculations, time comparisons, and the state of items external to the current process are all suitable things for `while` loops. A menu system that keeps displaying options and reading user input would be a good candidate for a `while` loop; it could exit when the user selects the "quit" option. On the other hand, if you have a set list of things to operate on, a `for` loop could be more useful.

Ways to Use While Loops

This section shows that `while` loops are quite versatile and can be used in a wide variety of ways. The most commonly used feature of `while` loops is for the loop to test something that the loop itself is changing, like the following code, which tests a /24 (class C) network for ping results. The test is to check whether the final octet is still under 255 (there's no point testing the broadcast address, and there can't be any IPv4 address octets over 255). The final statement of the body of the loop increments the octet; otherwise the loop would keep pinging 192.168.1.1 eternally. This essentially reproduces the for loop behavior that you saw earlier.

```
$ cat while-ping.sh
#!/bin/bash

PREFIX=192.168.1
OCTET=1
while [ "$OCTET" -lt "255" ]; do
  echo -en "Pinging ${PREFIX}.${OCTET}..."
  ping -c1 -w1 ${PREFIX}.${OCTET} >/dev/null 2>&1
  if [ "$?" -eq "0" ]; then
    echo " OK"
  else
    echo "Failed"
  fi
  let OCTET=$OCTET+1
done
```

while-ping.sh

Another common use for while is to read the contents of a text file, line by line. The following script reads a file line by line and displays useful information about the file, too. The entire while read/do/done command is treated by the shell as a single command (which it is) so the redirection from $filename works in exactly the same way as read < $filename.

```
$ cat readfile.sh
#!/bin/bash

filename=$1

if [ ! -r "$filename" ]; then
  echo "Error: Can not read $filename"
  exit 1
fi

echo "Contents of file ${filename}:"
while read myline
do
  echo "$myline"
done < $filename
echo "End of ${filename}."
echo "Checksum: `md5sum $filename`"
$ ./readfile.sh
Error: Can not read
$ ./readfile.sh /etc/shadow
Error: Can not read /etc/shadow
$ ./readfile.sh /etc/hosts
Contents of file /etc/hosts:
```

```
127.0.0.1        localhost

# The following lines are desirable for IPv6 capable hosts
::1     localhost ip6-localhost ip6-loopback
fe00::0 ip6-localnet
ff00::0 ip6-mcastprefix
ff02::1 ip6-allnodes
ff02::2 ip6-allrouters

192.168.1.3      router
192.168.1.5      plug
192.168.1.10     declan
192.168.1.11     atomic
192.168.1.12     jackie
192.168.1.13     goldie   smf      spo  sgp
192.168.1.227    elvis

192.168.0.210    dgoldie ksgp
End of /etc/hosts.
Checksum: 785ae781cf4a4ded403642097f90a275  /etc/hosts
$
```

readfile.sh

This is a fairly simplistic example and it does not really do anything more useful than cat. while can do more than this in a few ways, one of which is by reading multiple words from the line. This uses the read tool, which matches each word to a variable. Any spare words are assigned to the final variable, so in the example that follows you read the IP address, hostname, and then any aliases.

```
$ cat readhosts.sh
#!/bin/bash

while read ip name aliases
do
  echo $ip | grep "[0-9]*\.[0-9]*\.[0-9]*\.[0-9]*" > /dev/null
  if [ "$?" -eq "0" ]; then
    # Okay, looks like an IPv4 address
    echo "$name is at $ip"
    if [ ! -z "$aliases" ]; then
      echo "  ... $name has aliases: $aliases"
    fi
  fi
done < /etc/hosts          THE ORIGINAL /ETC/HOSTS FILE FOR REFERENCE
$ cat /etc/hosts  ◄────┘
127.0.0.1        localhost

# The following lines are desirable for IPv6 capable hosts
::1     localhost ip6-localhost ip6-loopback
fe00::0 ip6-localnet
ff00::0 ip6-mcastprefix
ff02::1 ip6-allnodes
ff02::2 ip6-allrouters

192.168.1.3      router
```

```
192.168.1.5      plug
192.168.1.10     declan
192.168.1.11     atomic
192.168.1.12     jackie
192.168.1.13     goldie smf spo sgp
192.168.1.227    elvis
192.168.0.210    dgoldie ksgp
$ ./readhosts.sh
localhost is at 127.0.0.1
router is at 192.168.1.3
plug is at 192.168.1.5
declan is at 192.168.1.10
atomic is at 192.168.1.11
jackie is at 192.168.1.12
goldie is at 192.168.1.13
   ... goldie has aliases: smf    spo   sgp
elvis is at 192.168.1.227
dgoldie is at 192.168.0.210
   ... dgoldie has aliases: ksgp$
```

readhosts.sh

This is a more intelligent processing of the hosts file; cat would not be able to interpret the file in this way at all. I mentioned this form in Chapter 3, and it is not necessarily intuitive as to why the loop actually exits when it has reached the end of the file. The read built-in command returns 0 (success) when it has read a line, but returns –1 (remember that any non-zero value indicates failure) when it encounters the end-of-file marker. If read didn't return a different value when it had reached the end of the file, you would never exit this loop.

The implication of this is that a while loop can use any command that will return different values in different circumstances. The test (or its alias, [) and read built-ins are the most common utilities used with a while loop, but you can use any command at all. The command date | grep 12:15 returns success (return code 0) if the time is 12:15, but not if it is 12:16. This loop does not really do anything at all — I've used the sleep command to show that the body of the loop is being executed. The output of the date command is shown as a side effect of the grep command matching the string it searches for.

```
$ while date | grep 12:15
> do
>    sleep 5
> done
Tue Dec 28 12:15:48 GMT 2010
Tue Dec 28 12:15:53 GMT 2010
Tue Dec 28 12:15:58 GMT 2010
$
```

Related to the capability to redirect the input of a loop from a file is the capability to redirect all of the output of a loop to a file rather than each of the individual commands. This can simplify the code quite dramatically in a complicated loop. The following example just lists the partitions /dev/sda[1-4] to demonstrate that the outputs of the echo and ls commands are all directed to the `partitions.txt` file. There is no need to append to the file; a single > suffices as the entire loop is one single command, and therefore one write operation.

```
$ cat while-tofile.sh
#!/bin/bash

i=1
while [ $i -lt 5 ]
do
  echo "`date` : Partition $i"
  ls -ld /dev/sda$i
  sleep 1.5
  let i=$i+1
done > partitions.txt
$ ./while-tofile.sh
$ cat partitions.txt
Tue Jan  4 21:54:48 GMT 2011 : Partition 1
brw-rw---- 1 root disk 8, 1 Jan  4 18:39 /dev/sda1
Tue Jan  4 21:54:49 GMT 2011 : Partition 2
brw-rw---- 1 root disk 8, 2 Jan  4 18:39 /dev/sda2
Tue Jan  4 21:54:51 GMT 2011 : Partition 3
brw-rw---- 1 root disk 8, 3 Jan  4 21:43 /dev/sda3
Tue Jan  4 21:54:53 GMT 2011 : Partition 4
brw-rw---- 1 root disk 8, 4 Jan  4 18:39 /dev/sda4
$
```

while-tofile.sh

Another useful command is the builtin : command, or the /bin/true command, both of which always return a value of zero, which indicates success. This can make a loop execute forever. Consider the following two alternative loops, which test to see if a remote host is alive via the ping command. The first, like the date loop shown previously, runs until the host stops responding. The second keeps going, and detects when the host has come up again.

```
$ cat ping1.sh
#!/bin/bash
host=${1:-declan}

while ping -c3 -w4 $host
do
  sleep 30
done
echo "$host has stopped responding to pings"
$ ./ping1.sh
PING declan (192.168.1.10) 56(84) bytes of data.
64 bytes from declan (192.168.1.10): icmp_req=1 ttl=64 time=1.50 ms
64 bytes from declan (192.168.1.10): icmp_req=2 ttl=64 time=1.73 ms
64 bytes from declan (192.168.1.10): icmp_req=3 ttl=64 time=1.77 ms

--- declan ping statistics ---
3 packets transmitted, 3 received, 0% packet loss, time 2003ms
rtt min/avg/max/mdev = 1.502/1.671/1.775/0.120 ms
```

```
PING declan (192.168.1.10) 56(84) bytes of data.
64 bytes from declan (192.168.1.10): icmp_req=1 ttl=64 time=2.26 ms
64 bytes from declan (192.168.1.10): icmp_req=2 ttl=64 time=1.41 ms
64 bytes from declan (192.168.1.10): icmp_req=3 ttl=64 time=1.44 ms

--- declan ping statistics ---
3 packets transmitted, 3 received, 0% packet loss, time 2001ms
rtt min/avg/max/mdev = 1.417/1.707/2.265/0.395 ms
PING declan (192.168.1.10) 56(84) bytes of data.

--- declan ping statistics ---
4 packets transmitted, 0 received, 100% packet loss, time 2998ms

declan has stopped responding to pings
$
```

ping1.sh

This might be exactly what is wanted; to keep testing forever, it can be more useful to have a never-ending while loop. This way, you also know when the target has come back online. You have to end this loop by pressing Ctrl-C, shown here as ^C.

```
$ cat ping2.sh
#!/bin/bash
host=${1:-declan}

while :
do
  ping -c3 -w 4 $host > /dev/null 2>&1
  if [ "$?" -eq "0" ]; then
    echo "`date`: $host is up"
  else
    echo "`date`: $host is down"
  fi
  sleep 30
done
$ ./ping2.sh
Wed Dec 29 12:10:57 GMT 2010: declan is up
Wed Dec 29 12:11:29 GMT 2010: declan is up
Wed Dec 29 12:12:03 GMT 2010: declan is down
Wed Dec 29 12:12:36 GMT 2010: declan is down
Wed Dec 29 12:13:08 GMT 2010: declan is up
^C
$
```

ping2.sh

A cleaner way to control the loop is for it to test for some condition completely external to the loop. This could be something involving the reason for the loop running in the first place, or it could be something as simple as a control file for the explicit purpose of controlling this loop. The following code uses a control file that contains a list of host names to be tested. If the host name is not found in the file, testing stops. In this sample run, I removed declan from /tmp/hosts-to-ping.txt after four minutes of testing.

```
$ cat ping3.sh
#!/bin/bash
host=${1:-declan}

while grep -qw $host /tmp/hosts-to-ping.txt
do
  ping -c3 -w 4 $host > /dev/null 2>&1
  if [ "$?" -eq "0" ]; then
    echo "`date`: $host is up"
  else
    echo "`date`: $host is down"
  fi
  sleep 30
done

echo "Stopped testing $host as it has been removed from /tmp/hosts-to-ping.txt"
$ echo declan > /tmp/hosts-to-ping.txt
$ ./ping3.sh declan
Wed Dec 29 12:41:19 GMT 2010: declan is up
Wed Dec 29 12:41:53 GMT 2010: declan is down
Wed Dec 29 12:42:25 GMT 2010: declan is down
Wed Dec 29 12:42:57 GMT 2010: declan is down
Wed Dec 29 12:43:29 GMT 2010: declan is up
Wed Dec 29 12:44:01 GMT 2010: declan is up
Wed Dec 29 12:44:33 GMT 2010: declan is up
Wed Dec 29 12:45:05 GMT 2010: declan is up
Stopped testing declan as it has been removed from /tmp/hosts-to-ping.txt
$
```

ping3.sh

You may notice that although you use a sleep 30 command to space out the messages, the timestamps show a gap of over 30 seconds. This is because the ping command itself takes a few seconds to run. The -c3 flag tells ping to send three packets, whereas -w 4 tells it to wait for up to four seconds to get a response. When the target is up, the three ping packets add about two seconds to the loop. When it is down, it adds four seconds to the loop, as it waits the full four seconds before timing out.

NESTED LOOPS

It is possible to put one loop inside another, even to put different kinds of loops within one another. Although there is no real limit to the number of loops that can be nested, the indentation becomes complicated, and it soon gets difficult to keep track of where all of the loops end. Nested loops are useful because you can use the best attributes of any type of loop that you need. Here, the while loop is best suited for running continuously until the user types the word "quit" to exit the loop. Inside the while loop, the for loop is best suited to iterating over a fixed set of items (fruits in the case of the code that follows). Although $myfruit is listed at the end of the loop, on the first iteration it is blank (`myfruit=""`) so the first run lists only three fruits. Subsequent runs include the user's favorite fruit at the end of the list.

```
$ cat nest.sh
#!/bin/sh
myfruit=""

while [ "$myfruit" != "quit" ]
do
   for fruit in apples bananas pears $myfruit
   do
     echo "I like $fruit"
   done # end of the for loop
   read -p "What is your favorite fruit? " myfruit
done # end of the while loop
echo "Okay, bye!"
$ ./nest.sh
I like apples
I like bananas
I like pears
What is your favorite fruit? grapes
I like apples
I like bananas
I like pears
I like grapes
What is your favorite fruit? plums
I like apples
I like bananas
I like pears
I like plums
What is your favorite fruit? quit
Okay, bye!
$
```

nest.sh

BREAKING AND CONTINUING LOOP EXECUTION

Although the preceding features can provide very neat and controlled execution of loops, sometimes it is more practical to break out of a loop when partway through it. It is possible to do this with the `break` command. This shell builtin gets you out of the innermost loop that it is in; you can specify greater levels by passing it a numerical argument. The default is 1, which indicates the current loop. `break 2` will break out of the innermost loop, and also out of the loop that contains it. `break 3` will also break out of the loop around the second loop, and so on. This example has two `for` loops; the outer loop counts from 1 to 6, while the inner loop runs through a,b,c,d,e,f. As demonstrated by the first test run, the inner loop exits when you press 1, continuing with the next number in sequence. When you press 2, both loops are broken out of, and the execution continues after the final `done`, with the `echo "That's all, folks"`.

```
$ cat break.sh
#!/bin/bash
for number in 1 2 3 4 5 6
```

```
do
  echo "In the number loop - $number"
  read -n1 -p "Press b to break out of this loop: " x
  if [ "$x" == "b" ]; then
    break
  fi
  echo
  for letter in a b c d e f
  do
    echo
    echo "Now in the letter loop... $number $letter"
    read -n1 -p "Press 1 to break out of this loop, 2 to break out totally: " x
    if [ "$x" == "1" ]; then
      break
    else
      if [ "$x" == "2" ]; then
        break 2
      fi
    fi
  done
  echo
done
echo
echo "That's all, folks"
$ ./break.sh
In the number loop - 1
Press b to break out of this loop: z

Now in the letter loop... 1 a
Press 1 to break out of this loop, 2 to break out totally: z
Now in the letter loop... 1 b
Press 1 to break out of this loop, 2 to break out totally: z
Now in the letter loop... 1 c
Press 1 to break out of this loop, 2 to break out totally: 1
In the number loop - 2
Press b to break out of this loop: z

Now in the letter loop... 2 a
Press 1 to break out of this loop, 2 to break out totally: z
Now in the letter loop... 2 b
Press 1 to break out of this loop, 2 to break out totally: z
Now in the letter loop... 2 c
Press 1 to break out of this loop, 2 to break out totally: 1
In the number loop - 3
Press b to break out of this loop: z

Now in the letter loop... 3 a
Press 1 to break out of this loop, 2 to break out totally: z
Now in the letter loop... 3 b
Press 1 to break out of this loop, 2 to break out totally: z
Now in the letter loop... 3 c
Press 1 to break out of this loop, 2 to break out totally: 2
That's all, folks
$
```

This second test run shows how pressing b (which causes break to be called with no arguments) when in the outer loop gets you to the same point as when pressing 2 in the inner loop (which causes break 2 to be called).

```
$ ./break.sh
In the number loop - 1
Press b to break out of this loop: z

Now in the letter loop... 1 a
Press 1 to break out of this loop, 2 to break out totally: z
Now in the letter loop... 1 b
Press 1 to break out of this loop, 2 to break out totally: z
Now in the letter loop... 1 c
Press 1 to break out of this loop, 2 to break out totally: z
Now in the letter loop... 1 d
Press 1 to break out of this loop, 2 to break out totally: z
Now in the letter loop... 1 e
Press 1 to break out of this loop, 2 to break out totally: z
Now in the letter loop... 1 f
Press 1 to break out of this loop, 2 to break out totally: z
In the number loop - 2
Press b to break out of this loop: b
That's all, folks
$
```

break.sh

The partner of the break command is the continue command. This is also a shell builtin. continue is related to break, but instead of exiting the current loop, it jumps straight to the test which controls the loop. As with break, you can specify a numerical argument to continue some level of outer loop. The first recipe shows a typical use of continue; when continue is executed, the rest of the current run through the loop is omitted, and you go back to the first line again. The end of this loop contains an echo statement, which says "This is the end of the loop." When you press r to repeat the loop immediately, the script calls continue, and that statement is skipped. Otherwise, that echo statement is executed and the loop continues as normal.

```
$ cat continue.sh
#!/bin/bash
i=1
while [ "$i" -lt "5" ]; do
  echo "i is $i"
  read -p "Press r to repeat, any other key to continue: " x
  let i=$i+1
  if [ "$x" == "r" ]; then
    echo "Skipping the end of the loop."
    continue
  fi
  echo "This is the end of the loop."
done
echo "This is the end of the script."
```

```
$ ./continue.sh
i is 1
Press r to repeat, any other key to continue: r
Skipping the end of the loop.
i is 2
Press r to repeat, any other key to continue: a
This is the end of the loop.
i is 3
Press r to repeat, any other key to continue: r
Skipping the end of the loop.
i is 4
Press r to repeat, any other key to continue: b
This is the end of the loop.
This is the end of the script.
$
```

continue.sh

The following code shows a slightly less obvious use; because you loop back before you have incremented the counter i, you can repeat this part of the loop without having to change anything — it is effectively creating an extra loop within the main loop.

```
$ cat continue-backwards.sh
#!/bin/bash
i=1
while [ "$i" -lt "5" ]; do
  echo "i is $i"
  read -p "Press r to repeat, any other key to continue: " x
  if [ "$x" == "r" ]; then
    echo "Going again..."
    continue
  fi
  let i=$i+1
done
$ ./continue-backwards.sh
i is 1
Press r to repeat, any other key to continue: a
i is 2
Press r to repeat, any other key to continue: r
Going again...
i is 2
Press r to repeat, any other key to continue: b
i is 3
Press r to repeat, any other key to continue: r
Going again...
i is 3
Press r to repeat, any other key to continue: c
i is 4
Press r to repeat, any other key to continue: d
$
```

continue-backwards.sh

WHILE WITH CASE

A common use of the case statement that you saw in Chapter 5 is to place it within a while loop. The case statement is then a useful tool which decides what to do on each iteration around the loop. The loop itself is then usually exited with the break statement introduced previously. This can be useful when you want to keep reading through some input until you either find a certain condition on the current line or until you get to the end of the input. This recipe implements a very simplistic command parser, which takes four commands: echo, upper, lower, and quit. The first echoes the input exactly, the second converts to uppercase, and the third converts to lowercase. When the quit command is found, it uses break to get out of the loop.

```
$ cat while-case.sh
#!/bin/bash

quit=0
while read command data
do
  case $command in
    echo)
        echo "Found an echo command: $data"
        ;;
    upper)
        echo -en "Found an upper command: "
        echo $data | tr '[:lower:]' '[:upper:]'
        ;;
    lower)
        echo -en "Found a lower command: "
        echo $data | tr '[:upper:]' '[:lower:]'
        ;;
    quit)
        echo "Quitting as requested."
        quit=1
        break
        ;;
    *)
        echo "Read $command which is not valid input."
        echo "Valid commands are echo, upper, lower, or quit."
        ;;
  esac
done

if [ $quit -eq 1 ]; then
  echo "Broke out of the loop as directed."
else
  echo "Got to the end of the input without being told to quit."
fi
$ ./while-case.sh
Hello
Read Hello which is not valid input.
Valid commands are echo, upper, lower, or quit.
echo Hello
Found an echo command: Hello
lower Hello
```

```
Found a lower command: hello
upper Hello
Found an upper command: HELLO
quit
Quitting as requested.
Broke out of the loop as directed.
```

In this second test run, instead of typing "quit," I pressed Ctrl-D (^D) to provide an end-of-file, so the loop ended of its own accord. Because the script had the opportunity to set the $quit flag in the case statement, it can detect the difference between the two exit conditions.

```
$ ./while-case.sh
hello
Read hello which is not valid input.
Valid commands are echo, upper, lower, or quit.
^D
Got to the end of the input without being told to quit.
$
```

while-case.sh

UNTIL LOOPS

The until loop is exactly like the while loop but the test is negated. This can improve readability and in certain circumstances makes a string of conditionals easier to write. Here, the code in until.sh is a clear description of how long the loop should run for: until $a is greater than 12, or $b is less than 100. On each iteration of the loop, $a is incremented by 1, and 10 is taken away from $b.

```
$ cat until.sh
#!/bin/bash

read -p "Enter a starting value for a: " a
read -p "Enter a starting value for b: " b
until [ $a -gt 12 ] || [ $b -lt 100 ]
do
  echo "a is ${a}; b is ${b}."
  let a=$a+1
  let b=$b-10
done
$ ./until.sh
Enter a starting value for a: 5
Enter a starting value for b: 200
a is 5; b is 200.
a is 6; b is 190.
a is 7; b is 180.
a is 8; b is 170.
a is 9; b is 160.
a is 10; b is 150.
a is 11; b is 140.
a is 12; b is 130.
$ ./until.sh
```

```
Enter a starting value for a: 10
Enter a starting value for b: 500
a is 10; b is 500.
a is 11; b is 490.
a is 12; b is 480.
$ ./until.sh
Enter a starting value for a: 1
Enter a starting value for b: 120
a is 1; b is 120.
a is 2; b is 110.
a is 3; b is 100.
$
```

until.sh

To write this in a `while` loop, everything has to be negated: `-gt` becomes `-le`, `-lt` becomes `-ge`, and `||` becomes `&&`. The description of the code changes too; `without-until.sh` continues incrementing a and reducing b by 10 for as long as a is less than (or equal to) 12 and b is also greater than (or equal to) 100. The description is less clear, and when the problem space is harder to describe, it is harder to write code for.

```
$ cat without-until.sh
#!/bin/bash

read -p "Enter a starting value for a: " a
read -p "Enter a starting value for b: " b
while [ $a -le 12 ] && [ $b -ge 100 ]
do
  echo "a is ${a}; b is ${b}."
  let a=$a+1
  let b=$b-10
done
$ ./without-until.sh
Enter a starting value for a: 5
Enter a starting value for b: 200
a is 5; b is 200.
a is 6; b is 190.
a is 7; b is 180.
a is 8; b is 170.
a is 9; b is 160.
a is 10; b is 150.
a is 11; b is 140.
a is 12; b is 130.
$ ./without-until.sh
Enter a starting value for a: 10
Enter a starting value for b: 500
a is 10; b is 500.
a is 11; b is 490.
a is 12; b is 480.
$ ./without-until.sh
Enter a starting value for a: 1
Enter a starting value for b: 120
a is 1; b is 120.
```

```
a is 2; b is 110.
a is 3; b is 100.
$
```

SELECT LOOPS

A very useful tool for menus is called select. It originally comes from the Kornshell, but is also found in bash. One interesting aspect of the select loop is that it has no conditional test at all; the only way out of the loop is to use break or exit. select continuously loops around, displaying a prompt, and sets its variable to the value provided by the loop. It also sets $REPLY to the actual number typed in by the user. If the user presses the ENTER key, select redisplays the list of items accepted by the loop. If an invalid option is typed in by the user, the variable is not set, so you can also easily see if a chosen item was valid or not. The best way to understand select is to see it in action.

Available for download on Wrox.com

```
$ cat select1.sh
#!/bin/bash

select item in one two three four five
do
  if [ ! -z "$item" ]; then
    echo "You chose option number $REPLY which is \"$item\""
  else
    echo "$REPLY is not valid."
  fi
done
$ ./select1.sh
1) one
2) two
3) three
4) four
5) five
#? 1
You chose option number 1 which is "one"
#? 4
You chose option number 4 which is "four"
#? (enter)
1) one
2) two
3) three
4) four
5) five
#? two
two is not valid.
#? 6
6 is not valid.
#? ^C
$
```

This simple loop tells `select` what the menu items are (the words "one" to "five" in this case) and all it does is test each time whether or not the `$item` variable has been set. If so, it is certain to be one of the words in the list, corresponding with the number entered by the user. Whatever the user typed, valid or not, goes into the reserved variable `$REPLY`. If the entry was not valid, `$item` is blank, so that is easily tested for. This simple script appears to be a relatively intelligent though terse menu system.

The `select` loop is capable of more polish than this simple example might suggest. It can use the `PS3` variable as a prompt, which makes the user experience far more understandable. If the `PS3` variable is not set, `select` displays "#? " as a prompt. This second script uses more of the options available in a `select` loop, including setting the `PS3` prompt, and reading `$REPLY` as well as the `$movie` variable as appropriate. The `select` loop wraps these longer items much as `ls` outputs columnar data when appropriate. This script also shows how `select` and `case` work very well together.

```
$ cat select2.sh
#!/bin/bash

echo "Please select a Star Wars movie; enter \"quit\" to quit,"
echo "or type \"help\" for help. Press ENTER to list the options."
echo

# Save the existing value of PS3
oPS3=$PS3
PS3="Choose a Star Wars movie: "
select movie in "A New Hope"            \
    "The Empire Strikes Back"  \
    "Return of the Jedi"       \
    "The Phantom Menace"       \
    "Attack of the Clones"     \
    "Revenge of the Sith"      \
    "The Clone Wars"
do
  if [ "$REPLY" == "quit" ]; then
    # This break must come before other things are run in this loop.
    echo "Okay, quitting. Hope you found it informative."
    break
  fi
  if [ "$REPLY" == "help" ]; then
    echo
    echo "Please select a Star Wars movie; enter \"quit\" to quit,"
    echo "or type \"help\" for help. Press ENTER to list the options."
    echo
    # If we do not continue here, the rest of the loop will be run,
    # and we will get a message "help is not a valid option.",
    # which would not be nice. continue lets us go back to the start.
    continue
  fi

  if [ ! -z "$movie" ]; then
    echo -en "You chose option number $REPLY, which is \"$movie,\" released in "
    case $REPLY in
      1) echo "1977" ;;
      2) echo "1980" ;;
```

```
        3) echo "1983" ;;
        4) echo "1999" ;;
        5) echo "2002" ;;
        6) echo "2005" ;;
        7) echo "2008" ;;
      esac
    else
      echo "$REPLY is not a valid option."
    fi
done

# Put PS3 back to what it was originally
PS3=$oPS3
$ ./select2.sh
Please select a Star Wars movie; enter "quit" to quit,
or type "help" for help. Press ENTER to list the options.

1) A New Hope              5) Attack of the Clones
2) The Empire Strikes Back 6) Revenge of the Sith
3) Return of the Jedi      7) The Clone Wars
4) The Phantom Menace
Choose a Star Wars movie: 2
You chose option number 2, which is "The Empire Strikes Back," released in 1980
Choose a Star Wars movie: 0
0 is not a valid option.
Choose a Star Wars movie: help

Please select a Star Wars movie; enter "quit" to quit,
or type "help" for help. Press ENTER to list the options.

Choose a Star Wars movie: (enter)
1) A New Hope              5) Attack of the Clones
2) The Empire Strikes Back 6) Revenge of the Sith
3) Return of the Jedi      7) The Clone Wars
4) The Phantom Menace
Choose a Star Wars movie: 5
You chose option number 5, which is "Attack of the Clones," released in 2002
Choose a Star Wars movie: quit
Okay, quitting. Hope you found it informative.
$
```

select2.sh

Again, a very short script is made to look far smarter than it really is. This example also adds an additional action — displaying the release year of each movie. An alternative implementation could be to set a few variables (release date, box office takings, and so on) for each movie and then have a single "display" section echo out the current values of those variables.

What you can really do with select loops is far more open than that — you can associate absolutely any action with each option. This final example shows some basic host table lookup facilities as a simplistic example of how a menu can be easily written to manage various system administration or other, end-user tasks. Notice that some of the options prompt the user for more data; you are not tied to the menu structure for obtaining input from users.

```
$ cat select3.sh
#!/bin/bash

# Save the existing value of PS3
oPS3=$PS3
PS3="Please choose a task (ENTER to list options): "
select task in Quit "View hosts" "Edit hosts" "Search hosts"\
            "Nameservice Lookup" "DNS Lookup"
do
  if [ ! -z "$task" ]; then
    case $REPLY in
      1) echo "Goodbye."
         break
         ;;
      2) cat /etc/hosts
         ;;
      3) ${EDITOR:-vi} /etc/hosts
         ;;
      4) read -p "Enter the search term: " search
         grep -w $search /etc/hosts || echo "\"$search\" Not Found."
         ;;
      5) read -p "Enter the host name: " search
         getent hosts $search || echo "\"$search\" Not Found."
         ;;
      6) read -p "Enter the host name: " search
         nslookup $search || echo "\"$search\" Not Found."
         ;;
    esac
  else
    echo "$REPLY is not a valid option."
  fi
done

# Put PS3 back to what it was originally
PS3=$oPS3
$ ./select3.sh
1) Quit              3) Edit hosts       5) Nameservice Lookup
2) View hosts        4) Search hosts     6) DNS Lookup
Please choose a task (ENTER to list options): 4
Enter the search term: sgp
192.168.1.13    goldie  smf     spo  sgp
Please choose a task (ENTER to list options): 6
Enter the host name: google.com
Server:        192.168.0.1
Address:       192.168.0.1#53

Non-authoritative answer:
Name:   google.com
Address: 173.194.37.104

Please choose a task (ENTER to list options): (enter)
```

```
1) Quit                3) Edit hosts          5) Nameservice Lookup
2) View hosts          4) Search hosts        6) DNS Lookup
Please choose a task (ENTER to list options): 5
Enter the host name: wwwgooglecom
"wwwgooglecom" Not Found.
Please choose a task (ENTER to list options): 1
Goodbye.
$
```

select3.sh

select is a useful and flexible tool, not too widely used but very powerful for building simple but consistent and resilient user interfaces. It can be useful in a wide variety of situations. Like for, it is also possible to use select without the "in (x)" syntax, in which case it will use the $* parameters of the script or function it finds itself in.

SUMMARY

The bash shell offers four loops: for, while, until, and select, although while and until are almost identical in practice. These loops offer almost all of the features of more powerful languages, and when the right one is chosen for the task, they make even quite complicated flow control easy to write and maintain.

The addition of break and continue make the formal, structured aspects of loops more useful in the real world where shell scripts are often required to be rather more pragmatic than other languages that end up with more complicated control structures to deal with these situations.

Probably the hardest thing when using loops in a script is determining which type of loop to use. for loops are best at iterating over a predefined list of items; while and until loops are better at continuing to execute code until some test condition changes. The select loop makes for really quick and easy menuing systems.

The next chapter is an in-depth look at variables, particularly some of the useful features that do not exist in the original Bourne shell but are added by bash, such as ksh and zsh.

7

Variables Continued

Variables exist in virtually every programming language; without them, there is not a lot a program can do other than simply execute a sequence of commands. With variables in a language, programs can store data that enables them to loop through iterations, take user input, and do different things depending on the values of the variables. This chapter covers in more depth what the bash shell in particular can do with variables; the standard Bourne shell was quite limited in what it could do, but bash and other shells have moved things forward a long way.

USING VARIABLES

When assigning a variable, the name is not preceded by a dollar sign: `variable=value`. When referencing a variable, it is preceded by a dollar sign: `echo $variable`. Actually, the `$variable` syntax is a special case, but it is sufficient most of the time. Variables are properly referenced as `${variable}`, as this allows the shell to differentiate between `${var}iable` (the variable `$var` followed by the text "iable") and `${variable}` (the variable `$variable`). This can be useful when applying suffixes to variables, such as "`${kb}Kb is $bytes bytes, or approx ${mb}Mb`":

```
$ cat mb2.sh
echo -n "Enter a size in Kb: "
read kb
bytes=`expr $kb \* 1024`
mb=`expr $kb / 1024`
echo "${kb}Kb is ${bytes} bytes, or approx ${mb}Mb."
$ ./mb2.sh
Enter a size in Kb: 12345
12345Kb is 12641280 bytes, or approx 12Mb.
$
```

If the curly brackets were not there, then `${kb}Kb` would become `$kbKb`, and as a variable called `kbKb` has not been defined, it will evaluate to the empty string.

In the context of a string, an undefined variable is interpreted as an empty string. If it were being treated as a number, it would be interpreted as zero.

With the curly brackets removed, the script runs like this:

```
$ cat mb1.sh
echo -n "Enter a size in Kb: "
read kb
bytes=`expr $kb \* 1024`
mb=`expr $kb / 1024`
echo "$kbKb is $bytes bytes, or approx $mbMb."
$ ./mb1.sh
Enter a size in Kb: 12345
  is 12641280 bytes, or approx .
$
```

It's hard to show in a book, but there is a space before the word "is." The blank variables simply boil down to nothing. $bytes is fine because it is surrounded by whitespace and therefore treated as the variable $bytes, as intended. The references to $kb and $mb have become references to the undefined variables $kbKb and $mbMb. The shell has no way of knowing that you meant anything different.

There are not many rules about variable names; they must start with a letter or underscore and can contain letters, numbers, and underscores. Periods, commas, spaces, and any other characters are not valid in variable names. Also, the first character of the variable name must be a letter or an underscore (not a digit).

Traditionally, system variables are all uppercase, with words separated by the underscore character: BASH_EXECUTION_STRING, LC_ALL, LC_MESSAGES, *and so on.*

Although there is no technical reason to do this, non-system variables are then usually lowercase, although some shell script writers follow the example of the system variables and use uppercase for all variables.

Often, variables that contain constants, strings, and sometimes also filenames are uppercase, whereas variables that contain numbers, user input, or other "data" variables are lowercase:

```
MESSAGES=/var/log/messages
LOGFILE=/tmp/output_log.$$
echo "$0 Started at `date`" > $LOGFILE
while read message_line from $MESSAGES
do
   echo $message_line | grep -i "USB" >> $LOGFILE
done
echo "$0 Finished at `date`" >> $LOGFILE
```

There is no "right" or "wrong" method, although it is good to be consistent.

Variable Types

In most programming languages, there is a difference between a string, an integer, a float, a char, and so on. In the shell, no real distinction is made in terms of how the variable is stored.

Some utilities do require a distinction, however — when a numeric value is expected, non-numeric values are treated as zero. This is most clearly demonstrated by doing some simple math — first, with only integers to demonstrate the expected behavior:

```
$ echo $((1 + 2))
3
$ x=1
$ y=2
$ echo $(($x + $y))
3
$
```

An alternative method, for shells such as the Bourne shell, which do not have the builtin `$((...))` syntax for simple mathematical operations, is to use `expr` to do calculations:

```
$ x=1
$ y=2
$ expr $x + $y
3
$
```

 Throughout this book, simple math is often done using expr *for portability, but the* $((...)) *syntax and the* let *keyword are also used. In this section, all three types are used.*

Again, this works perfectly because this is still doing numerical operations on numbers, so everything is nice and clear-cut. Substituting text in to the variable, the shell replaces the text with the value zero.

```
$ x=hello
$ y=2
$ echo $(($x + $y))
2
$
```

The shell has replaced `hello` with zero, so this becomes equivalent to the following:

```
$ echo $((0 + 2)
2
$
```

Similarly, using `let` has the same effect. Because it is processed by the shell, the `let` keyword knows that $x evaluates to the number 0 in this context, and not the string `hello`.

```
$ x=hello
$ y=2
$ let z=$x+$y
```

```
$ echo $z
2
$
```

However, if you use `expr` to do the calculation for you, the shell does not have any builtin knowledge that `expr`, as an external tool, expects numbers, not strings, so it does not do the substitution.

```
$ x=hello
$ y=2
$ expr $x + $y
expr: non-numeric argument
$
```

The shell has left `hello` as is, so it remains valid shell syntax, but not valid input for the `expr` utility.

```
$ expr hello + 2
expr: non-numeric argument
$
```

It is also worth noting that quotes around the variable when it is declared are not retained, as the variable is treated identically however it was declared (unless it has spaces in its value, in which case the quotes are required):

```
$ x="hello"
$ y=2
$ echo $(($x + $y))
2
$ expr $x + $y
expr: non-numeric argument
$ x="hello world"
$ echo $x+$y
hello world+2
$ expr $x + $y
expr: syntax error
$ let z=$x+$y
$ echo $z
0
$
```

Length of Variables

To count the number of characters in the variable, the `${#variable}` structure is used. This is equivalent to `strlen()` and similar functions in other languages. The Bourne shell does not have this feature, but most other shells do.

```
$ myvar=hello
$ echo ${#myvar}
5
```

The curly brackets `{}` are necessary for this feature; `$#myvar` expands to `$#` and the string `myvar`. `$#` is the number of parameters the shell has been called with, and `myvar` is just text, so instead of what you may have expected, `0myvar` is displayed.

```
$ echo $#myvar
0myvar
```

It is worth noting here that unlike some operations in the shell, the existence of spaces in the variable's contents does not affect the result. This is again because of the curly brackets, which provide sufficient structural information to the shell without the need for double quotes.

```
$ myvar=hello
$ echo ${#myvar}
5
$ myvar="hello world"
$ echo ${#myvar}
11
$
```

The following script will trim text to fit a certain length, marking any part-finished lines with a \ line-continuation character:

```
$ cat trimline.sh
#!/bin/bash

function trimline()
{
  MAXLEN=$((LINELEN - 3)) # allow space for " \ " at end of line
  if [ "${#1}" -le "${LINELEN}" ]; then
    echo "$1"
  else
    echo "${1:0:${MAXLEN}} \\"
    trimline "${1:${MAXLEN}}"
  fi
}

LINELEN=${1:-80} # default to 80 columns
while read myline
do
  trimline "$myline"
done
$ cat gpl.txt | ./trimline.sh 50
Developers that use the GNU GPL protect your ri \
ghts with two steps: (1) assert copyright on th \
e software, and (2) offer you this License givi \
ng you legal permission to copy, distribute and \
/or modify it.
$
```

trimline.sh

This reads each line in one at a time and passes it to the `trimline` function. `trimline` checks the line it has received to see if any further processing is required. If the total line is shorter than `${LINELEN}`, it simply `echoes` it out and continues. Otherwise, it `echoes` `${MAXLEN}` characters, followed by a space and a backslash (\\ — two backslashes are required, as \" is a literal double quotation mark). It then passes on the remainder of the line to a new instance of `trimline` for further processing, in case the line is more than two "lines" long.

Special String Operators

When a variable is treated as a string, there are a few special operators that can be used for the string. The same applies if the string happens to be 123 or 3.142, but this is basically string operation, not numeric operation. In the bash shell, > and < can be used to compare strings. This feature uses the [[...]] syntax specific to the bash shell — it does not exist in the external /usr/bin/ test program, nor in the Bourne shell, but if you are sure of using bash or ksh, this syntax can be used. Note the final test: Alphabetically, 20 comes before 4, so this is not a universal type-agnostic comparison; it is a string comparison only.

 ksh has the same feature using the same syntax.

Available for download on Wrox.com

```
$ cat sort.sh
#!/bin/bash

if [[ "$1" > "$2" ]]; then
  echo "$2 $1"
else
  echo "$1 $2"
fi
$ ./sort.sh def abc
abc def
$ ./sort.sh hello world
hello world
$ ./sort.sh world hello
hello world
$ ./sort sh 4 20
20 4
```

sort.sh

The shell can be thought of as internally storing variables as strings but occasionally treating them as integers. The rest of this chapter treats variables as strings, because that is where the interesting string manipulation happens.

 These features are specific to bash (and ksh, as noted previously); trying to use this syntax on Bourne shell systems will not work. Be careful if you are writing scripts to be used across a variety of platforms to check what features are available.

Stripping Variable Strings by Length

Many languages (or their associated libraries) include a function called (or equivalent to) substr(), which will cut a string down by character position. The bash (though again, not Bourne) shell provides this feature as part of its variable manipulation syntax.

The bash documentation refers to variables as parameter *and special operators to it as* word *so* ${myvar:-default} *is referred to in the abstract as* ${parameter:-word}. *This naming isn't particularly intuitive for the user of the shell; in my experience, people find it much easier to understand what is going on when* parameter *is replaced with a more clearly understood word,* variable. *Using the word* parameter *is relevant from the perspective of a bash developer — that is, somebody working on the source code of bash itself — but unhelpful for those who are actually using the shell.*

The definition of the traditional `substr` call is `substr(string, offset [,length])`, like this (in C):

```
myvar = "foobar";
substr(myvar, 3);          // foobar becomes bar
substr(myvar, 3, 2);       // foobar becomes ba
```

The first `substr` digs three characters into the string and outputs from the fourth character. The second does the same but limits the output to two characters. As the bash implementation doesn't use a function, the syntax is slightly different, for equivalent results:

```
${variable:3}              # foobar becomes bar.
${variable:3:2}            # foobar becomes ba.
```

One real-world use for this is when you are interested only in lines from a log file which contain certain text in a given place: You might want to change the format output by the `diff` command, for example. The `diff` command compares two files and shows what differences exist, marking lines only in `file2` with > and files only in `file1` with <.

```
$ cat file1
ABC
def
$ cat file2
ABC
DEF
$ diff file1 file2
2c2
< def
---
> DEF
$
```

`diff` is a useful tool for generating patches, but it adds a bit of clutter around its output. If you are only interested in added or removed lines, and not the extra `diff` syntax, you could do this:

```
$ cat diff1.sh
#!/bin/bash

diff $1 $2 | while read diffline
do
  if [ "${diffline:0:2}" == "< " ]; then
    echo "Remove line: ${diffline:2}"
  fi
```

```
    if [ "${diffline:0:2}" == "> " ]; then
      echo "Add line: ${diffline:2}"
    fi
done
$ ./diff1.sh file1 file2
Remove line: def
Add line: DEF
$
```

diff1.sh

A less verbose presentation is to use the symbols + and – to signify the addition or removal of a line from the file. diff2.sh does this simply by replacing the text in the echo statements. The output is quite a bit clearer.

```
$ cat diff2.sh
#!/bin/bash

diff $1 $2 | while read diffline
do
  if [ "${diffline:0:2}" == "< " ]; then
    echo "-: ${diffline:2}"
  fi
  if [ "${diffline:0:2}" == "> " ]; then
    echo "+: ${diffline:2}"
  fi
done
$ ./diff2.sh file1 file2
-: def
+: DEF
```

diff2.sh

> /bin/sh *is a symbolic link to dash (not bash) in some GNU/Linux distributions — Ubuntu (since 6.10, "Edgy Eft") and Debian GNU/Linux (since 5.0, "Lenny"). Dash is a smaller, faster shell than bash, but with fewer features. Although it was somewhat controversial when Ubuntu made the change, all it really means is that if your script requires bash features, it needs to start with* #!/bin/bash, *not* #!/bin/sh, *as* #!/bin/sh *implies POSIX compliance and nothing more. Dash does not support substrings.*

Stripping from the End of the String

Bash also has the ability to cut from the end of the string, not just from the start of the string. Notice the space between the : and the –4. This space is essential; otherwise, it would be the same as :-, which, as you will see in the section "Providing Default Values," provides a default value if the variable is unset. This quirk is one of a very few signs that the syntax has grown and changed over time to add new features.

```
${variable: -4}        # foobar becomes obar
```

This takes the same approach as the `${variable:4}` syntax, but from the other end of the string. You can search back to get the final n characters from the string. In this case, `foobar -4` becomes `obar`, just as `${variable:4}` gives `foob`.

Stripping Strings with Patterns

Often, data comes with superfluous padding — leading zeroes, spaces, and so on, which can be inconvenient. Bash contains a feature for removing patterns from either the start or the end of the string. It can do it in two different ways: what is known as "greedy" and "non-greedy" pattern matching. Greedy pattern matching means that the longest possible pattern that matches the expression will be selected. Non-greedy pattern matching means that the shortest possible pattern that matches the expression will be selected.

➤ The `${variable#word}` syntax uses non-greedy pattern matching at the start of the string.

➤ The `${variable##word}` syntax uses greedy pattern matching at the start of the string.

➤ The `${variable%word}` syntax uses non-greedy pattern matching at the end of the string.

➤ The `${variable%%word}` syntax uses greedy pattern matching at the end of the string.

Because this syntax uses pattern matching and not just plain text, this is quite a flexible feature. To strip out the first section of a phone number in xxx-xxx-xxxx format, the `${phone#*-}` syntax matches suitable patterns.

Stripping from the Start of a String with Patterns

Think of `#*-` as "strip until the first -." This is the non-greedy start-of-string search, which will get rid of the area code but leave the final two sections of the phone number:

```
$ phone="555-456-1414"
$ echo ${phone#*-}
456-1414
$
```

To strip out all sections but the last one, the `${phone##*-}` syntax strips out everything until the final -. Think of `##*-` as "strip until the last -."

```
$ echo ${phone##*-}
1414
$
```

To strip out the first two sections, leaving any others in place, use the non-greedy search with the pattern `*-*-`. This will match 555-456- and leave the final section alone.

```
$ echo ${phone#*-*-}
1414
```

Alternatively, a greedy search for `*-*-` will also leave the final section because there is only one way in which this pattern can be matched with this string:

```
$ echo ${phone##*-*-}
1414
```

Stripping from the End of a String with Patterns

Think of `%-*` as meaning "strip from the final - onwards." This gets rid of the final `-*`, leaving the area code and middle part of the phone number:

```
$ echo $phone
555-456-1414
$ echo ${phone%-*}
555-456
```

Similarly, a greedy search will strip out everything from the first `-*` pattern in the string. This is the forward equivalent of `${phone##-*}`.

```
$ echo ${phone%%-*}
555
```

Again, a non-greedy method can strip the final two parts of the string. This matches 456-1414, leaving the area code behind.

```
$ echo ${phone%-*-*}
555
$
```

At first glance, this can seem to be a confusing feature, with limited usefulness, and as such, it is very rarely used by the average shell scripter, even when he knows that bash will be available as an interpreter. (Sometimes you will see bash scripts that clearly go out of their way to avoid using bash features; while this sometimes means that the script writer wasn't aware of the feature, it can indicate that the script is intended to be portable to systems where bash isn't available.)

However, this can be a really useful tool. Perl is incredibly strong with regular expressions; this syntax brings the shell somewhat closer, although Perl will always have the advantage in this particular area. If what you really need is to match text against complicated regular expressions, then do seriously consider Perl. Otherwise, this feature makes bash very useful.

One practical example is a script that installs one of a number of different versions of the Veritas Volume Manager, which has different installation requirements for different versions. Here, the need is to differentiate between any release of 5.0, or some other release. The set of 5.0 releases available are known as 5.0, 5.0MP3, 5.0MP3RP3, and 5.0MP4. To match any of those, you need a match of 5.0, followed by an optional MP string and then arbitrary other text after that. You do this with non-greedy pattern matching. It will simply remove any MP* string after the 5.0. If that leaves 5.0, then the original string started with 5.0.

```
if [ "${vxvm_version%MP*}" == "5.0" ]; then
  ; # do the necessary to install VxVM 5.0
else
  ; # do the necessary to install another version
fi
```

For a more detailed example, let's take a list of URLs gathered from various sources. Although there is a strict definition of what makes a URL, there are many different forms in which people express URLs. Sometimes the protocol is stated with `http://`, `https://`, `ftp://`, and so on. Sometimes a particular port is specified (`https://example.com:8443/`). Sometimes a path is specified, other times just the domain. This script can filter out only the domain part of the URL.

```
$ cat url.sh
#!/bin/bash

getdomain()
{
  url=$1

  url_without_proto=${url#*://}
  echo "$url becomes $url_without_proto"

  domain_and_port=${url_without_proto%%/*}
  echo "$url_without_proto becomes $domain_and_port"

  domain=${domain_and_port%:*}
  echo "$domain_and_port becomes $domain"

  getent hosts $domain | head -1
}

for url in $*
do
  getdomain $url
done
$
```

url.sh

The `url_without_proto` variable matches the value of the URL without any leading `*://`, such as `http://`, `https://`, and `ftp://`, by stripping out any `*://` that it should find at the start of the string. Note that an invalid URL, such as `amazon.comhttp://ebay.com`, would be stripped down to `ebay.com` by this operation. If no protocol is specified, no match is made, and no change happens.

Second, the `domain_and_port` variable strips off any slashes from the end of the string. This will strip `en.wikipedia.org/wiki/Formula_One` down to `en.wikipedia.org`. (Any `http://` protocol header has already been removed from the `url_without_proto` variable). However, `en.wikipedia.org:8080` is a valid part of a URL, and this does not get rid of that.

The third and final substitution is to get rid of any port number trailing after the domain name. There is no need to use a greedy pattern matching; the first will suffice as a colon is not valid in the domain name itself.

 An IPv6 URL can contain colons; `http://fc00:30:20` could be port 20 at IP address `fc00:30`, or it could be port 80 (the default for http) at IP address `fc00:30:20`. IPv6 gets around this by putting square brackets around the IP part, so `http://[fc00:30:20]:80/` is more clearly port 80 at `fc00:30:20`.

In what is effectively three lines of code, this script handles all these apparently complicated URLs. The inconsistent style of each line of input is brought under control and an IP address for each site is returned to show that a valid domain was found. First of all, `http://flickr.com/` gets the leading protocol and the trailing slash removed. Similarly, `http://del.icio.us` is handled with no trailing data at all after the domain name.

```
$ ./url.sh http://flickr.com/
http://flickr.com/ becomes flickr.com/
flickr.com/ becomes flickr.com
flickr.com becomes flickr.com
68.142.214.24   flickr.com
$ ./url.sh http://del.icio.us
http://del.icio.us becomes del.icio.us
del.icio.us becomes del.icio.us
del.icio.us becomes del.icio.us
76.13.6.175     del.icio.us
$
```

For something more ambitious, Google URLs can become quite complicated. A simple search is easy enough; there are not too many wild characters here.

```
$ ./url.sh www.google.com/search?q=shell+scripting
www.google.com/search?q=shell+scripting becomes www.google.com/search?q=shell+scrip
    ting
www.google.com/search?q=shell+scripting becomes www.google.com
www.google.com becomes www.google.com
74.125.230.115  www.l.google.com www.google.com
$
```

A Google mailbox has a more complicated URL, but again the script is unfazed. The simple rules hold up against some hard-to-predict input:

```
$ ./url.sh https://mail.google.com/a/steve-parker.org/#inbox/12e01805b72f4c9e
https://mail.google.com/a/steve-parker.org/#inbox/12e01805b72f4c9e becomes mail.goo
    gle.com/a/steve-parker.org/#inbox/12e01805b72f4c9e
mail.google.com/a/steve-parker.org/#inbox/12e01805b72f4c9e becomes mail.google.com
mail.google.com becomes mail.google.com
209.85.229.19   googlemail.l.google.com mail.google.com
$
```

A more complicated URL requires quotes around the parameter, or the shell will interpret the `&` as a background command before it even gets to the script. Once passed successfully to the script, however, the presence of strange characters, including the colons in `ADME:B:ONA:GB:1123`, do not confuse it:

```
$ ./url.sh "http://cgi.ebay.co.uk/ws/eBayISAPI.dll?ViewItem&item=270242319206&ssPag
eName=ADME:B:ONA:GB:1123"
http://cgi.ebay.co.uk/ws/eBayISAPI.dll?ViewItem&item=270242319206&ssPageName=ADME:B
:ONA:GB:1123 becomes cgi.ebay.co.uk/ws/eBayISAPI.dll?ViewItem&item=270242319206&ssP
    ageName=ADME:B:ONA:GB:1123
cgi.ebay.co.uk/ws/eBayISAPI.dll?ViewItem&item=270242319206&ssPageName=ADME:B:ONA:GB
:1123 becomes cgi.ebay.co.uk
```

```
cgi.ebay.co.uk becomes cgi.ebay.co.uk
66.135.202.12   cgi-intl.ebay.com cgi.ebay.co.uk
$
```

As one final test, let's look at an https URL with a port and trailing data. This simple script is capable of string parsing that would otherwise seem to be the exclusive domain of Perl.

```
$ ./url.sh https://127.0.0.1:6789/login.jsp
https://127.0.0.1:6789/login.jsp becomes 127.0.0.1:6789/login.jsp
127.0.0.1:6789/login.jsp becomes 127.0.0.1:6789
127.0.0.1:6789 becomes 127.0.0.1
127.0.0.1        localhost
$
```

With all three of these commands, if there is no match, then no change is made. That's not a bad result; a lot of scenarios have been correctly processed, and demonstrably so, with just three lines of code.

SEARCHING STRINGS

sed, the "stream editor," provides a flexible search-and-replace facility, which can be used to replace text. For example, you can upgrade your datacenter in one fell swoop by replacing Wintel with Linux:

```
sed s/Wintel/Linux/g datacenter
```

sed is extremely powerful, but the basic search-and-replace functionality is also a feature of bash. Spawning additional processes takes time, which is exacerbated in a loop that runs 10, 100, or 1,000 times. Because sed is a relatively large program to fire up just to do some simple text replacement, using the builtin bash functionality is a lot more efficient.

The syntax is not too dissimilar from the sed syntax. Where $datacenter is the variable, and the mission is — again — replacing Wintel with Linux, the sed from the previous line of code would be equivalent to:

```
echo ${datacenter/Wintel/Linux}
```

Using Search and Replace

Consider a line in /etc/passwd for a user called Fred. This syntax can be used to change the pattern fred to wilma.

```
$ user=`grep fred /etc/passwd`
$ echo $user
fred:x:1000:1000:Fred Flintstone:/home/fred:/bin/bash
$ echo ${user/fred/wilma}
wilma:x:1000:1000:Fred Flintstone:/home/fred:/bin/bash
$
```

This has only changed the first instance of the word `fred`. To change all instances of `fred` to `wilma`, change the first `/` to a double `//` (or, as the documentation explains it, add an extra slash to the beginning of the search string). This replaces every instance of the search pattern with the new text.

```
$ echo ${user/fred/wilma}
wilma:x:1000:1000:Fred Flintstone:/home/fred:/bin/bash
$ echo ${user//fred/wilma}
wilma:x:1000:1000:Fred Flintstone:/home/wilma:/bin/bash
$
```

This has changed the username field and the home directory field from `fred` to `wilma`. It has still not changed the GECOS field (the human-readable part, which still says `Fred Flintstone`). This is unfortunately not possible directly with this feature.

If the pattern must match at the very start of the variable's value, the standard regular expression syntax would be to use `/^fred/wilma`. However, the shell does not do regular expressions, and the carat (`^`) is used in variable modification for changing the case of a variable. The syntax for this is to use `#` instead of `^`. Here, the final search tries to replace 1000 with 1001, but it does not match because it is not at the start of the line:

```
$ echo ${user/^fred/wilma}
fred:x:1000:1000:Fred Flintstone:/home/fred:/bin/bash
$ echo ${user/#fred/wilma}
wilma:x:1000:1000:Fred Flintstone:/home/fred:/bin/bash
$ echo ${user/1000/1001}
fred:x:1001:1000:Fred Flintstone:/home/fred:/bin/bash
$ echo ${user/#1000/1001}
fred:x:1000:1000:Fred Flintstone:/home/fred:/bin/bash
$
```

Similarly, to match the end of the line, use `%` at the start of the search string, rather than `$` at the end of the search string as you would when using regular expressions. Here, the shell is changed from bash to ksh:

```
$ echo ${user/%bash/ksh}
fred:x:1000:1000:Fred Flintstone:/home/fred:/bin/ksh
$
```

This can be used in a more practical way to change the extensions of filenames, which may contain anything, including the pattern being searched for, any number of times in the name itself. To rename all `*.TXT` files to a more Unix-like `*.txt`, use `/%.TXT/.txt`:

```
#!/bin/bash
for myfile in *.TXT
do
  mynewfile=${myfile/%.TXT/.txt}
  echo "Renaming $myfile to ${mynewfile} ..."
  mv $myfile $mynewfile
done
```

Because the list of files could include `FILE.TXT.TXT`, the inclusion of the `%` symbol makes sure that only a final `.TXT` is replaced. `FILE.TXT.TXT` would be renamed `FILE.TXT.txt`, not `FILE.txt.txt`. Keeping the period ensures that `fileTXT` is not changed to `filetxt` but `file.TXT` does get changed to `file.txt`.

Replacing Patterns

Wildcards are also possible in the search pattern, but only the "greedy matching" style is possible. Replacing `f*d` with `wilma` will match the asterisk with as much as possible; in this case, `red:x:1000:1000:Fred Flintstone:/home/fre`. Instead, `fred` can be matched with `f??d`.

```
$ echo $user
fred:x:1000:1000:Fred Flintstone:/home/fred:/bin/bash
$ echo ${user/f*d/wilma}
wilma:/bin/bash
$ echo ${user/f??d/wilma}
wilma:x:1000:1000:Fred Flintstone:/home/fred:/bin/bash
$
```

Deleting Patterns

When you just need to delete the pattern, simply don't provide any replacement text (and the final / is optional, too). The same pattern-matching rules apply, with a single / matching only the first instance, /# matching only at the start of the line, /% matching only the end of the line, and // matching all instances:

```
$ echo ${user/fred}
:x:1000:1000:Fred Flintstone:/home/fred:/bin/bash
$ echo ${user/#fred}
:x:1000:1000:Fred Flintstone:/home/fred:/bin/bash
$ echo ${user//fred}
:x:1000:1000:Fred Flintstone:/home/:/bin/bash
$ echo ${user/%bash}
fred:x:1000:1000:Fred Flintstone:/home/fred:/bin/
$
```

Changing Case

The bash shell also provides for changing between uppercase and lowercase. To convert to uppercase, use `${variable^^}`; to change to lowercase, use `${variable,,}`.

```
$ echo ${user^^}
FRED:X:1000:1000:FRED FLINTSTONE:/HOME/FRED:/BIN/BASH
$ echo ${user,,}
fred:x:1000:1000:fred flintstone:/home/fred:/bin/bash
$
```

There is another syntax where `${variable^pattern}` changes a pattern to uppercase and `${variable,,pattern}` changes it to lowercase. However, this only works on a word basis, and not across the entire variable.

PROVIDING DEFAULT VALUES

Often, you need to have a variable contain a value, but you don't know whether or not it is currently set. It can be useful to define a default value if the variable in question is not set.

If you write a script that requires the user to edit a file, you could do this:

```
echo "You must now edit the file $myfile"
sleep 5
vi "${myfile}"
echo "Thank you for editing $myfile"
```

But not everybody likes vi. They might want to use emacs, or nano, or gedit, or kate, or anything else.

One way to do this is to allow the user to set a variable (by convention this is called EDITOR) to define their favorite editor. The following:

```
vi "${myfile}"
```

becomes:

```
${EDITOR} "${myfile}"
```

which solves the problem nicely; the user defines whatever he or she wants in EDITOR, and the script is much more flexible. But what if EDITOR is not set? Because variables do not need to be declared, no error will occur; $EDITOR will just silently be replaced with the empty string:

```
 "${myfile}"
```

If $myfile is /etc/hosts, then the system will try to execute /etc/hosts, which will fail, because /etc/hosts doesn't (or at least, it shouldn't!) have the executable bit set:

```
$ ls -l /etc/hosts
-rw-r--r-- 1 root root 1494 2008-05-22 00:44 /etc/hosts
```

If $myfile is "rm -rf /" then it will be executed, not edited, which is far from the intended action. To avoid this, supply a default value for the variable. The syntax for this is ${*parameter*:-*word*}. The curly brackets are required, and *word* can be expanded by the shell if necessary. Therefore, this will do the job, providing /usr/bin/vim as a default, if no other editor has been set:

```
${EDITOR:-/usr/bin/vim} "${myfile}"
```

If you are not sure that vim will always be located at /usr/bin/vim, you might want to use the `which` command to find out where vim is located. The shell will expand commands within backticks, so this is a more robust version:

```
${EDITOR:-`which vim`} "${myfile}"
```

It would be clumsy to do this every time, so the shell also allows you to set the default if necessary, by using ${*parameter*:=*word*}. That way, subsequent references to the variable don't need the special treatment:

```
${EDITOR:=`which vim`} "${myfile}"
${EDITOR} "${yourfile}"
```

It can be useful in scripts to give meaningful names to arguments that the script was called with, as it helps to make the script more readable. For example, this script will check how full a given filesystem is, but default to the root (/) filesystem:

```
#!/bin/sh
FILESYS=${1:-/}
df -h ${FILESYS}
```

On a more practical level, you may want a script to store logs with customizable filenames but provide a default unique (or reasonably unique) name for the log file if one is not provided. The current time is a common way to do this, but the script cannot reevaluate the date and time every time it writes to the log file — it would end up writing to a different file every minute. Default values are perfect for this situation. Here, LOGFILE is set to the current date and time by default, or it takes whatever path is given on the command line instead.

```
$ cat default.sh
#!/bin/bash

LOGFILE=${1:-/tmp/log.`basename $0`-`date +%h%d.%H%M`}
echo "Logging to $LOGFILE"
$ ./default.sh
Logging to /tmp/log.default.sh-Feb13.2313
$ ./default.sh /tmp/logfile.txt
Logging to /tmp/logfile.txt
$
```

default.sh

"Unsetting Variables" looked at ways to unset a variable. You can test the status of a variable with the -z test to see if it is of zero length:

```
$ myvar=hello
$ if [ -z "${myvar}" ]
> then
>   echo "myvar is empty"
> else
>   echo "myvar is set to $myvar"
> fi
myvar is set to hello
```

The test works as expected. Set the variable to be empty and test it again.

```
$ myvar=
$ if [ -z "${myvar}" ]
> then
>   echo "myvar is empty"
> else
>   echo "myvar is set to $myvar"
> fi
myvar is empty
```

Compare this with unsetting the variable. It does not have any length, but this time that is because it does not exist in the environment.

```
$ unset myvar
$ if [ -z "${myvar}" ]
> then
>    echo "myvar is empty"
> else
>  echo "myvar is set to $myvar"
> fi
myvar is empty
```

Ah — the -z test can't tell the difference between a blank and a variable which is not set. For this special condition, the ? operator on the variable can come in handy. This can display alternate text (such as "goodbye" in this example) if the variable is not set. Notice that it does not display the text alone, but with a reference to the variable that is not set:

```
$ myvar=hello
$ echo ${myvar?goodbye}
hello
$ myvar=
$ echo ${myvar?goodbye}

$ unset myvar
$ echo ${myvar?goodbye}
bash: myvar: goodbye
$
```

A similar situation can be dealt with by the + operator. Here, if $myvar has a value, the expression after the plus sign is evaluated. If not, an empty string is returned. The expression after the plus sign can be a string such as goodbye or an expression like $x.

```
$ myvar=hello
$ echo ${myvar+goodbye}
goodbye
$ unset myvar
$ echo ${myvar+goodbye}

$ x=1
$ echo ${myvar+$x}

$ myvar=hello
$ echo ${myvar+$x}
1
$
```

This can be used to substitute a given value only in certain situations. For example, if an installer has an optional graphical mode that should only be invoked if the DISPLAY variable is set, this call will launch graphical mode only if it is likely to succeed. This demonstration uses echo to show the command that would have been launched.

```
$ unset DISPLAY
$ echo ./installer ${DISPLAY+"--display $DISPLAY"}
./installer
```

```
$ DISPLAY=127.0.0.1:0
$ echo ./installer ${DISPLAY+"--display $DISPLAY"}
./installer --display 127.0.0.1:0
$
```

INDIRECTION

One particularly useful trick in the bash shell is indirection. You'll have to be a little bit careful when using it, as it's easy to get confused as to which variable is which, but it can be a real life-saver.

It is possible to use the value of one variable as the name of anther variable. For example, the following:

```
for mything in PATH GDMSESSION HOSTNAME
do
  echo $myvar is ${!myvar}
done
```

will run like this:

```
PATH is /usr/bin:/bin:/usr/local/bin:/home/steve/bin:/usr/games
GDMSESSION is gnome
HOSTNAME is declan
```

Not terribly useful, at first glance. But it means that you can create your own variable names on-the-fly and then access the data within that name:

```
$ cat empdata.sh
#!/bin/bash
# Employee Data
Dave_Fullname="Dave Smith"
Dave_Country="USA"
Dave_Email=dave@example.com

Jim_Fullname="Jim Jones"
Jim_Country="Germany"
Jim_Email=jim.j@example.com

Bob_Fullname="Bob Anderson"
Bob_Country="Australia"
Bob_Email=banderson@example.com

echo "Select an Employee:"
select Employee in Dave Jim Bob
do
  echo "What do you want to know about ${Employee}?"
  select Data in Fullname Country Email
  do
    echo $Employee                 # Jim
    echo $Data                     # Email
    empdata=${Employee}_${Data}    # Jim_Email
    echo "${Employee}'s ${Data} is ${!empdata}"    # jim.j@example.com
    break
```

```
    done
  break
done
```

```
$ ./empdata.sh
Select an Employee:
1) Dave
2) Jim
3) Bob
#? 2
What do you want to know about Jim?
1) Fullname
2) Country
3) Email
#? 3
Jim
Email
Jim's Email is jim.j@example.com
$
```

This script uses the `select` loop to provide a basic menu just to get the data from the user in a simple way. The clever bit is in the line that defines the `$empdata` variable from the values of two other variables, and then the following line, which indirectly accesses the value of a variable with that name.

SOURCING VARIABLES

A useful method for storing data, particularly configuration options, is to store a text file with entries that are actually variable definitions. This is easy to edit and very easy for a shell script to read. Often, users may not even realize how the file is used. One such example is the `/etc/sysconfig` directory in Red Hat-based Linux distributions. There is a common `/etc/sysconfig/network` file with the basic network configuration, which is read by a lot of system scripts. There is then a set of program-specific files, such as `/etc/sysconfig/ntpd`, which contains specific options for the Network Time Protocol daemon. Consider the start of `/etc/init.d/ntpd`, which is run when the system boots; it sources both of these files, and subsequently uses the values within them:

```
# Source function library.
. /etc/init.d/functions

# Source networking configuration.
. /etc/sysconfig/network

if [ -f /etc/sysconfig/ntpd ];then
      . /etc/sysconfig/ntpd
fi
```

The configuration files themselves look like the following example. These files are easily edited by the systems administrator, or by software, and when required during system boot the variables contain all of the relevant options.

```
root@redhat# cat /etc/sysconfig/network
NETWORKING_IPV6=no
HOSTNAME=redhat.example.com
NETWORKING=yes
GATEWAY=192.168.32.1
root@redhat# cat /etc/sysconfig/ntpd
# Drop root to id 'ntp:ntp' by default.
OPTIONS="-u ntp:ntp -p /var/run/ntpd.pid"

# Set to 'yes' to sync hw clock after successful ntpdate
SYNC_HWCLOCK=no

# Additional options for ntpdate
NTPDATE_OPTIONS=""
root@redhat#
```

The /etc/init.d/ntpd script then calls the ntpd binary with $OPTIONS, a variable which in this case has the value "-u ntp:ntp -p /var/run/ntpd.pid". The systems administrator can edit the text file and does not have to edit the init script itself. This is easier for the systems administrator, and because the init script itself has not been changed, the settings will not be lost if the distribution updates the init script as part of a system update.

SUMMARY

Variables are an essential part of any programming language, and while the shell's syntax is sometimes complicated, it provides powerful capabilities, which in other languages are treated as arithmetic or string specific features. The shell's variable syntax allows you to get substrings, do basic regular expressions, and so on with variables, by operating directly on the variables themselves. This means that there is no need for many functions, such as substr(), strlen(), and the like.

Chapter 3 explored almost all of the predefined variables, including variables such as PATH and PS1; COLUMNS and ROWS; RANDOM, $0, $1, $2, and so on; $* and $@, and all the things that they can be used for. This chapter has gone further into what can be done with user-defined variables, and the powerful transformations that the shell itself can do to their values.

Variables are used in any non-trivial script, so a good understanding of the basics is essential. For the more complex syntax, it is useful to have a basic reference to hand.

The next chapter looks at functions and libraries, which regularly make great use of variables. By combining variables with functions, serious computation is possible.

8

Functions and Libraries

Functions are a very useful feature of any programming language. By defining a specific section of code as a function, that code can be reused in different parts of the script, providing the same functionality for consistency, readability, and maintainability. Often, it is useful to bundle up a set of functions into libraries, providing a set of related functions in one convenient place. This chapter covers various uses of functions, defines what a shell function is (and isn't), and then covers libraries of functions.

FUNCTIONS

Functions are a way of separating out particular pieces of a script into smaller, more manageable chunks of code. Functions make your code modular, which is a good design principle because a function

- ➤ Hides implementation details from the main script, simplifying the shell script's main body of code

- ➤ Allows consistent reuse of code from within the script, or even between several shell scripts

- ➤ Can be replaced if the underlying detail it works with is changed

- ➤ Can be tested over and over again as a small piece of a larger script, with changing input values to prove that the code is correct

This all helps to keep your code more flexible, readable, and maintainable.

 When developing a piece of code as a function, it can be useful to put it in a file by itself, and have the "main" part of the script call the function repeatedly with different test values. This can speed up the development and testing cycle significantly.

Defining Functions

It is conventional to define functions at the start of the file, although this is not strictly necessary. It is helpful for debugging and maintenance to include a comment marking where the function definitions end and the actual code execution begins, to save readers from having to read through all the definitions before getting to the main code. The block of code defined as a function can be declared in one of three different ways, depending on the exact shell in use. The standard Bourne shell syntax uses the function name followed immediately by a pair of parentheses () and curly brackets {} around the code itself.

```
$ cat myfunction.sh
#!/bin/bash

myfunction()
{
    echo "This is the myfunction function."
}

# Main code starts here

echo "Calling myfunction..."
myfunction
echo "Done."
$ ./myfunction.sh
Calling myfunction...
This is the myfunction function.
Done.
$
```

myfunction.sh

There is a second syntax, which is not accepted by the Bourne shell, although bash and ksh both accept it. Instead of following the function name by a pair of parentheses, the function name is preceded by the keyword `function`:

```
function myfunction
```

Yet another syntax, accepted by bash alone, is to combine both elements.

```
function myfunction()
```

Because the Bourne syntax is accepted by all shells, that is the most common one in use. The second syntax is also used frequently and by using the `function` keyword, it provides a more clear declaration that it is a function.

Function Output

Some languages differentiate between procedures and functions; functions return a value, and should not have any other side effects, whereas procedures do not return a value but are likely to have side effects. Like C, the shell does not make this distinction — there are no procedures, although a function may choose not to return a value (in which case it effectively returns zero), or the caller may simply decide not to check its return value, so there is little practical benefit in having both procedures and functions. However, shell functions are, in practice, more often used as procedures than as functions. Part of the reason for this is that they can only return a single byte, which is returned in the $? variable as an integer between 0 and 255, which limits the mathematical usefulness of a function. Instead, as with programs and shell scripts, the return code is often used to indicate whether or not the function succeeded in its task.

Return Codes

The simplest and most common way to get a value from a function is to use a simple number — sometimes expressed as a negative — as a return value indicating success (0) or failure (non-zero). This function returns relevant diagnostic information depending on what error conditions it may come across. The script tries to find the IP addresses relating to eth0, eth1, and eth2. The way this function works is specific to the Red Hat Linux style of network interface definitions, which are stored in /etc/sysconfig/network-scripts/ifcfg-eth*. The variable IPADDR is defined in these files, so if it is available the function finds it and reports it.

```
debian$ cat redhat-nics.sh
#!/bin/sh

getipaddr()
{
  cd /etc/sysconfig/network-scripts || return 1
  if [ -f ifcfg-$1 ]; then
    unset IPADDR
    . ifcfg-$1
    if [ -z "$IPADDR" ]; then
      return 2
    else
      echo $IPADDR
    fi
  else
    return 3
  fi
  # Not strictly needed
  return 0
}

for thisnic in eth0 eth1 eth2
do
  thisip=`getipaddr $thisnic`
  case $? in
    0) echo "The IP Address configured for $thisnic is $thisip" ;;
    1) echo "This does not seem to be a RedHat system" ;;
    2) echo "No IP Address defined for $thisnic" ;;
    3) echo "No configuration file found for $thisnic" ;;
  esac
done
```

redhat-nics.sh

Because different Linux distributions use different mechanisms for configuring networks, this script does not work on a system that doesn't use the Red Hat style of network configuration. A good technique is to check for the existence of /etc/redhat-release, which should exist on any Red Hat or derivative system, such as CentOS or Oracle Linux.

```
debian$ ./redhat-nics.sh
cd: 29: can't cd to /etc/sysconfig/network-scripts
This does not seem to be a RedHat system
cd: 29: can't cd to /etc/sysconfig/network-scripts
This does not seem to be a RedHat system
cd: 29: can't cd to /etc/sysconfig/network-scripts
This does not seem to be a RedHat system
debian$
```

As you might expect, this function fails every time it is run on a Debian system; Debian stores network configuration in /etc/network/interfaces, an entirely different system. When run on a Red Hat–based system, it reports the values for eth0 and eth1, but eth2, while it exists, does not have an IP address defined.

```
rhel6$ ./redhat-nics.sh
The IP Address configured for eth0 is 192.168.3.19
The IP Address configured for eth1 is 10.201.24.19
No IP Address defined for eth2
rhel6$
```

> *Because this loop may run more than once, it is vital to unset $IPADDR every time the loop is run. Otherwise the [-z "$IPADDR"] test could pass for eth2 but it would still contain the IP address of eth1.*

Returning a String

It may be noted that the preceding example, when it did find a match, responded by echoing the value of $IPADDR. This was then picked up by the calling script because the function call was made as thisip=`getipaddr $thisnic`. What happens here is that the variable thisip is assigned with any and all output from the function; the function is deliberately silent other than outputting an IP address if it finds one; it is therefore managing to provide two channels of communication with its caller. The return code tells the caller whether or not an IP address was found (and the reason for the failure if it was not found), but the output itself is the actual data that the caller was looking for.

Writing to a File

A function can write its output to a file. This recipe shows a function that simply writes its second parameter (a number) to its first parameter (the name of a file). The calling script first tells it to write 1, 2, 3 to file1, and 2, 3, 4 to file2. It then wipes file1, and calls the function again, writing 11, 12, 13 to file1, and 12, 13, 14 to file2.

In this example, file2 has a randomly generated unique filename from mktemp; file1 is always called /tmp/file.1. Another process can be attached to the file assuming it knows the name of the file to access. In a separate window, run `tail -F /tmp/file.1` before running the script, and observe the output. The `tail -F` output is shown below the output of the script itself.

```sh
$ cat writetofile.sh
#!/bin/sh

myfunc()
{
  thefile=$1
  echo Hello number $2 >> $thefile
}

file1=/tmp/file.1
file2=`mktemp`

for i in 1 2 3
do
  myfunc $file1 $i
  myfunc $file2 `expr $i + 1`
done

echo "FILE 1 says:"
cat $file1
echo "FILE 2 says:"
cat $file2

> $file1

for i in 11 12 13
do
  myfunc $file1 $i
  myfunc $file2 `expr $i + 1`
done

echo "FILE 1 says:"
cat $file1
echo "FILE 2 says:"
cat $file2

rm -f $file1 $file2
$ ./writetofile.sh
FILE 1 says:
Hello number 1
Hello number 2
Hello number 3
FILE 2 says:
Hello number 2
Hello number 3
Hello number 4
FILE 1 says:
Hello number 11
Hello number 12
Hello number 13
FILE 2 says:
Hello number 2
```

```
Hello number 3
Hello number 4
Hello number 12
Hello number 13
Hello number 14
$
```

> tail -F *does comment when the file doesn't exist, but it keeps on going. Also,*
> *If the* tail *process only started after the* 11, 12, 13 *had been written to the file,*
> *it would not get the* 1, 2, 3 *output because the script had already truncated the*
> *file by that stage.*

```
$ tail -F /tmp/file.1
tail: cannot open `/tmp/file.1' for reading: No such file or directory
tail: `/tmp/file.1' has become accessible
Hello number 1
Hello number 2
Hello number 3
tail: /tmp/file.1: file truncated
Hello number 11
Hello number 12
Hello number 13
tail: `/tmp/file.1' has become inaccessible: No such file or directory
```

Other, more sophisticated languages allow for the return of complex sets of values from a function. The shell does not provide this functionality, but something similar can often be simulated by writing output to a file. This simple function calculates the square and the cube of a supplied number and writes the results to a temporary file. Because two lines are written to the file, a simple "head -1" and "tail -1" will suffice to get the two items of data from the function. These can be read into variables to achieve the same effect as if they had been set directly by the function. It is not as elegant, but it can achieve the required result.

```
$ cat square-cube.sh
#!/bin/bash

squarecube()
{
  echo "$2 * $2" | bc > $1
  echo "$2 * $2 * $2" | bc >> $1
}

output=`mktemp`
for i in 1 2 3 4 5
do
   squarecube $output $i
```

```
    square=`head -1 $output`
    cube=`tail -1 $output`
    echo "The square of $i is $square"
    echo "The cube of $i is $cube"
done
rm -f $output
$ ./square-cube.sh
The square of 1 is 1
The cube of 1 is 1
The square of 2 is 4
The cube of 2 is 8
The square of 3 is 9
The cube of 3 is 27
The square of 4 is 16
The cube of 4 is 64
The square of 5 is 25
The cube of 5 is 125
$
```

squarecube.sh

Redirecting the Output of an Entire Function

Instead of having the function itself deliberately write to a file, it can be more appropriate for the function to write to `stdout` as normal, and direct the entire function to a file. This also means that the function can be run with or without redirection, just by the way it was called. This short function takes the format of `lspci` (which for each PCI device on the system shows the PCI path, a space, and then the vendor's identification string) and `lscpu` (which displays various attributes of the CPU as feature: value. By replacing the first space of `lspci` and the first colon of `lscpu`, a Comma-Separated Values (.csv) file can be created, which can be nicely formatted when viewed in a spreadsheet. Figure 8-1 shows how a spreadsheet displays the generated data.

```
$ cat pci.sh
#!/bin/bash

getconfig()
{
  echo "PCI Devices,"
  lspci | sed s/" "/','/1
  echo "CPU Specification,"
  lscpu | sed s/":"/','/1 | tr -d ' '
}

echo -en "Getting system details..."
getconfig > pci.csv
echo "Done."
ls -l pci.csv
```

pci.sh

```
$ ./pci.sh
Getting system details...Done.
-rw-rw-r-- 1 steve steve 2297 Jan 24 21:14 pci.csv
$ oocalc pci.csv ◄
```

THIS COMMAND LAUNCHES THE OPENOFFICE.ORG SPREADSHEET SOFTWARE.

pci.csv

	A	B
1	**PCI Devices**	
2	00:00.0	Host bridge: Intel Corporation Mobile 4 Series Chipset Memory Controller Hub (rev 09)
3	00:02.0	VGA compatible controller: Intel Corporation Mobile 4 Series Chipset Integrated Graphics Controller (rev 09)
4	00:02.1	Display controller: Intel Corporation Mobile 4 Series Chipset Integrated Graphics Controller (rev 09)
5	00:1a.0	USB Controller: Intel Corporation 82801I (ICH9 Family) USB2 UHCI Controller #4 (rev 03)
6	00:1a.7	USB Controller: Intel Corporation 82801I (ICH9 Family) USB2 EHCI Controller #2 (rev 03)
7	00:1b.0	Audio device: Intel Corporation 82801I (ICH9 Family) HD Audio Controller (rev 03)
8	00:1c.0	PCI bridge: Intel Corporation 82801I (ICH9 Family) PCI Express Port 1 (rev 03)
9	00:1c.1	PCI bridge: Intel Corporation 82801I (ICH9 Family) PCI Express Port 2 (rev 03)
10	00:1c.2	PCI bridge: Intel Corporation 82801I (ICH9 Family) PCI Express Port 3 (rev 03)
11	00:1d.0	USB Controller: Intel Corporation 82801I (ICH9 Family) USB UHCI Controller #1 (rev 03)
12	00:1d.1	USB Controller: Intel Corporation 82801I (ICH9 Family) USB UHCI Controller #2 (rev 03)
13	00:1d.2	USB Controller: Intel Corporation 82801I (ICH9 Family) USB UHCI Controller #3 (rev 03)
14	00:1d.3	USB Controller: Intel Corporation 82801I (ICH9 Family) USB UHCI Controller #6 (rev 03)
15	00:1d.7	USB Controller: Intel Corporation 82801I (ICH9 Family) USB2 EHCI Controller #1 (rev 03)
16	00:1e.0	PCI bridge: Intel Corporation 82801 Mobile PCI Bridge (rev 93)
17	00:1f.0	ISA bridge: Intel Corporation ICH9M LPC Interface Controller (rev 03)
18	00:1f.2	SATA controller: Intel Corporation ICH9M/M-E SATA AHCI Controller (rev 03)
19	00:1f.3	SMBus: Intel Corporation 82801I (ICH9 Family) SMBus Controller (rev 03)
20	04:00.0	Network controller: Atheros Communications Inc. AR928X Wireless Network Adapter (PCI-Express) (rev 01)
21	05:00.0	Ethernet controller: Atheros Communications AR8132 Fast Ethernet (rev c0)
22	**CPU Specification**	
23	Architecture	x86_64
24	CPUop-mode(s)	32-bit, 64-bit
25	CPU(s)	2
26	Thread(s)percore	1
27	Core(s)persocket	2

FIGURE 8-1

When the output of the function could be of direct interest to the caller, as well as being stored to a file, the `tee` command can direct output to `stdout` as well as to a file. This can be useful when the operator needs to see the output, but you also want to store the output to a file so that a log exists of the state of the system when the script was run.

Available for download on Wrox.com

```
$ cat pid.sh
#!/bin/bash

process_exists()
{
  pidof "$1" && echo "These $1 process(es) were found." || \
      echo "No $1 processes were found."
}

echo "Checking system processes..."
```

```
process_exists apache2 | tee apache2.log
process_exists mysqld | tee mysql.log
process_exists squid | tee squid.log
$ ./pid.sh
Checking system processes...
2272 1452 1451 1450 1449 1448 1433
These apache2 process(es) were found.
No mysqld processes were found.
No squid processes were found.
$ cat apache2.log
2272 1452 1451 1450 1449 1448 1433
These apache2 process(es) were found.
$ cat mysql.log
No mysqld processes were found.
$ cat squid.log
No squid processes were found.
$
```

pid.sh

It is often useful to define a generic logging function for taking diagnostic log reports as the script executes. This can be useful in any script but particularly when doing systems administration where a common task is to run multiple commands (or sets of commands) and log the results. The output here is deliberately messy to make a point. The script does not have to worry about the tidiness of the output at all; it just logs the results and keeps going. The script's author may not have time to write an elegant script that displays the results of every command beautifully, but does want to have a log of what happened. These simple functions provide the ability to do that without overly complicating the main script. The fact that a line such as uname -a, when added to the script name, date, and time goes over the 80-character column limit is not really important for a log file of this nature. In this case, the output of uname -a alone is 81 characters, so this cannot always be avoided.

Available for
download on
Wrox.com

```
$ cat debugger.sh
#!/bin/bash

LOGFILE=/tmp/myscript.log
# The higher the value of VERBOSE, the more talkative the log file is.
# Low values of VERBOSE mean a shorter log file;
# High values of VERBOSE mean a longer log file.
VERBOSE=10
APPNAME=`basename $0`

function logmsg()
{
  echo "${APPNAME}: `date`: $@" >> $LOGFILE
}

function debug()
{
  verbosity=$1
  shift
  if [ "$VERBOSE" -gt "$verbosity" ]; then
    echo "${APPNAME}: `date`: DEBUG Level ${verbosity}: $@" >> $LOGFILE
```

```
  fi
}

function die()
{
  echo "${APPNAME}: `date`: FATAL ERROR: $@" >> $LOGFILE
  exit 1
}

logmsg Starting script $0
uname -a || die uname command not found.
logmsg `uname -a`
cat /etc/redhat-release || debug 8 Not a RedHat-based system
cat /etc/debian_version || debug 8 Not a Debian-based system
cd /proc || debug 5 /proc filesystem not found.
grep -q "physical id" /proc/cpuinfo || debug 8 /proc/cpuinfo virtual file not found
.
logmsg Found `grep "physical id" /proc/cpuinfo | sort -u | wc -l` physical CPUs.
unset IPADDR
. /etc/sysconfig/network-scripts/ifcfg-eth0 || debug 1 ifcfg-eth0 not readable
logmsg eth0 IP address defined as $IPADDR
logmsg Script $0 finished.
$
```

```
$ ./debugger.sh
Linux goldie 2.6.32-5-amd64 #1 SMP Fri Dec 10 15:35:08 UTC 2010 x86_64 GNU/Linux
cat: /etc/redhat-release: No such file or directory
6.0
./debugger.sh: line 39: /etc/sysconfig/network-scripts/ifcfg-eth0: No such file or
Directory
```

debugger.sh

If you run the script and look at the output in `/tmp/myscript.log`, you'll see how the different functions provide a standardized logfile format with minimal effort for the developer:

```
$ cat /tmp/myscript.log
debugger.sh: Mon Jan 24 23:46:40 GMT 2011: Starting script ./debugger.sh
debugger.sh: Mon Jan 24 23:46:40 GMT 2011: Linux goldie 2.6.32-5-amd64 #1 SMP Fri D
ec 10 15:35:08 UTC 2010 x86_64 GNU/Linux
debugger.sh: Mon Jan 24 23:46:40 GMT 2011: DEBUG Level 8: Not a RedHat-based system
debugger.sh: Mon Jan 24 23:46:40 GMT 2011: Found 1 physical CPUs.
debugger.sh: Mon Jan 24 23:46:40 GMT 2011: DEBUG Level 1: ifcfg-eth0 not readable
debugger.sh: Mon Jan 24 23:46:40 GMT 2011: eth0 IP address defined as
debugger.sh: Mon Jan 24 23:46:40 GMT 2011: Script ./debugger.sh finished.
$
```

 The die() *function is part of the Perl language. For quick and dirty scripts, its functionality is well worth borrowing.*

This script defines three functions — logmsg, which simply logs all messages passed to it; debug, which logs messages passed to it if the script-wide VERBOSE variable allows it; and die, which logs a message and ends the script. The main body of the script then attempts a variety of commands, most of which get logged, and some of which are bound to fail. Notice the following line:

```
logmsg Found `grep "physical id" /proc/cpuinfo | sort -u | wc -l` physical CPUs.
```

This shows that anything can be passed to a function, including a mix of predefined text and the outputs of system commands. Counting the unique physical IDs of installed CPUs gives a total count of physical CPUs — with multi-core chips becoming more and more common, it is often useful to determine exactly how many actual chips are installed in the system.

Functions with Trap

trap is a useful call for a shell script to define early on. It can take other forms, too, but the most common use is for a script to define a cleanup function for trap to call if the script gets interrupted. If your script uses temporary files, you can remove them with a generic function, whatever the reason for the script being interrupted. This script trawls a directory looking for files in which ldd can find links to libraries. If it finds libraries, ldd displays those libraries and sends a return code of zero (success).

```
$ ldd /bin/ls
        linux-vdso.so.1 =>  (0x00007fff573ff000)
        libselinux.so.1 => /lib/libselinux.so.1 (0x00007f5c716a1000)
        librt.so.1 => /lib/librt.so.1 (0x00007f5c71499000)
        libacl.so.1 => /lib/libacl.so.1 (0x00007f5c71291000)
        libc.so.6 => /lib/libc.so.6 (0x00007f5c70f30000)
        libdl.so.2 => /lib/libdl.so.2 (0x00007f5c70d2c000)
        /lib64/ld-linux-x86-64.so.2 (0x00007f5c718d2000)
        libpthread.so.0 => /lib/libpthread.so.0 (0x00007f5c70b0f000)
        libattr.so.1 => /lib/libattr.so.1 (0x00007f5c7090b000)
$
```

This trawling of the filesystem can take a long time so it is sensible to allow for the possibility that the script will be killed before it gets the chance to complete. This means that the filesystem is kept tidy even if it has been started many times but never finished. It can also ensure that subsequent runs of the script do not pick up old, part-complete files from earlier runs.

```
$ cat ldd.sh
#!/bin/bash
# mktemp will give a pattern like "/tmp/tmp.U3XOAi92I2"
tempfile=`mktemp`
echo "Temporary file is ${tempfile}."
logfile=/tmp/libraries.txt
[ -f $logfile ] && rm -f $logfile

# Trap on:
# 1 = SIGHUP (Hangup of controlling terminal or death of parent)
# 2 = SIGINT (Interrupted by the keyboard)
# 3 = SIGQUIT (Quit signal from keyboard)
# 6 = SIGABRT (Aborted by abort(3))
```

```
# 9 = SIGKILL (Sent a kill command)

trap cleanup 1 2 3 6 9

function cleanup
{
  echo "Caught signal - tidying up..."
  # Tidy up after yourself
  rm -f ${tempfile}
  echo "Done. Exiting."
}

find $1 -type f -print | while read filename
do
  ldd ${filename} > ${tempfile}
  if [ "$?" -eq "0" ]; then
    let total=$total+1
    echo "File $filename uses libraries:" >> $logfile
    cat $tempfile >> $logfile
    echo >> $logfile
  fi
done
echo "Found `grep -c "^File " $logfile` files in $1 linked to libraries."
echo "Results in ${logfile}."
```

ldd.sh

```
$ ./ldd.sh /bin
Temporary file is /tmp/tmp.EYk2NnP6QW.
Found 78 files in /bin linked to libraries.
Results in /tmp/libraries.txt.
$ ls -l /tmp/tmp.EYk2NnP6QW
ls: Cannot access /tmp/tmp.EYk2NnP6QW: No such file or directory.
$
```

THE LS COMMAND SHOWS THAT THE TEMPORARY FILE HAS BEEN REMOVED.

Running the script again, but pressing ^C before it completes, results in a SIGINT. The ls command once more confirms that the temporary file was removed, even though the script had not finished. The /tmp/libraries.txt file does still exist; it is only the temporary file that is deleted.

```
$ ./ldd.sh /bin
Temporary file is /tmp/tmp.nhCOS9N3WE.
^CCaught signal - tidying up...
Done. Exiting.
Found 21 files in /bin linked to libraries.
Results in /tmp/libraries.txt.
$ ls -ld /tmp/tmp.nhCOS9N3WE
ls: /tmp/tmp.nhCOS9N3WE: No such file or directory
$ ls -ld /tmp/libraries.txt
-rw-rw-r-- 1 steve steve 16665 Mar  9 14:49 /tmp/libraries.txt
$
```

Recursive Functions

A recursive function is one that calls itself as part of its own execution. A simple example to demonstrate this is the mathematical factorial function. The factorial of an integer is the product of all the integers between 1 and itself. So the factorial of 6 (also written as 6!) is 1×2×3×4×5×6, which is 720. It is possible to do this non-recursively, but because 6! is (5! × 6), and 5! is (4! × 5), and so on, a simple factorial function can actually be written like this:

```
$ cat factorial.sh
#!/bin/bash
factorial()
{
  if [ "$1" -gt "1" ]; then
    previous=`expr $1 - 1`
    parent=`factorial $previous`
    result=`expr $1 \* $parent`
    echo $result
  else
    echo 1
  fi
}

factorial $1
$ ./factorial.sh 6
720
```

factorial.sh

It is not necessarily obvious what happens with this script. Adding a bit of logging and some `sleep` calls (so that the timestamps more clearly indicate what happens when) really help to demonstrate what happens to function output, and what the side effects are. `factorial` gets called before the `echo` statement, which says what happens when. The calculations are done just before the debugging statements. The first six lines of the log show that `factorial 6` calls `factorial 5`, which calls `factorial 4`, and so on down to `factorial 1` at 11:50:12, which returns 1. The log then starts working its way out of the recursion, calculating `factorial 2` at 11:50:18, `factorial 3` at 11:50:20, all the way up to the final step, calculating `factorial 6` at 11:50:26.

```
$ cat recursive-string.sh
#!/bin/bash

LOG=/tmp/factorial-log.txt
> $LOG

factorial()
{
  echo "`date`: Called with $1" >> $LOG
  sleep 1
  if [ "$1" -gt "1" ]; then
    previous=`expr $1 - 1`
    parent=`factorial $previous`
    result=`expr $1 \* $parent`
```

```
      echo "`date`: Passed $1 - the factorial of $previous is ${parent}. "\
           "$1 * $parent is ${result}." >> $LOG
      echo "`date`: Sleeping for 2 seconds." >> $LOG
      sleep 2
      echo $result
   else
      echo "`date`: Passed $1 - returning 1." >> $LOG
      echo "`date`: Sleeping for 5 seconds." >> $LOG
      sleep 5
      echo 1
   fi
}

read -p "Enter a number: " x
echo "Started at `date`"
factorial $x
echo "Here is my working:"
cat $LOG
rm -f $LOG
echo "Finished at `date`"
$ ./recursive-string.sh
Enter a number: 6
Started at Wed Jan 26 11:50:07 GMT 2011
720
Here is my working:
Wed Jan 26 11:50:07 GMT 2011: Called with 6
Wed Jan 26 11:50:08 GMT 2011: Called with 5
Wed Jan 26 11:50:09 GMT 2011: Called with 4
Wed Jan 26 11:50:10 GMT 2011: Called with 3
Wed Jan 26 11:50:11 GMT 2011: Called with 2
Wed Jan 26 11:50:12 GMT 2011: Called with 1
Wed Jan 26 11:50:13 GMT 2011: Passed 1 - returning 1.
Wed Jan 26 11:50:13 GMT 2011: Sleeping for 5 seconds.
Wed Jan 26 11:50:18 GMT 2011: Passed 2 - the factorial of 1 is 1.  2 * 1 is 2.
Wed Jan 26 11:50:18 GMT 2011: Sleeping for 2 seconds.
Wed Jan 26 11:50:20 GMT 2011: Passed 3 - the factorial of 2 is 2.  3 * 2 is 6.
Wed Jan 26 11:50:20 GMT 2011: Sleeping for 2 seconds.
Wed Jan 26 11:50:22 GMT 2011: Passed 4 - the factorial of 3 is 6.  4 * 6 is 24.
Wed Jan 26 11:50:22 GMT 2011: Sleeping for 2 seconds.
Wed Jan 26 11:50:24 GMT 2011: Passed 5 - the factorial of 4 is 24.  5 * 24 is 120.
Wed Jan 26 11:50:24 GMT 2011: Sleeping for 2 seconds.
Wed Jan 26 11:50:26 GMT 2011: Passed 6 - the factorial of 5 is 120.  6 * 120 is 720
.
Wed Jan 26 11:50:26 GMT 2011: Sleeping for 2 seconds.
Finished at Wed Jan 26 11:50:28 GMT 2011
$
```

recursive-string.sh

The preceding script is called `recursive-string.sh` because it passes the numbers around as strings; the following script is called `recursive-byte.sh` because it uses return values from the function to return the actual number calculated. Because Unix return codes are bytes, they can only hold a value between 0 and 255. You can see that this script works fine with input up to 5, but fails when passed a value of 6 to calculate, because factorial 6 is 6*120=720, which is greater than 255.

```
$ cat recursive-byte.sh
#!/bin/bash

LOG=/tmp/factorial-log.txt
> $LOG

factorial()
{
  echo "`date`: Called with $1" >> $LOG
  sleep 1
  if [ "$1" -gt "1" ]; then
    previous=`expr $1 - 1`
    factorial $previous
    parent=$?
    result=`expr $1 \* $parent`
    echo "`date`: Passed $1 - the factorial of $previous is ${parent}. " \
         "$1 * $parent is ${result}." >> $LOG
    echo "`date`: Sleeping for 2 seconds." >> $LOG
    sleep 2
    return $result
  else
    echo "`date`: Passed $1 - returning 1." >> $LOG
    echo "`date`: Sleeping for 5 seconds." >> $LOG
    sleep 5
    return 1
  fi
}

read -p "Enter a number: " x
echo "Started at `date`"
factorial $x
echo "Answer: $?"
echo "Here is my working:"
cat $LOG
rm -f $LOG
echo "Finished at `date`"
$ ./recursive-byte.sh
Enter a number: 5
Started at Wed Jan 26 11:53:49 GMT 2011
Answer: 120
Here is my working:
Wed Jan 26 11:53:49 GMT 2011: Called with 5
Wed Jan 26 11:53:50 GMT 2011: Called with 4
Wed Jan 26 11:53:51 GMT 2011: Called with 3
Wed Jan 26 11:53:52 GMT 2011: Called with 2
Wed Jan 26 11:53:53 GMT 2011: Called with 1
Wed Jan 26 11:53:54 GMT 2011: Passed 1 - returning 1.
Wed Jan 26 11:53:54 GMT 2011: Sleeping for 5 seconds.
Wed Jan 26 11:53:59 GMT 2011: Passed 2 - the factorial of 1 is 1.  2 * 1 is 2.
Wed Jan 26 11:53:59 GMT 2011: Sleeping for 2 seconds.
Wed Jan 26 11:54:01 GMT 2011: Passed 3 - the factorial of 1 is 2.  3 * 2 is 6.
Wed Jan 26 11:54:01 GMT 2011: Sleeping for 2 seconds.
```

```
Wed Jan 26 11:54:03 GMT 2011: Passed 4 - the factorial of 1 is 6.  4 * 6 is 24.
Wed Jan 26 11:54:03 GMT 2011: Sleeping for 2 seconds.
Wed Jan 26 11:54:05 GMT 2011: Passed 5 - the factorial of 1 is 24.  5 * 24 is 120.
Wed Jan 26 11:54:05 GMT 2011: Sleeping for 2 seconds.
Finished at Wed Jan 26 11:54:07 GMT 2011
$
```

recursive-byte.sh

When you pass the number 6 to this script, it produces the value 208, because 720 modulo 256 is 208. Showing the working, bc gets the answer right, but when the shell function passes that value back, it is compressed down into a single byte, and the significant bits of 720 make 208.

 Because a byte is made up of 8 bits, numbers over 255 wrap around. In binary, 120 is 1111000, which is 8 bits, which is fine. 720 is 1011010000, which is 10 bits. The first two are dropped, leaving 1101000, which is 208 in decimal.

```
$ ./recursive-byte.sh
Enter a number: 6
Started at Wed Jan 26 11:54:46 GMT 2011
Answer: 208
Here is my working:
Wed Jan 26 11:54:46 GMT 2011: Called with 6
Wed Jan 26 11:54:47 GMT 2011: Called with 5
Wed Jan 26 11:54:48 GMT 2011: Called with 4
Wed Jan 26 11:54:49 GMT 2011: Called with 3
Wed Jan 26 11:54:50 GMT 2011: Called with 2
Wed Jan 26 11:54:51 GMT 2011: Called with 1
Wed Jan 26 11:54:52 GMT 2011: Passed 1 - returning 1.
Wed Jan 26 11:54:52 GMT 2011: Sleeping for 5 seconds.
Wed Jan 26 11:54:57 GMT 2011: Passed 2 - the factorial of 1 is 1.  2 * 1 is 2.
Wed Jan 26 11:54:57 GMT 2011: Sleeping for 2 seconds.
Wed Jan 26 11:54:59 GMT 2011: Passed 3 - the factorial of 1 is 2.  3 * 2 is 6.
Wed Jan 26 11:54:59 GMT 2011: Sleeping for 2 seconds.
Wed Jan 26 11:55:01 GMT 2011: Passed 4 - the factorial of 1 is 6.  4 * 6 is 24.
Wed Jan 26 11:55:01 GMT 2011: Sleeping for 2 seconds.
Wed Jan 26 11:55:03 GMT 2011: Passed 5 - the factorial of 1 is 24.  5 * 24 is 120.
Wed Jan 26 11:55:03 GMT 2011: Sleeping for 2 seconds.
Wed Jan 26 11:55:05 GMT 2011: Passed 6 - the factorial of 1 is 120.  6 * 120 is 720
.
Wed Jan 26 11:55:05 GMT 2011: Sleeping for 2 seconds.
Finished at Wed Jan 26 11:55:07 GMT 2011
$
```

Recursion is a flexible technique when used carefully. It is essential to understand when the calls will be made and how the loop will exit. It is also important to be careful not to overuse resources — if every instance of the function will open a file, you could end up with more open files than allowed by the system.

VARIABLE SCOPE

Functions traditionally return only a single value. The shell is not quite as straightforward as that, so some side effects can occasionally be surprising. There is only one shell executing the script so any variables within a function continue to exist outside it. This script has three variables, GLOBALVAR, myvar, and uniquevar. In some languages, GLOBALVAR would be treated as global in similar circumstances because it has been defined outside of the function itself. In some languages, myvar within the function would be local to the function and separate from the myvar variable outside the function. In many languages, uniquevar would fail when it is first called because it has never been defined before that point. In the shell, this is okay. uniquevar would still not be seen outside of the function, because it has never existed beyond the function.

These occasionally conflicting but widely understood standards are common across many programming languages. The shell is a little different because it is not a strict programming language. Try to predict the outcome of the following script before running it, and be prepared to explain why the results will be as you predict. You can use Table 8-1 for this.

TABLE 8-1: Predicted final values of GLOBALVAR, myvar, and uniquevar

VARIABLE	INITIAL VALUE	PREDICTED FINAL VALUE, WITH REASONS
$GLOBALVAR	1	
$myvar	500	
$uniquevar	undefined	

```
$ cat scope.sh
#!/bin/sh

the_function()
{
  echo "  This is the_function. I was passed $# arguments: "\
      "\"$1\", \"$2\", \"$3\"."
  myvar=100
  echo "    GLOBALVAR started as $GLOBALVAR;"
  GLOBALVAR=`expr $GLOBALVAR + 1`
  echo "    GLOBALVAR is now $GLOBALVAR"
  echo "    myvar started as $myvar;"
  myvar=`expr $myvar + 1`
  echo "    myvar is now $myvar"
  echo "uniquevar started as $uniquevar"
  uniquevar=`expr $uniquevar + 1`
  echo "uniquevar is $uniquevar"
  echo "  Leaving the_function."
}

GLOBALVAR=1
myvar=500
```

```
echo "This is the main script."
echo "GLOBALVAR is $GLOBALVAR"
echo "myvar is $myvar"
echo "I was passed $# arguments: "\
    "\"$1\", \"$2\", \"$3\"."
echo "***************************"
echo

echo "Calling the_function with 1 2 3 ..."
the_function 1 2 3
echo "GLOBALVAR is $GLOBALVAR"
echo "myvar is $myvar"
echo
echo "Calling the_function with 3 2 1 ..."
the_function 3 2 1
echo "GLOBALVAR is $GLOBALVAR"
echo "myvar is $myvar"
echo
echo "Calling the_function with $1 $2 $3 ..."
the_function $1 $2 $3
echo "GLOBALVAR is $GLOBALVAR"
echo "myvar is $myvar"
echo
echo "All Done."
echo "GLOBALVAR is $GLOBALVAR"
echo "myvar is $myvar"
echo "uniquevar is $uniquevar"
$
```

scope.sh

First, GLOBALVAR is part of the environment that gets passed to the_function when the_function gets called, so it is to be expected that the_function knows the initial value of GLOBALVAR. Because it is all in one shell, GLOBALVAR gets incremented as any global variable would, and on subsequent calls to the_function, GLOBALVAR is incremented again.

Second, myvar is different from GLOBALVAR because it gets defined within the_function itself. This can suggest to the language that myvar here is different from myvar elsewhere. This is not the case with the shell, however; if myvar is assigned a value, then that is the value for the running process (in this case the shell) of that variable, whether the process considers itself to be within a function or in any other state; this is a straightforward Unix system variable, which has no concept of functions, shells, or scope.

Finally, uniquevar has the most obvious potential issues because it has never been defined. That is okay; the shell will treat it as the empty string, and the first time it is referenced, it is as uniquevar=`expr $uniquevar + 1`. This is passed to expr as uniquevar=`expr  + 1`, which expr is quite happy to evaluate as 1. uniquevar is 1 from now on, and the next time it is referred to it will increment to 2, and so on. uniquevar even retains its value outside of the function when echoed at the end of the main script.

```
$ ./scope.sh a b c
This is the main script.
```

```
GLOBALVAR is 1
myvar is 500
I was passed 3 arguments:  "a", "b", "c".
******************************

Calling the_function with 1 2 3 ...
   This is the_function. I was passed 3 arguments:  "1", "2", "3".
     GLOBALVAR started as 1;
     GLOBALVAR is now 2
     myvar started as 100;
     myvar is now 101
uniquevar started as
uniquevar is 1
   Leaving the_function.
GLOBALVAR is 2
myvar is 101

Calling the_function with 3 2 1 ...
   This is the_function. I was passed 3 arguments:  "3", "2", "1".
     GLOBALVAR started as 2;
     GLOBALVAR is now 3
     myvar started as 100;
     myvar is now 101
uniquevar started as 1
uniquevar is 2
   Leaving the_function.
GLOBALVAR is 3
myvar is 101

Calling the_function with a b c ...
   This is the_function. I was passed 3 arguments:  "a", "b", "c".
     GLOBALVAR started as 3;
     GLOBALVAR is now 4
     myvar started as 100;
     myvar is now 101
uniquevar started as 2
uniquevar is 3
   Leaving the_function.
GLOBALVAR is 4
myvar is 101

All Done.
GLOBALVAR is 4
myvar is 101
uniquevar is 3
$
```

The fact that myvar is treated as global can be a particular problem. A function often needs to use its own variables without the risk of clobbering the values of the caller, without the function necessarily knowing anything about the caller. Naming the local variables the_function_variable_one, the_function_variable_two, and so on, or even the_function_stock and the_function_price, soon becomes unwieldy. The bash shell addresses this issue by adding the keyword `local`. When you add the line `local myvar` to `the_function`, the outcome is different.

```
the_function()
{
  echo "  This is the_function. I was passed $# arguments: "\
       "\"$1\", \"$2\", \"$3\"."
  local myvar=100
  echo "    GLOBALVAR started as $GLOBALVAR;"
  GLOBALVAR=`expr $GLOBALVAR + 1`
  echo "    GLOBALVAR is now $GLOBALVAR"
  echo "    myvar started as $myvar;"
  myvar=`expr $myvar + 1`
  echo "    myvar is now $myvar"
  echo "uniquevar started as $uniquevar"
  uniquevar=`expr $uniquevar + 1`
  echo "uniquevar is $uniquevar"
  echo "  Leaving the_function."
}
```

scope2.sh

This additional keyword tells bash that `myvar` is not the same as the external variable of the same name. Anything that happens to `myvar` within `the_function` does not affect the other variable, which also happens to be called `myvar`. This means that `the_function` can confidently use whatever variable names it wants. The `scope2.sh` script below shows the difference made by declaring `myvar` as `local`.

> Obviously, if `the_function` *needs to refer to the value of the other* `myvar` *variable, it must use a different name for its local variable.*

```
$ ./scope2.sh a b c
This is the main script.
GLOBALVAR is 1
myvar is 500
I was passed 3 arguments:  "a", "b", "c".
*****************************

Calling the_function with 1 2 3 ...
  This is the_function. I was passed 3 arguments:  "1", "2", "3".
    GLOBALVAR started as 1;
    GLOBALVAR is now 2
    myvar started as 100;
    myvar is now 101
uniquevar started as
uniquevar is 1
  Leaving the_function.
GLOBALVAR is 2
```

```
myvar is 500

Calling the_function with 3 2 1 ...
  This is the_function. I was passed 3 arguments:  "3", "2", "1".
    GLOBALVAR started as 2;
    GLOBALVAR is now 3
    myvar started as 100;
    myvar is now 101
uniquevar started as 1
uniquevar is 2
  Leaving the_function.
GLOBALVAR is 3
myvar is 500

Calling the_function with a b c ...
  This is the_function. I was passed 3 arguments:  "a", "b", "c".
    GLOBALVAR started as 3;
    GLOBALVAR is now 4
    myvar started as 100;
    myvar is now 101
uniquevar started as 2
uniquevar is 3
  Leaving the_function.
GLOBALVAR is 4
myvar is 500

All Done.
GLOBALVAR is 4
myvar is 500
uniquevar is 3
$
```

The addition of the `local` keyword makes bash a practical shell for writing more complex functions and libraries. The standard behavior, where a function can change the value of any variable, should also be clearly understood, or debugging can become very difficult.

Functions are a useful way to repeat code without writing it out again, or writing every block of code as a separate shell script to call. They can be made even more useful when grouped together into libraries of related functions.

LIBRARIES

The shell has no real concept of libraries in the way that Perl and C use libraries. In C, you can bring in the Math library by including its header file and linking against the library (simply called "m," hence -lm in the following gcc call). Additional functions, including cos(), sin(), and tan(), are then available to the program.

```
$ cat math.c
#include <stdio.h>
#include <math.h>

int main(int argc, char *argv[])
{
```

```
    int arg=atoi(argv[1]);
    printf("cos(%d)=%0.8f\n", arg, cos(arg));
    printf("sin(%d)=%0.8f\n", arg, sin(arg));
    printf("tan(%d)=%0.8f\n", arg, tan(arg));
    return 0;
}
$ gcc -lm -o math math.c
$ ./math 30
cos(30)=0.15425145
sin(30)=-0.98803162
tan(30)=-6.40533120
$ ./math 60
cos(60)=-0.95241298
sin(60)=-0.30481062
tan(60)=0.32004039
$ ./math 90
cos(90)=-0.44807362
sin(90)=0.89399666
tan(90)=-1.99520041
$
```

math.c

This sample C code does no sanity tests on its input and is only here to show how linking to a library works in the C language. Also, if its results look wrong, that is because it is working in radians and not degrees.

The shell has a few ways of defining standard settings — aliases, variables, and functions, which create an environment almost indistinguishable from a set of libraries. When your shell is invoked interactively, it reads ~/.profile, and (depending on the exact shell in use) ~/.bashrc, ~/.kshrc, or similar. Using the same method, your script can invoke (source) other files to gain their contents, without running any actual code. The functions defined in those files will then be available to your script.

Much as ~/.bashrc defines things but does not typically actually execute any code, libraries really should do nothing on execution, other than reading in the function definitions they contain.

If your shell script can read in its own set of variables, and — most usefully — functions, then it can benefit from a customized environment and gain the modularity benefits mentioned at the start of this chapter.

Taking this to its logical conclusion, a library of shell scripting functions can be defined in your environment and made available for the use of all shell scripts and interactive sessions, or just a set of libraries for a particular script.

Creating and Accessing Libraries

Creating a library is the same as creating a shell script, except that there is no actual starting point — all you do with a library is define functions. The actual calls will go in the main shell script, plus of course functions may call other functions in the same library, or even functions from other libraries.

> It might seem obvious that a function cannot call another function defined later in the same library file. However, because the functions are not executed until later, as long as the code makes syntactic sense, it does not matter if a function defined earlier in the library calls a function defined later in the library because by the time the main script calls them, both functions are already defined in the environment. This is the same as a script calling a missing binary. The syntax is fine so the shell parses it correctly.

Shell script filenames often end in `.sh` (or even `.bash`, `.ksh`, and so on if it is helpful to make explicit that the script requires a particular shell). Libraries do not have to be marked as executable, and do not normally have any extension at all. Libraries also should not start with the `#!/` syntax, as they will not be executed by the operating system, but only read in by the shell itself.

To include a library in a shell script, the `.` or `source` command is called with the name of the library file. If the shell option `shopt sourcepath` is set, bash searches the `$PATH` for a file with that name and then looks in the current directory. Otherwise, it just looks in the current directory. The `source` command reads everything in the file into the current environment so any function definitions in the library will be taken on by the currently executing shell. Similarly, any variables defined there will be set in the current shell.

Library Structures

When writing a reasonably large set of scripts, it is worth setting up a `lib/` directory to contain functions that you expect to use on a regular basis. This provides the benefits of consistency, readability, and maintainability which were mentioned at the start of this chapter and the reusability of calling those same functions from multiple scripts. For generic libraries, `${HOME}/lib` may be a suitable location; for a script in `/usr/local/myapp/`, then `/usr/local/myapp/bin` and `/usr/local/myapp/lib` would be more suitable locations.

Libraries can call each other, and inheritance works in a predictable manner: if `lib1` sources `lib2`, then anything that sources `lib1` inherits `lib2` also.

```
$ cat calling.sh
#!/bin/sh

. ./lib1

func1

echo "I also get func2 for free..."
func2
```

calling.sh

```
$ cat lib1
. ./lib2

func1()
{
  echo func1
  func2
}

anotherfunc()
{
  echo More stuff here.
}
```

lib1

```
$ cat lib2
func2()
{
  echo func2
}
```

lib2

```
$ ./calling.sh
func1
func2
I also get func2 for free...
func2
$
```

These libraries can't all source each other, however, or you get the error message "too many open files" as the shell recursively opens both files again and again until it is out of resources. Getting func2 to call anotherfunc requires that lib2 has the definition of anotherfunc (although the calling.sh script now knows all of the function definitions, lib2 itself does not), which means that lib2 has to source lib1. Because lib1 also sources lib2, the shell ends up in a recursive loop, which results in the following error:

 The maximum number of files that can be open at any time is set by the nofile *parameter in* /etc/security/limits.conf.

```
$ ./calling.sh
.: 1: 3: Too many open files
$
```

One solution is to get `calling.sh` to `source` both libraries; that way, `lib2` will know about `anotherfunc` by the time it gets called. That does work; as long as neither library file sources the other, and the calling script sources any library file required, then the overall environment is set up correctly. This does mean that `calling.sh` has to know about any changes to the structure of the library. This is easily fixed by adding a meta-library file, here called `lib`:

```
$ cat calling.sh
#!/bin/sh

. ./lib

func1

echo "I also get func2 for free..."
func2
$ cat lib
. ./lib1
. ./lib2
```

lib

```
$ ./calling.sh
func1
func2
More stuff here.
I also get func2 for free...
func2
More stuff here.
$
```

A more flexible way to manage interdependencies like this is to mimic the C header structure, which has a very similar problem. In C, a header such as `stdio.h` starts by checking if `_STDIO_H` has already been defined. If it has, then `stdio.h` has already been included. If not defined, then it goes on to declare everything that `stdio.h` is capable of.

```
#ifndef _STDIO_H
# define _STDIO_H        1

    ... stdio declarations go here ...

#endif
```

The shell can do something similar, and even a little bit more tidily. By defining a variable with the same name as the library, the shell can find out if the library has already been sourced in this environment. That way, if multiple libraries all try to reference one another, the shell will not get caught in an infinite loop.

Notice that this example also mimics the C convention of starting a system (or library) variable name with an underscore. There is no technical difference between a variable starting with an underscore and any other variable, but it makes it stand out as a system variable or metavariable, not to be confused with something storing user data. When these example libraries are called lib1 *and* lib2, *this might not seem to pose a problem. If the script deals with stock control, one library might be called* stock *and another library might be called* store. *These are also very likely candidates for data variables, so by following this convention, you avoid the risk of overlapping metadata variables* $_stock *and* $_store *with actual data variables* $stock *and* $store.

```
$ cat calling.sh
#!/bin/sh

. ./lib1

func1

echo "I also get func2 for free..."
func2
$ cat lib1
_lib1=1
[ -z "$_lib2" ] && . ./lib2

func1()
{
  echo func1
  func2
}

anotherfunc()
{
  echo More stuff here.
}
$ cat lib2
_lib2=1
[ -z "$_lib1" ] && . ./lib1

func2()
{
  echo func2
  anotherfunc
}
$ ./calling.sh
func1
func2
More stuff here.
I also get func2 for free...
func2
More stuff here.
$
```

calling.sh

This is a more robust solution to the problem. If it is possible to use a single library file, or to keep dependencies between libraries to a minimum, that is preferred. If this isn't possible, setting a flag variable in this way keeps the dependencies under control.

Network Configuration Library

Now that you've seen how libraries work, let's formulate a more solid script. This script includes a centralized script that configures a new network interface. It depends upon a library that determines how to accomplish this task for the appropriate operating system it finds itself on. Notice that as long as the centralized script remains generic enough, this structure can be expanded a long way, resulting in an extensible, maintainable cross-platform shell script library. This library contains four files and one shell script:

➤ `network.sh`

➤ `definitions`

➤ `debian-network`

➤ `redhat-network`

➤ `solaris-network`

The first two files define the basic library structure: generic definitions are in the `definitions` file, and the `network.sh` is top-level script itself.

```
$ cat definitions
# Various error conditions. It is better to
# provide generic definitions so that the
# individual libraries are that much clearer.
_WRONG_PLATFORM=1
_NO_IP=2
_NO_CONFIG=3

# Success is a variant on failure - best to define this too for consistency.
SUCCESS=0
$
```

definitions

```
$ cat network.sh
#!/bin/bash

[ -z "$_definitions" ] && . definitions
[ -f /etc/redhat-release ] && . ./redhat-network
[ -f /etc/debian_version ] && . ./debian-network
[ `uname` == "SunOS" ] && . ./solaris-network

for thisnic in $*
do
  thisip=`getipaddr $thisnic`
  case $? in
    $SUCCESS) echo "The IP Address configured for $thisnic is $thisip" ;;
```

```
    $_WRONG_PLATFORM) echo "This does not seem to be running on the expected platfo
rm" ;;
    $_NO_IP) echo "No IP Address defined for $thisnic" ;;
    $_NO_CONFIG) echo "No configuration found for $thisnic" ;;
  esac
done
$
```

network.sh

There are then three different library files, each containing a definition of `getipaddr`, but only the appropriate instance will be defined on any running system. Each system has a totally different implementation of `getipaddr`, but this does not matter to the library.

```
$ cat redhat-network
[ -z "$_definitions" ] && . definitions

# RedHat-specific getipaddr() definition
getipaddr()
{
  [ -d /etc/sysconfig/network-scripts ] || return _$WRONG_PLATFORM
  if [ -f /etc/sysconfig/network-scripts/ifcfg-$1 ]; then
    unset IPADDR
    . /etc/sysconfig/network-scripts/ifcfg-$1
    if [ -z "$IPADDR" ]; then
      return $_NO_IP
    else
      echo $IPADDR
    fi
  else
    return $_NO_CONFIG
  fi
  # Not strictly needed
  return $SUCCESS
}
$
```

redhat-network

```
$ cat debian-network
[ -z "$_definitions" ] && . ../definitions

# Debian-specific getipaddr() definition
getipaddr()
{
  [ -f /etc/network/interfaces ] || return $_WRONG_PLATFORM
  found=0
  while read keyword argument morestuff
  do
    #echo "Debug: k $keyword a $argument m $morestuff"
    if [ "$keyword" == "iface" ]; then
      if [ "$found" -eq "1" ]; then
```

```
            # we had already found ours, but no address line found.
            return $_NO_IP
        else
          if [ "$argument" == "$1" ]; then
            found=1
          fi
        fi
      fi
      if [ "$found" -eq "1" ]; then
        if [ "$keyword" == "address" ]; then
          # Found the address of this interface.
          echo $argument
          return $SUCCESS
        fi
      fi
  done < /etc/network/interfaces
  if [ "$found" -eq "0" ]; then
    return $_NO_CONFIG
  fi
  # Not strictly needed
  return $SUCCESS
}
```

debian-network

```
$ cat solaris-network
[ -z "$_definitions" ] && . ./definitions

# Solaris-specific getipaddr() definition
getipaddr()
{
  uname | grep SunOS > /dev/null || return $_WRONG_PLATFORM
  [ -f /etc/hostname.${1} ] || return $_NO_CONFIG
  [ ! -s /etc/hostname.$1 ] && return $_NO_IP
  getent hosts `head -1 /etc/hostname.${1} | cut -d"/" -f1 | \
        awk '{ print $1 }'` | cut -f1 || cat /etc/hostname.${1}
  return $SUCCESS
}
$
```

solaris-network

The main script can then comfortably call the function from its library without having to know anything about the differences between the operating systems or the way in which the library deals with them. It simply calls getipaddr and gets the results back that it needs. On a Debian system, with only eth0 defined, the result looks like this:

```
debian# ./network.sh eth0 eth1 bond0 bond1 eri0 qfe0 wlan0
The IP Address configured for eth0 is 192.168.1.13
No configuration found for eth1
No configuration found for bond0
No configuration found for bond1
No configuration found for eri0
```

```
No configuration found for qfe0
No configuration found for wlan0
debian#
```

On a Red Hat system with `eth1` and `bond0` configured, and `eth0` configured but with no IP address (being part of `bond0`), the result of the script looks like this:

```
redhat# ./network.sh eth0 eth1 bond0 bond1 eri0 qfe0 wlan0
No IP Address defined for eth0
The IP Address configured for eth1 is 192.168.44.107
The IP Address configured for bond0 is 192.168.81.64
No configuration found for bond1
No configuration found for eri0
No configuration found for qfe0
No configuration found for wlan0
redhat#
```

On a Solaris system with `eri0` and `qfe0` configured, the result of the script looks like this:

```
solaris# ./network.sh eth0 eth1 bond0 bond1 eri0 qfe0 wlan0
No configuration found for eth0
No configuration found for eth1
No configuration found for bond0
No configuration found for bond1
The IP Address configured for eri0 is 192.168.101.3
The IP Address configured for qfe0 is 192.168.190.45
No configuration found for wlan0
solaris#
```

This makes for a simple interface — `getipaddr` can be called without the calling script needing to know anything about the implementation. The finishing touch is to turn `network.sh` itself into a library so that a calling script does not even need to know about the `redhat-network`, `debian-network`, and `solaris-network` libraries; it can just `source` the `network` library and call `shownetwork` to display network information. The way in which `$*` works within a function means that no change to the code is required to migrate it from a script to a function, or vice-versa.

```
$ cat network
[ -f /etc/redhat-release ] && . ./redhat-network
[ -f /etc/debian_version ] && . ./debian-network
[ `uname` == "SunOS" ] && . ./solaris-network

shownetwork()
{
  for thisnic in $*
  do
    thisip=`getipaddr $thisnic`
    case $? in
      $SUCCESS) echo "The IP Address configured for $thisnic is $thisip" ;;
      $_WRONG_PLATFORM) echo "This does not seem to be running " \
              "on the expected platform" ;;
      $_NO_IP) echo "No IP Address defined for $thisnic" ;;
      $_NO_CONFIG) echo "No configuration found for $thisnic" ;;
```

```
      esac
   done
}
$
```

network

```
$ cat client.sh
#!/bin/bash

. ./network

shownetwork $@
```

client.sh

```
$ ./client.sh eth0
The IP Address configured for eth0 is 192.168.1.13
$
```

Use of Libraries

Libraries are very useful things to build up; many systems administrators collect their own tool-boxes of scripts, functions, and aliases that make day-to-day life easier and more efficient. Use of task-specific libraries in more involved scripts makes the development, debugging, and maintenance much simpler, too. Sharing libraries across teams can be a useful form of knowledge sharing, although in practice most administrators tend to maintain their own sets of tools independently, with a more robust set of shared tools maintained by the team. This can help to formalize standards, speed up delivery of common tasks, and ensure consistency of delivery.

GETOPTS

Functions, scripts, and other programs are all passed their arguments in the same way — $1 is the first argument to a program, to a script, or to a function. It is difficult for a calling script to tell whether it is calling an external program, script, or function. So it makes sense for a function to act much like a script.

This mkfile script is a wrapper to dd, which provides syntax similar to the mkfile binary in Unix. It uses getopts in the main script to parse its parameters, which shows the basic usage of getopts. Valid options for this script are:

➤   -i infile (name of a file to copy input from; the default is /dev/zero)

➤   -b blocksize (the size of each block read and written; the default is 512KB)

➤   -q for the script to operate quietly

➤   -? for usage information

For any other input, the usage information will be displayed. The -i and -b options require a parameter; -q and -? do not. This is all expressed quite succinctly to getopts with the statement 'i:b:q?'. The colon (:) indicates a required parameter, so i: and b: show that -i and -b require a parameter, and it is an error condition if one is not supplied. The other two characters are not followed by a colon so they are standalone flags without parameters. When a parameter is passed, its value is put into the variable OPTARG.

> *Although most shell scripts in this book have a filename extension of* .sh, mkfile *is an existing binary for which this script provides workalike functionality. Therefore, it makes sense in this instance for the script to have the same name as the original.*

```
$ cat mkfile
#!/bin/bash
# wrapper for dd to act like Solaris' mkfile utility.

function usage()
{
    echo "Usage: mkfile [ -i infile ] [ -q ] [ -b blocksize ] size[k|m|g] filename"
    echo "Blocksize is 512 bytes by default."
    exit 2
}

function humanreadable ()
{
  multiplier=1
  case $1 in
    *b)    multiplier=1           ;;
    *k)    multiplier=1024        ;;
    *m)    multiplier=1048576     ;;
    *g)    multiplier=1073741824  ;;
  esac
  numeric=`echo $1 | tr -d 'k'|tr -d 'm'|tr -d 'g'|tr -d 'b'`
  expr $numeric \* $multiplier
}

# mkfile uses 512 byte blocks by default - so shall I.
bs=512
quiet=0
INFILE=/dev/zero

while getopts 'i:b:q?' argv
do
  case $argv in
        i) INFILE=$OPTARG      ;;
        b) bs=$OPTARG          ;;
        q) quiet=1             ;;
        \?) usage              ;;
  esac
```

```
done

for i in `seq 2 ${OPTIND}`
do
  shift
done

if [ -z "$1" ]; then
  echo "ERROR: No size specified"
fi
if [ -z "$2" ]; then
  echo "ERROR: No filename specified"
fi
if [ "$#" -ne "2" ]; then
  usage
fi

SIZE=`humanreadable $1`
FILENAME="$2"

BS=`humanreadable $bs`

COUNT=`expr $SIZE / $BS`
CHECK=`expr $COUNT \* $BS`
if [ "$CHECK" -ne "$SIZE" ]; then
  echo "Warning: Due to the blocksize requested, the file created will be"\
       "`expr $COUNT \* $BS` bytes and not $SIZE bytes"
fi

echo -en "Creating $SIZE byte file $FILENAME...."

dd if="$INFILE" bs=$BS count=$COUNT of="$FILENAME" 2>/dev/null
ddresult=$?
if [ "$quiet" -ne "1" ]; then
  if [ "$ddresult" -eq "0" ]; then
    echo "Finished:"
  else
    echo "An error occurred. dd returned code $ddresult."
  fi
  # We all know that you're going to do this next - let's do it for you:
  ls -l "$FILENAME" && ls -lh "$FILENAME"
fi

exit  $ddresult
```

mkfile

```
$ ./mkfile -?
Usage: mkfile [ -i infile ] [ -q ] [-b blocksize ] size[k|m|g] filename
Blocksize is 512 bytes by default.
$ ./mkfile -i
./mkfile: option requires an argument -- i
Usage: mkfile [ -i infile ] [ -q ] [ -b blocksize ] size[k|m|g] filename
```

```
Blocksize is 512 bytes by default.
$ ./mkfile 10k foo
Creating 10240 byte file foo....Finished:
-rw-rw-r-- 1 steve steve 10240 Jan 28 00:31 foo
-rw-rw-r-- 1 steve steve 10K Jan 28 00:31 foo
$
```

The first of these three runs of mkfile show, first, the -? option, which takes its own path through the code, displaying the usage message and exiting. The second shows invalid input; -i must be followed by the name of a file or device to read from. getopts displays the error message "option requires an argument -- i" but continues executing. The usage message is displayed when the script later checks if $# is equal to 2, which in this case is not true. Finally, the third run shows a successful execution of the mkfile script.

Handling Errors

If you do not want getopts to display its own error messages, you can set OPTERR=0 (the default value is 1). You cannot export this variable to change an existing shell script; whenever a new shell, or a new shell script, is started, OPTERR is reset to 1. Setting OPTERR to 0 can help the script to appear more slick by displaying only more relevant messages; it would be better if the script reported the error by saying "Input file not specified; please specify the input file when using the -i option."

> *An alternative to the OPTERR variable is to set the first character of the definition as a colon, so use ':i:b:q?' instead of 'i:b:q?'.*

This simple change makes for much more streamlined shell scripts. Because the option is put into the OPTARG variable, a customized error message can be given depending on the missing value. A nested case statement is used here to process the new value of OPTARG. Note that like the question mark, the colon has to be escaped with a backslash or put in quotes. Both styles are shown here, the question mark with a backslash and the colon in quotes:

```
while getopts ':i:b:q?' argv
do
    case $argv in
        i) INFILE=$OPTARG          ;;
        b) bs=$OPTARG              ;;
        q) quiet=1                 ;;
        \?) usage                  ;;
        ":")
          case $OPTARG in
            i) echo "Input file not specified."
               echo "Please specify the input file when using the -i option."
               echo
               usage
               ;;
            b) echo "Block size not specified."
               echo "Please specify the block size when using the -b option."
               echo
```

```
                    usage
                    ;;
              *) echo "An unexpected parsing error occurred."
                 echo
                 usage
                 ;;
          esac
          exit 2
    esac
done
```

mkfile2

```
$ ./mkfile -i
./mkfile: option requires an argument -- i
Usage: mkfile [ -i infile ] [ -q ] [ -b blocksize ] size[k|m|g] filename
Blocksize is 512 bytes by default.
$ ./mkfile2 -i
Input file not specified.
Please specify the input file when using the -i option.

Usage: mkfile [ -i infile ] [ -q ] [ -b blocksize ] size[k|m|g] filename
Blocksize is 512 bytes by default.
$
```

Getopts within Functions

getopts can also be used within a function; this function converts temperatures between Centigrade and Fahrenheit, but takes various options to control how it works. Because getopts increments the OPTIND variable as it works through the parameters, this must be reset every time the function is called. OPTIND is the counter that getopts uses to keep track of the current index. This is not normally an issue when parsing the arguments only once, but as this function is called many times, it has to reset OPTIND every time.

```
$ cat temperature.sh
#!/bin/bash

convert()
{
  # Set defaults
  quiet=0
  scale=0
  error=0
  source=centigrade

  # Reset optind between calls to getopts
  OPTIND=1
  while getopts 'c:f:s:q?' opt
  do
    case "$opt" in
      "c") centigrade=$OPTARG
           source=centigrade ;;
```

```
      "f") fahrenheit=$OPTARG
            source=fahrenheit  ;;
      "s") scale=$OPTARG ;;
      "q") quiet=1 ;;
      *) echo "Usage: convert [ -c | -f ] temperature [ -s scale | -q ]"
         error=1
         return 0 ;;
    esac
  done

  if [ "$quiet" -eq "1" ] && [ "$scale" != "0" ]; then
    echo "Error: Quiet and Scale are mutually exclusive."
    echo "Quiet can only return whole numbers between 0 and 255."
    exit 1
  fi

  case $source in
    centigrade)
      fahrenheit=`echo scale=$scale \; $centigrade \* 9 / 5 + 32 | bc`
      answer="$centigrade degrees Centigrade is $fahrenheit degrees Fahrenheit"
      result=$fahrenheit
      ;;
    fahrenheit)
      centigrade=`echo scale=$scale \; \($fahrenheit - 32\) \* 5 / 9 | bc`
      answer="$fahrenheit degrees Fahrenheit is $centigrade degrees Centigrade "
      result=$centigrade
      ;;
    *)
      echo "An error occurred."
      exit 0
      ;;
  esac
  if [ "$quiet" -eq "1" ]; then
    if [ "$result" -gt "255" ] || [ "$result" -lt "0" ]; then
      # scale has already been tested for; it must be an integer.
      echo "An error occurred."
      echo "Can't return values outside the range 0-255 when quiet."
      error=1
      return 0
    fi
    return $result
  else
    echo $answer
  fi
}

# Main script starts here.

echo "First by return code..."
convert -q -c $1
result=$?
if [ "$error" -eq "0" ]; then
  echo "${1}C is ${result}F."
```

```
fi

convert -f $1 -q
result=$?
if [ "$error" -eq "0" ]; then
  echo "${1}F is ${result}C."
fi

echo

echo "Then within the function..."
convert -f $1
convert -c $1

echo

echo "And now with more precision..."
convert -f $1 -s 2
convert -s 3 -c $1
```

temperature.sh

```
$ ./temperature.sh 12
First by return code...
12C is 53F.
An error occurred.
Can't return values outside the range 0-255 when quiet.

Then within the function...
12 degrees Fahrenheit is -11 degrees Centigrade
12 degrees Centigrade is 53 degrees Fahrenheit

And now with more precision...
12 degrees Fahrenheit is -11.11 degrees Centigrade
12 degrees Centigrade is 53.600 degrees Fahrenheit
```

 The second test fails because the answer (12F = -11C) cannot be expressed in the return code of a function, which at 1 byte can only be in the range 0–255. Strangely, functions are not always the most suitable method for returning numerical output!

SUMMARY

Functions are a convenient way to package sections of code in a flexible, modular, and reusable format. Functions are called in much the same way as shell scripts and other commands, and parse their arguments in exactly the same way as a shell script — $1, $2, $3, $*, as well as getopts all work the same way in a function as in a shell script. This makes it quite easy to convert an existing script into a function, and vice-versa.

Putting groups of related functions together in libraries extends the language and effectively provides customized commands tailored for the particular task at hand. Libraries make programming easier, more abstract, and more convenient, taking implementation detail away from the script and hiding it in a more suitable location. This makes changing the way the library works transparent, making changes and upgrades to the underlying methods seamless.

Arrays are a special type of variable which can be very flexible, although they do not work very well with functions. This is all covered in the next chapter.

Arrays

An array is a special type of variable that contains a set of values, accessed by a key (also known as an index). Unless otherwise specified, arrays in bash are indexed from zero, so the first element in the array is `${array[0]}`, not `${array[1]}`. This is not intuitive to all, but it comes from the fact that bash is written in the C programming language, which also works in this way.

It is possible to have sparse arrays, so for non-contiguous data such as mapping a few PIDs to their process names, you can store `pid[35420]=httpd -k ssl` without having to have all of the other 35,419 items stored in the array. This can be useful, although it is difficult to know which index(es) might actually have values stored with them.

Arrays in the shell are only one-dimensional. This means that if you want to model a chess board, it is not possible to access square c6 as `${chessboard[2][5]}`. Instead, you would have to find some way to flatten out the board into a linear 64-item line, so `${chessboard[0]}` through `${chessboard[7]}` are the first row, `${chessboard[8]}` through `${chessboard[15]}` are the second row, and so on. The alternative is to have 8 arrays of 8, which is how Recipe 17-1 deals with multiple rows of characters.

New to bash version 4 are associative arrays. These arrays have text instead of a number as their index, so you can keep track of race results using `${points[Ferrari]}` and `${points[McLaren]}` rather than `${points[0]}` and `${points[1]}` and then having a lookup table mapping 0 to "Ferrari" and 1 to "McLaren." This chapter discusses the different types of arrays available, what they can be used for, and how they are accessed and manipulated.

ASSIGNING ARRAYS

There are quite a few different ways to assign values to arrays. Some are variations on a theme, but there are three main ways to assign values, which are broken down here into "one at a time," "all at once," or "by index," which is partway in between the other two. You can also assign values to an array from a variety of sources, including wildcard expansion and program output.

If the array is declared via the "one at a time" or "all at once" method, the shell automatically detects that an array is being declared. Otherwise, the `declare -a myarray` statement is necessary to declare to the shell that this variable is to be treated as an array.

One at a Time

The simplest and most straightforward way to set the values of an array is to assign each element one at a time. Just like regular variables, there is no dollar ($) symbol when assigning a value, only when referring to it. At the end of the variable name, the index number goes in square brackets:

```
numberarray[0]=zero
numberarray[1]=one
numberarray[2]=two
numberarray[3]=three
```

In addition to its simplicity and clarity, an additional advantage of this form is that you can define sparse arrays. In the following example, there is no third item ("two") in the array:

```
numberarray[0]=zero
numberarray[1]=one
numberarray[3]=three
```

As with regular variables, you can include spaces in the value, but it will need to be quoted, whether with quotes or a backslash:

```
country[0]="United States of America"
country[1]=United\ Kingdom
country[2]=Canada
country[3]=Australia
```

All at Once

A more efficient way to assign arrays is to list all of the values in a single command. You do this by simply listing the values in a space-separated list, enclosed by parentheses:

```
students=( Dave Jennifer Michael Alistair Lucy Richard Elizabeth )
```

One downside of this is that sparse arrays cannot be assigned in this way. Another is that you must know the values required up front, and be able to hard-code them into the script or calculate them within the script itself.

Any character in IFS can be used to separate the items, including a newline. It is perfectly valid to split the array definition over multiple lines. You can even end the line with comments. In the following code, the students are split into individual lines with a comment by each subset of the list saying which year each group of students represents.

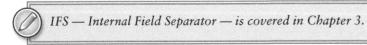

IFS — Internal Field Separator — is covered in Chapter 3.

```
$ cat studentarray.sh
#!/bin/bash

students=( Dave Jennifer Michael      # year 1
    Alistair Lucy Richard Elizabeth   # year 2
```

```
        Albert Roger Dennis James Roy      # year 3
        Rory Jim Andi Elaine Clive         # year 4
        )

    for name in ${students[@]}
    do
      echo -en "$name "
    done
    echo
$ ./studentarray.sh
Dave Jennifer Michael Alistair Lucy Richard Elizabeth Albert Roger Dennis James Roy
 Rory Jim Andi Elaine Clive
$
```

studentarray.sh

In practice, it would typically be impractical to hard-code the names of the students into the script if it were for anything other than a one-off task. Other, more flexible ways of reading in data are covered later in this section.

By Index

A shorthand version of the "one at a time" method, or depending on how you look at it, possibly a more explicit version of the "all at once method," is to specify the values together within one set of parentheses, but to state the index along with the value. This is mainly useful when creating sparse arrays, but can also be useful as a way of making clear what elements go where without the long-winded "one at a time" method, which requires you to provide the name of the variable every time. This method is also particularly useful when using associative arrays, which are discussed later in this chapter. The following snippet assigns the names of the first 32 ASCII characters (see man ascii) to an array. This is useful for confirming that the names are in the right place. For example, you can easily see that CR is at index 13 without having to count the 13 items before it.

```
nonprinting=([0]=NUL [1]=SOH [2]=STX [3]=ETX [4]=EOT [5]=ENQ
  [6]=ACK [7]=BEL [8]=BS [9]=HT [10]=LF [11]=VT [12]=FF [13]=CR
  [14]=SO [15]=SI [16]=DLE [17]=DC1 [18]=DC2 [19]=DC3 [20]=DC4
  [21]=NAK [22]=SYN [23]=ETB [24]=CAN [25]=EM [26]=SUB [27]=ESC
  [28]=FS [29]=GS [30]=RS [31]=US)
```

All at Once from a Source

This is a special case of "all at once" — the contents of the parentheses can be supplied by the shell itself, whether through filename expansion or the output of any command or function. To read in the values of a process's status table, assigning each of the values to an element in an array, simply call ($(cat /proc/$$/stat)). Each item in the output will be assigned to an element of the array.

```
$ cat /proc/$$/stat
28510 (bash) S 28509 28510 28510 34818 28680 4202496 3094 49631 1 1 6 14 123 28 20
0 1 0 27764756 20000768 594 18446744073709551615 4194304 5082140 140736253670848
 140736253669792 140176010326894 0 69632 3686404 1266761467 0 0 0 17 0 0 0 92 0 0
$ stat=( $(cat /proc/$$/stat) )
```

```
$ echo ${stat[1]}
(bash)
$ echo ${stat[2]}
S
$ echo ${stat[34]}
0
$ echo ${stat[23]}
594
$
```

To read in a file line by line, set the IFS to the newline character and read it in. This is a particularly useful technique for reading text files into memory.

```
$ cat readhosts.sh
#!/bin/bash
oIFS=$IFS

IFS="
"

hosts=( `cat /etc/hosts` )
for hostline in "${hosts[@]}"
do
   echo line: $hostline
done

# always restore IFS or insanity will follow...
IFS=$oIFS
$ ./readhosts.sh
line: 127.0.0.1 localhost
line: # The following lines are desirable for IPv6 capable hosts
line: ::1     localhost ip6-localhost ip6-loopback
line: fe00::0 ip6-localnet
line: ff00::0 ip6-mcastprefix
line: ff02::1 ip6-allnodes
line: ff02::2 ip6-allrouters
line: 192.168.1.3      sky
line: 192.168.1.5      plug
line: 192.168.1.10     declan
line: 192.168.1.11     atomic
line: 192.168.1.12     jackie
line: 192.168.1.13     goldie  smf
line: 192.168.1.227    elvis
line: 192.168.0.210    dgoldie ksgp
$
```

Readhosts.sh

The source can also be a list of files from wildcard expansion. In the following code, every file that matches the pattern *.mp3 is added to the mp3s array:

```
$ mp3s=( *.mp3 )
$ for mp3 in "${mp3s[@]}"
> do
```

```
>     echo "MP3 File: $mp3"
> done
MP3 File: 01 - The MC5 - Kick Out The Jams.mp3
MP3 File: 02 - Velvet Underground - I'm Waiting For The Man.mp3
MP3 File: 03 - The Stooges - No Fun.mp3
MP3 File: 04 - The Doors - L.A. Woman.mp3
MP3 File: 05 - The New York Dolls - Jet Boy.mp3
MP3 File: 06 - Patti Smith - Gloria.mp3
MP3 File: 07 - The Damned - Neat Neat Neat.mp3
MP3 File: 08 - X-Ray Spex - Oh Bondage Up Yours!.mp3
MP3 File: 09 - Richard Hell & The Voidoids - Blank Generation.mp3
MP3 File: 10 - Dead Boys - Sonic Reducer.mp3
MP3 File: 11 - Iggy Pop - Lust For Life.mp3
MP3 File: 12 - The Saints - This Perfect Day.mp3
MP3 File: 13 - Ramones - Sheena Is A Punk Rocker.mp3
MP3 File: 14 - The Only Ones - Another Girl, Another Planet.mp3
MP3 File: 15 - Siouxsie & The Banshees - Hong Kong Garden.mp3
MP3 File: 16 - Blondie - One Way Or Another.mp3
MP3 File: 17 - Magazine - Shot By Both Sides.mp3
MP3 File: 18 - Buzzcocks - Ever Fallen In Love (With Someone You Shouldn't've).mp3
MP3 File: 19 - XTC - This Is Pop.mp3
MP3 File: 20 - Television - Marquee Moon.mp3
MP3 File: 21 - David Bowie - 'Heroes'.mp3
$
```

 Notice all of the potentially troublesome characters in these filenames; there are spaces, commas, ampersands, single quotes, brackets, and periods in filenames. The array structure manages to deal with these easily in this simple example; later in this chapter, it does more complicated operations on these strings without the programmer having to worry about any particularly special quoting.

Read from Input

The bash shell builtin command `read` can read elements into an array when called with the -a flag. This is a really easy way to define an array, whether from user input or from a file.

```
$ read -a dice
4 2 6
$ echo "you rolled ${dice[0]} then ${dice[1]} then ${dice[2]}"
you rolled 4 then 2 then 6
$
```

The `read -a` command can be incredibly useful in a lot of situations, but it can become even more useful when combined with the IFS variable. The following example tells the shell that the IFS is something different from its default value of <space><tab><newline>, so to read /etc/passwd, which has fields separated by colons, simply set IFS=: before the read command. Note that it is best whenever possible to use IFS= in the same line as the command for which you want IFS to be modified, because it then only applies to the read command and not to the other commands within the loop.

The GECOS field may contain trailing commas; by convention it should say something like Steve Parker,The Lair,202-456-1414,Author but here it just says Steve Parker,,, which doesn't look so good, so the trailing commas are stripped using the %%,* syntax. Some system accounts do not have GECOS fields defined at all, so this script falls back to the login name to define the $user variable from the first field (login name) if the fifth field (GECOS) is not set.

```
$ cat user.sh
#!/bin/bash

while IFS=: read -a userdetails
do
  unset user
  gecos=${userdetails[4]%%,*}
  username=${userdetails[0]}
  user=${gecos:-$username}
  if [ -d "${userdetails[5]}" ]; then
    echo "${user}'s directory ${userdetails[5]} exists"
  else
    echo "${user}'s directory ${userdetails[5]} doesn't exist"
  fi
done < /etc/passwd
$ ./user.sh
root's directory /root exists
daemon's directory /usr/sbin exists
bin's directory /bin exists
sys's directory /dev exists
sync's directory /bin exists
games's directory /usr/games exists
man's directory /var/cache/man exists
lp's directory /var/spool/lpd doesn't exist
mail's directory /var/mail exists
news's directory /var/spool/news doesn't exist
uucp's directory /var/spool/uucp doesn't exist
proxy's directory /bin exists
www-data's directory /var/www exists
backup's directory /var/backups exists
Mailing List Manager's directory /var/list doesn't exist
ircd's directory /var/run/ircd doesn't exist
Gnats Bug-Reporting System (admin)'s directory /var/lib/gnats doesn't exist
nobody's directory /nonexistent doesn't exist
libuuid's directory /var/lib/libuuid exists
messagebus's directory /var/run/dbus exists
Avahi autoip daemon's directory /var/lib/avahi-autoipd exists
festival's directory /home/festival doesn't exist
Gnome Display Manager's directory /var/lib/gdm exists
Hardware abstraction layer's directory /var/run/hald exists
usbmux daemon's directory /home/usbmux doesn't exist
sshd's directory /var/run/sshd exists
saned's directory /home/saned doesn't exist
HPLIP system user's directory /var/run/hplip exists
Steve Parker's directory /home/steve exists
Avahi mDNS daemon's directory /var/run/avahi-daemon exists
ntp's directory /home/ntp doesn't exist
```

```
Debian-exim's directory /var/spool/exim4 exists
TiMidity++ MIDI sequencer service's directory /etc/timidity exists
$
```

user.sh

The bash shell builtin command `readarray` reads in text files in an even more flexible manner than that shown in the preceding script for reading /etc/hosts. The initial index value can be specified (-O), as can the maximum number of lines to be read (-n). Lines can also be skipped (-s) from the start of the input.

```
$ readarray -n 4 -s 2 food
porridge
black pudding
apples
bananas
cucumbers
burgers
eggs
$ printf "%s" "${food[@]}"
apples
bananas
cucumbers
burgers
$
```

The first two items were skipped because of the -s 2 parameter. Only four actual parameters were read because of the -n 4 parameter, although this means that six were read in total; the size of the array is 4. The seventh item in the input does not get read at all.

One common way to display the items of an array is the `printf "%s\n" "${food[@]}"` notation; this iterates through the values of the array, printing each as a string followed by a newline. Because the trailing newlines were added into the elements of the array, the \n was not required in the preceding example. The -t flag to `readarray` strips these trailing newline characters, which is almost always what is required.

ACCESSING ARRAYS

The basic method for accessing the values of arrays is much the same as the first method shown of assigning values to arrays. The curly brackets are compulsory. If an index is omitted, the first element is assumed.

Accessing by Index

Reusing the `numberarray` array from earlier in this chapter, the following code adds some `echo` statements to display the values after the assignments. Note that the sparse array means that no `numberarray[2]` exists.

```
$ numberarray[0]=zero
$ numberarray[1]=one
```

```
$ numberarray[3]=three
$ echo ${numberarray[0]}
zero
$ echo ${numberarray[2]}

$ echo ${numberarray[3]}
three
$
```

If you try to access $numberarray[1] without the curly brackets, the shell will interpret $numberarray as the first element within numberarray, and [1] as a literal string. This results in the literal string zero[1] being returned, which is not what was wanted.

```
$ echo $numberarray[1]
zero[1]
$
```

Length of Arrays

Finding the number of elements in an array is very similar to finding the length of a regular variable. While ${#myvar} gives the length of the string contained in the $myvar variable, ${#myarray[@]} or ${#myarray[*]} returns the number of elements in the array. With a sparse array, this still only returns the number of actual elements assigned to an array, which is not the same thing as the highest index used by the array.

Note also that ${#myarray} returns the length of the string in ${myarray[0]} and not the number of elements in the $myarray array. To get the length of the third item within an array, the syntax is ${#array[2]} because arrays are zero-indexed. The length of the first item is ${#array[0]} and ${#array[1]} is the length of the second item.

```
$ fruits=( apple banana pear orange )
$ echo ${#fruits[@]}
4
$ echo ${#fruits}
5
$ echo ${#fruits[0]}
5
$ echo ${#fruits[1]}
6
$ echo ${#fruits[2]}
4
$ echo ${#fruits[3]}
6
$
```

Accessing by Variable Index

The index does not have to be a hard-coded integer; it can also be the value of another variable. So you can iterate through a (non-sparse) array with a variable, or even just randomly access any element in an array by its index. This example shows the iteration through the four Beatles, which are indexed 0–3. The command seq 0 $((${#beatles[@]} - 1)) counts from 0 to 3, or more precisely, from 0 to (4–1) where 4 is the length of the array, but because it is zero-indexed, the four elements have indices 0 through 3.

The script then adds a fourth element, with index 5, creating a sparse array (element 4 is missing) so Stuart Sutcliffe (or should that be Pete Best?) is not picked up by this loop.

```
$ cat index.sh
#!/bin/bash

beatles=( John Paul Ringo George )
for index in $(seq 0 $((${#beatles[@]} - 1)))
do
   echo "Beatle $index is ${beatles[$index]}."
done

echo "Now again with the fifth beatle..."
beatles[5]=Stuart

for index in $(seq 0 $((${#beatles[@]} - 1)))
do
   echo "Beatle $index is ${beatles[$index]}."
done
echo "Missed it; Beatle 5 is ${beatles[5]}."
$ ./index.sh
Beatle 0 is John.
Beatle 1 is Paul.
Beatle 2 is Ringo.
Beatle 3 is George.
Now again with the fifth beatle...
Beatle 0 is John.
Beatle 1 is Paul.
Beatle 2 is Ringo.
Beatle 3 is George.
Beatle 4 is .
Missed it; Beatle 5 is Stuart.
$
```

index.sh

As long as the array is not associative, you can also do basic math within the [] brackets. This can keep the code more readable in addition to making it easier to write. The bubblesort algorithm compares elements with their neighbors, and this code is a bit easier to read than if it had to include additional lines calculating j-1. The use of the C-style for makes it look hardly shell-like at all.

```
$ cat bubblesort.sh
#!/bin/bash

function bubblesort()
{
  n=${#data[@]}
  for i in `seq 0 $n`
  do
    for (( j=n; j > i; j-=1 ))
    do
      if [[ ${data[j-1]} > ${data[j]} ]]
```

```
        then
          temp=${data[j]}
          data[j]=${data[j-1]}
          data[j-1]=$temp
        fi
    done
  done
}


data=( roger oscar charlie kilo indigo tango )

echo "Initial state:"
for i in ${data[@]}
do
  echo "$i"
done

bubblesort

echo
echo "Final state:"
for i in ${data[@]}
do
  echo "$i"
done
$ ./bubblesort.sh
Initial state:
roger
oscar
charlie
kilo
indigo
tango

Final state:
charlie
indigo
kilo
oscar
roger
tango
$
```

bubblesort.sh

The downside of this form is that the variable ${n} *had to be calculated outside of the* for *loop.*

Selecting Items from an Array

It is one thing to select a single item from an array, but sometimes it is useful to retrieve a range from an array. This is done in a `substr`-like way, providing the starting index and the number of items to retrieve. A simple `${food[@]:0:1}` gets the first item; `:1:1` gets the second, `:2:1` gets the third, and so on. That is the same as using `${food[0]}`, `[1]`, and `[2]`, and not apparently very useful.

 As shown in the 7:1 example, accessing the nonexistent eighth element of the array (`${food[@]:7:1}`) doesn't cause any errors; it simply returns the blank string.

```
$ food=( apples bananas cucumbers dates eggs fajitas grapes )
$ echo ${food[@]:0:1}
apples
$ echo ${food[@]:1:1}
bananas
$ echo ${food[@]:2:1}
cucumbers
$ echo ${food[@]:7:1}

$
```

Extending the reach makes for a more flexible mechanism. By replacing the final `:1` in the preceding code with a different number, you can retrieve a set of results from the array.

```
$ echo ${food[@]:2:4}
cucumbers dates eggs fajitas
$ echo ${food[@]:0:3}
apples bananas cucumbers
$
```

If you take this a little further, the initial number can be omitted. This will retrieve the elements of the array from the provided offset onwards.

```
$ echo ${food[@]:3}
dates eggs fajitas grapes
$ echo ${food[@]:1}
bananas cucumbers dates eggs fajitas grapes
$ echo ${food[@]:6}
grapes
$
```

Displaying the Entire Array

To display the entire variable, a simple `echo ${array[@]}` will suffice, but it is not particularly appealing:

```
$ echo ${distros[@]}
Ubuntu Fedora Debian openSuSE Sabayon Arch Puppy
```

A more flexible option is to use `printf` to add text and formatting to the output. `printf` will format each item in the array with the same formatting string, so this almost emulates a loop:

```
$ printf "Distro: %s\n" "${distros[@]}"
Distro: Ubuntu
Distro: Fedora
Distro: Debian
Distro: openSuSE
Distro: Sabayon
Distro: Arch
Distro: Puppy
$
```

ASSOCIATIVE ARRAYS

The associative array is a new feature in bash version 4. Associative arrays link (associate) the value and the index together, so you can associate metadata with the actual data. You can use this to associate a musician with his instrument. An associative array must be declared as such with the uppercase `declare -A` command.

```
$ cat musicians.sh
#!/bin/bash

declare -A beatles
beatles=( [singer]=John [bassist]=Paul [drummer]=Ringo [guitarist]=George )

for musician in singer bassist drummer guitarist
do
   echo "The ${musician} is ${beatles[$musician]}."
Done
$ ./musicians.sh
The singer is John.
The bassist is Paul.
The drummer is Ringo.
The guitarist is George.
$
```

musicians.sh

Before associative arrays were introduced to bash, it was obvious that
`${beatles[index]}` did not make sense; it was automatically interpreted as
`${beatles[$index]}`. However, because an associative array can have text as the
index, `${beatles["index"]}` can now be valid, so the dollar sign is compulsory
for associative arrays. If the dollar sign was omitted, the word "index," and not the
value of the variable `$index`, would be interpreted as the index of the array.

What makes associative arrays even more useful is the ability to reference back to the name of the index. This means that given the name of the instrument, you can get the musician's name, but also given the name of the musician, you can determine his instrument. To do this, use the `${!array[@]}` syntax.

```
$ cat instruments.sh
#!/bin/bash

declare -A beatles
beatles=( [singer]=John [bassist]=Paul [drummer]=Ringo [guitarist]=George )

for instrument in ${!beatles[@]}
do
  echo "The ${instrument} is ${beatles[$instrument]}"
done
$ ./instruments.sh
The singer is John
The guitarist is George
The bassist is Paul
The drummer is Ringo
$
```

instruments.sh

MANIPULATING ARRAYS

The fact that arrays are structurally different from other variables means that some new syntax is required to manipulate arrays. Wherever possible, doing things to arrays is syntactically very similar to doing the equivalent thing to a string, but there are instances where that syntax is not flexible enough.

Copying an Array

Copying one array to another is simple. It is important for quoting and spacing that the `${array[@]}` format (rather than `${array[*]}`) is used, and also that double quotes are put around the whole construct. These demonstrations are probably the clearest way to show what can happen when other forms are used.

```
$ activities=( swimming "water skiing" canoeing "white-water rafting" surfing )
$ for act in ${activities[@]}
> do
>   echo "Activity: $act"
> done
Activity: swimming
Activity: water
Activity: skiing
Activity: canoeing
Activity: white-water
Activity: rafting
Activity: surfing
$
```

What happened here is that because there were no double quotes around the list, "swimming," "water," and "skiing" were all treated as separate words. Placing double quotes around the whole thing fixes this:

```
$ for act in "${activities[@]}"
> do
>    echo "Activity: $act"
> done
Activity: swimming
Activity: water skiing
Activity: canoeing
Activity: white-water rafting
Activity: surfing
$
```

Similarly, the * is not suitable either with or without quotes. Without quotes, it does the same as the @ symbol. With quotes, the whole array is boiled down into a single string.

```
$ for act in ${activities[*]}
> do
>    echo "Activity: $act"
> done
Activity: swimming
Activity: water
Activity: skiing
Activity: canoeing
Activity: white-water
Activity: rafting
Activity: surfing
$ for act in "${activities[*]}"
> do
>    echo "Activity: $act"
> done
Activity: swimming water skiing canoeing white-water rafting surfing
$
```

Thus, to copy an array, define a new array with the values of `"${activities[@]}"`. This will preserve whitespace in the same way as the `for` loop in the preceding code got the correct treatment of whitespace. This is shown in the following code.

```
$ hobbies=( "${activities[@]}" )
$ for hobby in "${hobbies[@]}"
> do
>    echo "Hobby: $hobby"
> done
Hobby: swimming
Hobby: water skiing
Hobby: canoeing
Hobby: white-water rafting
Hobby: surfing
$
```

This does not work properly for sparse arrays, however. The actual value of the index is not passed on in this way, so the `hobbies` array cannot be a true copy of the `activities` array.

```
$ activities[10]="scuba diving"
$ hobbies="( ${activities[@]} )"
$ for act in `seq 0 10`
> do
>   echo "$act : ${activities[$act]} / ${hobbies[$act]}"
> done
0 : swimming / swimming
1 : water skiing / water skiing
2 : canoeing / canoeing
3 : white-water rafting / white-water rafting
4 : surfing / surfing
5 :  / scuba diving
6 :  /
7 :  /
8 :  /
9 :  /
10 : scuba diving /
$
```

Appending to an Array

Appending to an array is much the same as copying it. The simplest way to append to an array is to extend the syntax for copying an array.

```
$ hobbies=( "${activities[@]" diving )
 $ for hobby in "${hobbies[@]}"
> do
>   echo "Hobby: $hobby"
> done
Hobby: swimming
Hobby: water skiing
Hobby: canoeing
Hobby: white-water rafting
Hobby: surfing
Hobby: scuba diving
Hobby: diving
$
```

Earlier in this chapter you saw how `seq 0 $((${#beatles[@]} - 1))` was used to get the final actual element of the array. The fact that the array is indexed from zero made this task a little bit awkward. When appending a single item to the array, the fact that the array is zero-indexed actually makes it easier.

```
$ hobbies[${#hobbies[@]}]=rowing
$ for hobby in "${hobbies[@]}"
> do
>   echo "Hobby: $hobby"
> done
Hobby: swimming
```

```
Hobby: water skiing
Hobby: canoeing
Hobby: white-water rafting
Hobby: surfing
Hobby: scuba diving
Hobby: diving
Hobby: rowing
$
```

The bash shell does have a builtin syntax to combine two arrays. With the C-like notation of +=, this method is concise and allows for very clear code.

```
$ airsports=( flying gliding parachuting )
$ activities+=("${airsports[@]}")
$ for act in "${activities[@]}"
> do
>   echo "Activity: $act"
> done
Activity: swimming
Activity: water skiing
Activity: canoeing
Activity: white-water rafting
Activity: surfing
Activity: scuba diving
Activity: climbing
Activity: walking
Activity: cycling
Activity: flying
Activity: gliding
Activity: parachuting
$
```

Deleting from an Array

Deleting an item from an array is the same as deleting a variable; you can use `myarray[3]=` or `unset myarray[3]`. Similarly, you can unset the whole array. However, `myarray=` by itself will only clear the value of the first item in the array. All of these situations are demonstrated in the code that follows.

```
$ for act in `seq 0 $(((${#activities[@]} - 1))`
> do
>   echo "Activity $act: ${activities[$act]}"
> done
Activity 0: swimming
Activity 1: water skiing
Activity 2: canoeing
Activity 3: white-water rafting
Activity 4: surfing
Activity 5: scuba diving
Activity 6: climbing
Activity 7: walking
Activity 8: cycling
Activity 9: flying
Activity 10: gliding
```

```
Activity 11: parachuting
$ activities[7]=
$ for act in `seq 0 $((${#activities[@]} - 1))`
> do
>    echo "Activity $act: ${activities[$act]}"
> done
Activity 0: swimming
Activity 1: water skiing
Activity 2: canoeing
Activity 3: white-water rafting
Activity 4: surfing
Activity 5: scuba diving
Activity 6: climbing
Activity 7:
Activity 8: cycling
Activity 9: flying
Activity 10: gliding
Activity 11: parachuting
$
```

The effect of this is to make a sparse array. Using `unset activities[7]` has largely the same effect. As discussed in Chapter 7, there is a difference between setting a variable to the empty string and unsetting it entirely, but it is obvious only when the `${variable+string}` or `${variable?string}` forms are used.

```
$ echo ${activities[7]

$ echo ${activities[7]+"Item 7 is set"}
Item 7 is set
$ unset activities[7]
$ echo ${activities[7]+"Item 7 is set"}

$
```

Once more, references to the array without an index are interpreted as references to the first element in the array. So clearing the array in this way only removes the first item.

```
$ activities=
$ for act in `seq 0 $((${#activities[@]} - 1))`
> do
>    echo "Activity $act: ${activities[$act]}"
> done
Activity 0:
Activity 1: water skiing
Activity 2: canoeing
Activity 3: white-water rafting
Activity 4: surfing
Activity 5: scuba diving
Activity 6: climbing
Activity 7:
Activity 8: cycling
Activity 9: flying
Activity 10: gliding
Activity 11: parachuting
```

If you unset the activities array itself, the whole thing disappears. This is the correct way to unset an array, although you can also use unset myarray[*].

```
$ unset activities
$ for act in `seq 0 $((${#activities[@]} - 1))`
> do
>   echo "Activity $act: ${activities[$act]}"
> done
$
```

ADVANCED TECHNIQUES

In the "all at once from a source" section earlier in this chapter, a set of MP3 files was listed with a clear pattern, which while almost useful for sorting, is not quite ideal. Those hyphens delimiting the artist and the track number would make an all-but-perfect way to automatically tag the MP3 files, but a cut or awk command to strip them would be a bit awkward. The colon is a better way to separate fields than space-dash-space. No character is perfect because a colon could appear in a song title or artist name, but this short script reduces the more complicated list of filenames down to the basics.

The for statement itself strips the trailing .mp3 from the filename, in the same way shown in Chapter 7, although this time it is working on the entire array. After that, when echo accesses the ${mp3} variable it also replaces the dash (-) with a colon at the same time. This does not necessarily mean that the code runs any faster than doing these tasks separately, but it is certainly a clear and simple way to write code. What is often most important is that the code is easy to understand.

```
$ for mp3 in "${mp3s[@]/%.mp3}"
> do
>   echo ${mp3// - /:}
> done
01:The MC5:Kick Out The Jams
02:Velvet Underground:I'm Waiting For The Man
03:The Stooges:No Fun
04:The Doors:L.A. Woman
05:The New York Dolls:Jet Boy
06:Patti Smith:Gloria
07:The Damned:Neat Neat Neat
08:X-Ray Spex:Oh Bondage Up Yours!
09:Richard Hell & The Voidoids:Blank Generation
10:Dead Boys:Sonic Reducer
11:Iggy Pop:Lust For Life
12:The Saints:This Perfect Day
13:Ramones:Sheena Is A Punk Rocker
14:The Only Ones:Another Girl, Another Planet
15:Siouxsie & The Banshees:Hong Kong Garden
16:Blondie:One Way Or Another
17:Magazine:Shot By Both Sides
18:Buzzcocks:Ever Fallen In Love (With Someone You Shouldn't've)
19:XTC:This Is Pop
20:Television:Marquee Moon
21:David Bowie:'Heroes'
$
```

SUMMARY

Arrays are a powerful feature of the shell that can be used in many different ways. They expand the power of the shell quite considerably, although requiring arrays as a supported feature restricts the portability of a shell script to systems that support arrays. Sparse arrays can be very useful, too, with none of the memory management necessary for lower-level languages such as C.

Associative arrays are even more flexible than regular arrays. They are, in effect, like sparse arrays with a name instead of a number as an index. This allows you to store metadata within the data's key itself. The ability to treat each element in an array as an individual string and use the more advanced bash features on those strings makes for great levels of flexibility, where one would otherwise reach for `perl`, `awk`, or `sed`.

The next chapter looks at processes and how the kernel manages them. This covers foreground and background processes, signals, `exec`, as well as I/O redirection and pipelines. The kernel is responsible for controlling all the processes on the system, how they run and how they interact with each other. The Linux kernel also exposes a lot of its internal workings via the `/proc` pseudo-filesystem, which is a very useful way for shell scripts to get access to internal kernel data structures.

10

Processes

One of the main tasks of an operating system is to run processes on behalf of its users, services, and applications. These are tracked in a process table inside the kernel, which keeps track of the current state of each process in the system, and the system scheduler decides when each process will be assigned to a CPU, and when it is taken off the CPU again. The ps command interrogates the process table. Following the Unix model of doing one thing and doing it well, ps has a set of switches to fine-tune exactly what is to be displayed from the full process tree.

The /proc pseudo-filesystem provides further insight into the running kernel; there is a directory under /proc for every process currently in the process table. In that directory can be found the state of the process — its current directory and the files it currently holds open. The Linux kernel exposes far more of the operating system than just the process table; /proc includes mechanisms for reading and writing kernel state directly, including networking settings, memory options, hardware information, and even the ability to force the machine to crash.

This chapter looks into processes, what they are, how they are managed, and how they can be manipulated. This is one of the oldest concepts of Unix and not much has changed in 40 years, but the Linux kernel in particular has brought a fresh relevance to the way in which the /proc filesystem provides real two-way interaction between the kernel and userspace.

THE PS COMMAND

The ps command is inconsistent between different flavors of Unix. The System V Unices use the normal dash (-) symbol to mark options, so ps -eaf is a common command to list all current processes, while BSD Unices do not, and also recognize different switches; ps aux is a common way to list all current processes on a BSD system. As is often the case, GNU/Linux straddles both traditions, and the GNU implementation of ps accepts System V and BSD options, as well as its own GNU options, such as --user. System V is probably the most widely used format, and the System V style is used in this chapter.

```
$ ps -fp 3010
UID        PID  PPID  C STIME TTY          TIME CMD
mysql      3010 2973  0 Oct24 ?        00:11:23 /usr/sbin/mysqld --basedir=/usr --d
atadir=/var/lib/mysql --user=mysql --pid-file=/var/run/mysqld/mysqld.pid --skip-ext
ernal-locking --port=3306
```

The headings are a little cryptic; UID, PID, and PPID are the Username, Process ID, and Parent PID, respectively. STIME is the time (or date) that the process was started. If associated with a terminal, the terminal is reported under TTY. TIME is the amount of CPU time that the process has used, and CMD is the full name of the executable. C is a rough figure to represent the percentage of CPU time the process is responsible for consuming.

> Many ps *options can be selected on the command line; to display all processes associated with the third pseudo terminal,* ps -ft /dev/pts/3 *shows only those processes. Similarly,* ps -fu oracle *shows only the processes owned by the user "oracle."*

The -F flag gives more detail; these columns are all described in the ps man page, but this adds the SZ, RSS, and PSR fields. SZ is the number of pages (usually 4KB on x86) of the whole process; RSS is the amount of physical RAM (not including swapped-out data) the process holds. PSR is the ID of the current CPU that the process is running on.

```
$ ps -Fp 3010
UID        PID  PPID  C    SZ   RSS PSR STIME TTY          TIME CMD
mysql      3010 2973  0 40228 22184   0 Oct24 ?        00:11:23 /usr/sbin/mysqld --
basedir=/usr --datadir=/var/lib/mysql --user=mysql --pid-file=/var/run/mysqld/mysql
d.pid -skip-external-loc king --port=3306
```

ps Line Length

ps will limit the length of its output to the width of your terminal. When writing to something that is not a terminal (tty), it will not limit the width of its output, but instead display the full command line. This means that scripts will get the full detail; for example, ps -fp 18611 | grep jrockit will see the full command line. If you are using an interactive terminal to test something, ps -fp 18611 may not display enough of the command line for the jrockit part of process 18611's command line to be visible, even though it is there.

Instead, running ps -fp 18611 | cat - will ensure that ps itself is running in a pipeline (not outputting to a tty), and is probably also the only justifiable reason for using the syntax | cat -. In the screenshot in Figure 10-1, the first ps command does not even have enough space to display the full directory path of the java executable, let alone what program it has actually been called to run. The second ps command sees the whole command line because although the output is ultimately going to the terminal device, what ps sees is that it is writing into a pipe, not a tty, so it displays the full command.

Parsing the Process Table Accurately

In the SysV style, ps -ft <terminal> and ps -fu <user> are the best way to get per-terminal and per-user records, respectively, from the in-kernel process table. However, not everything can be filtered by choosing options to the ps command. More creative techniques are required. These have been found, over time, not to be 100 percent effective, so newer commands have also been created to provide accurate parsing of the process table.

```
steve@weblogic:~                                                         _ □ ×
steve@weblogic$ ps -fp 18611
UID        PID  PPID  C STIME TTY         TIME CMD
dmtdev    18611    1  0 Jun20 ?       00:29:41 /opt/weblogic/middleware/jrockit
steve@weblogic$ ps -fp 18611 | cat -
UID        PID  PPID  C STIME TTY         TIME CMD
dmtdev    18611    1  0 Jun20 ?       00:29:41 /opt/weblogic/middleware/jrockit
-jdk1.6.0_20-R28.1.0-4.0.1/jre/bin/java -classpath /opt/weblogic/middleware/jroc
kit-jdk1.6.0_20-R28.1.0-4.0.1/jre/lib/rt.jar:/opt/weblogic/middleware/jrockit-jd
k1.6.0_20-R28.1.0-4.0.1/jre/lib/i18n.jar:/opt/weblogic/middleware/wls_1033/patch
_wls1033/profiles/default/sys_manifest_classpath/weblogic_patch.jar:/opt/weblogi
c/middleware/wls_1033/patch_ocp353/profiles/default/sys_manifest_classpath/weblo
gic_patch.jar:/opt/weblogic/middleware/jrockit-jdk1.6.0_20-R28.1.0-4.0.1/lib/too
ls.jar:/opt/weblogic/middleware/wls_1033/wlserver_10.3/server/lib/weblogic_sp.ja
r:/opt/weblogic/middleware/wls_1033/wlserver_10.3/server/lib/weblogic.jar:/opt/w
eblogic/middleware/wls_1033/modules/features/weblogic.server.modules_10.3.3.0.ja
r:/opt/weblogic/middleware/wls_1033/wlserver_10.3/server/lib/webservices.jar:/op
t/weblogic/middleware/wls_1033/modules/org.apache.ant_1.7.1/lib/ant-all.jar:/opt
/weblogic/middleware/wls_1033/modules/net.sf.antcontrib_1.1.0.0_1-0b2/lib/ant-co
ntrib.jar:/opt/weblogic/middleware/wls_1033/utils/config/10.3/config-launch.jar:
/opt/weblogic/middleware/wls_1033/wlserver_10.3/common/derby/lib/derbynet.jar:/o
pt/weblogic/middleware/wls_1033/wlserver_10.3/common/derby/lib/derbyclient.jar:/
opt/weblogic/middleware/wls_1033/common/derby/lib/derbytools.jar -
DListenAddress=a-dmtdev-d.bc.jsplc.net -DNodeManagerHome=/var/opt/weblogic/domai
ns/dmtdev1/nodemanager -DQuitEnabled=true -DListenPort=16006 weblogic.NodeManage
```

FIGURE 10-1

 For scripts that automatically kill *processes, it is extremely important to be able to accurately identify only the processes that you are interested in, especially if the script will be run as the "root" user.*

It used to be that the way to find (for example) all of your Apache web server processes was to run:

$ **ps -eaf | grep -w apache**

but that would (sometimes, and unpredictably) return:

```
root      1742     1  0 19:46 ?        00:00:00 /usr/sbin/apache2 -k start
www-data  1757  1742  0 19:46 ?        00:00:00 /usr/sbin/apache2 -k start
www-data  1758  1742  0 19:46 ?        00:00:00 /usr/sbin/apache2 -k start
www-data  1759  1742  0 19:46 ?        00:00:00 /usr/sbin/apache2 -k start
www-data  1760  1742  0 19:46 ?        00:00:00 /usr/sbin/apache2 -k start
www-data  1761  1742  0 19:46 ?        00:00:00 /usr/sbin/apache2 -k start
steve     2613  2365  0 20:11 pts/0    00:00:00 grep apache
```

which includes the grep command itself — its command line does indeed include the word "apache." By running the search, you have changed the process table! One of the traditional ways to get around this is:

```
ps -eaf | grep -w apache | grep -v grep
```

which is okay, unless grep happens to be part of the ps output that you are looking for. (If your web server is for progress reports, and runs as a user called "progrep," all of those processes will be omitted.) The other traditional way, and a slightly more sophisticated alternative, is to use regular expressions:

```
ps -eaf | grep -w ap[a]che
```

which will match `apache` but won't match itself! The downside is that this will also match any processes that you may have called `apche`. If you are going to automatically kill any matching processes, it is wise to be sure that you are not matching any other processes at all.

Linux (and modern Unices) has a set of useful commands for identifying processes based on various criteria. Unlike `grep`ping through the output of `ps`, `pgrep` by default only matches the actual process name. This means that you won't accidentally match a process running as the "progrep" user from the preceding example. (The `-f` flag to `pgrep` does cause it to match the full command line, but this is rarely useful.) Because `pgrep` returns just a list of PIDs, in a shutdown script, you could just run the following (the `-x` means that it has to have an exact match):

```
kill -9 `pgrep -x apache2`
```

`pgrep` is even more flexible than that, however. You can specify that you only want certain user(s), so if you have multiple instances of a program running as different userids, you can identify just one set, using `pgrep -u devtest iidbms` to list the Ingres database instances run by the `devtest` user. You can go the other way, too, and just find all processes belonging to that user, regardless of process name, with `pgrep -u devtest`.

Because `pgrep` is so often used to kill processes, it is symbolically linked to a very similar command called `pkill`. `pkill` takes almost exactly the same syntax, but instead of just listing the PIDs, it kills the processes, too. So the `kill 9` shown previously is equivalent to `pkill -x apache2`. You can feed `pkill` a different signal to use, with the same syntax as `kill`: `pkill -1 -x apache2` will send a signal 1 to the process.

Table 10-1 shows the most common signals sent to processes.

TABLE 10-1: Commonly Used Signals

NUMBER	SIGNAL	MEANING
0	0	Caught on exit from shell
1	SIGHUP	Clean, tidy up; reread configuration files and continue
2	SIGINT	Interrupt
3	SIGQUIT	Quit
6	SIGABRT	Abort
9	SIGKILL	Kill the process immediately
14	SIGALRM	Alarm clock
15	SIGTERM	Terminate cleanly

When shutting down a machine, an OS will normally call any shutdown scripts registered, send a SIGTERM to any remaining processes, and finally send a SIGKILL to any processes that are still running.

There are many other flags to `pgrep`, all documented in the man page. One useful flag, mainly useful when outputting a list for human consumption, is `-1` to include the process name. Here, searching for processes that include "ii" in their names, instead of just getting the list of PIDs, also gets the process name.

```
$ pgrep -1 ii
8402    iimerge
8421    iigcc
8376    iimerge
8439    iigcd
8387    iimerge
8216    iigcn
```

Another commonly used flag for `pgrep` is the `-d` switch to specify a delimiter. Normally each PID is displayed on a line by itself; with `-d ' '` you can get them space-delimited such as `pidof`, or `-d ','` for comma-separated. Note that the order of the PIDs is reversed in the two commands.

```
$ pidof apache2
2510 2509 2508 2507 2502 1536 1535 1534 1533 1532 1495
$ pgrep -d',' apache2
1495,1532,1533,1534,1535,1536,2502,2507,2508,2509,2510
$
```

KILLALL

A useful shortcut for `killing` all processes is `killall`. `killall` kills processes that match a supplied criteria. Much like `pgrep` and friends, `killall` is very flexible. First, a word of warning: You should never consider running `killall` without the `-e` (exact match) option, unless you really know what you are doing and exactly what processes could ever be running on the system. The other very common switch is `-u`, which allows you to specify the user ID to which to limit the search. If your apache process runs as the user www, then by specifying `-u` www you can be sure that no other users' processes will be affected, as with the preceding `pgrep` example. `killall -u` www by itself will kill every process run by the www user — again, exactly the same as `pgrep`. You can specify different signals to pass with the `-s` switch — so `killall -1 -u` www sends a SIGHUP signal to the www processes, telling them to restart.

A simple application startup/shutdown script looks like this:

```
$ cat /etc/init.d/myapp
#!/bin/bash
case "$1" in
    "start") su - myapp /path/to/program/startall
        # This may spawn a load of processes, whose names and PIDs may not be known.
```

```
        # However, unless suid is involved, they will be owned by the myapp user
        ;;
    "stop") killall -u myapp
        # This kills *everything* being run by the myapp user.
        ;;
    *) echo "Usage: `basename $0` start|stop"
        ;;
esac
$
```

Many services start a set of processes, whose names you, as a systems administrator, may not even be aware of, which may change from version to version of the application, and so on. It may also be the case that the application users log in as myapp and run interactive shells, which they do not want to be killed when you shut down the service.

The script can be more fine-grained, if you know that all of the main processes owned by your application contain "myapp_" (myapp_monitor, myapp_server, myapp_broker, and so on) by specifying: killall -u myapp myapp_.

Beware when on a Unix (not GNU/Linux) system — killall will kill every single process on the system (other than kernel tasks and its own parents). GNU/Linux provides killall5 for this. killall5 is the same program as pidof. pgrep finds only the name of the binary itself, whereas pidof finds it by its identity. If Apache is listed in the process table as /usr/sbin/apache2, then pidof apache2 and pidof /usr/sbin/apache2 match, but pgrep /usr/sbin/apache2 finds nothing. Conversely, where gnome-terminal is in the process table without a path, pgrep will not find it as /usr/bin/gnome-terminal, while pidof will match either.

```
$ ps -eaf | egrep "(apache|gnome-terminal)"
root      1476     1  0 18:36 ?        00:00:00 /usr/sbin/apache2 -k start
www-data  1580  1476  0 18:36 ?        00:00:00 /usr/sbin/apache2 -k start
www-data  1581  1476  0 18:36 ?        00:00:00 /usr/sbin/apache2 -k start
www-data  1582  1476  0 18:36 ?        00:00:00 /usr/sbin/apache2 -k start
www-data  1583  1476  0 18:36 ?        00:00:00 /usr/sbin/apache2 -k start
www-data  1584  1476  0 18:36 ?        00:00:00 /usr/sbin/apache2 -k start
steve     2461     1  0 18:37 ?        00:00:02 gnome-terminal
$ pgrep /usr/sbin/apache2
$ pgrep apache2
1476
1580
1581
1582
1583
1584
$ pidof /usr/sbin/apache2
1584 1583 1582 1581 1580 1476
$ pidof apache2
1584 1583 1582 1581 1580 1476
$ pgrep /usr/bin/gnome-terminal
$ pgrep gnome-terminal
2461
$ pidof gnome-terminal
```

```
2461
$ pidof /usr/bin/gnome-terminal
2461
$
```

THE /PROC PSEUDO-FILESYSTEM

The kernel's process table, and the state of the processes in it, are available in the /proc pseudo-filesystem, identified by their PIDs. If you want information about PID 28741, then /proc/28741/ contains the relevant information. There is also a special symbolic link, called /proc/self: To any process that refers to /proc/self, it will appear as a symbolic link to the running process. This is not always easy to spot:

```
$ echo $$
2168
$ ls -ld /proc/self /proc/$$
dr-xr-xr-x 7 steve steve  0 Nov 12 16:06 /proc/2168
lrwxrwxrwx 1 root  root  64 Nov 12 15:56 /proc/self -> 2171
```

What is happening here is not necessarily intuitive. The shell has a PID of 2168, and the shell passes the value of $$ to ls. In the ls program, /proc/self is /proc/2171 because ls is running as PID 2171. So these two are not the same number.

This script uses the /proc virtual filesystem to get the state of a given process along with the CPU that it was most recently run on. This can be useful for correlating with what top says about I/O Wait states, for example. Of course, you can use it to display almost anything about the process; in the Linux kernel source, /fs/proc/array.c contains the do_task_stat() function, which is what writes /proc/<pid>/stat.

```
$ cat stat.sh
#!/bin/sh
# Example on RHEL5 (2.6.18 kernel):
#23267 (bash) S 23265 23267 23267 34818 23541 4202496 3005 27576 1 6 4 3 45 16 15 0
 1 0 1269706754 72114176 448 18446744073709551615 4194304 4922060 140734626075216
 18446744073709551615 272198374197 0 65536 3686404 1266761467 18446744071562230894 0
 0 17 2 0 0 23
PID=${1}
if [ ! -z "$PID" ]; then
   read pid tcomm state ppid pgid sid tty_nr tty_pgrp flags min_flt cmin_flt
 maj_flt cmaj_flt utime stime cutime cstime priority nice num_threads
it_real_value start_time vsize mm rsslim start_code end_code start_stack eis eip
pending blocked sigign sigcatch wchan oul1 oul2 exit_signal cpu rt_priority
policy ticks < /proc/$PID/stat
   echo "Pid $PID $tcomm is in state $state on CPU $cpu"
fi
```

stat.sh

This will display something along the lines of the following:

```
Pid 2076 (bash) is in state S on CPU 1
```

Because of the development model of the Linux kernel, it does not provide an API guarantee, so things such as /proc/*/stat will change over time. It is never difficult, however, to find documentation, or even the part of the kernel that writes to these files in /proc, and work out the changes for yourself. In practice, an API such as /proc/*/stat tends to stay compatible, adding new values to the end. For example, when it_real_value was removed from the 2.6.17 kernel, it was replaced with a zero (see http://lkml.org/lkml/2006/2/14/312) so that start_time and the fields following it keep the same position that they have always had.

You can tweak the output to display any of the variables in the pseudo-file /proc/$$/stat. For example:

```
echo "Pid $PID $tcomm is in state $state on CPU $cpu. Its parent is Pid $ppid."
echo "It is occupying $vsize bytes."
```

This will display something like the following:

```
Pid 3053 (bash) is in state S on CPU 1. Its parent is Pid 2074.
It is occupying 19763200 bytes.
```

PRTSTAT

The prtstat utility is a very useful utility that provides the same information as the script in the preceding section, but is an external binary. It is part of the psmisc project, which also provides fuser, killall, and pstree. You could get the CPU number from prtstat by piping it through grep and awk, which is easier than taking responsibility for correct parsing of a relatively long and complicated set of variables, although it does look a little less tidy, and involves spawning three different binaries, whereas the shell script in the preceding section spawns no processes at all.

```
$ prtstat $$
Process: bash            State: S (sleeping)
  CPU#:  1             TTY: 136:1   Threads: 1
Process, Group and Session IDs
  Process ID: 2168          Parent ID: 2063
    Group ID: 2168          Session ID: 2168
  T Group ID: 2999


Page Faults
  This Process    (minor major):     4539         0
  Child Processes (minor major):   114675        55
CPU Times
  This Process    (user system guest blkio):  0.07  0.14  0.00  0.93
  Child processes (user system guest):         4.56  0.67  0.00
Memory
  Vsize:        19 MB
  RSS:        2412 kB          RSS Limit: 18446744073709 MB
  Code Start:  0x400000        Code Stop:  0x4d8c1c
  Stack Start: 0x7fffb27ae720
  Stack Pointer (ESP): 0x7fffb27ae300    Inst Pointer (EIP): 0x7fe37fa9a36e
Scheduling
  Policy: normal
  Nice:   0        RT Priority: 0 (non RT)
$
$ prtstat -r $$ | grep processor: | awk '{ print $2 }'
0
```

I/O REDIRECTION

Every process has three standard files open upon creation. These are called standard input, standard output, and standard error, and are given file descriptors 0, 1, and 2, respectively. These are commonly known as stdin, stdout, and stderr. `ls -l /proc/self/fd` shows the files open by the `ls` command itself; after these standard 0, 1, and 2, `ls` has also opened the directory `/proc/5820/fd` to list it (5820 being the PID of `ls` itself), with a file descriptor of 3.

```
$ ls -l /proc/self/fd
total 0
lrwx------ 1 steve steve 64 Jan 27 21:34 0 -> /dev/pts/1
lrwx------ 1 steve steve 64 Jan 27 21:34 1 -> /dev/pts/1
lrwx------ 1 steve steve 64 Jan 27 21:34 2 -> /dev/pts/1
lr-x------ 1 steve steve 64 Jan 27 21:34 3 -> /proc/5820/fd
$
```

Because everything is a file, even the concepts of input and output are also files. Here, the controlling terminal (`/dev/pts/1`) is the source of input, and also where output and errors must be redirected. `ls` does not really take interactive input, but its output, and any errors it has to report, go to the controlling terminal so that when users run the `ls` command, they see its output on their terminal.

Because these are files, they can be redirected to other files. The > operator is used to redirect output from one file to another. Running the `ls` command again, but directing its output to `/tmp/ls-output.txt` shows nothing on the terminal because all output has gone to the file in `/tmp` instead.

```
$ ls -l /proc/self/fd > /tmp/ls-output.txt
$
```

Displaying the contents of the file shows an interesting change in what the `ls` command has actually displayed. Standard input (0) and standard error (2) are both still links to `/dev/pts/1`, but standard output (1) is now pointing to the file that the `ls` command was creating at the time it was running.

```
$ cat /tmp/ls-output.txt
total 0
lrwx------ 1 steve steve 64 Jan 27 21:42 0 -> /dev/pts/1
l-wx------ 1 steve steve 64 Jan 27 21:42 1 -> /tmp/ls-output.txt
lrwx------ 1 steve steve 64 Jan 27 21:42 2 -> /dev/pts/1
lr-x------ 1 steve steve 64 Jan 27 21:42 3 -> /proc/5839/fd
$
```

Taking this example further, redirecting standard error (2) to a different file, is achieved by the syntax 2>. Redirecting the standard error file of `ls` to `/tmp/ls-err.txt` results in a further change to the standard output of `ls`.

 There must be no space between the 2 and the >, or the shell will interpret 2 as an argument to `ls`, and > as a redirection of standard output.

```
$ ls -l /proc/self/fd > /tmp/ls-output.txt 2> /tmp/ls-err.txt
$ cat /tmp/ls-output.txt
```

```
total 0
lrwx------ 1 steve steve 64 Jan 27 21:50 0 -> /dev/pts/1
l-wx------ 1 steve steve 64 Jan 27 21:50 1 -> /tmp/ls-output.txt
l-wx------ 1 steve steve 64 Jan 27 21:50 2 -> /tmp/ls-err.txt
lr-x------ 1 steve steve 64 Jan 27 21:50 3 -> /proc/5858/fd
$ cat /tmp/ls-err.txt
$
```

/proc/self is a useful way of demonstrating how the redirection works. Taking it to the extreme, you can also redirect standard input (0), and set things up so that ls will produce errors as well as output. The standard output goes to ls-output.txt, and the error about the nonexistent file goes to ls-err.txt.

```
$ ls -l /proc/self/fd /nosuchfile > /tmp/ls-output.txt 2> /tmp/ls-err.txt
$ cat /tmp/ls-output.txt
/proc/self/fd:
total 0
lrwx------ 1 steve steve 64 Jan 27 21:54 0 -> /dev/pts/1
l-wx------ 1 steve steve 64 Jan 27 21:54 1 -> /tmp/ls-output.txt
l-wx------ 1 steve steve 64 Jan 27 21:54 2 -> /tmp/ls-err.txt
lr-x------ 1 steve steve 64 Jan 27 21:54 3 -> /proc/5863/fd
$ cat /tmp/ls-err.txt
ls: cannot access /nosuchfile: No such file or directory
$
```

The final test for this is to use something as input; ls is a very useful tool for this test and does not read from standard input, but you can still direct its input from elsewhere. Even sending the contents of /etc/hosts to it is syntactically valid, if pointless. It is best to direct </etc/hosts first, then the > redirection of standard output, followed by the 2> redirection of standard error. With other combinations, complicated situations can arise that will result in unexpected output.

```
$ ls -l /proc/self/fd /nosuchfile < /etc/hosts \
>      > /tmp/ls-output.txt 2> /tmp/ls-err.txt
$ cat /tmp/ls-output.txt
/proc/self/fd:
total 0
lr-x------ 1 steve steve 64 Jan 27 22:52 0 -> /etc/hosts
l-wx------ 1 steve steve 64 Jan 27 22:52 1 -> /tmp/ls-output.txt
l-wx------ 1 steve steve 64 Jan 27 22:52 2 -> /tmp/ls-err.txt
lr-x------ 1 steve steve 64 Jan 27 22:52 3 -> /proc/2623/fd
$ cat /tmp/ls-err.txt
ls: cannot access /nosuchfile: No such file or directory
$
```

There is now no mention of the terminal device in any of the files that the ls command holds open. All input and output is redirected to other files. As it happens, other than /proc/self/fd, these are all outside of the /proc pseudo-filesystem.

Appending Output to an Existing File

The > syntax creates the target file with zero length; to append instead of overwriting, use >>, which will preserve any existing content but still create the file if it does not already exist.

```
$ cat names.txt
Homer
Marge
Bart
$ echo Lisa >> names.txt
$ cat names.txt
Homer
Marge
Bart
Lisa
$ echo Lisa > names.txt
$ cat names.txt
Lisa
$
```

 Another use of the > syntax is to deliberately blank out an existing file. One understandable mistake made when cleaning up a full filesystem is to remove a log file that is still in use by an application. The filesystem will not free the space until the file has been closed by the application. Using > to truncate the file brings its size down to zero without the application having to close the file.

Permissions on Redirections

Looking back on the permissions on the links above, you can see that these are not standard symbolic links. Symbolic links normally have 777 permissions — there is no real meaning to the concept of a symbolic link having permissions or an owner of its own. Because the kernel will enforce certain semantic permissions during redirection, these links do have restricted permissions: Standard input is not writeable, and neither standard output nor standard error are readable, as with a regular terminal. This is treated more deeply in the "Exec" section that follows.

A file opened read-only will have r-x permissions. A file opened for writing will have -rx permissions, and a file opened for both reading and writing will have rwx permissions. As standard, these will have no Group or Other permissions granted at all.

EXEC

The exec builtin calls the underlying exec(3) system call. It has two main purposes. The first is the way in which the system call is most commonly used — to replace the currently running process with a different process. That is, the shell itself will be replaced by a different program, be it another shell, or any other program. When the exec'd program terminates, control is not returned to the calling shell. The second use is to cause redirection to happen as a byproduct of the exec call.

Using exec to Replace the Existing Program

A typical login session is shown in the following example, when the user logs in to `node2` from `node1`. The hostnames are reflected in the shell prompts, and the `%` prompt reflects a csh session, while the `$` prompt reflects a bash session.

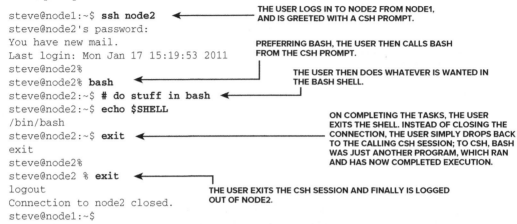

```
steve@node1:~$ ssh node2              ◄──── THE USER LOGS IN TO NODE2 FROM NODE1,
steve@node2's password:                     AND IS GREETED WITH A CSH PROMPT.
You have new mail.
Last login: Mon Jan 17 15:19:53 2011        PREFERRING BASH, THE USER THEN CALLS BASH
steve@node2%                                FROM THE CSH PROMPT.
steve@node2% bash              ◄──── THE USER THEN DOES WHATEVER IS WANTED IN
steve@node2:~$ # do stuff in bash  ◄──      THE BASH SHELL.
steve@node2:~$ echo $SHELL
/bin/bash                                   ON COMPLETING THE TASKS, THE USER
steve@node2:~$ exit   ◄───────────────      EXITS THE SHELL. INSTEAD OF CLOSING THE
exit                                        CONNECTION, THE USER SIMPLY DROPS BACK
steve@node2%                                TO THE CALLING CSH SESSION; TO CSH, BASH
steve@node2 % exit  ◄────────────           WAS JUST ANOTHER PROGRAM, WHICH RAN
logout                                      AND HAS NOW COMPLETED EXECUTION.
Connection to node2 closed.    THE USER EXITS THE CSH SESSION AND FINALLY IS LOGGED
steve@node1:~$                 OUT OF NODE2.
```

When the `exec` builtin is used, the user does not get returned to the csh session on exiting bash. The original csh process was replaced entirely with the bash executable.

```
steve@node1:~$ ssh node2
steve@node2's password:
You have new mail.                    THE CSH PROCESS IS REPLACED BY A
Last login: Mon Jan 31 11:23:43 2011  BASH PROCESS.
steve@node2% exec bash    ◄───────────
steve@node2:~$ # do stuff in bash
steve@node2:~$ echo $SHELL            WHEN THE USER EXITS THE BASH SHELL, THERE IS
/bin/bash                             NO CSH SESSION TO GO BACK TO; THE CONNECTION
steve@node2:~$ exit  ◄────────────    IS CLOSED.
exit
Connection to node2 closed.
steve@node1:~$
```

To boil this down to its logical conclusion, the session below simply execs a uname call. This is equivalent to (and as far as `node2` is concerned, in implementation almost exactly the same as) the command `ssh node2 uname -a`. This shows that `node1` has a 2.6.32-5 kernel, whereas `node2` has a 2.6.26-2 kernel.

```
steve@node1:~$ uname -a
Linux node1 2.6.32-5-amd64 #1 SMP Fri Dec 10 15:35:08 UTC 2010 x86_64 GNU/Linux
steve@node1:~$ ssh node2
steve@node2's password:
You have new mail.
Last login: Mon Jan 31 11:26:14 2011
steve@node2% exec uname -a
Linux node2 2.6.26-2-amd64 #1 SMP Sun Jun 20 20:16:30 UTC 2010 x86_64 GNU/Linux
Connection to node2 closed.
steve@node1:~$
```

More concisely, this is shown as a one-line `ssh` command.

```
steve@node1:~$ uname -a
Linux node1 2.6.32-5-amd64 #1 SMP Fri Dec 10 15:35:08 UTC 2010 x86_64 GNU/Linux
steve@node1:~$ ssh node2 uname -a
Linux node2 2.6.26-2-amd64 #1 SMP Sun Jun 20 20:16:30 UTC 2010 x86_64 GNU/Linux
steve@node1:~$
```

Using exec to Change Redirection

The second use of the `exec` builtin is to change the redirection settings of the currently executing shell. This is a more interesting use of `exec`, and while it can seem very obscure and confusing, it is actually quite clear-cut, once the principles are properly understood. Because most scripts that use this technique are generally quite complicated in themselves, the side effects can sometimes be hard to debug in place.

The best way to understand how `exec` redirection works is to work through some very simple examples, where the script is doing nothing more complicated than `exec`s to and from a few test files. This can still be confusing at times, and `exec` does not always act as you might have predicted in every situation. These examples work by looking at the `/proc/$$/fd` directory, which shows (as symbolic links) the files currently held open by the running shell.

```
$ ls -l /proc/$$/fd
total 0
lrwx------ 1 steve steve 64 Jan 31 11:56 0 -> /dev/pts/1
lrwx------ 1 steve steve 64 Jan 31 11:56 1 -> /dev/pts/1
lrwx------ 1 steve steve 64 Jan 31 11:56 2 -> /dev/pts/1
lrwx------ 1 steve steve 64 Jan 31 11:58 255 -> /dev/pts/1
$
```

The open files are 0 (stdin), 1 (stdout), and 2 (stderr). 255 is a little trick that bash uses to keep a copy of these for when they are redirected. This is specific to bash. Other shells will act the same for these tests, but will not have file descriptor 255.

The names stdin, stdout, and stderr are reflected in the `/dev` filesystem. These are symbolic links to `/proc/self/fd/0`, 1, and 2 respectively. This is just one of the many conveniences afforded by the fact that `/proc/self` always points to the currently running process because the `/proc` filesystem really is an interactive conversation with the running kernel, and not just some filesystem exposing some data about the kernel.

```
$ ls -l /dev/std*
lrwxrwxrwx 1 root root 15 Jan 31 08:17 /dev/stderr -> /proc/self/fd/2
lrwxrwxrwx 1 root root 15 Jan 31 08:17 /dev/stdin -> /proc/self/fd/0
lrwxrwxrwx 1 root root 15 Jan 31 08:17 /dev/stdout -> /proc/self/fd/1
$
```

Opening a File for Writing

When you run `exec 3> /tmp/testing`, a new file descriptor is created, pointing to `/tmp/testing`. The file `/tmp/testing` is also created, and opened for writing.

There can be no space between "3" and ">", or the command would be inter-preted as a request to exec *the command called "3" and redirect its stdout to* /tmp/testing. *"3>" (and indeed any number immediately followed by ">" or "<") is part of the syntax of the shell.*

```
$ exec 3> /tmp/testing
$ ls -l /proc/$$/fd
total 0
lrwx------ 1 steve steve 64 Jan 31 11:56 0 -> /dev/pts/1
lrwx------ 1 steve steve 64 Jan 31 11:56 1 -> /dev/pts/1
lrwx------ 1 steve steve 64 Jan 31 11:56 2 -> /dev/pts/1
lrwx------ 1 steve steve 64 Jan 31 11:58 255 -> /dev/pts/1
l-wx------ 1 steve steve 64 Jan 31 11:56 3 -> /tmp/testing
$
```

stdin, stdout, and stderr all work as before, but the command echo hello >&3 is directed to file number three, which is /tmp/testing. The file /tmp/testing can also be read as normal — it is just a file.

```
$ echo hello
hello
$ echo hello >&3
$ cat /tmp/testing
hello
$ echo testing >&3
$ cat /tmp/testing
hello
testing
$
```

Successive writes to &3 result in the text being appended, not overwritten. This is not the same as if &3 were replaced with /tmp/test-two because the single > for /tmp/test-two creates the file afresh every time. Writing to a file descriptor is more like writing to a network device or to a printer. Once data has been sent there, it cannot be truncated like a file in a filesystem can. To append to a regular file, the double >> must be used.

```
$ echo hello > /tmp/test-two
$ cat /tmp/test-two
hello
$ echo testing > /tmp/test-two
$ cat /tmp/test-two
testing
$
$ echo hello > /tmp/test-two
$ echo testing >> /tmp/test-two
$ cat /tmp/test-two
hello
testing
$
```

Opening a File for Reading

Writing to a file descriptor is all well and good, but input is just as important as output. Reversing the direction of the arrow reverses the data flow. The syntax exec 4< /tmp/testing creates file descriptor 4, also pointing to /tmp/testing, but as a file open for reading, not writing.

```
$ exec 4< /tmp/testing
$ ls -1 /proc/$$/fd
total 0
lrwx------ 1 steve steve 64 Jan 31 11:56 0 -> /dev/pts/1
lrwx------ 1 steve steve 64 Jan 31 11:56 1 -> /dev/pts/1
lrwx------ 1 steve steve 64 Jan 31 11:56 2 -> /dev/pts/1
lrwx------ 1 steve steve 64 Jan 31 11:58 255 -> /dev/pts/1
l-wx------ 1 steve steve 64 Jan 31 11:56 3 -> /tmp/testing
lr-x------ 1 steve steve 64 Jan 31 12:05 4 -> /tmp/testing
$ cat /tmp/testing
hello
testing
$ cat <&4
hello
testing
```

Keeping Track of File Position

There is a difference between reading from a regular file and reading from its file descriptor. You can read a regular file as many times as you like, and its content will not change. Reading from a file descriptor consumes the input, just as the read command keeps consuming its input when running in a while loop.

```
$ cat /tmp/testing
hello
testing
$ cat <&4
$
```

This is demonstrated by further reads to, and writes from, the file descriptors. Thinking of file descriptors as streams, not the actual file contents itself, should help to make this clear.

 It could be said that there is a hidden water analogy in Unix. Data flows from one place to another and is even transported along pipes. This analogy can also be used for the <, <<, >, and >> symbols; data flows through these funnels in the direction shown.

```
$ echo more testing >&3
$ cat /tmp/testing
hello
testing
more testing
$ cat <&4
more testing
$
```

Writing to file descriptor 3 appends to /tmp/testing, but because file descriptor 4 is already at line 3, the cat <&4 command only returns the new data, unlike cat /tmp/testing, which opens the file afresh on every invocation. The running shell knows its position in file descriptor 4 and maintains it at all times. This is true whether the file /tmp/testing is appended to, or the file descriptor 3 is written to.

```
$ echo append to the file itself >> /tmp/testing
$ cat /tmp/testing
hello
testing
more testing
append to the file itself
$ cat <&4
append to the file itself
$
```

If the file on the filesystem is cleared down and new data is written to it, the file descriptor 4 keeps its place even though the file has been truncated by the > redirection:

```
$ echo new data to the file > /tmp/testing
$ cat /tmp/testing
new data to the file
$ cat <&4
$
```

As more gets written to the file, the file length eventually catches up to the placement of file descriptor 4. It is in these situations that the way in which exec works can become confusing, and cause unexpected (possibly data-damaging) results. In the example below, the words "even more data" finally make the file longer than it had been before it was truncated; the extra characters "ore data" are displayed and the old file descriptor 4 has caught up with the current content.

```
$ echo lots more data >> /tmp/testing
$ echo more and more data >> /tmp/testing
$ cat <&4
$ echo even more data >> /tmp/testing
$ cat <&4
ore data
$
```

Similarly devastating consequences would happen if the file were removed. The kernel does keep track of this, and the word "(deleted)" is shown in the /proc/$$/fd/ listing.

```
$ ls -l /proc/$$/fd
total 0
lrwx------ 1 steve steve 64 Jan 31 11:56 0 -> /dev/pts/1
lrwx------ 1 steve steve 64 Jan 31 11:56 1 -> /dev/pts/1
lrwx------ 1 steve steve 64 Jan 31 11:56 2 -> /dev/pts/1
lrwx------ 1 steve steve 64 Jan 31 11:58 255 -> /dev/pts/1
l-wx------ 1 steve steve 64 Jan 31 11:56 3 -> /tmp/testing
```

```
lr-x------ 1 steve steve 64 Jan 31 12:05 4 -> /tmp/testing
$ rm /tmp/testing
$ ls -l /proc/$$/fd
total 0
lrwx------ 1 steve steve 64 Jan 31 11:56 0 -> /dev/pts/1
lrwx------ 1 steve steve 64 Jan 31 11:56 1 -> /dev/pts/1
lrwx------ 1 steve steve 64 Jan 31 11:56 2 -> /dev/pts/1
lrwx------ 1 steve steve 64 Jan 31 11:58 255 -> /dev/pts/1
l-wx------ 1 steve steve 64 Jan 31 11:56 3 -> /tmp/testing (deleted)
lr-x------ 1 steve steve 64 Jan 31 12:06 4 -> /tmp/testing (deleted)
$
```

This has significant ramifications for filesystem usage, among other things. The file has been deleted (possibly by a systems administrator because the /tmp filesystem was full and /tmp/testing was a large log file), but the bash process still holds it as an open file. This applies whether the owning process is a shell script, an Apache web server, an Oracle database, or any other program. Although the file has been removed from the filesystem, it still exists in the kernel's filesystem driver until the last process has closed it. The space in the filesystem has not been freed, either. The process keeps reading and writing the file as if had not been removed, even though an explicit call to the ls program shows that to other processes, the file does not exist.

```
$ ls -l /proc/$$/fd
total 0
lrwx------ 1 steve steve 64 Jan 31 11:56 0 -> /dev/pts/1
lrwx------ 1 steve steve 64 Jan 31 11:56 1 -> /dev/pts/1
lrwx------ 1 steve steve 64 Jan 31 11:56 2 -> /dev/pts/1
lrwx------ 1 steve steve 64 Jan 31 11:58 255 -> /dev/pts/1
l-wx------ 1 steve steve 64 Jan 31 11:56 3 -> /tmp/testing (deleted)
lr-x------ 1 steve steve 64 Jan 31 12:05 4 -> /tmp/testing (deleted)
$ echo line one >&3
$ echo line two >&3
$ echo line three >&3
$ cat <&4
line one
line two
line three
$ cat /tmp/testing
cat: /tmp/testing: No such file or directory
$ echo line four >&3
$ cat <&4
line four
$
```

Because of this, it is apparently impossible for the systems administrator to free the space without killing this process (or at least getting it to close its files). Actually, the administrator can free space in the filesystem by writing to the file; this is a symptom of what was seen in the file descriptor 4 example earlier in this section. If the following loop keeps writing to the disk, it will eventually fill up the filesystem.

For this example, it is necessary that the whole while *loop be a single process keeping* date.log *open; if, instead, each call to* date *opened the file to append to it each time around the loop, the behavior would be different. A typical application process like this will hold files open in this way, not opening them every time to append to them. If the application does close the file, it is an easy task to move it away or remove it.*

```
$ while :
> do
>    date
>    sleep 1
> done >> date.log
```

Time passes and eventually the disk fills up:

```
date: write error: No space left on device
date: write error: No space left on device
date: write error: No space left on device
date: write error: No space left on device
date: write error: No space left on device
date: write error: No space left on device
```

There is no point in removing the file because, as the preceding code shows, the process will hold its copy of the file open. The way to free the space is to write to the file.

```
[root@server]# tail date.log
Mon Feb  7 12:46:23 GMT 2011
Mon Feb  7 12:46:24 GMT 2011
Mon Feb  7 12:46:25 GMT 2011
Mon Feb  7 12:46:26 GMT 2011
Mon Feb  7 12:46:27 GMT 2011
Mon Feb  7 12:46:28 GMT 2011
Mon Feb  7 12:46:29 GMT 2011
Mon Feb  7 12:46:30 GMT 2011
Mon Feb  7 12:46:31 GMT 2011
Mon Feb  7 12:46:32 G[root@server]#
[root@server]# df -k .
Filesystem          1K-blocks      Used Available Use% Mounted on
/dev/sdb1              616636    616636         0 100% /var/datelog
```

At this stage, the filesystem is full, and the 12:46:32 line cannot even be finished. The operator resets date.log, freeing up eight blocks:

```
[root@server]# > date.log
[root@server]# df -k .
Filesystem          1K-blocks      Used Available Use% Mounted on
/dev/sdb1              616636    616628         8 100% /var/datelog
[root@server]# date
Mon Feb  7 12:46:58 GMT 2011
[root@server]# cat date.log
Mon Feb  7 12:46:53 GMT 2011
Mon Feb  7 12:46:54 GMT 2011
```

```
Mon Feb  7 12:46:55 GMT 2011
Mon Feb  7 12:46:57 GMT 2011
Mon Feb  7 12:46:58 GMT 2011
Mon Feb  7 12:46:59 GMT 2011
Mon Feb  7 12:47:00 GMT 2011
Mon Feb  7 12:47:01 GMT 2011
Mon Feb  7 12:47:02 GMT 2011
Mon Feb  7 12:47:03 GMT 2011
Mon Feb  7 12:47:04 GMT 2011
[root@server]# wc -l date.log
21 date.log
[root@server]#
```

Space is freed on the filesystem, the loop continues writing to the file, and nothing had to be restarted. As the date and wc commands show, the log file continues to be written to in real time.

PIPELINES

Pipelines are a central feature of Unix and Linux shells. A pipe connects two processes together, generally attaching the standard output of one process to the standard input of another. Instead of writing the output of the first command to a file and then running the second command, taking that file as input, the intermediary file can be bypassed entirely with this method. It is so central to shell scripting that it has already been mentioned in passing many times, but it is worth clarifying what actually happens when a pipe is set up. This example pipes the output of find into grep:

```
$ find / -print | grep hosts
/lib/security/pam_rhosts.so
/var/lib/ghostscript
/var/lib/ghostscript/CMap
/var/lib/ghostscript/fonts
/var/lib/ghostscript/fonts/cidfmap
/var/lib/ghostscript/fonts/Fontmap
find: `/var/lib/php5': Permission denied
find: `/var/lib/polkit-1': Permission denied
/var/lib/dpkg/info/denyhosts.postinst
```

What happens here is that grep is started first, followed by find. Once both processes exist, the output of the find process is linked to the input of the grep process. The find process can then run and its output gets sent to grep. As the preceding sample output shows, the standard error device for the find process is still the calling terminal, so that is displayed as normal. It has not been passed through grep. This is evident because the error lines do not include the text "hosts" anywhere in them. This, therefore, is the standard error of find and not the output from grep.

BACKGROUND PROCESSING

It is sometimes useful to get a command to run in the background, and return control to the shell immediately. If the script does not depend upon the results or status of the executed command, there is no need to wait for it to complete. The ampersand symbol (&) at the end of a command line does this. The PID of the backgrounded process is set in the variable $! and execution of the main script or interactive shell continues as normal. It can also monitor the activity of the backgrounded child process as it works. This dd command reads 512MB of random data from the /dev/urandom driver and writes it to a file named bigfile. The interactive shell lists bigfile as it grows, and uses the $! variable to monitor progress using ps and strace. The strace output shows the random data as it is being read from /dev/urandom and written to bigfile.

```
$ dd if=/dev/urandom of=bigfile bs=1024k count=512 &
[1] 3495
$ ls -lh bigfile
-rw-rw-r-- 1 steve steve 18M Jan 28 18:01 bigfile
$ ls -lh bigfile
-rw-rw-r-- 1 steve steve 196M Jan 28 18:02 bigfile
$ ps -fp $!
UID         PID  PPID  C STIME TTY          TIME CMD
steve       3495  3363 99 18:01 pts/1     00:00:44 dd if=/dev/urandom of=bigfile bs=10
24k count=512
$ strace -p $! 2>&1 | head -5
Process 3495 attached - interrupt to quit
write(1, "\251\0\322\335J\362\214\334\331\342\213\356\377\23%\371\353U\377H\262\225
'w\r`_\316\306\220\325g"..., 828440) = 828440
read(0, "znm9;\311}\344\21z\342\"\215n\272d8\24\321\215\363\340\327%\213\3623&\273;
\10\323"..., 1048576) = 1048576
write(1, "znm9;\311}\344\21z\342\"\215n\272d8\24\321\215\363\340\327%\213\3623&\273
;\10\323"..., 1048576) = 1048576
read(0, "\fq31\273\343c/\300\343\31\262V\263\222\351\310\310/\274t\223\330\217\223\
345H\221B\310\237\246"..., 1048576) = 1048576
$ ls -lh bigfile
-rw-rw-r-- 1 steve steve 288M Jan 28 18:02 bigfile
$ 509+3 records in
509+3 records out
53
[1]+  Done                    dd if=/dev/urandom of=bigfile bs=1024k count=512
$ rm bigfile
$
```

The next chapter covers the interactive tools bg and fg, which are very useful for dealing with multiple processes. bg causes a stopped job to continue executing in the background, whereas fg causes a backgrounded job to be brought to the foreground.

Wait

It is possible to wait for one, more, or all backgrounded processes to complete. This session downloads the md5sum.txt file, which is very small, and then the first two CD-ROM ISO images of CentOS 5.5. These are large files, so they are downloaded in the background so that control can be returned to the shell.

```
$ wget http://mirror.ox.ac.uk/sites/mirror.centos.org/5.5/isos/x86_64/md5sum.txt
--2011-02-12 22:27:46--  http://mirror.ox.ac.uk/sites/mirror.centos.org/5.5/isos/x8
6_64/md5sum.txt
Resolving mirror.ox.ac.uk... 163.1.2.224, 163.1.2.231
Connecting to mirror.ox.ac.uk|163.1.2.224|:80... connected.
HTTP request sent, awaiting response... 200 OK
Length: 788 [text/plain]
```

```
Saving to: `md5sum.txt'

100%[=======================================>] 788         --.-K/s   in 0s

2011-02-12 22:27:46 (50.8 MB/s) - `md5sum.txt' saved [788/788]
$ wget http://mirror.ox.ac.uk/sites/mirror.centos.org/5.5/isos/x86_64/CentOS-5.5-x8
6_64-bin-1of8.iso > /dev/null 2>&1 &
[1] 4572
$ wget http://mirror.ox.ac.uk/sites/mirror.centos.org/5.5/isos/x86_64/CentOS-5.5-x8
6_64-bin-2of8.iso > /dev/null 2>&1 &
[2] 4573
$ ps -f
UID         PID   PPID  C STIME TTY           TIME CMD
steve       4555  4554  0 22:26 pts/3     00:00:00 -bash
steve       4572  4555  2 22:27 pts/3     00:00:00 wget http://mirror.ox.ac.uk/site
steve       4573  4555  2 22:28 pts/3     00:00:00 wget http://mirror.ox.ac.uk/site
steve       4574  4555  0 22:28 pts/3     00:00:00 ps -f
$ jobs
[1]-  Running                 wget http://mirror.ox.ac.uk/sites/mirror.centos.org/5
.5/isos/x86_64/CentOS-5.5-x86_64-bin-1of8.iso > /dev/null 2>&1 &
[2]+  Running                 wget http://mirror.ox.ac.uk/sites/mirror.centos.org/5
.5/isos/x86_64/CentOS-5.5-x86_64-bin-2of8.iso > /dev/null 2>&1 &
$ wait
```

It would not be possible to foreground both of the active wget processes in the same terminal, but the final wait command has a similar effect. It waits until all of the caller's children have returned, and then passes control back to the calling shell. This is not so vital for an interactive session, but a script can use this method to retrieve all of the ISO images before then comparing the md5sums, which can only be done once the downloads have completed.

```
[1]-  Done                    wget http://mirror.ox.ac.uk/sites/mirror.centos.org/5
.5/isos/x86_64/CentOS-5.5-x86_64-bin-1of8.iso > /dev/null 2>&1
[2]+  Done                    wget http://mirror.ox.ac.uk/sites/mirror.centos.org/5
.5/isos/x86_64/CentOS-5.5-x86_64-bin-2of8.iso > /dev/null 2>&1
$ md5sum -c md5sum.txt
CentOS-5.5-x86_64-bin-1of8.iso: OK
CentOS-5.5-x86_64-bin-2of8.iso: OK
$
```

 For brevity, md5sum.txt *was trimmed to include only these two files. Otherwise, it would have displayed error messages about the other six missing ISO images 3–8.*

Catching Hangups with nohup

When running a long background process like the downloads in the previous section, it can be useful to ensure that the job will not be terminated if the user logs off his or her session, or is logged out because a network link has gone down. The nohup command runs processes in a wrapper, which protects them from receiving signals that would otherwise cause them to terminate. These don't always go together, but it is very common to background a nohup'd process, and similarly, it is very common to nohup a backgrounded process.

By default, the output of the command will go to nohup.out. However, if stderr and stdout are both redirected elsewhere, then nohup.out will not be created.

By tying these all together, a script can be created to download and verify the ISO images automatically. The following code logs its output to individual files, one file per image, and does a proper md5sum check at the end.

```
$ cat getisos.sh
#!/bin/bash
MIRROR=http://mirror.ox.ac.uk/sites/mirror.centos.org/5.5/isos/x86_64
IMAGE=CentOS-5.5-x86_64-bin-

wget ${MIRROR}/md5sum.txt > md5.out 2>&1
for image in ${IMAGE}{1,2,3,4,5,6,7,8}of8.iso
do
  nohup wget ${MIRROR}/${image} > ${image}.out 2>&1 &
  grep ${image} md5sum.txt >> files-to-check.txt
done

echo "Waiting for files to download..."
jobs
wait
echo "Verifying MD5 sums..."
md5sum -c files-to-check.txt
if [ "$?" -eq "0" ]; then
  echo "All files downloaded successfully."
else
  echo "Some files failed."
  exit 1
fi
$
```

getisos.sh

```
$ ./getisos.sh
Waiting for files to download...
[1]    Running                 nohup wget ${MIRROR}/${image} > ${image}.out 2>&1 &
[2]    Running                 nohup wget ${MIRROR}/${image} > ${image}.out 2>&1 &
[3]    Running                 nohup wget ${MIRROR}/${image} > ${image}.out 2>&1 &
[4]    Running                 nohup wget ${MIRROR}/${image} > ${image}.out 2>&1 &
[5]    Running                 nohup wget ${MIRROR}/${image} > ${image}.out 2>&1 &
[6]    Running                 nohup wget ${MIRROR}/${image} > ${image}.out 2>&1 &
[7]-   Running                 nohup wget ${MIRROR}/${image} > ${image}.out 2>&1 &
[8]+   Running                 nohup wget ${MIRROR}/${image} > ${image}.out 2>&1 &
```

There is then a long delay as the eight ISO images are downloaded in parallel. Eventually, once all the files have been downloaded, they are all checked by the md5sum utility.

```
Verifying MD5 sums...
CentOS-5.5-x86_64-bin-1of8.iso: OK
CentOS-5.5-x86_64-bin-2of8.iso: OK
```

```
CentOS-5.5-x86_64-bin-3of8.iso: OK
CentOS-5.5-x86_64-bin-4of8.iso: OK
CentOS-5.5-x86_64-bin-5of8.iso: OK
CentOS-5.5-x86_64-bin-6of8.iso: OK
CentOS-5.5-x86_64-bin-7of8.iso: OK
CentOS-5.5-x86_64-bin-8of8.iso: OK
All files downloaded successfully.
```

If the download was not successful, it is easy to see the output for that particular download. In this example, the download of image 6 failed. The output of wget is quite verbose, so a head checks that the download started successfully, and the tail shows that it completed properly.

 Also, wget is one of those programs that detects when its output is not going to a terminal, and it is even more verbose in that case. To a terminal, it would display a progress bar, but when redirected, it gives a more detailed update on the download progress.

```
Verifying MD5 sums...
CentOS-5.5-x86_64-bin-1of8.iso: OK
CentOS-5.5-x86_64-bin-2of8.iso: OK
CentOS-5.5-x86_64-bin-3of8.iso: OK
CentOS-5.5-x86_64-bin-4of8.iso: OK
CentOS-5.5-x86_64-bin-5of8.iso: OK
CentOS-5.5-x86_64-bin-6of8.iso: FAILED
CentOS-5.5-x86_64-bin-7of8.iso: OK
CentOS-5.5-x86_64-bin-8of8.iso: OK
md5sum: WARNING: 1 of 8 computed checksums did NOT match
Some files failed.
$ head CentOS-5.5-x86_64-bin-6of8.out
--2011-02-12 22:53:20--  http://mirror.ox.ac.uk/sites/mirror.centos.org/5.5/isos/x8
6_64//CentOS-5.5-x86_64-bin-6of8.iso
Resolving mirror.ox.ac.uk... 163.1.2.224, 163.1.2.231
Connecting to mirror.ox.ac.uk|163.1.2.224|:80... connected.
HTTP request sent, awaiting response... 200 OK
Length: 657436672 (627M) [application/x-iso9660-image]
Saving to: `CentOS-5.5-x86_64-bin-6of8.iso'

     0K .......... .......... .......... .......... ..........  0%  113K 94m42s
    50K .......... .......... .......... .......... ..........  0%  223K 71m23s
   100K .......... .......... .......... .......... ..........  0%  204K 65m6s
$ tail -4 CentOS-5.5-x86_64-bin-6of8.out
638200K .......... .......... .......... .......... .......... 99%  141M 0s
638250K .......... .......... .......... .......... .......... 99%  180M 0s
638300K .......... .......... .......... .......... ........  100%  173M=83s

2011-02-12 23:12:26 (115K/s) - `CentOS-5.5-x86_64-bin-6of8.iso' saved [653668352/65
3668352]
$
```

This shows that the file appeared to download successfully, so it must have been corrupted as it was transmitted over the Internet. Running the md5sum utility against that single file confirms it — the checksums do not match.

```
$ grep CentOS-5.5-x86_64-bin-6of8.iso md5sum.txt
f0b40f050e17c90e5dbba9ef772f6886  CentOS-5.5-x86_64-bin-6of8.iso
$ md5sum CentOS-5.5-x86_64-bin-6of8.iso
50ef685abe51db964760c6d20d26cf31  CentOS-5.5-x86_64-bin-6of8.iso
$
```

OTHER FEATURES OF /PROC AND /SYS

As mentioned previously, the /proc filesystem on Linux exposes a lot of detail about the kernel, which is not (as it may first seem) a static set of files created at boot, but is a direct hook into the kernel itself. Accordingly, some files can be written to, some can be read, and others can be read or written. A number of features in /proc are described in the proc(5) man page; run man 5 proc to read it. These files can be very useful for shell scripts because a shell script can get very close to the internals of the kernel itself, which is unusual for a Unix-like system.

Version

/proc/version is a read-only listing of the kernel version, including build details of how it was compiled. This can be a more complete, and more accurate, way to detect the actual kernel version than uname. Despite how it looks here, it is actually a single line of text.

```
$ cat /proc/version
Linux version 2.6.32-5-amd64 (Debian 2.6.32-29) (ben@decadent.org.uk) (gcc version
 4.3.5 (Debian 4.3.5-4) ) #1 SMP Fri Dec 10 15:35:08 UTC 2010
$ uname -a
Linux goldie 2.6.32-5-amd64 #1 SMP Fri Dec 10 15:35:08 UTC 2010 x86_64 GNU/Linux
$
```

SysRq

There is a little-used key on the PC keyboard, labeled SysRq. Its history goes back to mainframe computer systems, but it is used by the Linux kernel as a way to communicate with the kernel even when normal methods (such as echoing to /proc as most of these examples cover) are not possible. If enabled, when the user presses the "magic" combination Ctrl+Alt+SysRq, along with one other key to specify what the kernel is to do, the kernel can perform some of the most basic tasks available to it — synchronize the filesystems, report on memory usage, or even reboot the system. The list of tasks available appears in Table 10-2.

TABLE 10-2: Common SysRq Commands

KEY	PURPOSE
c	Crash the system.
m	Show the memory of the system.
h	Show help.
r	Set the console display to Raw mode.
s	Synchronize all filesystems.
i	Send a KILL signal to all processes (except init).
u	Unmount all filesystems.
b	Reboot the machine.
e	Send a TERM signal to all processes (except init).

There is a common mnemonic, "Raising Skinny Elephants Is Utterly Boring." To safely reboot a hung system, this will set the console to raw mode, sync the filesystems, send a TERM to all processes, unmount all filesystems, and reboot the machine. Figure 10-2 shows a console where the Control-Alt-SysRq and h combination has been pressed to display the SysRq help message, followed by Control-Alt-SysRq and s to sync the disks.

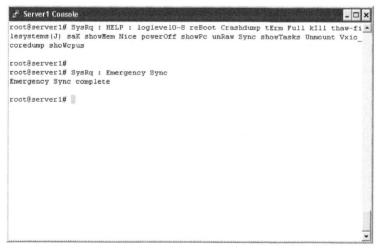

FIGURE 10-2

The sysrq feature has two files under /proc: /proc/sysrq-trigger and /proc/sys/kernel/sysrq. The latter enables or disables the sysrq feature and is readable by all users and writeable by the root user. A 1 means that the feature is enabled; 0 means that it is disabled.

The /proc/sysrq-trigger file takes one of the keys from Table 10-2 and behaves as if a user had pressed Ctrl+Alt+SysRq plus that key on the system console. This can be particularly useful when the console is in a remote datacenter.

```
declan:~# echo h > /proc/sysrq-trigger
declan:~# tail -1 /var/log/messages
Feb 13 22:17:44 declan kernel: [2328070.124615] SysRq : HELP : loglevel0-8 reBoot
Crashdump tErm Full kIll saK aLlcpus showMem Nice powerOff showPc show-all-timers(Q
)

unRaw Sync showTasks Unmount shoW-blocked-tasks
declan:~# echo m > /proc/sysrq-trigger
declan:~# tail -24 /var/log/messages
Feb 13 22:17:52 declan kernel: [2328078.469396] SysRq : Show Memory
Feb 13 22:17:52 declan kernel: [2328078.469396] Mem-info:
Feb 13 22:17:52 declan kernel: [2328078.469396] Node 0 DMA per-cpu:
Feb 13 22:17:52 declan kernel: [2328078.469396] CPU    0: hi:    0, btch:   1 usd:
  0
Feb 13 22:17:52 declan kernel: [2328078.469396] CPU    1: hi:    0, btch:   1 usd:
  0
Feb 13 22:17:52 declan kernel: [2328078.469396] Node 0 DMA32 per-cpu:
Feb 13 22:17:52 declan kernel: [2328078.469396] CPU    0: hi: 186, btch:  31 usd:
  81
Feb 13 22:17:52 declan kernel: [2328078.469396] CPU    1: hi: 186, btch:  31 usd:
140
Feb 13 22:17:52 declan kernel: [2328078.469396] Active:109030 inactive:364454 dirty
:35 writeback:0 unstable:0
Feb 13 22:17:52 declan kernel: [2328078.469396]  free:11420 slab:23854 mapped:9902
 pagetables:1888 bounce:0
Feb 13 22:17:52 declan kernel: [2328078.469396] Node 0 DMA free:8376kB min:28kB low
:32kB high:40kB active:124kB inactive:3032kB present:10788kB pages_scanned:0 all_un
reclaimable? no
Feb 13 22:17:52 declan kernel: [2328078.469396] lowmem_reserve[]: 0 2003 2003 2003
Feb 13 22:17:52 declan kernel: [2328078.469396] Node 0 DMA32 free:37304kB min:5708k
B low:7132kB high:8560kB active:435996kB inactive:1454784kB present:2051120kB pages
_scanned:0 all_unreclaimable? no
Feb 13 22:17:52 declan kernel: [2328078.469396] lowmem_reserve[]: 0 0 0 0
Feb 13 22:17:52 declan kernel: [2328078.469396] Node 0 DMA: 10*4kB 10*8kB 4*16kB 4*
32kB 4*64kB 1*128kB 2*256kB 2*512kB 2*1024kB 0*2048kB 1*4096kB = 8376kB
Feb 13 22:17:52 declan kernel: [2328078.469396] Node 0 DMA32: 2090*4kB 2250*8kB 280
*16kB 12*32kB 1*64kB 1*128kB 1*256kB 1*512kB 1*1024kB 0*2048kB 1*4096kB = 37304kB
Feb 13 22:17:52 declan kernel: [2328078.469396] 444427 total pagecache pages
Feb 13 22:17:52 declan kernel: [2328078.469396] Swap cache: add 214, delete 13, fin
d 0/0
Feb 13 22:17:52 declan kernel: [2328078.469396] Free swap  = 1951004kB
Feb 13 22:17:52 declan kernel: [2328078.469396] Total swap = 1951856kB
Feb 13 22:17:52 declan kernel: [2328078.469396] 523984 pages of RAM
Feb 13 22:17:52 declan kernel: [2328078.469396] 8378 reserved pages
Feb 13 22:17:52 declan kernel: [2328078.469396] 332107 pages shared
Feb 13 22:17:52 declan kernel: [2328078.469396] 201 pages swap cached
declan:~#
```

/proc/meminfo

`/proc/meminfo` provides a fairly detailed overview of the current status of memory and the virtual memory system. Some of the more immediately interesting elements are highlighted in the code that follows. `MemTotal` and `MemFree` are fairly self-explanatory; this is the physical memory available and free, respectively. The Virtual Memory subsystem includes swap space, and that is displayed here, too, as is the current state of filesystem buffers and caches. `/proc/meminfo` can be a useful source of system information and, like most of `/proc`, is designed to be easily parsed by humans and by scripts. The `/sys/devices/system/node` section later in this chapter shows a slightly more advanced equivalent.

```
MemTotal:      2062424 kB
MemFree:         46984 kB
Buffers:        201248 kB
Cached:        1575452 kB
SwapTotal:     1951856 kB
SwapFree:      1951004 kB
```

/proc/cpuinfo

The read-only file `/proc/cpuinfo` displays information about the processor(s) installed in the system. Strictly speaking, it displays the processing threads on the system, so a hyperthreaded, multi-core, multi-processor system may list a lot of CPUs. To work out how many physical CPUs are in a system, or how many cores a CPU has, is no longer straightforward. The "physical id" field counts the cores upward from 0, so if the highest physical ID is 3, then there are four actual chips inside the machine. Similarly, the "core id" field counts the number of cores, so if a CPU has cores 0–5, it is a six-core CPU. Hyperthreading doubles the number of execution threads available, but a hyperthreaded core is listed only once in `/proc/cpuinfo`.

The `cpuinfo.sh` script parses `/proc/cpuinfo` to give a human-readable description of the system processors.

```
$ cat cpuinfo.sh
#!/bin/bash
hyperthreads=1
grep -w "^flags" /proc/cpuinfo | grep -qw "ht" && hyperthreads=2
phys=`grep "physical id" /proc/cpuinfo | sort -u | wc -l`
cores=`grep "core id" /proc/cpuinfo | sort -u | wc -l`
threads=`expr $phys \* $cores \* $hyperthreads`
detail=`grep "model name" /proc/cpuinfo | sort -u | cut -d: -f2- \
  | cut -c2- | tr -s " " " " `
echo "`hostname -s` has $phys physical CPUs ($detail) each with $cores cores. "
echo "Each core has $hyperthreads threads: total $threads threads"
$ ./cpuinfo.sh
webserv has 2 physical CPUs (Intel(R) Xeon(R) CPU L5420 @ 2.50GHz) each with 4
cores.
Each core has 2 threads: total 16 threads
$
```

cpuinfo.sh

/sys

/sys is a pseudo-filesystem very closely related to /proc; there is even some overlap, as /proc has a /sys subdirectory that contains similar items. The cpu.sh script reads and writes the /sys/devices/system/node/ tree. The mem.sh script later in this chapter reads memory configuration from the same tree.

```
$ cat cpu.sh
#!/bin/bash

if [ ! -f /sys/devices/system/node/node0/cpu0/online ]; then
  echo "node0/cpu0 is always Online."
fi

function showcpus()
{
  cpu=${1:-'*'}
  for node in `ls -d /sys/devices/system/node/node*/cpu${cpu} | \
        cut -d"/" -f6 | sort -u`
  do
    grep . /sys/devices/system/node/${node}/cpu*/online /dev/null \
        | cut -d"/" -f6- | sed s/"\/online"/""/g | \
          sed s/":1$"/" is Online"/g |sed s/":0$"/" is Offline"/g
  done
}

function online()
{
  if [ ! -f /sys/devices/system/node/node*/cpu${1}/online ]; then
    echo "CPU$1 does not have online/offline functionality"
  else
    grep -q 1 /sys/devices/system/node/node*/cpu${1}/online
    if [ "$?" -eq "0" ]; then
      echo "CPU$cpu is already Online"
    else
      echo -en "`showcpus $cpu` - "
      echo -en "Onlining CPU$cpu ... "
      echo 1 > /sys/devices/system/node/node*/cpu${1}/online 2> /dev/null
      if [ "$?" -eq "0" ]; then
        echo "OK"
      else
        echo "Failed to online CPU$1"
      fi
    fi
  fi
}

function offline()
{
  if [ ! -f /sys/devices/system/node/node*/cpu${1}/online ]; then
    echo "CPU$1 does not have online/offline functionality"
  else
    grep -q 0 /sys/devices/system/node/node*/cpu${1}/online
    if [ "$?" -eq "0" ]; then
```

```
            echo "CPU$cpu is already Offline"
        else
            echo -en "`showcpus $cpu` - "
            echo -en "Offlining CPU$cpu ... "
            echo 0 > /sys/devices/system/node/node*/cpu${1}/online 2> /dev/null
            if [ "$?" -eq "0" ]; then
                echo "OK"
            else
                echo "Failed to offline CPU$1"
            fi
        fi
    fi
}

case $1 in
    show) showcpus $2
        ;;
    on)
        shift           # Lose the keyword
        for cpu in $*
        do
            online $cpu
        done
        ;;
    off)
        shift           # Lose the keyword
        for cpu in $*
        do
            offline $cpu
        done
        ;;
    *) echo "Usage: "
        echo "  `basename $0` show [ cpu# ] - shows all CPUs shared by that node"
        echo "  `basename $0` on cpu# ( cpu# cpu# cpu# ... )"
        echo "  `basename $0` off cpu# ( cpu# cpu# cpu# ... )"
        ;;
esac
```

cpu.sh

The main body of the script is a `case` statement that reads the first word passed to the script (of which `on`, `off`, and `show` are valid keywords) and calls the relevant function as required. For `show`, an optional parameter of CPU id restricts the output to a single CPU. If not provided, the `cpu=${1:-'*'}` at the start of the `showcpus` function sets the value of this parameter to an asterisk. This is later taken as a wildcard to match all CPUs in the system.

NUMA *stands for Non-Uniform Memory Architecture; it can mean large clusters of machines such as the Beowulf cluster.* NUMA *can also refer to multiple multi-core CPUs, where one part of the system RAM is tied to one CPU, and another part of the memory address space is tied to another.*

For the on and off keywords, a shift gets the keyword itself off the argument list, leaving only a list of CPU numbers. These are passed in turn to the relevant function, online or offline as appropriate, which echoes either a 0 (offline) or a 1 (online) to /sys/devices/system/node/ node*/cpu${1}/online. Because each CPU has a unique ID regardless of which NUMA node it is under, the * saves the script from working out which node to use; there is only one node*/cpu2 for example. Before doing that, these functions make two sanity checks. The first of these is to see if the online file exists for this CPU. On x86 systems, it is not possible to offline the first CPU; it does not have an online file. In that case, the message "CPU$i does not have online/offline functionality" is displayed and the rest of the function is not executed. The second test is to see if the CPU is already in the requested state; if it is, the cryptic message "write error: Invalid argument" is displayed, so it is best for the script to hide that, and instead display the more useful message "CPU$cpu is already Online" (or Offline, as appropriate). After the echo statement, the return code is tested to see if it was successful, and the script reports back to the user if an error was detected.

> *In such a short function, the nested if statements are acceptable; in a longer function, the first error test, which checks that the "online" file exists, could instead explicitly return from the function, leaving the rest of the function slightly less indented, as well as making it perfectly clear to a casual reader that the function does indeed do no more work if the "online" file does not exist.*

In these sample runs, the cpuinfo.sh script from earlier in this section is also used to help identify the CPUs available on each system. First, on a laptop, cpu.sh does not produce much of interest; CPU0 cannot be switched off, so only CPU1 can be switched on and off.

```
laptop# ./cpu.sh
node0/cpu0 is always Online.
Usage:
  cpu.sh show [ cpu# ] - shows all CPUs shared by that node
  cpu.sh on cpu# ( cpu# cpu# cpu# ... )
  cpu.sh off cpu# ( cpu# cpu# cpu# ... )
laptop# ./cpuinfo.sh
laptop has 1 physical CPUs (Pentium(R) Dual-Core CPU T4400  @ 2.20GHz) each w
ith 2 cores.
Each core has 2 threads: total 4 threads
laptop# ./cpu.sh show
node0/cpu0 is always Online.
node0/cpu1 is Online
laptop# ./cpu.sh off 1
node0/cpu0 is always Online.
node0/cpu1 is Online - Offlining CPU1 ... OK
laptop# ./cpu.sh show
node0/cpu0 is always Online.
node0/cpu1 is Offline
laptop# ./cpu.sh on 1
node0/cpu0 is always Online.
node0/cpu1 is Offline - Onlining CPU1 ... OK
laptop# ./cpu.sh show
node0/cpu0 is always Online.
```

```
node0/cpu1 is Online
laptop# ./cpu.sh off 0
node0/cpu0 is always Online.
CPU0 does not have online/offline functionality
laptop# ./cpu.sh show
node0/cpu0 is always Online.
node0/cpu1 is Online
laptop#
```

On a larger system, with eight cores, the script is more interesting. Individual processing cores can be enabled and disabled as required. Every core is still part of the same NUMA node, which essentially means that this is a totally non-NUMA architecture.

```
minnow# ./cpuinfo.sh
minnow has 2 physical CPUs (Intel(R) Xeon(R) CPU L5420  @ 2.50GHz) each with 4 core
s. Each core has 2 threads: total 16 threads
minnow# ./cpu.sh show
node0/cpu0 is always Online.
node0/cpu1 is Online
node0/cpu2 is Online
node0/cpu3 is Online
node0/cpu4 is Online
node0/cpu5 is Online
node0/cpu6 is Online
node0/cpu7 is Online
minnow# ./cpu.sh off 2 5 7
node0/cpu0 is always Online.
Offlining CPU2 ... OK
Offlining CPU5 ... OK
Offlining CPU7 ... OK
minnow# ./cpu.sh show
node0/cpu0 is always Online.
node0/cpu1 is Online
node0/cpu2 is Offline
node0/cpu3 is Online
node0/cpu4 is Online
node0/cpu5 is Offline
node0/cpu6 is Online
node0/cpu7 is Offline
minnow#
```

In case you do not always have immediate access to such a machine, the output from this SunFire X4640 with 128GB RAM and 8 CPUs totaling 48 cores could be useful for reference.

```
whopper# ./cpuinfo.sh
whopper has 8 physical CPUs (Six-Core AMD Opteron(tm) Processor 8435) each with 6 c
ores. Each core has 2 threads: total 96 threads
whopper# ./cpu.sh show
node0/cpu0 is always Online.
node0/cpu1 is Online
node0/cpu2 is Online
node0/cpu3 is Online
node0/cpu4 is Online
node0/cpu5 is Online
```

```
node1/cpu10 is Online
node1/cpu11 is Online
node1/cpu6 is Online
node1/cpu7 is Online
node1/cpu8 is Online
node1/cpu9 is Online
node2/cpu12 is Online
node2/cpu13 is Online
node2/cpu14 is Online
node2/cpu15 is Online
node2/cpu16 is Online
node2/cpu17 is Online
node3/cpu18 is Online
node3/cpu19 is Online
node3/cpu20 is Online
node3/cpu21 is Online
node3/cpu22 is Online
node3/cpu23 is Online
node4/cpu24 is Online
node4/cpu25 is Online
node4/cpu26 is Online
node4/cpu27 is Online
node4/cpu28 is Online
node4/cpu29 is Online
node5/cpu30 is Online
node5/cpu31 is Online
node5/cpu32 is Online
node5/cpu33 is Online
node5/cpu34 is Online
node5/cpu35 is Online
node6/cpu36 is Online
node6/cpu37 is Online
node6/cpu38 is Online
node6/cpu39 is Online
node6/cpu40 is Online
node6/cpu41 is Online
node7/cpu42 is Online
node7/cpu43 is Online
node7/cpu44 is Online
node7/cpu45 is Online
node7/cpu46 is Online
node7/cpu47 is Online
whopper# ./cpu.sh off 0 3 7 9 12 24 31 42 45
node0/cpu0 is always Online.
CPU0 does not have online/offline functionality
Offlining CPU3 ... OK
Offlining CPU7 ... OK
Offlining CPU9 ... OK
Offlining CPU12 ... OK
Offlining CPU24 ... OK
Offlining CPU31 ... OK
Offlining CPU42 ... OK
Offlining CPU45 ... OK
whopper# ./cpu.sh show
```

```
node0/cpu0 is always Online.
node0/cpu1 is Online
node0/cpu2 is Online
node0/cpu3 is Offline
node0/cpu4 is Online
node0/cpu5 is Online
node1/cpu10 is Online
node1/cpu11 is Online
node1/cpu6 is Online
node1/cpu7 is Offline
node1/cpu8 is Online
node1/cpu9 is Offline
node2/cpu12 is Offline
node2/cpu13 is Online
node2/cpu14 is Online
node2/cpu15 is Online
node2/cpu16 is Online
node2/cpu17 is Online
node3/cpu18 is Online
node3/cpu19 is Online
node3/cpu20 is Online
node3/cpu21 is Online
node3/cpu22 is Online
node3/cpu23 is Online
node4/cpu24 is Offline
node4/cpu25 is Online
node4/cpu26 is Online
node4/cpu27 is Online
node4/cpu28 is Online
node4/cpu29 is Online
node5/cpu30 is Online
node5/cpu31 is Offline
node5/cpu32 is Online
node5/cpu33 is Online
node5/cpu34 is Online
node5/cpu35 is Online
node6/cpu36 is Online
node6/cpu37 is Online
node6/cpu38 is Online
node6/cpu39 is Online
node6/cpu40 is Online
node6/cpu41 is Online
node7/cpu42 is Offline
node7/cpu43 is Online
node7/cpu44 is Online
node7/cpu45 is Offline
node7/cpu46 is Online
node7/cpu47 is Online
```

/sys/devices/system/node

The mem.sh script inspects the memory available to each CPU node. In a true NUMA system, if all of a node's CPUs were offline, the memory associated with that node would not be available. The way that Linux works on x86_64 architecture, the memory is still available, although the CPU is marked as being offline for processing duties.

```
$ cat mem.sh
#!/bin/bash

kb=`head -1 /proc/meminfo | awk '{ print $2 }'`
mb=`echo "scale=2; $kb / 1024"| bc`
gb=`echo "scale=2; $mb / 1024"| bc`
echo "Server has $gb Gb ($kb Kb)"

cd /sys/devices/system/node
grep MemTotal node/meminfo | while read name node memtotal kb kB
do
  mb=`echo "scale=2; $kb / 1024"| bc`
  gb=`echo "scale=2; $mb / 1024"| bc`
  echo "Node $node has $gb Gb. "\
  "`grep -w 1 /sys/devices/system/node/node${node}/cpu[0-9]*/online \
  | wc -l` CPUs online"
done
```

mem.sh

This script starts by displaying the total RAM available to the OS. This will be slightly lower than the total RAM actually installed as some is mapped at boot time by PCI cards and other system devices. Then it reads the `MemTotal` line from `/sys/devices/system/node/node*/meminfo`, and for each entry returned, which says something along the lines of `meminfo:Node 0 MemTotal: 3074028 kB`, it reads the variables `name node memtotal kb kB`. Not all of these are needed by the script; in fact, only `name` and `kb` are used, but the other variables help to parse the output without resorting to `awk`.

Finally, the script `greps` the number of "1"s in the `online` file for each of the CPUs associated with that node. This gives it the number of online CPUs for that node. This actually misses the fact that CPU0 does not have an `online` file. There are a number of workarounds for that, but the purpose of this script is to show how `/sys` works, and not to clutter up the script with too much error-checking.

```
whopper# ./mem.sh
Server has 125.91 Gb (132035676 Kb)
Node 0 has 15.76 Gb. 4 CPUs online
Node 1 has 15.78 Gb. 4 CPUs online
Node 2 has 15.78 Gb. 5 CPUs online
Node 3 has 15.78 Gb. 6 CPUs online
Node 4 has 15.78 Gb. 5 CPUs online
Node 5 has 15.78 Gb. 5 CPUs online
Node 6 has 15.78 Gb. 6 CPUs online
Node 7 has 15.78 Gb. 4 CPUs online
whopper# ./cpu.sh on `seq 0 50`
node0/cpu0 is always Online.
CPU0 does not have online/offline functionality
CPU1 is already Online
CPU2 is already Online
Onlining CPU3 ... OK
CPU4 is already Online
CPU5 is already Online
```

```
CPU6 is already Online
Onlining CPU7 ... OK
CPU8 is already Online
Onlining CPU9 ... OK
CPU10 is already Online
CPU11 is already Online
Onlining CPU12 ... OK
CPU13 is already Online
CPU14 is already Online
CPU15 is already Online
CPU16 is already Online
CPU17 is already Online
CPU18 is already Online
CPU19 is already Online
CPU20 is already Online
CPU21 is already Online
CPU22 is already Online
CPU23 is already Online
Onlining CPU24 ... OK
CPU25 is already Online
CPU26 is already Online
CPU27 is already Online
CPU28 is already Online
CPU29 is already Online
CPU30 is already Online
Onlining CPU31 ... OK
CPU32 is already Online
CPU33 is already Online
CPU34 is already Online
CPU35 is already Online
CPU36 is already Online
CPU37 is already Online
CPU38 is already Online
CPU39 is already Online
CPU40 is already Online
CPU41 is already Online
Onlining CPU42 ... OK
CPU43 is already Online
CPU44 is already Online
Onlining CPU45 ... OK
CPU46 is already Online
CPU47 is already Online
CPU48 does not have online/offline functionality
CPU49 does not have online/offline functionality
CPU50 does not have online/offline functionality
whopper#
```

Sysctl

The `sysctl` command controls most of these parameters; although echoing the appropriate value to /proc reconfigures a Linux system on the fly, and a reboot would bring in the changes in /etc /sysctl.conf, sysctl -p will dynamically reread all of /etc/sysctl.conf, too. This provides a major win over older Unices, which still require a reboot for kernel changes.

SUMMARY

The kernel manages all manner of detail about the running system; processes are one part of that and the process table has been exposed in the /proc pseudo-filesystem for a long time. The Linux kernel also exposes a lot of other kernel state into /proc. This makes for a more flexible system; hugepages, shared memory, and many other parameters can be configured on the fly without requiring a reboot.

Process control includes managing the file descriptors of a process, which can be redirected in a variety of ways to achieve different things. Input and output can be piped and redirected to and from other files and processes.

After this rather in-depth chapter, Chapter 11 finishes off Part I by looking at some of the different shells available, what they have in common, what features each offers, and also how they differ from one another.

11

Choosing and Using Shells

She sells seashells on the seashore
The shells she sells are seashells, I'm sure
So if she sells seashells on the seashore
Then I'm sure she sells seashore shells.

—Terry Sullivan, 1908

On traditional Unix systems, the standard shell (/bin/sh) for all users and for system scripts is the Bourne shell. On most GNU/Linux distributions, bash has always been the default shell. More recently, some GNU/Linux systems use dash as the system shell (/bin/sh) but retain bash for interactive shells, normally as /usr/bin/bash. There are many different shells, each written for a particular purpose and with its own history, which leads to each having a slightly different syntax and feature set.

This chapter looks at the shells available, where they came from, and what they do. This book focuses mainly on bash, with reference to the Bourne shell, but it is important to know about the other popular shells too. This chapter also hopes to give some of the flavor of the different environments in which a shell script might find itself running, and how that environment could affect the operation of the script.

There is no real need to use the same shell for interactive use as for shell scripting. The main benefit to using the same shell for both is that you can easily test your syntax or try out an idea interactively to see how to make it work before writing it in a script. On the other hand, it may be more beneficial to use an interactive shell that has the features you like to use for filesystem navigation, history recall, and so on, and you can always invoke another shell on the command line simply by typing its name.

THE BOURNE SHELL

When Unix was first born, it had a very basic shell written by Ken Thompson, one of the creators of Unix. The Bourne shell was written by Steve Bourne in 1979 as a scriptable Unix shell. All other shells have a prefix to qualify which shell they are — ksh, csh, zsh, and so on — but the Bourne shell does not call itself bsh because it simply is "the shell," so its canonical path is /bin/sh. Other shells came along later with more features, while staying generally compatible with the Bourne shell — some more compatible than others.

One of the most significant new concepts that the Bourne shell provided was the pipeline, the structure that allows one process to pass its output to the input of another process. This was a dramatic change in the capability of a shell command. Bourne also introduced variables and flow control, turning the shell from being a very basic command interpreter into a flexible scripting language.

THE KORNSHELL

The Kornshell (ksh) was written by David Korn in 1983. It is a very popular shell for scripting as well as interactive use, particularly on proprietary Unices. Like bash and dash, it is backward-compatible with the Bourne shell but adds new features and syntax. Ksh introduced cursor-key navigation of the shell history, as well as providing arrays and floating-point math. For a long time, ksh was proprietary Unix software of AT&T, so pdksh (now mksh, http://mirbsd.de/mksh) is a Free Software equivalent to ksh93. After ksh93 was released under IBM's Common Public License in 2005, most GNU/Linux distributions included ksh93 instead of pdksh or mksh, as did OpenSolaris. As a result, whenever you find ksh on a recent system, it is likely to be the genuine ksh93 and not a clone.

The common ground between ksh and Bourne functionality was used to define the POSIX standard for /bin/sh, so ksh is a significant shell scripting language. In traditional Unix systems, it is quite acceptable for the root user's shell to be set to /bin/ksh. It is the default shell on IBM's AIX Unix. /etc/init.d scripts will still be run under the Bourne shell, but the interactive root shell can be ksh (often with the -o vi option to provide vi-like history recall).

Microsoft's Services For Unix (SFU — now discontinued) provided an almost-compatible ksh shell for the Windows environment, although it was based on mksh, which at the time was not quite compatible with the original ksh. At http://lists.blu.org/pipermail/discuss/1998-August/002393.html, you can read the story of how David Korn queried a Microsoft product manager about his choice of Kornshell implementation during a presentation about SFU. Korn criticized the choice of implementation because it was incompatible with genuine ksh, and asked whether Microsoft had considered any of the more compatible ksh variants. Only after the poor Microsoft representative had tried to claim that their implementation of the Kornshell was fully compatible with the Kornshell was it eventually pointed out to him that the person asking the awkward questions about Kornshell compatibility was David Korn himself.

THE C SHELL

The C shell (csh) was written in the 1970s by Bill Joy, one of the founders of Sun Microsystems and also a very prolific BSD Unix hacker. One of the main attractions of csh was that its syntax looked a lot more like the C language, which many systems programmers are very familiar with. It was also a better interactive shell than the Bourne shell, providing the `history` command for the first time. It also added job control and the concept of using the tilde (~) to represent the current user's home directory. All of these features (but not the C-style syntax) have been taken on by all of the other shells listed here.

In 1996, Tom Christiansen wrote a widely distributed article entitled "Csh Programming Considered Harmful" (`http://www.faqs.org/faqs/unix-faq/shell/csh-whynot/`), which pointed out some of the ways in which csh syntax can be counterintuitive or limiting to the systems programmer. The issues that Christiansen raises are particularly focused around the areas of redirection and process control.

THE TENEX C SHELL

Tcsh is the Tenex Csh, and offers many improvements to the standard csh, while remaining totally compatible with csh. Its improvements over csh include better history control; `pushd` and `popd` for stacking directory positions; terminal locking; and `which`, `where`, and also read-only variables. It also provides spelling correction; an interactive tcsh will prompt the user with suggested options if it suspects that a typing error has been made.

In addition to automatic completion of commands and filenames, tcsh also adds automatic completion of variable names. It can be configured to do this in either case-sensitive or case-insensitive mode.

THE Z SHELL

The Z shell (zsh) was written by Paul Falstad in 1990. It was intended to be a ksh-like shell but also included some csh-like features because csh was a very popular interactive shell in the 1970s and 1980s. It is particularly good as an interactive shell. It does not claim full POSIX or Bourne compatibility, which allows it greater flexibility to add new features, although it does aim to be ksh compatible. It can change its behavior with the `emulate` command, or if called as `/bin/sh` or `/bin/ksh`, to act more like those shells.

Zsh is a lot like bash for interactive use, with similar, although in some ways more featureful, history recall and command completion. The `compctl` command can be used to customize just how the completion works. Globbing syntax is slightly different from ksh and Bourne shell, and arrays are indexed from 1, not 0.

THE BOURNE AGAIN SHELL

Bash is the standard interactive shell on most GNU/Linux and Mac OSX systems, and is becoming popular with traditional Unix users, too. It is also the default shell for the Cygwin environment, which provides GNU tools under Microsoft Windows. It is compatible with the Bourne shell, but adds a number of extra features, most of which are covered in this book. The name of the bash shell (the "Bourne Again shell") is a play on the name of the author of the Bourne shell.

Bash was initially written by Brian Fox in 1988 for the Free Software Foundation (FSF) and is currently maintained by Chet Ramey. It takes some ideas from various shells including csh and ksh. Most noticeably, bash uses [[...]], $(...), and ((...)) syntaxes from ksh.

Bash, if called as sh, acts more like the Bourne shell in the configuration files it reads. This is documented in more detail later in this chapter.

THE DEBIAN ALMQUIST SHELL

Dash started life in 1989 as the Almquist Shell (ash), written by Kenneth Almquist. It was ported for the Debian project in 1999 by Herbert Xu as the Debian Almquist Shell (dash). Like bash, it aims for POSIX compliance, but unlike bash, it tries nothing more; it aims only to be a POSIX-compliant shell. This makes it smaller, lighter, and faster than bash. It therefore replaces bash as the default /bin/sh in many GNU/Linux distributions, which generally retain bash for interactive use, using dash for system scripts, particularly startup scripts.

The longstanding availability of bash as /bin/sh on GNU/Linux caused some problems when migrating to dash, as a lot of system scripts called /bin/sh as their interpreter but expected to be able to use features of bash. The site https://bugs.launchpad.net/ubuntu/+source/dash/+bug/61463 provides a list of many of the problems experienced when Ubuntu 6.10 moved from bash to dash as the default /bin/sh in 2006.

DOTFILES

The operating system in its standard format provides various settings chosen by the distributor and by the projects responsible for the individual shells themselves. These can then be customized by the systems administrator by editing configuration files in the /etc directory. The main configuration file, which all Bourne-compatible shells honor, is /etc/profile. This provides some basic, sane settings for interactive shells; it typically sets the command prompt to $ or # depending on whether or not it is running as root; sets the umask; and sets PATH, TERM, and other useful variables. It may also do other useful things such as display the /etc/motd (Message of the Day) file, notify the user if she has new mail messages, and even display a "fortune cookie" message to amuse the user as she logs in. It can also call other scripts, often to be found in the /etc/profile.d/ directory. These can be used to customize specific features, applications, and tools in a way that allows the package manager to add or remove those tweaks along with the application, without having to edit the /etc/profile script itself.

 All of these configuration files are sourced and not simply executed. This means that any variables or functions defined by these files are inherited by the running shell.

Because individual users will want to customize their own shells in their own way, each user gets a set of files, which, unlike the global /etc files, they can edit in their own way. For system stability, the /etc files are parsed first, followed by the user's own files. Each shell tends to have its own set of filenames to read so, for example, bash-specific commands can be put into ~/.bashrc, which will not cause an error if the user chooses to run the ksh at some point because ksh will read ~/.kshrc instead. All Bourne-compatible shells refer to /etc/profile and ~/.profile regardless of their own conventions. Similarly, tcsh, which is based on csh, will read csh's /etc/.login and ~/.cshrc as appropriate for compatibility with csh.

Files whose names begin with a period are not shown up by a regular ls command. This provides no security whatever — ls -a displays them readily — but it helps to keep configuration files and data files separate. Home directories can often end up quite messy, so it can be useful for the user's own customization files to be hidden from display by default. All of these configuration files (even those in /etc, most of which are not hidden) are often commonly referred to overall as "the profile" or "the environment" but also simply as "dotfiles."

This provides great customization and flexibility, but the resulting mass of files — /etc/profile, /etc/login, /etc/bash.bashrc, /etc/csh.cshrc, /etc/ksh.kshrc, /etc/profile.d/*, ~/.profile, ~/.bashrc, ~/.kshrc, ~/.login, ~/.cshrc, ~/.tcshrc, and so on — causes a lot of confusion for many shell users and systems administrators. The tongue-twister "She sells sea-shells on the sea shore" is positively easy to deal with when compared with all of these different combinations. Which files are read when, and what should go into each one? The three different classes of shell invocation are interactive login shells, interactive non-login shells, and non-interactive shells. Each has its own definition, and each shell reads different files in each of these three situations. The sections that follow cover all of these combinations, organized by class and shell in the text that follows.

 Because dash acts the same as the Bourne shell (sh) for all of these, it is omitted from these tables.

Interactive Login Shells

A login shell is one that is executed as a result of a system login event; it is by nature interactive. Login shells are spawned for su - (but not su alone; that is just treated as an interactive shell, not a login shell) and for ssh sessions as well as for console and serial terminal login sessions. For interactive login shells, it is useful for the profile scripts to do things such as eval `ssh-agent`, which holds your private ssh keys for all commands in that login session (although in a graphical environment, the windowing system itself is likely to be configured as a client of ssh-agent itself), define aliases, and so on.

It can also be useful, when you have only non-root access to a system which provides you with a shell you do not want to use as your interactive shell, to use the suitable dotfile to replace the provided shell with the one of your choice. To ensure that your Bourne shell is replaced with a bash shell, this snippet at the very end of ~/.profile ensures that you get bash wherever it can be found.

```
if [ -x /usr/bin/bash ]; then
  echo "Replacing $SHELL with bash"
  exec /usr/bin/bash
fi
```

In Debian GNU/Linux systems, /etc/profile *is configured to call* /etc/bash.bashrc *and the default* ~/.profile *is configured to call* ~/.bashrc *so that the interactive login shell also picks up all of the files of the interactive non-login shell.*

Table 11-1 shows how each shell configures an interactive login shell.

TABLE 11-1: Interactive Login Shell Configuration Files

SHELL	CONFIGURATION FILES READ
bash	/etc/profile, then the first-found of ~/.bash_profile, ~/.bash_login, and ~/.profile.
csh	/etc/csh.cshrc, followed by /etc/csh.login, /etc/.login, /etc/login.std, or /etc/cshrc, depending on the operating system. After that, ~/.cshrc and ~/.login.
sh	/etc/profile then ~/.profile.
tcsh	As csh, but if ~/.tcshrc exists then it is used instead of ~/.cshrc.
ksh	/etc/profile, ~/.profile, /etc/ksh.kshrc, then ~/.kshrc.
zsh	/etc/zsh/zshenv, $ZDOTDIR/.zshenv, /etc/zsh/zprofile, $ZDOTDIT/.zprofile, /etc/zshrc, $ZDOTDIR/.zshrc, /etc/zsh/slogin, $ZDOTDIR/.zlogin.

Csh Compatibility

The csh combinations are actually even more complex than that; see the FILES section of the tcsh(1) man page for an exhaustive list covering how NeXT, Solaris, ConvexOS, Stellix, Intel, A/UX, Cray, and Irix all vary over csh, and how tcsh varies again on those combinations.

Zsh Compatibility

Depending on how zsh is built, /etc/zsh may actually be /etc. Solaris's zsh is built without the enable_etcdir configuration option, so /etc/zsh is just /etc on Solaris. This also occurs on other distributions' builds of zsh: Red Hat uses /etc, and Debian uses /etc/zsh. Also, if ZDOTDIR is not set, then $HOME is the default value used instead. The place to customize ZDOTDIR is /etc/zsh/zshenv, or if not set there, then in ~/.zshenv.

Interactive Non-Login Shells

A non-login shell is one that is spawned for an already-logged-in user but does not represent a new login instance. This happens when you just type "bash" into an existing interactive shell, for su (when not called as su -), and when a new terminal emulator window or tab is opened in a graphical session.

This is a good place to customize the PATH variable, set the PS1 prompt, and so on. Table 11-2 shows how each shell configures an interactive non-login shell.

TABLE 11-2: Interactive Non-Login Shell Configuration Files

SHELL	CONFIGURATION FILES READ
bash	`~/.bashrc`, or like sh if called as sh
csh	`/etc/csh.cshrc`, `~/.cshrc`
sh	`$ENV` if set, otherwise nothing
tcsh	`/etc/csh.cshrc`, then `~/.tcshrc` if found, otherwise `~/.cshrc`
ksh	`/etc/ksh.kshrc`, `~/.kshrc`
zsh	`/etc/zsh/zshenv`, `$ZDOTDIR/.zshenv`, `/etc/zshrc`, `$ZDOTDIR/.zshrc`

Here, the Bourne shell sources the file named by the environment variable $ENV if it is set. This is therefore similar to bash's `~/.bashrc` file, although slightly more flexible in that it gives the user the opportunity to source any file he chooses for a non-login shell session. If bash is called with the name sh, it will also source $ENV if it is set, for compatibility with the Bourne shell. This is useful for older scripts which assume that `/bin/sh` is Bourne and will read the $ENV file.

Non-Interactive Shells

A non-interactive shell is one that is not directly associated with a terminal. A shell script spawns a non-interactive shell session, as do tools such as cron and at. Table 11-3 shows how each shell configures a non-interactive shell. Notice that Bourne and compatible shells do not parse any system or user-level files when running non-interactive shells.

TABLE 11-3: Non-Interactive Shell Configuration Files

SHELL	CONFIGURATION FILES READ
bash	`$BASH_ENV` if set, or like sh if called as sh
csh	`/etc/csh.cshrc`, `~/.cshrc`
sh	None
tcsh	`/etc/csh.cshrc`, then `~/.tcshrc` if found, otherwise `~/.cshrc`
ksh	None
zsh	`/etc/zsh/zshenv`, `$ZDOTDIR/.zshenv`

As sh sources $ENV for an interactive non-login shell if set (and bash does the same if called as sh), bash also sources $BASH_ENV if it has been set, and if it has been called as bash. This allows bash to include additional configuration for non-interactive scripts that would not have been included for interactive scripts.

Logout Scripts

Bash, zsh, and csh also offer scripts that can be executed when an interactive shell (whether login or non-login) exits. This can be useful if the end of the session would mean that visibility of the window was lost (such as with a PuTTY session from Microsoft Windows) or if changes need to be made to terminal settings for the calling system.

For zsh, $ZDOTDIR/.zlogout and then /etc/zsh/zlogout are executed if they exist. For bash, ~/.bash_logout and /etc/bash_logout are called if they exist. For csh and tcsh, ~/.logout and then /etc/.logout, /etc/logout, /etc/csh.logout, or the appropriate equivalent are executed on exit. Again, the FILES section of the tcsh(1) man page has an excellent summary of what convention is used for the name of the global logout script by various different operating systems.

COMMAND PROMPTS

The shell has four different command prompts, called PS1, PS2, PS3, and PS4. PS stands for Prompt String. PS1 is almost always customized, the others are almost never customized.

The PS1 Prompt

PS1 was introduced in Chapter 2, "Getting Started." It is the standard prompt that you see at the start of every line. In the examples in this book, it is generally shown as the dollar symbol followed by a space ("$ "), which is the standard way to indicate an unprivileged user in the Bourne and bash shells. The root user's PS1 prompt by convention is set to, or at least ends with, "# ". PS1 may contain text, but most shells also expand various special characters in the PS1 variable. In bash, the default unprivileged prompt is \s-\v\$, which is the name (\s) and version (\v) of the shell — for example "bash-4.1$ ". Some of the most useful elements are \u (username), \h (hostname), \t (current time), and \d (date).

The full set of special characters for PS1 is described in the PROMPTING section of the bash(1) man page. One of the more interesting special characters provides allows you to set a colored prompt by entering octal character references using the standard \0xx notation. This PS1 sets a red prompt with a regular input line:

```
PS1="\033[1;31m\u@\h\w\$\033[0m "
```

The number 31 in the first \033[1;31m is the code for red; the final 0 in the \033[0m is gray, so it sets the input back to normal; only the prompt itself is red. Add 10 for a background color; so for a red background, use 41, not 31.

Tables 11-4 and 11-5 list the appropriate numbers for each color and style. Combine these as you wish to get the desired effect.

TABLE 11-4: Prompt Colors (y)

NUMBER (OCTAL)	COLOR
30	Black
31	Red
32	Green
33	Yellow
34	Blue
35	Magenta
36	Cyan
37	Gray
39	Default

TABLE 11-5: Appearance Settings (x)

NUMBER (OCTAL)	APPEARANCE
0	Dark
1	Bright
4	Underlined
5	Blinking
7	Inverse

These long strings are actually quite simple; \033[x;ym defines the color with y and the appearance with x. If x is 0, the output is dark, and 1 is bright. 4 is underlined text, 5 is blinking text (if your terminal supports it), and 7 is the opposite of the default. You can combine these options by including the full sequence. Grey text is 0;37, and on a red background it is 1;41 (red is 31 + 10), so you can combine the two with this prompt:

```
PS1="\033[0;37m\033[1;41m\u@\h:\w$ "
```

Although the shell does a good job of wrapping text properly at the end of the line, when these control characters are introduced, its calculations get messed up. As a result, you may find that it does not scroll down to the next line when you get to the far right hand side of the window, and the text wraps over itself.

The PS2, PS3, and PS4 Prompts

PS2 is the secondary prompt; this is mainly used in interactively written loops, such as for `while`. The default value is > and there is normally no reason at all to change it.

The PS3 variable is used by the `select` builtin loop. This was covered in Chapter 6. This variable only needs to be set when using the select builtin command. It can make an otherwise mundane menu system appear far more complete and appealing.

The PS4 variable is displayed when the -x option (for tracing execution of a script) is used in the shell. The default value is + and, like PS2, there is generally no need to change it. The following script shows you how the number of PS4 indentations is used to see the level of indirection; the script itself gets one +, and external commands (`expr`) get a double ++ identifier. Further commands (if -x is set again for them — this option is not inherited beyond the first child) would have a triple +++ prefix.

```
$ cat while.sh
#!/bin/bash

i=1
while [ "$i" -lt "100" ]
do
   echo "i is $i"
   i=`expr $i \* 2`
done
echo "Finished because i is now $i"
$ bash -x while.sh
+ i=1
+ '[' 1 -lt 100 ']'
+ echo 'i is 1'
i is 1
++ expr 1 '*' 2
+ i=2
+ '[' 2 -lt 100 ']'
+ echo 'i is 2'
i is 2
++ expr 2 '*' 2
+ i=4
+ '[' 4 -lt 100 ']'
+ echo 'i is 4'
i is 4
++ expr 4 '*' 2
+ i=8
+ '[' 8 -lt 100 ']'
+ echo 'i is 8'
i is 8
++ expr 8 '*' 2
+ i=16
+ '[' 16 -lt 100 ']'
+ echo 'i is 16'
i is 16
++ expr 16 '*' 2
+ i=32
+ '[' 32 -lt 100 ']'
+ echo 'i is 32'
```

```
i is 32
++ expr 32 '*' 2
+ i=64
+ '[' 64 -lt 100 ']'
+ echo 'i is 64'
i is 64
++ expr 64 '*' 2
+ i=128
+ '[' 128 -lt 100 ']'
+ echo 'Finished because i is now 128'
Finished because i is now 128
$
```

ALIASES

Aliases are peculiar to interactive shells. They are not expanded in shell scripts, which helps to ensure predictability for the script, and it means that you can confidently define aliases for interactive use, safe in the knowledge that it will not break any shell scripts. As such, aliases are an ideal way to save you keystrokes, enabling you to avoid repeatedly typing the same complicated words or command sequences, as well as enabling you to automatically tweak the behavior of popularly used commands.

Timesavers

Some timesaving aliases include shortcuts to ssh to particular hosts, edit certain files, and so on. One convenient timesaver is to set aliases for systems that you regularly log in to. With the aliases that follow, you can log in to the web server as the apache user, and log in to each of the DNS servers as the bind user, simply by typing web, dns1, or dns2.

```
$ alias web='ssh apache@web.example.com'
$ alias dns1='ssh bind@ns1.example.com'
$ alias dns2='ssh bind@ns2.example.com'
```

You can take this even further by adding more options. The following alias emulates a simple VPN, forwarding the intranet web server's port 80 to port 8080 at localhost. See the ssh documentation for more details about ssh port forwarding.

```
$ alias vpn='ssh -q -L 8080:192.168.1.1:80 steve@intranet.example.com'
$ vpn
steve@intranet.example.com's password:<enter password>
Linux intranet 2.6.26-2-amd64 #1 SMP Sun Jun 20 20:16:30 UTC 2010 x86_64
You have new mail.
Last login: Wed Mar 16 21:45:17 2011 from 78.145.17.30
steve@intranet:~$
```

Modifying Behaviors

Aliases can be useful ways to modify standard behaviors of commands. One convenient alias, particularly for newcomers to the command line, is `alias rm='rm -i'`, which forces the `rm` command to prompt before removing anything. It could be argued that this breaks the Unix model of keeping everything silent unless there is an actual error, but it is certainly useful for some users. As mentioned in Chapter 2, another convenient alias is `less -X`, which stops `less` from clearing the screen when it exits. Whatever sequences you find yourself typing regularly, just stop and think if it would make your life better if it was an alias. The `rm` alias can always be overridden via the `rm -f` format; you can also avoid alias expansion by preceding it with a backslash, as shown here:

```
$ alias echo='echo Steve Says: '
$ echo Hello World
Steve Says: Hello World
$ \echo Hello World
Hello World
$
```

Another useful alias is for `wget`; it can take a number of arguments, which can go in `~/.wgetrc` but may be more convenient as an alias. Some web servers try to customize their content depending on the browser requesting the page, so sending them a more useful User-Agent string than `Wget/1.12` (`linux-gnu`) may get better results. "Mozilla/5.0" is a useful string to pass; most standard web browsers mention Mozilla within their User-Agent strings.

```
$ alias download='wget -U"Mozilla/5.0" -nc '
$ download http://www.example.com/
--2011-03-16 21:52:06--  http://www.example.com/
Resolving www.example.com... 192.0.32.10, 2620:0:2d0:200::10
Connecting to www.example.com|192.0.32.10|:80... connected.
HTTP request sent, awaiting response... 302 Found
Location: http://www.iana.org/domains/example/ [following]
--2011-03-16 21:52:07--  http://www.iana.org/domains/example/
Resolving www.iana.org... 192.0.32.8, 2620:0:2d0:200::8
Connecting to www.iana.org|192.0.32.8|:80... connected.
HTTP request sent, awaiting response... 200 OK
Length: 2945 (2.9K) [text/html]
Saving to: `index.html'

100%[=====================================>] 2,945        --.-K/s   in 0s

2011-03-16 21:52:07 (83.8 MB/s) - `index.html' saved [2945/2945]

$ ls -l index.html
-rw-r--r-- 1 steve steve 2945 2011-02-09 17:13 index.html
$
```

 Some websites share all of their content with the Google search engine to get in the rankings, but when you try to access the site, they require you to register and log in. You can play them at their own game by setting your User-Agent string to `Googlebot/2.1 (+http://www.google.com/bot.html)`*.*

HISTORY

The `history` command lists what commands have been run before, either in the current shell session or in others (by the same user). It generally stores this information in the `.<shellname>_history` file in the user's home directory. This can be useful for auditing and for checking on what commands have been run, but it is not a security feature; the file is plain text and can easily be edited by anybody with permission to access the file.

Recalling Commands

You can recall commands in a number of ways; the standard, most basic way is to run the `history` command. That displays the commands stored in the current history buffer, with a number to the left of each one:

```
$ history | tail -7
  557  pwd
  558  cd
  559  cd bin
  560  ls
  561  cat dos2unix
  562  id
  563  history
$
```

These can be recalled with the bang, or pling, or exclamation mark (!) symbol, so typing !562 executes the `id` program again. Alternatively, `!-n` recalls the last-but-n command, so from this starting point, `!-1` (or its shortcut, `!!`) would call `history` again, `!-2` would call `id`, and `!-3` would call `cat dos2unix`.

Searching History

There are three main ways to interactively search through the history buffer. The first is with the arrow keys; press the up arrow to scroll backwards and the down arrow to scroll forwards. When you get to a command you want to execute again, either press Enter to execute it exactly as before, or press the left or right arrows to start editing the command before re-executing it.

Alternatively, if you know exactly how the command started, you can recall it by typing ! followed by the start of the command. To append extra text to the end of the command line, type that after the command you want to call. This works for commands only, not their arguments.

```
$ echo Hello World
Hello World
$ echo Goodbye          !E RECALLS THE LAST COMMAND THAT
Goodbye                 STARTED WITH AN "E"
$ !e   ◄
echo Goodbye            !ECHO RECALLS THE LAST ECHO
Goodbye                 COMMAND
$ !echo   ◄
echo Goodbye            !ECHO H DOES NOT RECALL THE ECHO HELLO
Goodbye                 WORLD COMMAND, IT SIMPLY APPENDS H TO
                        THE LAST ECHO
$ !echo H   ◄
echo Goodbye H
Goodbye H
$
```

The third way to search through history, which searches across the entire command line, is to press Control and then "r" (^R) and then type in the part of the command line you want to search for. This searches backwards through the history and finds the most recent line that contains the text you typed. From there, keep on pressing ^R again to get the next most recent matching line. As with the arrow-key browsing, you can press the left or right arrow to start editing a selected line before executing it.

Timestamps

If the HISTTIMEFORMAT variable is set, bash will save a timestamp in the history file along with the command line itself. Then, when you run history, it will include the time, in the format specified by the HISTTIMEFORMAT variable. The values for this variable are defined in the strftime(3) man page; %c uses the current locale's preferred format, %D is shorthand for %m/%d/%y (month/day/year), %F is %Y-%m-%d, and %T is %H:%M:%S (hours:minutes:seconds). There are many more (see the strftime(3) man page for the full list), but these are the most commonly used ones for HISTTIMEFORMAT.

If HISTTIMEFORMAT is not set, then no timestamps will be saved. Because this cannot be retrofitted, when HISTTIMEFORMAT has not been previously saved, it looks as if every earlier command was run at the same time as the last command before HISTTIMEFORMAT was set. In this example, HISTTIMEFORMAT has never been set for root, so when it is set at 21:19:19, all earlier events are timestamped at the time that the current shell started (21:19:08), although they were actually all executed earlier than that.

```
# history
    1  cd /boot/grub
    2  vi menu.lst
    3  cat menu.lst
    4  date
    5  ls
    6  cat /etc/hosts
    7  ssh steve@node4
    8  vi /boot/grub/menu.lst
    9  /sbin/reboot
   10  PS1="# "
   11  history
# date
Thu Mar 17 21:19:19 GMT 2011
# HISTTIMEFORMAT="%T %F "
# history
    1  21:19:08 2011-03-17 cd /boot/grub
    2  21:19:08 2011-03-17 vi menu.lst
    3  21:19:08 2011-03-17 cat menu.lst
    4  21:19:08 2011-03-17 date
    5  21:19:08 2011-03-17 ls
    6  21:19:08 2011-03-17 cat /etc/hosts
    7  21:19:08 2011-03-17 ssh steve@node4
    8  21:19:08 2011-03-17 vi /boot/grub/menu.lst
    9  21:19:08 2011-03-17 /sbin/reboot
   10  21:19:13 2011-03-17 PS1="# "
   11  21:19:14 2011-03-17 history
   12  21:19:19 2011-03-17 date
   13  21:19:30 2011-03-17 HISTTIMEFORMAT="%T %F "
   14  21:19:31 2011-03-17 history
#
```

The current shell's history is buffered until the shell exits, so you can't see the file being updated in real time. By logging out and then back in again, the history file shows some timestamped entries (starting with a hash and a number) and older, unstamped entries.

```
# cat .bash_history
cd /boot/grub
vi menu.1st
cat menu.1st
date
ls
cat /etc/hosts
ssh steve@node4
vi /boot/grub/menu.1st
/sbin/reboot
#1300396753          ←——————  THE TIMESTAMPS START HERE
PS1="# "
#1300396754
history
#1300396759
date
#1300396770
HISTTIMEFORMAT="%T %F "
#1300396771
history
#1300396789
cat ~/.bash_history
#
```

TAB COMPLETION

All of the modern shells have command and filename completion via the <TAB> key. Bourne shell and csh do not, but ksh, bash, tcsh, and zsh all have tab completion to varying degrees. The basic principle in all of these shells is the same; you type the start of the word, hit the <TAB> key twice, and the list of possible commands or files is displayed. The actual details differ in implementation, so a brief overview of how to get things done in each of these shells follows.

ksh

Typing ca and then hitting <TAB> twice results in a list rather like that produced by the select command. Each item is numbered so you simply enter the number that relates to your choice followed by another <TAB>. For example, ca could be the start of cancel, callgrind_annotate, or any of these other possibilities.

```
ksh$ ca<TAB><TAB>
 1) /usr/bin/cancel
 2) /usr/bin/callgrind_annotate
 3) /usr/bin/cameratopam
 4) /usr/bin/callgrind_control
 5) /usr/bin/cancel.cups
 6) /usr/bin/cal
 7) /usr/bin/captoinfo
 8) /usr/bin/catchsegv
```

```
 9) /usr/bin/card
10) /usr/sbin/cacertdir_rehash
11) /usr/sbin/callback
12) /bin/cat
6<TAB>
ksh$ /usr/bin/cal
      March 2011
Su Mo Tu We Th Fr Sa
       1  2  3  4  5
 6  7  8  9 10 11 12
13 14 15 16 17 18 19
20 21 22 23 24 25 26
27 28 29 30 31
$
```

Filename completion works in exactly the same way:

```
ksh$ cat /etc/host<TAB><TAB>
1) host.conf
2) hosts
3) hosts.allow
4) hosts.deny
4<TAB>
ksh$ cat /etc/hosts.deny
```

tcsh

tcsh acts in much the same way, but the options are displayed in a more efficient columnar format. Also, there is no need to press <TAB> twice; a single press of the <TAB> key is enough for tcsh. Filename completion is exactly the same as command completion.

```
goldie:~> ca<TAB>
cabextract          callgrind_annotate captoinfo         case.sh
cal                 callgrind_control  case              cat
calendar            canberra-gtk-play  case1a.sh         catchsegv
calibrate_ppa       cancel             case2.sh          catman
goldie:~> cal
      March 2011
Su Mo Tu We Th Fr Sa
       1  2  3  4  5
 6  7  8  9 10 11 12
13 14 15 16 17 18 19
20 21 22 23 24 25 26
27 28 29 30 31

goldie:~>
```

zsh

The display from zsh looks very similar to that of tcsh; when you press <TAB> once, the options are listed in columns under the cursor, but broken down into categories: external commands, reserved words, shell builtins, and so on. Each time you press <TAB>, the current command line cycles through the different commands in turn, so you can just press Enter to select the currently displayed option. When you do choose the command you want, the list of options is hidden, so the display is much cleaner.

```
steve@goldie> ca<TAB>                                               ~
Completing external command
cabextract            calibrate_ppa      canberra-gtk-play   cat
cal                   callgrind_annotate cancel              catchsegv
calendar              callgrind_control  captoinfo           catman
Completing reserved word
Case
steve@goldie> cal                                                  ~
      March 2011
Su Mo Tu We Th Fr Sa
       1  2  3  4  5
 6  7  8  9 10 11 12
13 14 15 16 17 18 19
20 21 22 23 24 25 26
27 28 29 30 31

steve@goldie>
```

bash

bash tab completion works in much the same way as the others. Consider the `cal` command again: Typing `ca<TAB><TAB>` looks just like the tcsh example earlier, although for bash, two <TAB>s are required. Filename completion works in just the same way; typing `cat /etc/ho<TAB>` expands to `/etc/host`, and then a double <TAB> lists all the options available. Keep typing to reduce the options.

```
$ ca<TAB><TAB>
cabextract        calibrate_ppa   captoinfo       catchsegv
cal               caller          case            catman
calendar          cancel          cat
$ cal
      March 2011
Su Mo Tu We Th Fr Sa
       1  2  3  4  5
 6  7  8  9 10 11 12
13 14 15 16 17 18 19
20 21 22 23 24 25 26
27 28 29 30 31

$ cat /etc/ho<TAB>st<TAB>
host.conf     hostname      hosts          hosts.allow  hosts.deny
$ cat /etc/hosts
```

bash completion is also programmable, through the `bash_completion` package. Both `/etc/bash_completion` and `/etc/bash_completion.d/` already contain scripts for all manner of commands. For example, ssh options are known to `bash_completion`, and it can expand them automatically. The snippet below shows some ssh options being automatically completed by the bash shell. This is far more impressive than mere filename completion, and it works specifically because the command is ssh; for gzip it offers options suitable for gzip, and so on.

```
$ ssh -o F<TAB>orward<TAB>
ForwardAgent=       ForwardX11=         ForwardX11Trusted=
$ ssh -o ForwardX<TAB>11<TAB><TAB>
ForwardX11=         ForwardX11Trusted=
$ ssh -o ForwardX11=no user@example.com
```

FOREGROUND, BACKGROUND, AND JOB CONTROL

Running interactive commands is useful, but to take advantage of the multitasking features of the OS, either a new terminal session is required for each command to be run, or some processes will have to execute without tying up the current terminal. This is achieved by running tasks in the background. These commands will then run as normal, but you get the PS1 prompt back immediately, and when the background process ends or is stopped, you get a notification message of its status if stopped, or otherwise of its exit code.

Backgrounding Processes

To execute a command in the background, you add the ampersand character (&) to the end of the line. The shell displays the job ID in square brackets and the PID of the backgrounded process. Also, you can access its Process ID in the $! variable. This means that you can kill the process before it completes, or even choose to wait for a particular process.

The wait shell builtin command can wait for all backgrounded processes to finish, which is its default action when called with no arguments. In this case, wait returns zero when all background processes belonging to the current shell have completed. If passed a Process ID (PID) or job spec that does not exist, or is not parented by the current shell, it immediately exits with a return code of 127. Otherwise, wait's return code is the same as the return code of the process or job being waited on. So an interactive user, or a script, could start a set of background tasks, choose one of them, and sleep until that task has completed. The following example shows how this works. By saving the value of $! in variables $one, $two, and $three, the second background task can be selected for kill, wait, or other commands.

```
$ sleep 600 &
[1] 13651
$ one=$!
$ sleep 600 &
[2] 13652
$ two=$!
$ sleep 600 &
[3] 13653
$ three=$!
$ echo PIDs are $one $two $three
PIDs are 13651 13652 13653
$ ps -fp $two
UID        PID  PPID  C STIME TTY          TIME CMD
steve    13652 13639  0 21:20 pts/6    00:00:00 sleep 600
$ kill -9 $two
```

```
$
[2]-  Killed                    sleep 600
$
```

Job Control

There is a better way to control processes. Job Control is a higher level of abstraction than Process Control. Every background process (or pipeline) is assigned the next sequentially available job number. Each running instance of a shell has its own list of jobs, so the first job run by the current shell will always be %1, the second is %2, and so on. When all jobs are complete, the next will be assigned to %1 again. The jobs builtin command lists the job number, status, and command line of all of the shell's jobs. Called as jobs -1, it also lists their PIDs. Where a "+" is shown after the job number, that is the job seen by the shell as the default, or "current" job, which can be referred to via the shortcuts %%, % or %+.

The fg and bg commands bring the specified job (or if none is specified, the current job) to the foreground and background, respectively. Pressing Control and "z" (^Z) stops the current foreground process, returning the user to the interactive shell prompt. A foreground job is one that is tied to the current terminal for input and output, so it can take interactive input from the keyboard and write to the screen. The following interactive session shows three gzip instances concurrently compressing three CD ISO images. This can take a few minutes, which provides plenty of time to play with changing and inspecting the status of these three background jobs. The sleep command can be useful for this kind of demonstration, but gzip is a more realistic example, and you can also see its progress if you stop and/or kill it as it is partway through working on a file by observing whether or not the resulting .gz file keeps on growing.

```
$ ls
OEL5-cd1.iso  OEL5-cd2.iso  OEL5-cd3.iso
$ gzip *cd1.iso & gzip *cd2.iso & gzip *cd3.iso &
[1] 3224
[2] 3225
[3] 3226
$ jobs -1
[1]   3224 Running              gzip *cd1.iso &
[2]-  3225 Running              gzip *cd2.iso &       BRING JOB %2 INTO THE
[3]+  3226 Running              gzip *cd3.iso &       FOREGROUND (FG)
$ fg %2
gzip *cd2.iso       THEN STOP IT
^Z
[2]+  Stopped               gzip *cd2.iso        THEN BACKGROUND IT
$ bg %2
[2]+ gzip *cd2.iso &
$ kill -9 %3
$
[3]+  Killed                gzip *cd3.iso
$ jobs -1                                            JOB 3 WAS KILLED BY ITS JOB
[1]-  3224 Running              gzip *cd1.iso &       SPEC; NOW KILL WHICHEVER IS THE
[2]+  3225 Running              gzip *cd2.iso &       CURRENT JOB
$ kill -9 %
[2]+  3225 Killed               gzip *cd2.iso
$ jobs -1
[1]-  3224 Running              gzip *cd1.iso &
```

```
$
$ fg
gzip *cd1.iso
^Z
[1]+  Stopped                 gzip *cd1.iso
$ bg
[1]+ gzip *cd1.iso &          WAIT FOR THE LAST JOB TO COMPLETE
$ wait  ◄─────────────────────┘
[1]+  Done                    gzip *cd1.iso
$ jobs -l
$
```

A backgrounded job may change state from Running to Stopped when it needs interactive input. You would then need to foreground that job and provide the required input. You can then stop it again by pressing Control and "z" together (^Z), and then re-background it with the bg command. The following short script sleeps for 3 seconds before asking the user for his name. It then sleeps another 3 seconds before responding. It is a simplification of a lot of scripts and programs, such as third-party software installation routines, which may suddenly and unexpectedly become interactive after a long period of silence.

```
# cat slowinstaller.sh
#!/bin/bash

sleep 3
read -p "What is your name? " name
sleep 3
echo Hello $name
# ./slowinstaller.sh
What is your name? Steve
Hello Steve
#
```

When run in the background, the job is stopped when it asks for interactive input. In the following code, the user sees the prompt, "What is your name?" and answers. However, the script is in the background, so the answer ("Bethany") goes straight to the interactive shell (which reports "Bethany: command not found").

```
# ./slowinstaller.sh &
[1] 10661
# What is your name? Bethany
-bash: Bethany: command not found

[1]+  Stopped                 ./slowinstaller.sh
```

The script is already stopped, and so it has to be brought to the foreground (fg) to accept the input. Here, the user realizes what has happened and foregrounds the process so as to continue the interactive session.

```
# ./slowinstaller.sh &
[1] 10683
# What is your name? fg
./slowinstaller.sh
Bethany
Hello Bethany
#
```

If the user realizes that the prompt has come from the backgrounded task, she can simply press ENTER to display the next prompt, at which stage the shell also displays the changed status of the background job. She can then foreground the job and interact with it until it ends, as shown in the code that follows. After that, it can safely be stopped (^Z) and backgrounded (bg) again until it needs further interactive input, or as in this case, it comes to a successful completion, as indicated with the [1]+ Done message.

```
# ./slowinstaller.sh
^Z
[1]+  Stopped                 ./slowinstaller.sh
#
# fg
./slowinstaller.sh
What is your name? Emily
^Z
[1]+  Stopped                 ./slowinstaller.sh
#
# bg
[1]+ ./slowinstaller.sh &
# Hello Emily

[1]+  Done                    ./slowinstaller.sh
#
```

nohup and disown

As standard, when a login shell exits, it sends a HUP (hangup) signal to all of its children. The effect of this is that all background tasks terminate when their interactive login shell terminates. bash can get around this with the huponexit shell option, but the standard way to deal with this in advance is to use the nohup (no-hangup) command. nohup ensures that the task does not get terminated when its owning shell exits, which can be particularly useful for long-running tasks; it is nice to be able to connect to a system, kick off a task, and disconnect again immediately. Without nohup, you would have to keep that interactive login shell active, which means ensuring that the network connectivity remains and that the machine you are connected from stays up and does not lose power, crash, or for any other reason end your interactive session.

```
$ nohup /usr/local/bin/makemirrors.sh > /var/tmp/mirror.log 2>&1 &
[1] 14322
$ cat /var/tmp/mirror.log
Wed Mar 16 22:27:31 GMT 2011: Starting to resync disk mirrors.
Do not interrupt this process.
$ exit
logout
Connection to node3 closed.
```

Related to nohup is disown; a command already running can be disowned in the same way that a nohup process is automatically disowned.

```
node1$ sleep 500 &
[1] 29342
node1$ disown %1
node1$ exit
logout
```

```
Connection to node1 closed.
node7:~$ ssh node1
steve@ node1's password:
Linux node1 2.6.26-2-amd64 #1 SMP Sun Jun 20 20:16:30 UTC 2010 x86_64
Last login: Wed Mar 16 22:30:50 2011 from 78.145.17.30
node1$ ps -eaf|grep sleep
steve     29342     1  0 22:30 ?        00:00:00 sleep 500
node1$
```

SUMMARY

A lot of different shells are available on Unix and Linux systems; this chapter looked at some of the most popular. They are all superficially very similar in that they all provide an interactive command-line interface to the system, and they all run basic shell scripts in the same way, but in practice there is a world of difference between them, which can make porting scripts from one shell to another very time-consuming and cumbersome.

Understanding the range of differences between systems is key to writing portable and robust shell scripts, as well as being comfortable with any customer's system however it is configured. Also, using aliases, prompts, and profile settings can make your home systems much more familiar and therefore productive, whether that is on a home network, an intranet, or company-wide.

The site `http://en.wikipedia.org/wiki/Comparison_of_command_shells` has an exhaustive comparison of all of the major shells available.

This chapter marks the end of the more theoretical part of this book. Part II looks in more depth at the individual tools available in Unix and Linux. Part III looks into uses of particular shell features more closely, and provides various practical recipes for typical real-life tasks.

PART II
Recipes for Using and Extending System Tools

12

File Manipulation

Part II, "Recipes for Using and Extending System Tools," explores the general tools available in a typical Unix/Linux system in more depth. This chapter covers the common features used on a daily basis, as well as some less well-known features, and provides a few hints and tips for ways that these tools can be used. These chapters will occasionally refer you to the man pages for more information on esoteric options because there is no point in reprinting man pages here. Many of the GNU commands, and particularly the coreutils package, have much better explanations in their info pages than in their respective man pages. If you have info installed on your system, the following is the syntax to read about stat (which is part of the coreutils package):

```
info coreutils 'stat invocation'
```

This chapter also covers input and output redirection, which is a reasonably well understood topic for basic redirections but gets a bit more involved when dealing with redirecting input from standard input using here documents, and diverting inputs and outputs from loops and other external commands.

STAT

stat is a fantastic utility that gives to shell users what C programmers have had access to since Unix began. The stat(2) system call calls the appropriate filesystem driver within the operating system's kernel and asks for the details stored in the file's inode. The stat(1) command exposes this kernel call to userspace. This gives the shell programmer lots of useful information about a file, which would otherwise have to be extracted from the output of programs such as ls. stat, instead, gives the whole inode in a form in which you can query any aspect of the inode directly.

```
$ stat /etc/nsswitch.conf
  File: `/etc/nsswitch.conf'
  Size: 513          Blocks: 8          IO Block: 4096    regular file
Device: 805h/2053d    Inode: 639428      Links: 1
```

```
Access: (0644/-rw-r--r--)  Uid: (    0/    root)   Gid: (    0/    root)
Access: 2011-03-30 19:35:48.000000000 +0100
Modify: 2010-06-05 19:52:18.000000000 +0100
Change: 2010-06-05 19:52:18.000000000 +0100
```

While this is quite interesting, and it would be possible to parse out the relevant details from this, `stat` takes a lot of format switches, which restrict its output to exactly the information you are looking for. This means that you can create your own super-`ls`, which reports on anything you like, in any way you like.

```
$ stat -c "%a %U %G %n" /etc/nsswitch.conf
644 root root /etc/nsswitch.conf
$ stat -c "%n is owned by %U and has permissions %a (%A)" /etc/nsswitch.conf
/etc/nsswitch.conf is owned by root and has permissions 644 (-rw-r--r--)
$
```

The RPM package format uses a spec file to describe the package. The top of this file is a simple list of Field: Value settings; these are really quite simple, as shown by this snippet from the OpenSSH spec file:

```
Name          : openssh
Version       : %{version}%{cvs}
Release       : %{release}
Group         : System/Network
```

RPM starts to get more complex with the file listings. Although it is possible to specify a default owner, a group, and permissions settings for all files, in practice any reasonably complex package will have different settings for different files. It is possible to craft this by hand, but more accurate (and easier) to trawl through an existing, properly configured system and read the attributes of each file. `stat` is the perfect tool to format this in exactly the way that the RPM spec file needs to be formatted; that is, the line should say `%attr (permissions,owner,group) filename`. Following best practices, although the RPM will install into `/opt`, this package is actually being built by an unprivileged user account from the packager's own home directory. Faking the root directory in this way is made easier by adding the slash before the filename (`/%n` rather than just `%n`) in the `stat` output format.

```
$ pwd
/home/steve/rpm
$ find . -ls
155660    4 drwxr-xr-x   3 steve   steve   4096 Mar 23 12:54 .
155661    4 drwxr-xr-x   3 steve   steve   4096 Mar 28 15:31 ./opt
155662    4 drwxr-xr-x   4 myapp   myapp   4096 Mar 30 12:52 ./opt/myapp
155663    4 drwxr-xr-x   2 myapp   myapp   4096 Mar 30 12:52 ./opt/myapp/etc
155664    4 -rw-------   1 myapp   myapp     12 Mar 30 12:52 ./opt/myapp/etc/myapp.conf
155665    4 drwxr-xr-x   2 myapp   myapp   4096 Mar 30 12:52 ./opt/myapp/bin
155666    8 -rwxr-x---   1 myapp   myapp   4368 Mar 30 12:52 ./opt/myapp/bin/myapp
155669    4 -rwxr-xr-x   1 steve   steve    111 Mar 30 12:54 ./packager.sh
$ cat packager.sh
#!/bin/bash

find opt/myapp -print | while read filename
do
  stat -c "%%attr (%a,%U,%G) /%n" "$filename"
done
```

```
$ ./packager.sh | tee -a myapp.rpm
%attr (755,myapp,myapp) /opt/myapp
%attr (755,myapp,myapp) /opt/myapp/etc
%attr (600,myapp,myapp) /opt/myapp/etc/myapp.conf
%attr (755,myapp,myapp) /opt/myapp/bin
%attr (750,myapp,myapp) /opt/myapp/bin/myapp
$
```

packager.sh

CAT

cat is one of the simplest tools in the Unix/Linux toolbox. It is very widely used and can do a lot more than the basic description of it would have you believe. We will start with the basic operation of cat, which is short for "concatenate." For example, the command cat file1 file2 will display the contents of all of the files passed as arguments.

```
$ cat file1
this is file1

it has four lines.
the second line is blank.
$ cat file2
this is file2

it has six lines in all (three blank),

of which this is the sixth.
$ cat file1 file2
this is file1

it has four lines.
the second is blank.
this is file2

it has six lines (three blank)

of which this is the sixth.
$
```

 The files do not have to be text files; cat *can work on binary files just as well.*

This may not seem a particularly useful feature, and indeed, it is probably the least common usage of the cat command! This section looks at a few scripts that use various different features of the cat utility. When designing a shell script, it can be useful to be aware of basic features such as these because using system tools to manipulate file contents for you is much more efficient and easier than doing it yourself in the shell script. Therefore, familiarity with some of these less widely used features can make shell scripting a much easier process.

Numbering Lines

When dealing with lines of code, configuration files, or many other text files, it can be useful to see the line numbers by each line. The -n option does this for you.

```
$ cat -n file1 file2
     1  this is file1
     2
     3  it has four lines.
     4  the second is blank.
     5  this is file2
     6
     7  it has six lines (three blank)
     8
     9
    10  of which this is the sixth.
$
```

To number each file individually, you would need one cat command per file. Commands can be separated with the semicolon, like this:

```
$ cat -n file1 ; cat -n file2
     1  this is file1
     2
     3  it has four lines.
     4  the second is blank.
     1  this is file2
     2
     3  it has six lines (three blank)
     4
     5
     6  of which this is the sixth.
$
```

Dealing with Blank Lines

Blank lines in a file are often uninteresting; they may be useful as padding in configuration files for humans to read, but they offer no purpose to the shell. This invocation using the -s flag retains blank lines to keep paragraphs as is, but squeezes out any duplicate blanks to avoid wasted space.

```
$ cat -s file1 file2
this is file1

it has four lines.
the second is blank.
this is file2

it has six lines (three blank)

of which this is the sixth.
$
```

You could also choose to number only the non-blank lines. This is much like cat -n in the preceding code, but it ignores the blanks:

```
$ cat -b file1 file2
    1 this is file1

    2 it has four lines.
    3 the second is blank.
    4 this is file2

    5 it has six lines (three blank)

    6 of which this is the sixth.
$
```

Non-Printing Characters

Not everything is a text file, and cat can cope with that usefully, too. This file contains control characters, which are only hinted at (by the #) when inspected with a regular cat.

```
$ cat file3
This is file3.  It contains various non-printing
characters, like the tab in this line,
and the #control#codes in this line.
$
```

The actual ASCII characters in the file are more clearly displayed with the -v flag, which displays most non-printing characters, and the -T flag, which explicitly displays tabs as ^I rather than expanding them inline.

```
$ cat -vT file3
This is file3.  It contains various non-printing
characters, like the tab ^Iin this line,
and the ^Bcontrol^Dcodes in this line.
$
```

 The ^B and ^D characters represent ASCII characters 1 and 3, respectively. In their proper context they mean Start of Heading and End Of Text, respectively, but in this case they represent data corruption. The cat command can make this clearly visible around the otherwise good text.

It can also be useful to see where the end of a line is, if there are extra spaces at the end of the line. The -e flag puts a $ symbol at the actual end of each line. Here it becomes obvious that file2 has some spaces at the end of the final line:

```
$ cat -e file2
this is file2$
$
it has six lines (three blank)$
$
```

```
$
of which this is the sixth.                    $
$
```

CAT BACKWARDS IS TAC

Another useful utility, inspired by cat, is tac. This is yet another play on words along the same lines as yacc, bash, GNU, and many other such self-consciously weak jokes.

```
$ tac file1 file2
the second is blank.
it has four lines.

this is file1
of which this is the sixth.


it has six lines (three blank)

this is file2
$
```

Although reversing the order of a file is not often useful, it can be useful in more subtle ways. It is easy to append data to a file, but to prepend data, tac can be very handy. Note that (tac alpha. txt ; echo Bravo ; echo Alpha) has to be done in a subshell so that the output of all three commands is written to tempfile.

```
$ cat alpha.txt
Delta
Echo
Foxtrot
Golf
Hotel
$ ( tac alpha.txt ; echo Bravo ; echo Alpha ) > tempfile
$ cat tempfile
Hotel
Golf
Foxtrot
Echo
Delta
Bravo
Alpha
$ tac tempfile > alpha.txt
$ cat alpha.txt
Alpha
Bravo
Delta
Echo
Foxtrot
Golf
Hotel
$ rm tempfile
$
```

REDIRECTION

There is another category of Input and Output when dealing with file input and output, and that is *redirection*. There is an implicit fluid metaphor in the Unix structure, as the flow of data through pipelines and arrowed brackets. Data flows from left to right through a pipe, and also in the direction of the arrow. Multiple arrows indicate appending instead of overwriting (or creating).

Redirecting Output: The Single Greater-Than Arrow (>)

The single-arrowed command > filename structure creates filename if it does not already exist. If filename does already exist, it is truncated to zero length, but its inode details remain as before. This structure is useful for writing to log files, creating data files, and performing most general file create-and-open tasks. If the file cannot be written to, the whole command line fails, and none of it is executed at all. The simple script that follows shows the file being created if it does not already exist, and truncated if it does exist. The date command shows that different data has been written to the file on the second time, but the original content has disappeared.

> *Although the file permissions are unchanged if the file already existed, if the file did not exist, it will be created with the standard permissions and ownership as dictated by the current value of* umask (2).

Available for download on Wrox.com

```
$ cat create.sh
#!/bin/bash

LOGFILE=/tmp/log.txt

function showfile
{
  if [ -f "${1}" ]; then
    ls -l "${1}"
    echo "--- the contents are:"
    cat "${1}"
    echo "--- end of file."
  else
    echo "The file does not currently exist."
  fi
}

echo "Testing $LOGFILE for the first time."
showfile $LOGFILE

echo "Writing to $LOGFILE"
date > $LOGFILE

echo "Testing $LOGFILE for the second time."
showfile $LOGFILE

sleep 10

echo "Writing to $LOGFILE again."
```

```
date > $LOGFILE

echo "Testing $LOGFILE for the third and final time."
showfile $LOGFILE

$ ./create.sh
Testing /tmp/log.txt for the first time.
The file does not currently exist.
Writing to /tmp/log.txt
Testing /tmp/log.txt for the second time.
-rw-rw-r-- 1 steve steve 29 Mar 28 14:45 /tmp/log.txt
--- the contents are:
Mon Mar 28 14:45:52 BST 2011
--- end of file.
Writing to /tmp/log.txt again.
Testing /tmp/log.txt for the third and final time.
-rw-rw-r-- 1 steve steve 29 Mar 28 14:46 /tmp/log.txt
--- the contents are:
Mon Mar 28 14:46:02 BST 2011
--- end of file.
$
```

create.sh

Appending: The Double Greater-Than Arrow (>>)

Instead of truncating, a pair of greater-than arrows appends to the file if it already exists. As with
the single arrow structure, if the file does not exist, it is created, and if there is no permission to create or append the file, then the whole command line fails without executing at all. Modifying the
preceding script shows a different result. The only difference between the create.sh and append.sh
scripts is that the echo statement says "Appending to" instead of "Writing to," and the date command uses a double-arrow structure, like this:

```
date >> $LOGFILE
```

> *There can be no space between the two arrows. They must be >>, not > >. The
> latter would fail as a syntax error.*

This time, with the /tmp/log.txt file removed before starting the run, the append.sh script creates
the file on the first run, as before. The second time around, however, it appends instead of truncating the file.

```
$ cat append.sh
#!/bin/bash

LOGFILE=/tmp/log.txt

function showfile
{
  if [ -f "${1}" ]; then
```

```
      ls -l "${1}"
      echo "--- the contents are:"
      cat "${1}"
      echo "--- end of file."
    else
      echo "The file does not currently exist."
    fi
}

echo "Testing $LOGFILE for the first time."
showfile $LOGFILE

echo "Appending to $LOGFILE"
date >> $LOGFILE

echo "Testing $LOGFILE for the second time."
showfile $LOGFILE

sleep 10

echo "Appending to $LOGFILE again."
date >> $LOGFILE

echo "Testing $LOGFILE for the third and final time."
showfile $LOGFILE
$ ./append.sh
Testing /tmp/log.txt for the first time.
The file does not currently exist.
Appending to /tmp/log.txt
Testing /tmp/log.txt for the second time.
-rw-rw-r-- 1 steve steve 29 Mar 28 14:53 /tmp/log.txt
--- the contents are:
Mon Mar 28 14:53:04 BST 2011
--- end of file.
Appending to /tmp/log.txt again.
Testing /tmp/log.txt for the third and final time.
-rw-rw-r-- 1 steve steve 58 Mar 28 14:53 /tmp/log.txt
--- the contents are:
Mon Mar 28 14:53:04 BST 2011
Mon Mar 28 14:53:14 BST 2011
--- end of file.
$
```

append.sh

This is particularly useful as it also preserves any other data that may have been in the file, whatever its format. Pre-seeding the file with arbitrary text shows that the existing contents are never affected. It also shows that the permissions are not changed when the file is appended.

```
$ echo "Hello, this is some test data." > /tmp/log.txt
$ chmod 600 /tmp/log.txt
$ ls -l /tmp/log.txt
-rw------- 1 steve steve 31 Mar 28 14:57 /tmp/log.txt
$ ./append.sh
```

```
Testing /tmp/log.txt for the first time.
-rw------- 1 steve steve 31 Mar 28 14:57 /tmp/log.txt
--- the contents are:
Hello, this is some test data.
--- end of file.
Appending to /tmp/log.txt
Testing /tmp/log.txt for the second time.
-rw------- 1 steve steve 60 Mar 28 14:58 /tmp/log.txt
--- the contents are:
Hello, this is some test data.
Mon Mar 28 14:58:00 BST 2011
--- end of file.
Appending to /tmp/log.txt again.
Testing /tmp/log.txt for the third and final time.
-rw------- 1 steve steve 89 Mar 28 14:58 /tmp/log.txt
--- the contents are:
Hello, this is some test data.
Mon Mar 28 14:58:00 BST 2011
Mon Mar 28 14:58:10 BST 2011
--- end of file.
$
```

Input Redirection: The Single Less-Than Arrow (<)

Pointing in the opposite direction, the command < filename structure redirects input rather than output. It is sometimes more convenient to feed data into a command in this way than to use a pipeline to feed it in from the left-hand side. One very common use for this is to feed a while loop with input from a text file. This allows the loop to read consecutive lines from the file and act on them accordingly. This simple script reads host names from standard input and tries to ping them.

```
$ cat readloop.sh
#!/bin/bash

while read -p "Host to check: " hostname
do
  if [ -z "$hostname" ]; then
    echo "Quitting due to blank input"
    break
  fi
  ping -c1 -w1 $hostname > /dev/null 2>&1
  if [ "$?" -eq "0" ]; then
    echo "Contact made with $hostname"
  else
    echo "Failed to make contact with $hostname"
  fi
done

$ ./readloop.sh
Host to check: localhost
Contact made with localhost
Host to check: example.com
Contact made with example.com
Host to check: nosuch.example.com
Failed to make contact with nosuch.example.com
```

```
Host to check:
Quitting due to blank input
$
```

readloop.sh

When run non-interactively, the `read` command does not display its prompt. Also, the loop never gets to `reading` a blank line because the EOF marker is found first, which causes the `while read` test to fail, so the interactive nicety of allowing the user to enter a blank line to exit is left alone. This script can be run with standard input redirected from a file, as shown:

```
$ cat hosts.txt
declan
192.168.0.1
localhost
$ ./readloop.sh < hosts.txt
Failed to make contact with declan
Contact made with 192.168.0.1
Contact made with localhost
$
```

Appending a blank line to the input means that the `[ -z "$hostname" ]` test passes, and the loop exits before www.example.com is parsed. This does somewhat change the working of the script. The URL `www.example.com` never gets tested because the blank line has been read and the loop has exited. Notice that this time, the "Quitting due to blank input" message is displayed, whereas it was not before because that test was never made.

```
$ echo >> hosts.txt
$ echo www.example.com >> hosts.txt
$ cat hosts.txt
declan
192.168.0.1          THE HOSTS.TXT NOW INCLUDES AN EXTRA BLANK LINE
localhost            AND WWW.EXAMPLE.COM. THESE WILL BE IGNORED.
←
www.example.com
$ ./readloop.sh < hosts.txt
Failed to make contact with declan
Contact made with 192.168.0.1
Contact made with localhost
Quitting due to blank input
$
```

Redirection can also be done within the file. Changing the final line to read `done < hosts.txt` hard-codes the loop to always read from the file `hosts.txt`. It could also read from $1, $HOSTS, or anything else required. This modified version reads the $HOSTS variable if defined, otherwise $1.

```
$ cat readloop2.sh
#!/bin/bash

HOSTS=${HOSTS:-$1}

while read -p "Host to check: " hostname
do
```

```
      if [ -z "$hostname" ]; then
        echo "Quitting due to blank input"
        break
      fi
      ping -c1 -w1 $hostname > /dev/null 2>&1
      if [ "$?" -eq "0" ]; then
        echo "Contact made with $hostname"
      else
        echo "Failed to make contact with $hostname"
      fi
done < $HOSTS

$ cat hosts2.txt
example.com
www.example.com
$ ./readloop2.sh hosts2.txt
Contact made with example.com
Contact made with www.example.com
$ HOSTS=hosts3.txt
$ export HOSTS
$ cat $HOSTS
bad.example.com
steve-parker.org
$ ./readloop2.sh
Failed to make contact with bad.example.com
Contact made with steve-parker.org
$
```

readloop2.sh

Here Documents: The Double Less-Than Arrow (<< EOF)

The <<EOF syntax does not read from a file, but from the current standard input, until the EOF
marker is found. The literal text EOF is not required; the pling, bang, or exclamation point (!) is
also commonly used. Whatever delimiting text is provided between the << and the end of that line
must be provided on a line by itself. The text in between <<EOF and the EOF marker itself is known
as a here document because instead of an external file, the file is provided inline in the shell session
(or, more commonly, the shell script). Variables are expanded, $(command) and backticks are hon-
ored, and arithmetic expansion is done as it would be in the rest of the script. This example shows
the working of a standard here document. It takes its command-line input and sends it to the named
web server.

```
$ cat heredoc.sh
#!/bin/bash
HOST=$1
shift
PORT=80
COMMAND=${@:-HEAD /}

echo "Sending \"$COMMAND\" to $HOST port $PORT"
netcat ${HOST} ${PORT} <<EOF
```

```
        ${COMMAND}

EOF
echo "Done!"
```

```
$ ./heredoc.sh example.com
Sending "HEAD /" to example.com port 80
HTTP/1.0 302 Found
Location: http://www.iana.org/domains/example/
Server: BigIP
Connection: close
Content-Length: 0

Done!
$ ./heredoc.sh www.iana.org HEAD http://www.iana.org/domains/example/ HTTP/1.0
Sending "HEAD http://www.iana.org/domains/example/ HTTP/1.0" to www.iana.org port 8
0
HTTP/1.1 200 OK
Date: Mon, 28 Mar 2011 21:35:20 GMT
Server: Apache/2.2.3 (CentOS)
Last-Modified: Wed, 09 Feb 2011 17:13:15 GMT
Content-Length: 2945
Connection: close
Content-Type: text/html; charset=UTF-8

Done!
$
```

heredoc.sh

The contents of the here document are sent exactly as is; it can be inconvenient to put this within a shell script because the indentation is messed up. You can choose to either send the indentation to the recipient program, which may or may not be acceptable, or left-justify all of the contents of the here document (and the EOF delimiter). Bash has a workaround for this; by adding a hyphen (<<-EOF) it will ignore any leading tab characters before the here document itself, or the EOF marker. This slight rewrite of the preceding script shows how this can improve presentation and readability. On the first attempt, the script is broken because no EOF is found at the start of a line:

```
$ cat manyhosts.sh
#!/bin/bash

function readhost
{
  HOST=$1
  shift
  PORT=80
  COMMAND="HEAD http://${HOST}/ HTTP/1.0"

  echo "Sending \"$COMMAND\" to $HOST port $PORT"
  netcat ${HOST} ${PORT} <<EOF
        ${COMMAND}

    EOF
```

```
    echo "Done!"
}

for host in $@
do
    readhost $host
done
$ ./manyhosts.sh example.com example.org
./manyhosts.sh: line 21: warning: here-document at line 11 delimited by end-of-file
(wanted `EOF')
./manyhosts.sh: line 22: syntax error: unexpected end of file
$ sed -i s/"<<EOF"/"<<-EOF"/1 manyhosts.sh
$ ./manyhosts.sh example.com example.org
Sending "HEAD http://example.com/ HTTP/1.0" to example.com port 80
HTTP/1.0 302 Found
Location: http://www.iana.org/domains/example/
Server: BigIP
Connection: close
Content-Length: 0

Done!
Sending "HEAD http://example.org/ HTTP/1.0" to example.org port 80
HTTP/1.0 302 Found
Location: http://www.iana.org/domains/example/
Server: BigIP
Connection: close
Content-Length: 0

Done!
$
```

THIS COMMAND DOES NOT WORK; NO EOF IS FOUND AT THE START OF A LINE.

THIS SED LINE SIMPLY REPLACES "<<EOF" WITH "<<-EOF"; THE SCRIPT WILL NOW WORK WITH INDENTATION.

manyhosts.sh

DD

The dd command streams bits from one file or device to another. It also reports to stderr how many records it read and wrote, and how long the whole process took. This makes it ideal for monitoring the performance of a storage device. If a device or path is suspected to be occasionally slow, regularly running a script like this can capture the evidence at any time of day or night:

```
# dd if=/dev/sda1 of=/dev/null bs=1024k count=1024
1024+0 records in
1024+0 records out
1073741824 bytes (1.1 GB) copied, 16.8678 s, 63.7 MB/s
#
```

The syntax for dd is a little obscure; if= specifies the input file, of= specifies the output file. bs= specifies the block size to copy, and count= specifies the number of said blocks to copy. The device used will affect the performance dramatically. Extreme examples are /dev/zero (fastest to read from), /dev/null (fastest to write to), and /dev/urandom, which can be a very slow device to read from, as it has to wait for sufficient entropy in the system in order to generate the random data.

Cache in the storage controller can have a huge impact; if you are doing performance testing (especially under Linux), the Linux system cache can also be huge; echo 3 > /proc/sys/vm/drop_caches before each read to make sure that the cache is properly flushed.

```
$ cat checkpaths.sh
#!/bin/sh
DEV1=${1:-sday}
DEV2=${2:-sdu}
DEV3=${2:-sdcc}
DEV4=${2:-sddg}

EXPECTED=350

cd /var/tmp
rm -f dd.pid

for DEV in $DEV1 $DEV2 $DEV3 $DEV4
do
  dd if=/dev/$DEV of=/dev/null bs=8192 count=1000000 2>&1|grep -w copied \
     >> dd.$DEV &
  echo $! >> dd.pid
done

sleep $EXPECTED
CHILDREN=2
while [ "$CHILDREN" -gt "0" ]
do
  echo "`date`: I have $CHILDREN children"
  sleep 5
  CHILDREN=`ps hfp $(cat dd.pid) | wc -l`
done

MAILOUT=0
for SECONDS in `awk '{ print $6 }' dd.$DEV1 dd.$DEV2 dd.$DEV3 dd.$DEV4 |\
  cut -d"." -f1`
do
  if [ "$SECONDS" -gt "$EXPECTED" ]; then
    MAILOUT=1
  fi
done

if [ "$MAILOUT" == "1" ]; then
  for DEV in $DEV1 $DEV2 $DEV3 $DEV4
  do
    msg=`cat dd.$DEV`
    logger -t storagespeed "Path Comparison: $DEV :$msg"
  done

  echo "It should take no more than $EXPECTED seconds to read 8Gb from a device."\
    "It took:\n`grep . dd.$DEV1 dd.$DEV2 dd.$DEV3 dd.$DEV4`" |\
    mailx -s "Slow I/O on `uname -n`" storage@example.com
fi
```

```
# grep storagespeed /var/log/messages
/var/log/messages:Mar 27 07:17:17 node42 storagespeed: Path
Comparison: sday :8192000000 bytes (8.2 GB) copied, 277.018 seconds,
29.6 MB/s
/var/log/messages:Mar 27 07:17:17 node42 storagespeed: Path
Comparison: sdu :8192000000 bytes (8.2 GB) copied, 428.881 seconds, 19.1
MB/s
/var/log/messages:Mar 27 07:17:17 node42 storagespeed: Path
Comparison: sdcc :8192000000 bytes (8.2 GB) copied, 176.26 seconds, 46.5
MB/s
/var/log/messages:Mar 27 07:17:17 node42 storagespeed: Path
Comparison: sddg :8192000000 bytes (8.2 GB) copied, 550.755 seconds,
14.9 MB/s
```

In this example, disk devices `/dev/sdu` and `/dev/sddg` both performed very badly, at 19.1 Mbps and 14.9 Mbps, respectively. This was logged to the system log file using the `logger` facility using the `storagespeed` tag. An e-mail was also automatically sent to the appropriate mailbox, reporting the issue and giving all of the relevant details. This can then be investigated by the storage experts upon receipt of the e-mail.

```
Subject: Slow I/O on node42
From: root <root@node42.example.com>
Date: Sun 27 Mar 2011 07:17:17 +0100
To: storage@example.com

It should take no more than 350 seconds to read 8Gb from a device. It took:
dd.sday:8192000000 bytes (8.2 GB) copied, 277.018 seconds, 29.6 MB/s
dd.sdu:8192000000 bytes (8.2 GB) copied, 428.881 seconds, 19.1 MB/s
dd.sdcc:8192000000 bytes (8.2 GB) copied, 176.26 seconds, 46.5 MB/s
dd.sddg:8192000000 bytes (8.2 GB) copied, 550.755 seconds, 14.9 MB/s
```

DF

`df` reports on the amount of disk space free on each mounted filesystem. It traditionally reports in kilobytes, but GNU `df` can also report in human-readable form, so 1024KB are shown as 1MB, 1024MB are shown as 1GB, and so on. Recent versions of `sort` are capable of sorting on this type of output, so it will understand that 1GB is greater than 900MB, for example, but at the time of writing this is not in very wide use, so it's safest to use KB for reporting and `sort -k` for sorting.

The brief script that follows uses `df` to determine which filesystem has the most available free space and whether or not that is large enough for a certain image. This can be used when planning an installation or piece of administrative work; if the server has no filesystems at all available for the install, then remedial work will be required before attempting the install. However, even if `/var` is full, if this script finds enough space in `/home`, the administrator may choose to do the install into that directory instead.

```
$ cat freespace.sh
#!/bin/bash

required=${1:-2131042}
```

```
        preferred=${2:-/var}

        available=`df -k /var | awk '{ print $4 }' | tail -1`
        if [ "$available" -gt "$required" ]; then
          echo "Good news. There is sufficient space in ${preferred}:"
          df -h $preferred
        else
          echo "Bad news. There is not enough space in ${preferred}:"
          df -h $preferred
          echo
          echo "Looking in other filesystems..."
          fs=`mktemp`
          df -k -x nfs | sort -k4 -n | awk '{ print $4,$6 }' | grep -v "Available" | \
            while read available filesystem
          do
          if [ "$available" -gt "$required" ]; then
            echo "Good news: $filesystem has $available Kb" | tee $fs
          fi
          done
          if [ ! -s $fs ]; then
            echo "No filesystems were found with sufficient free space."
            exit 1
          fi
          rm -f $fs
        fi
$ ./freespace.sh 3105613 /var
Bad news. There is not enough space in /var:
Filesystem             Size  Used Avail Use% Mounted on
/dev/sda5              28G   27G  417M  99% /

Looking in other filesystems...
Good news: /home/steve has 3387316 Kb
$ ./freespace.sh 14502 /var
Good news. There is sufficient space in /var:
Filesystem             Size  Used Avail Use% Mounted on
/dev/sda5              28G   27G  417M  99% /
$
```

freespace.sh

MKTEMP

It is often useful to be able to create a temporary file, which can be guaranteed to be unique. Many scripts use /tmp/programname.$$ for temporary files, where $$ is a special variable that returns the PID of the currently running process. This is often sufficient, but not truly robust. For example, if you read and write from /tmp/programname.$$, a malicious user could create lots of files in /tmp — programname.1, programname.2, and so on, such that creation of /tmp/programname.$$ fails (and that may not be easily checked for), the script writes data to a file owned by an untrusted user, or it reads data from a file provided by an untrusted user.

A truly robust solution must check that the filename is not in use and create that file for you before returning with the name of the file. `mktemp` does just that, creating either a file or a directory, whichever you require.

`mktemp` will, by default, create a file in the `/tmp` directory and return its name on standard output. However, you can specify your own template for the created file; the default template is `$TMPDIR/tmp.XXXXXXXXXX`, or `/tmp/tmp.XXXXXXXXXX` if `$TMPDIR` is not defined — that is, `/tmp/tmp.` followed by 10 randomly generated characters (upper and lowercase letters, and digits), but `mktemp /var/tmp/helloXXX` will create a file in `/var/tmp` with a name starting with "`hello`" followed by three random characters.

```
$ ls -l `mktemp`
-rw------- 1 steve steve 0 Oct  8 16:47 /tmp/tmp.9e0M1DJrFW
$
$ cat mktemp.sh
#!/bin/sh

TEMPFILE=`mktemp` || exit 1
ls -l $TEMPFILE
echo "This is definitely my temporary file" > $TEMPFILE
cat $TEMPFILE
rm -f $TEMPFILE
$ ./mktemp.sh
-rw------- 1 steve steve 0 Oct  8 16:49 /tmp/tmp.FqsOiJihvK
This is definitely my temporary file
$
```

You can also specify a suffix, either using the `--suffix` flag, or by ending the template with something other than `x`. This example creates a `.txt` file by providing `--suffix .txt` as an argument.

```
$ cat mktemp.sh
#!/bin/sh

TEMPFILE=`mktemp --suffix .txt` || exit 1
ls -l $TEMPFILE
echo "This is definitely my temporary file" > $TEMPFILE
cat $TEMPFILE
rm -f $TEMPFILE
$ ./mktemp.sh
-rw------- 1 steve steve 0 Oct  8 16:49 /tmp/tmp.AqaySc7mOc.txt
This is definitely my temporary file
$
```

 The directory in which `mktemp` *is to create the file or directory must exist for* `mktemp` *to succeed.* `mktemp` *does not create parent directories (although* `mkdir -p` *does).*

```
$ cat mktemp.sh
#!/bin/sh

TEMPDIR=`mktemp -d` || exit 1
```

```
echo "This is a file in my temporary directory" > $TEMPDIR/file1
echo "This is another file in my temporary directory" > $TEMPDIR/file2
ls -la $TEMPDIR
rm -rf $TEMPDIR
$ ./mktemp.sh
total 16
drwx------  2 steve steve 4096 Oct  8 16:50 .
drwxrwxrwt 10 root  root  4096 Oct  8 16:50 ..
-rw-rw-r--  1 steve steve   41 Oct  8 16:50 file1
-rw-rw-r--  1 steve steve   47 Oct  8 16:50 file2
$
```

mktemp.sh

 At most, the created file will have 0600 permissions — that is, readable and writable by the owner, but no other permissions available. If the umask is more restrictive than that, the more restrictive permissions will be applied.

JOIN

join is a utility that will combine two different files based on common keys in both files. Both files have to be sorted on the key for this to work, but that can usually be arranged, even if it means creating a temporary file from the original input. Another limitation is that there has to be a common delimiter used for both input files, and for the output. If you can live with those restrictions, join can be a very useful tool. Using the same input data as the paste section of the next chapter, join can be used to combine different databases. The code that follows shows two files, hosts and ethers. First they are sorted on key 2 (the hostname) so that they are in the same order as each other. The join command then combines these files by hostname.

```
$ cat hosts
127.0.0.1       localhost
192.168.1.5     plug
192.168.1.10    declan
192.168.1.11    atomic
192.168.1.13    goldie
192.168.1.227   elvis
$ cat ethers
0a:00:27:00:00:00 plug
01:00:3a:10:21:fe declan
71:1f:04:e3:1b:13 atomic
01:01:8d:07:3a:ea goldie
01:01:31:09:2a:f2 elvis
$ sort -k2 ethers > ethers.sorted
$ sort -k2 hosts > hosts.sorted
$ join -j2 -a1 hosts.sorted ethers.sorted
atomic 192.168.1.11 71:1f:04:e3:1b:13
declan 192.168.1.10 01:00:3a:10:21:fe
```

```
elvis 192.168.1.227 01:01:31:09:2a:f2
goldie 192.168.1.13  01:01:8d:07:3a:ea
localhost 127.0.0.1
plug 192.168.1.5 0a:00:27:00:00:00
$
```

Here the common field is the second field in both files, as specified by -j2. The -a1 flag tells join to display everything from the first file, even if there is no match in the second file. This can be useful for seeing what hosts do not have an entry in ethers; in this case, it is only localhost.

INSTALL

install is cp on steroids. It can set file permissions, create directories, take backups, and much more, all from a single command line. As its name suggests, it was written for software installation scripts, although it can be used for other purposes, too.

Because an existing copy of the file may already be installed, install can also take backups before installing the new files. This is specified by the -b flag, which creates backup files with a tilde (~) at the end of the filename. The --backup option can specify other policies for backups, which are:

➤ simple or never: The default tilde (~) backup only.

➤ numbered or t: Numbered backups, as .~1~, .~2~, and so on.

➤ existing or blank: simple or numbered, whichever is already in use (default is simple).

➤ none or off: Never take backups.

The -m flag specifies mode, either in octal format (0750 for a regular file, with rwx, r-x, and --- access for User, Group, and Other, respectively), or symbolic format, such as -m 'u=rwx,g=r'. Note that this flag is not applied to parent directories; they will be created with 755 permissions.

The -o and -g flags tell install which owner and group the file should have; these can only be used by the root user, as a non-privileged user would not have the permissions to do that. The -v flag tells install to be verbose about what it is doing, which can be useful for providing feedback as to what is happening.

This script shows a simple application's Makefile and installer. The installer itself is wrapped up into the Makefile logic, so a make install command will perform an intelligent installation, rather than putting mkdir, cp, chown, and chmod commands into the Makefile.

```
steve@goldie:~$ cd myapp
steve@goldie:~/myapp$ ls
installer.sh  Makefile  myapp.c  myapp.conf
steve@goldie:~/myapp$ cat Makefile
all:    myapp.c
        $(CC) -o myapp myapp.c

clean:  myapp
```

```
         rm -f myapp
```
THE INSTALL TARGET WILL RUN INSTALLER.
SH, WHICH IS LISTED BELOW.

```
install:        myapp
        ./installer.sh /opt/myapp myapp myapp
steve@goldie:~/myapp$ cat installer.sh
#!/bin/bash
ROOTDIR=${1:-/opt/myapp}
OWNER=${2:-myapp}
GROUP=${3:-myapp}

# Create bin and opt directories. Parents will be 755; if run
# as root, their ownership will be root:root. (any suid/sgid will be preserved)
install -v -m 755 -o $OWNER -g $GROUP -d $ROOTDIR/bin $ROOTDIR/etc
if [ "$?" -ne "0" ]; then
  echo "Install: Failed to create directories."
  exit 1
fi

# install the binary itself
install -b -v -m 750 -o $OWNER -g $GROUP -s myapp $ROOTDIR/bin
if [ "$?" -ne "0" ]; then
  echo "Install: Failed to install the binary"
  exit 2
fi

# Install the configuration file, only read-writeable by the owner.
install -b -v -m 600 -o $OWNER -g $GROUP myapp.conf $ROOTDIR/etc
if [ "$?" -ne "0" ]; then
  echo "Install: Failed to install the config file"
  exit 3
fi
```

THE SOFTWARE CAN BE BUILT AS A
NON-PRIVILEGED USER.

```
echo "Install: Succeeded."
steve@goldie:~/myapp$ make
cc -o myapp myapp.c
steve@goldie:~/myapp$ su -
```

IT IS THEN INSTALLED BY THE ROOT USER.

```
Password: root_password
root@goldie:~# cd ~steve/myapp
root@goldie:/home/steve/myapp# make install
./installer.sh /opt/myapp myapp myapp
`myapp' -> `/opt/myapp/bin/myapp' (backup: `/opt/myapp/bin/myapp~')
`myapp.conf' -> `/opt/myapp/etc/myapp.conf' (backup: `/opt/myapp/etc/myapp.conf~')
Install: Succeeded.
root@goldie:/home/steve/myapp# ls -1R /opt/myapp
/opt/myapp/:
total 8
drwxr-xr-x 2 myapp myapp 4096 Mar 28 11:52 bin
drwxr-xr-x 2 myapp myapp 4096 Mar 28 11:52 etc
```

AN LS IN THE RELEVANT
DIRECTORY SHOWS THE
ORIGINAL FILES (DATED
JANUARY) AND THE NEW
FILES (DATED MARCH)
THAT REPLACED THEM.
NOTICE THAT THE
DIRECTORIES' TIMESTAMPS
ARE FRESHENED ALSO.

```
/opt/myapp/bin:
total 16
-rwxr-x--- 1 myapp myapp 4368 Mar 28 11:52 myapp
```

```
-rwxr-x--- 1 myapp myapp 4368 Jan 12 09:21 myapp~

/opt/myapp/etc:
total 8
-rw------- 1 myapp myapp 12 Mar 28 11:52 myapp.conf
-rw------- 1 myapp myapp 12 Jan 16 17:34 myapp.conf~
root@goldie:/home/steve/myapp# exit
$
```

A clean install looks slightly different. In this case, it shows that it is creating the intermediate directories. Also, the comments about taking backups are missing. This part of the installation is shown in the code that follows.

```
root@goldie:/home/steve/myapp# make install
./installer.sh /opt/myapp myapp myapp
install: creating directory `/opt/myapp'
install: creating directory `/opt/myapp/bin'
install: creating directory `/opt/myapp/etc'
`myapp' -> `/opt/myapp/bin/myapp'
`myapp.conf' -> `/opt/myapp/etc/myapp.conf'
Install: Succeeded.
root@goldie:/home/steve/myapp# exit
```

myapp, makefile, and installer

GREP

grep is a vital part of the Unix/Linux toolbox. It searches its input for lines that match the regular expression passed to it. In its simplest (and most common) usage, it is used to search for a fixed string, in which case the flags are more significant than the regular expression functionality of grep. grep's regular expression grammar is described later in the chapter in the section "Grep Regular Expressions." grep is such a common command that you can find it in many of the code examples in this book, even when it is not being addressed directly. This section provides some examples of how it can be used in some more and less common ways, and explains what grep is capable of.

grep Flags

The four most commonly used flags to grep are -i (case-insensitive search), -l (list only the names of matching files), -w (which matches whole words only), and -v (invert; this lists only the lines that do not match the pattern). Another less well-known flag that is rather useful is -e. This can be used to pass multiple search patterns on a single command line. grep -e replaces egrep as the preferred way to search for many patterns at once. The following example uses a contacts list (contacts.txt) with a fixed structure, such that each contact has four lines associated with it and each line contains one field. Apart from that, nothing else is fixed — there could be any other text in the file, and spacing could be padded in any way. These four flags can be tested quite effectively.

```
$ head -4 contacts.txt
Name:Steve Parker
Phone:44 789 777 2100
Email:steve@steve-parker.org
```

```
Web:http://steve-parker.org/
$ grep -i sTEve contacts.txt          ◄──────── -I SPECIFIES A CASE-INSENSITIVE SEARCH.
Name:Steve Parker
Email:steve@steve-parker.org          THIS SHOWS THAT THERE IS ANOTHER FILE IN THE CURRENT
Web:http://steve-parker.org/          DIRECTORY THAT ALSO CONTAINS THE WORD STEVE.
$ grep -l Steve *          ◄────────────────┘
contacts.txt
users.txt
$ grep -v -e 0 -e Steve -e http contacts.txt  ◄────── THE MANY <-E EXPRESSION> CALLS
                                                       ARE ALL NEGATED BY THE -V FLAG.
                                                       NO LINE THAT MATCHES ANY OF
Name:Richard Stallman                                  THESE EXPRESSIONS IS LISTED.
Email:rms@stallman.org

Name:Linus Torvalds
Email:torvalds@osdl.org
```

Three other (but less commonly known) flags available in GNU `grep` are -A, -B, and -C. These provide a certain number of lines After, Before, and around (Context) the matching line, respectively. These can be used to effectively provide context around a search result.

```
$ grep -A2 Steve contacts.txt    ◄──────── THE TWO LINES AFTER THE MATCHING
Name:Steve Parker                          LINE ARE PHONE AND E-MAIL.
Phone:44 789 777 2100
Email:steve@steve-parker.org               THE FOUR LINES BEFORE THE LAST MATCH MAKE UP
$ grep -B4 steve-parker contacts.txt  ◄──┐ THE FULL RECORD FOR THIS CONTACT.
Name:Steve Parker                        │
Phone:44 789 777 2100                    │
Email:steve@steve-parker.org         ◄───┘
Web:http://steve-parker.org/
$
```

grep Regular Expressions

When passed regular expressions, `grep` uses the following rules to match the pattern. It will match the longest possible pattern (greedy matching).

?	The preceding item is optional and matched at most once.
*	The preceding item will be matched zero or more times.
+	The preceding item will be matched one or more times.
{n}	The preceding item is matched exactly n times.
{n,}	The preceding item is matched n or more times.
{,m}	The preceding item is matched at most m times.
{n,m}	The preceding item is matched at least n times, but not more than m times.

The `contacts.sh` script below uses the regular expression `^Name:.*${name}` to search for any line that starts with the label `Name:`, then `.*`, which matches any number of occurrences of any character, and which subsequently contains the string entered by the user. It also uses -i to perform a case-insensitive search for convenience.

```
$ cat contacts.sh
#!/bin/bash
CONTACTS=contacts.txt

PS3="Search For: "

select task in "Show All Information" "Show Phone" "Show Email" "Show Web"
do
  name=""
  if [ "$REPLY" -le "4" ] && [ "$REPLY" -ge "1" ]; then
    while [ -z "$name" ]
    do
      read -p "Enter a name to search for: " name
    done
    case $REPLY in
      1)
          grep -A3 -i "^Name:.*${name}" $CONTACTS
          ;;
      2)
          grep -A1 -i "^Name:.*${name}" $CONTACTS | cut -d: -f2-
          ;;
      3)
          grep -A2 -i "^Name:.*${name}" $CONTACTS | \
          grep -e "^Email:" -e "^Name:"| cut -d: -f2-
          ;;
      4)
          grep -A3 -i "^Name:.*${name}" $CONTACTS | \
          grep -e "^Web:" -e "^Name:"| cut -d: -f2-
          ;;
    esac
  fi
done

$ ./contacts.sh
1) Show All Information  3) Show Email
2) Show Phone            4) Show Web
Search For: 1
Enter a name to search for: steve
Name:Steve Parker
Phone:44 789 777 2100
Email:steve@steve-parker.org
Web:http://steve-parker.org/
Search For: 4
Enter a name to search for: s
Steve Parker
http://steve-parker.org/
Richard Stallman
http://stallman.org/
Linus Torvalds
http://www.cs.helsinki.fi/~torvalds
Search For: ^C
$
```

The first search finds the only "Steve" listed in the `contacts.txt` file. The second search looks for "`^Name:.*s`" anywhere in the file. It performs a `grep -A3 -i` for that regular expression, which matches Steve, Stallman, and Linus Torvalds. Each of those matching lines, and the three lines below it, are output, but before it gets to the display, a `grep -e` singles out only the Name and E-mail lines. Finally, for presentation purposes, the field name is stripped of the output when displaying only a single item per person.

SPLIT

When managing and transferring files, there are often limits to the size of files that can be transferred. Whether it's e-mail systems with 2MB or 10MB limits, or FAT filesystems with 4GB limits, or saving large amounts of data to 4.7GB DVDs, there are always problems when you are used to dealing with a flexible and powerful OS that is perfectly capable of handling much larger files than this, and then discover that a lot of the mainstream infrastructure is not as powerful as a modern Linux or Unix system.

The solution to this problem is the `split` utility; although it can split files based on line numbers, it is most often used to split a large file into smaller, regular chunks. The `-b` flag tells it to work in this way. You can specify the chunk size in K, M, G, T, P, E, Z, and even Y. These are in multiples of 1,024; adding a B suffix (KB, MB, GB, and so on) will work in multiples of 1,000.

The default options are quite widely recognized in that it creates a sequence of files called xaa, xab, xac, and so on (until it gets to xax, xay, xaz, xba, xbb, xbc, xbd . . .). However, it does have some more friendly options; the `-d` flag uses digits instead of letters — x01, x02, x03 instead of xaa, xab, xac — and you can also define your own prefix instead of the letter *x*. It is a good habit to add an underscore to the end of the prefix, so that you can more easily see the suffix.

The default size of the suffix is two characters; if the file will be broken into more than 100 chunks, you will need to specify a longer suffix length with the `-a` option: `-a3` for up to 1000 chunks, `-a4` for up to 10,000 chunks, and so on. Unfortunately, `split` will not calculate this for you, and will complain "output file suffixes exhausted" after it has used all available suffixes.

Consider the following example in which a Solaris 10 Update 9 virtual machine image (which is just over 4GB) is `split` into five files of at most 1GB (1024 * 1024 * 1024 bytes) using a prefix of Sol10u9 and a numerical suffix (01 to 05). As evidenced in the timestamps, this operation took around 4 minutes:

```
$ ls -l
-rwxrwxr-x 1 steve steve 4332782080 Oct 20 11:16 Solaris 10 u9.vdi
$ ls -lh
-rwxrwxr-x 1 steve steve 4.1G Oct 20 11:16 Solaris 10 u9.vdi
$ split -b 1G -d Solaris\ 10\ u9.vdi Sol10u9_
$ ls -l
total 8470776
-rw-rw-r-- 1 steve steve 1073741824 Dec  1 10:20 Sol10u9_00
```

```
-rw-rw-r-- 1 steve steve 1073741824 Dec  1 10:21 Sol10u9_01
-rw-rw-r-- 1 steve steve 1073741824 Dec  1 10:23 Sol10u9_02
-rw-rw-r-- 1 steve steve 1073741824 Dec  1 10:24 Sol10u9_03
-rw-rw-r-- 1 steve steve   37814784 Dec  1 10:24 Sol10u9_04
-rwxrwxr-x 1 steve steve 4332782080 Oct 20 11:16 Solaris 10 u9.vdi
$ ls -lh
total 8.1G
-rw-rw-r-- 1 steve steve 1.0G Dec  1 10:20 Sol10u9_00
-rw-rw-r-- 1 steve steve 1.0G Dec  1 10:21 Sol10u9_01
-rw-rw-r-- 1 steve steve 1.0G Dec  1 10:23 Sol10u9_02
-rw-rw-r-- 1 steve steve 1.0G Dec  1 10:24 Sol10u9_03
-rw-rw-r-- 1 steve steve  37M Dec  1 10:24 Sol10u9_04
-rwxrwxr-x 1 steve steve 4.1G Oct 20 11:16 Solaris 10 u9.vdi
$
```

You can put these files back together with the `cat` command, which works just as well with binary files as with text files. The example below shows this at work. The `diff` shows that the resulting file is identical to the original.

```
$ cat Sol10u9_* > Sol10.vdi
$ ls -lh
total 12.2G
-rw-rw-r-- 1 steve steve 1.0G Dec  1 10:20 Sol10u9_00
-rw-rw-r-- 1 steve steve 1.0G Dec  1 10:21 Sol10u9_01
-rw-rw-r-- 1 steve steve 1.0G Dec  1 10:23 Sol10u9_02
-rw-rw-r-- 1 steve steve 1.0G Dec  1 10:24 Sol10u9_03
-rw-rw-r-- 1 steve steve  37M Dec  1 10:24 Sol10u9_04
-rwxrwxr-x 1 steve steve 4.1G Oct 20 11:16 Solaris 10 u9.vdi
-rwxrwxr-x 1 steve steve 4.1G Dec 20 10:49 Sol10.vdi
$ diff Solaris\ 10\ u9.vdi Sol10.vdi
$ echo $?
0
$
```

TEE

`tee` is yet another one of those overlooked tools that can make your scripts do useful things very simply and cleanly. It passes its input to stdout, but it also writes it to a file at the same time. With the `-a` flag, it will append to the file. You could just have two `echo` statements writing to the standard output and to a log file, in which case you need to ensure that any changes to one output line are repeated in the matching line. Personal experience teaches that this does not happen, which causes massive confusion when the output and the log file differ slightly but significantly. The script that follows is simple enough, but the three differences between the two lines are not obvious to spot, and worse still, once identified, it is not obvious which line has the errors.

```
$ cat bad.sh
#!/bin/bash

for i in `seq -w 1 10` 14 19 13
do
    j=`expr $i \* $i`
    echo "`date`: I am `basename $0` and I can count to ${i}," \
        "which is not particularly impressive, especially as I get a bit" \
```

```
              "confused after ten. I do know that the prime factors of ${i} squared are" \
              "`factor $j | cut -d. -f2 | cut -c2- | tr ' ' 'x' | sed s/"^$"/"(none)"/1`" \
              "which is a bit more impressive."
      echo "`date`: I am `basename $0` and I can count to ${i}," \
              "which is not particularly impressive, especially as I get a bit" \
              "confused after ten. I do know that the prime factors of ${i} squared are" \
              "`factor $i | cut -d: -f2 | cut -c1- | tr ' ' 'x' | sed s/"^$"/"(none)"/1`" \
              "which is a bit more impressive." >> /tmp/count.log
      sleep 10
   done
   $
```

bad.sh

> The three errors introduced here are `factor $i`, `cut -d.`, and `cut -c1-`. There is no point in showing the output of this script, as both the stdout and the count.log are incorrect and wrongly formatted.

A second problem with running the same command line twice is that if the command (or pipeline) takes a long time to run, then within a loop like this, the total time taken would be doubled. Far better is to use the same command line and divert its output to both the output and the log file at the same time.

This simple script calculates MD5 checksums of a set of ISO CD images, which it writes to a log file. Because of `tee`, it can also produce useful output to the user at the same time as creating a log file that can be used directly as input to `md5sum --check`, with no duplication of code at all.

Available for
download on
Wrox.com

```
$ cat tee.sh
#!/bin/bash
LOGFILE=/tmp/iso.md5

> $LOGFILE
find /iso -type f -name "*.iso*" -print | while read filename
do
  echo "Checking md5sum of $filename"
  md5sum "$filename" | tee -a $LOGFILE
done

$ ./tee.sh
Checking md5sum of /iso/SLES-11-DVD-i586-GM-DVD1.iso.gz
5d7a7d8a3e296295f6a43a0987f88ecd  /iso/SLES-11-DVD-i586-GM-DVD1.iso.gz
Checking md5sum of /iso/Fedora-14-i686-Live-Desktop.iso.gz
6d07f574ef2e46c0e7df8b87434a78b7  /iso/Fedora-14-i686-Live-Desktop.iso.gz
Checking md5sum of /iso/oi-dev-147-x86.iso.gz
217cb2c9bd64eecb1ce2077fffbd2238  /iso/oi-dev-147-x86.iso.gz
Checking md5sum of /iso/solaris/sol-11-exp-201011-text-x86.iso.gz
05505ece2efc4a046c0b51da71b37444  /iso/solaris/sol-11-exp-201011-text-x86.iso.gz
Checking md5sum of /iso/solaris/sol-10-u9-ga-x86-dvd.iso.gz
80f94ce0f8ab3093ae1beafb8aef75d8  /iso/solaris/sol-10-u9-ga-x86-dvd.iso.gz
$ cat /tmp/iso.md5
5d7a7d8a3e296295f6a43a0987f88ecd  /iso/SLES-11-DVD-i586-GM-DVD1.iso.gz
6d07f574ef2e46c0e7df8b87434a78b7  /iso/Fedora-14-i686-Live-Desktop.iso.gz
217cb2c9bd64eecb1ce2077fffbd2238  /iso/oi-dev-147-x86.iso.gz
```

```
05505ece2efc4a046c0b51da71b37444   /iso/solaris/sol-11-exp-201011-text-x86.iso.gz
80f94ce0f8ab3093ae1beafb8aef75d8   /iso/solaris/sol-10-u9-ga-x86-dvd.iso.gz
$
```

tee.sh

TOUCH

touch is a way to create a file, or update its timestamp, without actually writing anything to it. That may seem a bit useless at first, but it is actually quite useful. Some tools simply check for the existence of a file; when Solaris reboots and finds a file called /reconfigure, it will automatically do a reconfiguration reboot. Many init scripts create files in /var/lock/subsys to indicate that the service is running. An empty file is often all that is needed there, too. It can also be useful to freshen a file with a current timestamp; the make command modifies its behavior depending on how new the source and binary files are. The find command can be told to report only files newer than a supplied sample file.

touch can also be used to make things appear different than they are. This can be useful for backup utilities, which restore files with their original timestamps. It can also be used for other purposes, not all of which are honorable. If a systems administrator accidentally made the wrong change to a file, it would appear to be possible for him to cover his tracks by not changing the timestamp.

```
# ls -l /etc/hosts
-rw-r--r-- 1 root root 511 Feb 25 12:14 /etc/hosts
# grep atomic /etc/hosts
192.168.1.15    atomic
# stat -c "%y" /etc/hosts
2011-02-25 12:14:12.000000000 +0000
# timestamp=`stat -c "%y" /etc/hosts`
# echo $timestamp
2011-02-25 12:14:12.000000000 +0000
# sed -i s/192.168.1.15/192.168.1.11/1 /etc/hosts
# ls -l /etc/hosts
-rw-r--r-- 1 root root 511 Mar 31 16:32 /etc/hosts
# date
Thu Mar 31 16:32:29 BST 2011
# grep atomic /etc/hosts
192.168.1.11    atomic
# touch -d "$timestamp" /etc/hosts
# ls -l /etc/hosts
-rw-r--r-- 1 root root 511 Feb 25 12:14 /etc/hosts
#
```

All is not quite what it seems, however. touch cannot let you modify the change time of a file, which is when its inode details were updated. The purpose of the touch command is to modify the inode details, so this cunning administrator would not be able to hide his tracks after all.

```
# stat -c "%z" /etc/hosts
2011-03-31 16:32:29.000000000 +0100
#
```

FIND

The `find` tool trawls filesystems, inspecting files (particularly their inodes), and can perform a variety of tests on them, and then perform certain actions on the files which match the specified tests. Although the syntax to `find` can be quite difficult to understand, it is almost always far more efficient to use `find` to trawl through the filesystem than to try to craft your own equivalent.

If you simply need to find a particular file by name, and the `updatedb` *command has been run on your system (usually invoked by* `cron` *on a regular basis) then the command* `locate name-of-file` *returns a result almost immediately. It depends on an up-to-date database of the names of files currently in the filesystem, but if that exists, and you are only interested in the name of the file,* `locate` *could be almost infinitely faster than* `find`*.*

The parameters to `find` are basically broken down into expressions and actions. The most common expressions are listed in Table 12-1.

TABLE 12-1: `find` Expressions

EXPRESSION	USED FOR
`-maxdepth levels`	Trawl only *levels* `levels` deep into the filesystem tree.
`-mount` (or `-xdev`)	Don't traverse into different filesystems.
`-anewer filename` or `-cnewer filename` or `-newer filename`	Find files that have been accessed (`-anewer`), changed (`-cnewer`), or modified (`-newer`) more recently than the reference file `filename`.
`-mmin n` or `-mtime n`	Find files that were modified *n* minutes (`-nmin`) or *n* days (`-mtime`) ago.
`-uid u` or `-user u`	Find files owned by user ID (`-uid`) or username (`-user`) u.
`-gid g` or `-group g`	Find files in the group ID (`-gid`) or group name (`-group`) g.
`-nouser` or `-nogroup`	Find files with no matching name of owner/group.
`-name n` or `-iname n`	Find files whose name matches *n* (`-iname` is case-insensitive).
`-perm -g=w`	Find files that have the group-writable bit set (regardless of other bits).
`-perm o=r`	Find files that have permissions 0500 exactly (owner can read, nothing else).

continues

TABLE 12-1 *(continued)*

EXPRESSION	USED FOR
`-size n`	Find files that have size n (suffixes b, k, M, G, the full list as well as others are allowed).
`-size +n` or `-size -n`	Find files that are larger (+n) or smaller (-n) than n.
`-type t`	Find files of type t, where t can be d(irectory), l(ink), f(ile), or b, c, p, s, D.

These expressions can be combined; the find(1) man page has some examples, although the code examples here should show you how expressions can be put together.

The commonly useful actions for find are somewhat easier to understand. -print simply names all matching files; -ls does the same but in an output very similar to that of the ls command. -print0 is covered in the xargs section of Chapter 14. There is also an -exec action, which is covered later in this section.

An incremental indexer can use find to identify files that have been modified since it last ran. For example, a website based on static files may be updated throughout the day by various contributors, but it would be inefficient to re-index the database every time a new file was uploaded. It would also be inefficient to re-index all files every night, as some may be very large and never change. By using the -newer option to find, an indexer can run on a regular basis (maybe once a day), identify the new or updated files, and re-index them overnight. This script identifies which files are suitable for indexing. It docs this with the find . -type f -newer $LASTRUN filter. This finds only regular files (not directories, block device drivers, and so on) that have been modified more recently than the timestamp on the $LASTRUN file. On the first invocation, or when $LASTRUN does not exist, it will index everything. On subsequent runs, only recently updated files will be indexed.

```
# cat reindexer.sh
#!/bin/bash
LASTRUN=/var/run/web.lastrun
WEBROOT=/var/www
# be verbose if asked.
START_TIME=`date`

function reindex
{
  # Do whatever magic is required to add this new/updated
  # file to the database.
  add_to_database "$@"
}

if [ ! -f "$LASTRUN" ]; then
  echo "Error: $LASTRUN not found. Will reindex everything."
  # index from the epoch...
  touch -d "1 Jan 1970" $LASTRUN
  if [ "$?" -ne "0" ]; then
    echo "Error: Cannot update $LASTRUN"
    exit 1
  fi
```

```
    fi

    cd $WEBROOT
    find . -type f -newer $LASTRUN -print | while read filename
    do
      reindex "$filename"
    done
    echo "Run complete at `date`."
    echo "Subsequent runs will pick up only files updated since this reindexing"
    echo "which was started at $START_TIME"
    touch -d "$START_TIME" $LASTRUN
    if [ "$?" -ne "0" ]; then
      echo "Error: Cannot update $LASTRUN"
      exit 1
    fi
    ls -ld $LASTRUN

    # ./reindexer.sh
    Error: /var/run/web.lastrun not found. Will reindex everything.
    Mon Mar 28 09:19:51 BST 2011:  Added to database: ./images/sgp_title_bg.jpg
    Mon Mar 28 09:19:52 BST 2011:  Added to database: ./images/vcss-blue.gif
    Mon Mar 28 09:19:53 BST 2011:  Added to database: ./images/shade2.gif
    Mon Mar 28 09:19:54 BST 2011:  Added to database: ./images/datacentrewide.jpg
    Mon Mar 28 09:20:00 BST 2011:  Added to database: ./images/shade1.gif
    Mon Mar 28 09:20:03 BST 2011:  Added to database: ./images/sgp_services.jpg
    Mon Mar 28 09:20:04 BST 2011:  Added to database: ./images/sgp_content_bg.jpg
     [ some output omitted for brevity ]
    Mon Mar 28 09:20:51 BST 2011:  Added to database: ./services.txt
    Mon Mar 28 09:20:53 BST 2011:  Added to database: ./sgp_style.css
    Mon Mar 28 09:20:54 BST 2011:  Added to database: ./i
    Mon Mar 28 09:20:55 BST 2011:  Added to database: ./common-services.txt
    Run complete at Tue Mar 28 09:20:57 BST 2011.
    Subsequent runs will pick up only files updated since this reindexing
    which was started at Tue Mar 28 09:19:49 BST 2011
    -rw-r--r-- 1 root root 0 Mar 28 09:19 /var/run/web.lastrun
    #
```

reindexer.sh

When the script runs the following morning, it picks up only the updated files. Notice that the script ran from 09:04 to 09:05, but the web.lastrun file is updated with the timestamp of the start time of 09:04, not the finish time of 09:05. That allows files that were updated while the script was running to be picked up by the subsequent run of the script.

```
    # ./reindexer.sh
    Tue Mar 29 09:04:46 BST 2011:  Added to database: ./images/shade2.gif
    Tue Mar 29 09:04:51 BST 2011:  Added to database: ./images/shade1.gif
    Tue Mar 29 09:04:58 BST 2011:  Added to database: ./services.txt
    Tue Mar 29 09:05:01 BST 2011:  Added to database: ./sgp_style.css
    Run complete at Tue Mar 29 09:05:02 BST 2011.
    Subsequent runs will pick up only files updated since this reindexing
    which was started at Tue Mar 29 09:04:46 BST 2011
    -rw-r--r-- 1 root root 0 Mar 29 09:04 /var/run/web.lastrun
    #
```

FIND -EXEC

The -exec flag to find causes find to execute the given command once per file matched, and it will place the name of the file wherever you put the {} placeholder. The command must end with a semi-colon, which has to be escaped from the shell, either as \; or as ";". In the following script, every file found has its md5sum taken and stored in a temporary file. This is achieved by this find -exec command in the script:

```
find "${DIR}" $SIZE -type f -exec md5sum {} \; | sort > $MD5
```

> *The* $SIZE *variable optionally adds* -size +0 *to the flags passed to* find, *as there is not a lot of point in taking the* md5sum *of a bunch of zero-length files; The* md5sum *of an empty file is always* d41d8cd98f00b204e9800998ecf8427e.

See the uniq section in Chapter 13 for a detailed explanation of how uniq filters the results. In short, -w32 tells it to look only at the checksums, and -d tells it to ignore truly unique lines, as they could not represent duplicate files.

The problem of efficiently locating duplicate files is not as simple as it might at first sound. With potentially gigabytes or terabytes of data, it is not efficient to use diff to compare each file against all of the other files. By taking a checksum of each file first, the up-front cost is relatively high, but then by using sort and uniq to good effect, the set of possible matches is quite easily and quickly obtained. The -c flag to this script goes the extra mile and still does a diff of any pair of files that have the same MD5 checksum. This is arguably the most inefficient way to do it, as diff can quickly spot two non-identical files, but it has to compare every single byte of two identical files before it can declare that they are indeed the same as each other. Given the incredibly low risk of two different files having the same checksum, whether or not it is worth using that option depends on the usage case.

As mentioned in the comments in the script, md5sum, like many commands, can take a set of file-names as its input, but when dealing with more files than the kernel is prepared to allocate for the command's arguments, it will fail to work at all. Therefore, find -exec is the perfect solution to this problem. Simply taking that relatively small amount of text and piping it through sort before dumping it into $MD5 means that the task is already nearly complete. All the padding around that one find - exec | sort pipeline is really just for sanity checking and providing tidier output.

```
$ cat check_duplicate_files.sh
#!/bin/bash
MD5=`mktemp /tmp/md5.XXXXXXXXXX`
SAMEFILES=`mktemp /tmp/samefiles.XXXXXXXXXX`
matches=0
comparisons=0
combinations=0

VERBOSE=1
SIZE=""
DIR=`pwd`
diff=0

function logmsg()
```

```
{
  if [ "$VERBOSE" -ge "$1" ]; then
    shift
    echo "$@"
  fi
}

function cleanup()
{
  echo "Caught signal - cleaning up."
  rm -f ${MD5} ${SAMEFILES} > /dev/null
  exit 0
}

function usage()
{
  echo "Usage: `basename $0` [ -e ] [ -v verbosity ] [ -c ] [ -d directory ]"
  echo " -e ignores empty files"
  echo " -v sets verbosity from 0 (silent) to 9 (diagnostics)"
  echo " -c actually checks the files"
  exit 2
}

# Parse options first
while getopts 'ev:l:cd:' opt
do
  case $opt in
    e) SIZE=" -size +0 " ;;
    v) VERBOSE=$OPTARG ;;
    d) DIR=$OPTARG ;;
    c) diff=1 ;;
  esac
done

trap cleanup 1 2 3 6 9 11 15

logmsg 3 "`date`: `basename $0` starting."
kickoff=`date +%s`

# Make sure that the temporary files can be created
touch $MD5 || exit 1

start_md5=`date +%s`
logmsg 3 "`date`: Gathering MD5 SUMs. Please wait."
find "${DIR}" $SIZE -type f -exec md5sum {} \; | sort > $MD5
#md5sum `find ${DIR} ${SIZE} -type f -print` > $MD5
# cutting out find is a lot faster, but limited to a few thousand files
done_md5=`date +%s`
logmsg 3 "`date`: MD5 SUMs gathered. Comparing results..."
logmsg 2 "md5sum took `expr $done_md5 - $start_md5` seconds"

uniq -d -w32 $MD5 | while read md5 file1
do
  logmsg 1 "Checking $file1"
  grep "^${md5} " $MD5 | grep -v "^${md5} .${file1}$" | cut -c35- > $SAMEFILES
```

```
      cat $SAMEFILES | while read file2
      do
        duplicate=0
        if [ "$diff" -eq "1" ]; then
          diff "$file1" "$file2" > /dev/null
          if [ "$?" -eq "0" ]; then
            duplicate=1
          else
            duplicate=2
          fi
        else
          duplicate=1
        fi
        case $duplicate in
          0) ;;
          1)
            if [ "$VERBOSE" -gt "5" ]; then
              echo "$file2 is duplicate of $file1"
            else
              echo $file2
            fi
            ;;
          2) echo "$file1 and $file2 have the same md5sum" ;;
        esac
      done
done
endtime=`date +%s`
logmsg 2 "Total Elapsed Time `expr $endtime - $kickoff` seconds."
logmsg 2 "`date`: Done. `basename $0` found $matches matches in $comparisons compar
isons."
logmsg 2 "Compared `wc -l $MD5 | awk '{ print $1 }'` files; that makes for $combina
tions combinations."
rm -f ${MD5} > /dev/null
$
```

check_duplicate_files.sh

The find command produces output like the code that follows. Piping the output through sort
shows what ends up in the $MD5 file.

```
$ find . -type f -exec md5sum {} \;
288be591a425992c4247ea5bccd2c929  ./My Photos/DCIM0003.doc
698ef8996726c92d9fbb484eb4e49d73  ./My Photos/DCIM0001.jpg
c33578695c1de14c8deeba5164ed0adb  ./My Photos/DCIM0002.jpg
ecca34048d511d1dc01afe71e245d8b1  ./My Documents/doc1.doc
288be591a425992c4247ea5bccd2c929  ./My Documents/cv.odt
619a126ef0a79ca4c0f3e3d061b4e675  ./etc/hosts
d41d8cd98f00b204e9800998ecf8427e  ./etc/config.txt
d265cc0520a9a43e5f07ccca453c94f5  ./bin/ls
619a126ef0a79ca4c0f3e3d061b4e675  ./bin/hosts.bak
da5e6e7db4ccbdb62076fe529082e5cd  ./listfiles
$ find . -type f -exec md5sum {} \; | sort
288be591a425992c4247ea5bccd2c929  ./My Documents/cv.odt
288be591a425992c4247ea5bccd2c929  ./My Photos/DCIM0003.doc
```

```
619a126ef0a79ca4c0f3e3d061b4e675   ./bin/hosts.bak
619a126ef0a79ca4c0f3e3d061b4e675   ./etc/hosts
698ef8996726c92d9fbb484eb4e49d73   ./My Photos/DCIM0001.jpg
c33578695c1de14c8deeba5164ed0adb   ./My Photos/DCIM0002.jpg
d265cc0520a9a43e5f07ccca453c94f5   ./bin/ls
d41d8cd98f00b204e9800998ecf8427e   ./etc/config.txt
da5e6e7db4ccbdb62076fe529082e5cd   ./listfiles
ecca34048d511d1dc01afe71e245d8b1   ./My Documents/doc1.doc
$ find . -type f -exec md5sum {} \; | sort | uniq -d -w32
288be591a425992c4247ea5bccd2c929   ./My Documents/cv.odt
619a126ef0a79ca4c0f3e3d061b4e675   ./bin/hosts.bak
```

A quick scan of the sorted output shows that hosts.bak and hosts have the same MD5 checksum, as do cv.odt and DCIM0003.doc . The uniq -d command strips out any truly unique entries, leaving only cv.odt and hosts.bak. These files' checksums are then located in the $MD5 file, revealing the duplicate entries.

```
$ find . -type f -exec md5sum {} \; \
      | grep 288be591a425992c4247ea5bccd2c929
288be591a425992c4247ea5bccd2c929   ./My Photos/DCIM0003.doc
288be591a425992c4247ea5bccd2c929   ./My Documents/cv.odt
$ find . -type f -exec md5sum {} \; \
      | grep 619a126ef0a79ca4c0f3e3d061b4e675
619a126ef0a79ca4c0f3e3d061b4e675   ./etc/hosts
619a126ef0a79ca4c0f3e3d061b4e675   ./bin/hosts.bak
$
```

As mentioned previously, it is then down to the level of security required as to whether or not to run diff against the identified matching files.

SUMMARY

While this chapter mainly looked at manipulating the files themselves, and their relationship with the underlying filesystem, the next chapter looks at manipulating the text within the file (or elsewhere).

13

Text Manipulation

In Unix and Linux, everything is a file. An awful lot of those files are plain ASCII text, and there are a lot of tools in Unix for manipulating text. This is another example of the principle that tools should "do one thing and do it well." This chapter introduces a mixture of some of the best-known text manipulating tools and some of the less well-known ones.

These text conversion filters can generally take their input either from stdin or from a file named on the command line. They then send their output to stdout. This means that although they can be used directly on files, they are often even more useful in a pipeline. So `cut -d: -f7 /etc/passwd | sort | uniq` will list all of the different shells configured in `/etc/passwd` in one single pipeline.

This chapter looks in detail at some of the best, most common, and most useful text manipulation tools available in the Unix and GNU/Linux environments. On the GNU side of things, most of these tools are now contained within the coreutils package; there used to be fileutils, shellutils, and textutils, until they were all merged into the coreutils package.

CUT

The `cut` command is used widely in shell scripts. It is the complement to `paste`, although "cut" and "paste" in this context have nothing to do with the GUI metaphor of moving data to a clipboard and then pasting it back again. Its advantage over more heavyweight alternatives such as `awk` is that it is much smaller and simpler and is therefore faster to execute. This might seem trivial, but it can make a noticeable difference within loops. It takes either one or two parameters. In its simplest form, `cut -c n` cuts out only column n, and `cut -c m-n` cuts out columns m to n in each line of the input, or of the file passed as an argument. It can also cut based on a delimiter, so, for example, `cut -d: -f5 /etc/passwd` will grab the fifth colon-delimited field from each line in `/etc/passwd`. The following script cuts the filename as the first field of a colon-delimited list, and then the title of the page from the first > onwards to the next <. It is far from foolproof, although the better understood the file format is, the more reliable this method is.

```
$ cat gettitle.sh
#!/bin/bash

grep "<title>" *.html | while read html
do
    filename=`echo $html | cut -d: -f1`
    title=`echo $html | cut -d">" -f2- | cut -d"<" -f1`
    echo "$filename = $title"
done
$ grep "<title>" *.html
Aliases.html:<title>Aliases - Bash Reference Manual</title>
ANSI_002dC-Quoting.html:<title>ANSI-C Quoting - Bash Reference Manual</title>
Arrays.html:<title>Arrays - Bash Reference Manual</title>
Bash-Builtins.html:<title>Bash Builtins - Bash Reference Manual</title>
Bash-Features.html:<title>Bash Features - Bash Reference Manual</title>
Bash-POSIX-Mode.html:<title>Bash POSIX Mode - Bash Reference Manual</title>
$ ./gettitle.sh
Aliases.html = Aliases - Bash Reference Manual
ANSI_002dC-Quoting.html = ANSI-C Quoting - Bash Reference Manual
Arrays.html = Arrays - Bash Reference Manual
Bash-Builtins.html = Bash Builtins - Bash Reference Manual
Bash-Features.html = Bash Features - Bash Reference Manual
Bash-POSIX-Mode.html = Bash POSIX Mode - Bash Reference Manual
$
```

gettitle.sh

ECHO

Most people are reasonably familiar with the echo command. It can be used for more than just displaying sequences of text to the terminal. These dial1 and dial2 scripts show you how to keep an interactive user updated and assured that something is still happening during long or slow periods when the script may be doing something complicated but cannot know how long it may take.

dial1

This first implementation of a "dial" actually just displays the current time, once per second, but without filling the screen with sequences of timestamps. It does this by sending a Control-M (^M) character to the terminal before the date itself, and disabling echo's default behavior of adding a \r\n sequence to the end of each line it displays, so that subsequent output will be at the start of a new line on the screen.

Control-M is the Carriage Return character (also commonly referred to as CR or \r), which is normally followed by the \n (New Line) character. Just sending Control-M by itself means that the cursor is brought back to the beginning of the line, then the date is displayed, and finally, the cursor stays where it is instead of going to the start of the next line, shifting up the current line if at the bottom of the terminal.

By default, the bash builtin echo *treats a backslash as a regular character. The* -e *switch to* echo *tells it to interpret backslash sequences as marking special character sequences. This is not strictly required in this script, but the two commonly go together. The Bourne* echo *does interpret backslash characters by default;* echo -e *effectively makes bash* echo *act like Bourne* echo.

A default behavior of echo is that it displays its input followed by \r\n. This is disabled with the -n switch. Experiment with these switches to get comfortable with what impact they have; the snippet that follows suggests some starting points.

```
$ echo "this line is followed by a newline"
this line is followed by a newline
$ echo -n "but this one is not."
but this one is not.$
$
$ echo "another way to omit the newline\c"
another way to omit the newline\c
$ echo -e "but it requires the -e switch\c"
but it requires the -e switch$
$
$ echo "backslash is nothing special.\r\n\r\n"
backslash is nothing special.\r\n\r\n
$ echo -e "unless you use the -e switch.\r\n\r\n"
unless you use the -e switch.


$
```

To enter the Control-M character into the script, the metacharacter Control-V is used. In vim, hold down the Control key and then press v; a carat (^) is displayed. Hold down Control again and press m. An uppercase M is displayed after the carat: echo -e "^M`date`". Here I have used the -v switch to cat so that it displays the non-printing characters in a legible format.

```
$ cat -v dial1.sh
#!/bin/bash

function stopdial
{
 if [ ! -z "$DIALPID" ]; then
   kill -9 $DIALPID
   unset DIALPID
   echo
 fi
}

function dial
{
  echo -en " "
  while :
  do
    echo -en "^M`date`"
```

```
      sleep 1
   done
   echo
}

# on any signal stop the dial subprocess
trap stopdial `seq 1 63`

echo Starting
echo "`date`: Doing something long and complicated..."

dial &
DIALPID=$!
sleep 10
stopdial

echo "`date`: Finished the complicated bit. That was hard!"
echo Done
$ ./dial1.sh
Starting
Fri Mar  4 17:26:48 GMT 2011: Doing something long and complicated...
Fri Mar  4 17:26:57 GMT 2011
Fri Mar  4 17:26:58 GMT 2011: Finished the complicated bit. That was hard!
Done
$
```

dial1.sh

It can't easily be shown on paper, but between 17:26:48 and 17:26:57 in the example above, the time was updated on the middle line, once every second. If the script gets killed partway through execution, the `trap` ensures that the dial gets killed, too. Otherwise, the terminal would keep getting updates of the current time as it goes on. Here is a shot of the script without the `trap` enabled.

 I increased the `sleep` *slightly to allow a bit of time to type messages to show what is happening. I also had the* `ps` *command in the history to save having to type too fast — type too slowly and the command line that you are typing in is interrupted by the date:* "ps Fri Mar 4 17:57:42 -eaf"

```
$ ./dial1.sh
Starting
Fri Mar  4 17:57:39 GMT 2011: Doing something long and complicated...
Fri Mar  4 17:57:43 GMT 2011^C
$
$ echo stopped it
stopped it
Fri Mar  4 17:57:51 GMT 2011
Fri Mar  4 17:57:59 GMT 2011
Fri Mar  4 17:58:07 GMT 2011
$ echo it came back
it came back
```

```
Fri Mar  4 17:58:15 GMT 2011
$ echo help
help
Fri Mar  4 17:58:19 GMT 2011
$ !ps
ps -eaf|grep dial1.sh
steve     4214     1  0 17:57 pts/3    00:00:00 /bin/bash ./dial1.sh
steve     4239  3699  0 17:58 pts/3    00:00:00 grep dial1.sh
Fri Mar  4 17:58:23 GMT 2011
$ kill -9 4214
$
```

 The final echo *statement in the* dial *function is not necessary because the* while *loop never terminates. However, it is tidy to put the terminal back in a consistent state, and if the loop was replaced with one that does terminate for whatever reason, then you would want the terminal to be tidy when it exits the function. In the* dial2 *script, this* echo *gets moved up into the* stopdial *function because that function does more to take care of cleaning up the display.*

dial2

The constantly updating date command is one way to assure the user that something is still happening. A slicker way is to have a spinning ASCII dial. This is a single character that displays each of the characters in the dial array in sequence. This gives the appearance of a dial constantly rotating clockwise.

There is another slight change to the dial function. It uses a counter, $d, to keep track of which character to display. It also sends the Control-H character, which is the backspace character, instead of Control-M, the Carriage Return character. This has the added benefit that unlike using Control-M, the dial can start from anywhere along the line, meaning that it is possible to have an introductory echo (again using the -n switch) introducing the dial.

```
$ cat -v dial2.sh
#!/bin/bash

function stopdial
{
 if [ ! -z "$DIALPID" ]; then
   kill -9 $DIALPID
   unset DIALPID
   echo -en "^H"
 fi
}

function dial
{
  dial=('/' '-' '\' '|' '/' '-' '\' '|' )
  echo -en " "
  d=0
```

```
      while :
      do
        echo -en "^H${dial[$d]}"
        d=`expr $d + 1`
        d=`expr $d % 8` # size of dial[] array
        sleep 1
      done
      echo
    }

    # on any signal stop the dial subprocess
    trap stopdial `seq 1 63`

    echo Starting
    echo "`date`: Doing something long and complicated..."

    echo -en "Here is a dial to keep you amused: "
    dial &
    DIALPID=$!
    sleep 10
    stopdial

    echo "`date`: Finished the complicated bit. That was hard!"
    echo Done
    $ ./dial2.sh
    Starting
    Fri Mar  4 18:05:51 GMT 2011: Doing something long and complicated...
    Here is a dial to keep you amused:
    Fri Mar  4 18:06:01 GMT 2011: Finished the complicated bit. That was hard!
    Done
    $
```

dial2.sh

Again, it is hard to show on paper, but after the "keep you amused: " message there was a dial that spun one-eighth of a circle every second. The extra echo -en "^H " in the stopdial function ensures that the cursor does a backspace over the dial and then writes a space over the top of it so that the last-displayed character does not stay onscreen after the dial has finished spinning. The final echo in the dial function has also been cleaned up to do the same.

FMT

fmt, part of the GNU coreutils package, is a classic example of a useful but little-known system tool. Its purpose is to format lines of text, much like the trimline.sh script in Chapter 7. In addition to being able to split lines and optionally merge shorter lines together, it has a very useful feature in the -p option, which is most useful for languages (such as the shell, with the # symbol, or C/C++ with its // notation), that use a marker for whole-line comments. fmt can also do some basic formatting; the -u flag tells it to make sure that there is exactly one space between each word and two spaces after a period.

This first one-line script invokes `fmt` with a small excerpt from *Gulliver's Travels*. As the `cat` command shows, the original `gulliver.txt` has no real formatting, but `fmt -ut` fixes word wrap, word spacing, and even indentation.

```
$ cat gulliver.txt
CHAPTER I.

The author gives some account of himself and family. His first inducements to tr
avel. He is shipwrecked, and swims for his life. Gets safe on shore in the count
ry of Lilliput; is made a prisoner, and carried up the country.

My father had a small estate in Nottinghamshire: I was the third of five sons. H
e sent me to Emanuel College in Cambridge at fourteen years old, where I resided
 three years, and applied myself close to my studies; but the charge of maintain
ing me, although I had a very scanty allowance, being too great for a narrow for
tune, I was bound apprentice to Mr. James Bates, an eminent surgeon in London, w
ith whom I continued four years.

$ fmt -ut gulliver.txt
CHAPTER I.

The author gives some account of himself and family. His first inducements
    to travel. He is shipwrecked, and swims for his life. Gets safe on
    shore in the country of Lilliput; is made a prisoner, and carried up
    the country.

My father had a small estate in Nottinghamshire: I was the third of
    five sons. He sent me to Emanuel College in Cambridge at fourteen
    years old, where I resided three years, and applied myself close
    to my studies; but the charge of maintaining me, although I had a
    very scanty allowance, being too great for a narrow fortune, I was
    bound apprentice to Mr. James Bates, an eminent surgeon in London,
    with whom I continued four years.

$
```

The second one-line script invokes `fmt` with the `-p` flag to format the comments in a shell script. With the `-s` flag, `fmt` would split only the lines that are too long, but without `-s`, it also wraps shorter lines together. Once `fmt` has tidied everything up, it makes sure that each of these comment lines starts with a hash. Non-comment lines are left totally as they were.

```
$ cat code.sh
#!/bin/bash
# this is a useful script that does far
# more than its comments
# might suggest at first glance.
#
# for one thing, it demonstrates the valid use of comments in a shell script in
a useful and practical manner.
# for another, it is very short and concise, unlike these comments, which are r
eally rather rambling at best.
# so it is useful
# to have a script
```

```
# like this in your arsenal.

echo "$@"
# That was fun.
# The end.
# fin
$ fmt code.sh -p "#"
#!/bin/bash
# this is a useful script that does far more than its comments might
# suggest at first glance.
#
# for one thing, it demonstrates the valid use of comments in a shell
# script in a useful and practical manner.  for another, it is very short
# and concise, unlike these comments, which are really rather rambling
# at best.  so it is useful to have a script like this in your arsenal.

echo "$@"
# That was fun.  The end.  fin
$ fmt -p"#" -w 40 code.sh
#!/bin/bash
# this is a useful script that does far
# more than its comments might suggest
# at first glance.
#
# for one thing, it demonstrates the
# valid use of comments in a shell
# script in a useful and practical
# manner.  for another, it is very
# short and concise, unlike these
# comments, which are really rather
# rambling at best.  so it is useful
# to have a script like this in your
# arsenal.

echo "$@"
# That was fun.  The end.  fin
$ fmt -p"#" -w 40 -s code.sh
#!/bin/bash
# this is a useful script that does far
# more than its comments
# might suggest at first glance.
#
# for one thing, it demonstrates the
# valid use of comments in a shell
# script in a useful and practical
# manner.
# for another, it is very short and
# concise, unlike these comments, which
# are really rather rambling at best.
# so it is useful
# to have a script
# like this in your arsenal.

echo "$@"
```

```
# That was fun.
# The end.
# fin
$
```

An even more powerful tool is `indent`, which can reformat entire C programs in a variety of styles, including the Kernighan and Ritchie style used in their seminal book, the GNU style, and the standard format for Linux kernel source code. This makes it easy for a developer to concentrate on the code using her own preferred format, and to share it with a multi-developer project in a standardized form. It also helps code from one project to be reused in another without breaking either project's style guidelines.

HEAD AND TAIL

The `head` and `tail` commands also do one thing and do it well. They work on text files, or in a pipeline, on a line-by-line basis, extracting lines from the start or end of the file or pipeline. By combining these two tools, individual lines or sets of lines can also be extracted from the middle of the file.

Prizes

This first script uses `shuf` with `head` and `tail` to first randomly sort the list of names and then extract the first three names from the resulting temporary file. Doing this randomization once and then repeatedly going back to the saved result, picking out different parts each time, ensures that the results are consistent, and there is no chance of the same person being mentioned twice. The first three people chosen get the Gold, Silver, and Bronze prizes. Positions 4, 5, and 6 each get a runners-up prize, and the person who came last as a result of the shuffling gets the booby prize.

Available for
download on
Wrox.com

```
$ cat prizes.sh
#!/bin/bash
PEOPLE=people.txt
temp=`mktemp`

shuf $PEOPLE > $temp
prizes=( Gold Silver Bronze )

position=0
head -3 $temp | while read name
do
  echo "The ${prizes[$position]} prize goes to $name"
  position=`expr $position + 1`
done
echo

echo "There are three runners-up prizes. In alphabetical order, the winners are:"
head -6 $temp | tail -3 | sort
echo
echo "The booby prize goes to `tail -1 $temp`. Bad luck `tail -1 $temp`!"
echo
echo "Congratulations to everybody who participated."
```

```
    rm -f $temp

$ ./prizes.sh
The Gold prize goes to Emily
The Silver prize goes to Bethany
The Bronze prize goes to Christopher

There are three runners-up prizes. In alphabetical order, the winners are:
Anthony
Mary
Daniel

The booby prize goes to John. Bad luck John!

Congratulations to everybody who participated.
$
```

prizes.sh

World Cup

The second head and tail script is a little more involved. It follows a similar principle, however; for the World Cup soccer tournament, each country is randomly assigned to a group, and then each country in the group plays one game against every other country in that group. Like the Prizes script in the preceding section, the countries are randomized using shuf, and then the for group in `seq 1 $NUMGROUPS` loop extracts the appropriate lines from the randomized file. If there are eight teams in a group (as there are with this test data from the 2010 World Cup), then on the first iteration, grouphead is 8, so head grabs the first 8 lines. tail then takes the last 8 lines of those 8, which is pointless the first time around, but makes sense on subsequent iterations. On the second iteration, grouphead is 16, so head grabs the first 16 lines, and tail then extracts the last 8 lines, so that /tmp/group2 gets lines 9–16 of the randomized file. The third time around, grouphead is 24, so the tail -8 results in lines 17–24. On the fourth iteration, grouphead is 32, so the head command returns the entire contents of the file, which are then run through tail -8 to get lines 25–32.

Once the script has sorted the groups, pr is used to display them in columnar format (to save a little space) and the arrangegames function arranges the members of each group to play against each other exactly once. Finally, the order of these group games is randomized to give a more natural feeling, as well as giving each team more chance of a rest between games. Finally, it is sorted by pr into two columns, again to save a little space.

```
$ cat worldcup.sh
#!/bin/bash

function arrangegames
{
  played=`mktemp`
  grep -v "^*** Group " /tmp/group${group} | while read team
  do
    # can't play against yourself
    grep -v "^${team}$" /tmp/group${group} | \
```

```
        grep -v "^*** Group " | while read opponent
     do
        grep "^${opponent} vs ${team}$" $played > /dev/null
        if [ "$?" -ne "0" ]; then
          echo "$team vs $opponent" | tee -a $played
        fi
     done
   done
   rm -f $played
}

################# Script Starts here ########################
TEAMS=teams.txt
RANDOMIZED=`mktemp`
NUMTEAMS=`wc -l $TEAMS | awk '{ print $1 }'`
NUMGROUPS=4

# Each group must have an even number of teams
TEAMSINGROUP=`echo "$NUMTEAMS / $NUMGROUPS" | bc`
echo "scale=1; $TEAMSINGROUP / 2" | bc | grep "\.0$" > /dev/null 2>&1
if [ "$?" -ne "0" ]; then
  echo "$NUMTEAMS does not divide into $NUMGROUPS groups neatly."
  exit 1
fi

shuf $TEAMS > $RANDOMIZED

for group in `seq 1 $NUMGROUPS`
do
  echo "*** Group $group ***" > /tmp/group${group}
  grouphead=`expr $group \* $TEAMSINGROUP`
  head -$grouphead $RANDOMIZED | tail -$TEAMSINGROUP >> /tmp/group${group}
done
echo "Groupings:"
pr -t -m /tmp/group*
echo

for group in `seq 1 $NUMGROUPS`
do
  echo "*** Qualifying games in Group $group ***"
  # Randomizing the order gives the teams more of a break.
  arrangegames $group | shuf | pr -t -c2
  echo
done
$ ./worldcup.sh
Groupings:
*** Group 1 ***    *** Group 2 ***    *** Group 3 ***    *** Group 4 ***
Ghana              Italy              Uruguay            Cameroon
Cote d'Ivorie      Mexico             Denmark            Japan
Greece             United States      Germany            South Korea
Brazil             Chile              Slovakia           Nigeria
Portugal           Netherlands        Spain              Switzerland
New Zealand        Slovenia           Argentina          Honduras
Australia          France             South Africa       Serbia
```

```
Paraguay          England          Algeria          North Korea

*** Qualifying games in Group 1 ***
Portugal vs Australia            Brazil vs New Zealand
Portugal vs New Zealand          Greece vs Paraguay
Ghana vs Brazil                  Cote d'Ivorie vs Portugal
Cote d'Ivorie vs New Zealand     Greece vs Portugal
Greece vs Australia              Cote d'Ivorie vs Greece
Cote d'Ivorie vs Paraguay        Ghana vs Paraguay
Greece vs Brazil                 Brazil vs Portugal
Brazil vs Paraguay               Cote d'Ivorie vs Australia
Brazil vs Australia              Cote d'Ivorie vs Brazil
New Zealand vs Australia         Ghana vs Greece
New Zealand vs Paraguay          Ghana vs Cote d'Ivorie
Ghana vs New Zealand             Ghana vs Portugal
Greece vs New Zealand            Ghana vs Australia
Australia vs Paraguay            Portugal vs Paraguay

*** Qualifying games in Group 2 ***
Italy vs United States           Mexico vs Slovenia
United States vs England         Italy vs France
Italy vs England                 Slovenia vs France
Italy vs Mexico                  United States vs Slovenia
France vs England                Netherlands vs Slovenia
Netherlands vs England           Italy vs Netherlands
United States vs Chile           Chile vs Netherlands
Mexico vs United States          Italy vs Chile
Mexico vs France                 Chile vs England
United States vs Netherlands     Italy vs Slovenia
Mexico vs Chile                  Mexico vs England
Slovenia vs England              Chile vs France
Chile vs Slovenia                Mexico vs Netherlands
United States vs France          Netherlands vs France

*** Qualifying games in Group 3 ***
Germany vs South Africa          Argentina vs South Africa
Argentina vs Algeria             Uruguay vs Spain
Uruguay vs Denmark               Denmark vs Spain
Slovakia vs South Africa         Germany vs Algeria
Germany vs Argentina             Uruguay vs Germany
Spain vs Argentina               Denmark vs Algeria
Uruguay vs Argentina             Slovakia vs Algeria
Spain vs Algeria                 Uruguay vs Algeria
Germany vs Slovakia              Slovakia vs Spain
South Africa vs Algeria          Uruguay vs Slovakia
Denmark vs Argentina             Denmark vs Slovakia
Germany vs Spain                 Spain vs South Africa
Denmark vs Germany               Uruguay vs South Africa
Denmark vs South Africa          Slovakia vs Argentina

*** Qualifying games in Group 4 ***
Switzerland vs Serbia            Nigeria vs North Korea
South Korea vs North Korea       South Korea vs Nigeria
South Korea vs Honduras          South Korea vs Switzerland
Japan vs Serbia                  Nigeria vs Serbia
Nigeria vs Switzerland           Honduras vs North Korea
Cameroon vs North Korea          Switzerland vs North Korea
```

```
Cameroon vs South Korea        Cameroon vs Japan
Cameroon vs Serbia             Japan vs Nigeria
Serbia vs North Korea          Switzerland vs Honduras
Japan vs Honduras              Cameroon vs Switzerland
Japan vs Switzerland           Japan vs South Korea
South Korea vs Serbia          Cameroon vs Nigeria
Honduras vs Serbia             Japan vs North Korea
Nigeria vs Honduras            Cameroon vs Honduras

$
```

The `tail` command can also be useful with its `-f` and `-F` options. These follow a file as lines are appended to it. `-F` differs from `-f` in that when using `-F` the file need not exist, or could be removed or truncated while `tail` is running, and `tail` will simply wait for it to come back. This is particularly useful interactively for monitoring log files, but it can also be used in a shell script, notably by backgrounding the `tail -F` process so that updates from the file being followed are shown to the user as they happen, but the script can continue processing. This script monitors the Apache access and error log files as it executes, so the user gets to see the results from the web server itself at the same time as the logs.

The `-n0` switch tells `tail` not to report any of the existing contents of the file (by default it displays the last 10 lines). The `-f` flag tells it to follow the file, displaying each new line as it arrives.

```
# cat apache.sh
#!/bin/bash

tail -n0 -f /var/log/apache2/access.log &
access=$!
tail -n0 -f /var/log/apache2/error.log &
error=$!

echo "Requesting HEAD of /..."
printf "HEAD / HTTP/1.0\n\n" | netcat localhost 80
echo
echo
echo "---- `date`"
sleep 10
echo "---- `date`"
echo "Requesting /nofile..."
printf "GET /nofile HTTP/1.0\n\n" | netcat localhost 80

kill -9 $access
kill -9 $error
# ./apache.sh
Requesting HEAD of /...
[Wed Mar 02 13:01:45 2011] [error] [client 127.0.0.1] PHP Notice:  Undefined variab
le: panelFile in /home/steve/sgp/newweb/php/layoutStart.php on line 25
[Wed Mar 02 13:01:45 2011] [error] [client 127.0.0.1] PHP Notice:  Undefined variab
le: panelTitle in /home/steve/sgp/newweb/php/layoutStart.php on line 25
HTTP/1.1 200 OK
Date: Wed, 02 Mar 2011 13:01:45 GMT
Server: Apache/2.2.16 (Debian)
X-Powered-By: PHP/5.3.3-7
Vary: Accept-Encoding
Connection: close
```

```
Content-Type: text/html

127.0.0.1 - - [02/Mar/2011:13:01:45 +0000] "HEAD / HTTP/1.0" 200 182 "-" "-"


---- Wed Mar  2 13:01:45 GMT 2011
---- Wed Mar  2 13:01:55 GMT 2011
Requesting /nofile...
[Wed Mar 02 13:01:55 2011] [error] [client 127.0.0.1] File does not exist: /home/st
eve/sgp/newweb/nofile
HTTP/1.1 404 Not Found
Date: Wed, 02 Mar 2011 13:01:55 GMT
Server: Apache/2.2.16 (Debian)
Vary: Accept-Encoding
Content-Length: 274
Connection: close
Content-Type: text/html; charset=iso-8859-1

<!DOCTYPE HTML PUBLIC "-//IETF//DTD HTML 2.0//EN">
<html><head>
<title>404 Not Found</title>
</head><body>
<h1>Not Found</h1>
<p>The requested URL /nofile was not found on this server.</p>
<hr>
<address>Apache/2.2.16 (Debian) Server at ksgp Port 80</address>
</body></html>
127.0.0.1 - - [02/Mar/2011:13:01:55 +0000] "GET /nofile HTTP/1.0" 404 477 "-" "-"
#
```

This can be helpful in debugging as the PHP errors are clearly shown as a result of the HEAD / request, and the 404 error is shown with the GET /nofile request. Similarly, the overall success (200 of the HEAD / request) is also seen at exactly the moment it happens.

OD

od stands for "octal dump" but it is capable of much more than just octal processing. It processes data and represents it in any one of a variety of useful formats. When comparing the GNU and non-GNU implementations of factor for the next chapter, I used od to confirm that the original (non-GNU) implementation uses two "space" characters to pad the results, which it displays one per line, unlike GNU which displays them all on one line. At first, if you look at the output, it looks like a pair of spaces, but it's impossible to tell if there's any whitespace after the numbers, or exactly what form the padding takes. Piping this through od -a gives a fairly human-readable interpretation: 6 followed by a newline, then two spaces, a 2 and a newline, followed by two spaces, a 3 and a final newline.

```
$ factor 6
6
  2
  3
$ factor 6 | od -a
0000000   6  nl  sp  sp   2  nl  sp  sp   3  nl
0000012
```

Piping the same through `od -x` gives the same information in hexadecimal format. Because this is a little-endian architecture, the bytes are swapped around; the 0a36 represents 0x36="6" then 0x0a=newline. The next byte-pair is two 0x20 characters, which are spaces. Then 0x32 is "2", and 0x0a is newline again. 0x2020 is two more spaces, then 0x33 is "3", and 0x0a is the final newline. The `ascii(7)` man page contains all of these ASCII characters with their decimal, hexadecimal, and octal representations.

```
$ factor 6 | od -x
0000000 0a36 2020 0a32 2020 0a33
0000012
```

There is also the `-t` "traditional" flag, which has a further `-x1` option that formats the hex in straight byte order, not as 2-byte words. This is easier to read than the `od -x` format, especially on little-endian hardware. Combining all of these shows some of the different ways that you can use od to display the same output.

```
$ factor 6
6
  2
  3
$ factor 6 | od -a
0000000   6  nl  sp  sp   2  nl  sp  sp   3  nl
0000012
$ factor 6 | od -x
0000000 0a36 2020 0a32 2020 0a33
0000012
$ factor 6 | od -t x1
0000000 36 0a 20 20 32 0a 20 20 33 0a
0000012
$
```

A more practical use for interrogating data at the byte-level is the Master Boot Record (MBR) of disks in x86 systems. If the MBR is damaged, the machine will not boot. The MBR is a well-documented structure of 512 bytes at the start of the disk. The first 440 bytes are executable code (the first part of the grub bootloader, or the Microsoft Windows boot loader, for example). The next six bytes are a disk signature and padding, so the first 446 bytes are not useful data in terms of the partition table. After this come four 16-byte records, one for each of the primary partitions. Finally, the two bytes 0xaa55 mark the end of the MBR, and are also used as a signature to confirm that the preceding 510 bytes are a genuine MBR and not just random data. This is useful for a BIOS to confirm before executing the 440 bytes of code, and it is also useful for this code to determine the condition of the MBR.

The following script uses the `-b` test to see if it has been passed a device (such as /dev/sda) or a regular file. This allows it to inspect the disk of a running machine by extracting the first 512 bytes using dd. For this script to be truly useful, however, it needs to be able to inspect the MBR of a broken system: By booting the broken machine from the CD-ROM or over the network, you can extract the MBR and pass it to a working machine for investigation. A regular file retrieved in this way can be processed without first invoking dd.

For each partition, the value for the first byte is either 0x00 (0; the partition is not bootable) or 0x80 (128; the partition is bootable). Anything else is invalid. The fifth byte contains the partition type — Linux, FAT32, LVM, NTFS, swap, and so on. The rest of this record is the start and end locations of the partition (f1, f2, f3, 11, 12, 13), the LBA of the first sector, and the number of sectors in the partition. The script uses bytes 0, 4, and 13–16 to show the bootable flag, partition type, and sector size, respectively.

A bit of fancy work from bc and printf converts the lowercase hexadecimal sector size into decimal bytes; this works on the basis that the sector size is 512 bytes, so two sectors make 1 kilobyte, which divided twice by 1,000 gives the number of gigabytes (in storage circles, 1GB is 1,000MB, not 1,024MB).

```
# cat mbr.sh
#!/bin/bash
if [ -b $1 ]; then
  mbr=`mktemp`
  echo "Reading MBR from device $1"
  dd if=$1 of=$mbr bs=512 count=1
  mbr_is_temporary=1
else
  mbr=$1
  if [ -r "$mbr" ]; then
    echo "Reading MBR from file $mbr"
  else
    echo "Readable MBR required."
    exit 1
  fi
fi

od -v -t x1 -An -j 510 $mbr |grep -q " 55 aa$"
if [ "$?" -ne "0" ]; then
  echo "MBR signature not found. Not a valid MBR."
  exit 1
fi

partnum=1
od -v -t x1 -An -j446 -N 64 $mbr | \
while read status f1 f2 f3 parttype 11 12 13 lba1 lba2 lba3 lba4 s1 s2 s3 s4
do
  if [ "$parttype" == "00" ]; then
    echo "Partition $partnum is not defined."
  else
    case $status in
      00) bootable="unbootable" ;;
      80) bootable="bootable" ;;
      *)  bootable="invalid";
    esac
    printf "Partition %d is type %02s and is %s." $partnum $parttype $bootable
    sectors=`printf "%02s%02s%02s%02s\n" $s4 $s3 $s2 $s1 | \
        tr '[:lower:]' '[:upper:]'`
    bytes=`echo "ibase=16; $sectors / 2" | bc`
    gb=`echo "scale=2; $bytes / 1000 / 1000" | bc`
    printf " Size %.02f GB\n" $gb
  fi
  partnum=`expr $partnum + 1`
done
if [ "$mbr_is_temporary" ]; then
  rm -f $mbr
fi
```

```
# ./mbr.sh /dev/sda
Reading MBR from device /dev/sda
1+0 records in
1+0 records out
512 bytes (512 B) copied, 7.5848e-05 s, 6.8 MB/s
Partition 1 is type 07 and is bootable. Size 25.70 GB
Partition 2 is type bf and is bootable. Size 32.95 GB
Partition 3 is type 05 and is unbootable. Size 58.55 GB
Partition 4 is not defined.
# fdisk -1 /dev/sda

Disk /dev/sda: 120.0 GB, 120034123776 bytes
255 heads, 63 sectors/track, 14593 cylinders
Units = cylinders of 16065 * 512 = 8225280 bytes
Disk identifier: 0x8b213c0c

   Device Boot      Start         End      Blocks   Id  System
/dev/sda1   *           1        3200    25703968+   7  HPFS/NTFS
/dev/sda2   *        3201        7303    32957347+  bf  Solaris
/dev/sda3            7304       14593    58556925    5  Extended
/dev/sda5   *        7304       10342    24410736   83  Linux
/dev/sda6           10343       10585     1951866   82  Linux swap / Solaris
/dev/sda7           10586       14593    32194228+  83  Linux
# ./mbr.sh /tmp/suspect-mbr.bin
Reading MBR from file /tmp/suspect-mbr.bin
Partition 1 is type 27 and is unbootable. Size 12.58 GB
Partition 2 is type 07 and is bootable. Size 0.10 GB
Partition 3 is type 07 and is unbootable. Size 58.59 GB
Partition 4 is type 05 and is unbootable. Size 172.91 GB
```

Solaris x86 `fdisk` partition tables are just the same as on Linux. While Linux systems tend to put one filesystem per `fdisk` partition, Solaris x86 uses one `fdisk` partition as a virtual disk (by default using the entire physical disk for this partition), which it chops into slices, and configures each slice as a filesystem. The special device for the first partition is c0t0d0p0, and the MBR can be found at the beginning of that device. This is different from Linux's more accurate representation, as c0t0d0p0 is equivalent to /dev/sda1, not /dev/sda.

```
solarisx86# ./mbr.sh /dev/dsk/c0t0d0p0
Reading MBR from device /dev/dsk/c0t0d0p0
1+0 records in
1+0 records out
Partition 1 is type 82 and is bootable. Size 143.23 GB
Partition 2 is not defined.
Partition 3 is not defined.
Partition 4 is not defined.
$
```

PASTE

The paste command is the opposite of cut; it pastes multiple files together, separated (by default) by tabs. This is not to be confused with the terms "cut" and "paste" when used in the context of a graphical user environment (GUI). The paste command creates tabular data from multiple files, so given three files it will put them together in three columns, the first from file1, the middle column from file2, and the final column from file3. It can take as input as many files as you like.

This script takes an input file `hosts`, which lists a set of hosts and uses that to store the IP and Ethernet address of each host. To ensure that the || structure fails if the `grep` or `getent` commands fail, the `pipefail` shell option is set. The script is therefore sure to write exactly one line to both $IPS and to $ETHERS, whether it succeeds or fails. This ensures that the files will be in step when pasted together. When `pipefail` is set, any failure anywhere in the pipeline causes the whole pipeline to fail. By default, the return value of the pipeline is the return value of the final command in that pipeline. This would mean that the success of `getent hosts | cut` is determined by the return code of `cut`, which pretty much always returns 0 to indicate success.

```
$ cat hosts
localhost
plug
declan
atomic
broken
goldie
elvis
$ cat /etc/ethers
0a:00:27:00:00:00 plug
01:00:3a:10:21:fe declan
71:1f:04:e3:1b:13 atomic
01:01:8d:07:3a:ea goldie
01:01:31:09:2a:f2 elvis
$ cat gethosts.sh
#!/bin/bash
HOSTS=hosts
ETHERS=ethers
IPS=ips

set -o pipefail
for host in `cat $HOSTS`
do
    echo -en "${host}..."
    getent hosts $host | cut -d" " -f1 >> $IPS || echo "missing" >> $IPS
    grep -w "${host}" /etc/ethers | cut -d" " -f2 >> $ETHERS \
        || echo "missing" >> $ETHERS
done
echo
paste $HOSTS $IPS $ETHERS
$ ./gethosts.sh
localhost...plug...declan...atomic...broken...goldie...elvis...
localhost     ::1        missing
plug    192.168.1.5      0a:00:27:00:00:00
declan  192.168.1.10     01:00:3a:10:21:fe
atomic  192.168.1.11     71:1f:04:e3:1b:13
broken  missing missing
goldie  192.168.1.13     01:01:8d:07:3a:ea
elvis   192.168.1.227    01:01:31:09:2a:f2
$
```

The default delimiter is the TAB character, although this can be changed with the -d flag. cut uses the first character in the delimiter to mark the first and second columns, the second character for the second and third columns, and so on. If there are more columns than delimiter characters, cut loops around the delimiter characters again. The -d, option gives Comma-Separated Values (CSV) output, editable by spreadsheet programs. The -s option pastes one file at a time, effectively shifting from columnar data to rows.

> *CSV as a file format is fundamentally flawed; it can't cope with commas within fields, or to do so it needs quotes around them. If it is to do that, then other quotes need to be quoted themselves.* The Art of Unix Programming *(ISBN 0131429019; Eric S. Raymond, 2008) discusses various text file formats and their implications at* http://www.catb.org/~esr/writings/taoup/html/ ch05s02.html. *Joel Spolsky has a good follow-up article at* http://www .joelonsoftware.com/articles/Biculturalism.html.

```
$ paste -d, hosts ips ethers > ip.csv
localhost,::1,missing
plug,192.168.1.5,0a:00:27:00:00:00
declan,192.168.1.10,01:00:3a:10:21:fe
atomic,192.168.1.11,71:1f:04:e3:1b:13
broken,missing,missing
goldie,192.168.1.13,01:01:8d:07:3a:ea
elvis,192.168.1.227,01:01:31:09:2a:f2
$ paste -d, -s hosts ips ethers >> ip.csv
$ oocalc ip.csv
```

Figure 13-1 shows the results of this script.

	A	B	C	D	E	F	G
1	localhost	::1	missing	regular paste produces columns			
2	plug	192.168.1.5	0a:00:27:00:00:00				
3	declan	192.168.1.10	01:00:3a:10:21:fe				
4	atomic	192.168.1.11	71:1f:04:e3:1b:13				
5	broken	missing	missing				
6	goldie	192.168.1.13	01:01:8d:07:3a:ea				
7	elvis	192.168.1.227	01:01:31:09:2a:f2				paste -s spins the axis
8	localhost	plug	declan	atomic	broken	goldie	elvis
9	::1	192.168.1.5	192.168.1.10	192.168.1.11	missing	192.168.1.13	192.168.1.227
10	missing	0a:00:27:00:00:00	01:00:3a:10:21:fe	71:1f:04:e3:1b:13	missing	01:01:31:09:2a:f2	01:01:8d:07:3a:ea
11							

FIGURE 13-1

> paste -s *can also be used to squash all of the carriage returns out of a file, as it pastes its first input file into a single line 1, and similarly the second input file into a single line 2, and so on.*

A more visible demonstration is found by placing parentheses around the hostname. Unfortunately, spaces would have to be added some other way.

```
$ paste -d"():" ips hosts ethers
::1(localhost)missing
192.168.1.5(plug)0a:00:27:00:00:00
```

```
192.168.1.10(declan)01:00:3a:10:21:fe
192.168.1.11(atomic)71:1f:04:e3:1b:13
missing(broken)missing
192.168.1.13(goldie)01:01:8d:07:3a:ea
192.168.1.227(elvis)01:01:31:09:2a:f2
$
```

Finally, the delimiter can also be used to group text into a fixed number of columns, by virtue of the \n character. The \n means newline and \t means TAB. So a delimiter of "tab tab tab newline," or \t\t\t\n, will split the first three columns by tabs, and put a newline after the fourth, grouping the items into four columns. This example takes a pipe from seq, which provides the numbers 1–27, so the file being processed is stdin, represented as -.

```
$ seq 1 27 | paste -s -d "\t\t\t\n" -
1       2       3       4
5       6       7       8
9       10      11      12
13      14      15      16
17      18      19      20
21      22      23      24
25      26      27
$
```

PR

pr is another of those less well-known formatting commands, but it is very useful in the right situation. The headers are not often useful, so pr -t is a good starting point. You can also omit all pagination with -T, which is often more useful when displaying onscreen rather than for print layout. As used in worldcup.sh, pr acts a bit like join, in that it was used to paste four columns of text together into a single page. It can also split single input into multiple columns, much like the ls command does when run interactively. Here a list of 30 rivers would be too much to list one by one, but pr can split them automatically into as many neat and tidy columns as required.

```
$ wc -l rivers.txt
30 rivers.txt
$ pr -T -4 rivers.txt
Alamance        Deschutes       Koochiching     Rappahannock
Asotin          Escambia        Latah           Scioto
Beaver          Greenbrier      Merrimack       Tallapoosa
Boise           Humboldt        Mississippi     Tensas
Brazos          Iowa            Neosho          Vermilion
Cassia          Judith Basin    Osage           Wabash
Chattahoochee   Kalamazoo       Platte          Yamill
Clearwater      Kankakee
$ pr -T -5 rivers.txt
Alamance        Chattahoochee Iowa          Merrimack     Scioto
Asotin          Clearwater    Judith Basin  Mississippi   Tallapoosa
Beaver          Deschutes     Kalamazoo     Neosho        Tensas
Boise           Escambia      Kankakee      Osage         Vermilion
Brazos          Greenbrier    Koochiching   Platte        Wabash
Cassia          Humboldt      Latah         Rappahannock  Yamill
$
```

If this goes too far, pr will trim the text to fit. The -J option can be used if all that is needed is columnar output, without necessarily lining up all of the output. There is insufficient room for a six-column output without trimming some of the text. With -J, pr manages to squeeze them all in.

```
$ pr -T -6 rivers.txt
Alamance    Cassia      Greenbrier  Kankakee    Neosho      Tallapoosa
Asotin      Chattahooch Humboldt    Koochiching Osage       Tensas
Beaver      Clearwater  Iowa        Latah       Platte      Vermilion
Boise       Deschutes   Judith Basi Merrimack   Rappahannoc Wabash
Brazos      Escambia    Kalamazoo   Mississippi Scioto      Yamill
$ pr -TJ -6 rivers.txt
Alamance         Cassia Greenbrier    Kankakee       Neosho Tallapoosa
Asotin    Chattahoochee Humboldt      Koochiching    Osage Tensas
Beaver    Clearwater    Iowa    Latah Platte Vermilion
Boise     Deschutes     Judith Basin  Merrimack      Rappahannock    Wabash
Brazos    Escambia      Kalamazoo     Mississippi    Scioto Yamill
$
```

PRINTF

printf is possibly more useful even than echo, although echo is a little bit more straightforward. One of the main features of printf is its ability to process C-style text-padding. This can be useful in displaying columnar data or just lining data up with other displayed elements. For example, the formatting string %-10s means a left-aligned string, at least 10 characters wide.

As an easy way to read entries from /etc/passwd, this script uses the IFS variable to tell read that the delimiter is the colon character, and then passes those variables to printf, which displays them with appropriate padding. Notice that the avahi-autoipd and Debian-exim accounts have more than ten characters, so the output is shifted along to the right and not trimmed. Similarly, the gnats and timidity GECOS ("name") fields are more than 30 characters, so their shells get shifted to the right.

```
$ cat printf1.sh
#!/bin/bash

printf "%-10s %-30s %-10s\n" "Username" "Name" "Shell"
cut -d: -f1,5,7 /etc/passwd | while IFS=: read uname name shell
do
  printf "%-10s %-30s %-10s\n" "$uname" "$name" "$shell"
done
$ ./printf1.sh
Username   Name                           Shell
root       root                           /bin/bash
daemon     daemon                         /bin/sh
bin        bin                            /bin/sh
sys        sys                            /bin/sh
sync       sync                           /bin/sync
games      games                          /bin/sh
man        man                            /bin/sh
lp         lp                             /bin/sh
gnats      Gnats Bug-Reporting System (admin) /bin/sh
nobody     nobody                         /bin/sh
```

```
libuuid                                  /bin/sh
messagebus                               /bin/false
avahi-autoipd Avahi autoip daemon,,,      /bin/false
festival                                 /bin/false
gdm          Gnome Display Manager       /bin/false
haldaemon    Hardware abstraction layer,,,  /bin/false
usbmux       usbmux daemon,,,            /bin/false
sshd                                     /usr/sbin/nologin
saned                                    /bin/false
avahi        Avahi mDNS daemon,,,        /bin/false
ntp                                      /bin/false
Debian-exim                               /bin/false
timidity    TiMidity++ MIDI sequencer service /bin/false
$
```

printf understands more than simple length of variables. It can align numerical output in useful ways, too. This little script displays the squares of 1–10 using echo, and then again using printf to highlight the difference.

Finally, it calculates the square roots of the numbers 1–10 to ten decimal places (scale=10). However, printf is fed the formatting string %0.4f, so exactly four decimal places are displayed, whether required or not.

```
$ cat printf2.sh
#!/bin/bash
for i in `seq 1 10`
do
  echo "$i squared is `expr $i \* $i`"
done

for i in `seq 1 10`
do
  printf "%2d squared is %3d\n" $i `expr $i \* $i`
done

for i in `seq 1 10`
do
  printf "The square root of %2d is %0.4f\n" $i `echo "scale=10;sqrt($i)"|bc`
done
$ ./printf2.sh
1 squared is 1
2 squared is 4
3 squared is 9
4 squared is 16
5 squared is 25
6 squared is 36
7 squared is 49
8 squared is 64
9 squared is 81
10 squared is 100
 1 squared is    1
 2 squared is    4
 3 squared is    9
 4 squared is   16
 5 squared is   25
```

```
 6 squared is  36
 7 squared is  49
 8 squared is  64
 9 squared is  81
10 squared is 100
The square root of  1 is 1.0000
The square root of  2 is 1.4142
The square root of  3 is 1.7321
The square root of  4 is 2.0000
The square root of  5 is 2.2361
The square root of  6 is 2.4495
The square root of  7 is 2.6458
The square root of  8 is 2.8284
The square root of  9 is 3.0000
The square root of 10 is 3.1623
```

SHUF

shuf is a useful sorter, which normally acts with random input to produce randomly shuffled output, although you can provide your own "random" source so that it produces repeatable results every time. It can work on input files or on numeric ranges. It can also be very useful when working on arrays.

Dice Thrower

This simple script throws three dice and gives you the total. This also shows you how putting something like this into a function makes it more flexible and easier to integrate into a script; not only is the main body of code simpler and easier to read, but you can change the implementation once and the effect ripples through the rest of the script.

```
$ cat dice.sh
#!/bin/bash

# could even do this as an alias.
function rolldice
{
  return `shuf -i 1-6 -n1`
}

total=0
rolldice
roll=$?
total=`expr $total + $roll`
echo "First roll was $roll"

rolldice
roll=$?
total=`expr $total + $roll`
echo "Second roll was $roll"

rolldice
roll=$?
```

```
        total=`expr $total + $roll`
        echo "Third roll was $roll"

        echo
        echo "Total is $total"

$ ./dice.sh
First roll was 5
Second roll was 3
Third roll was 2

Total is 10
$ ./dice.sh
First roll was 3
Second roll was 4
Third roll was 5

Total is 12
$ ./dice.sh
First roll was 4
Second roll was 2
Third roll was 2

Total is 8
$
```

dice.sh

Card Dealer

Slightly more advanced is a routine to pick random playing cards. This script uses `shuf` with two arrays to randomize the suit and the value of the card. It shows the randomization by rejecting the first three cards picked, and then sets the fourth as a variable so that its value does not get lost.

```
$ cat cards.sh
#!/bin/bash

suits=( diamonds clubs hearts spades )
values=( one two three four five
         six seven eight nine ten
         jack queen king )

function randomcard
{
  echo "the `shuf -n1 -e ${values[@]}` of `shuf -n1 -e "${suits[@]}"`"
}

echo "You rejected `randomcard` and put it back in the deck."
echo "You rejected `randomcard` and put it back in the deck."
echo "You rejected `randomcard` and put it back in the deck."
YOURCARD=`randomcard`
echo "You picked $YOURCARD."
echo "I remember $YOURCARD so it is no longer random."
```

```
echo "It will always be $YOURCARD."
```

```
$ ./cards.sh
You rejected the jack of clubs and put it back in the deck.
You rejected the seven of diamonds and put it back in the deck.
You rejected the four of hearts and put it back in the deck.
You picked the three of spades.
I remember the three of spades so it is no longer random.
It will always be the three of spades.
$ ./cards.sh
You rejected the ten of hearts and put it back in the deck.
You rejected the two of diamonds and put it back in the deck.
You rejected the queen of spades and put it back in the deck.
You picked the six of diamonds.
I remember the six of diamonds so it is no longer random.
It will always be the six of diamonds.
$
```

cards.sh

Because you can define your own random source, a small change to the code makes the randomness more or less predictable. A change to the `randomcard` function means that (on my system) it always picks the Jack of Clubs. Your system will have a different `/etc/hosts`, so the result will be different from mine but will always produce the same result each time you run it.

Available for
download on
Wrox.com

```
function randomcard
{
  echo "the `shuf --random-source=/etc/hosts -n1 -e ${values[@]}` of"\
      "`shuf --random-source=/etc/hosts -n1 -e "${suits[@]}"`"
}
$ ./cards-lessrandom.sh
You rejected the jack of clubs and put it back in the deck.
You rejected the jack of clubs and put it back in the deck.
You rejected the jack of clubs and put it back in the deck.
You picked the jack of clubs.
I remember the jack of clubs so it is no longer random.
It will always be the jack of clubs.
$
```

cards-lessrandom.sh

A totally predictable sequence can be rigged by creating a random source with fully known values. For example, the value 23549yer0tirgogti435r4gt9df0gtire (picked by tapping randomly on my keyboard) will always result in the Queen of Hearts being picked. Replace `/etc/hosts` in `randomcard` with `/tmp/random` to reproduce this.

```
$ echo 23549yer0tirgogti435r4gt9df0gtire > /tmp/random
$ ./cards-lessrandom.sh
You rejected the queen of hearts and put it back in the deck.
You rejected the queen of hearts and put it back in the deck.
You rejected the queen of hearts and put it back in the deck.
You picked the queen of hearts.
```

```
I remember the queen of hearts so it is no longer random.
It will always be the queen of hearts.
$
```

Travel Planner

Finally, a more involved script makes random travel plans with surprising consistency. When it suggests a trip to New York, it might suggest visiting the Statue of Liberty, but when it suggests Sydney it might suggest the Opera House, so the randomness is not truly random. This script uses a subdirectory called places/, which contains a text file named after each known destination. Each line of that file contains one tourist destination for that place. The while loop in tourism.sh makes sure that the final attraction is not preceded by the word "and," which means that you can change the number of days by supplying them on the command line, and the English grammar still works. It also places commas before the final join, and between the final pair, and behaves correctly when displaying a single day trip.

```
$ ls -l places/
total 32
-rw-rw-r-- 1 steve steve 46 Feb 19 12:04 Amsterdam
-rw-rw-r-- 1 steve steve 38 Feb 18 18:36 London
-rw-rw-r-- 1 steve steve 65 Feb 19 12:08 Microsoft
-rw-rw-r-- 1 steve steve 61 Feb 19 12:06 New York
-rw-rw-r-- 1 steve steve 38 Feb 18 18:49 Paris
-rw-rw-r-- 1 steve steve 53 Feb 19 12:08 Seattle
-rw-rw-r-- 1 steve steve 72 Feb 19 12:03 Sydney
-rw-rw-r-- 1 steve steve 47 Feb 19 12:08 Unix
$ cat places/Paris
the Eiffel Tower
Notre Dame
the Seine
$ cat tourism.sh
#!/bin/bash
cd places
place=$(shuf -e -n1 *)
days=${1:-2}

echo -en "Let's go to $place and check out "
count=1
shuf -n$days "$place" | while read trip
do
  let count=$count+1
  echo -en $trip
  if [ "$count" -le "`expr $days - 1`" ]; then
    echo -en ", "
  elif [ "$count" -le "$days" ]; then
    echo -en " and "
  else
    echo " "
  fi
done
```

```
$ ./tourism.sh
Let's go to Sydney and check out the Opera House and Sydney Harbour Bridge
$ ./tourism.sh 1
Let's go to New York and check out the Empire State Building
$ ./tourism.sh 3
Let's go to Paris and check out Notre Dame, the Eiffel Tower and the Seine
$ ./tourism.sh 4
Let's go to London and check out the London Eye, the Houses of Parliament, Big Ben
and Covent Garden
```

tourism.sh

SORT

sort is a very powerful utility in the Unix/Linux toolkit. It can sort on various criteria, it can check and merge sorted files, it can sort on different keys, and it can even sort on different characters within those keys. It can also strip out repetitions, which can eliminate the need for the sort file.txt | uniq syntax.

The switches for sort fall into two categories. There are switches that modify the behavior of sort; -u strips out duplicate results, and -c and -C only check whether or not the input is sorted. -t specifies a field separator other than whitespace, and -s leaves otherwise-equal lines in the order in which they were originally found in the input. The other switches modify the strategy that sort actually uses to sort its input. Table 13-1 summarizes the flags that sort can take to modify its sorting strategy.

TABLE 13-1: Sort Modifiers

FLAG	RESULT
-M	Sort by month; unknown < Jan < Dec (depending on locale).
-b	Ignore leading whitespace.
-d	Dictionary sort; ignore punctuation.
-f	Case-insensitive sort.
-g	General numerical sort. Use -n for most purposes.
-i	Ignore non-printable characters.
-h	Sort human-readable filesizes.
-n	Numerical sort; 9 before 10.
-R	Random sort.
-r	Reverse the results of the sort.
-V	A sorting algorithm that understands that software version numbers often look like foo-1.23a.093.

The sort -M *feature depends on the current locale, specifically the* LC_TIME *variable. You can see what locales are installed via the* locale -a *command.*

Sorting on Keys

The -k switch tells sort which field (or fields) to use as the sort keys. The default delimiter is any amount of whitespace, so given a rather messy input file like the following musicians.txt, the sort -k 2 command will alphabetically sort by surname. The fact that the fields are not tidily arranged does not matter; sort by default takes any amount of whitespace as the field delimiter.

 The format of the -k *switch changed many years ago, and the old format is seen so rarely it is not worth mentioning in a modern book.*

```
$ cat musicians.txt
Freddie Mercury         Singer    Queen       5 Sep 1946
Brian May          Guitarist    Queen     19 Jul 1947
John Deacon         Bass       Queen      19 Aug 1951
Roger Taylor        Drums      Queen       26 Jul 1949
Benny Andersson     Pianist    Abba     16 Dec 1946
Bjorn Ulvaeus        Guitarist        Abba      25 Apr 1945
Anni-Frid Lyngstad  Singer     Abba      15 Nov 1945
Agnetha Faltskog    Singer     Abba     5 Apr 1950
$ sort -k2 musicians.txt
Benny Andersson     Pianist    Abba     16 Dec 1946
John Deacon         Bass       Queen      19 Aug 1951
Agnetha Faltskog    Singer     Abba     5 Apr 1950
Anni-Frid Lyngstad  Singer     Abba      15 Nov 1945
Brian May          Guitarist    Queen     19 Jul 1947
Freddie Mercury         Singer    Queen       5 Sep 1946
Roger Taylor        Drums      Queen       26 Jul 1949
Bjorn Ulvaeus        Guitarist        Abba      25 Apr 1945
$
```

Sorting on multiple fields is also possible. To arrange these musicians by age, simply sort by year, then month, and then day of birth. Specify the keys in the order required, and specify for each one how you want the field to be sorted; day and year are numeric, so use the -n switch as per Table 13-1, while -M specifies the three-letter abbreviation of the month.

```
$ sort -k7n -k6M -k5n musicians.txt
Bjorn Ulvaeus        Guitarist        Abba      25 Apr 1945
Anni-Frid Lyngstad  Singer     Abba      15 Nov 1945
Freddie Mercury         Singer    Queen       5 Sep 1946
Benny Andersson     Pianist    Abba     16 Dec 1946
```

```
Brian May              Guitarist   Queen    19 Jul 1947
Roger Taylor           Drums       Queen    26 Jul 1949
Agnetha Faltskog       Singer      Abba    5 Apr 1950
John Deacon            Bass        Queen    19 Aug 1951
$
```

A more practical example is sorting the /etc/hosts file. Sorting this by hostname would not be very useful; it would be better to get the file sorted numerically by IP address. This is a bit more complex; the IP address is delimited by periods, so the -t switch can be used to specify the delimiter. The data can be sorted first by key 1, then by key 2, then key 3, and finally key 4. This is a little less intuitive because sort -t. -k1 -k2 -k3 -k4 does not do what you might expect. Key 1 is treated as the initial "127." followed by the entire rest of the line, so by the time sort gets to key 4, it re-sorts them by the final octet of the IP address (.1, .210, .227, and so on), totally undoing the previous three sorts.

```
$ cat hosts
127.0.0.1        localhost
192.168.1.3      sky
192.168.1.11     atomic
192.168.1.10     declan           declan.example.com
192.168.0.210    dgoldie ksgp dalston
192.168.1.5      plug
192.168.1.227    elvis
192.168.1.13     goldie  goldie.example.com smf  spo  sgp
$ sort -t. -k1 -k2 -k3 -k4 hosts
127.0.0.1        localhost
192.168.0.210    dgoldie ksgp dalston
192.168.1.10     declan           declan.example.com
192.168.1.11     atomic
192.168.1.13     goldie  goldie.example.com smf  spo  sgp
192.168.1.227    elvis
192.168.1.3      sky
192.168.1.5      plug
```

To get around this, you can tell sort which is the starting and ending field for each key. In this case, the first key is fields 1 to 1 inclusive, the second is fields 2 to 2 inclusive, and so on. This gets the desired result; the IP addresses are grouped together in their subnets and numerically sorted within them. The -n flag also tells sort to do a numerical sort (so that 5 comes before 10, which it wouldn't do on an alphabetical sort).

```
$ sort -t. -k1,1n -k2,2n -k3,3n -k4,4n hosts
127.0.0.1        localhost
192.168.0.210    dgoldie ksgp dalston
192.168.1.3      sky
192.168.1.5      plug
192.168.1.10     declan           declan.example.com
192.168.1.11     atomic
192.168.1.13     goldie  goldie.example.com smf  spo  sgp
192.168.1.227    elvis
$
```

Sorting Log Files by Date and Time

Breaking down fields can be taken even further, by sorting just on certain characters within a field. The standard Apache access log file stores the date and time of an access as [02/Mar/2011:13:06:17 -0800]. This is not easy to sort automatically; the first key here is 2011, the second is Mar, then 02. After that, it's 13, then 06, then 17. Apart from the values being out of sequence (2011/Mar/02/13:06:17 would be easier), the word Mar for the month of March comes before Apr but after Dec, which makes no sense alphabetically.

Fortunately, as you saw in the musicians example at the start of this section, sort can determine the names of months from the locale, so as long as your current locale uses the same names as in the log file, sort can use the -M flag to sort months in the order they come in the calendar year (Jan to Dec). To show how these are all sorted, take this typical example of a systems administrator inspecting three log files. The page in question (article 928, identified by the URL snippet art=928) appears in the two older log files, but not the current access_log. A simple grep, however, processes these files in the "wrong" order, as access_log.processed.1 comes alphabetically before the older access_log.processed.2, and the filename wildcard expansion sorts its results alphabetically. This means that the logs are displayed out of sequence.

```
$ ls -ltr access*
-rw-rw-r-- 1 steve steve 22429808 Mar  2 04:42 access_log.processed.2
-rw-rw-r-- 1 steve steve 45490104 Mar  4 04:49 access_log.processed.1
-rw-rw-r-- 1 steve steve 19457016 Mar  5 21:16 access_log
$ grep art=928 *
access_log.processed.1:77.88.31.247 - - [02/Mar/2011:13:06:17 -0800] "GET /urandom/
comment.php?art=928 HTTP/1.1" 200 11551 "-" "Mozilla/5.0 (compatible; YandexBot/3.0
; +http://yandex.com/bots)"
access_log.processed.1:77.88.31.247 - - [02/Mar/2011:16:30:34 -0800] "GET /urandom/
comment.php?title=Number+of+the+day&art=928 HTTP/1.1" 200 11599 "-" "Mozilla/5.0 (c
ompatible; YandexBot/3.0; +http://yandex.com/bots)"
access_log.processed.1:66.249.69.52 - - [04/Mar/2011:01:18:32 -0800] "GET /urandom/
comment.php?art=928 HTTP/1.1" 200 11584 "-" "Mozilla/5.0 (compatible; Googlebot/2.1
; +http://www.google.com/bot.html)"
access_log.processed.2:67.195.111.173 - - [01/Mar/2011:06:26:32 -0800] "GET /urando
m/comment.php?title=Number+of+the+day&art=928 HTTP/1.0" 200 11599 "-" "Mozilla/5.0
(compatible; Yahoo! Slurp; http://help.yahoo.com/help/us/ysearch/slurp)"
access_log.processed.2:218.213.130.168 - - [01/Mar/2011:07:25:41 -0800] "GET /urand
om/comment.php?art=928 HTTP/1.1" 200 11551 "-" "ichiro/4.0 (http://help.goo.ne.jp/d
oor/crawler.html)"
access_log.processed.2:218.213.130.168 - - [01/Mar/2011:07:33:54 -0800] "GET /urand
om/comment.php?title=Number+of+the+day&art=928 HTTP/1.1" 200 11599 "-" "ichiro/4.0
(http://help.goo.ne.jp/door/crawler.html)"
```

In this instance, because the timestamps on the files are correct, the administrator could use ls -lt to sort the files into the correct order with grep art=928 `ls -tr access_log*`, but in practice, the logs might have been downloaded from a remote server and all have the same timestamp, or their names may not follow a logical order. Instead, the code that follows shows the definitive way to sort these files by date. The following code uses a variation on the default syntax of sort. The type itself can be anything in Table 13-1, and can go with either the start or the end of the field, or both. 4.10n,4.13n is equivalent to 4.10n,4.13 or 4.10,4.13n.

In the following example, then, sort -k 4.10,4.13n tells sort that the first, most significant field is the year, which is found in characters 10–13 inclusive of the fourth field, and it tells it to sort these numerically. The second -k flag, -k 4.6,4.8M, tells sort that characters 6–8 of the fourth field should be treated as a three-letter Month abbreviation in the current locale. The rest is as described in the previous section: Year, Month, Day, Hour, Minute, Second. This produces the results in the required order:

```
$ grep art=928 * |   sort -k 4.10,4.13n -k 4.6,4.8M -k 4.3,4.4n\
>       -k 4.15,4.16n -k 4.18,4.19n -k 4.21,4.22n
access_log.processed.2:67.195.111.173 - - [01/Mar/2011:06:26:32 -0800] "GET /urando
m/comment.php?title=Number+of+the+day&art=928 HTTP/1.0" 200 11599 "-" "Mozilla/5.0
(compatible; Yahoo! Slurp; http://help.yahoo.com/help/us/ysearch/slurp)"
access_log.processed.2:218.213.130.168 - - [01/Mar/2011:07:25:41 -0800] "GET /urand
om/comment.php?art=928 HTTP/1.1" 200 11551 "-" "ichiro/4.0 (http://help.goo.ne.jp/d
oor/crawler.html)"
access_log.processed.2:218.213.130.168 - - [01/Mar/2011:07:33:54 -0800] "GET /urand
om/comment.php?title=Number+of+the+day&art=928 HTTP/1.1" 200 11599 "-" "ichiro/4.0
(http://help.goo.ne.jp/door/crawler.html)"
access_log.processed.1:77.88.31.247 - - [02/Mar/2011:13:06:17 -0800] "GET /urandom/
comment.php?art=928 HTTP/1.1" 200 11551 "-" "Mozilla/5.0 (compatible; YandexBot/3.0
; +http://yandex.com/bots)"
access_log.processed.1:77.88.31.247 - - [02/Mar/2011:16:30:34 -0800] "GET /urandom/
comment.php?title=Number+of+the+day&art=928 HTTP/1.1" 200 11599 "-" "Mozilla/5.0 (c
ompatible; YandexBot/3.0; +http://yandex.com/bots)"
access_log.processed.1:66.249.69.52 - - [04/Mar/2011:01:18:32 -0800] "GET /urandom/
comment.php?art=928 HTTP/1.1" 200 11584 "-" "Mozilla/5.0 (compatible; Googlebot/2.1
; +http://www.google.com/bot.html)"
$ grep art=928 `ls -tr access_log*`
```

A handy way to count the characters in the string is to echo a number line directly above or below a sample of the text that you want to compare. This technique enables you to avoid pointing at the screen while trying to keep count of characters.

```
$ echo " [02/Mar/2011:16:30:34 -0800]" ; echo "123456789012345678901234567890"
 [02/Mar/2011:16:30:34 -0800]
123456789012345678901234567890
$
```

 The characters in the field start from the first whitespace before the field starts, so "Mar" is characters 6 to 8 of the field (not 5–7 as you may expect). The -b flag can be used to disable this behavior.

Sorting Human-Readable Numbers

Many modern utilities conveniently display file sizes in human-readable form; 2.6GB is easier to read than 2751758391 bytes. Until summer 2010, however, sort was unable to parse these different forms; 2.6GB is clearly bigger than 3.0MB, but sort has to understand the units to know that. The following brief script gives a nice top-10 list of largest files in a directory. It takes the du -sh *, which provides the results in unsorted order, and sorts them into reverse numerical order. This gets the biggest at the top and the smallest at the bottom. Piping the results of that through head gets the top 10 (if there are at least 10 entries in the directory), and piping that through cat -n prepends the position number. This can be particularly useful when run from /home to see who is using all of the disk space.

```
# cat dirsize.sh
#!/bin/bash

cd "${1:-.}"
if [ "$?" -ne "0" ]; then
  echo "Error: Failed to change to directory $1"
  exit 2
fi
echo "The largest files/directories in $1 are:"
du -sh * | sort -hr | head | cat -n -
# ./dirsize.sh /var/log
The largest files/directories in /var/log are:
     1   1.3M    installer
     2   1.1M    kern.log.1
     3   780K    messages.1
     4   696K    apache2
     5   680K    wtmp.1
     6   572K    kern.log
     7   412K    messages
     8   380K    daemon.log.1
     9   288K    syslog.1
    10   284K    daemon.log
#
```

dirsize.sh

TR

The tr utility translates single characters into other characters. Called as echo frabacbable | tr 'a' 'b', whenever it sees the letter a it replaces it with b, resulting in the output frbbbcbbble. This script tunes the kernel as required by the installation instructions from the vendor. The exact details may change with the version so this has to be downloaded from the vendor each time, but two things remain constant:

➤ The vendor always supplies the kernel tunables as temporary changes as echo value > /proc, instead of as tunings for the sysctl.conf file.

➤ The vendor's typography is terrible, with spurious slashes and uppercase characters where they are not valid. This must be handled gracefully.

There are two ways to tune the Linux kernel; to set the maximum number of files a user may have open, you can echo 65536 > /proc/sys/fs/file-max, which makes the change instantly, although it is lost on reboot, or you can add the line sys.fs.file-max = 65536 to /etc/sysctl.conf. This will be applied whenever the system is booted. You will need to run sysctl -p to dynamically load the new values from /etc/sysctl.conf. Notice how sys.fs.file-max is represented in the /proc filesystem as sys/fs/file-max. This is ideal for tr; there is a single character, known to be used only as a delimiter, and the goal is to replace it with a different single character, which is also only to be used as a delimiter.

Another use for tr is to transpose a range of characters into the relevant position in a second range. This is commonly used to convert [A-Z] into [a-z], although it can convert any characters. It can also use predefined ranges, so [:alnum:] represents all letters and numbers, [:digit:] represents digits, [:space:] represents any whitespace, and so on. These are all listed on the tr(1) man page.

This script takes the current release notes (relnotes.txt) and extracts any echo value > /proc/tunable.subsys.subval commands, and turns them into suitable tunable.subsys.subval = value entries for /etc/sysctl.conf. It uses tr '[A-Z]' '[a-z]' to convert any uppercase text into lowercase, as all kernel tunables are lowercase. It converts the slashes into periods via tr '/' '.'. It also strips any duplicate slashes so that /pROc/sYs///kERnel//sHMMax as input is turned into the valid format sys.kernel.shmmax as output.

```
$ ls
installproduct.sh
$ cat installproduct.sh
#!/bin/bash
VERSION=${1:-"2.4.3"}
DOWNLOAD=downloads.vendor.com
URL=http://${DOWNLOAD}/product/v${VERSION}

echo "Retrieving release notes..."
wget -nd ${URL}/relnotes.txt

echo "Got release notes:"
echo "*** START OF RELEASE NOTES"
cat relnotes.txt
echo "*** END OF RELEASE NOTES"

grep "^echo " relnotes.txt | tr -s "/" | while read ignoreecho params
do
  value=`echo $params | cut -d">" -f1`
  proc=`echo $params | cut -d">" -f2 | cut -d"/" -f3-`
  sysctl=`echo $proc | tr '[A-Z]' '[a-z]' | tr '/' '.'`
  echo "Setting $sysctl to $value..."
  echo $sysctl = $value | tee -a /etc/sysctl.conf
done
echo "Loading new kernel values."
sysctl -p >/dev/null 2>&1
$ ./installproduct.sh
Retrieving release notes...
--2011-03-07 17:19:08--  http://downloads.vendor.com/product/v2.4.3/relnotes.txt
Resolving downloads.vendor.com... 192.168.1.13
Connecting to downloads.vendor.com|192.168.1.13|:80... connected.
HTTP request sent, awaiting response... 200 OK
Length: 292 [text/plain]
```

```
Saving to: `relnotes.txt'

100%[=======================================>] 292         --.-K/s   in 0s

2011-03-07 17:19:08 (21.9 MB/s) - `relnotes.txt' saved [292/292]

Got release notes:
*** START OF RELEASE NOTES
Before installLiNg This product, TUne the kernel as follows:

echo 65536 > ///Proc//sys/FS/fiLE-max
echo 2097152 > /prOC//sYs/kErnEl/SHmall
echo 2147483648 > /pROc/sYs///kERnel//sHMMax
echo 4096 > /prOc/syS/kerNel//shmMni
echo 250 32000 100 128 > /prOc//sYS/KERNEl/SEm

ThEn run thE instAller ROUtine.
*** END OF RELEASE NOTES
Setting sys.fs.file-max to 65536 ...
sys.fs.file-max = 65536
Setting sys.kernel.shmall to 2097152 ...
sys.kernel.shmall = 2097152
Setting sys.kernel.shmmax to 2147483648 ...
sys.kernel.shmmax = 2147483648
Setting sys.kernel.shmmni to 4096 ...
sys.kernel.shmmni = 4096
Setting sys.kernel.sem to 250 32000 100 128 ...
sys.kernel.sem = 250 32000 100 128
$
```

installproduct.sh

As mentioned previously, `tr` is capable of more than just uppercase/lowercase conversion. Using asymmetric sets, specified characters can be condensed down to allow for more restrictive requirements. This `access_log` from a website forum contains lots of relevant data, but it is not easily parsed. In this example, the `cut` statement just strips the URL request from the log:

```
$ cut -d'"' -f2 access_log
GET /forum/viewforum.php?f=2 HTTP/1.1
GET /forum/templates/subSilver/images/folder_lock_new.gif HTTP/1.1
GET /forum/templates/subSilver/images/folder_lock.gif HTTP/1.1
GET /forum/viewtopic.php?p=884&sid=a2738b9fc491726ac290aa7a9447291b HTTP/1.1
GET /forum/viewforum.php?f=2&sid=a705161ccdf318a111c67dcde0e1bd03 HTTP/1.0
GET /forum/profile.php?mode=register&sid=a705161ccdf318a111c67dcde0e1bd03 HTTP/1.0
GET /forum/viewtopic.php?p=840&sid=88c87f962c9ee6bdfff8b5fba9c728a8 HTTP/1.1
GET /forum/viewtopic.php?p=848 HTTP/1.1
```

This can be interpreted much more easily if the ?, &, and = symbols are stripped away. This simple `tr` statement replaces any such character with a space, making it easy now to pass the text into a `read` statement:

```
$ cut -d'"' -f2 access_log | tr '[?&=]' ' '
GET /forum/viewforum.php f 2 HTTP/1.1
GET /forum/templates/subSilver/images/folder_lock_new.gif HTTP/1.1
GET /forum/templates/subSilver/images/folder_lock.gif HTTP/1.1
```

```
GET /forum/viewtopic.php p 884 sid a2738b9fc491726ac290aa7a9447291b HTTP/1.1
GET /forum/viewforum.php f 2 sid a705161ccdf318a111c67dcde0e1bd03 HTTP/1.0
GET /forum/profile.php mode register sid a705161ccdf318a111c67dcde0e1bd03 HTTP/1.0
GET /forum/viewtopic.php p 840 sid 88c87f962c9ee6bdfff8b5fba9c728a8 HTTP/1.1
GET /forum/viewtopic.php p 848 HTTP/1.1
$ cut -d'"' -f2 access_log | tr '[?&=]' ' ' | while read METHOD PAGE ARGUMENTS
> do
>   echo Page requested was $PAGE
>   echo Arguments were $ARGUMENTS
> done
Page requested was /forum/viewforum.php
Arguments were f 2 HTTP/1.1
Page requested was /forum/templates/subSilver/images/folder_lock_new.gif
Arguments were HTTP/1.1
Page requested was /forum/templates/subSilver/images/folder_lock.gif
Arguments were HTTP/1.1
Page requested was /forum/viewtopic.php
Arguments were p 884 sid a2738b9fc491726ac290aa7a9447291b HTTP/1.1
Page requested was /forum/viewforum.php
Arguments were f 2 sid a705161ccdf318a111c67dcde0e1bd03 HTTP/1.0
Page requested was /forum/profile.php
Arguments were mode register sid a705161ccdf318a111c67dcde0e1bd03 HTTP/1.0
Page requested was /forum/profile.php
Arguments were mode register agreed true sid a705161ccdf318a111c67dcde0e1bd03 HTTP/
1.0
Page requested was /forum/posting.php
Arguments were mode newtopic f 2 sid a705161ccdf318a111c67dcde0e1bd03 HTTP/1.0
Page requested was /forum/login.php
Arguments were redirect posting.php mode newtopic f 2 sid a705161ccdf318a111c67dcde
0e1bd03 HTTP/1.0
Page requested was /forum/posting.php
Arguments were mode newtopic f 2 sid a705161ccdf318a111c67dcde0e1bd03 HTTP/1.0
Page requested was /forum/login.php
Arguments were redirect posting.php mode newtopic f 2 sid a705161ccdf318a111c67dcde
0e1bd03 HTTP/1.0
Page requested was /forum/viewtopic.php
Arguments were p 840 sid 88c87f962c9ee6bdfff8b5fba9c728a8 HTTP/1.1
Page requested was /forum/viewtopic.php
Arguments were p 848 HTTP/1.1
```

Another useful but less widely known switch for `tr` is the `-d` switch. That deletes any characters it is given. One of the many uses for this is to adapt Ethernet (MAC) addresses from their common colon-separated hex bytes format (70:5a:b6:2a:e8:b8) to the colonless format also commonly used (705ab62ae8b8). `tr -d` does this perfectly.

```
$ ifconfig -a|grep HW
eth0      Link encap:Ethernet  HWaddr 70:5a:b6:2a:e8:b8
pan0      Link encap:Ethernet  HWaddr 6e:b4:bc:3a:bd:2e
vboxnet0  Link encap:Ethernet  HWaddr 0a:00:27:00:00:00
wlan0     Link encap:Ethernet  HWaddr 70:1a:04:e3:1b:10
$ ifconfig -a|grep HW | tr -d ':' | cut -c1-10,38-
eth0      705ab62ae8b8
pan0      6eb4bc3abd2e
vboxnet0  0a0027000000
wlan0     701a04e31b10$
$
```

UNIQ

At first glance, uniq appears to be a tool that displays only unique lines in a file. In reality, it strips consecutive repeated lines, but if the same line occurs later in the input, it will be displayed again. Therefore, a common combination is sort | uniq, although that can be done slightly more efficiently using the sort -u command, as there is no need to spawn a second process and set up the pipe between them.

It may seem like a fair question to ask what uniq is useful for, and the answer is that uniq is actually quite flexible in what it can do. In the previous chapter, uniq was used with the -w and -d flags to find only those entries that had duplicate checksums. The -w flag tells it to parse only the first 32 characters (which are the checksum; the rest will inevitably be different), and the -d flag (if the input data is sorted) lists only those items that are not unique. This is a very useful way to filter the results, which would be cumbersome and time-consuming in a for or while loop in a shell script.

 The uniq *command is also rather unique in that if passed a second filename on the command line, it will write the output to that file instead of to stdout, overwriting it if it already exists.*

The complement of -d is -u; while uniq will normally print each line only once, with -u it will only print the unique lines; if an entry is listed twice, it will not be displayed at all. These three invocations — uniq alone, uniq -u, and uniq -d — provide a flexible way to filter almost any input for any purpose. The other major filters are used for skipping characters and for defining which fields to compare.

As you saw in the previous chapter, -w32 compares only the first 32 characters. The complement to -w N is -s N, which ignores the first N characters. There is also the -f N flag, which skips the first N fields, where fields are separated by spaces and/or tabs. Textual comparisons can be made case-insensitive with the -i flag. Also, uniq can give a count with each line output; with -uc this will always be 1; with -dc this will always be greater than 1.

This all goes to make uniq, which often seems like an old, simplistic, and single-purpose tool, actually very flexible. I have included additional code examples using uniq to demonstrate what uniq can do when pushed. Many people often write complicated and cumbersome scripts that could actually be made shorter and faster by judicious use of uniq.

A lowest unique bid auction, where instead of the highest bidder, the bidder with the lowest unique bid wins the auction, is a perfect candidate for the uniq -u flag. By first sorting the bids numerically, uniq -u -f1 skips the first field (the bidder's name) and strips out the non-unique bids, leaving only the unique bids. In the example that follows, Richard, Angela, and Fred made unique bids. Because the data has already been sorted by the time it gets to uniq, the first record must be the lowest unique bid. The lowest unique bid is quite a difficult concept to get your head around at first, but it is easily implemented in a simple one-line command because of uniq:

```
$ cat bidders
Dave 1.39
Bob 2.31
```

```
  Albert 0.91
  Elizabeth 1.39
  Angela 1.09
  Fred 3.13
  Caroline 2.31
  Rodger 0.91
  Richard 0.98
$ sort -k2 -n bidders | uniq -u -f1 | head -1
  Richard 0.98
$
```

WC

wc stands for Word Count, although it can also count characters and lines. This makes it a flexible tool for counting any kind of items. It is most commonly used to count the number of lines in a file, or (as with most Unix tools) in any other data sent to it, but it can count characters and words, too.

Although it is often used against only one file, or to parse standard input via a pipe, wc is also capable of counting and totaling multiple files at once. The three main flags to wc are -w (count words), -c (count characters), and -1 (count lines). Of these, by far the most commonly used is the line count. Counting the number of lines in a file is often useful; counting the number of results from a pipeline is also very useful. A lot of the code and recipes in this book use wc -1 as an automatic way of counting the number of results.

All implementations of wc pad their output when processing multiple files so that the columns line up nicely. This can be a pain when scripting, because " 14" is not so easily interpreted as the number fourteen as a simple "14" without the padding. The Unix implementation of wc always pads so a workaround is required; awk will happily strip the whitespace, so the command below using awk works fine. This snippet shows multiple files with padding and how this affects the common task of assigning a variable with the length of a file.

```
$ wc -1 /etc/hosts*
   18 /etc/hosts
   14 /etc/hosts.allow
   87 /etc/hosts.deny
  119 total
$ wc -1 /etc/hosts
   18 /etc/hosts
$ num_hosts=`wc -1 /etc/hosts | cut -d' ' -f1`
$ echo $num_hosts
18 /etc/hosts
$ num_hosts=`wc -1 /etc/hosts | awk '{ print $1 }'`
$ echo $num_hosts
18
$
```

The GNU implementation of wc does not do any padding if there is only stdin, or a single file, to list. This means that if there is only one file then the first, more naïve attempt to set num_hosts directly from the wc output will work under GNU. On other implementations of wc, the awk is necessary to retrieve the actual number, ignoring the padding.

In the World Cup script earlier in this chapter, the NUMTEAMS variable was defined in this way. To write portable scripts, it is safest to assume that the output from wc is not safely padded; the additional overhead is minimal if the script is to be run on a relatively modern machine and it is not in the middle of an intensive loop:

```
NUMTEAMS=`wc -l $TEAMS | awk '{ print $1 }'`
```

This example causes no major overheads at all and ensures greater cross-platform portability for the script. It is therefore best to use this method when parsing the output of wc unless you are certain that it will be run by the GNU implementation of wc on a single input. In that case, you can use the lighter cut tool, as in:

```
NUMTEAMS=`wc -l $TEAMS | cut -d ' ' -f1`
```

SUMMARY

Unix and Linux are very flexible when it comes to manipulating text. Most configuration settings are stored in text format, in a tool-independent way, so that any number of tools may be used to manipulate them. This gives the user and systems administrator great power, as they are not locked into a single tool for editing /etc/hosts and another custom tool for editing /etc/passwd. Instead, a whole suite of tools is available for manipulating just about anything, and those tools can be combined in all sorts of different ways. This clear design decision to make everything open and accessible is a key strength of the Unix model.

The next chapter builds on this and the previous chapter, and looks at practical systems administration tasks.

14

Tools for Systems Administration

System administration is the most common task to which shell scripting is put. Many of the commands in Unix and Linux exist to configure the system itself, so it is not surprising that the majority of scripts are written for that purpose. This chapter aims to give some real-world examples of how these commands can be used and, particularly, how they can be used effectively within shell scripts to automate, extend, and simplify system administration tasks. It also discusses some of the pitfalls and gotchas associated with the tools, and how they are actually used in real life. This should give a solid foundation for the rest of the book, which consists of full, in-depth recipes, focusing more on what the recipes actually do than on the underlying tools themselves.

BASENAME

basename returns the actual filename name of a file, stripped of any directory paths. It is by far most commonly used with the $0 variable for a script to find out how it was called. This can be useful for debugging and general output messages. The capability to determine the name that a program was called by is also used by some system utilities to modify their actual behavior. The mount and umount commands share a lot of common code, but the effect of running umount /home is very different — the opposite — from that of running mount /home. A single program deals with this by checking the name that it was called as and acting appropriately. This removes redundancy and keeps all of the filesystem mounting and unmounting code in the same program. A straightforward example of this is the dos2unix conversion utility mentioned later. The DOS (and Microsoft Windows) text file format uses CR+LF, whereas Unix (and Linux) use LF alone. This difference goes back a long way and is not likely to be reconciled ever. Two conversion utilities, unix2dos and dos2unix, exist to perform the simple conversions between the two text file formats. These are not always available on every platform, and there are various quirks that affect the apparently simple translation between these two very similar formats, but sed is a great way to perform the conversion. The page http://sed.sourceforge.net/sed1line.txt has a load of useful sed one-liners, including some that are used by this script.

> *The tofrodos package, which provides the* `fromdos` *and* `todos` *commands, is another way to do this.*

The initial `ls -il` shows that `dos2unix` and `unix2dos` are hard links; they are the same file with two directory entries and two different names. The `diff` confirms this. The script behaves differently depending on how it was called, however.

```
$ ls -il dos2unix unix2dos
5161177 -rwxr-xr-x 2 steve steve 613 Feb 21 14:55 dos2unix
5161177 -rwxr-xr-x 2 steve steve 613 Feb 21 14:55 unix2dos
$ diff dos2unix unix2dos
$ echo $?
0
$ cat dos2unix
#!/bin/bash
# from http://sed.sf.net/sed1line.txt:
# sed 's/.$//'                        # assumes that all lines end with CR/LF
# sed 's/$'"/`echo \\\r`/"            # command line under bash

if [ ! -f "$1" ]; then
  echo "Usage: `basename $0` filename"
  echo "  `basename $0` converts between DOS and UNIX formats."
  echo "  When called as unix2dos, it converts to DOS format."
  echo "  Otherwise, it converts to UNIX format."
  exit 1
fi

case `basename $0` in
  unix2dos)
    sed -i 's/$'"/`echo \\\r`/" $1
    exit $?
    ;;
  *) # Default to being dos2unix
    sed -i 's/.$//' $1
    exit $?
    ;;
esac
exit 0
```

dos2unix (the same file as unix2dos)

`cat -v` shows the spurious CR characters as `^M`. The same script converts in one direction or another depending on whether it was called as `unix2dos`, or — by default, if called by any other name — it will act as `dos2unix`.

```
$ cat -v hello.txt
line one^M
line two^M
```

```
line three^M
$ ./dos2unix hello.txt
$ cat -v hello.txt
line one
line two
line three
$ ./unix2dos hello.txt
$ cat -v hello.txt
line one^M
line two^M
line three^M
$
```

This means that a single file can embed a lot of hidden information about its subject, whether it is mounting and unmounting filesystems, or converting text files between Unix and DOS formats, and that detailed knowledge is contained in a single file. If the implementation detail changes (and simple as unix2dos/dosunix seems, the sed page lists 11 different invocations, depending on the environment), then only one file needs to be changed, and the chances of missing the other change are reduced, too.

DATE

The date command is a strangely useful tool. It is most commonly used to create timestamps, particularly when logging events that have happened. The syslog utility adds timestamps to events that it logs, so /var/log/messages, syslog, auth.log, and other such files all contain that key ingredient at the start of the line. This can be vital for working out the chain of events and how different events captured in different log files, or even on different machines, tie in with each other.

Typical Uses of date

The two most common uses of the date command in system administration are probably logging results and status messages, particularly when logging to a file, and creating temporary files with meaningful names. Scripts for both of these techniques are provided here, followed by some of the more complex things made possible by the advanced features of the date command. This first recipe emulates the logger facility described later in this chapter. The second uses the date to create a set of uniquely but informatively named log files. In this example, the timestamp is useful for tracking down the error in the web server. A common NTP source is also particularly useful, although even totally independent systems can be compared if the time difference between them can be established.

```
$ cat getuptime.sh
#!/bin/bash
LOG=/var/tmp/uptime.log
echo "`date`: Starting the $0 script." | tee -a $LOG
echo "`date`: Getting today's uptime reports." | tee -a $LOG
wget http://intranet/uptimes/index.php?get=today.csv >> $LOG 2>&1
echo "`date`: Getting this week's uptime reports." | tee -a $LOG
wget http://intranet/uptimes/index.php?get=thisweek.csv >> $LOG 2>&1
```

```
echo "`date`: Getting this month's uptime reports." | tee -a $LOG
wget http://intranet/uptimes/index.php?get=thismonth.csv >> $LOG 2>&1
echo "`date`: Getting this year's uptime reports." | tee -a $LOG
wget http://intranet/uptimes/index.php?get=thisyear.csv >> $LOG 2>&1
echo "`date`: Finished the $0 script." | tee -a $LOG
```

$ **./getuptime.sh**
```
Tue Mar 22 14:15:01 GMT 2011: Starting the ./getuptime.sh script.
Tue Mar 22 14:15:01 GMT 2011: Getting today's uptime reports.
Tue Mar 22 14:15:07 GMT 2011: Getting this week's uptime reports.
Tue Mar 22 14:15:13 GMT 2011: Getting this month's uptime reports.
Tue Mar 22 14:15:16 GMT 2011: Getting this year's uptime reports.
Tue Mar 22 14:15:22 GMT 2011: Finished the ./getuptime.sh script.
```
$ **cat /var/tmp/uptime.log**
```
Tue Mar 22 14:15:01 GMT 2011: Starting the ./getuptime.sh script.
Tue Mar 22 14:15:01 GMT 2011: Getting today's uptime reports.
--2011-03-22 14:15:01--  http://intranet/uptimes/index.php?get=today.csv
Resolving intranet... 192.168.0.210
Connecting to intranet|192.168.0.210|:80... connected.
HTTP request sent, awaiting response... 200 OK
Length: 4398 (4.3K) [text/html]
Saving to: `intranet/uptimes/index.php?get=today.csv'

    OK ....                                              100%  168M=0s

2011-03-22 14:15:07 (168 MB/s) - `intranet/uptimes/index.php?get=today.csv' saved [
4398/4398]


Tue Mar 22 14:15:07 GMT 2011: Getting this week's uptime reports.
--2011-03-22 14:15:07--  http://intranet/uptimes/index.php?get=thisweek.csv
Resolving intranet... 192.168.0.210
Connecting to intranet|192.168.0.210|:80... connected.
HTTP request sent, awaiting response... 200 OK
Length: 4398 (4.3K) [text/html]
Saving to: `intranet/uptimes/index.php?get=thisweek.csv'

    OK ....                                              100%  173M=0s

2011-03-22 14:15:13 (173 MB/s) - `intranet/uptimes/index.php?get=thisweek.csv' save
d [4398/4398]
```

THE "THISMONTH" REPORT FOR SOME REASON CAUSES AN INTERNAL SERVER ERROR AT 14:15:13.

```
Tue Mar 22 14:15:13 GMT 2011: Getting this month's uptime reports. ←
--2011-03-22 14:15:13--  http://intranet/uptimes/index.php?get=thismonth.csv
Resolving intranet... 192.168.0.210
Connecting to intranet|192.168.0.210|:80... connected.
HTTP request sent, awaiting response... 501 Internal Server Error
2011-03-22 14:15:16 ERROR 501: Internal Server Error.


Tue Mar 22 14:15:16 GMT 2011: Getting this year's uptime reports.
--2011-03-22 14:15:16--  http://intranet/uptimes/index.php?get=thisyear.csv
Resolving intranet... 192.168.0.210
Connecting to intranet|192.168.0.210|:80... connected.
HTTP request sent, awaiting response... 200 OK
```

```
Length: 4398 (4.3K) [text/html]
Saving to: `intranet/uptimes/index.php?get=thisyear.csv'

    OK ....                                               100%  185M=0s

2011-03-22 14:15:22 (185 MB/s) - `intranet/uptimes/index.php?get=thisyear.csv' save
d [4398/4398]

Tue Mar 22 14:15:22 GMT 2011: Finished the ./getuptime.sh script.
$ tail -4 /var/log/apache2/access.log
192.168.5.103 - - [22/Mar/2011:14:15:01 +0000] "GET /uptimes/index.php?get=today.cs
v HTTP/1.0" 200 4649 "-" "Wget/1.12 (linux-gnu)"
192.168.5.103 - - [22/Mar/2011:14:15:07 +0000] "GET /uptimes/index.php?get=thisweek
.csv HTTP/1.0" 200 4649 "-" "Wget/1.12 (linux-gnu)"
192.168.5.103 - - [22/Mar/2011:14:15:13 +0000] "GET /uptimes/index.php?get=thismont
h.csv HTTP/1.0" 501 229 "-" "Wget/1.12 (linux-gnu)"
192.168.5.103 - - [22/Mar/2011:14:15:16 +0000] "GET /uptimes/index.php?get=this yea
r.csv HTTP/1.0" 200 4649 "-" "Wget/1.12 (linux-gnu)"
$
```

THIS LINE IN THE SERVER'S ACCESS LOG SHOWS THE 501 AT 14:15:13.

getuptime.sh

This second script takes regular snapshots of the system's memory. More powerful system monitoring tools are, of course, available, but sometimes all that is needed is a simple shell script. This very short script grabs a copy of /proc/meminfo at one-minute intervals to see how memory is being used on a server. Each file is named mem.(year)(month)(day).(hour)(minutes).

Available for download on Wrox.com

```
$ cat monitor.sh
#!/bin/bash
while :
do
    cat /proc/meminfo > /var/tmp/mem.`date +%Y%m%d.%H%M`
    sleep 60
done
$
```

monitor.sh

The script above creates a new file every minute. This data can be easily parsed into something that can be read by a spreadsheet and shown as a graph.

```
/var/tmp# grep MemFree mem.*
mem.20110323.1715:MemFree:       131217092 kB
mem.20110323.1716:MemFree:       129300240 kB
mem.20110323.1717:MemFree:       124681904 kB
mem.20110323.1718:MemFree:       117881144 kB
mem.20110323.1719:MemFree:       120531736 kB
mem.20110323.1720:MemFree:       112337316 kB
mem.20110323.1721:MemFree:       110234640 kB
mem.20110323.1722:MemFree:       106036032 kB
mem.20110323.1723:MemFree:       91977924 kB
mem.20110323.1724:MemFree:       78725428 kB
```

```
mem.20110323.1725:MemFree:        78719628 kB
mem.20110323.1726:MemFree:        78720700 kB
mem.20110323.1727:MemFree:        78720376 kB
mem.20110323.1728:MemFree:        77418280 kB
mem.20110323.1729:MemFree:        73464744 kB
mem.20110323.1730:MemFree:        80239176 kB
mem.20110323.1731:MemFree:        78712968 kB
mem.20110323.1732:MemFree:        78717092 kB
mem.20110323.1733:MemFree:        66421840 kB
mem.20110323.1734:MemFree:        48610120 kB
mem.20110323.1735:MemFree:        36769560 kB
mem.20110323.1736:MemFree:        36693548 kB
mem.20110323.1737:MemFree:        36694500 kB
mem.20110323.1738:MemFree:        36694984 kB
mem.20110323.1739:MemFree:        36698632 kB
mem.20110323.1740:MemFree:        36703592 kB
mem.20110323.1741:MemFree:        36668052 kB
mem.20110323.1742:MemFree:        36681928 kB
mem.20110323.1743:MemFree:        36685028 kB
mem.20110323.1744:MemFree:        36686388 kB
mem.20110323.1745:MemFree:        36676812 kB
mem.20110323.1746:MemFree:        36684908 kB
mem.20110323.1747:MemFree:        36685308 kB
mem.20110323.1748:MemFree:        36685056 kB
mem.20110323.1749:MemFree:        36685088 kB
mem.20110323.1750:MemFree:        36685432 kB
mem.20110323.1751:MemFree:        36684512 kB
mem.20110323.1752:MemFree:        36684736 kB
mem.20110323.1753:MemFree:        36684564 kB
mem.20110323.1754:MemFree:        35108364 kB
```

This small `while` loop divides the KB down to MB and then down to GB, cuts out the time, and displays them separated by a comma. I have piped the result through `pr -T -4` for display purposes; in practice, this would end as `done > memory.csv` instead of `done | pr -T -4`. Spreadsheet software can then be used to turn this into a graph, showing available memory being consumed over time. Figure 14-1 shows how memory is used over time.

```
# grep MemFree *|cut -d. -f3-|cut -d: -f1,3| while read time mem kb
> do
>   echo "${time:0:4},`expr $mem / 1024 / 1024`"
> done | pr -T -4
1715,125        1725,75         1735,35         1745,34
1716,123        1726,75         1736,34         1746,34
1717,118        1727,75         1737,34         1747,34
1718,112        1728,73         1738,34         1748,34
1719,114        1729,70         1739,34         1749,34
1720,107        1730,76         1740,35         1750,34
1721,105        1731,75         1741,34         1751,34
1722,101        1732,75         1742,34         1752,34
1723,87         1733,63         1743,34         1753,34
1724,75         1734,46         1744,34         1754,33
#
```

Free Memory

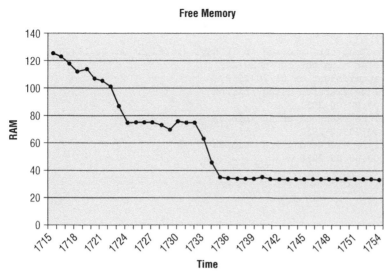

FIGURE 14-1

More Interesting Uses of date

date is actually a very flexible command, which can perform quite complicated time conversions, as can all of the GNU utilities that deal with dates (touch, at, batch, and so on). Visit http://www.gnu .org/software/tar/manual/html_chapter/Date-input-formats.html for an explanation of some of the more complicated features available. The following script deals with the nearlining, archival, and eventual deletion of sensitive data by calculating what the date will be in 30 days, 3 months, and 7 years, respectively. Doing this without date gets really quite complicated; if it's October, November, or December, then adding 3 months will change the year. If it's after the 29th of January, then adding 30 days may or may not take you into March, depending on whether it's a leap year, and so on. date can take care of all these things behind the scenes for you.

```
$ date
Sun Mar 20 15:23:19 EDT 2011
$ cat save_records.sh
#!/bin/bash
DATEFORMAT="%m/%d/%Y"

TODAY=`date +${DATEFORMAT}`
echo "Today is $TODAY"

# Get the three dates
LONGTERM=`date -d "30 days"  "+${DATEFORMAT}"`
ARCHIVAL=`date -d "3 months" "+${DATEFORMAT}"`
DELETION=`date -d "7 years"  "+${DATEFORMAT}"`

echo "Files will be moved to long-term storage in 30 days (midnight at $LONGTERM)."
echo "Files will be archived at midnight on $ARCHIVAL."
echo "They will be deleted at midnight on $DELETION."

at -f /usr/local/bin/longterm_records "$1" midnight $LONGTERM
at -f /usr/local/bin/archive_records  "$1" midnight $ARCHIVAL
```

```
at -f /usr/local/bin/delete_records   "$1" midnight $DELETION
$ ./save_records.sh /var/spool/data/todays_records/
Today is 03/20/2011
Files will be moved to long-term storage in 30 days (midnight at 04/19/2011).
Files will be archived at midnight on 06/20/2011.
They will be deleted at midnight on 03/20/2018.
warning: commands will be executed using /bin/sh
job 28 at Tue Apr 19 00:00:00 2011
warning: commands will be executed using /bin/sh
job 29 at Mon Jun 20 00:00:00 2011
warning: commands will be executed using /bin/sh
job 30 at Tue Mar 20 00:00:00 2018
$
```

save_records.sh

DIRNAME

In the same category but with opposite functionality to basename, dirname returns the directory name from a path. This is useful when a script does not know the exact location that files will be held in, for example when the script is part of a tarball that could be extracted into the user's home directory, or /tmp, or anywhere else. The following script uses dirname $0 quite extensively to produce its own relative paths to a fairly complex directory structure. It uses etc/install.cfg (relative to the location of the script) to determine whether or not to interactively ask the installer to accept the license terms.

```
$ cat install.sh
#!/bin/bash
ACCEPT_LICENSE=0   # may be overridden by the config file

echo "Reading configuration..."
CFG=`dirname $0`/etc/install.cfg
. $CFG
echo "Done."

mkdir `dirname $0`/logs 2>/dev/null || exit 1

if [ "$ACCEPT_LICENSE" -ne "1" ]; then
  ${PAGER:-more} `dirname $0`/LICENSE.TXT
  read -p "Do you accept the license terms?"
  case $REPLY in
    y*|Y*) continue ;;
    *) echo "You must accept the terms to install the software."
       exit 1 ;;
  esac
fi

rm -f `dirname $0`/logs/status
case `uname` in
```

```
    Linux)
      for rpm in `dirname $0`/rpms/*.rpm
      do
        rpm -Uvh $rpm 2>&1 | tee `dirname $0`/logs/`basename ${rpm}`.log
        echo "${PIPESTATUS[0]} $rpm" >> `dirname $0`/logs/status
      done
      ;;
    SunOS)
      for pkg in `dirname $0`/pkgs/*.pkg
      do
        pkgadd -d $pkg 2>&1 | tee `dirname $0`/logs/`basename ${pkg}`.log
        echo "${PIPESTATUS[0]} $pkg" >> `dirname $0`/logs/status
      done
      ;;
    *) echo "Unsupported OS. Only RPM and PKG formats available."
      exit 2 ;;
  esac


  echo
  # Check for errors... grep -v "^0 " returns 1 if there *are* any lines
  # which start with something other than "0 ".
  grep -v "^0 " `dirname $0`/logs/status
  if [ "$?" -ne "1" ]; then
    echo "Errors were encountered during installation of the above packages."
    echo "Please investigate before using the software."
  else
    echo "Software installed successfully."
  fi
```

install.sh

In this test run of the preceding install.sh script, the root user knows that the installer has been
downloaded into the user steve's home directory, which is not a path that the scripter who created
install.sh would have guessed. If root had changed into the funky-1.40/ directory, the correct
relative path for the config file would be etc/install.cfg. Because root actually called it from
/home/steve, the correct relative path would be funky-1.40/etc/install.cfg. By using dirname,
you do not need to worry about any of this, and certainly not about having to hardcode the absolute
path /home/steve/funky-1.40/etc/install.cfg into the script.

```
# cd ~steve
# pwd
/home/steve
# tar xzvf /tmp/funky-1.40.tar.gz
funky-1.40/
funky-1.40/install.sh
funky-1.40/rpms/
funky-1.40/rpms/fnkygroovyapps-1.40-1-x86_64.rpm
funky-1.40/rpms/fnkygroovycfg-1.40-1-x86_64.rpm
funky-1.40/rpms/fnkygroovy-1.40-1-x86_64.rpm
funky-1.40/pkgs/
funky-1.40/pkgs/FNKYgroovycfg.pkg
```

```
funky-1.40/pkgs/FNKYgroovyapps.pkg
funky-1.40/pkgs/FNKYgroovy.pkg
funky-1.40/etc/
funky-1.40/etc/install.cfg
funky-1.40/LICENSE.TXT
# cat funky-1.40/etc/install.cfg
ACCEPT_LICENSE=0
# echo ACCEPT_LICENSE=1 > funky-1.40/etc/install.cfg
# funky-1.40/install.sh
Reading configuration...
Done.
Preparing... ####################################### [100%]
1:fnkygroovy ####################################### [100%]
Preparing... ####################################### [100%]
1:fnkygroovyapps ######################################## [100%]
Preparing... ####################################### [100%]
1:fnkygroovycfg ######################################## [100%]
Software installed successfully.
#
```

funky-1.40.tar.gz

 dirname *just strips the final* /*, *which is not always very useful. It can be useful at times to run* cd `dirname $0`; BASEDIR=`pwd` *to get the absolute path of the directory.*

FACTOR

The factor tool is a reasonably clever (although limited for serious cryptographic work by the size of the numbers that it can work on) tool that produces the prime factors of a number. Prime numbers are divisible only by 1 and themselves, so the factors cannot be reduced down any further. This produces some rather surprising results; even a rather large number such as 43,674,876,546 has only five prime factors.

```
$ factor 43674876546
43674876546: 2 3 7 1451 716663
$ factor 716663
716663: 716663
$
```

The script that follows reformats the output of factor to appear rather clever. In its implementation, it is approaching that of a functional, rather than procedural, language. It starts with the pure list of answers (omitting the colon and anything before it), and each time, it multiplies the first two numbers together and passes that result, along with the remaining factors, to the next instance of itself. This is a nice use of recursion to loop through input of unknown length. If the factorize function is called with only one argument, that must be the final $sum, which means that all of the other factors have already been multiplied out. To make more sense of it, uncomment the "Parsing" line to see what it gets passed at each stage.

```
$ cat factorize.sh
#!/bin/bash

function factorize
{
  # echo "Parsing $@"
  if [ "$#" -gt "1" ];
  then
    sum=`expr $1 \* $2`
    echo "$1 x $2 = $sum"
    shift 2
    factorize $sum $@
  fi
}

# GNU says: 72: 2 2 2 3 3
# UNIX says:
#72
#  2
#  2
#  2
#  3
#  3
# So test for GNU vs non-GNU

factor --version | grep GNU > /dev/null 2>&1
if [ "$?" -eq "0" ]; then
  factorize `factor $1 | cut -d: -f2-`
else
  factorize `factor $1 | grep -v "^${1}" `
fi
```

factorize.sh

```
$ ./factorize.sh 72
2 x 2 = 4
4 x 2 = 8
8 x 3 = 24
24 x 3 = 72
$ ./factorize.sh 913
11 x 83 = 913
$ ./factorize.sh 294952
2 x 2 = 4
4 x 2 = 8
8 x 7 = 56
56 x 23 = 1288
1288 x 229 = 294952
$ ./factorize.sh 43674876546
2 x 3 = 6
6 x 7 = 42
42 x 1451 = 60942
60942 x 716663 = 43674876546
$
```

> *The GNU* `factor` *program displays all its output on the same line, with a colon between the final number and its factors. The Unix* `factor` *displays the final number at the start of the first line, then each factor on a line of its own, indented by two spaces. The script looks for GNU in the* `--version` *output (which actually exists only in the GNU version) to see how to reformat; either skip up to the first colon for GNU, or cut out the line that starts with the initial number for other implementations of* `factor`.

IDENTITY, GROUPS, AND GETENT

One common use of the `id` command is to ensure that a script is being run with the appropriate privileges. This is not particularly useful for enforcing security mechanisms, as scripts can easily be copied and edited, but sometimes it is useful to inform the user that the script will not work as expected if they are not root. For example, this short script displays configured network adapters and their current speeds. The `ethtool` command requires root privileges to perform its task, so it makes sense to bail out instead of failing to work properly.

```
$ cat nicspeed.sh
#!/bin/bash
# This script only works for the root user.
if [ `id -u` -ne 0 ]; then
  echo "Error: This script has to be run by root."
  exit 2
fi

for nic in `/sbin/ifconfig | grep "Link encap:Ethernet" | \
    grep "^eth" | awk '{ print $1 }'`
do
  echo -en $nic
  ethtool $nic | grep Speed:
done
$ ./nicspeed.sh
Error: This script has to be run by root.
# ./nicspeed.sh
eth0    Speed: 1000Mb/s
eth1    Speed: 100Mb/s
eth4    Speed: 1000Mb/s
#
```

**WHEN RUN AS AN UNPRIVILEGED
USER, IT REFUSES TO CONTINUE.**

WHEN RUN AS ROOT, THE SCRIPT WORKS.

nicspeed.sh

Another command related to name services in general, but including the password database, is `getent`. `getent` retrieves keyed values from certain naming services (as listed in `/etc/nsswitch .conf`). Some of these databases can be output in their entirety; `getent passwd` is equivalent to `cat /etc/passwd`, but is agnostic of the naming service in use. Others are not; `getent ethers` requires a parameter (either a name or a MAC address is accepted, as both are keys).

One of the benefits of Free and Open Source Software is that if you want to see exactly how it works, it is often very easy to get the source code and read what it does. In researching this topic, I wanted to check how getent group *copes with a group's name being totally numeric. Just go to* http://ftp.gnu.org/ gnu/glibc/glibc-2.13.tar.gz, *extract* getent.c, *and find the relevant code on line 224.*

```
224          gid_t arg_gid = strtoul(key[i], &ep, 10);
225
226          if (errno != EINVAL && *key[i] != '\0' && *ep ==
'\0')
227            /* Valid numeric gid.  */
228            grp = getgrgid (arg_gid);
229          else
230            grp = getgrnam (key[i]);
```

The preceding code checks if the key is valid as a group name, and if so, it treats it as a name; otherwise, it treats it as a number.

The following script uses the groups and id commands once each. For all of the other lookups, it uses getent group or getent passwd, respectively. This should be a useful library of code to gather various combinations of group membership information.

```
$ cat groups.sh
#!/bin/bash

function get_groupname
{
  [ ! -z "$1" ] && getent group $@ | cut -d: -f1
}

function get_groupid
{
  [ ! -z "$1" ] && getent group $@ | cut -d: -f3
}

function get_username
{
  [ ! -z "$1" ] && getent passwd $1 | cut -d: -f1
}

function get_userid
{
  [ ! -z "$1" ] && getent passwd $1 | cut -d: -f3
}

function get_user_group_names
{
  [ ! -z "$1" ] && groups $@ | cut -d: -f2
```

```
}

function get_user_group_ids
{
  get_user_group_names $@ | while read groups
  do
    get_groupid $groups
  done
}

function get_primary_group_id
{
  [ ! -z "$1" ] && getent passwd $1 | cut -d: -f4
}

function get_primary_group_name
{
  [ ! -z "$1" ] && get_groupname `get_primary_group_id $@`
}

function show_user
{
  [ $# -gt 0 ] && getent passwd $@ | cut -d: -f1,5
}

function show_groups
{
  for uid in $@
  do
    echo "User $uid : Primary group is `get_primary_group_name $uid`"
    printf "Additional groups: "
    for gid in `id -G $uid | cut -d" " -f2-`
    do
      printf "%s " `get_groupname $gid`
    done
    echo
  done
}

function show_group_members
{
  for sgid in `get_groupid $@`
  do
    echo
    echo "Primary members of the group `get_groupname $sgid`"
    show_user `getent passwd | cut -d: -f1,4 | grep ":${sgid}$" | cut -d: -f1`
    echo "Secondary members of the group `get_groupname $sgid`"
    show_user `getent group $sgid | cut -d: -f4 | tr ',' ' '`
  done
}
USERNAME=${1:-$LOGNAME}
echo "User $USERNAME is in these groups: `id -Gn $USERNAME`"
show_groups $USERNAME
```

```
    show_group_members `id -G $USERNAME`

$ ./groups.sh
User steve is in these groups: sysadm support
User steve : Primary group is sysadm
Additional groups: staff support

Primary members of the group sysadm:
steve:Steve Parker
bethany:Bethany Parker
Secondary members of the group sysadm:
www:Apache Web Server
dns:Bind Name Server

Primary members of the group staff:
hr:Human Resources
Secondary members of the group staff:
steve:Steve Parker
bethany:Bethany Parker
emily:Emily Parker
jackie:Jackie Parker

Primary members of the group support:
ops1:Operator Account 1
ops2:Operator Account 2
Secondary members of the group support:
steve:Steve Parker
emily:Emily Parker
$
```

groups.sh

LOGGER

logger is a command-line tool that uses the syslog facility present on most Unix and Linux systems. This has a few benefits, one of which is that it allows a non-privileged shell script to write to log files owned by the superuser. It also means that the actual file that gets written to is determined by the system administrator, not the author of the script. This provides additional flexibility and customization.

```
$ cat checkfs.sh
#!/bin/bash

logger -t checkfs -p user.info "Starting checkfs"
df | cut -c52- | grep -v "Use%" | while read usage filesystem
do
  if [ "${usage%\%}" -gt "85" ]; then
    logger -t checkfs -s -p user.warn "Filesystem $filesystem is at $usage"
  fi
done
logger -t checkfs -p user.info "Finished checkfs"
```

checkfs.sh

```
$ df -h
Filesystem              Size  Used Avail Use% Mounted on
/dev/sda5                28G   27G  395M  99% /
tmpfs                   1.5G     0  1.5G   0% /lib/init/rw
udev                    1.5G  248K  1.5G   1% /dev
tmpfs                   1.5G     0  1.5G   0% /dev/shm
/dev/sda3                56G   55G  1.8G  97% /iso
/dev/sda6               134G  124G  3.3G  98% /home/steve
$ ./checkfs.sh
checkfs: Filesystem / is at 99%
checkfs: Filesystem /iso is at 97%
checkfs: Filesystem /home/steve is at 98%
$
```

This results in the following log messages being added to the /var/log/messages file. Notice that although the script was run as an unprivileged user, who may not even have permission to read the file, they can still write to the file via the syslog facility.

```
Mar 29 20:14:08 goldie checkfs: Starting checkfs
Mar 29 20:14:08 goldie checkfs: Filesystem / is at 99%
Mar 29 20:14:08 goldie checkfs: Filesystem /iso is at 97%
Mar 29 20:14:08 goldie checkfs: Filesystem /home/steve is at 98%
Mar 29 20:14:08 goldie checkfs: Finished checkfs
```

MD5SUM

MD5 is a checksumming algorithm that generates fairly long (128-bit) checksums based on the contents of files. It can be useful for verifying that files have not silently become corrupted, whether on disk or, more commonly, when transmitted over unreliable networks such as the Internet. For example, Figure 14-2 shows the GNU.org FTP server with source code, binaries, documentation, and an md5sum file. In the bottom window, the md5sum --check command automatically reads the md5 checksums from the file and tests the downloaded files against the expected checksums.

It is possible for two different files to generate the same checksum; because there are a virtually infinite number of files that could exist, this is inevitable, although with MD5, it is very uncommon. For most cases, however, if the md5 checksum matches, it is safe to say that the files themselves match. It is also always true that if the md5 checksums do not match, the data is different.

One use for this is to monitor a file for changes. To detect if the contents of a file have changed even though the overall size has not changed, a checksum can be stored before and after the suspected change. If the checksum is different, then the file has definitely been modified. This can be particularly useful with large files, as it would be impractical to take snapshot copies of the file just to be able to observe that there has (or has not) been a change made to it. The md5 checksum of any file is always only 128 bytes, regardless of the size of the file itself. It is therefore possible to save regular snapshots of the checksum of a file, even when it is not practical to save multiple copies of the actual data itself.

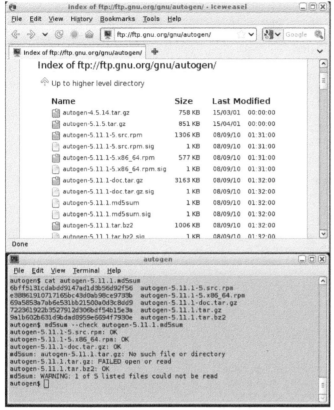

FIGURE 14-2

This script monitors a file and reports when it has been changed. It saves the md5sums of the files it is monitoring and sends an alert whenever any of those files change.

```
# cat monitorlogs.sh
#!/bin/bash
SAVEDIR=/tmp/log.save
mkdir -p ${SAVEDIR}
cd /var/log

NOW=`date +%d%b%Y%H%M%S`
mkdir -p "$SAVEDIR" 2>/dev/null
for FILE in messages syslog dmesg daemon.log
do
  md5sum "${FILE}" | cut -d" " -f1 > "${SAVEDIR}/${FILE}.md5"
done

while :
do
```

```
NOW=`date +%d%b%Y%H%M%S`
for FILE in messages syslog dmesg daemon.log
do
  prev=`cat "$SAVEDIR/${FILE}.md5" || echo 0`
  if [ -s "${FILE}" ]; then
    # it exists and has content
    md5=`md5sum ${FILE} | cut -d" " -f1 |tee "${SAVEDIR}/${FILE}.md5"`
    if [ "$prev" != "$md5" ]; then
      case "$prev" in
        0) echo "`date`: $FILE appeared." ;;
        *) echo "`date`: $FILE changed."
             ;;
      esac
      cp "${FILE}" "${SAVEDIR}/${FILE}.$NOW"
    fi
  else
    # it doesn't exist; did it exist before?
    if [ "$prev" != "0" ]; then
      echo "`date`: $FILE disappeared."
      echo 0 > "${SAVEDIR}/${FILE}.md5"
    fi
  fi
done
sleep 30
done

# ./monitorlogs.sh
Fri Feb 11 11:44:45 GMT 2011: messages appeared.
Fri Feb 11 11:44:45 GMT 2011: syslog appeared.
Fri Feb 11 11:44:45 GMT 2011: dmesg appeared.
Fri Feb 11 11:44:45 GMT 2011: daemon.log appeared.
Fri Feb 11 11:45:15 GMT 2011: messages changed.
Fri Feb 11 11:45:15 GMT 2011: syslog changed.
Fri Feb 11 11:46:15 GMT 2011: messages changed.
Fri Feb 11 11:46:15 GMT 2011: syslog changed.
^C
#
```

monitorlogs.sh

MKFIFO

A First-In First-Out (FIFO) file is known as a named pipe. Like regular pipes, which are used to tie together the input and output of otherwise independent commands, FIFOs manage the input and output between processes. However, any process at all may (if filesystem permissions permit) read and write to and from this pipe. This allows multiple processes to communicate with one another without even knowing who is receiving the data they send, or sending the data they are receiving. The mkfifo command sets up a FIFO, optionally setting permissions at the same time.

Master and Minions

This inter-process communication provides a very useful multitasking ability in a really easy-to-use-and-understand manner. This master script occasionally emits commands; one of its many minions picks it up and works on it. That work could take some time to complete (these clients have lots of `sleep` statements to make sure that it does!), but the master can dispatch the work to the queue and return to its loop. However, when all of its minions (or clients) are busy, its `echo` to the FIFO does not return until there is a client to pick it up, so the master then gets blocked. In Figure 14-3, when the first client (center left) picks up the "quit" command, it exits; when the remaining client exits in response to the second "quit" command, there are no more processes listening to the pipe, so the master does not get to display its prompt again until a client arrives to execute its previous command.

FIGURE 14-3

 These "commands" are, of course, a made-up language; the minions merely treat the first word they read as a command, and then echo *out any remaining words one at a time, with a one-second pause between each word.*

Available for download on Wrox.com

```
$ cat master.sh
#!/bin/bash
pid=$$
fifo=/tmp/fifo.$pid
log=/tmp/log.$pid
```

```
> $log

echo "My PID is $pid"
mkfifo $fifo

while :
do
  echo -en "Give me a command for one of my minions: "
  read cmd
  echo $cmd > $fifo
done

rm -f $log $fifo
```

master.sh

```
$ cat minion.sh
#!/bin/bash
master=$1
fifo=/tmp/fifo.$master
log=/tmp/log.$master

while :
do
  read cmd args < $fifo
  if [ ! -z "$cmd" ]; then
    if [ "$cmd" == "quit" ]; then
      echo "Very good, master." | tee -a $log
      exit 0
    fi
    echo "`date`: Executing \"${cmd}\" for the master." | tee -a $log
    if [ ! -z "$args" ]; then
      for arg in $args
      do
        echo -en "$arg " | tee -a $log
        sleep 1
      done
      echo | tee -a $log
    fi
  fi
  sleep 10
done
$
```

minion.sh

When run, the minions display to their output and also (via the underused but very convenient tee -a utility) to a log file. The bottom window watches what gets written there; notice in Figure 14-3 (presented previously) that the command "say a b c d e f g h" started executing slightly before the "count 1 2 3 4 5 6" had finished; the final echo from the count command is written to the log after the timestamp and initial a has been written by the say command. Figure 14-3 shows a sample run of these recipes.

There is no technical reason for the master and minions to use the master's PID in the names of the files they use. It could just as easily be called `/tmp/master.fifo` or anything else. It can also be a permanent part of the filesystem, in a specific location documented by the application such as `/opt/master/comms/master-minion`; using `/tmp` and PIDs as labels is often convenient to ensure that two concurrently running pairs of master-minion FIFOs can coexist without interfering with each other.

Reversing the Order

In the opposite direction, it is possible to have lots of independent processes writing to the FIFO, with a master (or even multiple masters) then reading from the other end of the pipe. One set of processes could collect pieces of work to be done, while the others pick up the next available task like the minions in the previous example. This recipe has multiple gatherers, each concurrently reading from a different filesystem and writing to the FIFO whenever it finds a zip archive. The master in this scenario is the script which reads from the FIFO. The following script reads zip files from the FIFO and looks for a filename containing the word "chapter."

Available for download on Wrox.com

```bash
#!/bin/bash
fifo=/tmp/zips.fifo
rm $fifo
mkfifo $fifo
searchstring=$@

while read filename
do
  unzip -l "${filename}" | grep $searchstring > /dev/null 2>&1
  if [ "$?" -eq "0" ]; then
    echo "Found \"$searchstring\" in $filename"
  fi
done < $fifo
echo "Finished."
```

zip-master.sh

The `zip-gatherer.sh` script contains a `searchfs` function, which does a `find` within the given filesystem (so searching `/` won't overlap into a separate `/home` filesystem, for example), and executes an instance of this function in the background for each filesystem it finds of type `crypt`, `ext`, or `fuseblk`.

Available for download on Wrox.com

```bash
#!/bin/bash
fifo=/tmp/zips.fifo

function searchfs
{
  temp=`mktemp`
```

```
    find ${1} -mount -type f -iname "*zip" -exec file {} \; \
        | grep "Zip archive data" | cut -d: -f1 > $temp
    cat $temp > $fifo
    rm -f $temp
    echo "Finished searching ${1}."
}

for filesystem in `mount -t crypt,ext3,ext4,fuseblk | cut -d" " -f3`
do
    echo "Spawning a child to search $filesystem"
    searchfs $filesystem &
done
# Wait for children to complete
wait
# send an EOF to the master to close the fifo
printf "%c" 04 > $fifo
```

zip-gatherer.sh

The searchfs function writes to a temporary file and then dumps that file to the FIFO. This helps consistency, as the find command can take a long time to run, and different instances of the function could overlap with each other, causing garbled filenames in the FIFO.

The zip-gatherer.sh script ends by sending a 04 (EOT) character to the FIFO. This closes the file, which causes the while read loop in zip-master.sh to exit. zip-gatherer.sh ensures that all of its children have finished their searches by executing a wait command with no arguments, which does not return until all of the script's children have completed.

The following shows the output of zip-gatherer.sh. Some directories under / are not available to the unprivileged user, so a Permission denied message is displayed. This can be easily hidden by directing stderr to /dev/null. The main script spawns a background process to trawl through each of the filesystems found, and each of those writes its findings to the same shared FIFO, ready to be processed by the master script.

```
$ ./zip-gatherer.sh
Spawning a child to search /
Spawning a child to search /windows
Spawning a child to search /home/steve
find: `/var/lib/php5': Permission denied
find: `/var/lib/polkit-1': Permission denied
find: `/var/lib/sudo': Permission denied
find: `/var/lib/gdm': Permission denied
find: `/var/cache/system-tools-backends/backup': Permission denied
find: `/var/cache/ldconfig': Permission denied
find: `/var/spool/exim4': Permission denied
find: `/var/spool/cups': Permission denied
find: `/var/spool/cron/atspool': Permission denied
find: `/var/spool/cron/atjobs': Permission denied
find: `/var/spool/cron/crontabs': Permission denied
find: `/var/run/exim4': Permission denied
```

```
find: `/var/run/cups/certs': Permission denied
find: `/var/log/exim4': Permission denied
find: `/var/log/apache2': Permission denied
find: `/home/steve/lost+found': Permission denied
find: `/etc/ssl/private': Permission denied
find: `/etc/cups/ssl': Permission denied
find: `/lost+found': Permission denied
find: `/root': Permission denied
Finished searching /.
Finished searching /home/steve.
Finished searching /windows.
$
```

The code snippet that follows shows the output of the `zip-master.sh` script. The `actionis.zip` file is not a valid zip file, so `unzip` displays an error. For flexibility, `zip-master.sh` takes `grep` arguments on its command line so that you can choose what to search for. This also means that the `-i` parameter can be passed on to `grep` for a case-insensitive search.

```
$ ./zip-master.sh -i chapter
Found "-i chapter" in /iso/E19787-01.zip
Found "-i chapter" in /home/steve/sc32/10_x86/125509-08.zip
Found "-i chapter" in /home/steve/Part I-3feb.zip
Found "-i chapter" in /home/steve/sc33/E19680-01.zip
Found "-i chapter" in /home/steve/Part I.zip
  End-of-central-directory signature not found.  Either this file is not
  a zipfile, or it constitutes one disk of a multi-part archive.  In the
  latter case, the central directory and zipfile comment will be found on
  the last disk(s) of this archive.
unzip:  cannot find zipfile directory in one of /home/steve/fonts/actionis.zip or
        /home/steve/fonts/actionis.zip.zip, and cannot find /home/steve/fonts/actio
nis.zip.ZIP, period.
Found "-i chapter" in /home/steve/Part I-jan3.zip
Finished.
$
```

NETWORKING

Networking is central to Unix and Linux systems. There are a lot of networking-related commands built in, all of which can be scripted, some more easily than others. `telnet` and `ping` are traditionally a bit cumbersome to script, so they are presented here with some techniques and also `netcat`, a cleaner and more scriptable alternative to `telnet`. This section also shows some basic techniques for talking to different types of Internet servers. Finally, secure communication is a key part of today's Internet, and even internal communications on trusted networks are encrypted more often than not. A lot of math is involved in encryption, but it does not have to be very complicated and difficult to work with. This section also includes various ways of using the OpenSSL suite of tools, not just the SSH protocol but also the lower-level SSL connections themselves, because these are actually a lot easier to use than is often assumed.

telnet

telnet is an old and insecure protocol for logging in to remote systems over the network. However, the telnet client is still a very useful network testing tool because all it does is send text back and forth between the two systems (although it does treat some characters as special protocol information, it is good enough for testing text-based protocols such as HTTP, SMTP, POP, and IMAP). It is very easy to test a web server with a simple telnet command; in the following example, the server at www.example.com gives a 302 status code, which indicates redirection to http://www.iana.org/domains/example/ (see http://www.w3.org/Protocols/rfc2616/rfc2616-sec10.html for the definitions of HTTP status codes), but in effect, you can take this to be a successful connection to the server. HTTP status codes in the 400s and 500s are generally problematic, indicating a problem with the request or with the server, respectively. Lower numbers are better; 200 means OK, indicating total success.

 When testing HTTP servers interactively, it is easiest to specify HTTP/1.0 rather than HTTP/1.1 as no additional headers are required for version 1.0 of the protocol. Also, remember to send a blank line after the request (that is, press the Return key twice) to indicate the end of the headers.

```
$ telnet www.example.com 80
Trying 192.0.32.10...
Connected to www.example.com.
Escape character is '^]'.
GET http://www.example.com/ HTTP/1.0

HTTP/1.0 302 Found
Location: http://www.iana.org/domains/example/
Server: BigIP
Connection: close
Content-Length: 0

Connection closed by foreign host.
$
```

You can also use a telnet client to talk directly with SMTP, POP, and IMAP servers, using their appropriate protocols, although these are increasingly becoming encrypted by default. See the "OpenSSL" section later in the chapter for communicating with encrypted services; it is not as difficult as commonly believed, and it is even quite easy to script.

netcat

The netcat tool transfers data over networks. It is quite similar to the telnet client, but it does not process special characters (such as EOF) differently. This means that it can be used to transfer binary data over the network and does not mangle any of the packets. There are a number of uses for netcat, including testing connections in the same way as a telnet client, port scanning, and file transfer.

Testing Connections with netcat

netcat can be used to communicate with servers of text-based protocols (such as HTTP, SNMP, POP, IMAP) in a similar way to telnet. It does not treat EOF differently, and does not display its own messages about escape characters and the like, so its output can be saved directly to a file.

```
$ telnet www.example.com 80
Trying 192.0.32.10...          ◄
Connected to www.example.com.          THE NEXT THREE LINES ARE FROM
Escape character is '^]'.               TELNET, NOT THE SERVER.
HEAD / HTTP/1.0

HTTP/1.0 302 Found
Location: http://www.iana.org/domains/example/
Server: BigIP
Connection: close
Content-Length: 0

Connection closed by foreign host.
$ netcat www.example.com 80          ALL OF THE OUPUT IS FROM THE
HEAD / HTTP/1.0                       SERVER ITSELF.

HTTP/1.0 302 Found          ◄
Location: http://www.iana.org/domains/example/
Server: BigIP
Connection: close
Content-Length: 0

$
```

Using netcat as a Port Scanner

nmap is a far more powerful tool for this job, but netcat can also be used as a port scanner. Again, its output is minimalist so it is much easier to parse the netcat output in an automated script.

```
$ nmap 192.168.0.210

Starting Nmap 5.00 ( http://nmap.org ) at 2011-03-24 19:41 GMT
Interesting ports on intranet (192.168.0.210):
Not shown: 997 closed ports
PORT    STATE SERVICE
22/tcp  open  ssh
80/tcp  open  http
111/tcp open  rpcbind

Nmap done: 1 IP address (1 host up) scanned in 0.08 seconds
$ netcat -vz 192.168.0.210 1-1024
intranet [192.168.0.210] 111 (sunrpc) open
intranet [192.168.0.210] 80 (www) open
intranet [192.168.0.210] 22 (ssh) open
$
```

Using netcat to Transfer Data

netcat can also be used to transfer data between systems. Because it takes data directly, it can write its output directly to a file. On the receiving end, launch netcat -l (listen) and specify a port number. Piping it through pv is not essential, but it does display a convenient progress status; pv -t shows the time that the pipe has been active; pv -b shows how many bytes have gone through it.

```
recipient$ netcat -l -p 8888 | pv -t > fedora.iso.gz
0:39:17
$
```

On the sending side, cat the file into netcat. Again, I have put pv into the pipeline because it conveniently displays progress. Otherwise, because netcat ignores EOF, there is no convenient way to tell that the transfer is complete. A Control-C is therefore necessary (from either end) to end the connection when the transfer is complete. Some distributions provide netcat with the -q option automatically enabled, but that would make it less useful for transfer of binary files.

```
sender$ cat /iso/Fedora-14-i686-Live-Desktop.iso.gz | pv -b | netcat recipient 8888
 669MB
^C
$
```

Taking this one step further, you can send entire tarballs or cpio archives over netcat. In the following example, I have used the -v flag to tar so that the files are shown at each end as they are put into, and extracted from, the archive.

```
recipient$ netcat -l -p 8888 | pv -t | tar xvf -
iso/:01
iso/debian-504-amd64-DVD-1.iso
iso/solaris-cluster-3_3-ga-x86.zip
iso/solaris-cluster-3_3-ga-sparc.zip
0:32:21
$
sender$ tar cvf - /iso | pv -b | netcat recipient 8888
tar: Removing leading `/' from member names
/iso/
/iso/debian-504-amd64-DVD-1.iso
/iso/solaris-cluster-3_3-ga-x86.zip
/iso/solaris-cluster-3_3-ga-sparc.zip
4.52GB
^C
$
```

ping

ping is a basic network diagnostic tool, which sends an ICMP packet to another host, requesting an echo response. If the remote host chooses to (and unless it is a fairly paranoid system, or a firewall, it should do), it sends an ICMP reply back in return. This is primarily useful to determine that the remote host is alive, although it has other side effects, too; the main side effect if they are on the same subnet is that the remote host's MAC (Ethernet) address is now known and added to the local system's ARP cache, as displayed by arp -a. One of the frustrations with traditional ping implementations is that they send four packets and wait a long time for a response. To test an entire Class C subnet used to mean that a script like this was required:

```
$ cat simpleping.sh
#!/bin/bash
LOG=ping.log
PREFIX=192.168.1
i=1

while [ "$i" -lt "8" ]
do
  echo "Pinging ${PREFIX}.$i"
  ping ${PREFIX}.$i  > /tmp/ping.$i 2>&1 &
  sleep 2
  kill -9 $!
  grep "^64 bytes from" /tmp/ping.$i
  if [ "$?" -eq "0" ]; then
    echo "${PREFIX}.$i is alive" | tee -a $LOG
  else
    echo "${PREFIX}.$i is dead" | tee -a $LOG
  fi
  rm -f /tmp/ping.$i
  i=`expr $i + 1`
done
```

```
$ ./simpleping.sh
Pinging 192.168.1.1
./ping.sh: line 20:  9641 Killed              ping ${PREFIX}.$i > /tmp/ping.$i 2>&1
192.168.1.1 is alive
Pinging 192.168.1.2
./ping.sh: line 20:  9651 Killed              ping ${PREFIX}.$i > /tmp/ping.$i 2>&1
192.168.1.2 is dead
Pinging 192.168.1.3
./ping.sh: line 20:  9658 Killed              ping ${PREFIX}.$i > /tmp/ping.$i 2>&1
192.168.1.3 is alive
Pinging 192.168.1.4
./ping.sh: line 20:  9665 Killed              ping ${PREFIX}.$i > /tmp/ping.$i 2>&1
192.168.1.4 is dead
Pinging 192.168.1.5
./ping.sh: line 20:  9675 Killed              ping ${PREFIX}.$i > /tmp/ping.$i 2>&1
192.168.1.5 is dead
Pinging 192.168.1.6
./ping.sh: line 20:  9682 Killed              ping ${PREFIX}.$i > /tmp/ping.$i 2>&1
192.168.1.6 is dead
Pinging 192.168.1.7
./ping.sh: line 20:  9689 Killed              ping ${PREFIX}.$i > /tmp/ping.$i 2>&1
192.168.1.7 is dead
$ cat ping.log
192.168.1.1 is alive
192.168.1.2 is dead
192.168.1.3 is alive
192.168.1.4 is dead
192.168.1.5 is dead
```

```
192.168.1.6 is dead
192.168.1.7 is dead
$
```

This has only tested the first seven devices on the network and has wasted an awful lot of screen real estate. It would be better to specify a timeout and a maximum packet count; GNU `ping` offers this feature, with the `-w` and `-c` options, respectively. This makes for a much simpler, cleaner, and faster `ping` test. The preceding test takes about eight minutes to run; the following takes about one second (normally less, as it is not common for a single ping request to take a full second). For even greater accuracy, increase `-w1` to `-w2`; this will take two seconds to complete but offers hosts two seconds to respond instead of one second. You could also use `-c2` to send two packets in case the first is lost. The `time` command shows the elapsed (real) time taken by the command, and shows in the test run below that the whole process took just over a quarter of a second.

```
$ cat ping2.sh
#!/bin/bash
LOG=ping.log
PREFIX=192.168.1

for i in `seq 1 254`
do
  ping -c1 -w1 ${PREFIX}.$i && \
    echo "${PREFIX}.$i is alive" | tee -a $LOG || \
    echo "${PREFIX}.$i is dead" | tee -a $LOG &
done
$

$ time ./ping2.sh > /dev/null 2>&1

real    0m0.255s
user    0m0.008s
sys     0m0.028s
$
$ wc -l ping.log
254 ping.log
$ grep alive ping.log
192.168.1.1 is alive
192.168.1.3 is alive
192.168.1.10 is alive
$
```

> *There is also a technique known as the Broadcast Ping (`ping -b`); this sends a single `ping` request over the local subnet addressed to the broadcast address. Every node on the subnet should respond to this `ping` request. That would be even simpler, although individual nodes can be configured to ignore broadcast requests even though they would respond to tailored `ping` requests.*

Scripting ssh and scp

Back in a different time, `rcp` was a useful utility for copying files between systems. It was easy to set up so that a shell script could easily copy a file from one machine to another without any awkward questions being asked. Networks are not trusted in the same way any longer, so `rcp`, `rlogin`, `rsh`, and their naîvely trusting friends (commonly known as the r-tools) are obsolete.

 Although its name starts with an "r" for "remote," the `rsync` tool is not one of the "r-tools," and can be configured to use SSH for secure authentication and encryption.

Many people are familiar with using `scp` interactively, but it can also be used to provide secure passwordless authentication. The key to this is public key infrastructure (PKI). PKI means that you can have asymmetric keys; that means that one is kept reasonably securely and is called the *private key*. The other key can safely be shared with anyone, even untrusted enemies, and is called the *public key*. Data encrypted with the public key can be decrypted with the private key, and vice versa. What this means, in effect, is that you can prove to the remote host that you are the owner of the private key, without ever having to reveal that key to anybody. This can be the basis for passwordless logins amongst many other features, including secure web browsing.

 Using a blank passphrase on the private key negates the whole authentication aspect of PKI. Sometimes, this is okay — if encryption is all that is required, then authentication does not matter — but for authentication purposes, it is essential that the private key has a good passphrase.

The `ssh-keygen` tool creates a pair of keys. All that you need to do then is to copy (or append) the public key (`id_rsa.pub`) to the remote server as `~/.ssh/authorized_keys`, and set the permissions correctly (0700 for the `~/.ssh,` directory and 0600 for `~/.ssh/authorized_keys`). The `ssh-copy-id tool` does all of this for you.

```
home$ ssh-keygen
Generating public/private rsa key pair.
Enter file in which to save the key (/home/steve/.ssh/id_rsa): <enter>
Created directory '/home/steve/.ssh'.
Enter passphrase (empty for no passphrase): ssh-password
Enter same passphrase again: ssh-password
Your identification has been saved in /home/steve/.ssh/id_rsa.
Your public key has been saved in /home/steve/.ssh/id_rsa.pub.
The key fingerprint
is:
28:17:fd:fe:df:60:8a:fa:9e:17:c0:94:8c:5f:e2:35
home$
home$ ssh-copy-id -i ~/.ssh/id_rsa.pub example.com
steve@example.com's password: example.com-password
```

```
Now try logging into the machine, with "ssh 'example.com'", and check in:

.ssh/authorized_keys

to make sure we haven't added extra keys that you weren't expecting.
home$ ssh example.com
Enter passphrase for key '/home/steve/.ssh/id_rsa': ssh-password
Last login: Fri Dec 11 11:01:33 2009 from home
example.com$ ls -l .ssh/authorized_keys
-rw------- 1 steve  user   395 Jun 3  2011 authorized_keys
example.com$
```

The next step is to add the key to your environment. If you are running a graphical session such as GNOME or KDE, the SSH agent should already be running for you. If not, you need to get your current shell to parse the output of the ssh-agent command. This gives your shell all the settings it needs to talk to the ssh-agent, which is automatically started in the background as a result of calling it. You can then manually add the key to the agent with the ssh-add command. This will prompt for the key's passphrase, and store the key in memory for future connections.

```
home$ eval `ssh-agent`
Agent pid 3996
home$ ps -fp 3996
UID        PID  PPID  C STIME TTY        TIME CMD
steve     3996     1  0 19:43 ?      00:00:00 ssh-agent
home$ ssh-add
Enter passphrase for /home/steve/.ssh/id_rsa:
Identity added: /home/steve/.ssh/id_rsa (/home/steve/.ssh/id_rsa)
home$ ssh steve@example.com
steve@example.com:~$ uname -n
example.com
steve@example.com:~$
```

This whole setup takes only a couple of minutes, and it gives you a secure infrastructure for connecting to remote machines. This can be used to provide rcp-like seamless copying of files between machines. The script that follows checks that the authentication mechanism works and displays an error message if it does not work. Once it has established that the infrastructure works, it uses scp to copy any files listed on the command line to the remote host. Because the calling shell has an active ssh-agent, no passwords are asked for at any stage in the process.

```
$ cat scp.sh
#!/bin/bash
user=$1
host=$2
shift 2
files=$@

echo "Testing connection to ${host}..."
ssh -n -o NumberOfPasswordPrompts=0 ${user}@${host}
if [ "$?" -ne "0" ]; then
   echo "FATAL: You do not have passwordless ssh working."
```

```
    echo "Try running ssh-add."
    exit 1
fi

echo "Okay. Starting the scp."
scp -B ${files} ${user}@${host}:
if [ "$?" -ne "0" ]; then
  echo "An error occurred."
else
  echo "Successfully copied $files to $host"
fi

echo "I can do ssh as well."
ssh ${user}@${host} ls -l ${files}

$ ./scp.sh wronguser example.com hosts scp.sh data
Testing connection to example.com...
Pseudo-terminal will not be allocated because stdin is not a terminal.
Permission denied (publickey,password,keyboard-interactive).
FATAL: You do not have passwordless ssh working.
Try running ssh-add.
$ ./scp.sh steve example.com hosts scp.sh data
Testing connection to example.com...
Pseudo-terminal will not be allocated because stdin is not a terminal.
Okay. Starting the scp.
hosts                                      100%  479      0.5KB/s   00:00
scp.sh                                     100%  436      0.4KB/s   00:00
data                                       100% 4096KB 105.0KB/s   00:39
Successfully copied hosts scp.sh data to example.com
I can do ssh as well.
-rw-r--r--  1 steve  user      479 Mar 21 14:51 hosts
-rw-r--r--  1 steve  user  4194304 Mar 21 14:52 data
-rwxr-xr-x  1 steve  user      501 Mar 21 14:51 scp.sh
home$
```

scp.sh

It really is that simple; you can set up automated copies, and even run commands on remote machines through a script, in a secure way with ssh. This is a very useful tool, and all that you need to do to keep it secure is to keep the passphrase secret and don't let anybody take over your login session.

OpenSSL

OpenSSL is the library that manages Secure Sockets Layer (SSL) connections. SSL provides two key benefits, authentication and encryption. This section mainly deals with the encryption side. For authentication, the key is signed by a Certificate Authority (CA), which is recognized by the client software (normally a web browser or mail client). The rest is the same whether signed by a CA or by yourself (known as a self-signed certificate). Adding SSL adds some additional complexity; there is no way to establish an SSL connection using `telnet`, for example. SSL connections are reasonably complicated to set up, but the `openssl` binary provides a useful wrapper with the `s_client` command. This implements all of the SSL protocol behind the scenes and provides a secure transport mechanism as painlessly as possible.

The `openssl s_client` tool does all of the SSL handshaking behind the scenes and displays the results. In the following code snippet, a connection to `www.google.com` on port 443 exchanges certificates and establishes a secure connection. The HTTP session is then just the same as the unencrypted session shown previously; a 302 status code redirects to another page at `google.com`. This time, however, all that an eavesdropper would see is the encrypted traffic.

 The same technique can be used to connect to secure SMTP, IMAP, POP, and other text-based services.

```
$ openssl s_client -connect www.google.com:443
CONNECTED(00000003)
depth=1 /C=ZA/O=Thawte Consulting (Pty) Ltd./CN=Thawte SGC CA
verify error:num=20:unable to get local issuer certificate
verify return:0
---
Certificate chain
 0 s:/C=US/ST=California/L=Mountain View/O=Google Inc/CN=www.google.com
   i:/C=ZA/O=Thawte Consulting (Pty) Ltd./CN=Thawte SGC CA
 1 s:/C=ZA/O=Thawte Consulting (Pty) Ltd./CN-Thawte SGC CA
   i:/C=US/O=VeriSign, Inc./OU=Class 3 Public Primary Certification Authority
---
Server certificate
-----BEGIN CERTIFICATE-----
MIIDITCCAoqgAwIBAgIQL9+89q6RUm0PmqPfQDQ+mjANBgkqhkiG9w0BAQUFADBM
MQswCQYDVQQGEwJaQTElMCMGA1UEChMcVGhhd3RlIENvbnN1bHRpbmcgKFB0eSkg
THRkLjEWMBQGA1UEAxMNVGhhd3RlIFNHQyBDQTAeFw0wOTEyMTgwMDAwMDBaFw0x
MTEyMTgyMzU5NTlaMGgxCzAJBgNVBAYTAlVTMRMwEQYDVQQIEwpDYWxpZm9ybmlh
MRYwFAYDVQQHFA1Nb3VudGFpbiBWaWV3MRMwEQYDVQQKFApHb29nbGUgSW5jMRcw
FQYDVQQDFA53d3cuZ29vZ2xlLmNvbTCBnzANBgkqhkiG9w0BAQEFAAOBjQAwgYkC
gYEA6PmGD5D6htffvXImttdEAoN4c9kCKO+IRTn7E0h8rqk41XXGOOsKFQebg+jN
gtXj9xVoRaELGYW84u+E593y17iYwqG7tcFR39SDAqc9BkJb4SLD3muFXxzW2k6L
05vuuWciKh0R73mkszeK9P4Y/bz5RiNQl/Os/CRGK1w7t0UCAwEAAaOB5zCB5DAM
BgNVHRMBAf8EAjAAMDYGA1UdHwQvMC0wK6ApoCeGJWh0dHA6Ly9jcmwudGhhd3Rl
LmNvbS9UaGF3dGVTR0NDQS5jcmwwKAYDVR0lBCEwHwYIKwYBBQUHAwEGCCsGAQUF
BwMCBglghkgBhvhCBAEwcgYIKwYBBQUHAQEEZjBkMCIGCCsGAQUFBzABhhZodHRw
Oi8vb2NzcC50aGF3dGUuY29tMD4GCCsGAQUFBzAChjJodHRwOi8vd3d3LnRoYXd0
ZS5jb20vcmVwb3NpdG9yeS9UaGF3dGVfU0dVfU0dDX0NBLmNydDANBgkqhkiG9w0BAQUF
AAOBgQCfQ89bxFApsb/isJr/aiEdLRLDLE5a+RLizrmCUi3nHX4adpaQedEkUjh5
u2ONgJd8IyAPkU0Wueru9G2Jysa9zCRo1kNbzipYvzwY4OA8Ys+WAi0oR1A04Se6
```

```
z5nRUP8pJcA2NhUzUnC+MY+f6H/nEQyNv4SgQhqAibAxWEEHXw==
-----END CERTIFICATE-----
subject=/C=US/ST=California/L=Mountain View/O=Google Inc/CN=www.google.com
issuer=/C=ZA/O=Thawte Consulting (Pty) Ltd./CN=Thawte SGC CA
---
No client certificate CA names sent
---
SSL handshake has read 1772 bytes and written 307 bytes
---
New, TLSv1/SSLv3, Cipher is RC4-SHA
Server public key is 1024 bit
Secure Renegotiation IS supported
Compression: NONE
Expansion: NONE
SSL-Session:
    Protocol  : TLSv1
    Cipher    : RC4-SHA
    Session-ID: 2E0A49E8A432E2EE45B1449744BFF2017F6AC0F7F2CB477F122770666D0FD5A7
    Session-ID-ctx:
    Master-Key: 1D0E53FDF5D5B4C50FD7040855DEAD1F59F4A31FADDFA95D33B53FB066FE54A1055
BD40C472CEF54BD0F67155C6609C2
    Key-Arg   : None
    Start Time: 1298235973
    Timeout   : 300 (sec)
    Verify return code: 20 (unable to get local issuer certificate)
---
GET https://www.google.com/ HTTP/1.0  ◄───────────────────────────────┐
                                                                        │
                                                  WHAT FOLLOWS AFTER THE SSL
HTTP/1.0 302 Found                                HANDSHAKE IS JUST LIKE THE TELNET
Location: https://encrypted.google.com/           SESSION SHOWN PREVIOUSLY.
Cache-Control: private
Content-Type: text/html; charset=UTF-8
Set-Cookie: PREF=ID=6d0ef1135c2f2888:FF=0:TM=1298235982:LM=1298235982:S=CukIbpibhIa
tYpgM; expires=Tue, 19-Feb-2013 21:06:22 GMT; path=/; domain=.google.com
Set-Cookie: NID=44=Rg2UzM1twCSAtpFrZwCB6niEX7vQjKa25eR3qkKaEtqP6Nx5Lb01PM9Rk11UgZ5u
XZ3sg4kEmp7lpoP2U8knxgZHPBM7Tz7kbD087T9iHSHpThgdtcMXeKIb7kItvnqO; expires=Mon, 22-A
ug-2011 21:06:22 GMT; path=/; domain=.google.com; HttpOnly
Date: Sun, 20 Feb 2011 21:06:22 GMT
Server: gws
Content-Length: 226
X-XSS-Protection: 1; mode=block

<HTML><HEAD><meta http-equiv="content-type" content="text/html;charset=utf-8">
<TITLE>302 Moved</TITLE></HEAD><BODY>
<H1>302 Moved</H1>
The document has moved
<A HREF="https://encrypted.google.com/">here</A>.
</BODY></HTML>
read:errno=0
$
```

The `openssl` binary is also capable of running a very basic secure web server. It passes files relative to the local directory in which it is running, so a request for `/README` when running in `/var/tmp` will return the file `/var/tmp/README`. This is not suitable for production use, but it is very useful for testing SSL clients' connectivity. This is not the place for a primer on SSL, but the following will get you a self-signed certificate (with a password of `welcome123`) for the OpenSSL server to use.

 You can throw away the `server.key` *and* `server.crt` *files after creating* `server.pem`*; only* `server.pem` *is required.*

```
$ openssl genrsa -des3 1024 > server.key
Generating RSA private key, 1024 bit long modulus
...........+++++
.............................+++++
e is 65537 (0x10001)
Enter pass phrase: welcome123
Verifying - Enter pass phrase: welcome123
$ openssl req -new -key server.key -x509 -days 3650 -out server.crt
Enter pass phrase for server.key: welcome123
You are about to be asked to enter information that will be incorporated
into your certificate request.
What you are about to enter is what is called a Distinguished Name or a DN.
There are quite a few fields but you can leave some blank
For some fields there will be a default value,
If you enter '.', the field will be left blank.
-----
Country Name (2 letter code) [AU]:US
State or Province Name (full name) [Some-State]:New York
Locality Name (eg, city) []:New York
Organization Name (eg, company) [Internet Widgits Pty Ltd]:Wrox
Organizational Unit Name (eg, section) []:Shell Scripting Recipes
Common Name (eg, YOUR name) []:Steve Parker
Email Address []:steve@steve-parker.org
$ cat server.crt server.key > server.pem
$ cat server.pem
-----BEGIN CERTIFICATE-----
MIID0TCCAzqgAwIBAgIJAMCjRE2qwt6vMA0GCSqGSIb3DQEBBQUAMIGiMQswCQYD
VQQGEwJVUzERMA8GA1UECBMITmV3IFlvcmsxETAPBgNVBAcTCE5ldyBZb3JrMQ0w
CwYDVQQKEwRXcm94MSAwHgYDVQQLExdTaGVsbCBTY3JpcHRpbmcgUmVjaXBlczEV
MBMGA1UEAxMMU3RldmUgUGFya2VyMSUwIwYJKoZIhvcNAQkBFhZzdGV2ZUBzdGV2
ZS1wYXJrZXIub3JnMB4XDTExMDMwMTIyMTkwNloXDTIxMDIyNjIyMTkwNlowgaIx
CzAJBgNVBAYTAlVTMREwDwYDVQQIEwhOZXcgWW9yazERMA8GA1UEBxMITmV3IFlv
cmsxDTALBgNVBAoTBFdyb3gxIDAeBgNVBAsTF1NoZWxsIFNjcmlwdGluZyBSZWNp
cGVzMRUwEwYDVQQDEwxTdGV2ZSBQYXJrZXIxJTAjBgkqhkiG9w0BCQEWFnN0ZXZl
QHN0ZXZlLXBhcmtlci5vcmcwgZ8wDQYJKoZIhvcNAQEBBQADgY0AMIGJAoGBAK4g
TJRXAha8mEWB/fwi7vWVsGrm9p+vYtANF4MmcMftyubAeN7fYSLk0vlyaqOjWDTo
aNTfdCPZRqNmf6NPGKUINu0ScTlCyarBSLMupIliv3Y4zj3s/XFU1zZnqYECynEw
DvpoxjwnSC/fQXIo4/fN9aRTuF256qsLkJLgiOJdAgMBAAGjggELMIIBBzAdBgNV
HQ4EFgQUiouy6g40AfzIlwwB1JDg8DWlI8AwgdcGA1UdIwSBzzCBzIAUiouy6g40
```

```
AfzIlwwB1JDg8DWlI8ChgaikgaUwgaIxCzAJBgNVBAYTAlVTMREwDwYDVQQIEwhO
ZXcgWW9yazERMA8GA1UEBxMITmV3IFlvcmxsxDTALBgNVBAoTBFdyb3gxIDAeBgNV
BAsTF1NoZWxsIFNjcmlwdGluZyBSZWNpcGVzMRUwEwYDVQQDEwxTdGV2ZSBQYXJr
ZXIxJTAjBgkqhkiG9w0BCQEWFnN0ZXZlQHN0ZXZlLXBhcmtlci5vcmeCCQDAo0RN
qsLerzAMBgNVHRMEBTADAQH/MA0GCSqGSIb3DQEBBQUAA4GBAET/0Rkhy7QLnOWW
pVrUXtnLy1Cg/gpsYFkLwhy5NNWOJ/d3hNMWfG2e1Ha64C/9bsPJz1p3itfhpK/g
Ff8ib2zRXctThNcmnGZbEylCF8svWus0Gjobe3+tkNn8orfFqj00Gi/JqTGDlCMl
EZgOjdaIjejA/p9uDhfjSvRnMGkx
-----END CERTIFICATE-----
-----BEGIN RSA PRIVATE KEY-----
Proc-Type: 4,ENCRYPTED
DEK-Info: DES-EDE3-CBC,D3A3DF183CADA55E

tA9ZENOT6sTOwKJAGk7vzhs1W3ZT5H96yDjcTFwrJ5m5mAJBNa7UxZuEeU+6vikG
ZK+X9DAfRU4MAzacSLCoGDQUcicAr43gpPqRmnS1oKCkCMe9/DszqpeHsXAWCX42
4/4iEsL3nctT1dNWrh90vJkNOgaw6I+4CjfxZa5OcgACQouIEjOz4CEg904c3oui
8UBWyTs/F5JI6v1RQ34r9X1irbj+ApJWz6poHPcsjT6L0RTDKWZx5u3VW3BS/WmU
jXFLsdrZleiK4+4aaGOqh0CC3yoMfVb4EJQliA4uYo/3NLq1lJ7QkC72GJWm2Q95
L2a5waHoMR6A5t8HbpfqkXEHRToNWypQCAEKhc9aR+l1rcVLml7/gqdqf+Dvc/Fx
xRcoifriuF31QiqcWRs4I/LtAPvzTmcTcWLRm4eMR+mQGK3WSVScRCoXJQ9WtLaj
aAhmDiz8tHWwP+9r2zy6dB51FJAx88h7AUe5YEPlBVQ5utgo/bVZUg/Ly7XlmmBl
Thsncq4J92c1sEOIbrEU+kYsyu5nfwRb54PUee3jovBaSZHUPEQw128Wc0msDQBs
DFE6m/PvMTLlt1snciPZ2Dp4sVZVgXtUbIvnFIoYzHl0LmerkbvjaxEphicBQ9Or
UHu3PZksPX1RbQrW+MLKdrdzEQRBh1qToTsHViTIVsT1RbzUUdZxMzyth271AdFx
kK2fxLTbMkwHobSnPHu9TPwNkdbw8Yfmry2aFbL8FwjRLXEv5PjCKeQUZgnn51nU
vCal0016DYNCF5DZ6RrFK7wr/8atsesanzjXnIc/6OM=
-----END RSA PRIVATE KEY-----
$
```

You are now ready to start your SSL web server. Create a text file in the current directory, call it README, and put some congratulatory text in it. I have used the message "Success! The Shell Scripting Recipes Self-Signed Key has worked!" Once set up, run `openssl s_server`, as shown in the code snippet that follows. Provide the key's passphrase when prompted.

 If `server.pem` *is not in the current directory, provide the* `-cert /var/tmp/server.pem`, *as in the example that follows. By default, it will use* `./server.pem`.

```
$ openssl s_server -cert /var/tmp/server.pem -accept 4433 -WWW
Enter pass phrase for server.pem: welcome123
Using default temp DH parameters
Using default temp ECDH parameters
ACCEPT
```

Now launch a web browser pointing at `https://localhost:4433/README`. (Be sure to specify `https`, not just `http`.) You should get a warning because the key is not signed by an authority known by the browser. It displays the details that you entered when you created your key. This is of no use in terms of proving identity — you could have entered any details you liked when creating the key. It is used by the SSL protocol for encryption, however. Figure 14-4 shows the certificate in the browser.

FIGURE 14-4

Accept this certificate and the browser should continue and retrieve the file README. This will be displayed in the browser window as it would display any other text file. The server shows the status of the connection, and the message FILE:README shows that the README file was requested. This is shown in Figure 14-5.

```
$ openssl s_server -accept 4433 -WWW
Enter pass phrase for server.pem:
Using default temp DH parameters
Using default temp ECDH parameters
ACCEPT
8413:error:14094418:SSL routines:SSL3_READ_BYTES:tlsv1 alert unknown ca:s3_pkt.c:11
02:SSL alert number 48
8413:error:140780E5:SSL routines:SSL23_READ:ssl handshake failure:s23_lib.c:142:
ACCEPT
FILE:README
ACCEPT
ACCEPT
ACCEPT
```

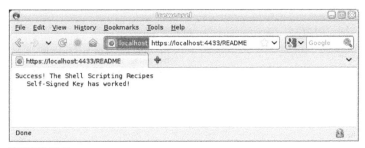

FIGURE 14-5

You can also use the `openssl s_client` to test your `openssl s_server` web server. The response from s_server (when in `-www` mode) is to send the appropriate HTTP headers followed by the README file. Again, the server will display the ACCEPT and FILE:README messages, but unlike the web browser, `s_client` did not query the fact that this test certificate is self-signed. It notes the verification error, but continues with the encrypted section.

```
$ openssl s_client -quiet -connect localhost:4433
depth=0 /C=US/ST=New York/L=New York/O=Wrox/OU=Shell Scripting Recipes/
CN=Steve Parker/emailAddress=steve@steve-parker.org      THE SELF-SIGNED CERTIFICATE
verify error:num=18:self signed certificate    ◄─────── IS NOTED HERE, BUT
verify return:1                                          PROCESSING CONTINUES.
depth=0 /C=US/ST=New York/L=New York/O=Wrox/OU=Shell Scripting Recipes/
CN=Steve Parker/emailAddress=steve@steve-parker.org
verify return:1
GET /README HTTP/1.0
HTTP/1.0 200 ok
Content-type: text/plain

Success! The Shell Scripting Recipes
    Self-Signed Key has worked!
read:errno=0
$
```

The preceding examples show the basic functionality of OpenSSL. Without the `-www` option, any text typed into the client is echoed by the server, and vice versa. This is an incredibly easy way to set up a `netcat`-type connection with encryption thrown in. On one server, you can start up the `openssl s_server`, listening for incoming data. On the remote server, send it a file, some data, or whatever you want. For true `scp`-type security, you would then need to plug in to PAM for authentication mechanisms and so on, but this is a very simple yet powerful tool for testing SSL connections in both directions.

The following example sets up a server (with the `server$` prompt) listening on port 4433 and writing whatever it received to `/tmp/data.bin`. The client (with the `client$` prompt) sends the binary file `/bin/ls` over the network to the server.

THE FILES ARE THE SAME SIZE.

```
server$ openssl s_server -quiet -accept 4433 > /tmp/data.bin
client$ cat /bin/ls | openssl s_client -quiet -connect server1:4433
server$ ls -lh /bin/ls /tmp/data.bin ◄─────┐
-rwxr-xr-x 1 root  root  106K Apr 28  2010 /bin/ls
```

```
-rw-rw-r-- 1 steve steve 106K Mar  1 23:14 /tmp/data.bin
server$ md5sum /tmp/data.bin /bin/ls  ◄
d265cc0520a9a43e5f07ccca453c94f5  /tmp/data.bin
d265cc0520a9a43e5f07ccca453c94f5  /bin/ls
$
```

THE CHECKSUM OF THE FILES IS THE SAME. THERE HAS BEEN NO CORRUPTION OVER THE NETWORK.

NOHUP

If you, whether interactively or as part of a shell script, want a process to run to completion without being `killed` because you have logged off, the `nohup` command informs the shell to ignore any "hangup" (HUP) signals that it would get sent when its controlling terminal logs off the system. It can still be `killed` with `kill -9`, but if a network glitch causes your link to the system to be dropped, or the client you are connecting from were to crash, or any of a million other reasons the connection could get broken, your process will continue to run.

This is mainly useful for executing long-running commands on a remote server, or even on multiple remote servers in parallel. Whether using automation or simply a sequence of `ssh` commands, you can log in to a machine, run `nohup /path/to/somecommand &` and log out again. The `&` puts the command in the background; generally, if you are not waiting around for the result of the command execution, it makes sense to run it as a background process. It also means that you get the shell prompt back so that you are able to log out.

By default, any input the process needs to read will be redirected from `/dev/null`, and output and errors will be written to a file `nohup.out` in the current directory. If stdout and stderr are both redirected elsewhere, `nohup.out` will not be created. This recipe simply spawns a long-running command in the background and returns to the menu. The file count appears to stay the same until the background job has completed; if it was written directly to `$thefile`, the count would be seen to increase over time until the job was complete. If this session were to be terminated for any reason, the `find` would keep on running, so that the next user of the menu would get the latest correct answer, and not a partial answer.

Available for download on Wrox.com

```
# cat menu.sh
#!/bin/bash
thefile=/var/log/filelisting.dat
tempfile=`mktemp`

select task in count recreate
do
  case $REPLY in
    1) wc -l $thefile ;;
    2) echo "Recreating the index. It will be ready in a few minutes."
        (nohup find / -print > $tempfile 2>&1 ; mv $tempfile $thefile) & ;;
  esac
done

# ./menu.sh
1) count
2) recreate
#? 1
895992 /var/log/filelisting.dat
#? 2
```

```
Recreating the index. It will be ready in a few minutes.
#? 1
895992 /var/log/filelisting.dat
#? 1
915128 /var/log/filelisting.dat
#?
```

SEQ

seq displays numbers in sequence, similar to how some implementations of the BASIC programming language implemented a for loop, with a start and an end number, and optional stepping. seq
can also take different printf-type formats, and also automatically pad output so that each item is
padded up to the maximum width used. This is helpful with fixed-width columns, where instead of
counting from 1 to 100, the output has to be 001 to 100.

Integer Sequences

The following script uses two seq statements. The outer loop uses seq 10 10 40 to feed the for
loop. seq 10 10 40 counts from 10 to 40 in increments of 10. These subnets are 192.168.10.0/24,
192.168.20.0/24, 192.168.30.0/24, and 192.168.40.0/24, for Production, Backup, Application, and
Heartbeat, respectively.

> *The /24 notation means that the first 24 bits (3 × 8-bit bytes, so 192.168.10,
> 192.168.20, and so on) are the network part of the address. This leaves the final
> byte to be the host address, that is, the part of the address that identifies the par-
> ticular host on that network.*

The inner loop then counts from 30 to 35, as these six nodes use the same host address on each network. Their hostnames are also tied to their host address, so node030 is also known as node030-prod,
node030-bkp, node030-app, and node030-hb, depending on which network is being used to access it.
For the production network, the raw name node030 is also associated with that IP address. A simple
if statement in the inner network takes care of this, adding an extra name to the output line.

```
$ cat hosts.sh
#!/bin/bash

for subnet in `seq 10 10 40`
do
  case $subnet in
    10) suffix=prod
        description=Production   ;;
    20) suffix=bkp
        description=Backup        ;;
    30) suffix=app
```

```
            description=Application  ;;
    40) suffix=hb
            description=Heartbeat    ;;
  esac
  cat - << EOF > /tmp/hosts.$subnet

# Subnet 192.168.${subnet}.0/24
# This is the $description subnet.
EOF
  for address in `seq 30 35`
  do
    # For Production network, also add the raw node name
    if [ "$suffix" == "prod" ]; then
      printf "192.168.%d.%d\tnode%03d\tnode%03d-%s\n" \
        $subnet $address $address $address $suffix >> /tmp/hosts.$subnet
    else
      printf "192.168.%d.%d\tnode%03d-%s\n" \
        $subnet $address $address $suffix >> /tmp/hosts.$subnet
    fi
  done
  cat /tmp/hosts.$subnet
done


$ ./hosts.sh

# Subnet 192.168.10.0/24
# This is the Production subnet.
192.168.10.30    node030 node030-prod
192.168.10.31    node031 node031-prod
192.168.10.32    node032 node032-prod
192.168.10.33    node033 node033-prod
192.168.10.34    node034 node034-prod
192.168.10.35    node035 node035-prod

# Subnet 192.168.20.0/24
# This is the Backup subnet.
192.168.20.30    node030-bkp
192.168.20.31    node031-bkp
192.168.20.32    node032-bkp
192.168.20.33    node033-bkp
192.168.20.34    node034-bkp
192.168.20.35    node035-bkp

# Subnet 192.168.30.0/24
# This is the Application subnet.
192.168.30.30    node030-app
192.168.30.31    node031-app
192.168.30.32    node032-app
192.168.30.33    node033-app
192.168.30.34    node034-app
192.168.30.35    node035-app

# Subnet 192.168.40.0/24
# This is the Heartbeat subnet.
```

```
192.168.40.30    node030-hb
192.168.40.31    node031-hb
192.168.40.32    node032-hb
192.168.40.33    node033-hb
192.168.40.34    node034-hb
192.168.40.35    node035-hb
$
```

hosts.sh

To write directly to /etc/hosts, the preceding script could either be called as ./hosts.sh >>
/etc/hosts, or the cat statement at the end of the loop could be written to append to /etc/hosts.
The script could also take a switch, which provides the name of the file (if any) to append (or write)
to. The way that it is presented above is more flexible, as the output could be written to any file (or
none at all, and display to stdout).

Floating Point Sequences

seq works on more than just integers. This simple script displays fractions of miles in kilometers.

```
$ cat miles.sh
#!/bin/bash
# 1m ~= 1.609 km

for miles in `seq 1 0.25 5`
do
    km=`echo "scale=2 ; $miles * 1.609" | bc`
    printf "%0.2f miles is %0.2f kilometers\n" $miles $km
    #echo "$miles miles is $km km"
done


$ ./miles.sh
1.00 miles is 1.61 kilometers
1.25 miles is 2.01 kilometers
1.50 miles is 2.41 kilometers
1.75 miles is 2.82 kilometers
2.00 miles is 3.22 kilometers
2.25 miles is 3.62 kilometers
2.50 miles is 4.02 kilometers
2.75 miles is 4.42 kilometers
3.00 miles is 4.83 kilometers
3.25 miles is 5.23 kilometers
3.50 miles is 5.63 kilometers
3.75 miles is 6.03 kilometers
4.00 miles is 6.44 kilometers
4.25 miles is 6.84 kilometers
4.50 miles is 7.24 kilometers
4.75 miles is 7.64 kilometers
5.00 miles is 8.05 kilometers
$
```

miles.sh

SLEEP

As used widely in this book, `sleep` and `date` combined can provide invaluable debugging information. The GNU implementation can also take decimal fractions, as well as the suffixes `m` for minutes, `h` for hours, and `d` for days. By inserting `sleep` statements into a script, you can effectively pause execution at that stage and see what is happening when. The `timeout` section later in this chapter makes good use of the `sleep` command to emulate the different scenarios of an application shutdown script.

Another common use for `sleep` is within a loop; to execute a set of commands once a minute, a simple `sleep 60` is easier than scheduling the task in `cron`. To run a task once every 90 seconds is far more difficult in `cron`, but again, the `sleep` statement fits this task perfectly.

```
$ cat memory.sh
#!/bin/bash

LOGFILE=/var/tmp/memory.txt
while :
do
  RAM=`grep MemFree /proc/meminfo | awk '{ print $2 }'`
  echo "At `date +'%H:%M on %d %b %Y'` there is $RAM Kb free on `hostname -s`" \
        |tee -a $LOGFILE
  sleep 60
done


$ ./memory.sh
At 12:45 on 25 Mar 2011 there is 500896 Kb free on goldie
At 12:46 on 25 Mar 2011 there is 441336 Kb free on goldie
At 12:47 on 25 Mar 2011 there is 213736 Kb free on goldie
At 12:48 on 25 Mar 2011 there is 82936 Kb free on goldie
At 12:49 on 25 Mar 2011 there is 96996 Kb free on goldie
At 12:50 on 25 Mar 2011 there is 87240 Kb free on goldie
At 12:51 on 25 Mar 2011 there is 493826 Kb free on goldie
```

memory.sh

Often overlooked, `sleep` is one of those small and trivial tools that it would be impossible to manage without. The GNU extensions make it a little more manageable; `sleep 1h` is more readable than `sleep 3600`; `sleep 2d` is much easier to understand than `sleep 172800`. The capability to `sleep` for a fraction of a second is maybe not quite so useful, because without a real-time operating system, the only thing that `sleep` can guarantee is that it will not return sooner than the requested time (unless it is `killed`). Recipe 17-1 later in the book does make use of sub-second sleeps to speed up the game as it progresses.

TIMEOUT

The `read` and `select` commands honor the variable `TMOUT`, which defines the maximum number of seconds they should wait for interactive input. Other commands do not have this functionality built in, but it can be an essential feature, particularly for scripted operations. This simple script is useful for demonstrating just what `timeout` does because it does not always do exactly what you might expect.

```
$ cat longcmd.sh
#!/bin/bash
trap 'echo "`date`: ouch!"' 15

echo "`date`: Starting"
sleep 20
echo "`date`: Stage Two"
sleep 20
echo "`date`: Finished"
```

longcmd.sh

On the first run, `-s 15 3` tells `timeout` to send a SIGTERM (signal 15) to the script after 3 seconds. This is `trap`ped by the script, but it has the effect of `kill`ing the first `sleep` command. So, 3 seconds after starting, at 13:33:46, the `ouch!` message is displayed as the script handles the `trap`. Execution resumes with the next command in the script, which `echo`es the date (still 13:33:46), `sleep`s for 20 seconds, and finishes at 13:34:06.

```
$ timeout -s 15 3 ./longcmd.sh ; date
Thu Mar 24 13:33:43 GMT 2011: Starting
Terminated
Thu Mar 24 13:33:46 GMT 2011: ouch!
Thu Mar 24 13:33:46 GMT 2011: Stage Two
Thu Mar 24 13:34:06 GMT 2011: Finished
Thu Mar 24 13:34:06 GMT 2011
```

 GNU coreutils did not have a `timeout` *tool until version 7. Until then, many distributions included a* `timeout` *tool from The Coroner's Toolkit (*`http://www.porcupine.org/forensics/tct.html`*). This has different syntax and more verbose output. There is no* `-s` *flag; instead of* `-s 15 3`*, use* `-15 3`*. The* `-k` *option does not exist at all. The GNU coreutils version of* `timeout` *is included since RHEL6, Debian 6, Ubuntu 11.04, and SuSE 11.*

If the script did not trap the SIGTERM, it would be terminated immediately on receiving the signal. `timeout` is particularly useful when dealing with particularly stubborn code that fails to exit quite so easily.

```
$ timeout -s 15 3 ./longcmd-notrap.sh ; date
Thu Mar 24 20:12:45 GMT 2011: Starting
Thu Mar 24 20:12:48 GMT 2011
$
```

Adding the `-k 12` switch tells `timeout` to send a SIGKILL to the process 12 seconds after the initial SIGTERM. Again, the `ouch!` message is displayed after 3 seconds as a result of the SIGTERM signal. Twelve seconds after that, the whole script is `kill`ed. It does not complete the second 20-second sleep, and it does not display the Finished message after it. This is a more forceful way of dealing with the timeout.

```
$ timeout -s 15 -k 12 3 ./longcmd.sh ; date
Thu Mar 24 13:34:09 GMT 2011: Starting
Terminated
Thu Mar 24 13:34:12 GMT 2011: ouch!
Thu Mar 24 13:34:12 GMT 2011: Stage Two
Killed
Thu Mar 24 13:34:24 GMT 2011
```

Similarly, the first signal can be a SIGKILL by specifying 9 (or KILL) to the -s flag. This has the effect of killing the process as soon as the specified timeout has expired.

```
$ timeout -s 9 3 ./longcmd.sh ; date
Thu Mar 24 13:34:35 GMT 2011: Starting
Killed
Thu Mar 24 13:34:38 GMT 2011
$
```

One practical use of timeout is calling hard-to-control applications, which are either poorly written, or depend upon uncontrollable external factors. An example of the former is writing shutdown scripts for applications that find themselves hung and unable to exit in a tidy manner. An example of the latter is when a download from an external network server hangs or fails to complete as expected. Given that you don't need to write any cumbersome structure to handle these cases, timeout is a perfect tool for managing them. The next two sections deal with each of these examples, and show how timeout can be used to provide a more manageable service.

Shutdown Script

A shutdown script can handle an awkward process by wrapping it with timeout. This provides a clear, known maximum time that the shutdown procedure can take. The sample shutdown program here, /usr/local/bin/stop.myapp, takes up to 50 seconds to finish (with a return code of 20), and if it catches a signal, it will sleep for up to 20 seconds before exiting with a return code of 20.

> *If it gets timed out (after 20 seconds), it will exit with a return code of 124, and if it gets* killed *(after 20 seconds plus 10 seconds), it will exit with a return code of 139. Because the* stop.myapp *program is designed to calmly stop the application, if it fails, the* myapp.sh *init script will forcibly kill the actual application, by killing the PID stored in* /var/run/myapp.pid. *The application cannot avoid this signal, but by this stage, the init script has done everything it possibly can to allow the system to shut itself down cleanly.*

The timeout *man page says that it will exit with a code of 124 if the command times out. However, if the command times out and has to be killed with SIGKILL (9), the* timeout *command itself dies, with an exit code of 137 (which is 128 plus the value of the signal sent to kill it). Therefore, it is more useful to check for 137 than for 124.*

Such problematic applications can be hard to nail down, so this script also logs the return code to /var/log/myapp.log every time it shuts down, so that the frequency of timeouts can be logged. Also, notice that the exit 10 can never happen. Once it gets to that part of the code, it has already been classed as having timed out, so timeout will return 124 or 139 depending on whether or not it has to kill the program.

Available for
download on
Wrox.com

```
$ cat /etc/init.d/myapp.sh
#!/bin/bash

function killapp
{
   # if we get here, the application refused to shut down.
   kill -9 `cat /var/run/myapp.pid`
}

case $1 in
   start)
        echo "Starting myap..."
        /usr/local/bin/myapp &
        echo $! > /var/run/myapp.pid
        ;;
   stop)
        echo "Stopping myapp..."
        timeout -s 15 -k 10 20 /usr/local/bin/stop.myapp
        res=$?
        echo "`date`: myapp returned with exit code $res" >> /var/log/myapp.log
        case "$res" in
          0)   echo "NOTE: myapp stopped by itself." ;;
          124) echo "NOTE: myapp timed out when stopping."
               killapp ;;
          137) echo "NOTE: myapp was killed when timing out."
               killapp ;;
           *)  echo "Note: myapp exited with return code $res" ;;
        esac
        rm -f /var/run/myapp.pid
        ;;
   *)
        echo "Usage: `basename $0` start | stop"
        exit 2
   esac
```

myapp.sh

```
$ cat /usr/local/bin/stop.myapp
#!/bin/bash
trap may_die 1 3 9 15

function may_die
{
  SLEEP=`expr $RANDOM % 20`
  echo "Sleeping for $SLEEP seconds (but you don't know that)"
  sleep $SLEEP && exit 10
}

TIME=`expr $RANDOM % 50`
echo "STOPPING MYAPP. (likely to take $TIME seconds, but you don't know that!)"
for i in `seq 1 $TIME`
do
  echo -en "."
  sleep 1
done

exit 20
$
```

stop.myapp

An 18-second shutdown is not affected by the `timeout`:

```
$ ./myapp.sh stop
Stopping myapp...
STOPPING MYAPP. (likely to take 18 seconds, but you don't know that!)
.................Note: myapp exited with return code 20
```

A 44-second shutdown is bound to be `timed` out. Because the further shutdown takes more than the permitted 10 seconds, the shutdown program is killed:

```
$ ./myapp.sh stop
Stopping myapp...
STOPPING MYAPP. (likely to take 44 seconds, but you don't know that!)
...................Terminated
Sleeping for 11 seconds (but you don't know that)
./myapp.sh: line 3:  6071 Killed                timeout -s 15 -k 10 20 /usr/local
/bin/stop.myapp
NOTE: myapp was killed when timing out.
```

A `timeout` followed by a shorter final `exit` still gets classed as a timeout, but it is saved from the `kill`.

```
$ ./myapp.sh stop
Stopping myapp...
STOPPING MYAPP. (likely to take 26 seconds, but you don't know that!)
...................Terminated
Sleeping for 2 seconds (but you don't know that)
NOTE: myapp timed out when stopping.
$
```

Network Timeout

The second example given in the previous section was of a system or process that is dependent upon something totally external to the system, such as a download from a remote server. If that server, or the network to it, is slow, the script itself cannot do anything about that, but it can use `timeout` to manage the situation. For example, if the expected time for a transfer is 10 seconds, `timeout` can be used to abort the transfer if it has not completed after a minute has passed.

```
$ cat downloader.sh
#!/bin/bash

for file in file1.zip file2.zip file3.zip
do
  timeout -s 9 60 wget http://unreliable.example.com/${file}
  if [ "$?" -ne "0" ]; then
    echo "An error occurred when downloading $file"
  fi
done
```

downloader.sh

```
$ ./downloader.sh
--2011-03-25 13:06:58--  http://unreliable.example.com/file1.zip
Resolving unreliable.example.com... 192.0.32.10
Connecting to unreliable.example.com|192.0.32.10|:80... connected.
HTTP request sent, awaiting response... 200 OK
Length: 84263304 (80M) [application/zip]
Saving to: `unreliable.example.com/file1.zip'

100%[=====================================>] 84,263,304  9.8M/s   in 8.0s

2011-03-25 13:07:06 (9.8 MB/s) - `unreliable.example.com/file1.zip' saved [84263304
/84263304]

--2011-03-25 13:07:06--  http://unreliable.example.com/file2.zip
Resolving unreliable.example.com... 192.0.32.10
Connecting to unreliable.example.com|192.0.32.10|:80... connected.
HTTP request sent, awaiting response... 200 OK
Length: 413396910 (394M) [application/zip]
Saving to: `unreliable.example.com/file2.zip'

59% [=======================>                ] 245,297,152 36.9M/s eta 6s    ./do
wnloader.sh: line 3:  3482 Killed                 timeout -s 9 60 wget http://unre
liable.example.com/${file}
An error occurred when downloading file2.zip
--2011-03-25 13:08:07--  http://unreliable.example.com/file3.zip
Resolving unreliable.example.com... 192.0.32.10
Connecting to unreliable.example.com|192.0.32.10|:80... connected.
HTTP request sent, awaiting response... 200 OK
Length: 701084434 (669M) [application/zip]
Saving to: `unreliable.example.com/file3.zip'

17% [=====>                                  ] 121,831,424 22.0M/s  eta 51s    ./do
```

```
wnloader.sh: line 3:  3484 Killed                timeout -s 9 60 wget http://unre
liable.example.com/${file}
An error occurred when downloading file3.zip
$
```

UNAME

uname is related to hostname but more flexible. On x86 architecture, it is less informative than on vendor-designed hardware; the SunFire E25k reports itself through uname -i as SUNW, Enterprise-25000, and the T5240 reports SUNW, T5240. By itself, uname reports the basic name of the running kernel, such as Linux or SunOS or FreeBSD. With other switches, it reports on the hostname (-n), kernel release (-r) and version (-v), CPU architecture (-m), operating system (-o), processor (-i), and hardware platform (-i). These are combined with the -a switch, which is normally equivalent to uname -snrvmpio.

uname is a useful way for a script to tailor itself to the platform it finds itself running on. This snippet determines the capability of the CPU and reports back accordingly. The dirname section earlier in this chapter also used uname to determine which OS it is running on, and makes a (rather broad) assumption about which package management system to use.

```
$ cat uname.sh
#!/bin/sh
case `uname -m` in
  amd64|x86_64)   bits=64 ;;
  i386|i586|i686) bits=32 ;;
  *) bits=unknown          ;;
esac
echo "You have a ${bits}-bit machine."
```

uname.sh

```
$ ./uname.sh
You have a 64-bit machine.
$
```

It is useful to know what to expect from uname, so Table 14-1 presents a few samples from different operating systems and architectures. The first three in the table are different flavors of Linux, the next two are Solaris SPARC, the next is Solaris on x86, and the final one is an OpenBSD server.

TABLE 14-1: uname Output on Different Operating Systems

OS	UNAME -S	UNAME -N	UNAME -R	UNAME -M
RedHat 6	Linux	hattie	2.6.32-71.el6.i686	i686
Debian 5	Linux	goldie	2.6.32-5-amd64	x86_64
Ubuntu 10.10	Linux	elvis	2.6.35-25-generic	x86_64
Solaris 10	SunOS	db9	Generic_142900-02	sun4u

OS	UNAME -S	UNAME -N	UNAME -R	UNAME -M
Solaris 10	SunOS	webapp	Generic_137137-09	sun4v
Solaris 10x86	SunOS	appserver	Generic_142901-02	i86pc
OpenBSD 4.8	OpenBSD	saga	4.8	i386

It is a little ironic that the uname command itself is so inconsistent between architectures and operating systems; Solaris, SCO, and others also have the -x option, which displays mostly the same information, but also the number of CPUs, bus architecture, and other information. BSD has no -i at all, and the GNU implementation does not get a sensible answer for uname -i on x86.

UUENCODE

uuencode, part of the sharutils package, encodes binary files so that they are suitable for transmission as e-mail attachments. Because e-mail is a text-based protocol, certain binary characters can disrupt the e-mail itself, so encoding down to a 7-bit safe text encoding ensures that the e-mail can get through. The recipient's e-mail client should detect the format and show the attachment as such, not as part of the text of the e-mail. uuencode is a little peculiar in that although it can read from either stdin or a file, when passed with just a filename as a parameter, it still assumes that it will be receiving the data from stdin. The last (or in this case, the only) filename it is passed is used as the name given to the file being attached. When processing stdin, this makes sense; the file has no name, but the recipient needs a name in order to be able to save or open it. Therefore, when processing a file, it is normally best to give the filename twice. The first is the name of the file, and the second is the name that the recipient will receive it as. The header is as shown in the following example. The first three words are "begin," then the octal permissions of the file (not terribly useful in e-mail attachments), and finally the filename as it will be presented to the recipient. Here, the local file sample.odt will be sent as recipient.odt.

```
$ uuencode sample.odt recipient.odt | head
begin 664 recipient.odt
M4$L#!!0``@``@``$&3<SY>QC(,,P)```"'``''''('''';6EM971Y<&55A<'!L:6-6-A
M=&EO;B;V]V;V0;B:7,:7,:,A;W!E;F108W5M96YT+G1E='102P,$%%``('''@`09-S
M/@@``''''''''''''''L''!C;VYT96YT+GAM;C*5778_B-A1][Z^(LM*^&0]#
M5UK2@56KJ_JFf:K:H=6^>FP'k/57;4/@w_?:(28p9"85$@+%]]P/GWM\'1Z^
M[)4L=M%*Q>8'B^[NR&$$[:RH]K:8;IC0ZT7Y]^Hw]+G\LOSA=2UH+QBAFx5Up%1HP/\
M%%N"M?=5:%^76:<H0+WREB>*^"K0ER._^."":8'^CJJ2K7?'A($>^)W#?;]&#!.!<
MK6>^^Y&5\Y@3N>S-'F
K'.$0nd]MUk,]9Y[r6j#;"n+`GbHHJ]%/K[hmr$8"n,
MFZ;:9-+.)<6l\g<_g.%ESP33c[-;)a&(4<\ec,h^gdrgnl(h',k:^b.v7i+?j
MA;01U)!`7G75[]:c%;%;#U!#-\2-UD8"G[=WQL:W=\;ZOHJ$S4!//N,G,*:0
```

The unmanageable binary of the LibreOffice document is now safely encoded as printable (if not human-readable!) 7-bit text. This can be appended to the body of an e-mail to be safely transmitted to the recipient. Here, I send the document to myself by displaying the document message ("Here is the document you wanted. Regards, Steve") and running uuencode in a subshell, the output of which all gets piped as a single text stream into the `mailx` command.

```
sender$ ( echo "Here is the document you wanted."; \
> echo "Regards, Steve."; \
> uuencode sample.odt mydocument.odt ) | \
> mailx -s "Document attached" steve@steve-parker.org
sender$
```

> *Configuring a machine to send e-mail is often as easy as setting* DSmailhost
> .example.com *(where* mailhost.example.com *is the name of your internal*
> *e-mail server).*

If the local machine is properly configured to send e-mail, this message is then e-mailed to the recipient named on the command line. Because of the nature of e-mail, the `mailx` command will return success so long as the syntax is correct; it is not capable of detecting any problems with delivery of the e-mail. You will need to check that yourself. The received e-mail is displayed in Figure 14-6.

FIGURE 14-6

XARGS

When a command is called with many arguments (which are often filenames), the kernel has to put that data somewhere for the command to reference it. Sometimes (often when using the `find` command to trawl through large filesystems), this list is longer than the kernel will allow. This results in messages such as "rm: Argument list too long." Many people are quite used to this and know the workaround is to use `xargs`, but not everybody understands quite how it works, which can have some significant implications.

```
$ rm `find . -name "*.core*" -print`
bash: /bin/rm: Argument list too long
$ find . -name "*.core*" -print0 | xargs -0 rm
$
```

To get around the problem, xargs will read its standard input (which has no such restrictions) and pass those on in manageable chunks to the command it has been told to pass them to. This simple listfiles script shows the effect of this on the command being run. Here, the -L 3 option tells xargs to break the input down into three files per call. This is not how everybody thinks that xargs works, so the result may be surprising.

```
$ cat listfiles
#!/bin/bash
echo "Listfiles (PID $$) was called with $# arguments:"
i=1
while [ -a "$1" ]
do
  echo "${i}: $1"
  ((i++))
  shift
done
```

listfiles

```
$ find . -print
.
./etc
./etc/hosts
./etc/config.txt
./bin
./bin/ls
./sh
./listfiles
$ find . -print | xargs -L 3 ./listfiles
Listfiles (PID 17088) was called with 3 arguments:
1: .
2: ./etc
3: ./etc/hosts
Listfiles (PID 17089) was called with 3 arguments:
1: ./etc/config.txt
2: ./bin
3: ./bin/ls
Listfiles (PID 17090) was called with 2 arguments:
1: ./sh
2: ./listfiles
$
```

The first three results from the find command were passed to listfiles as three arguments:

1. .

2. ./etc

3. ./etc/hosts.

Then the next three files were passed to another instance of listfiles, which is clearly a different instance because its PID is different. Finally, there are only two files left, so they are passed to the final call of listfiles.

This is all fine, until filenames start to contain strange characters, like the innocent space symbol. Adding My Photos and My Documents folders to the directory confuses xargs greatly. The first instance is called with three arguments:

1. .

2. ./My Photos

3. ./My Photos\DCIM0001.jpg

However, it interprets these as five different words:

1. .

2. ./My

3. Photos

4. ./My

5. Photos\DCIM0001.jpg

Of these, only the first is an actual file (well, a directory, as it happens). The other four fail the [-a "$1"] test, so no output is displayed for them at all. The confusion continues until it gets back to the paths with no spaces in them whatsoever.

```
$ find . -print
.
./My Photos
./My Photos/DCIM0001.jpg
./My Photos/DCIM0002.jpg
./My Documents
./My Documents/doc1.doc
./My Documents/cv.odt
./etc
./etc/hosts
./etc/config.txt
./bin
./bin/ls
./sh
./listfiles
$ find . -print | xargs -L 3 ./listfiles
Listfiles (PID 17096) was called with 5 arguments:
1: .
Listfiles (PID 17097) was called with 6 arguments:
Listfiles (PID 17098) was called with 4 arguments:
Listfiles (PID 17099) was called with 3 arguments:
1: ./etc/config.txt
2: ./bin
3: ./bin/ls
Listfiles (PID 17100) was called with 2 arguments:
1: ./sh
2: ./listfiles
$
```

To get around this confusion, xargs -0 expects files to have the ASCII zero character separating their names, and treats any other kind of whitespace as part of the file's name. The find -print0 and `locate -0` syntax of those respective commands also supports this method of listing filenames. This is far more robust and is well worth using by default.

```
$ find . -print0 | xargs -0 -L 3 ./listfiles
Listfiles (PID 17129) was called with 3 arguments:
1: .
2: ./My Photos
3: ./My Photos/DCIM0001.jpg
Listfiles (PID 17130) was called with 3 arguments:
1: ./My Photos/DCIM0002.jpg
2: ./My Documents
3: ./My Documents/doc1.doc
Listfiles (PID 17131) was called with 3 arguments:
1: ./My Documents/cv.odt
2: ./etc
3: ./etc/hosts
Listfiles (PID 17132) was called with 3 arguments:
1: ./etc/config.txt
2: ./bin
3: ./bin/ls
Listfiles (PID 17133) was called with 2 arguments:
1: ./sh
2: ./listfiles
$
```

This passes all of the arguments to the command, but some commands want the filenames to be passed to them in a different way. If you want to search for each file found in a log file, `grep -nw "^${filename}$" /tmp/interesting` would be the command to use; this will search for only an exact match of the full filename. However, this command is not quite what is required:

```
find . -print0 | xargs -0 grep -n /tmp/interestingfiles
```

Rather, the filename needs to go between the `-n` and `/tmp/interestingfiles`. The standard placeholder for the filename is `{}`, although this can be changed with the `-I` flag. This command line puts the filename in the appropriate part of the `grep` command's arguments. `xargs` is also intelligent enough to infer `-L1`, so that each instance of `grep` is called with exactly one filename to search for.

```
$ cat /tmp/interestingfiles
./bin/ls
./My Documents/cv.odt
./usr/bin/sleep
$ find . -print0 | xargs -0 -I{} grep -nw "^{}$" /tmp/interestingfiles
2:./My Documents/cv.odt
1:./bin/ls
$
```

YES

A lot of utilities, such as `fsck`, have a `-y` option to say "yes" to all questions that they may ask. The good ones are then written so that "yes" to any question means basically the same thing — whether it's to mark superblocks clean or to remove inodes, the `-y` flag to `fsck` indicates that it should do whatever is necessary to fix the filesystem. This can be very useful for scripts as it means that they do not have to interact with the user. Some tools do not have this option, and yes can be useful when using these interactively. What yes does is spew out a continuous supply of the letter *y*. These two commands are equivalent:

```
# fsck -y /dev/sdf1
# yes | fsck /dev/sdf1
```

 As an alternative, yes can take any other text as a parameter, and it will display that instead.

One use for yes that may not look too obvious at first glance is this one-line command:

```
$ yes no | cp -i * /tmp
```

This pipes the word "no" into the cp command, which, when called as cp -i, will always query before overwriting a file. The net result of this is that existing files will not be replaced, but other files will be copied into /tmp. Not often required, but it is at least entertaining for the way it looks as well as being occasionally useful, too.

SUMMARY

System administration requires the mastery of a complex and interrelated set of tools. I hope this chapter has presented some of the ways in which these tools can be used in shell scripts to automate common system administration tasks, to make complex tasks easier, quicker, and repeatable, and also to help make basic operations more flexible and useful.

The first parts of this book covered more theory, concepts, and details of how particular tools and features in the Unix and GNU/Linux ecosystem work. The rest of the book consists of recipes, with a focus on the tasks themselves and how and why they are done in a certain way. These recipes build upon the knowledge and information presented earlier to build up a set of solid, practical shell scripts that can be used as is or modified for particular uses. These recipes also provide useful examples of how the tools and features of the shell can be put together for a variety of purposes.

PART III
Recipes for Systems Administration

15

Shell Features

This chapter looks at three specific tasks: installing an init script onto any distribution of Linux or Unix, reporting on installed RPM packages, and a Kickstart postinstall script.

The first recipe points out some techniques for dealing with portability issues. Probably the most important thing to take from this recipe is that it is broken into four distinct steps as outlined in the Structure section. Although it might seem more efficient to copy the script to the relevant location as soon as the distribution has been determined, the code is made much more maintainable by realizing that these are separate tasks and doing only one step at a time.

The RPM Report recipe uses arrays from Chapter 9 and some of the more complicated variable structures from Chapter 7 to produce a fairly short and simple script to perform a common task. It also shows how some simple HTML formatting can be applied in a shell script in order to exploit the greater display capabilities of a graphical web browser for a more professional-looking presentation than you get with plain text output.

The Kickstart postinstall recipe sources libraries of functions and also uses here documents and redirection to make for a simple and maintainable Kickstart environment. It also demonstrates how different forms of conditional execution can be used to match the situation; sometimes testing the return code in `$?` makes for neater code, sometimes `[ command ] && command` is more readable. A lot of this is down to personal taste, but with time and experience the choice of syntax for a given expression becomes more intuitive.

RECIPE 15-1: INSTALLING INIT SCRIPTS

This recipe uses conditional execution — `if`, `test`, and `case` — to determine how to start up a process automatically at boot time. Most GNU/Linux systems today install init scripts into `/etc/init.d`, but not all, and the method of actually registering (if at all) and starting the process up differ between distributions. In Chapter 16, Recipe 16-1, "Init Scripts," describes the init script itself.

Technologies Used

➤   if, else, elif

➤   case

➤   [expression] && command

Concepts

An init script is a simple shell script that starts up a service when the system boots up and shuts it down cleanly when the system is going down. This recipe is for a generic software installation routine to automatically install an init script when the software is installed outside of a package management system. http://lwn.net/Distributions lists over 500 different distributions. Most fall into one of a few categories (Red Hat–based, Debian-based, and so on) but a few are quite unique.

Potential Pitfalls

There are a few pitfalls for the script itself; the worst scenario is to fail without recognizing it and reporting the failure to the user. This script does make guesses on distros it does not successfully detect, but in its defense, it does display a message saying what it is doing. Following the normal Unix tradition, it is a very quiet script, totally silent on success, and displaying messages only when there is something to warn the user about or if something goes seriously wrong.

Another more specific pitfall is to get the requirements for a distro wrong; this is not always as easy to avoid as it sounds because many distributions are available, and any of them may change the way that they do anything at all for whatever reason they like. The larger, more stable ones are less likely than others to change things arbitrarily, but Upstart and SMF are two notable changes in Ubuntu and Solaris, respectively, to the system startup facility, which has otherwise been stable for decades. The structure of this recipe is specifically designed to prevent these kinds of problems from creeping into the script over time.

Structure

The structure of a script like this can have a very strong impact on how well it works and is maintained over time. Because it is a pretty insignificant infrastructure script, it is not likely to get the same level of attention to detail or quality control as the actual piece of software that it is in charge of starting up. This is not even the init script; this is just a disposable script that is used once to install the init script. The obvious question is "Why bother about its quality at all then?" The reason is that it will get so badly mistreated over time that scripts like this become ugly and unmaintainable chunks of code, which soon become unmanageable and buggy. These are the kinds of script where adding support for a new distribution inadvertently breaks support for another, and fixing one part of the code breaks another. Getting the structure right from the start means that the script will be flexible and maintainable in the future, and new developers coming to change the code can see what they are supposed to do and where. The temptation might well be to detect Red Hat (for example) and immediately copy the init script into /etc/init.d, run chkconfig, and be done with it. This will indeed work for Red Hat, but it ignores the more complex subtleties that the script also has to deal with.

This script is broken down into four distinct steps:

1. Determine the distribution.
2. Install into the appropriate init directory.
3. Register the service.
4. Start the service.

Determine the Distribution

Most distributions provide a convenient way to determine that the system is provided by that particular distribution; often this is a file in /etc, the presence of which confirms the distribution. The contents of that file then normally provide more detailed information, so if, for example, you rely on a feature in SuSE 10.0 and newer, parsing /etc/SuSE-release will tell you programmatically whether or not that feature should work. This step determines only what distro is in use; other distro-specific work is not done at this stage, but in Step 2 instead. This allows the script to bundle similar distributions together for that task.

When determining the distribution, the if / elif / elif / else structure is ideal, as each distro may have its own work to do, whether that is checking for the presence of a particular file or doing some other similar processing task. The final else statement sets distro=unknown, which again is useful for later processing.

Install into Init Directory

Having determined the distribution, the second section installs into the appropriate directory based on the distribution. For many modern GNU/Linux distros, a simple init_dir=/etc/init.d is sufficient here, but others have their own quirks.

This stage uses the case construct to iterate through the different possible distributions. It also has a catchall * clause, which on an unknown distribution will loop through various commonly found directories, and if it finds that one of those directories exists, it will assume that that is the right place to install the init script. This allows it to show a little common sense, which might prove useful. It is important to let the user know that some guesswork has happened here because, if that guesswork turns out to be wrong, the user has some indication of where the problem might lie.

Register the Service

Before it can be started, the service must be registered with the system. Traditionally, this meant installing symbolic links from /etc/init.d into rcN.d, where N is the runlevel being changed to. Some of these links would be called SXXservice, where S means Start, and XX is a number indicating the order in which the services should be started, lowest number to highest. These scripts will be called with a single start parameter. Other links would be KXXservice, where K means Kill, and these will be called with a single stop parameter to allow the service to shut down cleanly when rebooting the machine or changing runlevels. Some more recent GNU/Linux distros use chkconfig instead, which parses comments in the init script itself to determine which runlevels and bootorder are needed.

Start the Service

The final action is to actually start the service. For many modern Linux distros, this is now `chkconfig $service on`; for others, it still involves calling the init script directly. The `autostart` variable is set to `yes` if the first parameter passed to the script was `-a`. This variable was defined at the start of the script, with a simplistic alternative to `getopt`. This is achieved by checking if `$1` is `-a`, and if it is, then `service=$2` instead of `service=$1`, and `autostart` get set as appropriate. Using `$2` for autostart would be easier for the script, but the syntax would be less natural and consistent with other Unix/Linux scripts.

The whole multi-line `case` statement is executed only if the `[ autostart == yes ]` test succeeds. This test uses the `cmd1 && cmd2` structure of the shell, using this common variant where `cmd1` is actually `test` (which is linked to `[`, as discussed in Chapter 5), and `cmd2` is the command to run if the test succeeds. If `autostart` is set to `yes`, then the `case` statement that follows it will be executed. Otherwise, script execution continues after the `esac`, which ends the `case` statement.

Recipe

```bash
#!/bin/bash

# service is the name of the init script
# as well as the name of the application.
if [ "$1" == "-a" ]; then
  autostart=yes
  service=$2
else
  autostart=no
  service=$1
fi
distro=unknown
init_dir=unknown
rc_dir=/etc/rc.d

# Step 1: Determine the Distribution
if [ -f /etc/redhat-release ]; then
  # Also true for variants of Fedora or RHEL
  distro=redhat
elif [ -f /etc/debian_version ]; then
  # Also true for Ubuntu etc
  distro=debian
elif [ -f /etc/SuSE-brand ] || [ -f /etc/SuSE-release ]; then
  distro=suse
elif [ -f /etc/slackware-version ]; then
  distro=slackware
else
  distro=unknown
fi

# Step 2: Install into the appropriate init directory
case $distro in
  redhat|debian|suse)
    # /etc/rc.d/ is a link to /etc/init.d
```

```
      # SuSE and RedHat don't need rc_dir.
      init_dir=/etc/init.d
      rc_dir=/etc
      ;;
  slackware)
      init_dir=/etc/rc.d
      rc_dir=/etc/rc.d
      ;;
  *)
      echo -n "Unknown distribution; guessing init directory... "
      for init_dir in /etc/rc.d/init.d /etc/init.d unknown
      do
        [ -d ${init_dir} ] && break
      done
      if [ "$init_dir" == "unknown" ]; then
        echo "Failed"
      else
        echo "Found ${init_dir}."
        rc_dir=$init_dir
      fi
esac

if [ $init_dir != unknown ]; then
  cp $service ${init_dir}
else
  echo "Error: Can not determine init.d directory."
  echo "Initialization script has not been copied."
  exit 1
fi

# Step 3: Register the service
case $distro in
  suse|redhat)
    chkconfig --add $service
    ;;
  *)
    ln -sf ${init_dir}/$service ${rc_dir}/rc2.d/S90$service
    ln -sf ${init_dir}/$service ${rc_dir}/rc3.d/S90$service
    ln -sf ${init_dir}/$service ${rc_dir}/rc0.d/K10$service
    ln -sf ${init_dir}/$service ${rc_dir}/rc6.d/K10$service
    ;;
esac

# Step 4: Start the Service
[ $autostart == yes ] && case $distro in
  suse|redhat)
    chkconfig $service on
    ;;
  unknown)
    echo "Unknown distribution; attempting to start up..."
    ${init_dir}/$service start
    ;;
  *)
    # Debian, Slackware
```

```
        ${init_dir}/$service start
        ;;
esac
$
```

Invocation

This script would normally be invoked by another script, such as an installation routine, but the (almost totally silent) invocation is shown here for completeness. The "`starting the application!`" message is displayed by the `myapp` init script itself, not by `install-init.sh`.

```
# ./install-init.sh -a myapp
/etc/init.d/myapp called with start; starting the application!
# ls -l /etc/init.d/myapp
-rwxr-xr-x 1 root root 429 Apr 11 12:56 /etc/init.d/myapp
# ls -l /etc/rc3.d/S90myapp
-rwxr-xr-x 1 root root 429 Apr 11 12:56 /etc/rc3.d/S90myapp
#
```

Summary

Different distributions have taken slightly different approaches over time to address the problem of starting and stopping system services. These are all basically the same, but they have the kind of small, subtle differences that can be harder to work around than the big, more obvious differences which tend to attract more attention. Abstracting all of this complexity into a single shell script means that the rest of the system (the installation routine of the application, in this case) does not need to worry about all these different implementations or how the shell script takes care of them all. Also, any change to the implementation details in this script can be easily tested in isolation from the main installer.

This recipe uses different flow control structures in the shell to achieve the individual parts of the script. Often when you see `if` being used a lot, particularly when it uses multiple `elif` statements, it should be replaced by `case`. In this instance, `if` is the ideal tool for identifying the distro, and `case` is the best tool for taking specific action, depending on which distro was identified.

RECIPE 15-2: RPM REPORT

This recipe does a useful task in that it compares RPMs installed on different machines and produces a reasonably easy-to-read report on the findings. This is often made more difficult by the way that RPM filenames work: a dash is a valid (and fairly common) part of the package name, as well as being used to separate the name, version, and release from one another.

This report takes the output from the `rpm -qa` command as input, which can be run on multiple different machines, or on the same machine at different times, to see how the package list compares either between machines or over time, respectively. Packages that are the same across all input files are shown as black text on a white background. Packages that have a variety of different versions installed are shown on a gray background for easy identification.

Technologies Used

➤ Parameter expansion, in particular `%` and `##`

➤ Associative arrays (these only work in bash version 4 or later)

➤ Functions

➤ Here documents

➤ HTML

Concepts

RPM filenames contain a lot of information but are not particularly easy to parse. For example, `gnome-panel-2.16.1-7.el5` is version `2.16.1` of the software, but release number `7.el5` of that version. Because parts of the filename are split with hyphens, and hyphens are quite common in package names, it becomes difficult to work out what part of the filename is what. The only way to do it is to work from the back; the version and release fields cannot contain hyphens. This means that the code that takes the version-and-release string has to strip out the name and version (`gnome-panel-2.16.1`) by taking out everything after the last hyphen, and then take out everything before the last hyphen in that string to get 2.16.1. It can easily get the release by stripping everything before the last hyphen. Concatenating the release and version back together again gets the version and release together in a single variable.

Displaying simple data in HTML is very easy and no particularly deep knowledge of HTML or CSS is required. This recipe produces HTML 4.01–compliant HTML code, basically just using the `<table>` element and some simple CSS. Each row starts with `<tr>` (table row) and ends with `</tr>`. Each heading cell within the row begins with `<th>` (table heading) and ends with `</th>`. Each data cell begins with `<td>` (table data) and ends with `</td>`.

Potential Pitfalls

The main pitfall with this task is dealing with the hyphens in package names. When faced with names such as `dbus-x11-1.1.2-12.el5`, `xorg-x11-fonts-75dpi-7.1-2.1.el5`, and `xorg-x11-drv-vesa-1.3.0-8.1.el5`, it seems impossible to get coherent data out of these names without the `%`, `%%`, `#`, and `##` syntaxes. Careful consideration of the input format and how to process it is key here. Making sure that this is read in and interpreted correctly in `readrpms` means that the data is coherent and therefore the code is simple in the rest of the script.

Structure

The two main functions are `readrpms` and `showrpms`. Around calls to these, `starthtml` and `endhtml` put out the basic structure required to start and end an HTML document. The other function in the recipe is `rpmnames`, which simply provides a sorted list of all of the rpm names, with version and release information stripped off the end. This is called by `showrpms` to get an ordered list from which to create the HTML report.

starthtml and endhtml

These two functions display the HTML code to start and end the HTML output. `starthtml` defines a CSS style sheet and starts the table definition. It uses a here document to do this. Because `<<-EOF` tells the here document to strip the leading tab, the script can have nice formatting and indent the contents of the function, but the generated HTML is left-aligned, which looks better if editing the actual HTML code itself.

At the end of `starthtml`, and also in `endhtml`, a simple `for` loop displays a title row at the top and bottom of the table, with the name of each file that has been used as input. This could be the hostname, it could be a timestamp of when the data was gathered, or it could even be both, or some higher-level information such as "web server" and "database server."

The rest of these functions is just the HTML syntax required at the start and end of an HTML document. The style information defines three classes of table row: `heading`, `same`, and `notsame`. This defines the font size and background color to be used for each of these types of rows. This is then used by displaying `<tr class="notsame">` in the script. Different colors can be assigned to table cells, too; uninstalled packages could be highlighted in one color, older packages in another color, or whatever suits the need.

readrpms

`readrpms` is the function that reads in the `rpm -qa` files and assigns the version numbers to an array. Because multi-dimensional arrays do not exist, it is not possible to have an array such as `rpm[node1][kernel-debug]= 2.6.18-194.el5`. Therefore, the structure is that an array called `version` stores paired data, with `nodename_rpmname` as the index, and the version number as the data. This becomes `version[node1_kernel-debug]=2.6.18-194.el5`, which is close enough for the purposes of this script to the multi-dimensional array which might be more intuitive to use.

There is a twist; it is possible to have multiple versions of the same RPM installed, so `readrpms` tests with `-z` to see whether or not the array element of `node_rpmname` is empty to start with and appends the RPM to the list if there is already an RPM of that name listed for that machine.

As discussed in the "Concepts" section, to get the version and release, an intermediate variable is required so that the relevant data can be stripped from the end of the package name.

showrpms

`showrpms` is the function that displays the HTML code. It takes a sorted list from `rpmnames`, and takes a template from the first node's entry for the RPM. It loops through each node's entry for the RPM, and if they all match the template, then every machine has the same version of this package installed. If not, it is flagged, and that row can be marked with the appropriate CSS tag. The `break` in that loop is probably premature optimization but if comparing a great many systems, it could be a slight performance improvement not to continue checking when a discrepancy has been found. To keep the output brief, and also searchable, stdout displays the message "RPM MATCH" if they are all the same, and displays each node only if they are different.

A `for` loop then iterates through the values again, and basically echoes `<td>${version[$idx]}</td>` to the HTML file. This is complicated by two factors. The first is that if a package is not installed, it is better to say that clearly than to just leave the table cell blank. The second is that if multiple copies of an RPM are installed, it is tidier to put them on a line of their own, so a `<br />` tag is inserted where a space was added by the `readrpms` function. `readrpms` could have inserted that `<br />` tag itself, but it is best to keep data structures and output formats separate. That way, the same code can be used even if the final output is to be plain text, or RTF, or CSV, or some other suitable format.

Because the script displays to stdout as well as to the HTML file, the first output line goes to stdout, but only if the RPMs are not all identical. The next line writes the HTML. `${version[$idx]:-NotInstalled}` displays either the version number or "`NotInstalled`" if the array element is blank. Any spaces in the version number (indicating multiple versions) are then replaced by sed with `<br />` tags. Finally, the "`NotInstalled`" marker is converted back into "`Not Installed`".

Recipe

Available for
download on
Wrox.com

```bash
#!/bin/bash

declare -A version
HTML=report.html

function rpmnames
{
  for rpm in `cat $* | sort -u`
  do
    echo ${rpm%-*-*}
  done | sort -u
}

function readrpms
{
  for node in $*
  do
    while read rpm
    do
                                        # rpm is gnome-panel-2.16.1-7.el5
      rpmname=${rpm%-*-*}                # gnome-panel
      rpmnameversion=${rpm%-*}           # gnome-panel-2.16.1
      rpmversion=${rpmnameversion##*-}   # 2.16.1
      rpmrelease=${rpm##*-}              # 7.el5
      idx=${node}_${rpmname}
      if [ -z "${version[$idx]}" ]; then
        version[$idx]="${rpmversion}-${rpmrelease}"
      else
        version[$idx]="${version[$idx]} ${rpmversion}-${rpmrelease}"
      fi
    done < $node
  done
}

function showrpms
{
  for rpmname in `rpmnames $*`
  do
    idx=$1_${rpmname}
    template="${version[$idx]}"
    allsame=1
```

```
    for node in $*
    do
      idx=${node}_${rpmname}
      if [ "${version[$idx]}" != "${template}" ]; then
        allsame=0
        break
      fi
    done

    if [ $allsame -eq 1 ]; then
      echo "RPM MATCH: $rpmname $template"
      echo "<tr class=\"same\">" >> $HTML
    else
      echo "RPM $rpmname"
      echo "<tr class=\"notsame\">" >> $HTML
    fi
    echo "<th>${rpmname}</th>" >> $HTML
    for node in $*
    do
      idx=${node}_${rpmname}
      [ $allsame -eq 0 ] && echo "$node : ${version[$idx]:-Not Installed}"
      echo "<td>${version[$idx]:-NotInstalled}</td>" | \
          sed s/" "/"<br \/>"/g | \
          sed s/"NotInstalled"/"Not Installed"/g >> $HTML
    done
    echo "</tr>" >> $HTML
  done
}

function starthtml
{
  cat - <<-EOF > $HTML
      <!DOCTYPE HTML PUBLIC "-//W3C//DTD HTML 4.01 Transitional//EN"
              "http://www.w3.org/TR/html4/loose.dtd">

      <html>
      <head>
      <meta http-equiv="Content-Type" content="text/html;charset=utf-8" >
      <title>Report on $*</title>
      <style type="text/css">
        tr.heading { background-color: #f2f2f2; font-size: 1.2em; }
        tr.same    { background-color: white; }
        tr.notsame { background-color: #c2c2c2; }
        td { font-family: sans-serif; font-size: 0.8em; }
        th { font-family: serif; font-size: 0.8em; }
      </style>
      </head>
      <body>
      <table border="1">
      <tr class="heading"><th>RPM</th>
EOF

  for node in $*
  do
```

```
    echo "<th>$node</th>" >> $HTML
  done
  echo "</tr>" >> $HTML
}

function endhtml
{
  echo "<tr class=\"heading\"><th>RPM</th>" >> $HTML
  for node in $*
  do
    echo "<th>$node</th>" >> $HTML
  done
  echo "</tr></table>" >> $HTML
  echo "</body></html>"  >> $HTML
}

starthtml $*
readrpms $*
showrpms $*
endhtml $*
```

rpm-report.sh

Invocation

```
$ ./rpm-report.sh node1 node2 node3 node4 node5
RPM MATCH: a2ps  4.13b-57.2.el5
RPM acl
node1 :  2.2.39-3.el5
node2 :  2.2.39-6.el5
node3 :  2.2.39-3.el5
node4 :  2.2.39-3.el5
node5 :  2.2.39-3.el5
RPM acpid
node1 :  1.0.4-9.el5_4.2
node2 :  1.0.4-9.el5_4.2
node3 :  1.0.4-7.el5
node4 :  1.0.4-9.el5_4.2
node5 :  1.0.4-9.el5_4.2
RPM aide
node1 : Not Installed
node2 :  0.13.1-6.el5
node3 : Not Installed
node4 : Not Installed
node5 : Not Installed
RPM alchemist
node1 :  1.0.36-2.el5
node2 : Not Installed
node3 :  1.0.36-2.el5
node4 :  1.0.36-2.el5
node5 :  1.0.36-2.el5
RPM MATCH: alsa-lib  1.0.17-1.el5 1.0.17-1.el5
```

```
RPM MATCH: alsa-utils  1.0.17-1.el5

 . . . . .
RPM zenity
node1 :  2.16.0-2.el5
node2 : Not Installed
node3 :  2.16.0-2.el5
node4 :  2.16.0-2.el5
node5 :  2.16.0-2.el5
RPM MATCH: zip  2.31-2.el5
RPM MATCH: zlib  1.2.3-3 1.2.3-3
$ web-browser ./report.html
```

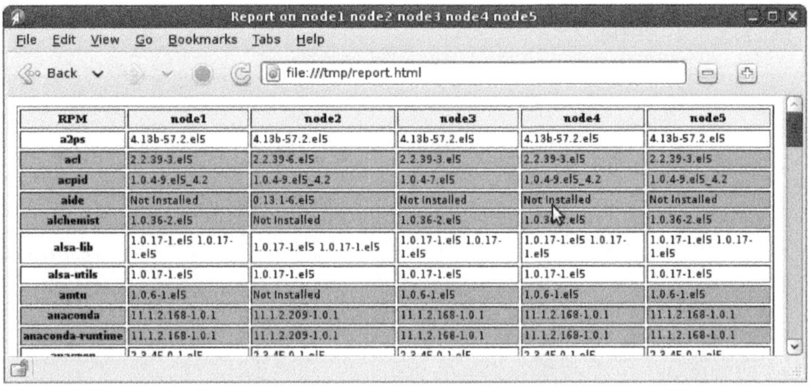

FIGURE 15-1

Summary

This report is quite useful in its own right, and the recipe to produce it is quite short and efficient because of the use of variable structures, particularly arrays and parameter expansion. Combining this with some very simple HTML produces a report that looks professional and can be pasted into documentation, put onto the intranet, or possibly even printed (although the test data used here comes to 42 printed landscape pages).

The structure of the code means that there is no limit to the number of hosts that can be compared, nor to the number of RPMs that can be compared. This is different from a lot of scripts that perform tasks like these, which often have hard-coded values of $node1, $node2, and $node3 and are therefore unable to process more. The output HTML may become harder to see all at once, but the output from the script, which displays lines starting with RPM, can be easily searched by other scripts for relevant information.

A few very simple techniques put together in the right way produce a script that is almost as straightforward as might first be assumed when taking on this task. It is not as simple as it could be if the data was supplied in a slightly different format, but it is quite simple, and broken down into separate read, display, and format sections for clarity and ease of further expansion.

RECIPE 15-3: POSTINSTALL SCRIPTS

Automated installation using Kickstart is a useful way to programmatically install many similar machines. One thing that is different for every machine is the IP addresses used; Kickstart can configure an IP address during the installation, but cannot configure additional networks or network bonding. This recipe can be fitted into the %post section of a Kickstart file to configure the network to start up with the new values on the next boot.

Technologies Used

➤ Kickstart

➤ Configuration of networking under Red Hat Enterprise Linux

➤ Network bonding

➤ Functions

➤ Here documents

➤ `ping`

Concepts

Networking is a critical part of computer configuration. If the system is not visible on the network, it does not matter how good everything else on the system is — it is not making its services available. Network bonding is a way to prevent certain common failures from taking the system entirely offline. Using two network adapters for the traffic means that if one fails anywhere along the route, the other can be used instead. It is best to use two different types of network adapter, so that they have different implementations and different kernel drivers. Of course, two different cables are required, and these should go to two separate network switches so that a failure in any of these devices can be tolerated by the system.

Linux has seven different bonding modes, each with its own properties. The mode is specified when the bonding module is loaded into the kernel.

➤ mode 0, or `balance-rr`: Round-robin, for load balancing and fault tolerance.

➤ mode 1, or `active-backup`: A failover mode for fault tolerance. It is this mode that is configured by this recipe. Two network adapters, of which one is active at any time, and a third (virtual) device, called `bond0`, are configured with the IP address.

➤ mode 2, or `balance-xor`: Uses XOR of the source and destination MAC address to determine which network adapter to use for each outbound packet.

➤ mode 3, or `broadcast`: Transmits on all interfaces at once, for fault tolerance.

➤ mode 4, or `802.3ad`: Link aggregation for fault tolerance and load balancing.

➤ mode 5, or `balance-tlb`: Transmits packets on the least-busy network adapter, for load balancing.

➤ mode 6, or `balance-alb`: Does load balancing of inbound packets, too, by tricking the remote ARP cache into sending to one adapter or the other.

There are a number of guides on the Internet, although the kernel documentation at `http://www.kernel.org/doc/Documentation/networking/bonding.txt` and in `/usr/share/doc/kernel-doc-*/Documentation/networking/bonding.txt` provides a lot of useful information very concisely. The options set by this recipe are `miimon=100`, which tells the bond to check the link once every 100 milliseconds (10 times a second), and `fail_over_mac=1`, which means that each network adapter keeps its own MAC address, and that remote ARP caches are updated after a failover. These options and many more are documented in the `bonding.txt` file which can be found at the locations mentioned above.

The state of a bond can be inspected while the system is running via `cat /proc/net/bonding/bond0`. This provides fairly detailed information about the status of the bond itself and its underlying slave devices.

Potential Pitfalls

One of the worst outcomes from automated network configuration is that the machine ends up being inaccessible via the network. Worse than that is if the machine is inaccessible because it is using an IP address that was already in use by something else. Bringing a new machine onto the network requires a few sanity checks, so this library performs a few basic checks before configuring the device.

Network device naming is not always totally predictable; there are various ways to configure the `udev` subsystem to force a particular port to always be called eth0, or eth1, or whatever is required.

Structure

The kickstart file defines a `%post` section, which is executed by bash. This can be used to tweak the system configuration in any way required. If you provide a simple library on the installation server, no complicated scripting needs to go into the `%post` section of each server's kickstart file.

The library provides three functions. The first in the file, `addroute`, adds a static network route to a device. This is done on Red Hat by the `route-NIC` file in `/etc/sysconfig/network-scripts`. There can be one such file per network adapter, and the route is added for that particular adapter. Although at the installation stage, you can safely assume that this file does not exist, appending to the file with >> is safer than simply writing to it with >, as no existing routes will be lost this way.

The second function in the file, `makeslave`, is just there to make the third function a little bit simpler. It uses a here document to create the configuration file for a network adapter to be configured as a slave to the virtual bond device. It takes two parameters, the network adapter to create and the bond that it will be a slave of. This time, it is best to use the single > to ensure that any existing configuration of that adapter is destroyed.

Because it is only called from within the library, it should be safe for `makeslave` *to assume that it is already running from the* `/etc/sysconfig/network-scripts` *directory. Scripts that provide an interface to other scripts or libraries should not make such assumptions.*

The third function is the main part of the library. This `addbond` function configures a virtual bond device with a floating IP address, which will be used by whichever NIC is most suitable at the time, and float from adapter to adapter in response to detected failures.

The start of the function reads in the variables it has been passed, and as a basic sanity test checks that all of the arguments expected have been provided. If $5 is not of zero length, then the others before it can be expected to have values also. This is not a user-facing script and it is not unreasonable to expect that the parameters provided are good. The script then performs another basic test; because networking has already been configured on the system (but with only one network adapter), it should be possible to confirm that no other host on the network is already configured with the IP address that is about to be assigned on the machine being installed. There is one exception to this — frequently, the IP address for the bond has already been used as the IP address to do the installation. The script therefore checks whether the `ip` command lists `inet` $IP in its output. If that IP address is not already being used by the machine being installed, then a quick `ping` should confirm that it is not already in use anywhere else on the network. This simple test ensures that the machine does not come back online with the IP address of another machine already on the network.

Because an installation environment is totally hands-off and can contain all sorts of unexpected configurations, even more sanity testing is done to ensure that the bond itself has not already been configured. If it has an `ifcfg-$BOND` file in `/etc/sysconfig/network-scripts`, or an entry in `/etc/modprobe.conf`, then the script also bails out because manual intervention is required.

To create the bond, two slave devices are required. The `makeslave` function mentioned previously deals with this and avoids repetition in the `addbond` function. A very similar here document is then used to create the entry for the bond device. This adds the IP address and netmask to the configuration. An entry is also added to `/etc/modprobe.conf`. This is needed to load the bonding module into the kernel at boot time, and to set the required options for the module.

Finally, the existing slave interfaces are brought down, the bonding module is loaded, and the newly configured bond device is brought online. This final stage is not strictly necessary, as the system was already capable of communicating with the kickstart server, and the new device will be brought online on the first reboot, which happens immediately after the `%post` section of the kickstart file has completed.

The `client-ks.cfg` file shows just the `%post` section of the kickstart file, here setting bond0 to use eth0 and eth4 (on a system with four onboard network ports, these should be the first port onboard and the first port of a PCI network card installed in the system), then bond1 using eth1 and eth5, which should be the two ports adjacent to the first two.

Recipe

Available for download on Wrox.com

```
# Library of networking functions
# Assumes RedHat Enterprise Linux style
[ -f /etc/redhat-release ] || return

function addroute
{
  # Add a route to a device
  # $1 = network adapter (eg eth0, bond0)
```

```
  # $2 = destination
  # $3 = router
  cd /etc/sysconfig/network-scripts
  echo "Adding $2 via $3 on $1"

  echo "$2 via $3" >> route-$1
}

function makeslave
{
  # $1 = network adapter
  # $2 = bond
  cat - > ifcfg-$1 <<EOF
DEVICE=$1
BOOTPROTO=none
ONBOOT=yes
MASTER=$2
SLAVE=yes
USERCTL=no
EOF
}

function addbond
{
  # $1 = bond, $2=network adapter 1, $3 = network adapter 2
  # $4 = IP address or name, $5 = netmask
  BOND=$1
  DEV1=$2
  DEV2=$3
  IP=`getent hosts $4 | awk '{ print $1 }'`
  NAME=`getent hosts $4 | awk '{ print $1 }'`
  NETMASK=$5

  if [ -z "$NAME" ] || [ -z "$5" ]; then
    echo "Usage: addbond bond dev1 dev2 ip netmask"
    return 1
  fi

  /bin/ip a | grep "^    inet ${IP}/" > /dev/null
  if [ "$?" -ne "0" ]; then
    if ping -c1 -w1 $IP > /dev/null 2>&1
    then
      echo "Error: $NAME ($IP) is responding to ping. Not configuring $IP"
      return
    fi
  fi

  cd /etc/sysconfig/network-scripts
  if [ -f ifcfg-$BOND ]; then
    echo "Error: $BOND is already configured"
  fi
  [ -f ifcfg-$DEV1 ] && mv ifcfg-$DEV1 bak.ifcfg-$DEV1
```

```
    [ -f ifcfg-$DEV2 ] && mv ifcfg-$DEV2 bak.ifcfg-$DEV2

    if grep $BOND /etc/modprobe.conf > /dev/null
    then
      echo "Error: $BOND is already defined in /etc/modprobe.conf"
      return
    fi

    echo "Creating bond device $BOND from $DEV1 and $DEV2"
    echo "with the IP address ${IP}/${NETMASK}"

    makeslave $DEV1 $BOND
    makeslave $DEV2 $BOND

    cat - > ifcfg-$BOND <<EOF
DEVICE=$BOND
BOOTPROTO=none
IPADDR=$IP
NETMASK=$NETMASK
ONBOOT=yes
EOF

    cat - >> /etc/modprobe.conf << EOF
alias $BOND bonding
options $BOND mode=1 miimon=100 fail_over_mac=1
EOF

    ifdown $DEV1
    ifdown $DEV2
    modprobe $BOND
    ifup $BOND
}
```

netlib

```
%post
. /mnt/source/netlib

makebond bond0 eth0 eth4 192.168.1.53 255.255.255.0
addroute bond0 192.168.9.0 192.168.1.1

makebond bond1 eth1 eth4 192.168.2.53 255.255.255.0
```

client-ks.cfg

Invocation

```
Creating bond device bond0 from eth0 and eth4
with the IP address 192.168.1.53/255.255.255.0
Adding 192.168.9.0 via 192.168.1.1 on bond0
Creating bond device bond1 from eth1 and eth4
with the IP address 192.168.2.53/255.255.255.0
```

Summary

The environment during installation is fairly minimal, but a lot of customization can be done during the postinstall stage of an installation. Network bonding can usefully be configured at this stage, and a library of code is a very useful way to do this because it enables you to keep the Kickstart file itself clean and simple. In addition, any fixes to the script have to be applied only to the copy on the Kickstart server, and not in hundreds (or even thousands) of client-specific Kickstart files.

16

Systems Administration

This chapter provides four recipes for common system administration tasks. The first is an example of an init script to start an application automatically when the system boots up. This shows the use of case, and uses the /var/run filesystem to store a PID file.

The second recipe provides two related CGI scripts, processing GET and POST requests. This will show how to handle these two methods of passing data from the browser to the server. The security implications of handling user-submitted data are also addressed.

The third recipe shows how configuration files can be used to provide default values and show them to the end user as well as remembering previous values selected by the user.

Finally, the fourth recipe implements a locking mechanism to ensure that multiple concurrent processes can share a critical resource without interfering with each other's use of it.

RECIPE 16-1: INIT SCRIPTS

System startup scripts are often called init scripts because they are normally started up by the init daemon from the /etc/init.d directory. This recipe provides a basic structure for such an init script. The process is started in the background and runs forever as a daemon, and the same process is killed to stop the daemon. This is not applicable to all applications; for example, it may be that $INSTDIR/$APP starts up another three processes and exits immediately. The Apache web server's apachectl command is a typical example of this. In that case, more detailed understanding of the application is required. How can those subprocesses be monitored, and stopped when required? For daemon type systems, however, this recipe should be a useful starting point.

 Background processes are often called demons or daemons.

Technologies Used

➤ `init`

➤ `chkconfig`

➤ `case`

Concepts

Recently some operating systems, notably Ubuntu and Solaris, began doing away with traditional init scripts in favor of more easily parallelized systems, using Upstart and SMF, respectively. Another flavor of Unix, BSD, has also always used a slightly different variant on the init scripts, and Slackware, too, uses a more BSD-like style, although Slackware also now supports the SysV initscripts style favored by most current Linux distributions.

The init script is responsible for starting and stopping, and more recently also monitoring and maintaining, the state of a particular application. The two standard options to the script are `start` and `stop`. When `chkconfig` is called to check the status of all installed init scripts, it calls each one with a `status` option. Very simplistic third-party startup scripts that start up their service by default unless called with the `stop` option would start a new copy of themselves every time the system state is tested.

The Linux Standard Base (LSB) also requires `restart`, `force-reload`, and `status` to be implemented. Others that LSB suggests are `try-restart` (which will restart the service only if it is already running) and `reload` (which will re-read the configuration without actually stopping and starting the service). You can read the full specifications online; the current 4.1.0 specification is at `http://refspecs.freestandards.org/LSB_4.1.0/LSB-Core-generic/LSB-Core-generic/tocsysinit.html`. This is not the place to go into what all of the fields mean, but the `lsb-ourdb` template shown in the section "Potential Pitfalls" later in this chapter should be suitable for the majority of applications. Simply edit the `Provides:` line to match the name of the service, and change the two `Description` lines to display something suitable.

Installing and registering the service is described in the "Register the Service" section of Recipe 15-1, "Installing Init Scripts."

Startup

When called with `start`, the script checks for an already-running instance and bails out if a PID file is found. Otherwise, it starts the application in the background, makes a note of the PID (in `$!`) and stores it in `$PIDFILE`.

Shutdown

When called with `stop`, the script checks the status of the application. If it is not running, `status` will exit with a non-zero return code, so `$0 status || exit 1` means that this instance will bail out if `status` fails to find a running copy. Because the script has confirmed via the `status` call that the application is running, it can get the PID from `$PIDFILE` and `kill` that PID. If the `kill` succeeds, then the script removes `$PIDFILE`; otherwise it `exits` with a return code of 1.

Status

To check the status, the script first checks the `$PIDFILE`. It then uses `ps -o comm= -p $PID` to get the name of the process running under that PID. If it is not the same as `$APP`, then it returns a non-zero exit code to indicate failure. Otherwise, it calls `ps -p $PID` and returns with whatever exit code `ps` returns (which will be zero on success, and non-zero otherwise).

> `ps -o comm` *displays a header as well as the actual process names.* `ps -o comm=` *does not display the header.*

Restart and Force-Reload

To restart, the script simply calls itself with the `stop` argument, and if that succeeds, then it calls itself again with the `start` argument. The `force-reload` implementation is also required by LSB, but in this case, it simply does the same as `restart`, so it calls `$0 restart`. A more specific implementation could be put under that placeholder at a later date if required.

Default

Because new parameters could be added or expected at any time, the catchall `*` option displays a message to standard output and exits with a return code of 2, which is a commonly used code for usage errors. Note that this block of code will also be executed if no parameters are passed at all.

Potential Pitfalls

Different implementations use different ways of registering services. The LSB defines specially formatted comments, which can be used by `chkconfig` to register services. The LSB standard suggests this format:

```
### BEGIN INIT INFO
# Provides: lsb-ourdb
# Required-Start: $local_fs $network $remote_fs
# Required-Stop: $local_fs $network $remote_fs
# Default-Start:  2 3 4 5
# Default-Stop: 0 1 6
# Short-Description: start and stop OurDB
# Description: OurDB is a very fast and reliable database
#         engine used for illustrating init scripts
### END INIT INFO
```

In real life, init scripts may contain some or all of these fields, and may contain other configuration data hidden in the comments as well. For example, on Red Hat Enterprise Linux 6, `/etc/init.d/sshd` has these additional special comment fields at the start. Red Hat also includes some other information in the header comments, but the comments between `### BEGIN INIT INFO` and `### END INIT INFO` are required to register the script.

```
# sshd            Start up the OpenSSH server daemon
#
# chkconfig: 2345 55 25
# description: SSH is a protocol for secure remote shell access. \
#              This service starts up the OpenSSH server daemon.
#
# processname: sshd
# config: /etc/ssh/ssh_host_key
# config: /etc/ssh/ssh_host_key.pub
# config: /etc/ssh/ssh_random_seed
# config: /etc/ssh/sshd_config
# pidfile: /var/run/sshd.pid

### BEGIN INIT INFO
# Provides: sshd
# Required-Start: $local_fs $network $syslog
# Required-Stop: $local_fs $syslog
# Should-Start: $syslog
# Should-Stop: $network $syslog
# Default-Start: 2 3 4 5
# Default-Stop: 0 1 6
# Short-Description: Start up the OpenSSH server daemon
# Description:       SSH is a protocol for secure remote shell access.
#                    This service starts up the OpenSSH server daemon.
### END INIT INFO
```

Structure

At its simplest, an init script contains a test of the first parameter, and with a `start` or `stop` argument will start or stop the application. As mentioned previously, `status restart` and `force-reload` should also be implemented at a minimum for LSB compliance.

chkconfig

For `chkconfig` use, the script starts with a header, which is formatted as shell script comments. These are ignored by the actual shell when processing them as scripts but are read by the `chkconfig` utility when installing and describing the services. On a system that does not have `chkconfig`, these comments are simply treated as comments and ignored.

Start and Stop

After the headers, the main body of code is usually implemented as a `case` statement, which runs the appropriate commands, either as a function or within the `case` statement itself, depending on the complexity. The LSB standards say that the init script should emit various different return codes depending on the outcome; many currently return zero whatever the status, while others return either 1 or –1 in case of an error.

Provides and Required-Start Elements

There is a field called Provides, which defines the name of the service provided by this init script. There are also fields called Required-Start and Required-Stop, which are used together with Provides to determine which order to run the scripts in. If /etc/init.d/udev declares Provides: udev, and /etc/init.d/network-manager declares Required-Start: $remote_fs dbus udev, then /etc/init.d/udev will be run before /etc/init.d/network-manager.

Another special field in there was $remote_fs. This is a system-defined facility, marked by the dollar sign at the start of its name. There are currently seven defined system facilities, as listed in Table 16-1.

TABLE 16-1: System Facilities

NAME	DESCRIPTION
$local_fs	All local filesystems have successfully mounted.
$network	The networking subsystem is available.
$named	IP / Hostname lookup (for example, DNS) is available.
$portmap	RPC services are available.
$remote_fs	Remote (network) filesystems are available.
$syslog	The system logger is available.
$time	The system clock is believed to be accurate.

Recipe

```
#!/bin/bash

### BEGIN INIT INFO
# Provides: myapp
# Required-Start: $local_fs $network $remote_fs
# Required-Stop: $local_fs $network $remote_fs
# Default-Start:  2 3 4 5
# Default-Stop: 0 1 6
# Short-Description: start and stop myapp
# Description: MyApplication is a great utility for
#        doing things with systems.
### END INIT INFO

INSTDIR=/usr/local/bin
PIDFILE=/var/run/myapp.pid
APP=myapp

case $1 in
  start)
        if [ -f $PIDFILE ]; then
          echo "Error: $PIDFILE already exists."
```

```
                  exit 1
              fi
              $INSTDIR/$APP &
              PID=$!
              echo $PID > $PIDFILE
              exit 0
              ;;
      stop)
              $0 status || exit 1
              PID=`cat $PIDFILE 2>/dev/null`
              if [ "$?" -eq "0" ]; then
                kill -9 $PID && rm -f $PIDFILE || exit 1
              else
                exit 1
              fi
              exit 0
              ;;
      status)
              PID=`cat $PIDFILE 2>/dev/null`
              if [ "$?" -ne "0" ]; then
                exit 1
              fi
              if [ -f $PIDFILE ]; then
                if [ "`ps -o comm= -p $PID`" != "$APP" ]; then
                  echo "Error: PID $PID is not $APP"
                  exit 1
                fi
                ps -p $PID > /dev/null 2>&1
                exit $?
              else
                exit 1
              fi
              ;;
      restart)
              $0 stop && $0 start
              ;;

      force-reload)
              $0 restart
              ;;

      *) echo "Argument \"$1\" not implemented."
         exit 2
         ;;
esac
```

Invocation

WHEN NOT RUNNING, THE STATUS
ARGUMENT RETURNS NON-ZERO.

STARTING THE APPLICATION RESULTS IN
THE PID BEING WRITTEN TO MYAPP.PID.

```
# /etc/init.d/myapp status   ◄────
# echo $?
1
# /etc/init.d/myapp start   ◄────
# cat /var/run/myapp.pid
```

```
9024
# ps -fp `cat /var/run/myapp.pid`
UID        PID  PPID  C STIME TTY          TIME CMD
root       9024     1  0 12:04 pts/3    00:00:00 /bin/bash /etc/init.d/myapp star
# /etc/init.d/myapp restart
# cat /var/run/myapp.pid
9040
# ps -fp `cat /var/run/myapp.pid`
UID        PID  PPID  C STIME TTY          TIME CMD
root       9040     1  0 12:09 pts/3    00:00:00 /bin/bash /etc/init.d/myapp star
# /etc/init.d/myapp stop
# cat /var/run/myapp.pid
cat: /var/run/myapp.pid: No such file or directory
# /etc/init.d/myapp restart
# cat /var/run/myapp.pid
cat: /var/run/myapp.pid: No such file or directory
```

RESTARTING THE APPLICATION RESULTS IN A NEW PID BECAUSE THE OLD INSTANCE WAS STOPPED AND A NEW ONE WAS STARTED AT 12:09.

STOPPING THE APPLICATION ALSO REMOVES MYAPP.PID.

IF THE APPLICATION IS NOT RUNNING, RESTART DOES NOT START IT.

Summary

Init scripts are normally fairly simple, but they do vary somewhat from system to system. This recipe provided a simple enough framework, which should work in most settings, but some systems can be more flexible in terms of parallel startup and dependency checking if provided with additional information in the comments at the start of the script.

RECIPE 16-2: CGI SCRIPTS

The Common Gateway Interface, or CGI, is the protocol that defines how data is passed to web servers, most recognizably in the form http://www.example.com/page?name=steve&shell=bash, but also, less noticeably, how forms are processed by web servers. This is often used with languages such as PHP, which require additional software on top of your web server, but these tasks can be performed using just a web server and the shell.

On today's Internet, CGI scripts need to be extremely robust and secure because anybody who can trick the script into doing something out of the ordinary can execute code on the web server with the permissions of the user account that runs the script. More complex systems such as PHP add more bloat and can hide the underlying details of what is happening, but they do add some additional security protection. For debugging problems with these more complicated systems, or in trusted or very simple environments, the shell can also be used for CGI scripts.

Technologies Used

➤ HTTP

➤ CGI; RFC 3875

➤ Apache mod_cgi

➤ eval, case, read

Concepts

The CGI protocol evolved faster than it could be documented, but RFC 3875 (`http://www.ietf.org/rfc/rfc3875`) has since been written to document the Common Gateway Interface. It allows the web server to receive additional data from the browser, using two protocols, GET and POST, which are defined by the HTTP protocol. DELETE and PUT are also in the Representational State Transfer (REST) architecture, although these are not used on the Web.

GET

The simplest form is GET, which embeds arguments in the URL itself. This is passed to the script as the environment variable `QUERY_STRING`. It is up to the script to parse this variable as best suits it, but the standard is that each `variable=value` pair is sent after an initial question mark, and they are then separated by ampersands (`&`). This is how variables are presented when a form is used to send the GET request. Some minor encoding is done, too; URIs can only contain certain characters, so spaces are replaced with `%20` (space is `0x20` in ASCII) although `+` can also be used to represent a space. A colon becomes `%3A`, a forward slash is `%2F`, and so on.

POST

The other common form is POST, which passes arguments within the body of the request. You can use POST to send files from the browser to the web server. Instead of the `QUERY_STRING` variable, POSTed data is processed on the script's standard input.

Forms

The form that sends the data is defined in HTML, with an `action` and `method` defined. The HTML itself is not necessarily CGI; it could be a plain HTML web page. The URL to the CGI script is defined in the `action` parameter, and the `method` specifies whether a GET or POST is to be used by the browser to send the data to the web server.

Potential Pitfalls

The main pitfall when processing user-submitted data is security. If you can avoid this pitfall, such as when testing local and entirely trusted systems, then using the shell as a debugging tool can be an excellent time-saver as it cuts out any complicated third-party bloat.

As discussed in the GET section below, and shown in Figure 16-5, editing the Location bar can be used to extract potentially sensitive data from the web server. Users can also direct `telnet` sessions at port 80 of your web server and send any kind of data that they choose directly to your CGI script, either in the `QUERY_STRING` variable (for GET requests) or in standard input (for POST requests). It can be very difficult for an administrator to secure against any possible attack, as has been shown over time, as CGI scripts have been attacked in a variety of ways. Ideally, a CGI script will know exactly what inputs it expects, and discard any other input without ever processing it. In practice, this is not often possible, so all input data must be treated as potentially malicious. Things to check for include:

➤ `$VARIABLE`

➤ `${VARIABLE}`

- ➤ cmd

- ➤ `cmd`

- ➤ $(cmd)

- ➤ cmd > file (or >>)

- ➤ cmd < file (or <<, <<-, or <<<)

Structure

First, assuming that you are using the Apache web server, add something like this to your Apache configuration to enable CGI. Depending on the exact setup, the names of files and directories will vary, but the important part is to define the /cgi-bin alias, and to set the +ExecCGI option for the directory that it is aliased to. Then install the index.html file anywhere in the web server's document directory and the two CGI files in the cgi-bin directory.

```
ScriptAlias /cgi-bin/ /var/www/cgi-bin/
<Directory "/var/www/cgi-bin">
        AllowOverride None
        Options +ExecCGI -MultiViews +SymLinksIfOwnerMatch
        Order allow,deny
        Allow from all
</Directory>
```

 To get these screenshots to use the example.com domain, I defined an entry in /etc/hosts and created a Virtual Host in Apache to respond to that name. You can see this in the sample raw /etc/hosts output in the POST section later on in this recipe.

Headers

The script must emit only HTML, all of which will be sent to the browser. This must start with a two-line header. The first line defines what the content is going to be, and the second is always a blank line. This marks the end of the headers and the beginning of the content.

```
Content-type: text/html
```

This header is sent by this recipe in the "Show the Header" section, including sending the initial HTML code to set the Title bar text and display an H1 heading.

GET

index.html contains two forms, shown in Figure 16-1 in the Invocation section that follows. The first is a GET form, which sends two text inputs, named one and two, and three checkboxes, named check1, check2, and check3. These names are not visible to the user other than in the page source and in the URL of the GET request. The table labels these fields as "First Text," "Second Text," and "Check These." The form is defined as action="/cgi-bin/hello.cgi" method="get".

hello.cgi parses the QUERY_STRING variable, first translating any ampersands into newlines. This turns one=hello+world&two=this+is+my+message&check1=on&check3=on into four separate lines, which are evaluated by eval. These four lines are:

➤ one=hello+world

➤ two=this+is+my+message

➤ check1=on

➤ check3=on

Notice that check2 is not sent at all because it was not set. This is unique to checkboxes; if the first text input was empty, it would be sent as one=; the QUERY_STRING would be one=&two=this+is+my+message. The script then translates the + symbols back into spaces (URLs can't contain spaces) to display the message. In the Invocation section that follows, Figure 16-2 shows hello.cgi interpreting and displaying the passed text and checkboxes.

This technique alone is inherently very insecure; passing untreated user input into eval is dangerous under any circumstances. In the Invocation section that follows, Figure 16-3 shows a malicious user entering the variable name $DOCUMENT_ROOT into the form. Figure 16-4 shows that the script seems to be perfectly safe; the dollar has been changed into the harmless text %24 ($ is 0x24 in ASCII). However, this conversion was done by the web browser, which is under the user's control. Figure 16-5 shows that the user can change the URL in the Location bar, and the web server's Document Root is displayed to the malicious user as part of the web page (/home/steve/book/web in this case). This information can then be used to launch further attacks; the user account "steve" is very likely to exist on the server, and is likely to be open to ssh, or on a web server, maybe even to ftp. Once you can get a remote server to interpret code on your behalf, you can pretty much control everything about it. This information is not secret, but this is not the place to provide any further examples — this is not a systems security book.

The second part of hello.cgi converts dollar symbols ($) into a harmless \$. This means that the lower part of Figure 16-5 shows the text $DOCUMENT_ROOT, which has not been interpreted by the script at all. This is still not guaranteed to be perfectly safe against all possible attacks, but it shows some of the issues that need to be guarded against.

POST

In the Invocation section that follows, Figure 16-6 shows the index.html page again, with the second form populated with the names of local files /etc/hosts and /etc/resolv.conf. POST data is sent from the browser to the script's standard input. The two protocols can't really be combined, although it is possible to use method="POST" and action="upload.cgi?foo=bar" to pass a GET request to the CGI script. This is shown in Figure 16-7, although this combination is not commonly used; POST forms normally use only the POST element and ignore QUERY_STRING. The encoding type has to be set to multipart/form-data to tell the browser that the files need to be encoded appropriately for sending over the HTTP protocol.

It is worth testing this script by commenting out the call to readfiles, *and uncommenting the* <pre> *tags and the* cat - *command at the end of the script. This shows the raw data that the script receives.*

The raw data as sent includes a randomly generated boundary string and some headers before each file containing filenames and variable names. An example of this output is shown here; understanding this structure is essential to understanding how the script interprets it.

```
----------------------------9254445291694807925741I075
Content-Disposition: form-data; name="fileone"; filename="hosts"
Content-Type: application/octet-stream

127.0.0.1       localhost www.example.com
192.168.1.3     router
192.168.1.5     plug
192.168.1.10    declan
192.168.1.11    atomic
192.168.1.13    goldie
192.168.1.227   elvis

----------------------------9254445291694807925741I075
Content-Disposition: form-data; name="filetwo"; filename="resolv.conf"
Content-Type: application/octet-stream

nameserver 192.168.1.3

----------------------------9254445291694807925741I075
Content-Disposition: form-data; name="filethree"; filename=""
Content-Type: application/octet-stream


----------------------------9254445291694807925741I075--
```

The upload.cgi script starts by reading the first line, which defines the boundary. This is used between the files as a marker. It is also used at the very end of the input, with "--" at the end to mark the very end of the input. The line boundary=${BOUNDARY%^M} strips the trailing Control-M from the boundary. This is necessary because the web browser sends the text in DOS format, which has an extra ^M at the end of each line due to the differences between the DOS and Unix text file formats.

The readfiles function reads the headers for the first file and creates a blank file in the uploads subdirectory. This is relative to the location of the upload.cgi script in the filesystem. The while loop then reads one line at a time, remembering the previous line read in the $previous_line variable. The ^M is stripped from each line as it is read. The function reads one line of input at a time, and uses a case statement to determine which of these three cases is found:

➤ When the boundary is found, the MD5 checksum of the completed file is taken, and the next set of headers is read in. If, for some reason, this fails, then the script exits.

➤ If the boundary followed by "--" is found, the md5sum of the last-read file is taken, and the function returns.

➤ In all other cases, the previous line is appended to the current file, and the $previous_line variable is set to the most recently read line.

The reason for the `$previous_line` hack is that, otherwise, the processing of each set of filename headers is made more complicated. Each line is sent with a blank line and then the boundary after it, so it is much cleaner if the `case` statement works one step behind the received input.

> *There is a `tee` commented out in the catch-all clause of the `case` statement. This could optionally be used to display the content of the uploaded file in the web browser. Displaying the file contents is not the purpose of this recipe, but it is provided to show how that task would be accomplished with one small and simple change to the script.*

Recipe

```html
<html>
  <head>
    <title>example.com</title>
  </head>
<body>
<h1>CGI Scripting</h1>
<table>
  <form action="/cgi-bin/hello.cgi" method="get">
    <tr><td colspan=2><h2>Submit Text (GET)</h2></td></tr>
    <tr><th>First Text:</th>
    <td><input type=text name=one></td></tr>
    <tr><th>Second Text:</th>
    <td><input type=text name=two></td></tr>
    <tr><th>Check These</th>
    <td>
      1<input type=checkbox name=check1>  
      2<input type=checkbox name=check2>  
      3<input type=checkbox name=check3>  
    </td></tr>
    <tr><td> </td><td>
    <input type=submit value="Submit Form">
    </td></tr>
  </form>
  <form action="/cgi-bin/upload.cgi?foo=bar"
        method="post" enctype="multipart/form-data">
    <tr><td colspan=2><h2>File Upload (POST)</h2></td></tr>
    <tr><th>File One:</th>
    <td><input type=file name=fileone></td></tr>

    <tr><th>File two:</th>
    <td><input type=file name=filetwo></td></tr>

    <tr><th>File Three:</th>
    <td><input type=file name=filethree></td></tr>

    <tr><td> </td><td>
    <input type=submit value="Upload Files">
    </td></tr>
  </form>
```

```
</table>
</body>
</html>
```

index.html

```
#!/bin/bash
echo "Content-type: text/html"
echo

cat - << EndOfHeaders
<html>
<head><title>Hello There!</title></head>
<body>
<h1>Hello There!</h1>
EndOfHeaders

echo "You said: $QUERY_STRING"

echo "<hr/>"
eval `echo ${QUERY_STRING} | tr '&' '\n'`
echo "one is ${one}" | tr '+' ' '
echo "<br/>"
echo "two is ${two}" | tr '+' ' '
echo "<br/>"
for check in check1 check2 check3
do
  if [ -z "${!check}" ]; then
    echo "${check} is not set<br/>"
  else
    echo "${check} is set<br/>"
  fi
done
echo "<hr/>"
eval `echo ${QUERY_STRING/'$'/'\\$'} | tr '&' '\n'`
echo "one is ${one}" | tr '+' ' '
echo "<br/>"
echo "two is ${two}" | tr '+' ' '
echo "<hr/>"

cat - << EOF
</body>
</html>
EOF
```

hello.cgi

```
#!/bin/bash

function readfiles
{
  read disposition data name filename
  read ct contenttype
  read blankline
  read previous_line
```

```
    eval `echo $filename | tr -d '^M'`
    echo "<hr/>"
    echo "Processing file \"$filename\" ($contenttype)<br/>"
    > uploads/$filename

  while read content
  do
    contentvalue=${content%^M}
    case $contentvalue in
      $boundary)
        # end of file.
        # First, show the summary of the previous file
        cd uploads
        md5sum $filename
        cd - > /dev/null
        echo "<br/>"
        # Now read in the headers of the next file
        read disposition data name filename
        read ct contenttype
        read blankline
        read previous_line
        eval `echo $filename | tr -d '^M'`
        if [ ! -z "$filename" ]; then
          echo "<hr/>"
          echo "Processing file \"$filename\" ($contenttype)<br/>"
          > uploads/$filename
        else
          # That was the end of the input. No proper notification
          # received (boundary--) but handle it gracefully.
          echo "<hr/>"
          return
        fi
        ;;

      ${boundary}--)
        # end of all input
        cd uploads
        md5sum $filename
        cd - > /dev/null
        echo "<hr/>"
        return
        ;;

      *)
        echo "$previous_line" >> uploads/$filename # | tee -a uploads/$filename
        previous_line=$content
        ;;
    esac
  done
}

# Show the Header
cat - << EndOfHeaders
Content-type: text/html

<html>
```

```
<head><title>Uploader</title></head>
<body>
<h1>File Uploads</h1>
EndOfHeaders

echo "Query String is $QUERY_STRING"

# Read the first line of input. This tells you the boundary
read BOUNDARY
boundary=${BOUNDARY%^M}

# Read and process the input
readfiles

# Use this instead for debugging and testing
# echo "<pre>"
# cat -
# echo "</pre>"

# Write the HTML footer
cat - << EOF
</body>
</html>
EOF
```

upload.cgi

Invocation

The initial web page is shown in Figure 16-1. This shows one GET and one POST form.

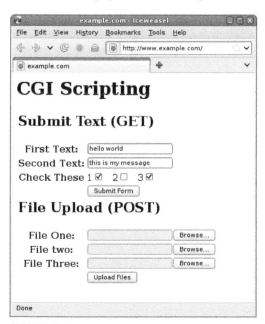

FIGURE 16-1

Figure 16-2 shows the results of the GET form being processed by `hello.cgi`. This simple test does not attempt to trick the CGI script in any way, but shows how the CGI script works.

FIGURE 16-2

Figure 16-3 shows the malicious user entering less sanitized data into the form. This simple attack does not work by itself because the web browser modifies the dollar symbol before sending it to the web server.

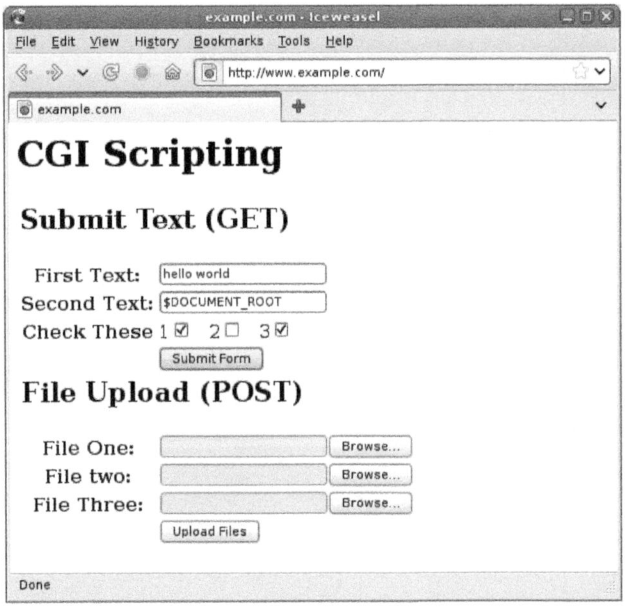

FIGURE 16-3

Figure 16-4 shows the result of the attempted attack. The dollar has been substituted with the harmless text "%24".

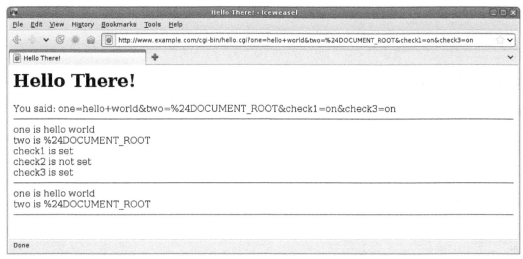

FIGURE 16-4

Figure 16-5 shows what happens when the user edits the query string directly by modifying the URL in the Location bar, changing %24 back to the dollar symbol. This time, the actual value of the $DOCUMENT_ROOT variable is displayed to the attacker.

FIGURE 16-5

Figure 16-6 shows the initial web page again, but populated, ready to send two files to the web server via the POST form. The names and contents of these files will be sent as part of the web request.

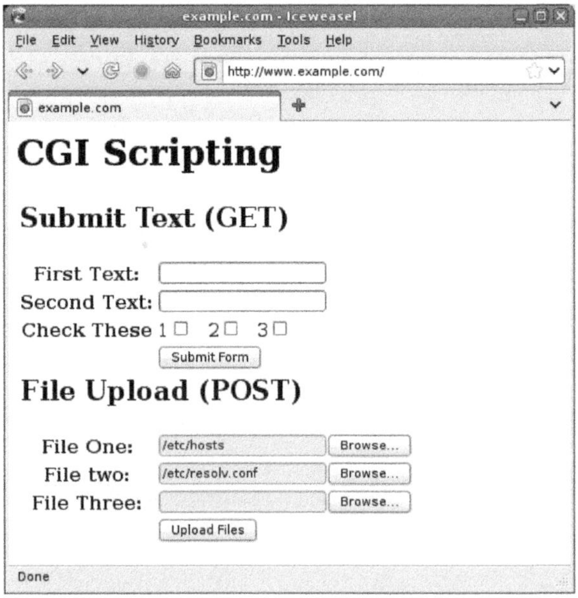

FIGURE 16-6

In Figure 16-7, the CGI script displays updates as it processes the files, and shows the MD5 checksum of each file.

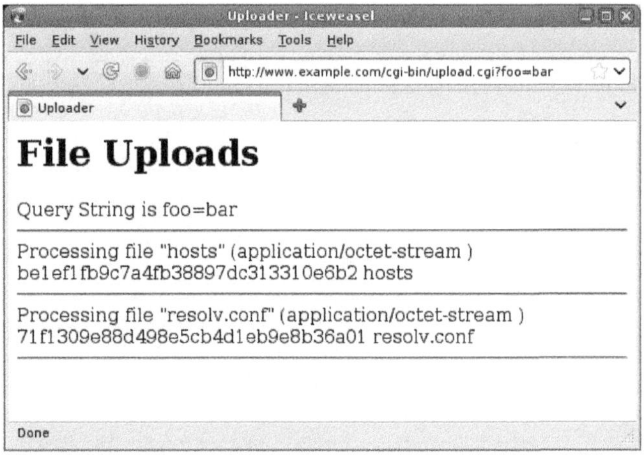

FIGURE 16-7

Summary

CGI is a useful tool, but it was designed with the assumption of a reasonably trustworthy Internet. As such, complex frameworks such as PHP or huge Perl libraries have been created to tame it. More recently, Ajax has been used to largely replace CGI by providing server-side processing in a more flexible and transparent manner. Still, CGI scripts written in the shell can be useful because they require no third-party software beyond the web server itself, are very quick and easy to put together, and can provide vital debugging information.

CGI allows you to programmatically change the response of the web server depending on the input sent. Two methods are available for processing CGI scripts: GET is more transparent and easier to debug, and POST allows files to be sent to the server. Browser plug-ins are available to convert POST forms to GET and vice-versa. Wireshark can also be used in tracing web traffic and debugging CGI connections.

RECIPE 16-3: CONFIGURATION FILES

Configuration files are common to almost every operating system and application. Some systems tend to favor binary files, as this is more convenient as a way of dumping the state of the application and reading the state back in. The Unix and GNU/Linux tradition is to use text files. This can be far more convenient for a shell script to use, and it also means that the files can be manipulated by human intervention, by other scripts and other software. It also means that there need be no lock-in to a particular application just because the data or configuration can only be read by one piece of software.

Technologies Used

- ➤ source (.)
- ➤ Variable assignment

Concepts

A shell script can be encompassed within a single file, including all of its code, data, and configuration. However, the script can be more flexible if these items are stored in separate files. The user can edit the configuration as a simple text file; this way the user does not ever have to see the implementation details of the script that reads and interprets them. This happens at all levels, from the application user at the high level down to system administration tasks such as editing /etc/hosts or /etc/sysconfig/network-scripts/ifcfg-eth0. These are all essentially configuration files, too.

One of the simplest formats for a configuration file is to use the same syntax that the shell uses. This way, you can use the source (.) command to bring the configuration into the environment directly. This is no accident; it is the way that the shell itself reads ~/.profile, ~/.bashrc, and other configuration files of its own.

Potential Pitfalls

The main pitfall with this technique is that escape and quotation characters can be a problem. For example, if a variable is assigned with the value a'b, then the shell will continue reading after the newline until it finds a closing single quotation mark.

```
$ cat eg.cfg
x=a'b
$ . eg.cfg
-bash: eg.cfg: line 1: unexpected EOF while looking for matching `''
-bash: eg.cfg: line 2: syntax error: unexpected end of file
$
```

Structure

This recipe shows various ways of assigning variables. At the start of the script, it sets the variables as blank. Then, using [-r $CFG], it reads in the configuration file if it exists and is readable. The -p switch to read includes the prompt in the read command, so read -p "Name: " name reads in the name variable with a prompt of Name:.

Adding ($NAME) to the prompt text suggests a default value that will be used if the user presses Return instead of typing in a value. This is achieved by the -z test, which tests if the variable is empty, and if so, sets the variable to the default value that had been read in. This mapping uses a convention of uppercase and lowercase variable names, so $name is the user-entered name, whereas $NAME is the value read in from the configuration file. This is not a defined standard in the shell, but a useful naming convention when it is convenient to have two different variables with the same name. In the "Invocation" section that follows, Bethany doesn't provide a value, so the default of "Manchester" is used.

Finally, the script writes out its current values to the configuration file. Because the file will be read in by the shell, standard shell syntax means that the comments beginning with a hash (#) will be ignored.

Recipe

```
DEBUG=0
NAME=Steve
LOCATION=Manchester

#!/bin/bash

DEBUG=3
NAME=
LOCATION=
COLOR=
CFG=`dirname $0`/name.cfg
[ -r $CFG ] && . $CFG

read -p "What is your name? ($NAME): " name
[ -z "$name" ] && name=$NAME
read -p "Where are you? ($LOCATION): " location
[ -z "$location" ] && location=$LOCATION
read -p "What is your favorite color? ($COLOR): " color
```

```
[ -z "$color" ] && color=$COLOR

echo "Hello ${name}, how is the weather in ${location}?"
echo "Can you see anything ${color}?"

echo "# Config file autogenerated by `id -nu` on `date`" > $CFG
echo "# Do not edit by hand, this file will be rewritten" >> $CFG
echo >> $CFG
echo DEBUG=$DEBUG >> $CFG
echo NAME=$name >> $CFG
echo LOCATION=$location >> $CFG
echo COLOR=$color >> $CFG
```

name.sh

name.cfg

Invocation

```
$ cat name.cfg
DEBUG=0
NAME=Steve
LOCATION=Manchester
$ ./name.sh
What is your name? (Steve): Bethany
Where are you? (Manchester):
What is your favorite color? (): Blue
Hello Bethany, how is the weather in Manchester?
Can you see anything Blue?
$ cat name.cfg
# Config file autogenerated by steve on Sun Apr 24 15:55:44 BST 2011
# Do not edit by hand, this file will be rewritten

DEBUG=0
NAME=Bethany
LOCATION=Manchester
COLOR=Blue
$ ./name.sh
What is your name? (Bethany): Emily
Where are you? (Manchester): the garden
What is your favorite color? (Blue): Pink
Hello Emily, how is the weather in the garden?
Can you see anything Pink?
$ cat name.cfg
# Config file autogenerated by steve on Sun Apr 24 15:56:07 BST 2011
# Do not edit by hand, this file will be rewritten

DEBUG=0
NAME=Emily
LOCATION=the garden
COLOR=Pink
$
```

Summary

Configuration files can be a useful way to store default values. They are easy to read in because the shell already contains the code to parse them; no additional code is required as it would be for Windows-style .ini files or for some other bespoke file format. This is not the only way to structure configuration files, but it is the most common, because it is so simple.

RECIPE 16-4: LOCKS

It can be useful to know that a process has exclusive access to a resource. For example, if a script takes a few minutes to process and update a critical file, leaving it in an inconsistent state until it has finished, it is not a good idea for other scripts to try to access that file while it is temporarily in a known-bad state.

A lock system provides such a mechanism, granting only one process at any time access to a particular resource. The resource itself can be anything at all; the lock is simply the barrier that stops multiple processes doing something at once. This can be used to ensure that init scripts do not start multiple copies of their processes (often using /var/run/app-name.pid as the lock file in this case), or anything else that requires guaranteed unique access.

The normal way to achieve locking in the shell is to put the PID of the running process into a common file. Any other instances of the script check that file before entering the critical section of code, and continue only if no other instance has already claimed the lock. In practice, it is not quite that simple. Processes have to allow for the possibility that the lock file has changed since they last checked its state. This cannot be fixed simply by checking the state again because the state after that is also unknown.

> *Although this recipe is fine for managing a resource among two processes, when there are more than two competing processes, there is a run of 9 system calls within* sed *which could potentially overlap. This recipe is a few hundred times safer than the alternative of doing this at the process level, but it is not possible to do completely robust locking without dedicated hardware support.*

Technologies Used

➤   sed -i for atomic changes to files

➤   > and >> for writing and appending to files

➤   Filesystem consistency

➤   Loops

Concepts

The concept of locking is fairly straightforward. The implementation is slightly more complicated, but not very. The lock file controls access to some critical resource. There is no actual link between the lock file and the resource itself; the lock file is just a voluntary mechanism that the script uses to ensure that it has clearance to use the critical resource.

The process gets the lock, then does some critical work, and then releases the lock. While one process has the lock, other processes that try to obtain it will be stuck in a loop until the lock is available. When the original process releases the lock, there may then be contention between multiple processes trying to acquire it. The solution to this problem is atomicity. Although atomicity is usually enjoyed only by very low-level components, such as hardware test-and-set calls implemented in CPU microcode, atomicity can be achieved through the internal consistency of the filesystem. Two different processes writing their PID (which is certain to be smaller than the smallest blocksize of the filesystem — typically 8KB) to the same file will not interfere with each other. By appending and not overwriting, all participating processes can see the state of the lock, which is key to the way that this script achieves practical locking, as explained in the "Structure" section later in this chapter.

Potential Pitfalls

The problem with implementing locks in the shell is that taking the lock has to be what is called an atomic process, but there is no single write-and-check function in the shell. If two instances of the script see that the lock is available, and then both instances go ahead and claim the lock, which one wins? This recipe has a while loop, which waits for the lock file to be removed and then takes the lock when it becomes available.

```
#!/bin/bash
LOCK=/tmp/myapp.lock

function get_lock
{
  MYPID=$1
  DELAY=2
  while [ -f "$LOCK" ]
  do
    sleep $DELAY
  done
  echo $MYPID > $LOCK
}

function release_lock
{
  rm -f $LOCK
}

echo "I am process $$"
get_lock $$
echo "$$: `date`" > /tmp/keyfile.txt
sleep 5
release_lock
cat /tmp/keyfile.txt
```

simplelock.sh

The problem is at the end of the `while` loop. If two instances are running at the same time, the scheduler could run or pause either process at any time. Most of the time, this is fine, but occasionally the execution order will be as shown in Table 16-2.

TABLE 16-2: A Non-Atomic Lock

SCRIPT ONE	SCRIPT TWO	LOCK FILE CONTENTS
	Read Lock	Empty
Read Lock		Empty
	Write Lock	PID #2
Write Lock		PID #1
Write to Critical File		PID #1
	Write to Critical File	PID #1

The second instance of the script ends up writing to the critical file, even though the lock contains the PID of the first instance. This is a bad thing, and it is exactly what the lock system was put in place to avoid. If it cannot stop this from happening, then the whole locking mechanism is really only a best-endeavors solution and not a fully robust one.

Because of the way this recipe works, it is possible for one process to "remove" itself from the lock, while two other processes are trying to remove themselves. If the first `sed` process is the last to complete (there is an overlap of only 9 system calls), it could write the PIDs of the other processes to the lock, apparently granting the lock to both of those processes at the same time. Those two processes could then continue, believing that they had exclusive access to the lock. This is incredibly unlikely to happen in practice, but without a write-and-check function in hardware, it is unavoidable.

Another weakness of the recipe provided here is that it could end up waiting indefinitely for access to a lock which will never be released. This could be worked around using the `timeout` utility, so that the script could at least give up gracefully and report the problem. However, `timeout` does not work with functions, only with scripts and programs which `timeout` (as an external program itself) can execute. This would be perfectly possible, it is just that `get_lock` would have to be implemented as a separate script, and not as a function.

Structure

This recipe shows two scripts, `domain-nolock.sh` and `domain.sh`. The task that they perform is the same. However, `domain.sh` uses a lock to control the main body of the script. This ensures that the resultant output file is coherent.

`domain.sh` shows the main working of the actual script. It is a very simplistic script, which does a whois lookup on an Internet domain name and retrieves the creation and expiration date as well as the list of authoritative DNS servers. It is inefficient in that it runs `whois` three times, which makes three separate lookups to the whois server. This can also get your IP address temporarily blocked from making further whois lookups. Even without the `sleep` statements inserted to ensure that the effect is clearly shown here, three whois searches take about 2 seconds, so it would be better to retrieve the whois record once and then search that local copy three times.

The script uses `tee -a` to write to the screen and also append to a log file. This has some significant consequences, which are addressed by the locking system.

 Whois records are not particularly well structured, so simply `grepping` through the output is not actually a very reliable way of getting information.

The `domain.sh` script has three functions, `get_lock`, `release_lock`, and `cleanup`. The main body of the script is just the same as `domain-nolock.sh`, except that it calls `get_lock` first, and `release_lock` after it has finished.

`get_lock` is the main function. It waits for the lock to become free, adds its PID to the lock, and then checks to make sure that it is the only PID in the lock file. The previous owner of the lock may have died without cleaning up the lock file, so it is also acceptable for that PID to be in the lock file. If the code has reached this stage, then it has already determined that the PID file has been released. If another PID is found in the lock file, it assumes that it lost the race. It removes its PID from the lock, backs off, and tries again. It keeps going around the outer `while` loop until `GOT_LOCK` has been set to 1.

The first part of `get_lock` loops `while [ -s "$LOCK" ]`. This loop waits until the lock file is of zero length, or ceases to exist. If this condition is already true, then the entire `while` loop is ignored. If a lock file is found, and has a length greater than zero, then it reads the PID from the lock file and uses `ps` to find the name of the process. If no name is found in the process table for that PID, the previous process may have finished without releasing the lock, so it removes that PID from the lock file by calling `release_lock` with the other process's PID. Releasing just that PID rather than removing the entire lock allows for the possibility that a third process has already noticed that the previous PID has finished, and has already taken the lock. The current instance makes no assumptions until the next time around the loop, when it should find that the file is empty. If the third process has already taken the lock by that stage, then this instance has to keep on waiting for the lock.

If the PID is still running, `get_lock` reports the status, increases its `sleep` delay, and goes around the loop again. What constitutes a suitable delay period depends very much on the application. It is probably useful to define an upper limit; if this loops around 360 times then the delay will be 6 minutes, then 6 minutes and 1 second, then 6 minutes and 2 seconds, and so on.

Once the initial `while` loop has been dealt with, there is no running process listed in the lock file. The script appends its own PID to the lock file and then checks to see if the lock contains anything else. If it does, then another process is doing exactly the same thing at the same time. However, because `grep` sets a return code, the `grep` and the subsequent `if` query can be seen as atomic. If the `grep` command fails to find another process listed in the file, then the file has been found in a clean state, and the lock has been taken. At the operating system level, `grep` is not a single atomic command; it is itself a process that takes time to run, and may get swapped out at any stage. The write-then-`grep` process, along with filesystem consistency, does ensure that this is effectively atomic, because another instance would back off anyway. Table 16-3 offers a more detailed look at the material from Table 16-2 and looks at what happens in the worst case scenario.

TABLE 16-3: Atomicity

SCRIPT ONE	SCRIPT TWO	LOCK FILE CONTENTS
`echo $$ >> $LOCK`		PID #1
`grep -vw $MYPID $LOCK` (interrupted)		PID #1
	`echo $$ >> $LOCK`	PID #1, PID #2
`grep` (continues, returns failure; no other processes found using the lock).		PID #1, PID #2
	`grep -vw $MYPID $MYLOCK` (succeeds; the lock has contained two PIDs since before this `grep` started)	PID #1, PID #2
Call to `if` checks return code of `grep`. Sees failure, knows that it has the lock, even though the other script has written to the lock file.		PID #1, PID #2
	Call to `if` checks return code of `grep`, and removes its own PID	PID #1
Writes its own PID to the lock file just to be sure. This should never be necessary.		PID #1

If the `grep` command succeeds, that means that it has found another process that is also trying to take the lock. The call to `release_lock` removes the current process's PID from the lock file, a random `sleep` (up to 5 seconds) tries to ensure that the two processes don't collide again, and the loop continues, as `GOT_LOCK` has not been set. It is possible that both instances remove themselves from the lock, but that causes no harm.

The `release_lock` function uses a simple `sed` command to remove one line from the lock file. The `^` and `$` around `$MYPID` indicate the start and end of the line, respectively, so the entire line has to exactly match the PID. Otherwise, removing PID 123 from the file would also remove another unrelated entry for PID 1234. Another common technique for removing a line from a file is to use `grep -v $PID $LOCK > /tmp/tempfile.$$`, and then `mv /tmp/tempfile.$$ $LOCK` to move the new file back over the top of the original file. This is not at all atomic, and another process could have written to the file between the `grep` and the `mv` commands. Those changes would then be lost. While `sed -i` effectively does the same thing, its overlap is at the system call level, hundreds of times faster than these processes could manage.

The `cleanup` function is called if the script gets interrupted. This is called via `trap` to remove the lock if the script is terminated before it has completed.

Recipe

```bash
#!/bin/bash
KEYFILE=/tmp/domains.txt
MYDOMAIN=$1

echo "$MYDOMAIN Creation Date:" | tee -a $KEYFILE
sleep 2
whois $MYDOMAIN | grep -i created | cut -d":" -f2- | tee -a $KEYFILE
sleep 2
echo "$MYDOMAIN Expiration Date:" | tee -a $KEYFILE
sleep 2
whois $MYDOMAIN | grep "Expiration Date:" | cut -d":" -f2- | tee -a $KEYFILE
sleep 2
echo "$MYDOMAIN DNS Servers:" | tee -a $KEYFILE
sleep 2
whois $MYDOMAIN | grep "Name Server:" | cut -d":" -f2- | \
        grep -v "^$" | tee -a $KEYFILE
sleep 2
echo "... end of $MYDOMAIN information ..." | tee -a $KEYFILE
```

domain-nolock.sh

```bash
#!/bin/bash

# LOCK is a global variable. For this usage, lock.myapp.$$ is not suitable.
# /var/run is suitable for root-owned processes; others may use /tmp or /var/tmp
# or their home directory or application filesystem.
# LOCK=/var/run/lock.myapp
LOCK=/tmp/lock.myapp
KEYFILE=/tmp/domains.txt
MYDOMAIN=$1
mydom=/tmp/${MYDOMAIN}.$$

# See kill(1) for the different signals and what they are intended to do.
trap cleanup 1 2 3 6

function release_lock
{
  MYPID=$1
  echo "Releasing lock."
  sed -i "/^${MYPID}$/d" $LOCK
}

function get_lock
{
  DELAY=2
  GOT_LOCK=0
  MYPID=$1

  while [ "$GOT_LOCK" -ne "1" ]
  do
    PID=
    while [ -s "$LOCK" ]
```

```
  do
    PID=`cat $LOCK 2>/dev/null`
    name=`ps -o comm= -p "$PID" 2>/dev/null`
    if [ -z "$name" ]; then
      echo "Process $PID has claimed the lock, but is not running."
      release_lock $PID
    else
      echo "Process $PID ($name) has already taken the lock:"
      ps -fp $PID | sed -e 1d
      date
      echo
      sleep $DELAY
      let DELAY="$DELAY + 1"
    fi
  done

  # Store our PID in the lock file
  echo $MYPID >> $LOCK

  # If another instance also wrote to the lock, it will contain
  # more than $$ and $PID
  # PID could be blank, so surround it with quotes.
  # Otherwise it is saying "-e $LOCK" and passing no filename,
  grep -vw $MYPID $LOCK > /dev/null 2>&1
  if [ "$?" -eq "0" ]; then
    # If $? is 0, then grep successfully found something else in the file.
    echo "An error occurred. Another process has taken the lock:"
    ps -fp `grep -vw -e $MYPID -e "$PID" $LOCK`
    # The other process can take care of itself.
    # Relinquish access to the lock
    # sed -i can do this atomically.
    # Back off by sleeping a random amount of time.
    sed -i "/^${MYPID}$/d" $LOCK
    sleep $((RANDOM % 5))
  else
    GOT_LOCK=1
    # Claim exclusive access to the lock
    echo $MYPID > $LOCK
  fi
  done
}

function cleanup
{
  echo "$$: Caught signal: Exiting"
  release_lock
  exit 0
}

# Main Script goes here.
# You may want to do stuff without the lock here.

# Then get the lock for the exclusive work
```

```
get_lock $$

############
# Do stuff #
############
echo "$MYDOMAIN Creation Date:" | tee -a $KEYFILE
sleep 2
whois $MYDOMAIN | grep -i created | cut -d":" -f2- | tee -a $KEYFILE
sleep 2
echo "$MYDOMAIN Expiration Date:" | tee -a $KEYFILE
sleep 2
whois $MYDOMAIN | grep "Expiration Date:" | cut -d":" -f2- | tee -a $KEYFILE
sleep 2
echo "$MYDOMAIN DNS Servers:" | tee -a $KEYFILE
sleep 2
whois $MYDOMAIN | grep "Name Server:" | cut -d":" -f2- | \
        grep -v "^$" | tee -a $KEYFILE
sleep 2
echo "... end of $MYDOMAIN information ..." | tee -a $KEYFILE
echo >> $KEYFILE

# Then release the lock when you are done.
release_lock $$

# Again, there may be stuff that you will want to do after the lock is released
# Then cleanly exit.
exit 0
```

domain.sh

Invocation

The following output shows two different interactive shells. The first shell has a prompt that says `Instance One` and it calls `domain-nolock.sh` with the domain "example.com" to look up. This runs to completion and everything seems fine.

```
Instance One$ ./domain-nolock.sh example.com
example.com Creation Date:
      1992-01-01
example.com Expiration Date:
 13-aug-2011
example.com DNS Servers:
 A.IANA-SERVERS.NET
 B.IANA-SERVERS.NET
... end of example.com information ...
Instance One$
```

The second instance has a prompt that says `Instance Two` and it calls `domain-nolock.sh` with the domain "steve-parker.org" to look up. Again, everything looks fine.

```
Instance Two$ ./domain-nolock.sh steve-parker.org
steve-parker.org Creation Date:
```

```
20-Jun-2000 13:48:46 UTC
steve-parker.org Expiration Date:
20-Jun-2011 13:48:46 UTC
steve-parker.org DNS Servers:
NS.123-REG.CO.UK
NS2.123-REG.CO.UK
... end of steve-parker.org information ...
Instance Two$
```

It is only when the output file is read back that the problem becomes apparent. Both scripts were writing to the same file at the same time, and it is now a jumbled mess:

```
Instance One$ cat /tmp/domains.txt
example.com Creation Date:
     1992-01-01
steve-parker.org Creation Date:
example.com Expiration Date:
20-Jun-2000 13:48:46 UTC
 13-aug-2011
steve-parker.org Expiration Date:
example.com DNS Servers:
20-Jun-2011 13:48:46 UTC
steve-parker.org DNS Servers:
 A.IANA-SERVERS.NET
 B.IANA-SERVERS.NET
NS.123-REG.CO.UK
NS2.123-REG.CO.UK
... end of example.com information ...
... end of steve-parker.org information ...


Instance One$
```

The better solution is to use locking. This time, domain.sh is called with the domain example.com. This runs to completion and again, nothing seems out of the ordinary at all, other than the comment Releasing lock at the end.

```
Instance One$ ./domain.sh example.com
example.com Creation Date:
     1992-01-01
example.com Expiration Date:
 13-aug-2011
example.com DNS Servers:
 A.IANA-SERVERS.NET
 B.IANA-SERVERS.NET
... end of example.com information ...
Releasing lock.
Instance One$
```

The second instance also calls domain.sh, this time with the domain steve-parker.org to look up. This instance keeps reading the lock file, and sleeps for 2 seconds, then 3 seconds, then 4 seconds, then 5 seconds until the lock has been released. The second instance then continues into the critical part of the code, writing to the screen and to the output file, which must not be written to by two concurrent processes.

```
Instance Two$ ./domain.sh steve-parker.org
Process 14228 (domain.sh) has already taken the lock:
steve    14228 12786  0 12:47 pts/7    00:00:00 /bin/bash ./domain.sh example.com
Fri Apr 22 12:47:11 BST 2011

Process 14228 (domain.sh) has already taken the lock:
steve    14228 12786  0 12:47 pts/7    00:00:00 /bin/bash ./domain.sh example.com
Fri Apr 22 12:47:14 BST 2011

Process 14228 (domain.sh) has already taken the lock:
steve    14228 12786  0 12:47 pts/7    00:00:00 /bin/bash ./domain.sh example.com
Fri Apr 22 12:47:17 BST 2011

Process 14228 (domain.sh) has already taken the lock:
steve    14228 12786  0 12:47 pts/7    00:00:00 /bin/bash ./domain.sh example.com
Fri Apr 22 12:47:21 BST 2011

steve-parker.org Creation Date:
20-Jun-2000 13:48:46 UTC
steve-parker.org Expiration Date:
20-Jun-2011 13:48:46 UTC
steve-parker.org DNS Servers:
NS.123-REG.CO.UK
NS2.123-REG.CO.UK
... end of example.com information ...
Releasing lock.
Instance Two$
```

The output file is now cleanly split into two sections: the first has example.com details and the second has details of steve-parker.org.

```
Instance One$ cat /tmp/domains.txt
example.com Creation Date:
      1992-01-01
example.com Expiration Date:
 13-aug-2011
example.com DNS Servers:
 A.IANA-SERVERS.NET
 B.IANA-SERVERS.NET
... end of example.com information ...

steve-parker.org Creation Date:
20-Jun-2000 13:48:46 UTC
steve-parker.org Expiration Date:
20-Jun-2011 13:48:46 UTC
steve-parker.org DNS Servers:
NS.123-REG.CO.UK
NS2.123-REG.CO.UK
... end of steve-parker.org information ...

Instance One$
```

Summary

Locks are a useful way to ensure that one instance of running code is treated differently from all the others, because it is the only one that holds the lock. Once the lock is held, there is no restriction on what that exclusive permission could be used for. It can be for writing to files, as shown in this recipe, or it can be used to make sure that there is only one instance of the process running at all. It can be used for any situation where it is desirable that the process doing some particular action knows that other processes will not interfere with it while it executes.

As the invocation examples showed, with or without locking, the first process carries on with no idea that another process is even running, let alone wanting to access the same resource that the first instance is using. The difference between the two is that the locking version knows that it has already arranged exclusive access to the resource.

17

Presentation

Presentation can make a big difference to the impression that users get about a shell script, and can also make it significantly easier to use. Not all shell scripts are temporary hacks to achieve a one-off task; some scripts remain in use for years, and will be used by a wide variety of people in that time. It is good, then, that scripts are not limited to printing out sequential lines of white text on a black background. This chapter shows some of the things that shell scripts are capable of, without any elaborate tricks or dependencies on other subsystems.

RECIPE 17-1: SPACE GAME

This recipe is inspired by the classic 1970s arcade game Space Invaders. The object is to kill the alien forces before they reach planet Earth (represented by the bottom of the screen). You can move your spaceship left and right using the "a" and "l" keys, and fire your cannon by pressing the "f" key. You get only one cannon shot at a time.

Technologies Used

- ➤ `kill`, `trap`, and `SIGALRM` for timing
- ➤ Advanced uses of `read` for timely response to keystrokes
- ➤ `tput` to control the terminal
- ➤ ANSI colors for display
- ➤ Arrays, particularly passing arrays to functions
- ➤ Basic mathematics to calculate position and collision detection

Concepts

The concepts behind the game itself are fairly simple. The aliens march from left to right and back again, and are coming down the screen toward you, so they move down one text row every time they get to the right-hand side of the screen. This is implemented by increasing the `ceiling` variable each time; the aliens are rendered at (row*2) + ceiling; multiplying by 2 means that there is a blank row between each wave of aliens, and adding the ever-increasing ceiling to this value means that the whole army gets lower over time.

You have a laser cannon, which is represented by a pair of variables, `cannonX` and `cannonY`, which keep track of where it is. `cannonX` is necessary because the laser keeps going in a vertical line even after you move, so it starts out the same as your ship's position, but remains independent of the ship after it is launched. This implementation means that you cannot fire another laser shot until the previous one has either hit an alien or reached the top of the screen. You can work around this by implementing an array of (cannonX, cannonY) pairs, but this would not be faithful to the original game and makes spraying the enemy with laser fire too easy.

The data structures are fairly simple; the ship and laser cannon have simple integer variables associated with their positions. Each row of aliens is represented internally by an array, which stores the point value of each alien when hit. This array is also used to keep track of which aliens are still alive — when an alien gets killed, its value in the array is used to increase the score, and the value in the array is then dropped down to zero, which is understood by the `drawrow` function to mean that the alien is not there, so it should not be drawn and should not be considered when doing collision detection.

The `aliens1` and `aliens2` arrays simply contain the encoding of what each row of aliens looks like. Each row has its own color and design, in simple ASCII art. Using two slightly different arrays, and the modulo 2 function `if (( $offset % 2 == 0 ))`, the aliens appear to be moving across the screen in a more animated fashion than if they simply moved from one screen position to another.

The real-time interactive reading of keypresses without the user having to press the Return key after each keystroke and the regular re-drawing of the screen are the two elements that make the shell appear to be an unsuitable language for such a game. The `read -n` syntax does not exist in older Unix systems, but GNU systems and Solaris 10 provide it. The real-time updating of the aliens is performed by the SIGALRM signal, which wakes the script up once every $DELAY seconds to refresh the display. Each time the script is awakened, the `move` function sets another alarm in $DELAY seconds' time, a bit like hitting the "snooze" button on your alarm clock.

The `sleep $DELAY` in the script assumes that `sleep` can take non-integer numbers; this is true for GNU `sleep` but not for traditional Unix `sleep`, which can't go lower than `sleep 1`, which sleeps for a full second. This makes the game rather slow to play on Unix, unfortunately. A possible workaround is to `sleep` once every X iterations, where just as $DELAY is gradually reduced, X is gradually increased. This, in time-honored fashion, is left as an exercise for the reader.

Because the loop reading the keyboard input is independent of the timed calls to the `move` function, you can get positive feedback on moves to the ship independent of the updates to the aliens' positions. This independence is vital for the game to feel interactive and not just turn-based.

One of the most frustrating things about arrays in bash is that they cannot be passed as arguments to functions, and they can't be sent back as return values. There is a workaround to this; calling the function with `"${a[@]}"`, and then processing `"$@"` (the quotes are essential in both cases) deals with this, including preservation of any space within the array elements.

```
$ cat func-array.sh
#!/bin/bash

a=( one "two three" four five )

function myfunc
{
  for value in "$@"
  do
    echo I was passed: $value
  done
}

myfunc "${a[@]}"


$ ./func-array.sh
I was passed: one
I was passed: two three
I was passed: four
I was passed: five
$
```

func-array.sh

Functions cannot pass arrays back as values, and although they can pass back the basic values, this method is not particularly robust and does not cope with whitespace at all. For reference, this snippet does as well as can be managed by bash, but it has limited usefulness.

```
$ cat array-func.sh
#!/bin/bash

a=( one two three four five )

function myfunc
{
  declare -a b
  i=0
  for value in "$@"
  do
    b[i]="abc.${value}.def"
    ((i++))
    shift
  done
  echo "${b[@]}"
}

for value in "${a[@]}"
```

```
do
  echo "Item is $value"
done
declare -a c
c=(`myfunc "${a[@]}"`)
for value in "${c[@]}"
do
  echo "Converted Item is $value"
done


$ ./array-func.sh
Item is one
Item is two
Item is three
Item is four
Item is five
Converted Item is abc.one.def
Converted Item is abc.two.def
Converted Item is abc.three.def
Converted Item is abc.four.def
Converted Item is abc.five.def
$
```

array-func.sh

Potential Pitfalls

Collision detection is the hardest thing to get right, particularly with the aliens being more than one cell wide. Keeping the screen clear also requires some vigilance; too many refreshes to the screen ruins the game because it causes excessive flickering. Calling the clear command takes a very long time, relatively speaking, and makes the display very flickery.

One of the most significant changes made to this script while writing it was to move the modulo function from a call to the external expr command within the for loop, which meant that expr was invoked for every single alien (whether dead or alive), and replace that with the builtin ((… %2)) construct. Changing from expr to the builtin method meant that changing the shapes of the aliens was possible; without this change it would be frustratingly slow. Moving the modulo out of the for loop is also slightly more efficient again, although less noticeably so.

Structure

First and last in the script is the tput command. This makes the cursor invisible (tput cinvis) before the game starts and makes it visible again (tput cvvis) after it exits. Another small touch is to unset the trap on SIGALRM when you quit the game so that the move function does not try to send a SIGALRM after the script has finished. These are only small details, but they improve the impression quite significantly. Or rather, without them, the impression is significantly worse.

This script is structured with four central functions as well as the main loop. Working from the bottom of the script upward, the main loop simply reads a single character (read -n 1) from the keyboard and if the key is the "left" or "right" instruction ("a" and "l" respectively) it updates the ship's location to match. The ship will be redrawn immediately. If the fire button ("f") is pressed, and the cannon is not already in use (cannonY -eq 0), then the cannonX variable is set relative to your ship's current X position, and cannonY is set to your ship's Y axis (fixed at the bottom of the screen).

The main loop calls drawship whenever a keypress moves your spaceship. This function clears out the whole bottom row with a printf statement and, as a decorative touch, color-codes the cannon within the ship to show whether it is armed or not. This, being separate from the move function, gives real-time updates to your ship movements unlike the monotonic updates of the slower alien spacecraft. drawship is also called as part of the move function so that cannon updates are regularly reflected even if the ship has not moved.

Above the main loop is the move function. The move function uses SIGALRM to call itself after $DELAY seconds. DELAY gets shorter over time, so the aliens move more quickly toward you. Every time move gets called, the aliens move one square further in the direction they were going. When they get to either edge of the screen, the direction variable is reversed so that they go back in the opposite direction. They also move down one row (by incrementing the ceiling) every time they hit the right-hand side of the screen.

move then calls the drawrow function once for every row of aliens. Because bash does not have multi-dimensional arrays, the number of rows of aliens is hard-coded into the script. Using a loop to iterate through the rows would be nice, but even with six rows of aliens, it is not too cumbersome to call the drawrow function six times. drawrow returns the index of any aliens that hit the cannon during rendering, or zero if no aliens on the current row were hit. This has an effect on the structure of the array; arrays are indexed from zero, but because zero has a special meaning in the return code of drawrow, the arrays row0 to row5, which store the aliens' points, do not use index[0], which is possibly a little clumsy, but it means that the next line after each call to drawrow simply sets rowX[$?]=0. If $? is zero, then the unused [0] index is updated, which has no effect on anything else. If $? is greater than zero, then it refers to an alien, so the array variable storing its score value is set to zero. This has the effect that subsequent calls to drawrow will not draw an alien at that location, and the collision detection will allow the cannon to shoot through that gap instead of stopping there. A cleaner implementation would require each call to drawrow to be followed by some more complicated code, which checks the return value and only updates the array if an alien was actually hit. The way used by this recipe is marginally faster to execute and, far more importantly, easier to read and maintain.

The number of aliens left alive is counted next, and if you have wiped out all of the invading forces, then a congratulatory message is displayed and the game exits. Possibly the game should continue with even faster aliens in the next wave; this would be easy to implement but would add some complexity and make the code slightly longer.

Finally, move calls the drawcannon function. This could be written inside the move function, but it is a bit cleaner to abstract it into its own function. drawcannon simply puts a space character over the top of the previous location, calculates the new position (one cell higher than before), and re-draws the cannon there.

The drawrow function does most of the heavy work. In addition to rendering the aliens, it performs collision detection to see if you have made a successful hit. Its first parameter tells it what type of alien to draw, and the rest are the values of the appropriate `rowX()` array. As mentioned previously, it is difficult to pass arrays to functions, and this is not the only way to do it, but it keeps the code simple. `shift` gets the `alientype` parameter out of the way: then the rest of `$@` is the list of values which tells `drawrow` which aliens are still alive, as well as how many points they are worth. This implementation also leaves it quite open to have aliens capable of surviving multiple hits; instead of reducing the value to zero, `drawrow` could simply subtract a fixed value from the alien's health, possibly leaving it above zero so that it will still be rendered on subsequent runs until it has been totally destroyed.

The function starts by working out if there are any aliens to draw on this row. If there are no aliens to draw on this line, then this row does not count toward the alien invasion attempt, so the function bails out before any further tests are done. If still running, it goes on to work out how high the current row is to be drawn. If this is the same as the `$bottom` variable, which defines the fixed Y location of your spaceship, then the invasion has succeeded, you have lost the game, and it exits with a suitable message. Otherwise, execution of the script continues.

For each alien, if it exists, the space taken up by the alien is compared with the position of the laser cannon. If they match, the alien's display icon, as defined by the `$avatar` variable, is replaced with three red stars to indicate the resulting explosion. The player's score is increased by the value stored in the array, and the `$killed` variable stores the index of this alien in the array so that it can be zeroed by the calling `draw` function. This saves `drawrow` from having to know the name of the array to update. If bash supported multi-dimensional arrays, this would not be necessary, but as each row is a separate array, it is easier for `drawrow` to return the index to the caller, and for the caller to maintain the state and update the appropriate array with the index of the deceased alien. Finally, the alien (or a corresponding space) is displayed, and the loop returns to draw the next alien in the row.

Recipe

```
#!/bin/bash
stty -echo

# Make the cursor invisible (man terminfo)
tput civis
clear

cat - << EOF



            SPACE

    LEFT:       a
    RIGHT:      l
    FIRE:       f

    QUIT:       q

                        Press any key.
EOF
read -s -n 1

row0=( 0 30 30 30 30 30 30 30 30 )
```

```
row1=( 0 20 20 20 20 20 20 20 20 )
row2=( 0 15 15 15 15 15 15 15 15 )
row3=( 0 10 10 10 10 10 10 10 10 )
row4=( 0 5 5 5 5 5 5 5 5 )
row5=( 0 1 1 1 1 1 1 1 1 )

aliens1=( '\033[1;32m|0|\033[0m' '\033[1;34m\-/\033[0m'
          '\033[1;35m:x:\033[0m' '\033[1;38m:#:\033[0m'
          '\033[1;33m!|!\033[0m' '\033[1;39m-:-\033[0m' )
aliens2=( '\033[1;32m:0:\033[0m' '\033[1;34m/-\\\033[0m'
          '\033[1;35m-x-\033[0m' '\033[1;38m-#-\033[0m'
          '\033[1;33m:|:\033[0m' '\033[1;39m-:-\033[0m' )

score=0

# farthest right that the *leftmost* alien can go to
MAXRIGHT=46
# furthest right that the ship can go to
FARRIGHT=73

# Ship's current position (x-axis)
ship=30
# Cannon column; remains the same even if ship moves
cannonX=$ship
# Cannon height; 0 means it's ready to fire
cannonY=0
# Positive direction to right, Negative to left
direction=1
offset=20
bottom=20
ceiling=4
MAXCEILING=6
DELAY=0.4

function drawrow
{
  # draw a row of aliens; return the index of any alien killed
  # note that only one alien can be killed at any time.
  alientype=$1
  shift
  let row="$alientype * 2 + $ceiling"
  aliensonrow=`echo $@ | tr ' ' '+' | bc`
  if [ $aliensonrow -eq 0 ]; then
    # Nothing to do here. In particular, do not detect failure.
    # Just clear the previous line (it may contain the final explosion
    # on that row) and return.
    tput cup $row 0
    printf "%80s" " "
    return 0
  fi
  if [ $row -eq $bottom ]; then
    tput cup `expr $bottom - 4` 6
    trap exit ALRM
    echo "YOU LOSE"
    sleep $DELAY
    stty echo
```

```
  tput cvvis
  exit 1
fi
declare -a thisrow
thisrow=( `echo $@` )

tput cup 0 0
printf "Score: %-80d" $score

killed=0
# Clear the previous line
tput cup `expr $row - 1` 0
printf "%80s" " "

tput cup $row 0
printf "%80s" " "
tput cup $row 0
printf "%-${offset}s"

# Don't do this calculation in the for loop, it is slow even without expr
if (( $offset % 2 == 0 )); then
  thisalien=${aliens1[$alientype]}
else
  thisalien=${aliens2[$alientype]}
fi

# there are 8 aliens per row.
for i in `seq 1 8`
do
  value=${thisrow[$i]}
  avatar=$thisalien

  if [ $value -gt 0 ]; then
    # detect and mark a collision
    if [ $row -eq $cannonY ]; then
      let LEFT="$i * 4 + $offset - 4"
      let RIGHT="$i * 4 + $offset - 1"
      if [ $cannonX -ge $LEFT ] && [ $cannonX -le $RIGHT ]; then
        killed=$i
        avatar='\033[1;31m***\033[0m'
        ((score=$score + $value))
        cannonY=0
      fi
    fi
  fi

  if [ $value -eq 0 ]; then
    printf "    "
  else
      echo -en "${avatar} "
  fi
done
  return $killed
}

function drawcannon
```

```
{
  # move the cannon up one
  if [ $cannonY -eq 0 ]; then
    # fell off the top of the screen
    return
  fi

  tput cup $cannonY $cannonX
  printf " "
  ((cannonY=cannonY-1))
  tput cup $cannonY $cannonX
  echo -en "\033[1;31m*\033[0m"
}

function drawship
{
  tput cup $bottom 0
  printf "%80s" " "
  tput cup $bottom $ship
  # Show cannon state by its color in the spaceship
  if [ $cannonY -eq 0 ]; then
    col=31
  else
    col=30
  fi
  echo -en "|--\033[1;${col}m*\033[0m--|"
}

function move
{
  # shift aliens left or right
  # move cannon, check for collision

  (sleep $DELAY && kill -ALRM $$) &

  # Change direction if hit the side of the screen
  if [ $offset -gt $MAXRIGHT ] && [ $direction -eq 1 ]; then
    # speed up if hit the right side of the screen
    DELAY=`echo $DELAY \* 0.90 | bc`
    direction=-1
    ((ceiling++))
  elif [ $offset -eq 0 ] && [ $direction -eq -1 ]; then
    direction=1
  fi

  ((offset=offset+direction))

  drawrow 0 ${row0[@]}
  row0[$?]=0
  drawrow 1 ${row1[@]}
  row1[$?]=0
  drawrow 2 ${row2[@]}
  row2[$?]=0
  drawrow 3 ${row3[@]}
  row3[$?]=0
```

```
  drawrow 4 ${row4[@]}
  row4[$?]=0
  drawrow 5 ${row5[@]}
  row5[$?]=0

  aliensleft=`echo ${row0[@]} ${row1[@]} ${row2[@]} ${row3[@]}\
        ${row4[@]} ${row5[@]} \
     | tr ' ' '+' | bc`
  if [ $aliensleft -eq 0 ]; then
    tput cup 5 5
    trap exit ALRM
    echo "YOU WIN"sleep $DELAY    tput echo
    tput cvvis
    echo; echo; echo
    exit 0
  fi

  drawcannon
  drawship
}

trap move ALRM

clear
drawship
# Start the aliens moving...
move
while :
do
  read -s -n 1 key
  case "$key" in
    a)
        [ $ship -gt 0 ] && ((ship=ship-1))
         drawship
         ;;
    l)
        [ $ship -lt $FARRIGHT ] && ((ship=ship+1))
         drawship
         ;;
    f)
        if [ $cannonY -eq 0 ]; then
          let cannonX="$ship + 3"
          cannonY=$bottom
        fi
        ;;
    q)
        echo "Goodbye!"
        tput cvvis
        stty echo
        trap exit ALRM
        sleep $DELAY
```

```
            exit 0
            ;;
    esac
done
```

Invocation

The game is run in the normal way, and with a color terminal should display a full-color game, with minimal flicker. Figure 17-1 shows the game in progress.

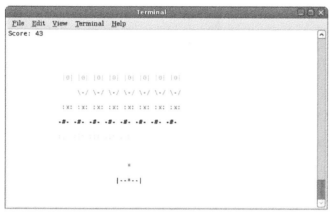

FIGURE 17-1

Figure 17-2 shows the explosion as an alien craft is hit. The three red asterisks mark the explosion.

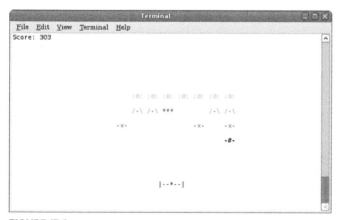

FIGURE 17-2

Figure 17-3 shows the end of the game as the alien craft land on Earth.

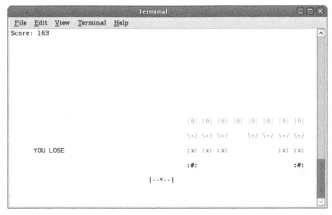

FIGURE 17-3

Figure 17-4 shows victory as the player vanquishes all comers.

FIGURE 17-4

Summary

Although just a bit of fun, this recipe shows that it is possible to create shell scripts that are far more interactive and involving than the regular "Press 1 to continue, Press 2 to exit" type menu systems that are usually passed off as interactive shell scripts. The shell can do much more than is regularly exploited, and although the shell is far from being the perfect language for game development, I hope this recipe will inspire more creative uses of shell scripts and particularly the newer features available in the bash shell (such as arrays) and in the GNU environment (like `sleep` being able to perform sub-second sleeps, without which this game is much less fun to play).

18

Data Storage and Retrieval

Retrieving, processing, and storing data is what computing is all about. This chapter looks at two different recipes which take on this task. The first processes HTML documents to identify and use any links contained in the document. This is not as easy as it first appears, so this recipe covers some of the work that has to be done to ensure that no links are missed and that regular text is not easily mistaken for a link. The second recipe parses kernel state from the Linux kernel's /proc pseudo-filesystem and converts this into CSV, which can be parsed by spreadsheet software and used to create graphs.

These two recipes balance each other, in that the first reads data which is really intended to be read by graphical desktop software in the form of a web browser. The second creates data which can be interpreted by desktop spreadsheet software. Although purely text-based, the shell can play a part in parsing as well as creating data for graphical software.

RECIPE 18-1: PARSING HTML

HTML is a very common markup language, but there is a lot of poorly written HTML out there, which makes parsing such a file quite difficult. This recipe shows a structure that strips the tags (`<a>`, `<li>`, and so on) from the HTML. The `downloader.sh` script acts on the `<a>` tags by saving the linked URL to a file named after the anchor text. Input of `<a href="http://www.example.com/">This is an example web site</a>` will download the index page of `www.example.com` to a file called "This is an example web site."

Technologies Used

> `tr`

> `((suffix++))`

> `wget`

Concepts

The actual action taken by this recipe is not particularly relevant; `wget -Fi` is capable of doing something very similar to what this script achieves, but this script is really about stripping tags from the HTML input.

Some HTML terminology is used in this recipe; in the input `<a href="/eg.shtml">example pages</a>`, `/eg.shtml` is the *link*, and `example pages` is the *anchor text*. By default, the anchor text is displayed in blue underlined text in the browser, and the link is the address of the page that will be displayed if the anchor text is clicked.

The recipe uses a very crude state machine to keep track of what position in the HTML input the script has reached. Without this, it would be necessary to make many more assumptions about the format of the input file.

Potential Pitfalls

There are a number of pitfalls in processing HTML; there is no single definition of the language, although most HTML today is either HTML 4.01, XHTML, or some unvalidated mess of tags, which roughly but not exactly corresponds to HTML 3. The recipe tries to structure the input into a set of tags in a sensible way, but it does make a number of implicit assumptions about the structure. If the input file is capable of being rendered by a web browser, then the recipe should also be able to strip the links out of it successfully.

Structure

The start of the recipe blanks out the key variables and sets the download directory, which is created if it does not already exist. The INFILE variable is set to `${HOME}/.mozilla/firefox/*/bookmarks.html`, which shows that variables can be used even inside the `${1:-default}` syntax.

The long list of `tr` statements structures the input into a long line of HTML, and then converts any < and > symbols into line breaks. After line breaks and spaces, the other class of whitespace is the tab character, so these are converted to spaces, and the `tr -s ' '` then squashes any sequences of spaces down into a single space character. This is how HTML expects whitespace to be treated. This does have one side effect, which is that anchor text with multiple spaces will also be squashed down; this is also what a web browser does with such input. `<a href="/eg.shtml">example pages</a>` becomes three lines of input:

➤   `a href="/eg.shtml"`

➤   `example pages`

➤   `/a`

The `while` statement can then expect to find input stripped into individual lines; the body of the `while` statement is a single `if ... else` statement, of which the `else` part is covered here first. The `else` part goes on to test if the tag is a (or A), and the current state of the very crude state machine is not already within an anchor (because, as the comment states, `<a href="#">a href</a>` is valid, if unlikely). The anchor text could equally be a `welcome page`, but just because the first word is "a" does not mean that this is the start of a link. If the tag is a and not already processing the anchor text, then the link is processed.

Interpreting the link itself can be troublesome; the Firefox bookmarks used as an example here include links such as A HREF="http://fxfeeds.mozilla.com/en-US/firefox/live-bookmarks/" FEEDURL="http://fxfeeds.mozilla.com/en-US/firefox/headlines.xml" ID="rdf:#$HvPhC3". To strip just the right part out of these, the recipe again breaks things into separate lines, and grabs just the line that includes href. It cuts from character 7 onward (to lose the a href=), and then cuts out any quotes that should be (but are not always) around the URL. Finally, if the retrieved link contains any text, the $state variable is set to anchor.

The other half of the if ... else statement deals with the other scenarios. The if statement itself tests if $state is anchor and $tag is not blank. If the tag is img, then the anchor "text" is actually an image; it would not be possible to save the image information as a filename, so the script will save as img.1, img.2, and so on. It does this simply by blanking out the rest of the line, so img src="/example.png" just becomes img.

Then, if the anchor text is multiple words, the $label variable will contain the rest of the words after the first one, so filename="$tag $label". Otherwise, the one and only word is the anchor text, so filename=$tag. The script then checks to see if that file already exists in the download directory. If it does, it checks ${filename}.1, ${filename}.2, and so on. The simple while loop does this by appending and incrementing the suffix until the $filename variable contains the name of a nonexistent file.

Finally, having read the link, set the state to anchor, and read in the anchor text; wget is called to download the file. The output is saved to a temporary file, and if the wget failed for any reason, its output is displayed. Otherwise, because it takes up a lot of space on the screen, the output is omitted if the command succeeds. The $state variable is then blanked out so that the whole process can start again.

Recipe

Available for download on Wrox.com

```
#!/bin/bash

INFILE=${1:-${HOME}/.mozilla/firefox/*/bookmarks.html}
state=
link=
download=/tmp/download
mkdir -p "$download" 2>/dev/null
BASE_URL=http://steve-parker.org

cat $INFILE | \
    tr '\n' ' ' | tr '<' '\n' | tr '>' '\n' | tr '\t' ' ' | tr -s ' ' | \
    while read tag label
do
  if [ "$state" == "anchor" ] && [ ! -z "$tag" ]; then
    if [ "$tag" == "img" ]; then
      label=
    fi
    if [ -z "$label" ]; then
      filename=$tag
    else
      filename="$tag $label"
    fi
    origname=$filename
```

```
        suffix=1
        while [ -f "${download}/${filename}" ]
        do
          filename="${origname}.${suffix}"
          ((suffix++))
        done
        echo "Retrieving $link as $filename"
        # Prepend BASE_URL if not otherwise valid
        firstchar=`echo $link | cut -c1`
        case "$firstchar" in
          "/") link=${BASE_URL}$link ;;
          "#") link=${BASE_URL}/$link ;;
        esac
        wget -O "${download}/${filename}" "$link" > /tmp/wget.$$ 2>&1
        if [ "$?" -eq "0" ]; then
          ls -ld "${download}/${filename}"
        else
          echo "Retrieving $link failed."
          cat /tmp/wget.$$
        fi
        state=
      else
        if [ "$tag" == "A" ] || [ "$tag" == "a" ]; then
          # Only do this if not already in an anchor;
          #   <a href="#">a href</a> is valid!
          if [ "$state" != "anchor" ]; then
            link=`echo $label| grep -i "href=" |tr [:blank:] '\n'| \
                grep -io "href.*"|cut -c6- | tr -d '"' |tr -d "'"`
            [ ! -z "$link" ] && state=anchor
          fi
        fi
      fi
    fi
done
rm /tmp/wget.$$ 2>/dev/null
```

downloader.sh

Invocation

```
$ cat eg.html
<a href="/eg.shtml">example pages</a>
<a href="/eg2.shtml">a       pages</a>

<a        href="/e+g.shtml">eg pages</a>
<a href="/imagelink1.html"><img src="/images/myimage1.png" alt="image here"></a>
<a href="/imagelink2.html"><img src="/images/myimage2.png" alt="image here"></a>
<a bar=foo>nono</a>
This is what <a href="#">a href</a> looks like
This is what <a href="#more">a marker</a> looks like
<a href='/e_g.shtml'>more
<a href="/moreimages.html"><img src="/images/myimage8.png" alt="image here"></a>
```

MULTIPLE SPACES CAN CAUSE PROBLEMS; THE RECIPE STRIPS THESE OUT WITH TR -S.

IMAGES AS ANCHOR TEXT CAN BE AWKWARD; THE RECIPE USES "IMG" AS THE FILENAME.

THIS LOOKS A LOT LIKE A LINK, BUT IT HAS NO HREF, SO IT IS IGNORED.

THE RECIPE WILL EFFECTIVELY CLOSE THIS TAG, AS IT DOES NOT ACTUALLY SEARCH FOR </A>

```
examples
</a>
<a class="pad" href="/examples.shtml" title="eg">further examples</a>
$ ./downloader.sh eg.html
Retrieving /eg.shtml as example pages
-rw-rw-r-- 1 steve steve 10421 May  1 12:58 /tmp/download/example pages
Retrieving /eg2.shtml as a pages
-rw-rw-r-- 1 steve steve 402 May  1 12:58 /tmp/download/a pages
Retrieving /e+g.shtml as eg pages
-rw-rw-r-- 1 steve steve 2409 May  1 12:58 /tmp/download/eg pages
Retrieving /imagelink1.html as img
-rw-rw-r-- 1 steve steve 94532 May  1 12:58 /tmp/download/img
Retrieving /imagelink2.html as img.1
-rw-rw-r-- 1 steve steve 1053 May  1 12:58 /tmp/download/img.1
Retrieving # as a href
-rw-rw-r-- 1 steve steve 3407 May  1 12:58 /tmp/download/a href
Retrieving #more as a marker
-rw-rw-r-- 1 steve steve 593 May  1 12:58 /tmp/download/a marker
Retrieving /e_g.shtml as more
-rw-rw-r-- 1 steve steve 548 May  1 12:58 /tmp/download/more
Retrieving /moreimages.html as img.2
-rw-rw-r-- 1 steve steve 5930 May  1 12:58 /tmp/download/img.2
Retrieving /examples.shtml as further examples
-rw-rw-r-- 1 steve steve 50395 May  1 12:58 /tmp/download/further examples
$ ./downloader.sh eg.html   ◄───────────     RUNNING THE SCRIPT AGAIN RESULTS
$ ./downloader.sh eg.html                     IN NEW FILENAMES BEING USED,
                                              RATHER THAN OVERWRITING.
Retrieving /eg.shtml as example pages.1
-rw-rw-r-- 1 steve steve 10421 May  1 13:04 /tmp/download/example pages.1
Retrieving /eg2.shtml as a pages.1
-rw-rw-r-- 1 steve steve 402 May  1 13:04 /tmp/download/a pages.1
Retrieving /e+g.shtml as eg pages.1
-rw-rw-r-- 1 steve steve 2409 May  1 13:04 /tmp/download/eg pages.1
Retrieving /imagelink1.html as img.3
-rw-rw-r-- 1 steve steve 94532 May  1 13:04 /tmp/download/img.3
Retrieving /imagelink2.html as img.4
-rw-rw-r-- 1 steve steve 1053 May  1 13:04 /tmp/download/img.4
Retrieving # as a href.1
-rw-rw-r-- 1 steve steve 3407 May  1 13:04 /tmp/download/a href.1
Retrieving #more as a marker.1
-rw-rw-r-- 1 steve steve 593 May  1 13:04 /tmp/download/a marker.1
Retrieving /e_g.shtml as more.1
-rw-rw-r-- 1 steve steve 548 May  1 13:04 /tmp/download/more.1
Retrieving /moreimages.html as img.5                     THE DEFAULT FILE, THE
-rw-rw-r-- 1 steve steve 5930 May  1 13:04 /tmp/download/img.5    FIREFOX BOOKMARKS
Retrieving /examples.shtml as further examples.1         FILE, IS USED IF NO HTML
-rw-rw-r-- 1 steve steve 50395 May  1 13:04 /tmp/download/further examples.1   IS PROVIDED.
$ ./downloader.sh   ◄──────────────────────────────────────────────────
Retrieving https://addons.mozilla.org/en-US/firefox/bookmarks/ as Get Bookmark Add-
ons
-rw-rw-r-- 1 steve steve 39564 May  1 13:13 /tmp/download/Get Bookmark Add-ons
Retrieving http://www.mozilla.com/en-US/firefox/central/ as Getting Started
-rw-rw-r-- 1 steve steve 41281 May  1 13:13 /tmp/download/Getting Started
Retrieving http://fxfeeds.mozilla.com/en-US/firefox/livebookmarks/ as Latest Headli
nes
-rw-rw-r-- 1 steve steve 17415 May  1 13:13 /tmp/download/Latest Headlines
Retrieving http://bad.example.com/ as This is a broken example
```

```
Retrieving http://bad.example.com/ failed.
--2011-05-01 23:03:11--  http://bad.example.com/
Resolving bad.example.com... failed: Name or service not known.
wget: unable to resolve host address `bad.example.com'
Retrieving http://www.mozilla.com/en-US/firefox/help/ as Help and Tutorials
-rw-rw-r-- 1 steve steve 25123 May  1 13:13 /tmp/download/Help and Tutorials
Retrieving http://www.mozilla.com/en-US/firefox/customize/ as Customize Firefox
-rw-rw-r-- 1 steve steve 35349 May  1 13:13 /tmp/download/Customize Firefox
Retrieving http://www.mozilla.com/en-US/firefox/community/ as Get Involved
-rw-rw-r-- 1 steve steve 5237 May  1 13:13 /tmp/download/Get Involved
Retrieving http://www.mozilla.com/en-US/firefox/about/ as About Us
-rw-rw-r-- 1 steve steve 22163 May  1 13:13 /tmp/download/About Us
$
```

Summary

This recipe processes input that is complicated and often poorly formatted, so following the documented standards is not sufficient. Taking some time to think about the variety of input that could be found, and how that can be forced into something standardized, makes the later processing a lot easier.

Keeping track of the state is also useful, particularly if items could be nested, such as the `<a href="#">a href</a>` mentioned in the comments. For other HTML elements, this state is also necessary; a `case` statement can be used to interpret each supported tag in turn.

RECIPE 18-2: CSV FORMATTING

Systems administration is often very reactive, and there often isn't time to design, write, and test a clean and tidy shell script. This recipe deals with a memory leakage problem; sometimes the best solution in this situation is to create a very quick and simple script that grabs the relevant data to be analyzed later. The important thing is to get timely data, not how tidy or nicely formatted the data (or even the script) is. `grab-meminfo.sh` is an example of such a script; it simply grabs the timestamp and a copy of `/proc/meminfo` three times a minute. It is better to save more data than you need than to discard details that will later be useful.

Technologies Used

- ➤ `/proc/meminfo`

- ➤ `((suffix++))`

- ➤ CSV

- ➤ bc

Concepts

`/proc/meminfo` is one of many files under `/proc` that appear to be text files but are actually a direct interface to the current running Linux kernel. These are an excellent resource for shell scripts to acquire raw data from the kernel in an easy-to-use format, without relying on additional utilities (such as `free`), which take the same data and reinterpret it.

The `plot-graph.sh` script takes the raw data from `/proc/meminfo` and formats it into a CSV file, which can be read by spreadsheet software such as Microsoft Excel, OpenOffice.org, or LibreOffice. This desktop software can be used to format the data into a graph, which can help to visualize the memory usage over time. It also saves the data out in a more concise format. Finally, `stats.sh` uses that output to do some longer-term analysis of peak and average memory usage over time, to identify the underlying cause of the problem.

Potential Pitfalls

Although time is of the essence, it pays to do a little bit of planning when writing a script like `grab-meminfo.sh`. The easier it is to parse output from this script the better, but it is well worth keeping as much data as possible, rather than calculating the total memory use and throwing the rest away. By keeping the full `meminfo` file, it is possible to plot memory usage against swap usage, which would have been lost if the script had only gathered memory usage statistics.

It would have been better if `grab-meminfo.sh` had created the log files in the format that `plot-graph.sh` saves; in reality, what gets logged is not as tidy as it could be, so this recipe deliberately shows transformation from the very crude initial snapshots to formatted graphs, rather than from tidily formatted snapshots.

Structure

`grab-meminfo.sh` is hardly structured at all; it is a `while` loop that grabs the contents of `/proc/meminfo`. `plot-graph.sh` takes this data and writes a CSV file from it. Because each snapshot is to a different file, `ls -tr` could be used to read these in order, using the timestamp of the file. If the timestamps have been lost (by copying the files to a remote server, perhaps) then `sort -n` is needed to order them by filename. The relevant data is taken from the file using `grep` (`meminfo`, like a lot of files under `/proc`, is designed to be simple to process), and the amount of physical memory and swap in use at the time is calculated and stored to a better-formatted log file for future use. It is also `echo`ed out to standard output; this can be redirected to a CSV file.

`bc` is used to convert the kilobytes reported by `/proc/meminfo` into more manageable gigabytes for the report. This recipe uses the `scale` feature of `bc`, which in this case is used to convert with an accuracy of two decimal places. For the sake of this graph, this is accurate enough, while ensuring that the labels on the graph are 0–18 GB and not 0–18,000,000 KB.

As shown in the Invocation section of this recipe, Figure 18-1 was produced in OpenOffice.org by selecting columns B, E, and F (Time, GB Memory Used, and GB Swap Used); selecting Chart from the Insert menu; choosing a Line graph; and adding a title in the Chart Elements section.

After some time, it would be desirable to understand more about how the memory is being used on the server. The third script, `stats.sh`, provides this higher-level overview, calculating the peak and mean memory usage per day. `stats.sh` strips out each date from the log file and processes it in turn. The mean may be skewed if the server is only in use during a 9:00 to 6:00 working day, as the statistics have been gathered 24/7. This can be alleviated by a simple `cut`; if the hour is before 9:00 a.m. or after 5:00 p.m., then the loop is skipped and the figures are ignored. This ensures that `stats.sh` will only show data gathered between 9:00 a.m. and 5:59 p.m.

Because `plot-graph.sh` formatted the data slightly better than `grab-meminfo.sh` did, `stat.sh`'s task is slightly easier. Each Memory line is followed by a Swap line, so within the `while` loop, a second `read` is done to get the associated Swap data. The totals and peaks are calculated, and the count is incremented. This data is then saved to a temporary file because the `while` loop itself is a subshell, and when the loop terminates, the subshell and all of its environment variables are lost. The main script therefore reads in the state of the loop from the temporary file, calculates the mean values, and writes the data to the CSV file. As shown in the Invocation section of this recipe, Figure 18-2 depicts clearly that there is a regular pattern with a spike every Monday. The top line is Peak RAM, then Mean RAM, Peak Swap, and Mean Swap at the bottom. This information can then be used to pinpoint exactly what is different on Mondays that causes the problem. It may be that Monday is the peak load, and the server simply needs more memory to cope with the load, or it could be that a part of the application that is only used on Mondays contains a memory leak that needs to be fixed.

Recipe

```bash
#!/bin/bash

count=1
while :
do
   date +%D:%H:%M > /var/tmp/$count.meminfo
   cat /proc/meminfo >> /var/tmp/$count.meminfo
   ((count++))
   sleep 20
done
```

grab-meminfo.sh

```bash
#!/bin/bash
LOG=/var/tmp/memory.log

echo "Date,Time,Memory Used,Swap Used,Gb Memory Used,Gb Swap Used"
for MEMINFO in `ls /var/tmp/*.meminfo | sort -n`
do
   timestamp=`head -1 $MEMINFO`
   memtotal=`grep "^MemTotal:" $MEMINFO | awk '{ print $2 }'`
   memfree=`grep "^MemFree:" $MEMINFO | awk '{ print $2 }'`
   swaptotal=`grep "^SwapTotal:" $MEMINFO | awk '{ print $2 }'`
   swapfree=`grep "^SwapFree:" $MEMINFO | awk '{ print $2 }'`

   ramused=$(( memtotal - memfree ))
   swapused=$(( swaptotal - swapfree ))

   date=`echo $timestamp | cut -d: -f1`
   time=`echo $timestamp | cut -d: -f2-`

   echo "$DATE Memory $ramused kB in use" >> $LOG
   echo "$DATE Swap $swapused kB in use" >> $LOG

   gbramused=`echo "scale=2;$ramused / 1024 / 1024"| bc`
```

```
    gbswapused=`echo "scale=2;$swapused / 1024 / 1024"| bc`

  echo "$date,$time,$ramused,$swapused,$gbramused,$gbswapused"
done
```

plot-graph.sh

```
#!/bin/bash
LOG=${1:-memory.log}
CSV=${2:-stats.csv}

echo "Date,Peak RAM,Peak Swap,Mean RAM,Mean Swap,Peak RAM (GB),\
Peak Swap (GB),Mean RAM (GB),Mean Swap (GB)" > $CSV

totals=/tmp/total.$$

for date in `cat $LOG | cut -d":" -f1 | sort -u`
do
  count=0
  peakram=0
  peakswap=0
  totalram=0
  totalswap=0
  echo "Processing $date"
  grep "^${date}:" $LOG | while read timestamp type ramused text
  do
    hour=`echo $timestamp|cut -d: -f2`
    if [ "$hour" -lt "9" ] || [ "$hour" -gt "17" ]; then
      continue
    fi
    read timestamp swaptype swapused text text
    ((count++))
    echo count=$count > $counter
    let totalram=$totalram+$ramused
    let totalswap=$totalswap+$swapused
    [ $ramused -gt $peakram ] && peakram=$ramused
    [ $swapused -gt $peakswap ] && peakswap=$swapused
    echo totalram=$totalram > $totals
    echo totalswap=$totalswap >> $totals
    echo peakram=$peakram >> $totals
    echo peakswap=$peakswap >> $totals
    echo count=$count >> $totals
  done
  . $totals
  meanram=`echo "$totalram / $count" | bc`
  meanswap=`echo "$totalswap / $count" | bc`

  peakramgb=`echo "scale=2;$peakram / 1024 / 1024"| bc`
  peakswapgb=`echo "scale=2;$peakswap / 1024 / 1024"| bc`
  meanramgb=`echo "scale=2;$meanram / 1024 / 1024"| bc`
  meanswapgb=`echo "scale=2;$meanswap / 1024 / 1024"| bc`

  echo "$date,$peakram,$peakswap,$meanram,$meanswap,$peakramgb,$peakswapgb,\
```

```
$meanramgb,$meanswapgb" >> $CSV
done
rm -f $totals
```

stats.sh

Invocation

```
$ nohup ./grab-meminfo.sh &
[1] 18580
$ nohup: ignoring input and appending output to `nohup.out'
```

```
$ ./plot-graph.sh > memory.csv
$ oocalc memory.csv
```

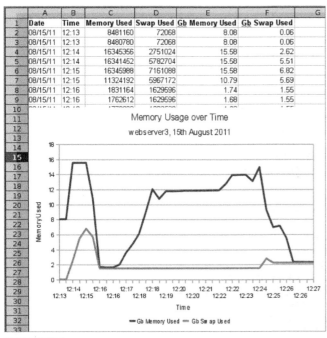

	A	B	C	D	E	F	G
1	Date	Time	Memory Used	Swap Used	Gb Memory Used	Gb Swap Used	
2	08/15/11	12:13	8481160	72068	8.08	0.06	
3	08/15/11	12:13	8480780	72068	8.08	0.06	
4	08/15/11	12:14	16345356	2751024	15.58	2.62	
5	08/15/11	12:14	16341452	5782704	15.58	5.51	
6	08/15/11	12:15	16345988	7161088	15.58	6.82	
7	08/15/11	12:15	11324192	5967172	10.79	5.69	
8	08/15/11	12:16	1831164	1629596	1.74	1.55	
9	08/15/11	12:16	1762612	1629596	1.68	1.55	

FIGURE 18-1

```
$ ./stats.sh
Processing 08/15/11
Processing 08/16/11
Processing 08/17/11
Processing 08/18/11
Processing 08/19/11
Processing 08/20/11
Processing 08/21/11
Processing 08/22/11
Processing 08/23/11
Processing 08/24/11
```

```
Processing 08/25/11
Processing 08/26/11
Processing 08/27/11
Processing 08/28/11
Processing 08/29/11
Processing 08/30/11
Processing 08/31/11
Processing 09/01/11
Processing 09/02/11
Processing 09/03/11
Processing 09/04/11
Processing 09/05/11
Processing 09/06/11
$ oocalc stats.csv
```

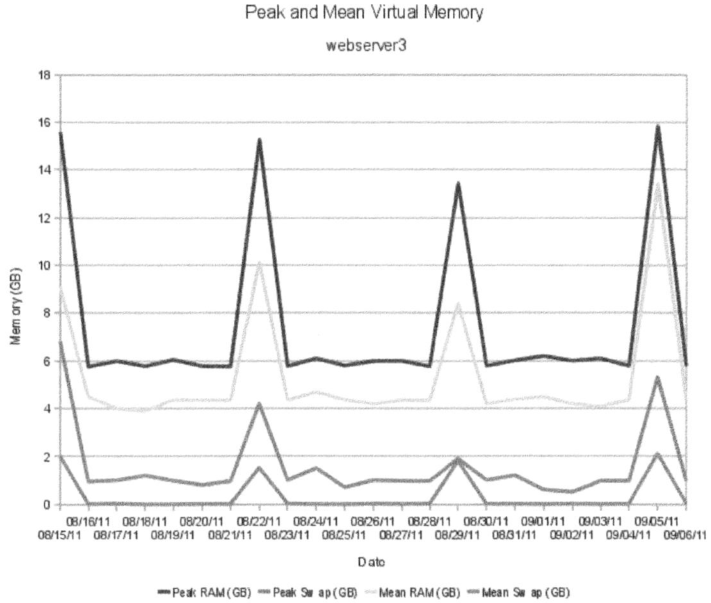

FIGURE 18-2

Summary

The shell is a useful tool to collect and massage data, but for formal presentation its text-only interface is limiting. Getting the shell to output data to desktop applications such as web browsers (as
you saw in Chapter 15, in Recipe 15-2) and spreadsheets (in this recipe) using text-based file formats
of HTML and CSV, respectively, makes the transition from text to graphical painless. This manipulation of data is not possible in other environments; if the data started out as an Excel spreadsheet
and macros, it is stuck in Excel forever. By using common text-based formats, the data can be
restructured and reformatted by any suitable tools and exported to more closed applications when
necessary. The humble shell script can be more powerful and flexible even than such large software
projects as Excel.

19

Numbers

Numbers are central to computing, but this chapter covers some of the problems that can be encountered when dealing with numbers in shell scripts. The first recipe looks at three different methods for listing the numbers in the Fibonacci Sequence. This uncovers some of the limitations on the size of numbers that the shell can deal with, and ways to work around them.

The second recipe deals with conversion of numbers between different bases. Although we normally express numbers in base 10 (the decimal system), base 2 (binary) is the native format used by the CPU. Base 16 (hexadecimal) is very commonly used because it is more compact than base 2, and one byte is neatly displayed in two hexadecimal characters. The `netboot.sh` recipe uses `printf` to convert between decimal and hexadecimal; the `bc` tool can convert numbers from any base to any other, but `printf` provides the easiest way to represent decimal numbers in both hexadecimal and octal.

RECIPE 19-1: THE FIBONACCI SEQUENCE

The Fibonacci Sequence is a very simple sequence of integers, where the value of each number in the sequence is calculated as the sum of the previous two numbers. It is traditionally started off with 0 and 1, so if F(0) is 0, and F(1) is 1, then F(2) is F(0) + F(1), which is 1. F(3) is F(1) + F(2), which is 2. F(4) is 3, F(5) is 5, F(6) is 8, F(7) is 13, and F(8) is 21. This number sequence gets bigger quite rapidly, so apart from being a rather aesthetically pleasing sequence, it is also a useful way to look at three different methods of doing calculations using large numbers with the shell.

Technologies Used

➤ Functions

➤ `((count++))`

➤   `$(( x + y ))`

➤   `[ x -lt y ]`

➤   `expr`

➤   `bc`

Concepts

The concept of continuing to add two numbers together is incredibly simple, but it is remarkably ubiquitous. Figure 19-1 shows the spiral that results from the way that the Fibonacci Sequence works. Each square has sides of the length of that position in the sequence, so the first two squares are 1×1, then a 2×2 square, then 3×3, 5×5, 8×8, 13×13, 21×21, and so on. By drawing a quarter-circle in each square, a spiral emerges. This spiral can be seen in nature, from pineapples to snail shells to sunflowers.

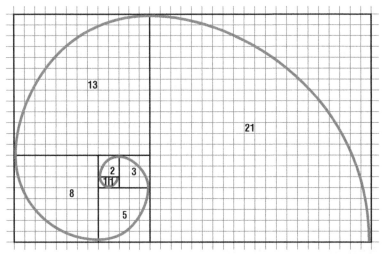

FIGURE 19-1

Potential Pitfalls

The main pitfall when dealing with large numbers is that the storage will "wrap around" itself. Computers use base 2 internally, where a bit is either on (1) or off (0). A single byte of 8 bits can represent a number up to 255. After that, it wraps around to zero again.

In normal base 10 math, the next number after 9,999 is 10,000, then 10,001, 10,002, and so on. On a calculator that only had the rightmost four digits of its display working, that would look like 9999 being followed by 0000, then 0001, and 0002. The same happens in the computer's internal representation of the numbers. After 1111 1111 (255) comes 1 0000 0000 (256), but the 8-bit byte can only see the 8 least-significant bits, which are all zeroes.

TABLE 19-1: Bit Wrapping

BINARY VALUE	DECIMAL VALUE
0000 0000	0
0000 0001	1
0000 0010	2
0000 0011	3
0000 0100	4
0000 0101	5
0000 0110	6
0000 0111	7
1111 1100	252
1111 1101	253
1111 1110	254
1111 1111	255
0000 0001 0000 0000	256 or 0
0000 0001 0000 0001	257 or 1
0000 0001 0000 0010	258 or 2

This problem is shown with single-byte accuracy in the recipe for method 1, and with 4-byte words in the subsequent recipes. The longest 4-byte word is made up of 32 consecutive ones, representing 4,294,967,295. After that, a 32-bit container wraps around to zero. In 64 bits, the maximum is 18,446,744,073,709,551,615, although, as shown in the recipe for method 2, this entire range is not necessarily available.

Structure for Method 1

The first recipe is structured slightly differently from the others; it uses a `for` loop using `seq` to count. Because it fails quickly, `seq` is a useful way to control it and make sure that it stops quite soon. The later, more robust versions use an infinite `while` loop (the colon in `while :` always evaluates to `true`) to allow them to keep on running until they get into the higher values when they, too, begin to fail.

The first recipe uses a `fibonacci` function, which returns the sum of its two arguments. This is the traditional computer science use of a function; it takes values as input, and returns a single value as a result of its calculations. Unfortunately, return codes are really intended as status reports and not as long integers, so this method is of no use in the shell when dealing with values over 255. The recipe includes a basic sanity test to see if it has wrapped around; the numbers should always be getting bigger. 144 + 233 = 377, which is 1 0111 1001 in binary. Losing the ninth bit leaves it as 0111 1001, which is 121 in decimal. 121 is smaller than the previous number, 233, so the answer 121 is clearly wrong. There must be a better way, and the subsequent methods demonstrate some alternative techniques.

A sleep for 0.1 seconds is called each time to make the output more easily readable; otherwise, the output would scroll past faster than you can read it. Of course, this artificial delay can be changed or removed as required. It makes little difference here with 15 runs but a bigger difference later when running through tens of thousands of iterations. As noted in Chapter 17, not all implementations of sleep will do sub-second delays, in which case a full second delay will have to be used instead, or none at all.

Recipe for Method 1

```
#!/bin/bash

function fibonacci
{
    return $(( $1 + $2 ))
}

F0=0
F1=1
echo "0: $F0,"
echo "1: $F1, "
for count in `seq 2 17`
do
   fibonacci $F0 $F1
   F2=$?
   if [ "$F2" -lt "$F1" ]; then
     echo "${count}: $F2 (WRONG!), "
   else
     echo "${count}: $F2,"
   fi
   F0=$F1
   F1=$F2
   sleep 0.1
done
fibonacci $F0 $F1
echo "${count}: $?"
```

fibonacci1.sh

Invocation of Method 1

```
$ ./fibonacci1.sh
0: 0,
1: 1,
2: 1,
```

```
3: 2,
4: 3,
5: 5,
6: 8,
7: 13,
8: 21,
9: 34,
10: 55,
11: 89,
12: 144,
13: 233,
14: 121 (WRONG!),
15: 98 (WRONG!),
16: 219,
17: 61 (WRONG!),
17: 24
$
```

Structure for Method 2

The second Fibonacci recipe ignores the return code of the function and simply gets the `fibonacci` function to `echo` the result. The shell itself can work with integers over 255; it is only the return codes that are limited to 1 byte. This bypasses the 1-byte limit, and the code that calls the function defines `F2=`fibonacci $F0 $F1`` so that F2 captures the stdout of the function, not the return code.

This recipe also replaces the `for` loop, which had a predetermined end-state, with an infinite `while` loop. It also provides and increments the `count` variable, as there is no `for` loop. This variable is incremented using the bash syntax of `((count++))`, which looks a lot like the C statement `count++`. This is shorthand for `let count=$count+1`. It is no more efficient, just easier to write and to read.

This recipe gets as far as the 92nd number in the sequence, 7,540,113,804,746,346,429, around seven and a half quintillion. The 93rd number is 4,660,046,610,375,530,309 + 7,540,113,804,746,346,429, which is 12,200,160,415,121,876,738, or 12 and a bit quintillion. This is at the limit of the shell's processing capability. The shell's implementation of an integer uses a system called *two's complement* to represent both negative and positive integers. This allows variables to store negative as well as positive numbers, at the expense of the range. A 1-byte (8-bit) two's complement variable can represent any integer from –127 to +128 rather than 0 to 255; a 64-bit two's complement variable could be any integer from –9,223,372,036,854,775,808 to +9,223,372,036,854,775,807. This recipe therefore fails after the 92nd number in the sequence, which, at 12 quintillion, is larger than the maximum 9.2 quintillion.

Replacing the shell math with `expr` makes no difference because the problem is with the internal representation of the number, not the technique used to add them. The `fibonacci3.sh` method replaces `echo` in the `fibonacci` function with `expr`, but it fails in almost exactly the same way as `fibonacci2.sh`. The only difference is that `expr` spits out an error message, while the shell implementation failed silently. Because `expr` did not give a value, the test `if [ "$F2" -lt "$F1" ]` expands to `if [ "" -lt "$F1" ]`, which does not make sense, so test (aka [) complains "integer expression expected."

Recipes for Method 2

```bash
#!/bin/bash

function fibonacci
{
   echo $(( $1 + $2 ))
}

F0=0
F1=1
echo "0: $F0, "
echo "1: $F1, "
count=2
while :
do
  F2=`fibonacci $F0 $F1`
  if [ "$F2" -lt "$F1" ]; then
    echo "${count}: $F2 (WRONG!),"
  else
    echo "${count}: $F2,"
  fi
  ((count++))
  F0=$F1
  F1=$F2
  sleep 0.1
done
fibonacci $F0 $F1
```

fibonacci2.sh

```bash
#!/bin/bash

function fibonacci
{
  #echo $(( $1 + $2 ))
  expr $1 + $2
}

F0=0
F1=1
echo "0: $F0, "
echo "1: $F1, "
count=2
while :
do
  F2=`fibonacci $F0 $F1`
  if [ "$F2" -lt "$F1" ]; then
    echo "${count}: $F2 (WRONG!),"
  else
    echo "${count}: $F2,"
  fi
  ((count++))
  F0=$F1
```

```
    F1=$F2
    sleep 0.1
done
fibonacci $F0 $F1
```

Invocations of Method 2

```
$ ./fibonacci2.sh
0: 0,
1: 1,
2: 1,
3: 2,
4: 3,
5: 5,
6: 8,
7: 13,
( 81 lines of output omitted )
89: 1779979416004714189,
90: 2880067194370816120,
91: 4660046610375530309,
92: 7540113804746346429,
93: -6246583658587674878 (WRONG!),
94: 1293530146158671551,
95: -4953053512429003327 (WRONG!),
96: -3659523366270331776,
97: -8612576878699335103 (WRONG!),
98: 6174643828739884737,
99: -2437933049959450366 (WRONG!),
^C
$ ./fibonacci3.sh
0: 0,
1: 1,
2: 1,
3: 2,
4: 3,
5: 5,
6: 8,
7: 13,
( 81 lines of output omitted )
89: 1779979416004714189,
90: 2880067194370816120,
91: 4660046610375530309,
92: 7540113804746346429,
expr: +: Numerical result out of range
./fibonacci3.sh: line 17: [: : integer expression expected
93: ,
expr: syntax error
./fibonacci3.sh: line 17: [: : integer expression expected
94: ,
expr: syntax error
./fibonacci3.sh: line 17: [: : integer expression expected
```

```
95: ,
expr: syntax error
./fibonacci3.sh: line 17: [: : integer expression expected
96: ,
expr: syntax error
./fibonacci3.sh: line 17: [: : integer expression expected
97: ,
^C
```

Structure for Method 3

The fourth recipe uses bc to do the math, and this is where the shell's strange relationship with variable types comes into play. Although the shell cannot deal with integers over 9,223,372,036,854,775,807, it can deal with strings that happen to look like integers. Because the shell is not doing the math, it can continue further than the previous recipes. However, the comparison of ["$F2" -lt "$F1"] does try to treat these large numbers as integers, and spits out error messages after the 92nd number in the sequence just as fibonacci3.sh did. For tidiness, then, this test is removed from fibonacci4.sh. The script then gets as far as the 324th number. For formatting purposes, after each 69th digit, bc prints a backslash (\\) and newline (\n), the standard line-continuation sequence. Appending | tr -d '\\\n' to the bc call strips these out, but the output without this fix is shown below, also. The example output continues after line 4374, but after that, the output starts to get a bit too long to put in a book.

Recipe for Method 3

```
#!/bin/bash

function fibonacci
{
   echo $1 + $2 | bc | tr -d '\\\n'
}

F0=0
F1=1
echo "0: $F0, "
echo "1: $F1, "
count=2
while :
do
   F2=`fibonacci $F0 $F1`
   echo "${count}: $F2,"
   ((count++))
   F0=$F1
   F1=$F2
   sleep 0.1
done
fibonacci $F0 $F1
```

fibonacci4.sh

Invocation of Method 3

```
$ ./fibonacci4-without-tr.sh
0: 0,
1: 1,
2: 1,
3: 2,
4: 3,
5: 5,
6: 8,
7: 13,
(316 lines omitted)
324: 23041483585524168262220906489642018075101617466780496790573690289968,
325: 37281903592600898879479448409585328515842582885579275203077366912825,
326: 60323387178125067141700354899227346590944200352359771993651057202793,
327: 97605290770725966021179803308812675106786783237939047196728424115618,
328: 15792867794885103316288015820804002169773098359029881919037948131841\
1,
(standard_in) 1: syntax error
329: ,
(standard_in) 1: illegal character: \
^C
$ ./fibonacci4.sh
0: 0,
1: 1,
2: 1,
3: 2,
4: 3,
5: 5,
6: 8,
7: 13,
(4364 lines omitted)
4372: 22104371486889933602618735961044632349577043348049549237830063379958351358033
11268917254596149645711206174771088398441721789053643030921941304454073026431478192
41390892330235850453528642957368751545308642998939685610815800594399228263960769129
21254068071415653174058777017937238760614372901733356868545935069969579993502736008
08716613231538450869710003373518827779200816776218994622421477019847855133314714546
18899014113986652857034659252548051809757752694982390345887265182046582236328217001
33763823103115778273585794003560474902759766584168221196134268569815826322073363147
428699925350910884706399169984309965059260700352426234305362961676292134793147315180
46138610752348150619982159457883646380864526446597385913849760882251106843955544650
97167798761562880904242190144594305156929701780458050593218239235282940068118503196
77599480281086457168264167341641925748865316857196662281426267110666547911046191378
6584739,
4373: 35765624365741963284919524730378813338126540562607632483122508004471265309976
21921732591032431764684384346503043840940743739673231228573220536605893452946866910
2466379672020110515798205692698064130753541939199360054474934714408493656406783979
93916754837161602464272387025650369909799845370879766002550803144584837747973615962
90818951240614280213820290475677516870911282615410106043042221375461525790866579223
58682302741351708415973899505187084097555426806237660513829820443468851292352812652
56208788452517468884050138332815587507021627661962415808212786797557853665691000413
38289519843703519722711363485632557273400445192109609864836613146184139760272144933
24088664108431699850825644193287950483122088101345491185485939837331355185435692969
4215718965955002159451023928160142130301689135398452673470238178668881272347228053
08054539175807683506731517912644386761586494590133000407819344010943092478942749225
2486693,
```

HERE, THE WIDTH OF THE NUMBER MEANS THAT THE FINAL DIGIT (1) IS PUT ON A LINE BY ITSELF, AFTER A BACKSLASH (\) AND NEWLINE. THIS HAS TO BE STRIPPED OUT FOR THE SHELL TO READ THIS AS A SINGLE STRING (BECAUSE AT THIS STAGE, THE SHELL IS TREATING THE OUTPUT AS A STRING, NOT AS A NUMBER).

```
4374: 5786999585263189688753826069142344568770358391065718172095257138442961666800933190649845628581410395590521274132239382465528726874259495161841059966479378345102660546890504369556115106998843548156760621849381390456652907353088077219203675531091517082290857725563833116404358760867041421827261312287109673821455441774147635197099535564472152731083530293849196344650112099391629100665463698395309380924181293769775813168553383612730085587577351359073131795012200508597170856255154335286810296538997261155563324715763593233637606240978139424613063700434705536737367998776436356081159445194614404429110533469942522332661145544535844170199574822476274553419460113702272748607798504708078036511715968639866145479428770993357007195824620293912376203932498842111290249875242942619571728723139091585650326668847741395182134046573124985654019456894140674995685254286312510451811447329662689245611121609640389988940603907143
```

Summary

There are various ways of getting results out of functions; the return code is a single byte and always will be for compatibility with Unix standards. This makes it a less than ideal method for passing values back to the caller. Instead, the result can be written to stdout, or to any other file as required. The downside to this method is that the function mustn't produce any other output because it will all be interpreted as being the result of the calculation.

The shell is capable of basic math at simple levels, but for very large numbers, more specialized tools such as bc have to be used. If doing a lot of complicated functions, bc itself is programmable, so a bc script rather than a shell script might be useful; bc's math library includes trigonometry and other more advanced functions, too.

RECIPE 19-2: PXE BOOTING

It used to be that a server would be installed by booting from a tape, floppy, CD, or DVD, and the operator would answer a set of questions in order to get the operating system installed as required. This still happens today, but large organizations do not have the time to do this low-level repetitive task for each of the thousands of servers they have installed. Small organizations also benefit from the fast, automated, and identical installs that this method provides. Automated, hands-off network installs are required for this, and DHCP and PXE are pretty much the only way to do this on x86 architecture. RedHat's Kickstart system is the most widely used automated installation infrastructure for Linux, and this recipe provides the most basic bare-bones setup to perform network installations.

This is not a systems administration book, so setting up DHCP, TFTP, and NFS servers is not covered here. This should provide a reasonable starting point for those topics, but its real purpose is to show how numbers such as IP addresses can be manipulated in shell scripts, even without apparently doing any math. The printf command can do a lot of conversion on-the-fly.

Technologies Used

➤   PXE

➤   Kickstart

➤   printf

Concepts

When a machine uses the PXE (Pre-eXecution Environment) to boot directly off the network, it needs to get an IP address from a DHCP server. The DHCP server can also give it the details of a TFTP server from which to retrieve an executable file. Typically for a Linux client, this file is called `/linux-install/pxelinux.0`. Once the client retrieves and executes `pxelinux.0`, it is hard-coded to look for a file from the `pxelinux.cfg/` subdirectory relative to where `pxelinux.0` was found. First, it will look for a file named after the MAC address, in the form 01-xx-xx-xx-xx-xx; then, it will look for a file named by the IP address as provided by the DHCP server.

The IP address is looked up in hexadecimal format. That is, 192 in hexadecimal is 0xC0, 168 is 0xA8, 1 is 0x01, and 42 is 0x2A, so 192.168.1.42 is 0xC0A8012A. This recipe sets up a very basic installation environment, and uses the formatting features of `printf` to display IP addresses in hexadecimal, without the script itself having to do any particularly heavy calculations.

Potential Pitfalls

There are no particular pitfalls, other than the wider issues of installing the wrong server, or using the wrong configuration. `bc` also can be used to convert between bases, and any base at all, rather than `printf`'s limited octal or hexadecimal output. 192.168.1.42 can be converted into its hex equivalent of 0xC0A8012A, but it takes a bit more interpretation than the `printf` solution used by the recipe.

```
$ IP=192.168.1.42
$ echo "obase=16;$IP" | tr '.' '\n' | bc
C0
A8
1
2A
$
```

Structure

In terms of number manipulation, the main part of the script is the line:

```
CLIENT_HEXADDR=$(printf "%02X%02X%02X%02X" `echo $CLIENT_IP | tr '.' ' '`)
```

This command `echo`es the `$CLIENT_IP` variable, which is in 192.168.1.42 format, and translates dots into spaces, which means that 192, 168, 1, and 42 are now separate arguments to the `printf` command. `printf` has been called with a formatting string of `%02X%02X%02X%02X`, which converts the four input numbers into two-character uppercase hexadecimal format, with padding zeroes. This is the file format that `pxelinux.0` is looking for.

`%x` converts any decimal number into its hexadecimal equivalent, with lowercase a-f for digits over 9. `%X` does the same, but uses uppercase A-F instead of a-f. The `%02X`, rather than simply `%X`, means that the number will be padded to be at least two characters wide. This ensures that "1" is turned into "01" and not just a "1." C0A8012A is not the same filename as C0A812A, and `pxelinux.0` is looking for each octet of the IP address as a distinct byte in the filename.

```
$ printf "%x%x%x%x\n" 192 168 1 42
c0a812a
```

```
$ printf "%02x%02x%02x%02x\n" 192 168 1 42
c0a8012a
$ printf "%02X%02X%02X%02X\n" 192 168 1 42
C0A8012A
$
```

The rest of the script creates the required files for the installation from some template files in $TFTPBOOT/messages/. The create_msgs function simply creates a pair of menu files for the client that include the names of the client and server in the display. create_kickstart creates a very short kickstart file, which can be used by the RedHat installer to configure the installation. In practice, kickstart files are longer than this and can include disk layout requirements, postinstall scripts, and lists of packages to install and to exclude, to enable a totally hands-off installation. To tweak your installation, add code to the %post section; this should be a fairly short piece of code, but it can launch a whole set of scripts to customize the client after it has been installed. This example adds a timeserver entry to /etc/hosts, and also calls a client-specific script (if it exists) on the NFS server to perform post-install tasks specific to that client. That can be the beginning of some very heavy-duty customization if required.

create_pxelinux_file creates the configuration file passed to pxelinux.0 to display a basic menu, which offers additional text (from client-f2.txt) when the user presses the F2 key, and basic text (from client.txt) on boot, or when the user presses the F1 key. The messages/ directory is relative to the $TFTPBOOT directory. Similarly, the ${OSNAME}/vmlinuz and ${OSNAME}/initrd.img files would point to /tftpboot/RHEL60/vmlinuz and /tftpboot/RHEL60/initrd.img on the server, respectively.

calc_client_details is the main function in this recipe. At the start of the script, the $CLIENT variable had been set to the first field (hostname) of the output of `getent hosts $1`. This gets the hostname whether the script was passed a hostname or an IP address because getent hosts always returns data in the same format, whichever key it was passed. calc_client_details then does a lookup of that name, and takes the second field, which is the IP address. It then processes that IP address as explained previously. If the result is an eight-character string, then it is assumed to have successfully looked up the name and IP address and converted it into a usable hexadecimal string. If apparently successful, it displays a one-line message containing all of this information, and continues. If not successful, it displays its calculations and quits before writing anything.

Recipe

```
#!/bin/bash

TFTPBOOT=/tftpboot/linux-install/pxelinux.cfg
NFS=/kickstart
CLIENT=`getent hosts $1 | awk '{ print $2 }'`
if [ -z "$CLIENT" ]; then
    echo "A failure occurred in looking up \"$1\""
    exit 2
fi
SERVER=`hostname`
OSNAME=RHEL60

function calc_client_details
{
```

```
    CLIENT_IP=`getent hosts $CLIENT | awk '{ print $1 }'`
    if [ -z "$CLIENT_IP" ] || [ -z "$CLIENT" ]; then
      echo "A failure occurred in looking up \"$CLIENT\""
      exit 2
    fi
    # 192.168.1.42 is C0 A8 01 2A
    CLIENT_HEXADDR=$(printf "%02X%02X%02X%02X" `echo $CLIENT_IP | tr '.' ' '`)
    if [ "`echo -n $CLIENT_HEXADDR | wc -c`" -ne "8" ]; then
      echo "An error occurred processing the Hex IP Address for \"$CLIENT\""
      echo "IPv4 Address detected: $CLIENT_IP"
      echo "Hex IP Address calculated: $CLIENT_HEXADDR"
      exit 1
    fi
    echo "Client details: $CLIENT is at IP address $CLIENT_IP ($CLIENT_HEXADDR)"
}

function create_pxelinux_file
{
  cat - > ${TFTPBOOT}/${CLIENT_HEXADDR} <<-EOF
        default boot
        timeout 600
        prompt 1
        display messages/${CLIENT}.txt
        F1 messages/${CLIENT}.txt
        F2 messages/${CLIENT}-F2.txt

        label boot
          localboot 0
        label install
          kernel ${OSNAME}/vmlinuz
          append initrd=${OSNAME}/initrd.img ks=nfs:${SERVER}:${NFS}/${CLIENT}.cfg
        EOF
  ls -ld ${TFTPBOOT}/${CLIENT_HEXADDR}
}

function create_kickstart
{
  mkdir -p ${NFS}
  if [ "$?" -ne "0" ]; then
    echo "Error creating ${NFS}"
    exit 1
  fi
  cat - > ${NFS}/${CLIENT}.cfg <<-EOF
        # Kickstart file for $CLIENT to boot from $SERVER
        text install
        # You would probably want to put more details here
        # but this is a shell scripting recipe not a kickstart recipe
        %post
        echo This is the postinstall routine
        printf "10.2.2.2\ttimeserver" >> /etc/hosts"
        /net/$SERVER/$NFS/${CLIENT}.postinstall
        EOF
  ls -ld ${NFS}/${CLIENT}.cfg
}

function create_msgs
```

```
{
  CLIENTFILE=${TFTPBOOT}/messages/client.txt
  CLIENTF2=${TFTPBOOT}/messages/client-f2.txt
  MYFILE=${TFTPBOOT}/messages/${CLIENT}.txt
  MYF2=${TFTPBOOT}/messages/${CLIENT}-f2.txt
  if [ ! -r "$CLIENTFILE" ]; then
    echo "Error reading $CLIENTFILE"
    exit 1
  fi

  sed s/CLIENT_NAME_HERE/$CLIENT/g $CLIENTFILE | \
      sed s/SERVER_NAME_HERE/$SERVER/g | \
      sed s/OSNAME/$OSNAME/g > ${MYFILE}
  sed s/CLIENT_NAME_HERE/$CLIENT/g $CLIENTF2 | \
      sed s/SERVER_NAME_HERE/$SERVER/g > ${MYF2}
  ls -ld ${MYFILE}
  ls -ld ${MYF2}
}

calc_client_details

create_msgs
create_kickstart
create_pxelinux_file
```

netboot.sh

```
    This is CLIENT_NAME_HERE, booted from SERVER_NAME_HERE.

    Type:

            boot            to boot from the local hard disk

            install         to install OSNAME over the network



    Press F1 for this screen
    Press F2 for information on the install process
```

client.txt

```
    This is CLIENT_NAME_HERE, booted from SERVER_NAME_HERE.

      This page provides information about the boot process.

      CLIENT_NAME_HERE will be installed over the network, destroying
```

the operating system currently installed on the internal disk.

This will be installed from SERVER_NAME_HERE. If this is not what you
want, type boot to boot from the internal disks.

Press F1 for the main install screen
Press F2 for this screen

client-f2.txt

Invocation

THE NAME "DELAN" DOES NOT
RESOLVE; THIS TYPO SHOULD
HAVE SAID "DECLAN."

```
goldie# ./netboot.sh delan
A failure occurred in looking up "delan"  ←
goldie# ./netboot.sh declan
Client details: declan is at IP address 192.168.1.10 (C0A8010A)
-rw-r--r-- 1 root root 219 Apr 26 12:21 /tftpboot/linux-install/pxelinux.cfg/messag
es/declan.txt
-rw-r--r-- 1 root root 419 Apr 26 12:21 /tftpboot/linux-install/pxelinux.cfg/messag
es/declan-f2.txt
-rw-r--r-- 1 root root 174 Apr 26 12:21 /kickstart/declan.cfg
-rw-rw-r-- 1 root root 245 Apr 26 12:21 /tftpboot/linux-install/pxelinux.cfg/C0A801
0A
goldie# cat /tftpboot/linux-install/pxelinux.cfg/messages/declan.txt
```

This is declan, booted from goldie.

Type:

    boot   to boot from the local hard disk

    install   to install RHEL60 over the network

Press F1 for this screen
Press F2 for information on the install process

```
goldie# cat /tftpboot/linux-install/pxelinux.cfg/messages/declan-f2.txt
```

This is declan, booted from goldie.

This page provides information about the boot process.

declan will be installed over the network, destroying
the operating system currently installed on the internal disk.

This will be installed from goldie. If this is not what you

```
                    want, type boot to boot from the internal disks.



            Press F1 for the main install screen
            Press F2 for this screen


goldie# cat /tftpboot/linux-install/pxelinux.cfg/C0A8010A
default boot
timeout 600
prompt 1
display messages/declan.txt
F1 messages/declan.txt
F2 messages/declan-F2.txt

label boot
    localboot 0
label install
    kernel RHEL60/vmlinuz
    append initrd=RHEL60/initrd.img ks=nfs:goldie:/kickstart/declan.cfg
goldie# cat /kickstart/declan.cfg
# Kickstart file for declan to boot from goldie
text install
# You would probably want to put more details here
# but this is a shell scripting recipe not a kickstart recipe
goldie#
```

Figure 19-2 shows the client declan once it has booted from the network. It displays the menu, and when the administrator types the word "install," it loads `vmlinuz` from the TFTP server, followed by `initrd.img`.

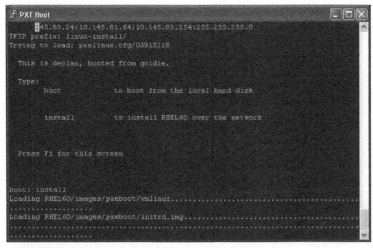

FIGURE 19-2

Summary

PXE Booting can be a slightly awkward thing to set up, but once the infrastructure is in place, it is a great way to automate the building of tens, hundreds, even thousands of servers quickly and easily. This recipe covered the mathematics involved in translating from one naming convention (192.168.1.42) to another (C0A8012A). This is necessary because most systems that work with IPv4 addresses use decimal representation, but `pxelinux.0` uses hexadecimal. Either system is fine, but translation between the two formats is required, and the role of the shell script is to accommodate these peculiarities and act as the glue between such similar but different systems.

Summary

20

Processes

Controlling processes is one of the key tasks of the operating system's kernel. The kernel also provides a signal-sending facility which enables one process to send a message to another. These can be handled by the `trap` facility of the receiving shell. Other methods are also available: for example, the mere existence of a file may be used to change a script's behavior. This recipe uses both of these methods. This recipe also makes use of the `pgrep` and `kill` commands to find running processes as well as sending signals to them.

RECIPE 20-1: PROCESS CONTROL

A number of commercial clustering products are available, which offer features such as monitoring and failing over network and storage services as well as processes. They also offer advanced protection against possible failure scenarios of multiple-node clusters, commonly known as "split brain" and "amnesia." This recipe is nowhere near that level of complexity, but it provides simple monitoring and restarting of services on a single server.

Technologies Used

- ➤ Associative arrays
- ➤ Signal processing
- ➤ Configuration files
- ➤ Process control: `pgrep`, `kill`
- ➤ `logger`
- ➤ Loops: `for`, `while`
- ➤ Conditional execution: `if`, `case`, `[ expression ] &&`

Concepts

Clustering and High Availability are huge topics in their own right. This recipe just looks at the monitoring and possible restarting of processes. At first, this seems a fairly trivial task, but there are a few subtleties to be dealt with. How to deal with a persistently failing process is one such issue; this recipe notes when the service last failed, and if it had already been restarted recently, then it disables the service and does not restart it again. Of course, just because something failed two weeks ago and has failed again since, that does not mean that it should be abandoned, so a timeout of 3 minutes (180 seconds) is defined in the script. By setting such hard-coded values as this and the debug value in the script just before its configuration file is read, the defaults are set if no other value is chosen, but the user can easily change those values by editing /etc/ha/ha.cfg.

The basic principle is to regularly check the PID of the monitored process. If the process has stopped, then restart it. If it has restarted under a different PID, that is treated as a failure, so the recipe logs the fact and leaves the new process to continue. This means that the process will not be restarted again on failure, but no direct intervention is taken by the script.

Different applications have different properties; some long-running processes (here sleep 600 is used as an example of a long-running process that is eventually bound to "fail") are straightforward: Start the process, monitor that its PID is still alive, and start off a new copy if it has died for whatever reason. Some services are not that simple. The Apache web server is started via the apachectl start directive, but that process itself terminates almost immediately, leaving a set of apache2 (possibly named apache, httpd, or httpd2, depending on how it was built) processes behind. For this scenario, the script waits a short while and then sees what PIDs are found. What Apache actually does here is to leave one root-owned process, which binds to the privileged port 80 and has children of its own, which run as a non-privileged user and actually serve up the requests when they come in.

The values for each application are configured by a .conf file for each service to be monitored. Along with some unused variables, which are included just to show what other kinds of things can be done, the main variables in these files are a flag to say whether or not the service is enabled, the startup command, the name of the process to look for in the process tree, and the delay after which the PIDs are to be gathered and monitored. There is also a flag to say whether or not a process should be stopped after multiple failures. As noted, the startup command and the name of the process that actually ends up running and being monitored could be totally different, or (as in the case of sleep) the same.

Finally, a special daemon process called Friar Tuck is monitored by the script. At http://www.catb .org/jargon/html/meaning-of-hack.html the Jargon File tells the apparently true story of a pair of processes called Robin Hood and Friar Tuck. These two processes monitored each other, and if one was killed, the other would restart it. Windows NT versions 3.5 and 4.0 also had a similar feature to stop users from changing the Registry to upgrade a Workstation to a Server; one thread monitors the registry setting, and another thread monitors the monitor. The same principle is used here; if the HA Monitor script was to suffer a failure, then the whole system would fail. This is called a Single Point of Failure (SPoF), and it is avoided by having a partner process that will monitor and restart the main monitor script. That makes the partner process a SPoF, too, so the main monitor script monitors its partner. This way, they both ensure that the other is running at all times. It would be possible for the Friar Tuck process to use the exact same code as the main monitor script, but Friar Tuck does not have to be as complicated as the main HA Monitor script. This means that Friar Tuck can be used to describe the basic operations of the monitoring process, while the main HA Monitor script can be used to go into a bit more depth and provide some more generic code for process monitoring and control.

Friar Tuck is also used as the communication point for the system; you start it by calling `friartuck.sh`, and you send signals to Friar Tuck to stop the service as well as to force it to refresh its configuration. Without this, it would be very difficult to stop the framework entirely; both processes have to be killed within a short period of time, before the other process recovers it. This is exactly what Robin Hood and Friar Tuck in the Jargon File story did. Sending signals to Friar Tuck is also how the main script is instructed to reread its configuration on the fly. This means that an enabled service, once disabled due to repeated failures, can be re-enabled by forcing the HA Monitor script to refresh its configuration.

Potential Pitfalls

There are a number of pitfalls with a system like this. One of the worst scenarios is that both of the processes can be killed at effectively the same time. At this level of clustering, there is simply nothing that can be done about this. More advanced clustering systems can hook directly into the OS kernel for all kinds of critical aspects of clustering, but this simple recipe just endeavors to keep its processes alive.

Another problem with the configuration of the system is the balance between abandoning and restarting failing processes. If a process keeps on failing because of a configuration problem, or regular memory leaks or other code failures, it can be counter productive to have the service occasionally available to external users but constantly going offline again. It can be better in this case to allow the service to fail and require manual intervention to fix the underlying problem.

An array storing timestamps of recent failures would provide more accurate diagnosis of problems in this case; if there have been two failures in the past 3 minutes but the last failure before that was 3 months ago, it is reasonable to restart the service again. However, if the service is constantly failing then it may be better to simply disable the service entirely. Shuffling the array of failure timestamps along every time would be fairly easy to implement.

Structure

The basic structure of this system is in HA Monitor, but a simpler version of it is embedded in the Friar Tuck process. Another key aspect of this recipe is the data structures involved. These are discussed in turn in the material that follows.

Data Structures

The main `hamonitor.sh` script makes extensive use of arrays to keep track of the different aspects of the unlimited number of processes that it can monitor. The Friar Tuck script does not need any of this, and is a lot simpler for it, but adding arrays makes the HA Monitor script much more flexible. Because the shell cannot do multi-dimensional arrays, each aspect of a process has its own array. The script does not use the `stopcmd`, `min`, and `max` arrays; these are listed here for completeness and to suggest other things that this script could easily enough be modified to do, should you so wish. The `pid` array keeps track of the PID(s) in use by the process; this is set to a negative value if there is to be a delay before the PIDs are gathered.

Another variable used by both scripts is tag; this is used by logger to identify the running process. Using logger -t "$tag", the script identifies itself accurately. The quotes around "$tag" are important; the colon goes after the tag, so without the quotation marks, it would say friartuck: (8357) ./ friartuck.sh FINISHING, which is not as clear as friartuck (8357): friartuck.sh FINISHING.

```
Apr 20 10:00:20 goldie friartuck (8357): ./friartuck.sh FINISHING. Signalling 8323
to do the same.
Apr 20 10:00:21 goldie hamonitor (8323): /etc/ha/hamonitor.sh FINISHING
Apr 20 10:00:25 goldie friartuck (8357): ./friartuck.sh FINISHED.
```

This can be particularly useful for debugging and diagnosing the script. As shown here, it is easy to see that friartuck.sh is signaling PID 8323, which is the hamonitor.sh script.

Friar Tuck

Friar Tuck controls everything, including starting the monitoring system and sending signals to the HA Monitor. Friar Tuck traps signals 3 and 4, and creates /tmp files to communicate these with HA Monitor. This coordinates a shutdown of the two processes when sent a SIGQUIT (3) or instructs HA Monitor to reread its configuration files when sent a SIGILL (4).

If pgrep doesn't find hamonitor.sh running as root, then start it. If it is found, but under an unexpected PID, log that fact and note the new PID. However, no special action will be taken if hamonitor.sh keeps on failing; friartuck.sh will always try to restart it. This is more simplistic behavior than hamonitor.sh, but it is just the crude and simple approach that friartuck.sh needs to take to ensure that hamonitor.sh is always running.

HA Monitor

The hamonitor.sh script is around 200 lines long; this is the second longest single script in this book, and about as long as it is sensible for one structured shell script to be. A simple sequence of commands can be much longer and stay manageable, but for a reasonably complex script, any longer than this and it would be worth splitting it out into different functions and libraries of code.

There is a while loop, which starts just over halfway down and continues to the end of the script. This is nearly 100 lines long and hard to see on the screen all at once, although the main part of it is an inner for loop which is a more manageable length.

This script can use the associative arrays available from bash version 4; if not available, configuration files have to be named 1.conf, 2.conf, and so on. Also, the declare -A statements will have to be changed to declare -a because -A is used to declare an associative array and does not exist in bash before version 4.

The script starts with a readconfig function. This reads the configuration files one by one into the arrays. This approach means that the number of processes monitored is effectively unlimited. The most noteworthy aspect of this function is that the variables expected to be read in from the configuration file are unset before the configuration file is read. If this was not done, and a configuration file omitted one of the variables, it would still have the value defined in the previous configuration file. This would be the wrong behavior and very difficult to track down. readconfig also does an initial check to see if the process is already running. If it is, it sets this element of the PID array to the list of PID(s) running that process as the specified user.

The function `failurecount` compares the process's `lastfailure` array element with the current timestamp. By using the GNU `date` formatting string of `%s`, which returns the number of seconds since January 1, 1970, calculating the difference between two times is easy. If this interval is less than the allowed failure window, then the process is marked as disabled. It is possible to put the line `STOPPABLE=0` in the configuration file; this is used for the Friar Tuck process, which should not be allowed to fail under any circumstances.

The first two arguments to the `startproc` function are the enabled flag and the username to run as. The rest of the arguments are used to start the process. This is achieved by processing the first two values and then disposing of them with the `shift 2` command, which leaves only the startup command and its arguments in `$@`.

The main `while` loop then starts up. This loop is split into two sections; the first part (before the `sleep $DELAY` line) checks for the existence of STOPFILE or READFILE. If these are found, and owned by root, the script will either shut down, removing the STOPFILE to indicate to Friar Tuck that it has received and acted on the message, or reread its configuration files and then remove READFILE so that it does not reread the configuration again on the next iteration of the loop.

After the `sleep $DELAY` command, the HA Monitor iterates through the `idx` array, which gives it the names of each of the keys to the arrays. With bash version 4, you can create this list without the `idx` array, using `${!process[@]}`, but in this case, it is clearer to use `idx` to list the keys. This method also works without associative arrays.

If the service is not enabled (either in the configuration file or because it has failed too many times), then it is ignored. `continue` goes back around the `for` loop to move on to the next process.

Next, the `pid` array is checked for a negative value. If negative, then the process has only recently started and may not have fully finished starting up yet. The variable is incremented (to bring it closer to zero) and again, `continue` is used to move on to the next process in the `for` loop. If the variable has got as high as `-1`, then `pgrep` is used to scan the process tree for the running process and assign that PID to the process's element in the `pid` array. If not found, then the process is labeled as having failed by calling the `failurecount` function. Otherwise, the new PID is logged and will be looked for on subsequent iterations around the loop.

The final 50 lines or so are the main substance of the script. Here, three different scenarios are tested for.

First, if the expected PID is not found when searching for the process, then the process has failed and must be either restarted or marked as failed. Skipping the second scenario for a moment, the third possibility that the script deals with is that the same process is still running under the same PID as before, and all is well.

The second possibility considered by the script is the more complicated scenario of the three. If the process was found to be running, but under a different PID, then one of two things has happened: Either the process has terminated and a new one has replaced it, or there are some other instances of the process running alongside the monitored one.

The list of PIDs are compared. If any previously monitored PIDs are not found in the currently running list of PIDs, then the `failed` variable is incremented. At the end of the loop, this variable determines the course of action. If no failed processes were found, then the additional PIDs are treated as harmless and unrelated to the monitored process.

If one or more previously monitored PIDs are found to be missing, the `failurecount` function is called. This will disable the process from further monitoring if it has already failed recently. The `pid` element is either set to the PID(s) of the process or to (0 - `startdelay`) if `startdelay` is non-zero. This gives the process time to stabilize if it needs to.

There is also a `stopha.sh` script provided. This simply sends signal number 3 (SIGQUIT) to the `friartuck.sh` process (or to another PID if passed one on the command line). Friar Tuck will trap this signal, shut down the HA Monitor, and then terminate itself.

Recipe

```bash
#!/bin/bash

function bailout
{
    logger -t $tag "$0 FINISHING. Signalling $pid to do the same."
    touch /tmp/hastop.$pid
    while [ -f /tmp/hastop.$pid ]
    do
      sleep 5
    done
    logger -t $tag "$0 FINISHED."
    exit 0
}

function reread
{
    logger -t $tag "$0 signalling $pid to reread config."
    touch /tmp/haread.$pid
}

trap bailout 3
trap reread 4

tag="friartuck ($$)"
debug=9
DELAY=10
pid=0
cd `dirname $0`
logger -t $tag "Starting HA Monitor Monitoring"

while :
do
  sleep $DELAY
    [ "$debug" -gt "2" ] && logger -t $tag "Checking hamonitor.sh"
    NewPID=`pgrep -u root hamonitor.sh`
    if [ -z "$NewPID" ]; then
      # No process found; child is dead.
      logger -t $tag "No HA process found!"
      logger -t $tag "Starting \"`pwd`/hamonitor.sh\""
      nohup `pwd`/hamonitor.sh >/dev/null 2>&1 &
      pid=0
    elif [ "$NewPID" != "$pid" ]; then
      logger -t $tag "HA Process rediscovered as $NewPID (was $pid)"
      pid=$NewPID
```

```
      else
        # All is well.
        [ "$debug" -gt "3" ] && logger -t $tag "hamonitor.sh is running"
      fi
done
```

```
#!/bin/bash

function readconfig
{
  # Read Configuration
  logger -t $tag Reading Configuration
  for proc in ${CONFDIR}/*.conf
  do
      # This filename can be web.conf if Bash4, otherwise 1.conf, 2.conf etc
      unset ENABLED START STOP PROCESS MIN MAX STARTDELAY USER STOPPABLE
      index=`basename $proc .conf`
      echo "Reading $index configuration"
      . $proc
      startcmd[$index]=$START
      stopcmd[$index]=$STOP
      process[$index]=$PROCESS
      min[$index]=$MIN
      max[$index]=$MAX
      startdelay[$index]=$STARTDELAY
      user[$index]=$USER
      enabled[$index]=$ENABLED
      idx[$index]=$index
      lastfailure[$index]=0
      stoppable[$index]=${STOPPABLE:-1}
      PID=`pgrep -d ' ' -u ${user[$index]} $PROCESS`
      if [ ! -z "$PID" ]; then
        # Already running
        logger -t $tag "${PROCESS} is already running;"\
          " will monitor ${USER}'s PID(s) $PID"
        pid[$index]=$PID
      else
        pid[$index]=-1
        if [ "$ENABLED" ]; then
          startproc $ENABLED $USER $START
        fi
      fi
  done
  logger -t $tag "Monitoring ${idx[@]}"

  # Set defaults
  DELAY=10
  FAILWINDOW=180
  debug=9
  . ${CONFDIR}/ha.cfg
}

# If Bash prior to version 4, use declare -a to declare an array
```

```
declare -A process
declare -A startcmd
declare -A stopcmd
declare -A min
declare -A max
declare -A pid
declare -A user
declare -A startdelay
declare -A enabled
declare -A lastfailure
declare -A stoppable
# Need to keep an array of indices for Bash prior to v4 (no associative arrays)
declare -A idx

function failurecount
{
  index=$1
  interval=`expr $(date +%s) - ${lastfailure[$index]}`
  lastfailure[$index]=`date +%s`
  if [ "$interval" -lt "$FAILWINDOW" ]; then
    if [ ${stoppable[$index]} -eq 1 ]; then
      logger -t $tag "${process[$index]} has failed twice within $interval"\
          " seconds. Disabling."
      enabled[$index]=0
    else
      logger -t $tag "${process[$index]} has failed twice within $interval"\
          " seconds but can not be disabled."
    fi
  fi
}

function startproc
{
  if [ "$1" -ne "1" ]; then
    shift 2
    logger -t "Not starting \"$@\" as it is disabled."
    return
  fi
  user=$2
  shift 2
  logger -t $tag "Starting \"$@\" as \"$user\""
  nohup sudo -u $user $@ >/dev/null 2>&1 &
}

CONFDIR=/etc/ha
tag="hamonitor ($$)"
STOPFILE=/tmp/hastop.$$
READFILE=/tmp/haread.$$
cd `dirname $0`
logger -t $tag "Starting HA Monitoring"
readconfig

while :
do
  if [ -f $STOPFILE ]; then
```

```
      case `stat -c %u $STOPFILE` in
        0)
          logger -t $tag "$0 FINISHING"
          rm -f $STOPFILE
          exit 0
        ;;
        *)
          logger -t $tag "$0 ignoring non-root $STOPFILE"
        ;;
      esac
  fi
  if [ -f $READFILE ]; then
    case `stat -c %u $READFILE` in
      0) readconfig
         rm -f $READFILE
         ;;
      *)
         logger -t $tag "$0 ignoring non-root $READFILE"
         ;;
    esac
  fi
  sleep $DELAY
  for index in ${idx[@]}
  do
    if [ ${enabled[$index]} -eq 0 ]; then
      [ "$debug" -gt "3" ] && logger -t $tag "Skipping ${process[$index]}"\
          " as it is disabled."
      continue
    fi

    # Check daemon running; start it if not.
    if [ ${pid[$index]} -lt -1 ]; then
      # still waiting for it to start up; skip.
      logger -t $tag "Not checking ${process[$index]} yet."
      pid[$index]=`expr ${pid[$index]} + 1`
      continue
    elif [ ${pid[$index]} == -1 ]; then
      pid[$index]=`pgrep -d' ' -u ${user[$index]} ${process[$index]}`
      if [ -z "${pid[$index]}" ]; then
        logger -t $tag "${process[$index]} didn't start in the allowed timespan."
        failurecount $index
      fi
      logger -t $tag "PID of ${process[$index]} is ${pid[$index]}."
      continue
    fi
    [ "$debug" -gt "2" ] && logger -t $tag "Checking ${process[$index]}"
    NewPID=`pgrep -d ' ' -u ${user[$index]} ${process[$index]}`
    if [ -z "$NewPID" ]; then
      # No process found; child is dead.
      logger -t $tag "No process for ${process[$index]} found!"
      failurecount $index
      startproc ${enabled[$index]} ${user[$index]} ${startcmd[$index]}
      if [ ${startdelay[$index]} -eq 0 ]; then
        pid[$index]=`pgrep -d ' ' -u ${user[$index]} ${process[$index]}`
      else
```

```
            pid[$index]=`expr 0 - ${startdelay[$index]}`
        fi
        [ "$debug" -gt "4" ] && logger -t $tag "Start Delay for "\
            "${process[$index]} is ${startdelay[$index]}."
    elif [ "$NewPID" != "${pid[$index]}" ]; then
        # The PID has changed. Is it just new processes?
        failed=0
        for thispid in ${pid[$index]}
        do
          echo $NewPID | grep -w $thispid > /dev/null
          if [ "$?" -ne "0" ]; then
            # one of our PIDs is missing
            ((failed++))
          fi
        done
        if [ "$failed" -gt "0" ]; then
          failurecount $index
          logger -t $tag "PID changed for ${process[$index]}; was \""\
              "${pid[$index]}\" now \"$NewPID\""
         # pid[$index]=-2 #SGP $NewPID
          if [ ${startdelay[$index]} -eq 0 ]; then
            pid[$index]=$NewPID
          else
            pid[$index]=`expr 0 - ${startdelay[$index]}`
          fi
        fi
      else
        # All is well.
        [ "$debug" -gt "3" ] && logger -t $tag "${process[$index]} is running"
    fi
  done
done
```

hamonitor.sh

```
#!/bin/bash
pid=${1:-`pgrep -u root friartuck.sh`}
kill -3 $pid
```

stopha.sh

```
# Apache is started with apachectl
# but the process is called apache2
START="/usr/sbin/apachectl start"
STOP="/usr/sbin/apachectl stop"
PROCESS=apache2
MIN=1
MAX=10
STARTDELAY=2
ENABLED=1
USER=root
```

apache.conf

```
START="nohup ./friartuck.sh >/dev/null 2>&1"
STOP=/bin/false
PROCESS="friartuck.sh"
MIN=1
MAX=1
STARTDELAY=0
ENABLED=1
USER=root
STOPPABLE=0
```

friartuck.conf

```
START="sleep 600"
STOP=
PROCESS=sleep
MIN=1
MAX=10
STARTDELAY=0
ENABLED=1
USER=steve
```

sleep.conf

Invocation

To start the framework, just run the `friartuck.sh` script. Here the `/var/log/messages` file logs the events as they happen. The `sleep` process is started, but the other two processes to be monitored are found to be already running. The `friartuck.sh` script is already running because it has just been launched from the command line, of course.

 Depending on how syslog is configured, the messages in this example may go to a different file.

```
# /etc/ha/friartuck.sh
Apr 20 11:03:36 goldie friartuck (10521): Starting HA Monitor Monitoring
Apr 20 11:03:46 goldie friartuck (10521): Checking hamonitor.sh
Apr 20 11:03:46 goldie friartuck (10521): No HA process found!
Apr 20 11:03:46 goldie friartuck (10521): Starting "/etc/ha/hamonitor.sh"
Apr 20 11:03:46 goldie hamonitor (10531): Starting HA Monitoring
Apr 20 11:03:46 goldie hamonitor (10531): Reading Configuration
Apr 20 11:03:46 goldie hamonitor (10531): apache2 is already running;  will monitor
root's PID(s) 7663
Apr 20 11:03:46 goldie hamonitor (10531): friartuck.sh is already running;  will mo
nitor root's PID(s) 10521
Apr 20 11:03:46 goldie hamonitor (10531): sleep is already running;  will monitor s
teve's PID(s) 10273
Apr 20 11:03:46 goldie hamonitor (10531): Monitoring friartuck sleep apache
Apr 20 11:03:56 goldie friartuck (10521): Checking hamonitor.sh
Apr 20 11:03:56 goldie friartuck (10521): HA Process rediscovered as 10531 (was 0)
```

```
Apr 20 11:03:56 goldie hamonitor (10531): Checking friartuck.sh
Apr 20 11:03:56 goldie hamonitor (10531): friartuck.sh is running
Apr 20 11:03:56 goldie hamonitor (10531): Checking sleep
Apr 20 11:03:56 goldie hamonitor (10531): sleep is running
Apr 20 11:03:56 goldie hamonitor (10531): Checking apache2
Apr 20 11:03:56 goldie hamonitor (10531): apache2 is running
```

The command-line invocation of `friartuck.sh` can now safely be killed. It will be restarted by the `hamonitor.sh` script. The whole thing is now running without a controlling terminal, and either script can restart the other autonomously.

```
Apr 20 11:04:36 goldie hamonitor (10531): Checking friartuck.sh
Apr 20 11:04:37 goldie hamonitor (10531): No process for friartuck.sh found!
Apr 20 11:04:37 goldie hamonitor (10531): Starting "nohup ./friartuck.sh >/dev/null
2>&1" as "root"
Apr 20 11:04:37 goldie hamonitor (10531): Start Delay for friartuck.sh is 0.
Apr 20 11:04:37 goldie hamonitor (10531): Checking sleep
Apr 20 11:04:37 goldie friartuck (10680): Starting HA Monitor Monitoring
Apr 20 11:04:37 goldie hamonitor (10531): sleep is running
Apr 20 11:04:37 goldie hamonitor (10531): Checking apache2
Apr 20 11:04:37 goldie hamonitor (10531): apache2 is running
Apr 20 11:04:47 goldie friartuck (10680): Checking hamonitor.sh
Apr 20 11:04:47 goldie friartuck (10680): HA Process rediscovered as 10531 (was 0)
```

Killing the `sleep` process then forces it to be restarted in much the same way as `friartuck.sh` was restarted. Due to the configuration preferences defined in its configuration file, `sleep` can only be restarted once in 3 minutes, or it will be marked as failed.

```
Apr 20 11:05:47 goldie hamonitor (10531): Checking sleep
Apr 20 11:05:47 goldie hamonitor (10531): No process for sleep found!
Apr 20 11:05:47 goldie hamonitor (10531): Starting "sleep 600" as "steve"
Apr 20 11:05:47 goldie hamonitor (10531): Start Delay for sleep is 0.
Apr 20 11:05:47 goldie hamonitor (10531): Checking apache2
Apr 20 11:05:47 goldie hamonitor (10531): apache2 is running
Apr 20 11:05:57 goldie friartuck (10680): Checking hamonitor.sh
Apr 20 11:05:57 goldie friartuck (10680): hamonitor.sh is running
Apr 20 11:05:57 goldie hamonitor (10531): Checking friartuck.sh
Apr 20 11:05:57 goldie hamonitor (10531): Checking sleep
Apr 20 11:05:57 goldie hamonitor (10531): sleep is running
```

Killing `sleep` again within the 3-minute window causes it to be disabled. The HA Monitor script will not attempt to restart it again until the configuration is re-read.

```
Apr 20 11:07:08 goldie hamonitor (10531): Checking sleep
Apr 20 11:07:08 goldie hamonitor (10531): No process for sleep found!
Apr 20 11:07:08 goldie hamonitor (10531): sleep has failed twice within 81  seconds
. Disabling.
Apr 20 11:07:08 goldie hamonitor (10531): Not starting "sleep 600" as it is disable
d.
Apr 20 11:07:08 goldie hamonitor (10531): Start Delay for sleep is 0.
```

Because `friartuck` has the property `STOPPABLE=0` in its configuration file, the array value `${stoppable[friartuck]}` has the value 0 also. Unlike the `sleep` process, however many times Friar Tuck is killed, it will always be restarted.

```
Apr 20 11:08:38 goldie hamonitor (10531): Checking friartuck.sh
Apr 20 11:08:38 goldie hamonitor (10531): No process for friartuck.sh found!
Apr 20 11:08:38 goldie hamonitor (10531): Starting "nohup ./friartuck.sh >/dev/null
2>&1" as "root"
Apr 20 11:08:38 goldie hamonitor (10531): Start Delay for friartuck.sh is 0.
. . . . . . . .
Apr 20 11:09:18 goldie hamonitor (10531): Checking friartuck.sh
Apr 20 11:09:19 goldie hamonitor (10531): No process for friartuck.sh found!
Apr 20 11:09:19 goldie hamonitor (10531): friartuck.sh has failed twice within 41
seconds but can not be disabled.
Apr 20 11:09:19 goldie hamonitor (10531): Starting "nohup ./friartuck.sh >/dev/null
2>&1" as "root"
Apr 20 11:09:19 goldie hamonitor (10531): Start Delay for friartuck.sh is 0.
```

At first glance, Apache appears to be treated in the same way; stopping Apache via the `apachectl stop` command causes all of its processes to terminate. The HA Monitor script restarts Apache just as it did with `sleep` and with `friartuck.sh`.

```
Apr 20 11:12:10 goldie hamonitor (10531): Checking apache2
Apr 20 11:12:10 goldie hamonitor (10531): No process for apache2 found!
Apr 20 11:12:10 goldie hamonitor (10531): Starting "/usr/sbin/apachectl start" as "
root"
Apr 20 11:12:10 goldie hamonitor (10531): Start Delay for apache2 is 2.
. . . . . . . .
Apr 20 11:12:20 goldie hamonitor (10531): Not checking apache2 yet.
. . . . . . . .
Apr 20 11:12:30 goldie hamonitor (10531): PID of apache2 is 11935.
. . . . . . . .
Apr 20 11:12:40 goldie hamonitor (10531): Checking apache2
Apr 20 11:12:40 goldie hamonitor (10531): apache2 is running
```

However, if `apachectl restart` is called independently of these scripts, Apache will reappear under a different PID without the HA Monitor framework knowing about it. So long as it is beyond the 3-minute window of the previous failure, this will be logged but execution will continue, monitoring the new PID.

```
Apr 20 11:17:32 goldie hamonitor (10531): PID changed for apache2; was "11935" now
"12868"
. . . . . . . .
Apr 20 11:17:42 goldie hamonitor (10531): Not checking apache2 yet.
. . . . . . . .
Apr 20 11:17:52 goldie hamonitor (10531): PID of apache2 is 12868.
. . . . . . . .
Apr 20 11:18:03 goldie hamonitor (10531): Checking apache2
Apr 20 11:18:03 goldie hamonitor (10531): apache2 is running
```

In this state, both `friartuck.sh` and `hamonitor.sh` can safely be killed, as either script will restart the other. As mentioned in the section "Potential Pitfalls," if they are killed at the same time, there is a possibility that neither script has the opportunity to restart the other, but the likelihood is that one will restart the other before both can be killed.

```
Apr 20 11:21:14 goldie hamonitor (10531): Checking friartuck.sh
Apr 20 11:21:14 goldie hamonitor (10531): No process for friartuck.sh found!
Apr 20 11:21:14 goldie hamonitor (10531): Starting "nohup ./friartuck.sh >/dev/null
2>&1" as "root"
Apr 20 11:21:14 goldie hamonitor (10531): Start Delay for friartuck.sh is 0.
Apr 20 11:21:14 goldie hamonitor (10531): Checking sleep
Apr 20 11:21:14 goldie friartuck (13564): Starting HA Monitor Monitoring
. . . . . . .
Apr 20 11:21:24 goldie friartuck (13564): Checking hamonitor.sh
Apr 20 11:21:24 goldie friartuck (13564): HA Process rediscovered as 10531 (was 0)
. . . . . . .
Apr 20 11:21:34 goldie friartuck (13564): Checking hamonitor.sh
Apr 20 11:21:34 goldie friartuck (13564): No HA process found!
Apr 20 11:21:34 goldie friartuck (13564): Starting "/etc/ha/hamonitor.sh"
Apr 20 11:21:34 goldie hamonitor (13620): Starting HA Monitoring
Apr 20 11:21:34 goldie hamonitor (13620): Reading Configuration
Apr 20 11:21:34 goldie hamonitor (13620): apache2 is already running;  will monitor
root's PID(s) 12868
Apr 20 11:21:34 goldie hamonitor (13620): friartuck.sh is already running;  will mo
nitor root's PID(s) 13564
Apr 20 11:21:34 goldie hamonitor (13620): Starting "sleep 600" as "steve"
Apr 20 11:21:34 goldie hamonitor (13620): Monitoring friartuck sleep apache
Apr 20 11:21:44 goldie friartuck (13564): Checking hamonitor.sh
Apr 20 11:21:44 goldie friartuck (13564): HA Process rediscovered as 13620 (was 0)
Apr 20 11:21:44 goldie hamonitor (13620): Checking friartuck.sh
Apr 20 11:21:44 goldie hamonitor (13620): friartuck.sh is running
Apr 20 11:21:44 goldie hamonitor (13620): PID of sleep is 13638.
Apr 20 11:21:44 goldie hamonitor (13620): Checking apache2
Apr 20 11:21:44 goldie hamonitor (13620): apache2 is running
```

So although both processes have been `killed`, operation continues as before. One change to note is that this time around, `sleep` has been restarted when `hamonitor.sh` started anew. The disabled state was only stored in the array of the running `hamonitor.sh` script. It would be easy to arrange for `hamonitor.sh` to write the updated state to the `sleep.conf` file or to some other discovered-state tracking file. However, the next test is to disable a command and then force `hamonitor.sh` to reread its configuration. This will re-enable it in just the same way. Killing Apache twice should do the job.

```
Apr 20 11:24:36 goldie hamonitor (13620): Checking apache2
Apr 20 11:24:36 goldie hamonitor (13620): No process for apache2 found!
Apr 20 11:24:36 goldie hamonitor (13620): Starting "/usr/sbin/apachectl start" as "
root"
Apr 20 11:24:36 goldie hamonitor (13620): Start Delay for apache2 is 2.
. . . . . . .
Apr 20 11:24:46 goldie hamonitor (13620): Not checking apache2 yet.
. . . . . . .
Apr 20 11:24:56 goldie hamonitor (13620): PID of apache2 is 14192.
. . . . . . .
```

```
Apr 20 11:25:06 goldie hamonitor (13620): Checking apache2
Apr 20 11:25:06 goldie hamonitor (13620): apache2 is running
. . . . . .
Apr 20 11:25:26 goldie hamonitor (13620): No process for apache2 found!
Apr 20 11:25:26 goldie hamonitor (13620): apache2 has failed twice within 50 second
s. Disabling.
Apr 20 11:25:26 goldie hamonitor (13620): Not starting "/usr/sbin/apachectl start"
as it is disabled.
Apr 20 11:25:26 goldie hamonitor (13620): Start Delay for apache2 is 2.
. . . . . .
```

Sending a `kill -4` signal to `friartuck.sh` causes Friar Tuck to create a file called `/tmp/`
`haread.$pid`, where `$pid` is the PID of the `hamonitor.sh` script. The `hamonitor.sh` script will
notice the existence of the file next time around its loop and reread its configuration files.

```
Apr 20 11:27:27 goldie hamonitor (13620): Skipping apache2 as it is disabled.
Apr 20 11:27:35 goldie friartuck (13564): ./friartuck.sh signalling 13620 to reread
config.
Apr 20 11:27:35 goldie friartuck (13564): Checking hamonitor.sh
Apr 20 11:27:35 goldie friartuck (13564): hamonitor.sh is running
Apr 20 11:27:37 goldie hamonitor (13620): Checking friartuck.sh
Apr 20 11:27:37 goldie hamonitor (13620): friartuck.sh is running
Apr 20 11:27:37 goldie hamonitor (13620): Checking sleep
Apr 20 11:27:37 goldie hamonitor (13620): sleep is running
Apr 20 11:27:37 goldie hamonitor (13620): Skipping apache2 as it is disabled.
Apr 20 11:27:37 goldie hamonitor (13620): Reading Configuration
Apr 20 11:27:37 goldie hamonitor (13620): Starting "/usr/sbin/apachectl start" as "
root"
Apr 20 11:27:37 goldie hamonitor (13620): friartuck.sh is already running;  will mo
nitor root's PID(s) 13564
Apr 20 11:27:37 goldie hamonitor (13620): sleep is already running;  will monitor s
teve's PID(s) 13638
Apr 20 11:27:37 goldie hamonitor (13620): Monitoring friartuck sleep apache
. . . . . .
Apr 20 11:27:47 goldie hamonitor (13620): PID of apache2 is 14711.
. . . . . .
Apr 20 11:28:07 goldie hamonitor (13620): Checking apache2
Apr 20 11:28:07 goldie hamonitor (13620): apache2 is running
```

Finally, to stop the entire framework, sending a `kill -3` signal to `friartuck.sh` causes Friar Tuck
to create `/tmp/hastop.$pid` and wait for `hamonitor.sh` to remove it. Both scripts will then cleanly
exit and not be restarted. This is also done by the `hastop.sh` script.

```
Apr 20 11:29:35 goldie friartuck (13564): ./friartuck.sh FINISHING. Signalling 1362
0 to do the same.
Apr 20 11:29:38 goldie hamonitor (13620): Checking friartuck.sh
Apr 20 11:29:38 goldie hamonitor (13620): friartuck.sh is running
Apr 20 11:29:38 goldie hamonitor (13620): Checking sleep
Apr 20 11:29:38 goldie hamonitor (13620): sleep is running
Apr 20 11:29:38 goldie hamonitor (13620): Checking apache2
Apr 20 11:29:38 goldie hamonitor (13620): apache2 is running
Apr 20 11:29:38 goldie hamonitor (13620): /etc/ha/hamonitor.sh FINISHING
Apr 20 11:29:40 goldie friartuck (13564): ./friartuck.sh FINISHED.
```

Summary

High Availability is a complex area, and complexity generally costs money. If unavailability of the application results in a cost to the business, then it is not unreasonable to spend money to mitigate against such a failure. You will get a more complete system capable of monitoring storage and network resources, restarting applications, as well as failing over between nodes to mitigate against total hardware failure.

However, when you are faced with an unreliable application that would be impractical to restart manually at all hours of day and night, this script will make reasonable attempts to keep the application running on your behalf and also cope with the basic problems that could hamper it, such as the High Availability script itself failing. It is also simple enough to understand and use without a week-long training course just to get you started with its core functionality.

21

Internationalization

Internationalization is often seen as something that can be done only by complex features of over-engineered programming environments. This is really not the case, and it is easy to produce internationalized shell scripts, as shown by this recipe. Dealing programmatically with human language is always tricky, and dealing with many different languages at once is even more complicated. The two key things are to keep shell syntax separate from the message strings, and to be aware of every instance of pluralization. An English script could get away with "I can see 1 aircraft" and "I can see 2 aircraft," but in another language the word "aircraft" would have a different plural form.

RECIPE 21-1: INTERNATIONALIZATION

Most shell scripts are written in American English, and the vast majority never get translated into any other language. Similarly, some scripts get written in the local language and are never translated into any other languages. Sometimes this is absolutely fine — an in-house script for a single-language workforce does not need to work in any other languages. At other times, however, you may run into a number of different problems unless the script is translated. The fact that a person can't use a script if he or she does not understand what it is saying is obviously a concern. If the script can communicate in somebody's first language, then his or her understanding of the information can be much clearer. Further, it can also be a legal or contractual requirement that certain languages be supported.

The discussion in this chapter assumes that the original script was written in English and translated into other languages from there, but there is no requirement for it to be that way at all. The original script can be written to display any language whatsoever; whatever the script emits becomes the `msgid`, which is then translated into `msgstr`.

The first script that I wrote which used internationalization, was a script to configure a particular USB-attached ADSL modem under GNU/Linux (`http://speedtouchconf.source-forge.net/`). At first, this script simply displayed some of the localization settings required for the modem to work with the user's ISP — each ISP has its own VPI/VCI pair for ADSL, which in the early days of ADSL customers were expected to know (or to run the ISP's Windows-only software, which had the values hard-coded). So Wanadoo in France used 8/35, other French ISPs used 8/67, all UK ISPs used 0/38, and so on. It soon became apparent that this modem was being used all over the world by people of widely varying technical abilities and very different levels of fluency in the English language. Along with collecting all of these VPI/VCI pairs, I started receiving offers to translate the script itself. Ultimately, it was translated by volunteers into Danish, Spanish, French, Italian, Norwegian, Polish, Portuguese, and Slovenian. This is all made possible — easy, even — by the GNU `gettext` facility. It is reasonably easy for a non-technical translator to provide translations, which means that it is quite easy to recruit volunteer translators. With `gettext`, the translator does not even need to read the shell script itself, only the strings to be translated. Having said that, it can be useful to see where in the script the message is used, and `gettext` does provide that context, as well as allowing the programmer to flag messages with comments to the translator.

Technologies Used

➤ Internationalization (i18n)

➤ Localization (L10n)

➤ `gettext`

➤ `eval_gettext`

➤ `eval_ngettext`

➤ `xgettext`

➤ `msgfmt`

Concepts

Translation is a four-step process. First the string is internationalized, then it is translated, potentially into many different languages, then compiled, and finally it is automatically localized into the required target language at run-time. Internationalization is commonly abbreviated to i18n, whereas localization is known as L10n. This comes from the fact that these are such long words to write; the '18' represents the 18 missing characters between "i" and "n", and '10' represents the 10 missing characters between "L" and "n."

Internationalization is the process of preparing a script to be used worldwide — internationally indeed. This involves marking any strings which will need to be translated, and in the case of shell scripts with `gettext`, making sure that the coding standards are suitably simple for `gettext` to identify variables within strings and translate them appropriately.

Second, translation is the process of taking the existing strings emitted by the shell script and translating them into different human languages. If a developer is fluent enough to translate the script into a different language, then all of the testing can be done quite easily with a fast turnaround time. If not, it could be awkward and time-consuming to rewrite code to work with `gettext`, get strings translated, compile the translations, and perform test runs, ideally with translators checking things over to ensure that the end result is as expected. One good workaround is to create a dummy language; in the late 1990s, the Red Hat Linux installer provided "Redneck" as one of the languages available for use during the installation process. This provides the North American developers with a language that they can test with, without developers having to be fluent in a foreign language. (It can be easy for politically incorrect text to slip into such a translation because, by definition, it is crossing linguistic/cultural boundaries, so remember always to be respectful.)

> *The Red Hat Linux 5.1 (note that this is not the same as RHEL 5.1) installation guide has a footnote on page 37, which explains the Redneck language thus:*
>
> The "Redneck" language entry represents a dialect of American English spoken by Red Hat Software's Donnie Barnes, and was used as a test case during the addition of internationalization support to the installation program. It is included solely for entertainment value (and to illustrate how difficult it is actually talking to Donnie).

Third, once the strings have been translated, the individual language text files are compiled into binary .mo files by the msgfmt utility for use with gettext. These can then be put in a locale-specific subdirectory under the $TEXTDOMAINDIR directory where the appropriate file will be used according to the current locale settings.

The text domain is what tells gettext which set of translations to use. If the system has two different applications installed, and they each have their own translations of the English phrase "No Change," the vending machine application will require different translations of that phrase (meaning "you won't get any coins back if you don't provide the exact amount of money required") than the status-tracking application (meaning "the status of this thing is the same as it was when last checked"). The text domain ensures that the relevant translation is used.

Localization is then the fourth and final step. This occurs on the user's machine, when the script is executed and control is passed over to gettext to quite literally get the relevant localized text to display to the user. In GUI systems, this may mean that menus, dialog boxes, and popup messages are displayed in the appropriate language. For a shell script, it means that the text is displayed in the correct language.

Potential Pitfalls

One of the less obvious pitfalls is not really technical at all. It is that, as the script evolves over time, the translations will need to be revisited for each change that produces new or different output. This can have significant impact, particularly on the percentage of languages that have complete translations. A single change to the script can break every language that until then had a 100 percent translation rate, and worsen further any languages that already had only partial support.

In a commercially driven project, if five languages are supported, five translators potentially need to be re-engaged to translate the new text. The time and cost of negotiating with them is likely to be very high compared to the lines of text they will be translating. In a community project, the same effort is required, although it may be that some of those translators are no longer interested in maintaining the script, so a replacement volunteer for that language has to be found, or the translation for that language will be incomplete. With 50 languages supported, there may be a need to find and encourage 50 translators, so the problem is tenfold, regardless of the motivation of the translators.

On the more technical side, one of the first things that people notice is that while echo ends output with a newline, gettext does not, so replacing echo statements with gettext directly does not produce the same result. Depending on the context, following the gettext with an echo by itself to insert a line break into the output is often the easiest fix. At other times, using other, more flexible output tools, such as printf, can produce cleaner, easier-to-read code than echo would have done alone.

More significantly, gettext does not know about any of the structures that the shell can use. This is not all bad; it means that translators don't need to know anything about shell scripting either. Looking at it from this angle helps when determining what is and is not suitable to be passed to gettext. However, gettext does have a big brother called eval_gettext, which can evaluate simple variable syntax so that values of variables can go into translatable strings. This can cope with simple variables, either $a or ${a}, but nothing more complicated, such as ${a:-1}. It also can't cope with other constructs, such as `pwd`. Any such shortcuts need to be done outside eval_gettext, which adds some small additional burden on the developer, but also means that it is easier for a non-technical translator to translate.

In the recipe, the short for loop, which doubles the numbers 2, 4, and 6, puts the answer into $ans, with the command ans=`expr $i \* 2`. This is then passed into eval_gettext, but the dollar symbols in $i and $ans have to be escaped so that they are not expanded by the shell. It is important that the exact text, including the dollar symbols, is passed on, because the msgid is "Twice $i is $ans," and not "Twice 2 is 4."

There is a further problem in pluralization. Some languages use the same word for plural as for singular items. For example in English, the word "sheep" is both the singular and plural of sheep. Conversely, the English plural of child is children, not childs. The structure is not logical and programmable, so it has to be translated depending on whether or not it is a plural. Some languages change the grammar entirely depending on whether singular or plural is being used. eval_ngettext can handle this discrepancy, as shown in the "I have n child[ren]" quote at the end of the script.

Structure

This recipe is just a very simple 33-line shell script. It creates a backup directory, ~/.savedfiles; welcomes the user to the script; echoes two random numbers; and then multiplies 2, 4, and 6 by 2. Finally, it claims to have 1, 2, or 3 children. None of this is particularly taxing, but it shows enough about internationalization for these purposes, and keeping the script itself as simple as possible helps to keep the focus on the translation.

First of all, xgettext finds all of the translatable strings in the script and creates messages.po, containing all of the strings in suitable format for translating. A copy of this file is taken for each language translated. Depending on the exact breakdown of labor, the developer will probably fill out most or even all of the header information, and the translator will read each msgid (English text) and populate its msgstr into the target language. This is represented in the recipe as vi po/de/script.po, where po is the directory named in the $TEXTDOMAINDIR variable. The msgfmt command may be run by the translator as part of his or her own testing, or by the developer after the translation has been submitted, or both. This creates the $TEXTDOMAIN.mo binary file, which contains the translation information. For the sake of demonstration, the text domain here is mynicescript, while the script itself is called script.sh. They could have the same or different names, but the difference is highlighted here to make the distinction clear. As a rule, the text domain is generally the name of the project, of which an individual script may be only a small part.

Recipe

```
steve@goldie:~/script$ cat script.sh
#!/bin/bash
. gettext.sh
export TEXTDOMAIN=mynicescript
cd `dirname $0`
export TEXTDOMAINDIR=`pwd`/po

savedir=`gettext "savedfiles"`
mkdir ~/.$savedir

gettext "Hello, world!"
echo
gettext "Welcome to the script."
echo

###i18n: Thank you for translating this script!
###i18n: Please leave $RANDOM intact :-)
eval_gettext "Here's a random number: \$RANDOM"
echo
eval_gettext "Here's another: \$RANDOM"
echo
echo
for i in 2 4 6
do
  ans=`expr $i \* 2`
  eval_gettext "Twice \$i is \$ans"
  echo
done
```

script.sh

First, xgettext grabs the text out of the script. This creates a messages.po file, which contains a header that should be completed by the developer and the translator in collaboration. It also contains a template containing every string found in the script, for translation by the translator.

```
steve@goldie:~/script$ xgettext --add-comments='##i18n' script.sh
steve@goldie:~/script$ cat messages.po
# SOME DESCRIPTIVE TITLE.
# Copyright (C) YEAR THE PACKAGE'S COPYRIGHT HOLDER
# This file is distributed under the same license as the PACKAGE package.
# FIRST AUTHOR <EMAIL@ADDRESS>, YEAR.
#
#, fuzzy
msgid ""
msgstr ""
"Project-Id-Version: PACKAGE VERSION\n"
"Report-Msgid-Bugs-To: \n"
"POT-Creation-Date: 2011-04-06 19:47+0100\n"
```

```
"PO-Revision-Date: YEAR-MO-DA HO:MI+ZONE\n"
"Last-Translator: FULL NAME <EMAIL@ADDRESS>\n"
"Language-Team: LANGUAGE <LL@li.org>\n"
"Language: \n"
"MIME-Version: 1.0\n"
"Content-Type: text/plain; charset=CHARSET\n"
"Content-Transfer-Encoding: 8bit\n"

#: script.sh:7
msgid "savedfiles"
msgstr ""

#: script.sh:10
msgid "Hello, world!"
msgstr ""

#: script.sh:12
msgid "Welcome to the script."
msgstr ""

#. ##i18n: Thank you for translating this script!
#. ##i18n: Please leave $RANDOM intact :-)
#: script.sh:17
#, sh-format
msgid "Here's a random number: $RANDOM"
msgstr ""

#: script.sh:19
#, sh-format
msgid "Here's another: $RANDOM"
msgstr ""

#: script.sh:25
#, sh-format
msgid "Twice $i is $ans"
msgstr ""
```

messages.po

```
steve@goldie:~/script$ mkdir -p po/de/LC_MESSAGES     ◄──────┐
steve@goldie:~/script$ cp messages.po po/de/script.po    SETTING UP THE GERMAN LOCALE (DE)
steve@goldie:~/script$ vi po/de/script.po
steve@goldie:~/script$ cat po/de/script.po
# My Nifty Script.
# Copyright (C) 2011 Steve Parker
# This file is distributed under the same license as the PACKAGE package.
# Steve Parker <steve@steve-parker.org>, 2011
#
#, fuzzy
msgid ""
msgstr ""
"Project-Id-Version: 1.0\n"
"Report-Msgid-Bugs-To: i18n@example.com\n"
"POT-Creation-Date: 2011-04-06 19:47+0100\n"
"PO-Revision-Date: 2011-05-11 12:32+0100\n"
```

```
"Last-Translator: FULL NAME <EMAIL@ADDRESS>\n"
"Language-Team: German Translator <de@example.org>\n"
"Language: de\n"
"MIME-Version: 1.0\n"
"Content-Type: text/plain; charset=iso-8859-1\n"
"Content-Transfer-Encoding: 8bit\n"
#: script.sh:7
msgid "savedfiles"
msgstr "gespeichertendateien"

#: script.sh:12
msgid "Hello, world!"
msgstr "Hallo Welt!"

#: script.sh:13
msgid "Welcome to the script."
msgstr "willkommen, um das Skript"

#. ##i18n: Thank you for translating this script!
#. ##i18n: Please leave $RANDOM intact :-)
#: script.sh:16
#, sh-format
msgid "Here's a random number: $RANDOM"
msgstr "Hier ist eine Zufallszahl: $RANDOM"

#: script.sh:17
#, sh-format
msgid "Here's another: $RANDOM"
msgstr "Hier ist eine andere: $RANDOM"

#: script.sh:22
#, sh-format
msgid "Twice $i is $ans"
msgstr "zweimal $i ist $ans"

#: script.sh:31
#, sh-format
msgid "I have $i child."
msgid_plural "I have $i children."
msgstr[0] "Ich habe $i Kind."
msgstr[1] "Ich habe $i Kinder."
```

script.po

COMPILING THE GERMAN STRINGS

```
steve@goldie:~/script$ msgfmt -o po/de/LC_MESSAGES/mynicescript.mo po/de/script.po
steve@goldie:~/script$ mkdir -p po/fr/LC_MESSAGES
steve@goldie:~/script$ cp messages.po po/fr/script.po       SETTING UP THE FRENCH LOCALE (FR)
steve@goldie:~/script$ vi po/fr/script.po
steve@goldie:~/script$ cat po/fr/script.po
# My Nifty Script.
# Copyright (C) 2011 Steve Parker
# This file is distributed under the same license as the PACKAGE package.
# Steve Parker <steve@steve-parker.org>, 2011
#
#, fuzzy
```

```
msgid ""
msgstr ""
"Project-Id-Version: 1.0\n"
"Report-Msgid-Bugs-To: i18n@example.com\n"
"POT-Creation-Date: 2011-04-06 19:47+0100\n"
"PO-Revision-Date: 2011-07-01 16:21+0100\n"
"Last-Translator: FULL NAME <EMAIL@ADDRESS>\n"
"Language-Team: French Translator <fr@example.org>\n"
"Language: fr\n"
"MIME-Version: 1.0\n"
"Content-Type: text/plain; charset=iso-8859-1\n"
"Content-Transfer-Encoding: 8bit\n"
#: script.sh:7
msgid "savedfiles"
msgstr "fichiersenregistrés"

#: script.sh:12
msgid "Hello, world!"
msgstr "Bonjour tout le monde!"

#: script.sh:13
msgid "Welcome to the script."
msgstr "Bienvenue sur le script."

#. ##i18n: Thank you for translating this script!
#. ##i18n: Please leave $RANDOM intact :-)
#: script.sh:16
#, sh-format
msgid "Here's a random number: $RANDOM"
msgstr "voici un nombre aléatoire: $RANDOM"

#: script.sh:17
#, sh-format
msgid "Here's another: $RANDOM"
msgstr "voici un autre: $RANDOM"

#: script.sh:22
#, sh-format
msgid "Twice $i is $ans"
msgstr "deux fois $i est de $ans"

#: script.sh:31
#, sh-format
msgid "I have $i child."
msgid_plural "I have $i children."
msgstr[0] "J'ai $i enfant."
msgstr[1] "J'ai $i enfants."
```

script.po

──────── **COMPILING THE FRENCH STRINGS**

steve@goldie:~/script$ **msgfmt -o po/fr/LC_MESSAGES/mynicescript.mo po/fr/script.po**

Invocation

Notice that in the examples that follow, the File exists message is reported by the mkdir command and not by the script. This is mkdir's own localization. For these test runs, I made sure that the directory already existed (in all three languages) to show this behavior. The directory name .savedfiles is purposefully translated into the local language by the script. If the script had decided that directory names would all be in English, then the message in German would be mkdir: kann Verzeichnis »/home/steve/.savedfiles« nicht anlegen: Die Datei existiert bereits. This is a decision to be made on a per-file basis; for obvious technical reasons, it is not possible to rename /etc/hosts to /stb/házigazdák just because you are in a Hungarian locale. This saved files directory in a user's home directory is, however, more suitable for translation, although it does depend on the application and how it will cope with the same user running the script again with a different locale setting.

```
steve@goldie:~/script$ ./script.sh
mkdir: cannot create directory `/home/steve/.savedfiles': File exists
Hello, world!
Welcome to the script.
Here's a random number: 17365
Here's another: 28848

Twice 2 is 4
Twice 4 is 8
Twice 6 is 12
I have 1 child.
I have 2 children.
I have 3 children.
steve@goldie:~/script$ export LANG=de_DE
steve@goldie:~/script$ ./script.sh
mkdir: kann Verzeichnis »/home/steve/.gespeichertendateien« nicht anlegen: Die Date
i existiert bereits
Hallo Welt!
willkommen, um das Skript
Hier ist eine Zufallszahl: 16618
Hier ist eine andere: 5870

zweimal 2 ist 4
zweimal 4 ist 8
zweimal 6 ist 12
Ich habe 1 Kind.
Ich habe 2 Kinder.
Ich habe 3 Kinder.
steve@goldie:~/script$ LANGUAGE=fr_FR
steve@goldie:~/script$ export LANGUAGE
steve@goldie:~/script$ ./script.sh
mkdir: impossible de créer le répertoire « /home/steve/.fichiersenregistrés »: Le f
ichier existe
Bonjour tout le monde!
Bienvenue sur le script.
voici un nombre aléatoire: 4944
```

```
voici un autre: 26037

deux fois 2 est de 4
deux fois 4 est de 8
deux fois 6 est de 12
J'ai 1 enfant.
J'ai 2 enfants.
J'ai 3 enfants.
```

Summary

Internationalization can be a complex topic but in practice, the actual translation comes down to a simple pairing of source and target languages in a simple text file. The developer can even easily strip out the msgid and msgstr strings if that helps the translator, and then put them in again after the translation is complete. All that is necessary is a simple text file.

```
msgid "Hello, world!"
msgstr "Bonjour tout le monde!"
```

Plurals can create additional complexity, and the script will need to be written so that the msgid strings fit neatly into the simplistic pattern required by gettext and eval_gettext. This all makes life easier for the translator, so these restrictions are actually a good thing.

Some of the greater challenges may be in recruiting and motivating translators and re-engaging them to update the translations when the messages in the script change. In a Free Software or Open Source project, making sure that potential translators feel comfortable with what is required of them is an important part of retaining and encouraging volunteers. You can make it very easy for translators to convert even one string at a time to the project; it would even be easy to set up a website that allows casual translators to arrive, select a language, be shown the current untranslated strings in that language, and provide their translations. You could even get away without doing any very serious authentication or checking. If 30 submissions for a string are received, and 28 of them correlate, then unless you are strongly in danger of being spoofed, it is likely that they are valid translations, even without any further checking.

Partial translations are also an option. If 100 percent translation is not an achievable goal, then in the interim a script can be published with partial translation, which will have the effect that some messages will be displayed in the native language, and others will be displayed in English. This is often better than no support at all for the language.

PART IV
Reference

- ▶ **APPENDIX:** Further Reading

- ▶ **GLOSSARY**

APPENDIX

Further Reading

There is a lot of information in the `man` and `info` pages for all of the software discussed in this book, particularly the bash `man` page and reference guide, and the `info` pages for the coreutils package. However, these are all incredibly densely packed documents, accurate but not particularly welcoming to the newcomer.

There are many tutorials and other, more verbose explanatory documents that are a much better way of getting into most of these topics. The lists which follow are some of those that I have found to be useful for my own uses, or to point people to for further information on a specific topic.

SHELL TUTORIALS AND DOCUMENTATION

Bash documentation can be found in two places: the GNU website (`gnu.org`) and the Cape Western Reserve University, home of the current maintainer, Chet Ramey.

➤ http://www.gnu.org/software/bash/

➤ http://www.gnu.org/software/bash/manual/bashref.html

➤ http://tiswww.case.edu/php/chet/bash/bashtop.html

➤ ftp://ftp.cwru.edu/pub/bash/FAQ

Mendel Cooper's *Advanced Bash-Scripting Guide* is available in PDF form at the webofcrafts .net website. It is also available in HTML; some links to particular highlights are included later in this appendix:

http://bash.webofcrafts.net/abs-guide.pdf

Andrew Arensberger's Ooblick site has a good page about the shell, including some slides:

> `http://ooblick.com/text/sh/`

Philip Brown's Bolthole website has lots of information, including a ksh tutorial:

> `http://www.bolthole.com/solaris/ksh.html`

Greg Wooledge's *Bash Guide* has a lot of good information:

> `http://mywiki.wooledge.org/BashGuide`

ARNnet has a rare interview with Steve Bourne:

> `http://www.arnnet.com.au/article/279011/a-z_programming_languages_bourne_shell_sh/`

Dotfiles is a resource with many examples of dotfiles:

> `http://dotfiles.org/`

The following are some direct links to general information in the *Advanced Bash-Scripting Guide*:

- ➤ `http://www.faqs.org/docs/abs/HTML/assortedtips.html`
- ➤ `http://www.faqs.org/docs/abs/HTML/contributed-scripts.html`

The Linux Documentation Project is home to a lot of good documentation, including the *Bash Beginner's Guide*, which, despite its name, covers quite a lot about shell programming:

> `http://www.tldp.org/LDP/Bash-Beginners-Guide/html/Bash-Beginners-Guide.html`

Finally, my own shell scripting tutorial focuses mainly on Bourne-compatible shell scripting, with occasional references to bash-specific features. My blog has occasional posts on specific points regarding the Unix and Linux shell:

- ➤ `http://steve-parker.org/sh/sh.shtml`
- ➤ `http://nixshell.wordpress.com/`

Arrays

Greg Wooledge has some very good information on bash arrays in his *Bash Guide*:

> `http://mywiki.wooledge.org/BashGuide/Arrays`

Tools

`find`, `sed`, and `awk` are some of the more complex tools called by shell scripts. The links that follow provide more detailed explanations of each of these. There are also entire books available on the `awk` and `sed` languages.

find

This page has some useful examples of using `find`:

> `http://www.kingcomputerservices.com/unix_101/using_find_to_locate_files.htm`

sed

The sed site at Sourceforge has links to a few recommended tutorials. The sed1line.txt file is also a very useful reference for quick ways to do common tasks with sed:

➤   http://sed.sourceforge.net/sed1line.txt

➤   http://sed.sourceforge.net/grabbag/tutorials/

➤   http://www.faqs.org/faqs/editor-faq/sed/

Lev Selector has a useful sed page, which includes links to other sed information:

http://www.selectorweb.com/sed_tutorial.html

awk

The IBM DeveloperWorks site has some useful awk information:

http://www.ibm.com/developerworks/linux/library/l-awk1/

Greg Goebel has a useful awk primer:

http://www.vectorsite.net/tsawk.html

Unix Flavors

Bruce Hamilton's *Rosetta Stone* is an excellent resource for, as it says on the website, "what do they call that in this world?" It covers most of the major Unix-like operating systems and how to do common tasks in each of them. You can also search it for something you do know (such as iptables) to find its equivalents in other operating systems (ipf, pfctl, and so on):

http://www.bhami.com/rosetta.html

SHELL SERVICES

There are two types of shell services; the traditional ones are shell hosts that allow you to have an account on their server, which you can ssh into. A newer form has come along more recently, such as http://anyterm.org/ — http://simpleshell.com/ is an instance of that — which uses AJAX to pass text between the browser and a shell on a server, turning a shell account into a web service. Fabrice Bellard (author of the QEMU emulator) has even written a Javascript-based 486 CPU emulator, which runs a native Linux in a browser at http://bellard.org/js-linux.

http://shells.red-pill.eu/ has a long list of shell providers, as does http://www.egghelp.org/shells.htm. Personally, I use silenceisdefeat.com occasionally (my username there is steveparker). They provide access to an OpenBSD server in return for a minimum one-off donation of USD $1.

It should go without saying that it is a privilege to be granted access to anybody else's system, and the terms of use always reflect that. It is only right to treat such a service as if you are a guest in someone's house. The only difference is that you should also expect and accept that your host has the right to inspect your files and activity however they please. It is not acceptable to use these services for sending spam, or for Denial of Service attacks, for portmapping, cracking, hosting warez, or for attempting anonymity, and all of the other obvious abuses that spring to mind, such as flooding the host's network either from within (for example, Bittorrent, DoS) or from without (for example, hosting), or using up too much CPU, memory, or other system resources. This is all largely automated anyway, so such attempts will be thwarted.

GLOSSARY

$ The dollar is used in the shell to reference variables. In regular expressions, it also signifies the end of a line of text.

| The pipe symbol is used to join commands in a pipeline.

**** The backslash is used to indicate that the character following it is to be taken literally and not expanded. There are a few exceptions to this; \\ is a literal backslash, so to embed the string \" the format is \\\". The other major exception is when a backslash is followed by a newline character. This indicates a line continuation, where the current line is joined to the following line. This can be useful for writing clearer, more easily read code.

The backslash does not escape a single quote when within single quotes; `echo 'That's all folks'` doesn't work, but nor does `echo 'That\'s all folks'`. To escape this, you have to include a \' outside of the other quotes: `echo 'That'\''s all folks'`.

#! The hash-bang (also known as she-bang) is a special pair of characters at the very start of the file, indicating that the executable that follows is the interpreter (and optional arguments) by which the script is to be executed.

& The ampersand tells the shell that the command preceding it is to be executed in the background. The shell remains in the foreground, and the $! variable is set to the PID of the background process.

[[is a synonym for the `test` program.

absolute path An absolute path starts with the slash character; /etc/hosts is an absolute path that indicates a specific file on the system wherever the referring process may be. *See also* relative path.

alias An alias is a shortcut for a command. These are honored only in interactive shell sessions, not in shell scripts.

array An array is a single variable with many values, each accessed by its index. Prior to bash version 4 and ksh93, indexes had to be integers. From bash 4 onward and ksh93 onward, associative arrays mean that indexes can also be character strings.

bash The Bourne Again SHell, the default shell on many Unix and Linux operating systems.

builtin A command built into the shell. For bash, these are listed in the bash `man` page under the heading "Shell Builtin Commands." They are mainly commands such as `cd`, which can't be run as an external process (the process would change directory without affecting the current shell) or `declare`, which defines how the current shell will treat the named variable. Similarly, the `source` (.) command has to be a part of the currently running shell process for it to have the required effect.

Some shell builtins override external equivalents. `echo` is one such builtin for reasons of efficiency.

The `type` command searches shell builtins before the `$PATH` environment variable, but `which` only looks in the `$PATH`. This means that `type kill` responds `kill is a shell builtin`, whereas `which kill` responds `/bin/kill`.

command substitution   The act of inserting the output of one command as another command. There are two forms of command substitution. The standard form uses backticks around the command line to indicate command substitution; the newer form uses `$(cmd)`. Command substitutions can be nested; backticks have to be escaped with a backslash. The following code snippets show the two forms; the quotes around the variable are required to keep the linebreaks between the output lines. The final linebreak is always removed.

```
$ foo=`ls -l \`which grep\` /usr/bin/test`
$ echo FOO is: "$foo"
FOO is: -rwxr-xr-x 1 root root 119288 Apr 22  2010 /bin/grep
-rwxr-xr-x 1 root root  30136 Apr 28  2010 /usr/bin/test

$ bar=$(ls -l $(which grep) /usr/bin/test)
$ echo BAR is: "$bar"
BAR is: -rwxr-xr-x 1 root root 119288 Apr 22  2010 /bin/grep
-rwxr-xr-x 1 root root  30136 Apr 28  2010 /usr/bin/test
$
```

compiled language   A compiled language is written as a text file, then parsed by a compiler to produce a binary file, which is executed by the operating system. The resulting binary is specific to the operating system and architecture that it was compiled on.

dash   The Debian Almquist SHell is now the default shell in Debian and other distributions that derive from it. It is a smaller, lighter shell than bash, but still POSIX-compliant.

device driver   Kernel code that deals with the implementation details of a particular class of device. Device drivers are normally found in the `/dev` directory, which may be an on-disk or virtual filesystem depending on the operating system. Device drivers are normally *block* or *character* devices. Block devices are things such as disk drives, which are written to block by block. Most other devices are character devices, such as terminals, audio drivers, memory, network devices, and so on. There are also special device drivers such as `/dev/random`, `/dev/zero`, and `/dev/null`, which are not associated with any physical piece of hardware — see *null*.

environment   The environment of a process is the name for its state; this includes its current working directory, the files that it holds open, its child processes, as well as the environment variables that are set for the process.

FIFO   A first-in first-out pipe. Examples of these are found in Chapter 14. Data represented by an entry in a filesystem; this is normally associated with data stored on a physical device, although this is not the case for virtual filesystems such as `/proc` and `/dev`. Files also have metadata, which is stored in its inode, and a name, which is stored in its directory entry.

FSF   The Free Software Foundation, founded by Dr. Richard M. Stallman, is the main sponsor of the GNU project, also founded by Dr. Stallman.

function   Functions are blocks of code that are not executed when defined (although the shell will report any syntax errors it finds when parsing a function) but effectively become additional commands available to the shell, and can be called as such. Chapter 8 covers functions in detail.

GNU   The GNU's Not Unix project has rewritten and expanded most of the original Unix tools as Free Software.

here document   A here document uses the << syntax to provide standard input to a command. The main use of this is in providing multiple lines of input to the command without having to first write those lines to a file, and then redirecting from that file. After the <<, you define a delimiter; that delimiter on a line by itself marks the end of the input. The code that follows shows a here document in use.

```
$ cat - > /tmp/output.txt << END_IT_HERE
> hello
> this is a test.
> END_IT_HERE
$ cat /tmp/output.txt
hello
this is a test.
$
```

here string   The syntax of a here string is <<<; it is like a here document except that instead of being a delimiter, the text to the right of the <<< is the command to execute. As shown in the following code, the text is taken literally, but command substitution can be used to provide the output of a command. To preserve the linebreaks in the output of the command, you must put the whole expression within double quotes. The script simply reads in two lines of input as $foo and $bar, and then displays them on the standard output.

```
$ cat /tmp/herestring.sh
#!/bin/bash
read foo
echo Foo is $foo
read bar
echo Bar is $bar
$ /tmp/herestring.sh <<< ls
Foo is ls
Bar is
$ /tmp/herestring.sh <<< `ls /tmp`
Foo is chris.txt herestring.sh keyring-vcxP9t MozillaMailnews orbit-steve
 sh-thd-1305760934 ssh-pQhaCK2245 virtual-steve.NqnWUy
Bar is
$ /tmp/herestring.sh <<< "`ls /tmp`"
Foo is chris.txt
Bar is herestring.sh
$
```

infinite recursion   *See* recursion, infinite

inode   Every file in a filesystem has one index node (inode), which stores key metadata about the file itself, including links to where the content of the file is found. The key data stored in the inode is:

➤ Owner

➤ Group

➤ Permissions

➤ File size

➤ Link count

➤ Time of last Change (ctime), Modification (mtime), and Access (atime)

This structure means that one file can appear in multiple directories and/or with multiple names; for each "copy" of the file, no additional disk space is required (other than the directory entry), and the link count is incremented. When all copies have been removed, the link count is reduced to zero and the space can be freed. However, if the file is open when the last link was removed, the inode reflects that fact; the file remains available to processes that had the file open when it was deleted, until all such processes have closed the file.

interpreted language   An interpreted (as opposed to compiled) language is parsed and executed one line at a time. A side effect of this is that the language can also often be used interactively. A program in an interpreted language can be executed on any system that supports that language (although subtle differences between systems can add some complexity to this). The shell is one such language. Contrast with *compiled language*.

kernel   The core of the operating system. The kernel is started before any other programs; it has full control of the hardware, including (for the x86 architecture on 80386 and newer) the exclusive ability to switch the CPU into its protected mode. This allows it to provide services such as preemptive multitasking, servicing of interrupts, and memory management.

ksh   The KornShell is written by David Korn as part of AT&T's Unix. It is now an open source project, and part of many GNU/Linux distributions as well as flavors of Unix.

Linux   A Unix-like operating system kernel, originally developed and still managed by Linus Torvalds.

null   The NULL byte is an ASCII character zero. /dev/null is known as the "bit bucket" — it discards anything sent to it. When read from, /dev/null outputs nothing. In contrast, /dev/zero provides a constant stream of NULL characters. Both of these /dev devices are special instances of device drivers in that they do not provide an interface to a particular piece of hardware.

process   An item being executed by the operating system. Each process has a Process ID (PID), and has an entry in /proc/PID, which contains the state of the process, such as the files that it has open. In a shell script, the shell is one process, and it executes built-in commands within itself. External commands, such as grep, spawn a new process, which executes and then sets a return code that is picked up by the shell in the $? variable.

recursion, infinite   *See* infinite recursion

redirection   The act of sending the contents of one file (most commonly an input or output stream, such as stdin or stdout) to another. This is covered in Chapter 10.

relative path   A relative path does not start with a slash; ../etc/hosts refers to the hosts file in the etc directory, which is in the same parent directory as the currently running process. etc/hosts refers to a hosts file in the etc directory immediately below the directory that the currently running process is in.

sh   The default system shell. This is often the Bourne shell, or other POSIX-compliant shell. Confusion over exactly what features `/bin/sh` has can cause great problems with shell portability.

shell   The shell is the default environment, command interpreter, and programming language in Unix and Linux systems. It is an interface between the user and the kernel.

Standard Input (stdin), Standard Output (stdout), Standard Error (stderr)   Standard Input, Output, and Error are the names of the three file descriptors that all processes are started with. These are file descriptors 0, 1, and 2, respectively. `echo hello` goes to stdout; `echo error >&2` goes to stderr.

Unix   A multiuser, multitasking enterprise-class operating system, first developed in 1969 and still in common use. Unix is a trademark of The Open Group (`http://opengroup.org/`).

whitespace   Space, tab, and newline are all classed as whitespace. By default, the Internal Field Separator (`$IFS`) is set to these three characters.

Index

INDEX

W

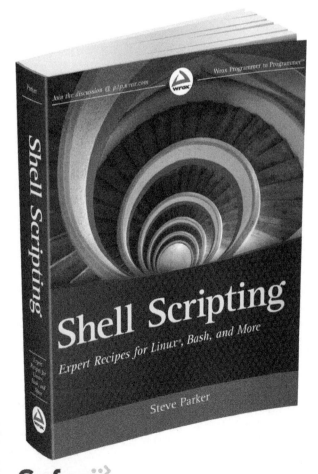

Printed and bound by CPI Group (UK) Ltd, Croydon, CR0 4YY

24/07/2023

03239180-0001